# GAY/LESBIAN ALMANAC

# GAY/LESBIAN ALMANAC

## A New Documentary

In which is contained,
in Chronological Order,
Evidence of the
True and Fantastical
**HISTORY**
of those Persons now called
**LESBIANS**
and
**GAY MEN,**
and of the
Changing Social Forms of
and Responses to those
Acts, Feelings, and Relationships
now called Homosexual,
in the Early American Colonies,
1607 to 1740,
and in the Modern United States,
1880 to 1950.

## Jonathan Ned Katz

1817

**HARPER & ROW, PUBLISHERS,** New York
Cambridge, Philadelphia, San Francisco,
London, Mexico City, São Paulo, Sydney

GAY/LESBIAN ALMANAC. Copyright © 1983 by Jonathan Ned Katz. All rights reserved. Printed in the United States of America. No part of this book may be used or reproduced in any manner whatsoever without written permission except in the case of brief quotations embodied in critical articles and reviews. For information address Harper & Row, Publishers, Inc., 10 East 53rd Street, New York, N.Y. 10022. Published simultaneously in Canada by Fitzhenry & Whiteside Limited, Toronto.

FIRST EDITION

Designed by C. Linda Dingler
Production Editors: Janet Goldstein, Bitite Vinklers
Copy Editors: Rodelinde Albrecht, Rosalyn Badalamenti
Proofreaders: Rodelinde Albrecht, Bernie Borok
Indexer: Jonathan Ned Katz

The author's research is ongoing and he would much appreciate learning of any additional documented sources. Communications may be sent to him in care of Harper & Row, Dept. 524, 10 E. 53rd St., New York, N.Y. 10022, though a reply may be impossible.

Library of Congress Cataloging in Publication Data

Katz, Jonathan.
  Gay/lesbian almanac.

  Bibliography: p.
  Includes index.
  1. Homosexuality, Male—United States—History.
2. Lesbianism—United States—History. I. Title.
HQ76.8.U5K37 1983    306.7′66′0973    81-48237    AACR2

ISBN 0-06-014968-X          83 84 85 86 87 10 9 8 7 6 5 4 3 2 1
ISBN 0-06-090966-8 (pbk.)    83 84 85 86 87 10 9 8 7 6 5 4 3 2 1

# Acknowledgments

Though I have learned much and received support from those listed below, none of the following persons necessarily agree with the ideas expressed in this book.

It is a special pleasure to acknowledge once again the able assistance of my mother, Phyllis Katz, who acted as my first "general reader," and whose years of editorial experience made her a most constructive, if demanding, critic.

Among those who read large parts of the manuscript at various stages, providing valuable responses that guided my work, are John D'Emilio, Lisa Duggan, Estelle Freedman, Philip Greven, Bert Hansen, and Jeffrey Weeks. Carole Vance and Paula Webster also provided valuable insights into the continuing struggle of women to affirm their own eros in the face of male-centered traditions.

Michael Dunn volunteered innumerable hours of research in the George Ives Papers, University of Texas, Austin, and other documents, for which I gratefully thank him. The section on the early colonial period might not have been undertaken without the hours of expert research volunteered by Robert Oaks, to whom I owe a huge debt of gratitude. Jaime Vidal also volunteered many hours of research on early colonial documents, for which I thank him.

My meetings with Allan Bérubé, Deborah Edel, Joan Nestle, Judith Schwarz, and James Steakley provided friendship, support, research tips, and a renewed sense of the value of this work. Stephen W. Foster and James Foshee again volunteered valuable long-distance research assistance.

I thank Barry D. Adam for research assistance; Carol Alpert for research assistance; Lisa Ben for copies of *Vice Versa;* John Boswell for research assistance; George Chauncey for research assistance; Liza Cowan for support; Louis Crompton for research assistance on early colonial laws; Dyan Dreisbach for picture research; James Fraser for the history conference; Eric Garber for informing me of *Norma Trist;* Barbara Grier for her bibliographies on lesbian literature; Rudy Grillo for research assistance; Ramón A. Gutiérrez for documents; Robert Haynes for the photo of Lisa Ben; Larry Van Heusen for informing me of James Baldwin's "Preservation of Innocence"; Joel Honig for research assistance; Penny House for support; Joseph Interrante for theoretical insights; James Kepner for copies of Henry Gerber's letters and research assistance; Lyle Koehler for research assistance; Steven Kowalik for research assistance; Alan Miller for the history conference; James Monahan for research assistance; Michael Moon for research assistance; Leland Moss for research assistance; Steve Nohling for research assistance; Harvey Perr for support; Arnold Pilling for research assistance; Charles Renslow for support; Wilhelm von Rosen for research in Denmark; Tony Segura for his collection of Henry Gerber's manuscripts; Laurence Senelick for research assistance; Christina Simmons for research assistance; Gregory Sprague for the dust jacket of *Strange Brother;* Ted Stroll for research assistance; Marshal Weeks for his postcards; Edmund White for support; Joseph Wortis for George Ives's letters; Robert B. Wyatt for support; Ian Young for his bibliography on gay male literature.

For their help and support I would also like to thank: April Adams, Chris Albertson, Patrick Barrett, Ellen Marie Bissert, Joseph Cady, Terry Collins, Patty Contaxis, Blanche Cook, Winston Davidson, Madeline Davis, Frances Doughty, Nick Ellison, Lillian Faderman, Karen Fetty, Terry Fonville, Richard George-Murray, Richard Goldstein, Pat Gozemba, Edward F. Grier, Larry Gross, Richard Hall, C. J. Hast, Barbara R. Henry (also known as J. R. Roberts), William M. Hoffman, Svend Hoiberg, Ross Irwin, Ed Jackson, Karla Jay, Walter Kendrick, Hubert Kennedy, Rudy Kikel, Don Knutson, Dennis Lampkowski, George Leigh, Barbara Levy, Barbara Love, Gordon McGregor, Toby Marotta, Robert K. Martin, MariJane Meaker, Cynthia Merman, Judith K. Myers, Ann Novotny, William Paul, John Perreault, Joan Raines, Rosalyn Richter, David Rothenberg, Vito Russo, Richard Schmiechen, Michael Seltzer, Richard Sennett, Herb Spiers, Judith Stein, Lester Strong, Tim Sweeney, Thurston Taylor, Kevin Thibideau, Doug Thompson, Daniel Tsang, Larry Volstad, Walter Williams, Bliss Woodruff, Allen Young.

For his special friendship, support, and continuing affection since June 28, 1976, I thank David Gibson; for their support and affection I thank Nan Bauer, Bill Cosgriff, Herbert Freudenberger, Becky Johnston, Carol Joyce, Robert Joyce, Jr., William Loren Katz, Seymour Kleinberg, Michael Lynch, Nicholas Patricca, Theodore Rauch, Michael Riordan, David Roggensack, James Schultz, J. Siegelaub, Ann Snitow, Edward Strug, Anthony Ward, Emily Rubin Weiner, Jeffrey Weinstein, Harold Wells, Scott Wirth, Albert Wolsky, and last, but not least, Walter Whitman, my cat, for his abundant love and kisses (see document dated 1920, January).

The Louis M. Rabbinowitz Foundation is thanked for its grant of $2500 to research the history of homosexual oppression and resistance.

# Contents

## NOTE

♀As in *Gay American History,* a female symbol has been placed beside the title of each document entry containing the most substantial references to women-loving women. Though this allows the most explicitly lesbian-relevant items to be distinguished at a glance, it should be noted that such selective symbolism reproduces the traditional sexist identification of the male with the universal. The symbols also suggest, incorrectly, that the documents not so marked are not relevant to lesbians. They may also suggest, incorrectly, that lesbian-relevant items are not relevant to gay men. Despite these problems positive response from lesbians in regard to the symbols in *Gay American History* results in my continuing their use here; but my hope is that males and females will both read this whole book, discovering by way of contrast or parallel how the history of the "other" sex illuminates their own.

# List of Documents

## PART II

### The Modern United States:
### The Invention of the Homosexual, 1880–1950

# Illustrations

# Preface

The present book extends the research begun in *Gay American History: Lesbians and Gay Men in the U.S.A.* (1976), introducing as many new documents as were there presented. The evidence is analyzed in essays introducing the two formative periods studied, "The Age of Sodomitical Sin, 1607–1740," and that modern era which included "The Invention of the Homosexual, 1880–1950." These two periods provide a study in contrasts, a comparison across time, illustrating basic changes in the social organization of sex.

This book offers a number of document discoveries. For the early colonial period these include the previously unpublished extensive testimony in a Connecticut sodomy trial of 1677; a Puritan minister's hell-fire and brimstone sermon of 1674 on the perils of leniency toward the "sins of Sodom"; and a large group of previously uncollected colonial sodomy laws—providing a new, broad perspective on the early colonists' death penalty and executions for the "abominable sin."

For the modern period, document discoveries include *Norma Trist* (1895), an early novel "of the Inversion of the Sexes," defending active lesbian relations, letters of love and appreciation written in 1921, from Detroit, by two male "inverts" to Edward Carpenter, the English defender of sexual "intermediate types"; Edith Ellis's public lecture in Chicago in 1915 in defense of sexual "abnormality" and Margaret Anderson's critique in *The Little Review;* a novel of 1936 by "crossing" woman Dr. Alberta Lucille/Alan Hart, in which a male "homosexual," hounded to his death, leaves a diary for publication because "he'd always wanted . . . to do something for people of his sort"; and FBI Director J. Edgar Hoover's private files reporting gossip concerning homosexuals in the 1930s and 1940s. The previously unpublished letters of Henry Gerber (1940–67), reveal the life and ideas of this little-known founder of the earliest homosexual emancipation organization in the United States, the Chicago Society for Human Rights (1924). And excerpts from Lisa Ben's *Vice Versa,* "America's Gayest Magazine" (1947–48), present reprints from the earliest periodical in America published specifically for lesbians.

In the present historical anthology a number of previously published documents take on a new resonance. See, for example, the love letters of F. O. Matthiessen to Russell Cheney, and those of Eleanor Roosevelt to Lorena Hickock. In addition, reproductions of a number of picture postcards, cartoons, photographs, and drawings illustrate the changing historical images of improper womanhood and manhood, of the female "queer" and male "fairy."

Analytical essays introducing the two sections of documents suggest new ways of looking at, understanding, and interpreting this evidence in its original social-historical context. A General Introduction to the whole volume discusses some theoretical and practical problems encountered in defining, researching, and interpreting lesbian and gay American history. But quoted passages from many not readily accessible sources allow readers to make up their own minds about the interpretations offered.

The dated entries that constitute the major text and substance of this book present information and documentary excerpts whose sources are given in back-notes. The excerpts are culled from autobiographies, letters, legal statutes, trial records, medical journals and books, theater, movie, and book reviews, news reports, editorials, obituaries, novels, songs, photos, drawings, and cartoons. The gathering together here of such diverse documents, in chronological order, suggests inner connections between apparently unrelated sources and themes. Studied in temporal sequence, even evidence that was previously known reveals unperceived facets, providing, finally, a "sense" of a particular historical era. Reading the dated entries in chronological order suggests the contours of an historically specific culture. Those entries make up a volume of unique and hybrid form, an intermediate type: part original documentary anthology; part analytical commentary, part popular historical encyclopedia, part annotated bibliography, part chronological description of events, part biographical record. Called an "Almanac," this volume is intended to evoke those popular early American compendiums of interesting and useful information. My aim has been to contribute to the ongoing cooperative recovery of lesbian and gay American history, and to present this history in a form accessible to all.

The evidence is presented chronologically, with materials on a particular theme only occasionally grouped together. This stress on chronology is intended to help situate homosexual history precisely in a particular society at a specific stage of development. This chronological ordering is a response to that present early stage of research in lesbian and gay history in which we are still establishing the most basic sense of what happened, before and after what. A linear, temporal arrangement of seemingly disparate bits of evidence suggests correlations to be explored and associations to be interpreted between phenomena which may at first have seemed unconnected. Establishing such a basic chronology helps us move on to more complex qualitative questions about the determinative impact of various conditions, the causative effect of various persons' acts.

Since the chronological ordering of evidence separates sources of similar type, and documents of similar theme, the introductions to the sections on the early colonies and the modern period discuss those reappearing sources and themes. Code words beside each document heading also identify at a glance that excerpt's basic character or theme. For example, the documents of the early colonial period include the tags "Statute," "Legal case," "Commentary," "Black American," "Intimacy," and "Resistance." A female symbol (♀) identifies major lesbian-relevant references. If readers follow one of these tagged themes or sources across time they can trace the changing, historically specific response to particular aspects of homosexual history. The exact source of quotes and information referred to in the text is cited in backnotes for the convenience of those who wish to pursue this research further. No backnote source citations are listed when the text refers to a dated document excerpted later in this volume.

As in my earlier *Gay American History*, I stress the documentation of oppression and resistance. In one sense, two women's or two men's achievement of an intimate relationship was a form of resistance to that modern society whose spokespersons decreed that true "sex love" could exist only between married male and female. But there is also a history of more explicit acts of resistance to the oppression of homosexuals: a written literature of homosexual self-assertion. This literature of resistance includes explicit essays in defense of homosexuality, and it also appears in fiction and letters. Various reports were also made (often by outraged medical writers) of acts in defense of embattled loves and lives. Excerpts from these documents are presented in juxtaposition to news reports, book and play reviews, medical commentaries, and other documents suggesting the larger historical context of this resistance. This record of explicit, active defiance, which first emerged in the United States in the mid-1880s, reveals a growing and resistant consciousness among lovers of the same sex.

Certain social patterns of response to same-sex intimacy also emerge when one particular kind of source is surveyed over a long period of time. For the early colonial era the statutes penalizing sodomy and other capital crimes constitute such a source, as do court records of actual punishments. The close study of a large number of these statutes and records reveals patterns in the naming and conceptualizing, and in the specific penalties provided in the 1600s and 1700s.

In the years 1880 to 1950 I focus on two major sources—American medical journal articles and *The New York Times*—allowing readers to trace these publications' changing responses to sexual "perversion," "inversion," and later, "homosexuality," over sixty years. *New York Times* reports of the Cleveland Street scandal in London, the Oscar Wilde and Count Eulenberg trials, the Alice Mitchell case, and later events provide clues to historical changes in the naming, the ways of thinking about, and the social treatment of homosexuals, as well as hints of homosexuals' own responses. *Times* obituaries, editorials, and reviews of books, plays, and movies document the response to same-sex intimacy in one of the nation's and world's most famous mass-circulation newspapers.

*The Times* is an especially interesting popular source to explore, as its columns record not only this one middle-class newspaper's response but reflect the expansion of other influential commercial media (book publishing, theater, and film production). In *The Times'* book, play, and film reviews published between

1880 and 1950, we can begin to trace the production and distribution of those images of "the lesbian" and "homosexual" which have for so long served as the major means by which such persons were known to the general public. A *Times* review of the play *A Florida Enchantment* in 1896 mentioned the role of financial speculators in putting risqué, formerly unspeakable themes before the public. Such reviews record the continued expansion of the entertainment business, an economic force fostering the public portrayal and discussion of a previously taboo area of human experience—the erotic (including the same-sex erotic).

Medical journal articles published between 1880 and 1950, and written almost exclusively with a condemnatory bias, now paradoxically turn out to be one of the richest early sources providing a glimpse into the social and emotional life of those who often called themselves "the intermediate sex." A survey of more than a hundred medical journal essays and books by doctors provides another source reflecting historical changes in the social response to, and forms of, same-sex love.

In the 1980s these old documents begin to provide a sense of past persons, acts, feelings, relationships, and conditions—a sense of the historically specific social organization of same-sex eroticism and intimacy.

# GAY/LESBIAN ALMANAC

# General Introduction:
# Lesbian and Gay History—Theory and Practice

In the beginning is a word. As we start to think about "lesbian and gay history" we necessarily employ some term or phrase to name our object of study. Each of those words, our tools of thought, has its own shape, implications, and histories. Those words decisively affect our most basic perception of the histories of "lesbians" and "gay men."

In the earliest era of American colonization the French and Spanish referred to native persons they called *amarionados* (effeminates); *bardaches* (catamites); *éffeminés; hermaphrodites;* and *hombres mariones impotentes* (impotent effeminate men). In the same era, the English referred to persons they called *amatores puerorum* (boy lovers); monsters in human shape; offending parties; sinners; Sodomites; Sodomitical boys; men who lie with men as with a woman; women who change the natural use into that which is unnatural; women who with women work wickedness; those who consent; those who do it.[1]*

Later Americans referred to persons called *Joyas;* Sapphists; tribades; pederasts; catamites; pathics; sissies; tomboys; bachelors; spinsters; old maids; friends; companions; comrades; comerados; Urnings; Uranians; Uraniads; gynanders; androgynes; feminosexuals; similisexuals; contrasexuals; homosexuals; bisexuals; transsexuals; transvestites; the third sex; intermediate sex; intersexes; inverts; perverts; queers; fairies; fags; faggots; faygelehs; pansies; Mary Anns; dykes; bulldikers; lady lovers; lesbos; lesbics; anomalies; obscenities; criminals; the insane; sick; pathological; immoral; contrary; temperamental; degenerate; fixated; deviant; abnormal; variant; homophile; lesbian; gay; a minority; oppressed group; a people; women-loving women; men-loving men.

Each of those words gives material body to a particular historical concept. Each term is a concrete clue to the often fundamentally different ideas and judgments about those who, in the United States since the 1890s, have been called "homosexual." That word and each of those words cited above summarize one of the historical ways in which we have been known, and perhaps have known ourselves. Each of those words locates us in a particular historical universe—of terms, concepts, persons, acts, feelings, relationships, of institutions and power.

*In this and the introductions to Parts I and II no citation is given for data and sources referred to again in the documentary sections.

All those terms express not only a particular idea about us but also a judgment of our value. Paying close attention to the words that have marked our presence here, we can begin to dig down, below the subjective level of concepts, judgments, attitudes, feelings, and consciousness, toward the objective historical situation of our predecessors, the changing social, political, and economic structures and responses amidst which they lived. The names we have been called, and those we have called ourselves, can be studied as one key to the objective character of our changing social and historical condition.

"Homosexual." "Lesbian." "Gay." "Same-sex intimacy." "Female-female eroticism." "Male-male sexuality." We are speechless without one or another of those terms. When we even provisionally speak of "homosexuality" and "homosexual history," we already assume the object of our thought has something to do with "same" and (by implication) "different sexes" ("females" and "males," "feminines" and "masculines"), that it involves the "sexes," and "sexuality," and that this "same-sex sexuality" has a "history." We have already equated the histories of "lesbians" and "gay men" under the rubric of the "same sex." We have already assumed a great deal, even before making our first effort at practical investigation.

At first thought, such assumptions may seem innocuous—but accepted as basic, unexamined givens they contaminate our perception, limiting, extending, and influencing it without our knowing it. The concepts of "homosexuality" and "heterosexuality," of "same" and "different sexes," of "lesbians" and "gay men," of "sexuality," "eroticism," and "intimacy" are among the major ones whose assumptions and implications we need to begin to question if we are to resist becoming agents of paradox—investigators who assume we know the basic character of that whose basic character we wish to know.

The projection of present terms, concepts, and forms of eroticism and intimacy on the past may seem an obvious error. But though recent researchers in sexual history have commonly noted the pitfalls of such an anachronism they have not always or even usually avoided it in practice. (At a time when the social histories of procreation and eroticism, of heterosexuality and homosexuality, and of women and men are still waging battles for legitimacy and funding, it is necessary to affirm the importance of a number of works that it is, in another context, important to criticize.)

In 1973, Vern Bullough and Martha Voght published an article titled "Homosexuality and Its Confusion with the 'Secret Sin' in Pre-Freudian America."[2] The authors emphasized that from the 1600s through the early 1900s (but especially in the 1800s), "homosexuality" was "confused" with "masturbation"; both were equated as forms of non-procreative sex. This "confusion" was the main focus of the essay.

The author's reference to confusion implied that there existed some universal, ahistorical, correct, true way of perceiving, categorizing, and naming "homosexuality," "masturbation," and other forms of sex. The authors assumed that those who in the 1880s associated masturbation and what is now called "homosexuality" were confused and mistaken; those who in the 1970s viewed masturbation and homosexuality as two different acts were clear-sighted, scientifically precise, and correct. But that assumption of past confusion and present truth short-circuited the authors' exploration of how and why, under a procreative standard, masturbation and homosexuality were associated as non-procreative. These researchers usefully described a particular historical association between what now, under a different standard, are usually considered different forms of sex. But the authors' naïve empiricism and present-centeredness made their analysis superficial and circular; they ended by explaining the "confused" association of homosexuality and masturbation by reference to terminological "confusion." The social basis for the association of terms and sexual acts was not explored; the specific social-historical organization of procreation and production was not examined.

The importance of understanding the culturally relative forms of "same-sex friendship" and the social response to them was stressed in a sophisticated, pioneering, and influential essay, Carroll Smith-Rosenberg's "The Female World of Love and Ritual" (1975).[3] Here Smith-Rosenberg suggested guidelines for analyzing the "deeply-felt, same-sex friendships" which she argued were "casually accepted" in America until the late 1800s. From the late 1700s through the mid-1880s, she said, a "female world" of close, "structured relationships appears to have been an essential aspect of American society." Such "relationships ranged from the supportive love of sisters, through the enthusiasms of adolescent girls, to sensual avowels of love by mature women."[1-2]* Many female-female intimacies appear to have been "both "sensual and Platonic," that is, deeply emotional, even physical in expression, though not "genital."[24]

Smith-Rosenberg suggested that historical analysis of same-sex intimacy should break with Freudian theories of "individual psychosexual development," "psychopathology," and the conceptual opposition between "normal" and "abnormal." Historians should focus, not on "deviance," but on accepted nineteenth-century "norms"—including those common, "normal" intimate relationships of females with females. Past same-sex intimacies should be viewed, she suggested, within a culturally specific setting, including particular family structures, "sex-role divisions," "male-female relationships," and the whole social organization of same-sex relationships.

"The essential question," argued Smith-Rosenberg, was not whether the partners to nineteenth-century female-female intimacies "had genital contact and can therefore be defined as heterosexual or homosexual." This historian thereby simultaneously agreed to define the "heterosexual" and "homosexual" by the "genital," and denied the appropriateness of applying that standard to the analysis of earlier eras' relationships. She relegated the question of the genital (and

---

*Bracketed superior numbers in the text specify page numbers on which quoted passages or information appear in sources listed in the backnotes. Such page numbers appear in the text only when the exact location of information or quote would be difficult to specify in the backnote.

a genitally-related eroticism) to nonessential importance, a judgment to which I shall return. Even while questioning the use of "genital" to define earlier intimacies, this historian remained trapped within the terms of the traditional medical concept of "homosexuality," defined essentially by the "genital." As we will see, Smith-Rosenberg's agreement to define the "heterosexual" and "homosexual" by the "genital" later allowed her essay to be cited as authority to deny the name "homosexual" or "lesbian" to several historic female-female intimacies.

Smith-Rosenberg stressed that early-nineteenth-century women's intimacies with women were not perceived in their own time according to twentieth-century distinctions between "deviance and normality, genitality and platonic love." Nineteenth-century female-female intimacies existed "in a particular historical context"—one in which "heterosocial" and "homosocial" worlds were complementary, the passionate love and close relationship of woman and woman provoked no fear of impropriety.[8]

Smith-Rosenberg proposed that traditional "psychosexual" analysis of intimacy be replaced by a "cultural or psychosocial" interpretation. Her essay focused on the existence of women's intimacies within a socially structured separate women's sphere of activity. That separate culture was contrasted with a modern society in which close female-female relationships had been made problematic.

She also suggested that modern psychiatric concepts of "homosexuality" and "heterosexuality" as absolutely opposed be replaced by a "relativistic model," positing a "continuum or spectrum" of "sexual and emotional impulses," with a "committed heterosexuality" at one pole, "uncompromising homosexuality" at the other.[28–29] She thus maintained the old homosexual/heterosexual polarity, though suggesting that the traditional concept of these as mutually exclusive be modified to include a sexual, emotional spectrum (implying an analysis in terms of degrees of "heterosexuality" and "homosexuality").

Since Kinsey, in 1948, first publicized the idea of a "continuum" of behaviors and feelings polarized between the "heterosexual" and "homosexual," in opposition to the earlier idea of a mutually exclusive "heterosexuality" and "homosexuality," the idea of an erotic continuum has become a popular mainstay of a liberal sexual pluralism.[4] The earliest sexual pluralists suggested a three-part division: heterosexual, bisexual, and homosexual. Other tri-partists have more recently preached "androgyny" as an alternative to an absolutely polarized "femininity" and "masculinity," suggesting that we'd all be greatly liberated by a hint of the "feminine," a touch of the "masculine."[5] The most recent sexual pluralists have postulated an infinity of erotic "variations," "sexualities," "homosexualities," and "heterosexualities" as alleged alternatives to the older hetero/homo dualism.[6]

All those pluralisms, however, simply extended the range of the original polarities without radically questioning them, without asking what it could mean to completely transcend the old oppositions. The new sexual pluralisms do not break in thought the old social links between female or male biology and particular human qualities, emotions, and behavior. Using any version of the concepts "homosexual" or "heterosexual" we cannot think clearly about a past society in which human lust and intimacy were not categorized on the basis of gender—or a future society in which the sex-biology of one's partners in lust and love was of no special concern and remained unnamed. If we wish to transcend the old hetero/homo world view it is not enough to think in terms of a "continuum" of eroticisms or intimacies divided between any number of "homosensual" or "heteroerotic" varieties; we must construct ways of completely bypassing the old mode of thought. I will later suggest how the history of the invention of the hetero/homo dichotomy can help us imagine a world without it.*

Though a genitally-defined "homosexuality" and a non-genital intimacy were discussed by Smith-Rosenberg in her study of women's friendships with women, the word "lesbian" was never mentioned. That terminological silence is indicative of a deeper, substantive silence about a specifically female-female intimacy which, though not necessarily involving genital contact or feeling, is nevertheless appropriately called "lesbian." The definition and appropriate historical application of the terms "lesbian," "gay," and "homosexual" have, since Smith-Rosenberg's essay was first published, become a matter of intellectual debate and political struggle. Various biographers and historians, the anxious agents of a defensive heterosexuality, have tried to hold on to their revered personages, while the first openly lesbian and gay researchers have tried to broaden and deepen their knowledge of their own pasts.

In 1978, Anna Mary Wells published a joint biography of Jeannette Marks, a teacher and writer, and Mary Woolley, a president of Mount Holyoke College, a book based largely on the two women's letters, left to the college archives by Marks.[7]

Wells recalled her discovery, while reading that previously unexamined correspondence for the first time, that the items she had casually picked up "were ardent love letters expressed in terms that both shocked and embarrassed me." Her "immediate impulse," she reported, was to abandon her biography of Mary Woolley: "It seemed to me impossible to ignore or suppress the content of the letters, impertinent to continue to read them, and quite unthinkable to publish them." She slowly realized, she claimed, "how deeply my own prejudices were involved" when she discovered what she called "sexual deviation" in "women I admired and respected." Finally, hearing rumors that there was "something 'vaguely scandalous'" about Mary Woolley, Wells decided "It's high time to set the record straight"—and proceeded with her biography.[xii] That she did not begin to understand the depths of her prejudice is clear from her book.

Discussing the evidence of Marks's and Woolley's "sexual deviation" with other Mount Holyoke graduates, Wells said she was "careful to avoid the use of

*See pp. 147–50, 171–74.

the words 'lesbian' or 'homosexual,' since both seem to me imprecise as well as pejorative." ("Sexual deviation" she considered exact and neutral.) It also seemed "impertinent" to Wells "to attempt to discover exactly how far the two women had permitted themselves physical expression of their affection." However, after *not* attempting "to discover exactly how far the two women had permitted themselves physical expression," Wells offered the opinion that Marks's and Woolley's

> relationship began in the childlike ignorance of sexual matters in which many young women of their generation were kept before marriage, and that when they became more sophisticated they voluntarily renounced all [!] physical contact. The emotional relationship . . . continued for the rest of their lives . . . steadily deepening until death parted them.[xi]

Wells reminded her readers that "it is very difficult to understand the past from the viewpoint of the present."[xii] She stressed that "the language of personal letters must be interpreted in the context of the social customs of the period in which they were written," and cited Carroll Smith-Rosenberg's essay "discussing affectionate letters between women in nineteenth-century America."[xiii–xiv]

In 1979, Marjorie Housepian Dobkin edited the journals and letters of feminist M. Carey Thomas, the first Dean of Bryn Mawr College, and included interpretive chapters on Thomas's life.[8]

Thomas's college years, Dobkin noted, included numbers of "strong emotional and romantic attachments" to other females, relationships then called "smashes." Thomas's later life also included close relationships with Mamie Gwinn and, following that, with Mary Garrett.

Dobkin explained that "the term 'lesbianism' is today used to imply both emotional and physical involvement, and Carey Thomas has been assumed, in print and out, to have been a lesbian in terms of her sexual preference and practice." This historian, therefore, found it necessary "to clarify the nature of Carey Thomas's relationships with and attitudes toward her close friends." Dobkin found it "hard to understand why anyone should care very much" about Thomas's personal relationships except as such knowledge "throws light on public behavior and achievements." The historian thereby accepted a traditional judgment denigrating the value of the personal at the expense of the public. She dwelled only on the "relatively inconsequential matter" of Thomas's close female friendships because, said Dobkin, "at least one reputable historian" had "gone so far" as to attribute Thomas's massive achievement to her " 'sexual preference.' "[79] (The historian was Frederick Rudolph, and his comment appeared in a history of education.[9])

Dobkin decried "The tendency to perceive relationships of another era in terms of contemporary attitudes, whereby nineteenth-century 'smashes' take on a uniform coloration in favor of lesbianism." Historical relativism was thus employed again as an argument against the attribution of "lesbianism" to past relationships. In opposition to such lesbian attributions, Dobkin cited Carroll Smith-Rosenberg's essay on "intense friendships" between women "which studies these relationships within the context of the existing cultural norms and moral strictures."[78] Dobkin also cited a study of a nineteenth-century village by Anthony Wallace, arguing that Carey Thomas's "idealized friendships with women fit the pattern Wallace describes of intense emotional and romantic attachments that were free of sexuality, although not of physical as well as of spiritual intimacy."[10] Though Dobkin assumed a distinction between "sexuality" and "physical" and "spiritual intimacy," she nowhere specified the difference, which is, by no means, self-evident.

That Carey Thomas's relationships did not harbor any "tendency" to even "latent homosexuality," Dobkin claimed, was indicated by her enjoyment of and, often, preference for men's company. (?!) But Thomas's liking men did not "in itself make a case for her heterosexual preference," said Dobkin. (Here I will interject that only the shoddiest analysis employs historical relativism to deny the "lesbian" or "homosexual" while affirming "heterosexual preference," a term and concept just as historically specific.) The "case" for Thomas's "heterosexual preference," Dobkin continued, was also bolstered by the "indisputable fact" that Thomas's feminist "rebellion was not against men as a class and was not psychosexually oriented."[80] Dobkin implied that any feminist who opposed men "as a class" was doing so out of some psychosexual antagonism associated with lesbianism. In contrast, Thomas's rebellion had been "against the social role assigned to women, and the limitations imposed on their lives," especially limitations on their intellectual opportunities. "But," said Dobkin, still arguing against the attribution of lesbianism, Thomas "at no time indicated her desire to have been born a man." She had even said she "preferred to be a woman." Dobkin thus implicitly equated lesbian feelings with the desire to be male, a primitive sexology, to put it kindly. Dobkin also argued that Thomas's general "aversion to sex would have applied to homosexuality" even more than to female-female relations, since she was essentially a conventional woman.[80–81]

Dobkin ended her brief for Thomas's "heterosexual preference" by citing an interesting, terse notation in Thomas's diary of January 21, 1927, reporting that she had seen the play *The Captive*—" 'about infatuation 2 women—vile play all people horrible.' " Thomas's niece also told of her aunt's "sadness in the late 1920s after having seen a play about homosexuality" which she thought was " 'the sort of thing that would make it difficult for women to develop the warm and close relationships some of them needed so very much.' "[87] Dobkin presented this response as evidence of Thomas's objection to lesbianism. It may be interpreted in a quite opposite sense, as an objection to the portrayal of lesbianism as captivity, and the social use of such portrayals to keep women apart.

That Dobkin's attempt to save Carey Thomas from the imputation of "lesbianism" was presented as a "feminist" analysis is shocking at this late date. For, since the early 1970s, a body of incisive writings by feminist women has carefully analyzed the deficiencies of any "feminism" fearful of the word "lesbian" being applied to those special female friendships which have so often supported women working for the liberation of their sex.[11] Nothing more need be said here about the intellectual poverty of Dobkin's assumption that if a woman loved a woman she necessarily wished to be or even identified with a man.

In 1980, Doris Faber published *The Life of Lorena Hickock,* the "Friend" (as the subtitle put it) of Eleanor Roosevelt.[12] This was based, in large part, on a collection of the two women's letters left by Hickock to the Franklin D. Roosevelt Library, a branch of the National Archives.

After her first look at the newly accessible Roosevelt–Hickock letters Faber left the research room she said, "in something like a classic state of shock." She immediately spoke to the Library's director, asking him "why couldn't this collection be locked up again, at least for several decades?" The next day Faber's husband and the Library director discussed the "implications" if the National Archives, a public institution, "were to suppress any sort of material against the stated wish of the donor." The "two men did most of the talking." But Doris Faber "emotionally" interrupted the men's philosophical debate to urge that "Eleanor Roosevelt was a great woman and her effusively affectionate letters should be removed [from the public archives] until the year 2000."[30-31] Faber's wish that Eleanor Roosevelt's love letters to Hickock had been destroyed or suppressed was reiterated throughout the book she finally based on these letters.

While the head of the Roosevelt Library took a week to "re-review" the letters, Doris Faber hoped, she said, that "a way would be found to justify sequestering at least the most ardent letters."[30-31] When the Library head decided not to suppress the letters, Faber, realizing that the story of the Roosevelt–Hickock relationship would eventually become public, asked herself whether she should not "tell it as fairly as possible." With "very mixed emotions," Faber "set out, after all," to write *The Life of Lorena Hickock.*[332] Numerous comments throughout this biography indicate that Faber despised Hickock for preserving those love letters which threatened Faber's reverence for Eleanor Roosevelt.

What Faber called the "homosexual implications" of the Roosevelt–Hickock relationship were most explicitly discussed in her backnotes, though comments were also scattered through her text. She "downplayed the question" of homosexuality, she said, "not merely from my personal reluctance to speculate about anybody else's private affairs, let alone Eleanor Roosevelt's, but mainly because . . . I do not believe that either of these women can be placed in the contemporary gay category."[353-54] In trying to clarify this problem of "categories," Faber had not found useful an unnamed "large tome" on gay life. She did find helpful Anna Mary Wells's account of the "emotional attachment" between Jeannette Marks and Mary Woolley—especially Wells's emphasis on the "cultural setting within which the attachment must be considered." Faber, like Wells, stressed "the unfairness of using contemporary standards to characterize the behavior of women brought up under almost inconceivably different standards."

Faber also cited "Havelock Ellis's analysis of the 'borderline' aspect of many female attachments," Carroll Smith-Rosenberg's "thoughtful scholarly article about feminine friendships," and E. M. Forster's portrait in his novel *Maurice* of what Faber called "a 'pure' affair between two men," paralleling, Faber thought, the Roosevelt–Hickock relationship. Faber concluded that Forster's picture of "a love between two persons of the same sex, transcending friendship, that has definite sexual nuances, and yet stops short of sexual activity," was the "key to interpreting" Roosevelt and Hickock. (Faber evidently referred to the "love" between Maurice and Clive which, Forster says, "though including the body" did "not gratify it." However, there is no question in the novel that this love was an illicit emotion tabooed by society and later called "homosexual."[13])

Commenting on Faber's volume in *The New York Times Book Review* (February 17, 1980), historian Arthur Schlesinger, Jr., agreed that "the basic point" about naming and characterizing the Roosevelt–Hickock relationship was that the words used in one era did not apply to the relationships of another. Roosevelt and Hickock, he said

> were both children of the Victorian age. Their correspondence [starting in 1932], with its romantic avowals and physical references, fits into a well-established tradition.

Roosevelt's and Hickock's was a traditional love, both "sensual and platonic" (Schlesinger quoted Smith-Rosenberg), but, he implied, this love was not lesbian.[3, 25]

Little need be said of the ethics, empathy, and charity, nor of the subtlety of thought to be expected from biographers who write of persons whose love letters, as Anna Mary Wells said, "shocked and embarrassed" her, or whose intimate correspondence sent them into "a classic state of shock," as Doris Faber reported. If a biographer admitted being equally distraught to discover a revered individual's Jewish or Black heritage we would, with cause, question that author's ability to write of that individual with humanity, feeling, or depth of insight. Studies of lesbian and gay persons' relationships, acts, and feelings are still, however, often mean-spirited, small-minded hackworks. Perhaps someday the stories of women-loving women and men-loving men will be composed by those empathetic and understanding enough to clearly and feelingly convey the full humanity, complexity, and contradictions of their subjects.

I have quoted at some length from Wells's, Dobkin's, Faber's, and Schlesinger's comments because these examples of a defensive heterosexuality so well express the dismay of present-day sexual traditionalists at the discovery of lesbian and gay history. Wells's unabashed report of her initial shock and embarrassment, and Faber's account of her own classic state of shock, constitute what I am irresistibly tempted to call (in the old psychiatric mode) "homosexual panic," a state of anxious terror provoked by a close encounter of an unexpected kind with the same-sex erotic in a beloved figure. Historian Lisa Duggan suggests that the three books in question represent a new field of research and an original literary genre: "not-lesbian history."[14] Those books would simply be pathetic and ephemeral if they did not succeed, for the time being, in defusing the explosive ironies and deadening the passionate poetry of their subject's lives and loves. For that they are despicable.

The books in question, and the very different Bullough and Voght, and Smith-Rosenberg articles, have also been discussed here in some detail because they raise a number of political and intellectual problems central to my own development of a historically relative view of lust and intimacy.

The authors of the three books affirmed a cultural and historical relativism for the purpose of denying the appropriateness of applying the modern names "lesbian," "gay," or "homosexual" to particular past same-sex intimacies, relationships clearly displaying an erotic emotion and deep feeling that have been in the twentieth century commonly associated with those names. These authors invoked the social and temporal character of sexual categories as a means of preserving intact the pantheon of notable heterosexuals. Because homosexuals have often been criticized for claiming as their own persons of achievement, it is curious to now find heterosexuals taking up a similar project. (It should be noted that, though most of the works cited focused on lesbians, the historical issues raised apply equally to gay men.)

The writers of the books cited, who confidently assure their readers that the relationship of X and Y was definitely "not lesbian," "not gay," "not homosexual," have to their own satisfaction, at least, positively identified the "lesbian," "gay," or "homosexual." These researchers in "not-lesbian" history refer to a prior "lesbianism," defined by genital contact or some "psychosexual," erotic emotion. These writers not-so-arbitrarily choose one of the (apparently) clearer contemporary concepts of the "homosexual" in order to save X and Y from that category worse than death. But, unfortunately for these anxious definitionists, it is by no means so easy to say what the "lesbian," "gay," or "homosexual" include and exclude.

A thoroughgoing historical relativism indicates that "lesbian," "gay," "homosexual," and "heterosexual" have no universal, unchanging, ahistorical meaning or reference. And even a cursory survey of current lesbian and feminist writings, and other psychological theorizing, suggests that there is no one, simple, unambiguous contemporary definition of those words. The most common, generally accepted (that is, establishment) definitions refer to some use of the genitals or some "sexual," "erotic" emotion which, in practice, is not so easy to distinguish from the "non-sexual." Especially at its more amorphous emotional perimeters, it is by no means easy to observe where the "lesbian," "gay," or "homosexual" erotic ends and the "non-lesbian," "non-gay," "non-homosexual" begins. One starts to suspect, finally, that the present enterprise of including and excluding persons and relationships from the category "homosexual" is mainly of concern to those who wish to be sure that they and their revered others do not fall into the class of the terrible tabooed. The pressure for precise categories, at this early stage of lesbian and gay history research, has the effect of diverting us from more substantial endeavors. The dire poverty of sexual categorizing as a primary project, and on a theoretically dubious and empirically inadequate basis, is well illustrated by the complex, fanciful, and now irrelevant classifications spun out in the late 1800s by Dr. Krafft-Ebing.[15]

Yet, for the pragmatic, practical purpose of researching the present book, I have had to adopt some broad, tentative, working definition of "lesbian" and "gay" and of "lesbian and gay history." It should be immediately noted that our present problem of defining an object of historical research and "relevant" surrounding "field" is quite different from that of ascertaining how a particular past human relationship, act, or feeling was thought of and responded to in its own time. For the purpose of this book I have defined "lesbian" and "gay" as referring to all manifestations of female-female and male-male eroticism, an erotic purposely left vague. This sensuality is documented in as diverse phenomena as the intense, passionate, physical, but seemingly non-genital friendships of women with women discussed by Carroll Smith-Rosenberg and Lillian Faderman, and in the most impersonal, brief, genital contacts of some present-day gay males.

In addition, "lesbian and gay history," as I have conceived it, includes a group of phenomena which are "lesbian relevant" and "gay relevant" without themselves being "lesbian" or "gay." Just as the history of women and Black people include essential references to those who were not women and not Black, so lesbian and gay history includes important references to those who were intimate without necessarily being erotic. Thus, "lesbian and gay history" is a broader, more inclusive category than "lesbian" and "gay"; this history is a study not limited to the erotic, but including reference to such varieties of female-female and male-male intimacy as the relationship of women with their "sisters" in the feminist movement, the relationship of men with their "brothers" in the labor movement.[16]

My concept of lesbian and gay as defined by an essential eroticism differs from definitions offered in recent years by a number of lesbian feminists. For example, historian Blanche Wiesen Cook defined "lesbians" as "Women who love women, who choose women to nurture and support and to form a living environment in which to work creatively and independently." That concept of "lesbian" made its essential element love, nurture, and support. Other lesbians have similarly defined "lesbian" as referring, essentially, to a female's "woman-loving," "woman-identification," or "woman-centeredness"—as referring to women whose "primary emotional commitment" is (or was) to women.[17] Stressing love as the essence of "lesbian," those definitions either deny that this love necessarily includes the erotic or are ambiguous on the subject of lust.

As tools for historical research and analysis, such general definitions present some unresolved difficulties, even as tentative working concepts. If all "intimate" relationships of women with women are called "lesbian," we then have no

specific name for those female-female relationships which did (or do) involve
genital contact and/or some sort of erotic emotion. (The same objection applies
to the definition of "gay" as referring to all male-male "intimacies.") To be sure,
the traditional medical definition of "homosexual" and "lesbian" has reduced
these to genital act and/or "psychosexual" emotion. But in response to such
reductionism it would be a mistake, I think, for lesbians and gay men to in any
way deny or de-emphasize the specifically "genital," "sexual," or "erotic" in
researching their histories. My concept of lesbian and gay history, therefore,
definitely includes the genital and erotic, as well as that which is relevant to such
relationships but has no identifiable "sexual" component.

At this early stage of lesbian and gay history research it seems better to err
on the side of a broad, vaguely defined inclusive concept. As we are just starting
to think about and explore this history, it seems best to be open-minded about
what it might include. This is a time, I think, when we are most usefully concerned, not with precise categorizing, but with researching, describing, and
analyzing the subtle differences between historically situated and changing forms
of human being, feeling, acting, and relating. To specify more precisely the
sometimes subtle differences between those historical forms we do need to become more aware of the assumptions inherent in the terms and concepts we use
as tools of thought.

In the title of this book, *Gay/Lesbian Almanac*, and in this Introduction, I use
the terms "gay" and "lesbian" in reference to the whole past history of "intimate"
relationships of males with males and females with females. This usage does
involve the present projection of modern terms on the past. The phrase "lesbian
and gay history," as used in this Introduction is a transhistorical, overall term; it
is used in the same sense as we sometimes employ "United States history" to refer
to the whole past development of this nation, including a time when there was
no United States as such. These projections of more recent terms on the past are
not anachronistic because they involve no equation of present and past, no
assertion that the exact present shape of phenomena actually existed in the past.
"Lesbian and gay history" gives a recent name to "intimacies" preceding the
historical invention and general use of those terms as appellations for specifically
"erotic" "same-sex" relationships.

Lesbian and gay history, as I conceive it, is a history both of eroticism and
of a more general intimacy. Because it is "homosexuals" who are supposedly
defined by and obsessed with sex, it is curious to note that it is, in fact, heterosexist apologists who have been and remain bewitched by the erotic as the basic
element distinguishing human relationships; it is now lesbians and gay men who
are breaking with that old mode of thought, to affirm a standard in which the
erotic may be an essential, though not the only, element. Our new stress on
intimacy by no means denigrates the erotic; quite the opposite. Instead of isolating an autonomous history of "sex," the history of the erotic can now be given
its full importance in relation to others aspects of human life. We can now stop

thinking of the erotic as "curiosa," consigned as the second-hand booksellers arrange it, to a separate shelf. The historical forms of the erotic can be studied in relation to a specific social organization of intimacy and alienation, of pleasure and procreation, of consumption and production. That there have existed inter-related social-historical modes of procreation, pleasure, and production, of intimacy and alienation, is itself an insight that can lead to further clarity about the changing forms of human relations.

It is not surprising that those lesbians and gay men now concerned with discovering the history of intimacy between females and between males should also raise critical questions about the history of female-to-male and male-to-female relations. Analysis of lesbian and gay history is also leading to searching questions about the historical invention of "heterosexuality" and the modern obsession with gender as it relates to eroticism and intimacy. Thinking about intimacy as historical also raises questions about the relation of human to human, apart from that sexual biology and socially constructed masculinity and femininity upon which our society bases so many other distinctions.

For the purpose, then, of informally naming a general female-female and male-male eroticism the terms "lesbian" and "gay" are perfectly legitimate and satisfactory. For the purpose of historical analysis, however, I do not think it clarifying to refer to a transhistorical eroticism or intimacy called "lesbian" or "gay." In the analytical sections of this book I have usually found it clearer to avoid the words "lesbian" and "gay," with their ambiguous reference to an intimacy which may or may not be erotic, and an intimacy with particular present forms. It has seemed clearer to me to use a descriptive terminology unambiguous in its reference to the specifically erotic, or to a more inclusive intimacy. I, therefore, usually employ some such descriptive term as the "female-female erotic," "woman-to-woman intimacy," "male-male eroticism," or "men-loving men."

In the analytical introductions to the early colonial era and to the "modern" period, and in the brief interpretive introductions to the documents, I have tried to avoid the use of terms and concepts not actually current at a particular time and place. When I analyze the documents of the early colonies, I do not use the modern terms "lesbian," "gay," "homosexual," or "heterosexual." I do refer to "sodomy," the "sodomitical," women who "change the natural use into that which is against nature," and women who "work wickedness with women." I also sometimes use more purely descriptive modern terms like "same-sex intimacy," the "procreative" and "non-procreative." When I have found it expedient in the analysis of the early colonies to refer to "same-sex eroticism" I have tried to do so in such a way as to indicate that this term (a synonymn for "homosexual") involves the projection of a modern concept on the past; the early colonists did not distinguish lust in terms of its "same sex" or "different sex" object. Likewise, when I refer to "same-sex intimacy" between colonial males or females, I intend a conscious projection of a current interest. That some such "intimacy" existed in the colonies, apart from our naming it, seems obvious. Yet by what conceptual means we grasp it affects substantially our perception of its particular historical contours.

Historical analysis using only the terms and concepts specific to the past remains locked within the intellectual boundaries of that past. So, while paying close attention to past terms and concepts as objects of analysis, it is necessary to apply to the interpretation of the past those modern categories which can illuminate bygone social modes of eroticism and intimacy. Analyzing the early colonies I, therefore, speak, for example, of the specific social-historical "organization of procreation," an institution which then had a determinative impact on the response to all forms of lust.

When stylistic considerations required, or when some clarification was to be made by introducing a term or concept foreign to the era analyzed, I have tried to do so self-consciously, in such a way that the reader will be aware of the verbal, conceptual, and historical discrepancy. Too often, I think, in works on "sexual history," the anachronistic use of terms and concepts has obscured the historically-specific qualities of the phenomena being studied. For example, my present circumspect use of terms and concepts is meant to correct my own earlier usage in *Gay American History,* where the word "homosexual" was employed in reference to phenomena of the early colonial era, and the specific historical character of early colonial "sodomy" was thereby obscured. In this book, I use the terms "homosexual" and "heterosexual" only when discussing that time period in which those words were actually introduced, and only in reference to those types of document sources in which they actually appeared; those terms and concepts were used in American medical journals, for example, long before they were in *The New York Times,* each use recording an important change in the social recognition of "homosexuals." My point in this careful application of terms derives from my new sense of how deeply the words we use and concepts with which we think affect our vision of the past, and limit our vision of the future.

In the analytical sections of this book referring to the early colonial era and to the "modern" period I have not thought it clarifying to use the word "gay." Before the 1960s, "gay" (for homosexual) appeared only sporadically in the respectable mass media, although it was earlier in common verbal use in the subculture. My reticence with regard to the use of "gay" differs from the practice of John Boswell in this book *Christianity, Social Tolerance and Homosexuality,* a monumental contribution to the history of male-male eroticism and intimacy.[18]

In that book, Boswell used the word "gay" to refer to "persons who are conscious of erotic inclination toward their own gender as a distinguishing characteristic." He applied this definition of gay universally, suggesting that such "gay persons" as he had specified constituted a "substantial minority in every age."[5] He theorized that, though social "tolerance" of gay persons changed historically, they and their consciousness of their beloveds' gender as erotically differentiating remained the same. His own evidence, however, indicated that persons conscious of being distinguished by their erotic inclination toward their own gender are by no means universal. Gender, Boswell pointed out, was *not* the basis for the categorization and social response to the erotic in ancient Greece or Rome.[58–59] My own empirical research and interpretation of the early American colonies also indicates that a consciousness of gender as differentiating did not then characterize the dominant response to eroticism. The use of gender as the criterion of two opposed eroticisms, "homosexual" and "heterosexual," "same sex" and "different sex," became socially dominant in the U.S. only about 1930.

The historical use of the word "gay," and such words as "temperamental" (for homosexual, documented in 1927) and "kiki" (for a lesbian "at ease with either a passive or aggressive partner," documented in 1947)—a special language particular to a specific group of persons—indicates the existence of a subculture with a fairly developed communications network, cohesion, stage of self-conscious differentiation from "others," and urban places of meeting, a subculture at a specific historical stage of development. The word "gay" (for homosexual) was first used in *The New York Times* in 1963, first in a book review, later that year in that paper's earliest survey of the city's homosexual society. The word "gay" first appeared in *The Times* in reference to the development of a militant homosexual liberation movement in 1970, when the paper reported a demonstration of the "Gay Liberation Front."[19] (In the early 1980s *Times* editors' refusal to adopt "gay" and "lesbian" instead of "homosexual," like their refusal to use "spokesperson" or "spokeswoman" instead of "spokesman" when referring to female speakers, are daily reminders of a power discrepancy between those who control the mass means of naming and significant groups of those named. If such relatively slight terminological changes are so vehemently resisted, even more substantive alterations in power relationships will certainly be.) Those *Times* usages mark two historical points in the modern development of gay men and lesbians in America. The use of the word "gay," first as a secret code known only to initiated members of the subculture and their friends, then, after 1969, as the publicly proclaimed self-designation of members of a militant liberation movement, reflects a homosexual culture at two very different historical points of development.

Since the mid-1970s, the common use in the political subculture of the terms "lesbian" and "gay," to stress the different social experience of women-loving women and men-loving men, reflects the historical existence of a vocal lesbian feminist movement. My reference in this book to "lesbian and gay history" reflects that present lesbian feminist consciousness concerning the importance of differentiating the histories of women-loving women and men-loving men.

The relationship between the specific historical character of terms and concepts, and the social organization in which they are produced, is well illustrated by the fairly recent invention of the opposition between the "homosexual" and "heterosexual." The earliest recorded use of the term "homosexuality" (in the form of the German *Homosexualität*) dates to 1869, when Dr. Károly Mária Benkert (under the pseudonym Kertbeny) used the word in an open letter to the Prussian Minister of Justice, arguing for the decriminalization of sexual relations between men (those between women were not illegal).[20] The term "homosexual" first appeared in American medical books and journals in the early 1890s, and came into general, popular use as part of "standard" American–English only in the 1920s. The word "homosexuality" is first known to have been used in *The New York Times* in 1926 (see October 24). The earliest use of "heterosexual" found in that paper was in 1930 (see April 20).

The term "heterosexual" first appeared in American medical texts in the early 1890s, where it referred to persons with "inclinations to both sexes" (now called "bisexual"). But by the mid-1890s "heterosexual" and "homosexual" were beginning to be used by American doctors to characterize a "normal" eroticism absolutely opposed to an "abnormal perversion." Contrary to Alfred Kinsey's and others' common assumption, the term "heterosexual" apparently followed the introduction of "homosexual." (The "deviant" was seemingly given nominal existence before the "norm," surprising only because we are used to thinking of the "norm" or "normative" as actively determining the "deviant."[21])

Although various persons, acts, feelings, and relationships similar to those later called "homosexual" and "heterosexual" probably did exist before the invention of those specific names and concepts, it is now by no means clear how such persons named, thought of, and evaluated themselves, or their acts, feelings, and relations, or how they were perceived and responded to by others. The essay by Smith-Rosenberg, discussed earlier, was important as a first attempt to discover the specific historical qualities of relationships existing before the epochal introduction and popularization of the terms and concepts "homosexual" and "heterosexual." But that historical problem will not even occur to us if we start by assuming the universal, unchanging existence of "homosexual" and "heterosexual"—or the "lesbian" and "gay"—persons just like us, who act, feel, and have relationships shaped and situated just like ours.

That "modern" American era from 1880 to 1950, in which the "homosexual" and "heterosexual" made their social debuts, was an age whose ideologists and citizens were obsessed with the relation of eroticism, "femininity," and "masculinity." That dominant "modern" preoccupation with lust and gender differed from the central concern of the early colonists, whose main worry was about lust, procreation, and the failure to so produce. Put another way, the "modern" United States institutionalized a response to the erotic whose dominant terms were "womanhood" and "manhood." In contrast, the early colonial organization of sex gave precedence to a standard whose dominant term was baby-making. In the early colonial economy of lust, procreativity was primary, gender secondary. The modern invention of the "homosexual" and "heterosexual" as the dominant modes of naming, perceiving, and socially reacting to the erotic, constituted one particular, temporally specific response—the response of a society obsessed with differentiating the "feminine" female from the "masculine" male, the intimacies of a "same sex" and a "different sex."

The idea of a "same sex," "different sex," and of "opposite sexes" by no means simply reflects that physiology unique to females or males. The concept of females and males as the "same," "different," or "opposite" records a changing historical comparison and judgment, based on different criteria. The judgments "same," "different," and "opposite," applied to the sexes, do not reflect some unchanging, ahistorical relationship of female and male biologies. Nor do the concepts of "same," "different," or "opposite sexes" simply reflect those unique characteristics bred into females or males in the historical process of engendering them as "feminine" or "masculine." The concepts of "same," "different," and "opposite sexes," accepted without question as mirroring a "natural," biological relationship of females and males, have themselves been important means in the social organization and production of an historical "femininity" and "masculinity."

The analytical introductions to the colonial and "modern" eras touch in more detail on some of the other terms and categories which have been applied historically to intimacies between men and between women: "natural" and "unnatural," "normal" and "abnormal," "active" and "passive," "minority" and "majority." Though long taken for granted as given, mechanical reflections of a relatively unchanging biology or "nature," all these terms and concepts turn out to be historically particular constructions, signifying historically changing forms of human feeling, activity, and relationship. In the documents it is possible to observe one term and concept emerging, another receding, a history suggesting the nonexistence of any absolute erotic.

In recent years, it has become common for those few historians interested in studying sex and intimacy to speak of different historical "ideas" about and "attitudes" toward "homosexuality," as well as the historical development of a "homosexual," "lesbian," or "gay consciousness," "identity," and prescriptive social "role."[22] Most contemporary researchers in the history of sex now probably agree that attitudes toward, subjective responses to, and the objective conditions of "lesbians" and "male homosexuals" are changing, as are their "identities," "self-consciousness," and "role." The same historians, however, have spoken of "homosexual behavior" as universal.[23] As allegedly universal, this "homosexual behavior" was the same, for example, in the American colonies in the 1680s as it is in Greenwich Village in the 1980s. I don't think so.

It is only the most one-dimensional, mechanical "behaviorism" that suggests that that act of male with male called "sodomy" in the early colonies was identical to that behavior of males called "homosexual" in the 1980s. It is only the most vulgar technological determinism of sexual organs that suggests their "contact" sums up that complex of intimate acts, behaviors, feelings, and relationships now called "lesbian" and "gay." It is, similarly, only the most foolish pseudoscience that refers to mouse behavior as "homosexual" or "heterosexual" depending on the sex-biology of mice humping partners.

But why all this stress, finally, on words and concepts? Are not these ultimately surface phenomena, our real object of interest being the relations, feelings, and acts of persons located in a specific time and social place, part of a particular social mode of pleasure, procreation, and production, a particular structure of action and power? Are we not, for example, less interested, finally, in the word and concept "homosexual," than in that power structure which allowed a group of medical entrepreneurs to define and affect the lives of a group called "homosexuals"?

I have stressed words and concepts here because they intervene between us and our perception of the specific historical qualities of past relations, feelings, acts, persons, and societies. Only, I think, by being more conscious of the historical specificity of the terms we use, and ideas that constitute our tools of thought, will we be able to perceive more clearly those peculiar temporal, transitory qualities of phenomena, that precise period quality, that has differentiated one historical form of eroticism and intimacy from another.

A temporal view, showing us that the terms and concepts defining us are historical inventions, the way we love socially constructed, can help us make the final intellectual break with psychiatrists, psychologists, and other "scientific" and professional "experts," authorities still often looked to for legitimation and respectability. (I would not, incidentally, replace heterosexual professionals by their gay and lesbian counterparts, or replace medical and psychological experts by historians.) An historical view throws us back on ourselves, as the definers of ourselves, responsible actors within a particular society and time. Our history suggests that the way we lust is not a "scientific" matter, and so has no scientific "answer." Our socially structured mode of loving is a matter of feeling, of value judgment, of moral choices. And that, finally, is up to us. Our historians, sociologists, anthropologists, and, yes, even our psychologists, may help us clarify our social situation and possibilities. But no expert can tell us how best to live.

Who we love, and how we love them, is a matter of aesthetics. The fact that we may employ particular bodily organs of lust as means of expression no more makes our intimacies a concern of medicine men or women than does the fact that we use our ears to listen to music, our eyes to enjoy a painting makes doctors experts on those arts. The physiology of art and music loving, like the biology of human loving, their chromosomal, gonadal, hormonal, and anatomical components, however much may ever be discovered about them, will never tell us what music or paintings we should enjoy, what persons to love, or how we should use our ears, eyes, minds, or other bodily parts in the practice of loving. Unfortunately for those who wish for biology or nature to stand behind and justify their own behavior and feelings, there exists an essential break between the world of biology and the world of human judgments and emotions, such that we human beings are forever left alone here, together to conceive and give birth to our own various social and historical modes of pleasure.

Thinking more clearly about sex and intimacy as historical can help us all free ourselves from those old biological modes of thought which assert that eroticism and other human relationships are given and relatively unchangeable. The history of eroticism and intimacy can be radicalizing, if it helps us see that "lesbian" and "gay," "homosexual" and "heterosexual," are not determined by anyone's genes, chromosomes, hormones, clitorises, penises, or other physical structures, apertures, instruments, or juices, but refer to relations, feelings, acts, and persons always in the process of becoming, within a particular historical context. If the "lesbian," "gay," "homosexual," and "heterosexual" are not given biologically, but constructed historically, we can together work to reconstruct ourselves and our society in radically new, more satisfying forms. Viewed historically, "lesbian" and "gay," "homosexual" and "heterosexual," are ways of loving which we together make, and can struggle to remake, according to our changing needs.

# PART I
# Early Colonial Exploration, Agriculture, and Commerce: The Age of Sodomitical Sin, 1607–1740

# Introduction

## *Native Americans*

After their first look at the New World, Spanish and French military men, missionaries, and surveyors of the earliest period of American exploration often brought back astonished reports. Among the native population were males who dressed and worked as women, and who participated in "sodomy" with other men, the latter of apparently unremarkable appearance and demeanor.*[1]

Spanish and French accounts dating from the early 1500s refer to cross-dressing, cross-working, and same-sex erotic activities among Native Americans, in particular the Indians of Florida and Illinois. During this period, representatives of Spain and France traveled to these areas of proprietary interest, propelled by acquisitive desire and reforming zeal, the eager agents of imperial states and proselytizing churches. As military and spiritual servants of colonial powers, these Europeans arrived on the American continent with the aim of converting the heathen, possessing their land, its rumored metals and animal pelts—motives scarcely calculated to make these foreigners empathetic, accurate observers of the natives' sexual behavior and emotional lives. But these early reports, vague and ambiguous as they are, do suggest the existence of institutionalized "sodomy" (the Europeans' name for it), and several other forms of male-male intimacy, among the natives of what are now Florida, Illinois, California, and Louisiana.

The greatest number and most striking of these reports refer to males whom the Spaniards and French called, variously, *amarionados, bardaches, éffeminés, hermaphrodites,* and *mariones.* These terms referred, it seems, not to males of anomalous physiology, but to those who lived as females, persons now usually described as "homosexual transvestites"—although it is not clear to what extent cross-dressing and cross-working existed apart from, or in association with, same-sex erotic activity. Sometimes educated from youth to adopt the work and dress customary for females, these males also sometimes adopted women's customary sexual role with other men.

*This analysis of Native American cultures as documented in mostly Spanish and French reports, from the 1500s to 1740, is based on a careful reexamination of the original texts quoted or cited in *GAH*, pp. 281–334, 610–19. These sources are listed in the index to *Gay American History*.

The French and Spanish observers' emphasis upon such "effeminate" cross-dressing, cross-working males should not blind us to the evidence of other, less immediately visible participants in male-male sexual and emotional relationships. For example, the numerous reports of "effeminate" males say almost nothing about those males with whom the "effeminates" were alleged to have sex, leaving the distinct impression that such men were quite unremarkable, even typical native males. Lafitau's report of 1724 referred to "special friendships" among native men, institutionalized relationships, deeply loving, committed, and lifelong, whose sexual component, if any, was not specified, and remains unclear. Some reports suggest the existence of sexual relationships between cross-dressing "boys" and conventional, adult males. Liette's report of 1702 suggests that cross-dressing, sodomy-practicing Illinois males had sexual relationships with females as well as males (as did the partners of the cross-dressers). Liette's exact comment is that cross-dressing Illinois males were bred from childhood to practice "sodomy" with those other males who were unable to satisfy all their passions with women. Liette added: "The women and girls who prostitute themselves to these wretches [the cross-dressers, apparently] are dissolute creatures." Liette's statement warns us not to assume any exclusiveness of erotic behavior or feeling among males in early Native American societies.

The possibility of sexual relations between Native American women is referred to directly in only one document, Pareja's *Confessional* of 1613, in which native females were asked about sexual contacts with other females.

Among the early documents of Native American same-sex erotic activity, cross-working, and cross-dressing, one reference appears to what we may call "cross-being," the belief of an individual that he or she (in this case, he) belonged to the "other" sex. Between 1678 and 1680 Hennepin observed a teen-age native boy who "dreamed that he was a girl," afterward giving "such credit" to the dream that "he believed himself to be" a female. He reportedly then "dressed as a girl" and did women's work.

The crossing of conventional sexual boundaries, not only in erotic relationships and activity, manners, and dress, but also in a person's basic sense of being, is that phenomenon which in the 1950s began to be called "transsexualism"— a phenomenon named and defined by doctors according to a medical model, as a problem requiring surgical and hormonal intervention. Here it must suffice to point out that all such sexual crossing, whether cross-working, -dressing, -feeling, or -being, is premised upon a social organization that includes a strict sexual division of activity, apparel, emotion, and character. The evidence suggests that Native American societies of the early colonial period did include such strict and institutionalized sexual divisions. However, the example cited does not suggest that a native who experienced a sense of cross-being had, in this era, to undergo any process of bodily alteration to assume his new sex-linked character, feelings, and activities. His society permitted him, apparently, to move from a sense of himself as male to a sense of himself as female, with associated role changes.

(Such a social solution to an individual's experience of a problematic cross-sexual being might be possible in our own society if the medical definition and "treatment" of "transsexualism" did not reproduce the sexist idea that certain feelings and acts are "female" or "male," and thus proper only to the inhabitants of female or male bodies.[2])

Analyzed in terms of geographic location, most of these early reports are seen to refer to natives of either the Florida or Illinois areas. A chronological summary of these reports by geographic region provides an overview of the known documents.

Some time between 1528 and 1536, Cabeza de Vaca observed Indian men of Florida who were "married" to each other, and described cross-dressing, cross-working *amarionados* (effeminate men) who "carry great burdens." Between 1562 and 1567, Laudonniere saw "hermaphrodites" who carried provisions when the Florida Indians went to war. In 1564, Le Moyne also observed that in Florida "hermaphrodites" were common; these, he said, worked hard and were "considered odious" by their fellow Indians. Spanish reports of the murder, in Florida, in 1566, of Guillermo, a Frenchman accused of being a "sodomite," also indicated, in passing, that Guillermo lived with a local Indian, who loved the Frenchman "very much"—suggesting the possible existence of an early interracial affectional relationship between men. About 1609, Torquemada wrote of *mariones* (effeminate men) among the natives of Florida, who cross-dressed, cross-worked, and married other men. In 1613, Pareja, a missionary with the Florida Indians, posed confessional questions about "sodomy" between men, between boys, and about sex acts between women. In the late 1600s, Coreal explored North America, later writing that, among the Florida Indians, the men were much inclined to sodomy, that effeminate boys also "abandon themselves" to it, did women's work, performed various servile functions, and were held in great contempt. Coreal thought these effeminate boys were confused by other observers with hermaphrodites.

Another group of early Spanish and French reports referred to the Indians of the Illinois area. Between 1673 and 1677, Marquette was mystified by cross-dressing Illinois men who "do everything that the women do," who played important political and ceremonial roles, and who "pass for Manitous, . . . or persons of Consequence." About 1678, in the Mississippi Valley area, Hennepin observed the teen-age boy (earlier cited) who dreamed that he was a girl, then dressed and worked as a woman. Hennepin also noted that "Hermaphrodites" were common, and that Indian men, guilty of "Sodomy," kept boys dressed as women for this activity. About 1680, Membré observed that "Hermaphrodites are numerous" among the Illinois, and mentioned cross-working Indian boys dressed as women, used for "infamous purposes." In the late 1600s, Lahonton traveled in North America, his report describing two groups of Illinois Indians: "Bachelors" and "Hermaphrodites," each group manifesting different characteristic behaviors. Lahonton also reported that the Illinois and other Indians who lived near the

Mississippi were all "strangely given to Sodomy." In 1687, Barcia casually mentioned a "hermaphrodite" traveling on the Mississippi with La Salle's party. In
1697, a report attributed to Tonti spoke of the Illinois and described cross-
dressing, cross-working boys, looked upon by the natives with contempt. These
boys were apparently the sexual objects of other males—a vice said to be outlawed by the natives, even though apparently indulged in. The report added that
"Hermaphrodites" were "common" among the Indians. In 1699, St. Cosme
reported seeing an Illinois Indian, "one of those wretches who from their youth
dress as girls and pander to the shameful of all vices." And in 1702, after spending
four years in the area now known as Chicago, Liette reported that there "sodomy
prevails," with males being "bred for this purpose" from childhood.

The cross-dressing, cross-working, and same-sex erotic activity reported by
Spaniards and Frenchmen was spoken of by them as "sinful," "abominable,"
"beastly," "dissolute," "infamous," "lewd," "loathsome," "shameful," and "unnatural." These observers unabashedly judged Native American practices according to the tenets of Christian morality. The Europeans' reports thus clearly reveal
at least as much about Spanish and French values as about Native American
customs. In these reports it is, in fact, often difficult to separate the European
observers' judgments from the evaluations ascribed to the Indians themselves, so
that the actual status and character of "sodomy" within native groups remains
ambiguous.

On the one hand, Marquette, in 1673, said that cross-dressing Illinois Indians performed important religious functions and "pass for . . . persons of Consequence." On the other hand, the report of 1697, attributed to Tonti, said that
cross-dressing, cross-working Illinois boys were looked upon by their fellow
natives with contempt. It is impossible to know from such reports whether Native
American or European values were reflected in Marquette's contradictory statement that cross-dressing males "glory in demeaning themselves." Similarly difficult to interpret is Lafitau's comment, in 1724, that Indian males who did
women's work were "honored by debasing themselves."

The known reports suggest the existence, at this time, among the Indians
of Florida and Illinois, of a definite sexual division of work and dress. Cross-
working and cross-dressing were often, though not always, associated with same-
sex erotic activity. The sources examined do not make clear whether the reported
sexual division of work and dress implied a parallel sexual division of power and
status. These early native cultures might have included a strict sexual division of
activity and dress, but not an unequal sexual division of power. Sexual distinctions in activity, power, and status exist in complex interrelation.

It is also difficult to be sure why almost all the presently known reports of
this period are by Spanish and French authors. Is our present knowledge biased
in favor of reports by those nations' writers? Or were early Spanish and French
observers engaged in some unique relationship with the American natives which

allowed these Europeans, in particular, intimate insights into native sexual life? Were those nations particularly "sodomy" conscious, or especially sensitive to sex role nonconformity? Or were sodomitical customs and sexual crossing especially prevalent among the natives of Florida and Illinois, those with whom the French and Spaniards came in contact? Perhaps those nation's observers, as Catholics, had a special interest in native "morality" and sexual practices. Perhaps the Spaniards and French, more interested in trade with the natives than in permanent settlement, found it expedient to be especially observant of native ways; perhaps such trade involved more intimate interaction with the natives than was customary for the early English and Dutch.

But were there really no sodomitical customs at this time among the natives in the areas of the English colonies, southern, middle, and northern? Or was the early relationship of English settlers and Native Americans so fraught with conflict that the English never got to know much about those whom they were displacing and exterminating? Or does the present lack of such reports for the areas of early English settlement reflect, alternately, a selective blindness in the vision of English observers, an unwillingness to write about what they felt to be unspeakably sinful practices? Perhaps future research will tell.

Spanish debates about South and Central American natives are suggestive for our understanding of their attitudes toward the inhabitants of North America. Spanish allegations concerning "irrational" native practices (sodomy, bestiality, incest, human sacrifice, cannibalism, drug-taking) were intimately connected with that country's colonialism. Spanish debates about native customs and the "rationality" of those conquered were closely tied to debates about that ideology justifying the Spanish Conquest. If the American natives were essentially "irrational," some argued that Spaniards had the right to the natives' land, property, and even persons. Others argued that if the American natives were "irrational," they were unfit to receive that Christian faith which justified the Spaniards' mission to America. The "rationality" of Native Americans was thus an important question for early apologists of Spanish imperialism.[3]

In 1526 and 1535, the Spanish historian and civil servant Fernandez de Oviedo published works attacking the natives of South America, alleging that sodomy was widespread among them. Oviedo's attack may have led Bishop Bartolome de Las Casas to begin his own famous defense of the South American Indians, a defense that dismissed charges of native vices, specifically sodomy. Published in 1552, Las Casas's first work also accused Spanish colonizers of great cruelties.[4]

Those Spaniards who continued to report the "unholy" practices of the North American natives did so in connection with their own imperial vision, in the service of their nation's colonial schemes. Their reports were well designed to buttress colonial policy. Yet the quantity of seemingly informed reports of sodomy and cross-dressing make it unlikely such accounts were a figment of the imperial imagination, the Old World proprietor's desire to proclaim publicly the very worst, most scandalous stories about the New World's "barbarians" in order to justify their colonization.

The eradication of sodomy and other indigenous Native American customs shocking to the Christian conscience was one early aspect of the Spanish and French mission in America. In 1613, the Confessional by Franciscan missionary Pareja was intended to detect and suppress sex between native women and between native men. In 1724, Jesuit missionary Lafitau, discussing "special friendships" among native men, said that at "one of our missions" the Fathers "suppressed attachments of this kind on account of the abuses that they feared would result from them." These Fathers worried, apparently, that intense friendship might lead to sodomy. Whether or not such special friendships actually involved sexual relations, the Jesuits, suspecting the worst, took steps to eradicate such intimacies.

Lafitau's comment is the only one of this period to refer directly to clerical "suppression" of North American native customs because of their suspected kinship with sodomy. Yet it seems reasonable to speculate that the elimination of native sodomy, cross-dressing, and cross-working was early a common part of the Europeans' conversion mission, that genocidal enterprise by which white men in the employ of church and state systematically forced their own "civilization" upon the original inhabitants of America, exterminating them in the name of Christian morality and the rights of empire.

In the 1980s it is possible to begin to separate the descriptive aspects of the early Spanish and French reports from the values that informed them, and the imperial aim that motivated them. If we reject the negative evaluation of sodomy held by both the natives' European defenders and their colonialist castigators, we can admit the natives' indigenous sexual customs without thereby condemning them.

The content of these early reports will remain obscure until much more empirical research and analytical effort is devoted to the subject of early Native American sexuality and intimacy, enabling us to view the customs these documents describe within the whole contemporary structure of Indian tribal life. The Europeans' observations need also to be studied in the context of their own societies and values.

The early European colonizers spoke of a Native American "hermaphrodite" and "bardache," analogizing those natives to the "sodomitical" and to current European sexual categories. Modern European-Americans referred to a Native American who was "transvestite," "homosexual," "gay," or "lesbian," thus analogizing such natives to their own culture, time, and sexual world view. But all such translations of one society's customs into the terms of another—all such analogies across cultures and time—may distort more than clarify. To understand Native American and each society's sexual customs in their own context and time, we need to invent new tools of speech and thought.[5]

### *The Southern, Middle, and New England Colonies: Sources*

What we know now about sodomy and other acts in the early English and Dutch colonies is based on several kinds of documents: legal case records, the texts of statutes, commentaries on law and legal cases, sermons on Sodom and sodomy, and in one instance a diary.

The legal reports of early colonial prosecutions for sodomy and other acts are among the most revealing extant documents. Unlike the texts of sodomy statutes, reports of charges, prosecutions, verdicts, and punishments record not only attitudes, but the treatment legally accorded those accused. For example, the discovery of the extensive record of the testimony in the sodomy trial of Nicholas Sension, in Connecticut, in 1674, the transcription and publication here of these manuscripts, provides rare, revealing, and relatively detailed evidence of the response to a man whose sodomitical attempts spanned more than thirty years.

Such trial records help us distinguish between actual prosecutions and the formal, legally enacted prescriptions for punishment, a distinction especially revealing in the case of adultery. Though this crime, like sodomy, was legally declared capital, it was hardly ever actually punished by execution (though it was often charged, and was, no doubt, much more common than sodomy).[6] By themselves, the statutory death penalties for sodomy and a number of other crimes suggest that early legislators considered these acts of equal moral gravity and social consequence. But the selective prosecution of these capital crimes documents practical distinctions in the evaluation of their danger.

The records now known document almost twenty legal cases involving charges of "sodomy" or other erotic acts between men or between women, in the period from 1607 to 1740 in the New England, Middle, and Southern colonies.[7] There is good evidence of four men being executed for "sodomy" in that era, in those colonies, and two or three others may have been executed for the crime in these years. (One more male is now known to have been executed extra-legally in 1566, in Spanish-held Florida, after being called a "sodomite."[8])

A second major type of evidence for this era are the legal statutes. The sodomy laws of the English colonies reveal how the crime was spoken of, and what punishments were officially mandated. These statute texts, a form of prescriptive literature, document the terms, concepts, and judgments then referring to sodomy; they do not reveal how often the penalties were actually carried out. And they do not usually reveal exactly what acts were defined as "sodomy." Just what acts the colonists called "sodomy," and prosecuted as such, is an important question to which I shall return.

The early colonial laws presented in this volume include all the major statutes of this period referring to what was then variously called "sodomy," "buggery," and "man lying with man." The usual absence of any statutory penalty for erotic activity between females is a silence that, upon analysis, reveals a universe—a legal world defined by some powerful males in such a way that female-female eroticism did not exist. The logic behind that exclusion, and the social structure behind that logic, will be explored.

This survey of sodomy statutes covers the years from the settlement of Jamestown, Virginia, in 1607, to 1740. The later abolition of the death penalty for the crime is also discussed. The chronological presentation of statute texts emphasizes overall historical trends, rather than developments within each colony or geographical region. Some important changes over time in the content of the sodomy laws may be noted: the gradual deletion from statute texts of citations to specific biblical passages, an alteration in which the original, explicit religious justification for the penalty was replaced by an implicit secular judgment. Also evident is a trend toward qualifying whom the sodomy laws were to punish. Clauses exempting persons under a specific age, and persons forced, were gradually added to some sodomy laws, qualifying the absolute, biblically inspired death penalty for both parties to sodomy.

The original texts of the sodomy statutes are reprinted, along with the whole list of crimes receiving the same capital penalty. The sodomy statute of each colony can thus be considered in relation to other, equally penalized acts. Only in this broad context can we begin to understand by what logic, and with what social purpose, early colonial lawmakers placed sodomy among the dozen or so crimes penalized by death.

Early colonial sodomy laws are included here because they are among the major existing sources for this era. But these law texts make difficult reading; of all the documents in this volume these early statutes most stubbornly withhold their implications from a modern reader. Because their language is difficult, and because the legislators who enacted them are foreign to us, their world remote, these statutes and other of this era's texts required the relatively extensive analysis presented here. This analysis is intended to clarify the historically particular implications of the terms referring to sodomy, the temporally specific character of the concepts, and the historically relative form of this crime itself in the early American colonies.

Another major kind of evidence for the early English colonies is here collectively called "commentary"; this includes comment on laws and legal cases, and sermons referring to Sodom's various sins. These texts include the legal-theological commentaries of three New England ministers (on a case of 1641–42), the religious commentary of the Reverend Thomas Shepard (1641), the historical commentary of the governor of the Plymouth Colony, William Bradford (about events of 1642), the legal commentary of the influential English jurist, Edward Coke (1644), and the theological exhortations of the Reverends Samuel Danforth (1674) and Cotton Mather (1701).

A close look at all the English and Dutch sources now available suggests some basic patterns in the terms, ideas, feelings, acts, relationships, persons, and in the social organization of sex specific to the early colonies. Since most of the evidence discovered, and the analysis, refers to New England, not to the southern or middle colonies, further studies of those colonies are needed and will, no doubt, modify some of my conclusions.

### Terms, Concepts, Sodomy, Society, and Time

The language and ideas of the early English colonists provide clues to their responses to licit and illicit intercourse. Analyzing the early colonists' terms and concepts provides a way into their heads, hearts, and lives—a way out of our own time-bound minds. The colonists' language and modes of thought are analyzed here as tools with which they named, organized, and produced their social world. Their words and ideas are seen, not simply as reflections of a particular social-historical structure, but as material and conceptual means by which they shaped it. Analysis reveals links between early colonial modes of speech, the thought behind that speech, and that society's organization of procreation, pleasure, and desire, of production, religious salvation, and legal control.

### Sin Against the "Family and Posterity": Crime Against the State

A number of early colonial documents speak of sodomy as a sin specifically against marriage, the family, and procreation. In 1642, the Reverend John Rayner of Plymouth declared that sodomy should be punished by death even though it might not involve quite the same "degree of sinning against the family and posterity" as some other "capital sins of uncleanness" (see 1641–42, Mass. Bay). As a sin against the "family and posterity," sodomy was quite serious enough to warrant death. Describing the execution of William Plaine in the New Haven Colony in 1646, John Winthrop explained that Plaine, though "a married man," was guilty of sodomy in England, as well as of inciting the youth of Guilford, Connecticut, to "masturbations." Plaine's crime was "dreadful" because it "tended to the frustrating of the ordinance of marriage and the hindering the generation of mankind." In 1674, the Reverend Danforth condemned sodomy and other carnal transgressions as violations of the marriage ordinance, an institution decreed by God to quench "boiling and burning lusts."

As a sin against marriage and posterity, sodomy, in the early colonies, violated the legally established and strictly enforced social organization of procreation and family life—institutions with significantly different social functions, meanings, value, and legal status than they have in America in the 1980s. Understanding that marriage, family, and procreation were the major productive institutions of early colonial society, we can see why sodomy, considered a threat to those institutions, was made a mortal sin and capital crime, and why that death penalty was enforced.

As a sin against marriage and the family, sodomy was also a sin against the household. The households of married couples were often the legally established places of residence for all persons, providing living space for both single and married. At least three New England colonies, Massachusetts Bay, Plymouth, and Connecticut, passed laws requiring unmarried people to live in "well ordered" families, as servants or boarders. But even before such laws were passed, town officials acted to discourage persons from living outside the household of a married couple.

In 1636–37, Connecticut magistrates provided that "no young man" who was unmarried, had no servants, and held no public office, "shall keep house by himself, without the consent of the Town where he lives."[9] (The wording suggests a class distinction: A single man with a servant, or holding office, probably a citizen of more than average property, might apparently obtain permission to form his own household.)

In 1639, the Plymouth Colony court prosecuted Anthony Bessie for "living alone disorderly," and "for taking in an inmate" (a male, undoubtedly) without permission—indicating the difficulties facing men who might wish to establish a living arrangement outside the household of a married couple.[10]

In 1639, Plymouth magistrates did license two unmarried men, John Carew and Edmund Weston, to live together and cooperate "in working and planting." But a qualification is revealing: Carew was allowed "to be for himself upon the continuance of the good report of his carriage & demeanor. . . ."[11]

In 1653, a Plymouth court ordered Teage Joanes, Richard Berry, and others "to part their uncivil living together." (Three years earlier, Joanes and Berry had been mentioned in this court's records when Berry had lodged, and later withdrawn, a "sodomy" charge against Joanes; see 1649, Oct. 29.)

In early Plymouth, although a good deal of suspicion was attached to households composed of unmarried men, such households were sometimes established. But in 1669, Plymouth law compelled unmarried persons to live in the household of a married couple. Legislators then cited the "grave Inconvenience [which] hath arisen by single persons . . . being for themselves," and not living in "well Governed families." The lawmakers declared: "No single person [shall] be suffered to live of himself," or in any family not approved by the Selectmen of the town.[12]

In 1672, the Essex County, Massachusetts, court was "informed that John Littleale of Haverhill" was living "in a house by himself, contrary to the law of the country, whereby he is subject to much sin and iniquity, which ordinarily are the companions and consequences of a solitary life." Littleale was ordered to "settle himself in some orderly family in the town."[13]

The household of a married couple not only provided the approved abode for all, but this living arrangement was consciously intended as a means of supervising and controlling behavior. The legal enforcement of familial living suggests the difficulties facing two persons of the same sex who might have wished to set up a household. Two men were certainly discouraged from living together; two women doing so was even more unfeasible.

As a sin against the family household, sodomy was also a sin against the major unit of production. As historian John Demos summed it up in his study of the Plymouth Colony, the colonial family was "an absolutely central agency of economic production and exchange." Each family household served as the primary productive unit, and as school, place of vocational and religious training, house of correction, and welfare institution.[14] As a threat to the family and sin against production, sodomy was subversive to the economy.

As a sin against marriage and posterity, sodomy was also a sin against the legally established and enforced social organization of procreation. Sodomy, and other forms of non-procreative sex, were seen as fundamental threats to the reproduction and increase of the colonial population, in particular, the reproduction of badly needed new laborers. In this primitive economy, the manufacture of offspring was a major, essential branch of production, analogous to farming, which, with hunting, fishing, and trading, were the dominant kinds of work.

Procreation was at this time informed by an agricultural metaphor: Sperm was "seed," a female was a "ripe" or "unripe vessel." Procreative activity was thought of as a kind of "planting," and children as a valuable crop of future producers, a particularly useful and perishable "fruit." A man's seed was spoken of as if it were scarce, limited, and precious, like grain; for a man to "spill," "spend," or "waste" his seed in any form of non-reproductive sex was, in this necessarily frugal economy, analogous to wasting or destroying the grain from which new crops would grow and on which survival depended.[15] In this agricultural economy, a "husband" was not only the partner of a wife, but also usually a "husbandman" or farmer, as well as one who husbanded his resources, spermatic as well as productive. A recent study indicates that in the colonies, human sexual activity resulting in conception (as measured by the recorded months of birth) followed an agricultural cycle.[16] The "planting" of the early settlements on the shores of America involved the implanting of sperm, the fertilization of females, and the procreation of new planters, as much as it did the planting of crops.

This was a period of extreme labor scarcity and of primitive technology; new producers were valued for their labor, labor power, and as a basic means of production. The manufacture of a large number of offspring was encouraged to supply the labor-intensive economy, and the colonial American birth rate was soon higher than any in Europe. The high birth rate of the early American colonists is often mentioned by historians.[17] But this fecundity is not often linked to a specific social-historical mode of procreation, a particular, institutional organization of intensive baby-making, a social system with strict negative sanctions against non-procreative sex. Maximized procreation in the early colonies was connected closely with survival—in a way that baby production is not in present-day America.

That the early Puritans linked non-procreative and non-productive acts seems clear. What is not so clear is the character of that conceptual connection. Did the Puritans think that the amount of male "seed" was so physically limited that its expenditure in a non-procreative act would mean an inadequate supply for procreative purposes and a decrease in the birth rate? Did their sodomy taboo reflect a belief in a physical conflict between the use of sperm for procreation or for pleasure?

Because the early colonists valued maximum procreation, it would follow that they strongly devalued any form of birth limitation. At the same time, a pressure for non-procreative intercourse may have originated with colonial women. Although the death of women in childbirth was lower in the early colonies than in Europe, this cause of female demise was still the major reason for the greater longevity of colonial men. Women's desire for life then conflicted with their desire to create life.[18]

In this nonindustrial, agricultural society, male-female anal intercourse may have been one form of limiting births, and the sodomy taboo as much a ban on male-female anal intercourse as on male-male acts. One law, written by John Cotton and enacted by New Haven legislators in 1656, did explicitly prohibit "abusing the contrary part of a grown woman"—in a provision against men lying with men, women changing the "natural use" and other forms of "going after strange flesh." While that reference to male-female anal intercourse indicates the act was known, the uniqueness of the reference prevents any generalization. The exact nature of the perceived conflict between maximized procreation and sodomy remains to be discovered. But it does seem that the capital punishment of sodomy was linked to a taboo against any form of birth limitation.

The legally enforced institutions of marriage and family were also the means by which male owners of private property in land, houses, implements, and agricultural product transferred this property to their children.[19] Sodomy, as an act against marriage and the family, was also an act against the system of property inheritance. The function of colonial marriage and family as a means of property transfer is strikingly different from the function of these institutions in present-day America. Now, if anything is passed from parents to children, it is usually property in consumption goods and money, not in the basic means of work. In the early colonies, that inheritance passed from fathers to their children was usually land, the major means of economic production necessary for family existence. Sodomy, as a sin against family and marriage, was a sin against the basic institution of private property.

In the 1980s, it may be difficult to understand why sodomy was once thought of as so destructive as to be penalized by death; in the 1980s, even religious fundamentalists do not usually believe "homosexuality" is a crime of such magnitude as to actually merit execution. In the United States now, when pressing problems are inflation, unemployment, boring work, inequality and dissatisfaction of the races, sexes, and sexual orientations, alienation among family members, discontent among young and old, inadequate and too expensive health care, when the gratification of consumer goods consumption is offered as a major consolation, and the pleasures of the senses are objects of marketing, "homosexuality" hardly seems to most people to be among the dozen or so most socially destructive acts.

In contrast, in the early colonies, "sodomy" was thought of as a major crime against the state. This, I argue, was because sodomy was seen as a fundamental threat to early colonial marriage, family, household, property, and procreation. Why sodomy was seen as such a threat is further clarified by the following considerations.

### Sinful Sodomy

The New England colonies were founded by English men and women who, reacting against increasing secularization, sought theological purity in biblical text; their laws, therefore, spoke of "sodomy" while those of the southern colonists spoke of "buggery" (the secular word for the crime). The New England colonies (Massachusetts Bay, Plymouth, Connecticut, New Haven, Rhode Island, and New Hampshire) were all established as secular settlements, theologically distinct from Old England, and each passed its own laws. While Puritan colonists broke with the terminology of the English "buggery" statute, New Englanders did maintain the death penalty for the crime, in conformity with English statute, though citing biblical authority. The language and provisions of the early Puritan sodomy laws, unlike the English law, were borrowed directly from the Bible; early New England laws often cited particular biblical passages. The Old Testament was the most common authority cited, though the laws of Rhode Island and New Haven cited New Testament passages. Though the early Puritans stressed the legal separation of religious and civil authorities by prohibiting ministers from holding legislative or judicial office, the wording of Puritan sodomy laws reflected the actual close association between churchmen and statesmen. The first New England sodomy laws clearly expressed a substantial link between religious and civil rulers. The sodomy laws of the Middle colonies (New York, New Jersey, Pennsylvania, and Delaware) were, with a few exceptions, generally modeled on the laws of New England.

The Southern colonies (Virginia, Maryland, North and South Carolina, and Georgia), intended by their English founders as profitable business investments, maintained a definite continuity with the legal tradition of the home country. And so the English "buggery" statute was usually either assumed to be in effect or was actually cited in legislation as in force. The English statute thus also became the southern colonists' statute. The southern colonists' adoption of the English "buggery" law reflected their founders' conception of their settlements as extensions and outposts of the British empire, rather than as new societies with their own theologically derived rules of conduct. When the English buggery law became operative in the southern colonies, the history of that statute became relevant to the development of American sodomy law.

## *"Buggery" in England*

The first English civil statute to criminalize "buggery" drew on French law and English popular use of the word "buggery" for the act clerics usually called "sodomy." The English word "buggery" derived from the French words *bougre* and *bougrerie,* referring, respectively, to heretics and heresy and, it seems, usurers and usury. In the 1200s, it was said the French then called usurers *bougres.*[20]

English popular sexual folklore also associated sodomy with usury and, specifically, with Italians from Lombardy. As early as 1376, the English Parliament, expressing old complaints of London traders against these Italians, requested that

> all the Lombards who practice no profession than that of Moneychanger quit this land as soon as possible; given that wicked Usury and all underhanded strategems are devised and maintained by them. . . . [These Lombard moneychangers] are of no use except to do evil: given that some among them who are considered Lombards are Jews, Saracens [Moslems], and private Spies; and have lately practiced in this land a very horrible vice which should not be named. By which the Kingdom cannot fail shortly to be destroyed, if stiff punishment be not speedily ordained for it. . . .[21]

That early association between Lombards and unnameable "vice" became part of English sexual folklore; it was repeated 157 years later in the English "buggery" law of 1533.

That English law was the first civil statute of the country to make a secular crime of an act which, up to then, had been only an infraction of church law. The "buggery" law of 1533 was passed as one legal step in that Reformation by which Henry VIII, as head of the English state, expropriated the Roman Catholic Church's large landholdings, and the Italian Church's monopoly of the means of moral judgment and spiritual salvation.

In 1529, Henry, with the Crown's economic needs in mind, was already contemplating the expropriation of the Roman Catholic Church's monasteries in England. In 1531, he declared himself the head of the Catholic Church in England, an act of religious devotion ensuring that large revenues no longer needed to be paid to the Roman pope. The "buggery" law of 1533 was one of the first in a series of Reformation acts cutting the English Church off from the Italian. Three years later, Henry VIII's investigator's accused some of the Catholic monasteries in England of being centers of "manifest sin, vicious carnal, and abominable living." Henry used these charges to convince Parliament to allow him to actually expropriate these monasteries. Part of the church land confiscated was later redistributed to a new class of landowners and commercial farmers, who thus owed title to their property, and their allegiance to the king.[22]

Until 1533 in England, "sodomy" was a sin, judged and punished by ecclesiastical authorities. Only in 1533 did "buggery" become a crime, to be punished by civil courts—by death and loss of property, with, significantly, no exception made for "clergy."

The first English "buggery" law stated that as there was no adequately severe punishment provided in civil statute "for the detestable and abominable Vice of Buggery committed with mankind or beast," it might therefore please the king, his spiritual and temporal Lords, and the Parliamentary Commons, to make the offense a "felony"—a crime graver than a "misdemeanor." Offenders under the new law were to suffer death and such "losses and penalties of their goods, chattels, debts, lands, tenements," and other transferable property, as felons were accustomed to under common law. The convicted party was to suffer the dispossession of estate and death, with no appeal to that ritual called "benefit of clergy," by which persons in holy orders were exempted from the usual penalties of the criminal law, and were subjected to less harsh church proceedings.[23]

Henry VIII's "buggery" law thus originated in the political and economic struggles of church and state. The terminological change in England from "sodomy" as sin to "buggery" as crime expressed an increasing secularization of power and control. The word "sodomy" evoked Sodom and Gomorrah, the Bible, theology, and God's earthly representatives. "Buggery" was a term adopted by the Crown from the language of the people, a popular, secular word, distinguished from "sodomy," the word of God as retailed by the clergy. The terminological change from "sodomy" to "buggery" thus expressed a change in the balance of political and economic power between church and state. The conceptual change from sin to sin-crime similarly expressed, in the realm of ideas, a change in the property relations of Roman pope and English king.

In all the early American colonies, as in England, the sin of sodomy was made one of the highest crimes, penalized by death. The Massachusetts Bay code (see 1641, Nov.) for example, provided death for heresy, witchcraft, blasphemy, three varieties of murder, bestiality, man lying with man as with a woman, adultery, male "carnal copulation" with a "woman-child" under ten years, male rape of a married or engaged female, male rape of a single female over ten, the stealing of a servant, false witness with intent to take a life, and treason. Other laws provided death for such crimes as idolatry, kidnapping, arson, robbery, and children over sixteen cursing, smiting, or rebelling against their parents. The unique New Haven law of 1656 provided death for male-female anal intercourse, incitement to masturbation, and undefined acts of women "against nature."

The moral-theological-legal concept of sodomy as a sin-crime was openly expressed in early colonial laws in the frequent use of evaluative terms, usually of biblical origin. A "detestable and abominable Vice" was the phrase characterizing "buggery" in the English law operative in the southern colonies. Sodomy was explicitly called an "unnatural sin" in the Pennsylvania law of 1683; sodomy was among the "Offenses against God" in the East New Jersey law of the same year. Early colonial statutes overtly expressed religious judgments made covert in the laws of later, ostensibly secular periods. This early expression in civil law of religious morality, and the universal death penalty for sodomy operative in all the colonies, and several times carried out, reflected clerics' monopoly of other-world connections, their this-world power. But the ministers' power was not unlimited.

In practice, colonial ministers defined sodomy more broadly than colonial magistrates; the ministers included a greater variety of acts under the nomenclature of "sodomy." And the ministers' more inclusive definition was not enacted into law by the magistrates. A conflict over the definition of sodomy existed in the early colonies between religious and civil authorities. But even the magistrates' narrower, operative definition was derived directly, often even word for word, from the Old Testament. Though ministers could not be magistrates, and the opinions of the two groups might differ, close working relations generally existed between them; churchmen were asked to help define legal categories and penalties. Men of God were the chief ideologists, religion the dominant ideology. This all-pervasive sway of God contrasts with America of the late 1800s in which medical men and "science" competed for influence with legal authorities and their ideas.

The sin of sodomy was occasionally spoken of as having the ability to "infect." Referring to an outbreak of sodomy, bestiality, adultery, and fornication in 1642, William Bradford warned that "one wicked person may infect the many." In 1677, a witness in the sodomy trial of Nicholas Sension reported being worried about Sension's attempted sodomy "infecting the rising generation." Although the word "infect" did already refer to physical disease, it also referred to a metaphorical, moral contagion, and it is not clear in the documents cited whether the term was used in one or the other (or both) senses. In any case, the idea of sodomy and other "sexual perversions" as actual diseases became the dominant concept only with the rise to power of professional physicians of the mind in the late 1800s, and the publicity given their medical definition of "homosexuality" in the 1920s and '30s.

Colonial sodomy was not a disease, and no one thought of consulting a doctor about it. (The Reverend Wigglesworth did, however, consult a doctor about an imagined venereal ailment seemingly inspired by sodomitical guilt; see 1653, February). In the early colonies, as sin and crime, sodomy might be prosecuted, charged, confessed, admitted, denied, judged, proved, punished, repented, or affirmed; it was not "treated" or "cured." As sin, sodomy was an act "committed" or not "committed," an act (and inclination) for which one was "guilty" or "not guilty," ashamed or unashamed. As sin, the act of sodomy might be taught by "bad" example, but no one thought (as did late-Victorian doctors) of distinguishing between "acquired" sodomy and "congenital." A sodomitical impulse was an inherent potential of all fallen male descendants of Eve and Adam. Only in the twentieth century would the doctors' allegedly objective and scientific concept of "homosexuality" hide the negative value judgment explicit in the colonial concept of sodomy as sin.

In the early colonies, sodomy included feeling as well as act. But sodomy was not essentially psychological; it was not a "psychosexual disturbance," "mental illness," "fixation of emotional development," nor the sympton of such, as "homosexuality" was perceived in the twentieth century. Colonial sodomy had no individual psychological "etiology." As sin, sodomy was said to originate in the unfortunate propensity of all human beings to follow the tempting immoral example. Since sodomitical and other lustful inclinations were universal, it was not their subjective "cause," but the objective stimulus to action that was of prime concern. "Sodomy," said Edward Coke, was "brought into" England by corrupt Italians. "Sodomy," suggested William Bradford, was brought into New England by "untoward servants." Sodomy, testified a witness at a Connecticut trial of 1677, was a "trade" which a sodomitical colonist had "taken up"—at school. Colonial sodomy, an inborn impulse and an act one learned, was like other nasty habits.

Only with the institutionalization of Enlightenment ideas after the American Revolution did the earlier, direct moral-theological condemnation of sodomy begin to give way to the legal condemnation of sodomy as "crime against nature," a "nature" alleged to determine sodomy's objective and moral character. Only in the late 1700s would the term "sodomy" be superseded by the phrase "crime against nature."* That secularization of thought in the late 1700s—the competition of a new legal philosophy of "natural rights" with the old theological morality of natural sin—reflected the relative loss of power of the clergy, the relative gain in power of lawyers. By the late 1700s, men of the bar were replacing men of the cloth as the major ideologists of a more fully developed commercial society. In the late 1700s, the institutionalizing of a new legal ideology ("constitutionalism") and a new interpretation of "natural law" ("natural rights" and the "crime against nature"), were linked to the rise of lawyers and a powerful commercial class.

Although the dominant early colonial ideology was theological, several kinds of evidence disprove the operation of a biblical or ecclesiastical determinism. A biblical death penalty does not "explain" the legal enactment of that penalty, or its enforcement. The usual failure of New England legislators to enact St. Paul's death penalty for women who changed the "natural use" is one example of the colonists' selectivity in regard to New Testament injunction. The lawmakers' inclusion in their sodomy statutes of clauses concerning force and age were also colonial emendations of the absolute Old Testament mandate of death for both men who lay with each other as they lay with women (Leviticus 20:13). The colonists' usual failure to carry out the statutory death penalty for "adultery" is another example of their failure to practice Old Testament precept. And the usual early colonial death penalty for rape also had only ambiguous biblical sanction.[24]

*See further discussion of the "crime against nature," p. 44.

## Speakable Sodomy

In 1629, Francis Higgeson referred, privately, in his journal, to "5 beastly Sodomitical boys" who had committed the "wickedness not to be named." In an historical account unpublished in his lifetime, William Bradford referred to sodomitical events of 1642 as "things fearful to name." In 1644, the English jurist Edward Coke published a legal commentary that influenced Americans. Coke referred to sodomy (or "buggery" as he usually called it) as a sin "amongst Christians not to be named," a phrase he said was used in the "usual Indictment" for the crime in England. In March 1653, the records document the prosecution of sundry New Haven "youths" for committing "much wickedness in a filthy corrupting way one with another." Their private confessions were so "filthy" they were "not fit to be made known in a public way."

But in the public discourse and legislative acts of the early American colonists, sodomy was a sin that these Christians often named. About 1642, in Massachusetts Bay, a broadside announcing the capital crimes (including "sodomy") was purportedly printed, and probably publicly posted for all to see.* The early colonists were supposed to be able to read and to understand (and were sometimes legally required to know) their settlement's list of capital crimes—and sodomy was on all those lists. A Plymouth Colony law specifically provided that children be made to understand "the Capital Laws"—and "sodomy" was among Plymouth's capital crimes.[25] During the first one hundred and fifty years of American colonial existence, this sinful activity had not just one, but three different public names: "buggery," "sodomy," and "men lying with men"; the sin of "women with women" was also occasionally publicly named. Such phrases as "unspeakable crime" or "unnameable among Christians" rarely appeared in the sodomy statutes or recorded court proceedings of the early colonies.

In this period, among these Christians, sodomy was not a secret, not unspoken, not unnamed. Sodomy, raised to capital status, was also raised to a relatively high degree of public consciousness. From almost the first years of English settlement on this continent, sodomy was publicly named as one of the major crimes against the state, one of the few infractions meriting death, one of those acts most meriting public naming. This is stressed because of our present tendency to attribute to seventeenth-century Puritans ideas and values specific to nineteenth-century Victorians—those who did make sodomy "unspeakable."

## Political Sodomy

There was no question in the early colonies that sodomy, and other forms of non-reproductive and reproductive copulation were of pressing civil concern. The

*See p. 77 for a picture of this broadside.

association of procreation with social survival made it a clear matter of political interest, legislative enactment, and judicial judgment. However, though sodomy, bestiality, rape, and adultery might often be placed next to each other on early colonial lists of capital crimes, there was usually no explicit emphasis on their carnal character; they were not called lust crimes. There was no category of legal infractions known as "sex crimes." In only one law (that of Rhode Island, 1647) were sodomy, bestiality, rape, adultery, and fornication grouped together in a legal provision "Touching Whoremongers." The early colonists believed that a pervasive lust needed to be strictly regulated; but "sexuality" was not yet isolated as a separate entity, an individual problem. Sodomy was not a "sexual" as opposed to a "social" infraction; as carnal, sodomy was a social offense, one of many.

In contrast, the mid-twentieth-century medical concept of "homosexuality" made "sexuality" essential. "Homosexuality" was "sexual" not "social"; "personal" not "political"; "private" not public"; an "individual problem," not a "social issue." Those modern medical oppositions did not inform the early colonists' concept of sodomy; they would not have understood the shock caused in 1969 by the link proclaimed in the title of Kate Millett's *Sexual Politics*. A colonial politics of lust was assumed.

## Sodom and Sodomy

In his sermon, the "Cry of Sodom," published in 1674, the Reverend Samuel Danforth drew an explicit parallel between the city of Sodom and the settlements of New England. Danforth warned New Englanders that their failure to punish by death such sins as sodomy and bestiality would bring God's vengeance on everyone. The early colonists lived with an ever-present fear that an angry God would punish their entire society for the sins of some inhabitants. All colonists were thought of as mutually dependent, not as autonomous individuals. The behavior of one affected the fate of all. Rooting out sin was a means of self-preservation, maintained William Bradford in his analysis of an outbreak, in 1642, of sodomy and other such "wickedness."

In the early colonies, the term and concept "sodomy" had connotations that they do not generally have for present-day Americans. For the colonists struggling to survive in the wilderness, the word "sodomy," no doubt, evoked the destruction of Sodom and Gomorrah, as much or more than illicit sex. For those early settlers perched precariously on the edge of a hostile continent, the term "sodomy" provoked thoughts of Sodom, that archetypal settlement destroyed for sin. Living from day to day with the threat of social dissolution, the early colonists no doubt felt a special kinship with that particular ancient city.

The early colonists found themselves at the mercy of natural, life-threatening forces which, personified as "God," seemed angry, vengeful, and punishing. The biblical Sodom and Gomorrah story likewise reflected an era of social development in which natural disasters were seen as God's punishment for human moral error. Inhabited by a vindictive God, the early Puritan universe also included an active, malicious Devil, an often evoked hell, and occasional malevolent witches. Early colonial lists of capital crimes included both sodomy and witchcraft. Only as colonial society became more secure, the survival and reproduction of the colonial labor force more assured, did sodomy gradually lose its previous, direct association with Sodom and social cataclysm.

### The Puritan Ethic, Sodomy, and Early Colonial Capitalism

Two early colonial sermons made clear connections between Puritan attitudes toward labor, idleness, the sins of Sodom, and, specifically, sodomy—between Puritan sexual morality and that work ethic congruent with a primitive period of technological development, of laborer and labor scarcity, and a system of private property in land.[26]

A sermon, in 1674, on the "sins of Sodom" by the Reverend Danforth, warned readers to "Beware of Sloth and Idleness." When "men are sluggish" in the work that God calls them to, the "Devil" sets them about his work. Don't lie in bed when you should be "in the Field," commanded Danforth, quoting two old maxims: "Laziness breeds Lewdness," and "No business, debauchery." The cleric warned that social destruction and disruption followed when the various "sins of Sodom" were not severely punished. Danforth went on to link "sodomy" (defined as "filthiness" committed by males with males or females with females) with idleness, the violation of the marriage ordinance and family life, the disobedience of children to parents, and of servants to masters.

In a classic Puritan sermon on a Christian's "Personal Calling," in 1701, Cotton Mather declared that one's worldly work kept one from idleness, and from all "the Sins of Sodom." Mather argued that an idle man, a man without a "calling" at which he spent most of his time, was "Impious towards God . . . , for he is Unrighteous towards his *Family,* towards his *Neighborhood,* towards the *Commonwealth.*" Mather linked the Puritans' high valuation of the family and socially useful work, their devaluation of idleness, and "the sins of *Sodom.*" For this Puritan, the various sins of Sodom all referred back to the one great sin of idleness; sexual sins and all the other vices of Sodom, arose from, and were subsumed under, that one grand Puritan sin, "sloth."

The Puritan work ethic informed the Puritan sex ethic. Although the early Puritans inveighed against celibacy, associated with that "popery" from which they vehemently dissented, these early Americans placed definite limits upon sexual expression, even within marriage. Sex and affection between husband and wife were not to become so important that they distracted from the couple's proper concentration upon God. Puritan laws against frivolous entertainments paralleled their laws against sex merely for pleasure. The Puritans' devaluation of play paralleled their distrust of "lust"—the danger of the unrestrained erotic was that it distracted from the full attention due one's God-given work, and God himself.

The early colonial work ethic contrasts with that early twentieth-century consumption ethic, influential in the United States by the 1920s. To spend in the early colonies was to use up scarce resources—the associations were generally negative. In contrast, in the early twentieth century, The Big Spender became one ideal of manhood, The Consumer one definition of proper womanhood. And those positive valuations of consumption were linked to a new valuation of sex as pleasure, quite apart from its procreative product. In contrast, the early colonists condemned all non-procreative seminal expenditures as non-productive.

### Natural/Unnatural; Procreative/Non-procreative

In the early colonies, the opposition between the "natural" and "unnatural" was the major polarity in whose terms sodomy was condemned. In 1636, for example, the prominent New England minister John Cotton referred to a man's carnal connection with a man, or a woman's with a woman, as "unnatural filthiness." In 1642, several colonial ministers referred to the "unnatural lusts of men with men, or woman with woman," "unnatural uncleanness," acts "against nature," and acts "against the Light of Nature." The New Haven statute of 1656 outlawed any "unnatural and shameful filthiness," providing death for any woman who changed the "natural use, into that which is against nature." A Massachusetts law of 1697 prohibited sodomy as "contrary to the very Light of Nature." That "Light" which "Nature" gave off in the early colonies was a kind of moral radiance determining the relative value of human copulations according to a procreative standard.

The "natural"/"unnatural" opposition expressed a basic distinction between procreative and non-procreative acts. But though that procreative/non-procreative opposition suggests a simple, absolute counterposing of good and bad, the matter was more complex. Procreation was an unqualified good, whereas lust in procreation was, at best, an unavoidable necessity. Even that "natural" lust experienced in procreation within marriage was not cleansed of sinfulness. Such natural, procreative lust was good only in comparison to that "unnatural" lust associated with non-procreative acts.*

Puritans emphatically condemned the Roman Church's adulation of virginity, its rule of absolute celibacy and chastity for the clergy, its denial of marriage to God's earthly ministers. Puritans praised marriage in the name of mutual aid and spiritual comfort, for its procreative results, and as a relief for lust. Marriage

---

*My reading of the documents, and my stress on the Puritans' negative valuation of erotic lust (as opposed to child production), contradicts the now generally accepted interpretations offered by Edmund Morgan, William and Mallerville Haller, and other historians responsible for the revisionist line that the Puritans were not as "puritanical" as the popular stereotype would have it. The stereotype, I think, is closer to reality than the prevailing revisionism.[27]

was a means, then, of channeling, controlling, limiting and, finally, extinguishing lust, not license to indulge it. "Chaste Marriage," continency within conjugal union, was the Puritan ideal. "Marriage is the Preservation of Chastity," said one Puritan divine. Marriage was honorable and valued, the marriage bed undefiled —if sexual intercourse was procreative in intent, the erotic indulged only in the name of offspring, and its own annihilation.[28]

According to the prevailing standard, "unnatural," non-procreative acts were, morally speaking, the worst. But even "natural," procreative acts within marriage were spoken of as sinful to the extent that they involved the arousal of lust. For early orthodox Puritans everyone was naturally "conceived in sin." The infant child of the early colonists was not the innocent, asexual angel of the Victorians. As the Reverend Shepard put it in 1641, "Every natural man and woman is born full of sin." For the early Puritans, the "natural man and woman" was corrupt, the state of nature a state of sin. "Original sin" was a "natural corruption." God sent dragons to inhabit colonist Joseph Pike's soul to bring him "nearer to the Lord, by . . . mortifying the natural and fleshly part"; taking up Christ's cross, Pike's own sinful "natural will and affections became much broken." That breaking of the "natural will" was a condition sought after and valued by Puritans.[29]

In the early Puritan colonies, "natural" and "unnatural" did not signify sin-free and sinful. Although the "natural" act of conception required colonial men, at least, to experience some lust, even this procreative lust involved sin, a sin, however, not as sinful as those "unnatural" acts and lusts having no possible procreative result.

### Sin Against God; Sin Against Nature

Although the early colonists declared sodomy "against nature," and a serious crime, they never in any of the documents I have seen termed sodomy a "crime against nature."* Sodomy was first of all a "sin against God." Only secondarily was this sin said to be "against nature" and declared a crime. Only in the Revolutionary era would sodomy be declared a "crime against nature." Only then would "nature" be spoken of as the prime determiner of moral character, with "God" relegated to the background as first, but no longer direct, active moral mover. The invention of "the crime against nature" in the late 1700s was not merely a matter of words, but of changes in world-views, and in the actual social world, changes in the relation of Americans to nature, and to each other.[30]

The early colonists thought of God's "natural," moral ordering of human relationships as hierarchical: The faithful Puritan was subordinate to God, the parishioner to minister, subject to monarch, wife to husband, female to male,

*For "crime against nature" see p. 39.

child to parent, younger to elder, single to married, student to teacher, servant to master, non-propertied to propertied. This idea of a proper, natural hierarchical order reflected and supported the actual organization of property, power, and control, the moral economy. Violations of any of the "natural," "God-given" relationships were seen as subversive to the whole hierarchy. Indulgence in copulation solely for pleasure, with no possible procreative result, was a violation of that "natural" relationship of husband and wife in which the act of child-production was valued as work essential to survival. Sodomy, as one form of non-procreative copulation, was viewed as an act against God's "natural," procreative, productive, marital, familial, religious, and civil orders.

Just as the social relationships and organization of the early colonists were hierarchical, so was their moral universe. A moral hierarchy of sins paralleled the social hierarchy of human relationships. The worst sins were those perceived as most dangerous to the colonists' continued existence; social destruction and construction constituted the standard in terms of which the early settlers judged the character of sodomy and other acts. That colonial concern with the social effect of acts contrasts with the present modern focus on "self-development" and individual "happiness" as the standard of morality. In the early colonies, those crimes punished by death included a variety of different acts whose only common denominator was their allegedly destructive effect on social reproduction.

In the colonial moral hierarchy of carnal acts, male-female procreative activity within marriage topped the list as the standard by which all other copulations were judged. Those acts which seemed least akin to proper procreativity were judged the worst. This implicit idea of a sexual-moral hierarchy was made explicit when, in 1642, the Reverend Rayner referred to sodomy and bestiality as "more" against the light of nature than some other capital crimes of uncleanness. Rayner also speculated that sodomy might not involve quite the same "degree of sinning against the family and posterity" as some other crimes, implying a moral hierarchy based on a familial, procreative standard.

### "Sodomy" or "Sodomite"; Act or Person

Not until the 1890s do American documents mention a person called "a homosexual" or "a lesbian." Not until the 1920s does "a homosexual" or "a lesbian" person become fairly common in American literature.

Though in the early colonies there was much mention of an act called "sodomy," rarely do we read in that era's documents of a person called a "sodomite," an individual named after the act. The term "Sodomites" was used in the early colonies to refer to Sodom's sinful citizens and their whole array of vices, but rarely to refer to persons guilty specifically and only of sodomy.

The early English settlers, following the Bible, did refer to "men lying with men as with a woman" and to women changing the "natural use" into that which is "against nature." But such persons' acts were not spoken of as transforming them into "a man-who-lies-with-men," or "a woman-who-changes-the-natural-use." Similarly, though American documents of this early period often referred to the act of "buggery" (meaning, usually, bestiality, and, sometimes, sodomy), no American reference has been found to a person called a "buggerer."[31]

In early New England, sodomitical sinners were not thought of as differing in their essential natures from Puritan saints. All persons' "cursed Natures" inclined them to every variety of wickedness—the "holiest man hath as vile and filthy a Nature, as the Sodomites," said Reverend Danforth in 1674. Even the most outwardly respectable Puritan might be inwardly guilty of "heart sodomy" or "heart buggery"—as well as "heart whoredom," "heart blasphemy," and "heart drunkenness"—warned Reverend Shepard in 1641. No Puritan was perfectly pure. Only a deep faith in God distinguished the saved from the damned; both were equally corrupted by "original sin," both were potential committers of sodomy—and other sins. In today's terms, original sin was "normal," not "deviant."

The Puritans did not punish sodomitical sinners because they were "deviant," "different," "abnormal," or a "minority." As sinners, committers of sodomy belonged to the Puritan majority. Those graced by faith and salvation were the minority. Given this social situation, the idea of a "sodomitical minority" would have made no sense to the early settlers. In a society in which an elite few were the "elect," and the many were the damned, no democratic political ideology had yet influenced the social response to carnal intercourse. For the Puritans the numbers of persons who performed certain numbers of acts had no bearing on those acts' "naturalness" or "unnaturalness." An absolute, qualitative, procreative standard determined what was considered "natural," not a quantitative norm. It is anachronistic to speak of a "gay," "homosexual," or even a "sodomitical minority" as if it existed for the early colonists. Projecting modern concepts on the past prevents us from understanding those settlers' responses to copulation.[32]

The detestable committer of sodomy was not thought of as a unique, distinct character type, a sodomitical being. The enactor of sodomy was perceived as kissing cousin of, and partner in sin to, those other major colonial malefactors —the committers of treason, murder, witchcraft, arson, idolatry, blasphemy, rape, bestiality, adultery, those who stole indentured servants, and those who smote their parents—those most abominable of sinners, penalized by death.

In the early colonies, one's work was of the essence, not some essential character trait, not one's "person." While good works definitely did not determine a Puritan's preordained salvation, such works were the earthly evidence, a present, reassuring sign, of an individual's future place in heaven. The political economy of the early colonies was not composed of "rugged individuals," "single entrepreneurs," or "self-made men." Nor was a prominent virtue "self-reliance" or a prominent activity "self-help." Self-annihilation, not self-aggrandizement, was the Puritan ideal. The family, not the individual, was the primary productive unit. This society was composed of a community-conscious population whose shared, precarious condition of life in the wilderness produced the sure knowledge that the survival of each depended on the effort of all, a population knowing in their bones that social survival was a communal work. Under such primitive conditions of economic cooperation no great emphasis was placed on the "individual." The focus was not on the "sodomite," but on "sodomy," and other sinful acts.

### Sinful Feelings, Sinful Acts

As the Reverend Shepard suggested, the early Puritans were as concerned about inner acts of the "heart" as about outward acts of the body. Lusting inwardly and fornicating outwardly were both acts, although differing perhaps in degree of transgression. "Feeling," for the early Puritans, was not commonly, or absolutely distinguished from "act"; feeling was an act, the inner movement of the soul. So sodomy as feeling was not distinguished essentially from sodomy as act. Only in the late 1800s would American doctors speak of a "sexual perversion" defined essentially by emotion, not by act. Only in the twentieth century would a "homoerotic" feeling be insistently distinguished from "homosexual" act—the modern judgment being that it is not quite so bad to feel it as to do it. In the early colonies, it was almost as bad to feel it as to do it.

The documents of the early colonial era, especially those of Puritan origin, vividly evoke a biblically defined universe of sinful emotions and sinful acts. These documents refer to "burning lusts, set on fire of hell," "boiling lusts," "unnatural lusts," "carnal lusts," "filthy lusts," and "infamous passions." To be sure, colonial laws and legal cases document the penalty for, and punishment of, only those caught in overt acts. But that was no doubt due to the technical difficulty of capturing, jailing, prosecuting, proving, and executing illicit lust. Such wayward desire was not reported to the authorities. It might, however, be secretly confessed to one's diary—in code—as proof to God, and to oneself, of one's private self-chastisement, moral struggle, and atonement. The Reverend Michael Wigglesworth's journal, written partly in code in the 1650s, recorded that "too much doting affection" for his male pupils (at Harvard) stimulated him to "filthy lust." But the possession of such immoderate affection, such dirty emotional secrets, made him not a "sodomite," but simply a "sinner."

Neither Wigglesworth nor any other known early colonial writer referred to "sodomitical lust," an emotion specific to sodomy. There was no sodomeroticism. In the early colonies there was "sensual lust." But no special sodomitical desire opposed an "other," "different," or "opposite" lust. No "homoerotic" feeling for a "same sex" opposed a "heteroerotic" feeling for a "different sex," no "homosexual" emotion opposed a "heterosexual." "Filthy lusts" and "infamous passions" included a variety of feelings associated with fornication, adultery, and a variety of other sins, not just sodomy, and not just sexual. The "lust" of early evangelical Puritans did not refer just to the erotic; they condemned all forms of lusting, desiring, willing, and wanting, all self-assertion, playfulness, and enjoyment. Thomas Shepard, for example, recalled his youthful sins of "lust and pride and gaming and bowling and drinking." Cotton Mather sought to "become a Man dead unto this World; crucified unto all Worldly Enjoyments." Michael Wigglesworth referred to his "carnal lusts," thus implicitly distinguishing between fleshly and other lusts. Wigglesworth prayed to God for "power over my still prevailing lusts, principally pride and sensuality, want of love to thee and fervent desires after communion with thee."[33]

Lusts for the early Puritans were multiple and various. Sensual lust was only one variety of those passions and appetites condemned as sinful; only in renouncing human desire, in doing "God's will" and "God's work" was one demonstrating one's faith and pursuing a relatively sinless path. Lusting was a particularly intense form of desiring, and carnal lust was a variety of desiring requiring special legal controls. But the Puritans' condemnation of carnal lust was secondary to their condemnation of desire in general. Sodomy was punished primarily as socially destructive, only secondarily as a specifically carnal crime.

The original Puritans did not focus repressively on the carnal in the same single-minded way as late-Victorian doctors, for example, focused on "sexuality." Lust was not equated with "sexuality," a thing cordoned off, a secret underworld of acts, a secret unconscious world of the mind. Carnal lusts and carnal acts existed in the everyday, ordinary Puritan universe, concupiscence was not relegated to a hidden erotic, exotic ghetto. The term and concept "sexuality," an entity which is sex, was a Victorian, not a Puritan, invention.[34] Our contemporary use of "Puritanism" to refer to a specifically sexual repression was an invention of the anti-Victorians of the early twentieth century.

The Puritans' focus on desiring and doing, on subjective feeling and objective act, reflected a society in which mental and manual activity was not completely divided, and organized in essentially different ways. Even the major colonial producer of ideas, the minister, worked at all those tasks necessary for survival, tasks as much manual as mental. Inner feeling was not radically alienated from overt act; no greater reality and value were assigned to act; feeling was as important and "real" as act. (Both act and feeling, however, alienated from the human, were experienced as God's doing.) Human activity was not yet divided and organized into waged acts called "labor," non-waged acts called "feeling."

### Man with Man, Woman with Woman

The early Puritans spoke often of the "abominable sin" that male might commit with male, and spoke occasionally of an analogous sin that female might commit with female. But they rarely spoke of "same" and "different" sexes, and never (as far as is known) of "opposite" sexes.[35] (Sodomy was an act committed by parties of the "same sex," said the Reverend Danforth in 1674; women were referred to as "the different sex" in a book published in 1724 [see]; those are the first uses of such phrases noted in the early colonial documents studied.)

The colonists' reference to acts of "man with man" and "woman with woman" did implicitly refer to men as the "same" as other men, women as the "same" as other women. The reference to a "Female with Females" working wickedness did imply the biological "sameness" of females; it did not stress any "difference" between males and females. The phrase about women changing the "natural use" into that which is "against nature" made no reference to the sex of the parties with whom women changed the "natural use." The terms "buggery" and "sodomy" made only ambiguous or implicit reference to the sex of the parties.

Compared to the Victorians, the early colonists placed relatively little explicit emphasis on the idea of sexual "sameness" and "difference." The late-Victorian concepts of "homo-" and "heterosexuality," stressing a "same-sex"/"different-sex" eroticism, were foreign to the early settlers.

As we have seen, the basic distinction between the early colonial concept of sodomy and of licit copulation was that between procreative and non-procreative. That distinction did not refer primarily to the anatomical similarity and dissimilarity of sexual actors; it applied equally to acts of females with males. Under that procreative standard, it was not the physiological "sameness" of actors that made sodomy seem like such a threat; sodomy was not punished because it violated boundaries of sexual "difference," standards of "masculinity" and "femininity."

Anal intercourse of males with males *or* males with females, like masturbation, the intercourse of women or men with animals, and adult males with pre-pubescent girls, were sins because they were non-reproductive. Sexual intercourse of human males with female beasts was condemned as not properly procreative; such relations were thought to result, possibly, in the birth of deformed, part-human, part-bestial creatures.[36] The "adultery" of a male, either married *or single,* with a married or engaged female, as well as the rape of a female by a male were sins because, as violations of the legally established and strictly enforced social mode of procreation, they were seen as socially disruptive and threats to colonial survival.

Evidence suggests that, just as the early English colonists did not associate sexual "sameness" or "difference" with sodomy, neither did they associate sodomy with any concept of "femininity" or "masculinity." An accusation, in 1707, against Lord Cornbury, Governor of New York and New Jersey, for his public cross-dressing, did not so much as hint that Cornbury's behavior might be associated with sodomitical activity or illicit carnality, though it is reasonable to suppose sodomitical rumors would have been spread about this despised colonial ruler, if such associations had occurred to Cornbury's many enemies.

In this period, only Spanish and French reports of male-male sodomy among Native Americans are known to have linked sodomitical copulation with "effeminacy" of dress, speech, and manner. The known colonial documents of the first period of English settlement suggest no association between "effeminacy" and male-male sodomy.

Similarly, in 1629, the Virginia magistrate's official resolution of a case of alleged hermaphroditism suggests that even the categories "man" and "woman" were not then necessarily considered mutually exclusive, an absolute opposition. On the one hand, the neighbors of one Thomas/Thomasine Hall demonstrated a most persistent curiosity about his/her sex, even several times making their own physical examinations of Hall's person. On the other hand, the Virginia governor resolved the public dispute about Hall's sex by declaring that Hall was "a man and woman." The magistrate also provided that Hall wear "man's apparel" *and* items of clothing traditional for women. Such gender specific clothing was a visual indicator of the social differentiation of the sexes. But the official decision to allow Hall to wear items of both sexes' clothing, and the official decision to recognize Hall's mixed sex, contrasts with nineteenth-century American doctors' responses to alleged hermaphroditism, cross-dressing, and other forms of sexual crossing. Those Victorian documents suggest that medical distinctions between men and women had then become more emphatic, the categories man and woman mutually exclusive.[37]

The early colonists' relative lack of stress on sexual differentiation is referred to in several recent historical analyses of the period.

Historian Mary P. Ryan, in her book *Womanhood in America* maintains that in the first period of settlement, within the social-economic unit of the household, "Colonial culture did not parcel out a whole series of temperamental attributes according to sex." There was no "full-fledged feminine stereotype." The "concepts of masculinity and femininity remained ill-defined in agrarian America," at least within the important sphere of household production. The cultural construction of sexual stereotypes was inhibited by an "agrarian frontier economy [which] kept the sexual division of labor simple and primitive"; the household system of production "precluded the isolation of women in a private and under-valued sphere."[38]

A recent survey by Laurel Thatcher Ulrich of seventy works about women, published by New England ministers between 1668 and 1735, reveals the qualities publicly praised at this time by one group of Puritan males.[39] Their virtuous woman sought God early, prayed and fasted, read, conversed, wrote, managed well, and submitted meekly and humbly to the will of God. But those virtues were not sex-linked; they applied equally to men and women. Qualities like "meekness," "submissiveness," and "piety" were no more specific to females than to males, Ulrich found. The literature on marriage stressed an ethic of "mutual responsibility, mutual caring," and reciprocal duties between near-equals.[64, 65]

The existence of few works on childbirth suggested to Ulrich the reluctance of ministers "to stress 'feminine' or 'masculine' themes over a common Christianity." And even the pregnancy literature stressed "similarities between men and women": an "analogy, not a contrast between the sexes" informed one Puritan's advice to husbands concerning the care of their pregnant wives. Men in sickness were said to need as much care as pregnant women. Puritan ministers, said Ulrich, acknowledged "the reproductive role of women" without attributing a "sexual content to the psyche and soul." They "upheld the spiritual oneness of the sexes" in the sphere of marital, familial, household relationships, though not in the polity or church.[67, 68] Early New England ministers "promoted the same asexual qualities" for both men and women: "prayerfulness, industry, charity, modesty, serious reading, and godly writing."

The virtuous woman, concluded Ulrich, "possessed no inherently female spiritual qualities, and her deepest reality was unrelated to her sex." Only later, about 1700, did a "subtle shift" begin to appear in the literature referring to women. Then appeared the first embryonic formulation of the ideal of the "genteel lady" dominant in the late 1700s, and of the ideal of the "tender mother" characteristic of the 1800s. These new, "gradually developing sexual definitions of the psyche," Ulrich suggested, were linked to the "increasingly mercantile," "secular," and "prosperous" society of the 1700s. Ulrich argued that overemphasizing the fates of "deviant women," such as Anne Hutchinson, prevented our acknowledging those common attitudes toward women and men which stressed equality.[59–60]

## Early Colonial Patriarchy

The early colonists did sometimes make emphatic distinctions between those activities appropriate exclusively for women or men. In the spheres of church and state, preaching, legislating, judging, and voting were exclusively men's work. Within those spheres a sharp sexual division of activity existed, a strict distinction between acts proper for women or men. Anne Hutchinson's attempt to preach is the most famous example of the harsh response to women's violation of men's control of ministerial activity.

Historian Lyle Koehler shows that the prosecution of Anne Hutchinson and other "American Jezebels," in Massachusetts, between 1636 and 1638, stressed those women's threat to the male monopoly of the means of religious salvation. One Puritan male complained that "the weaker Sex" had set up Anne Hutchinson as "a Priest" and "thronged" after her. Another reported he daily heard a "clamor" that "New England men usurpt over their wives, and keep them in survile subjection." Governor John Winthrop blamed Anne Hutchinson for causing "divisions between husband and wife . . . till the weaker give place to the stronger, otherwise it turns to open contention."[40]

At Anne Hutchinson's heresy hearing in November 1637, Winthrop said that her criticism of the ministers and her holding religious meetings in her home were acts not "fitting for your sex."[27] Hugh Peter told Hutchinson she had "stept out of you[r] place, you have rather been a Husband than a Wife and a preacher than a Hearer; and a Magistrate than a Subject."[28] The Reverend John Cotton warned that Hutchinson's teaching would provoke "promiscuous and filthie comings together of men and Women without Distinction or Relation of Marriage."[41] Koehler reports that the Reverend Thomas Shepard warned that Hutchinson was likely "to seduce and draw away many, especially simple woman of her own sex."[31] Shepard praised his own wife for her "incomparable meekness of spirit, toward myself especially."[23] Puritan men lamented the "madness" of those who would hold "silly women laden with their lusts" in higher esteem than men, who were "honoured of Christ" and imbued "with power and authority from him to Preach." Anne Hutchinson's husband was criticized as a "man of very mild temper and weak parts, and wholly guided by his wife."[35] Anne Hutchinson and her follower, Mary Dyer, were alleged by Puritan men to have given birth to deformed offspring. One explained: As Hutchinson "had vented misshapen opinions, so she must bring forth deformed monsters."[34] (The monstrous births also thought to result from human-bestial couplings reveal a similar concept of procreative catastrophe as punishment for improper intercourse.)

Although males dominated the religious and political spheres of early colonial patriarchy, within those spheres differences did exist in the activities, property, and power of men. Although religious, political, legislative, and judicial posts were limited to men, those positions were effectively limited to a few males. Though property distribution varied widely in different colonies, its distribution was such that those men with the most wealth had the most power. A division between classes intersected that between women and men, so that certain religious and political activities then closed to women were also effectively closed to most men. In the context of early colonial agricultural production, that activity prohibited to women and allowed to some men, was of relatively little importance compared to the necessary work of both sexes.

Within the sphere of domestic agricultural production, the male was spoken of as "head" of the household and family, the husband as "governor" of the wife, and the "patriarchs" of the Old Testament might be cited as the models for males in a society which was, in its own time called "patriarchal." But the functional importance of the productive and procreative work of women undermined, to some degree, the sexual division of power favoring men. The essential, valued activity of women in production and procreation modified the character of early colonial patriarchy. Within the basic unit of production, the family household, women and men cooperated in similarly organized and essential work. There did exist a sexual division of work, legal power, and social status within the family and out. But no distinction then existed between wage-work and non-waged housework, between the basic organization of women's work and men's work. The cooperative mode of early colonial work resulted in much less stress on male-female difference than was later typical of middle-class Victorians, with their separate and differently organized male and female spheres.

## Male/Female; Stronger/Weaker

In the early colonial economy of production and procreation, when a male/female distinction was made, it was relative, between "stronger" and "weaker," not between active and passive. Women were often called the "weaker sex" and the "weaker vessel"; they were "weaker," but not "weak." The relative strengths and weaknesses of men and women, as manifested in agricultural work and child-bearing, field work and housework, were the basis of the prevailing distinction. Women's physical vulnerability in child-bearing then constituted a particular "weakness" perceived as distinguishing women and men.[42] The political economy of the early colonies made the male/female relationship dominant/subordinant, not active/passive. In the early colonies everyone was active. Even the owner of a large southern plantation kept busy as farm manager, his wife as house manager. Though the ideal relationship of colonial women to men might be that of follower and initiator, passivity and inactivity were not defined as female. In striking contrast, late-Victorian doctors reiterated over and over again the association of male/active, female/passive. The absence of this opposition in the early colonies had major implications for the colonial economy of procreation, and for the colonial response to sodomy and other non-procreative acts.

In the sphere of sodomitical intercourse the colonists did not associate male with active sodomite, female with a passive sodomized. Both parties to procreative and non-procreative intercourse were considered active. And so for such acts both parties were thought of as responsible and punished. (Distinctions in degree of punishment *were* made with reference to force, consent, and age.)

Within the colonial social organization of human procreation, the activity of both women and men was valued as necessary and essential to this major branch of production. But the female was thought of as a procreative "vessel," a conductor of "seed," the male as seed-giver. As a vessel a woman was thought of as accepting the male seed and carrying it as it ripened, a "fruitful vine." Women's work in human reproduction was transportive, men's originative, initiative, "seminal." Men who indulged in non-procreative seminal acts were spoken of as using up scarce productive means—in biblical phrase, as "spilling" or "wasting" their seed. Women who participated in non-reproductive acts were not said to be wasting any such essential procreative substance. To be sure, when females with females worked wickedness, they were said to be actively putting their bodies to use "against nature." Such women were temporarily diverting their bodies from their proper use; they were not "wasting" their substance in non-reproductive acts.

That particular patriarchal concept of male as seeder, female as seed carrier,

was reflected in the differential punishment of women and men for non-procreative copulation. The seminal import attached specifically to the male in procreation was reflected in the fact that sodomy, for practical, legal purposes, was
generally considered an act exclusively of males with males. Only the unique New
Haven law of 1656 included male-female anal intercourse and (undefined) acts
of women "against nature" as forms of sodomy. The social dominance of a
male-defined, male-centered concept of sodomy meant that the few early references of ministers to sexual acts of female with female were not embodied in legal
statute.

### Penetration, Emission, and Patriarchy

Complex questions of interpretation are raised by the colonists' executions
for "sodomy," other, lesser punishments for acts they spoke of as "sodomy"—
related, and still other acts which seem to us related, but did not seem so to
colonial legislators and judges. Those who have studied the records of American
colonial law enforcement differ about the relative frequency with which the statutory death penalty for "sodomy" was actually carried out, and even about the
manner of analyzing these prosecutions.

In 1942, a pioneering essay on "The Puritans and Sex," by Edmund Morgan, was one of the earliest of the few works discussing colonial American sexuality.[43] In this influential study Morgan claimed that the colonists "usually" punished sodomy by death, and immediately added: "Rape, adultery, and
fornication" were regarded by the colonists "as pardonable weaknesses"—suggesting that the three latter acts (unlike sodomy) were not usually punished as
harshly as statute required. (Some confusion was introduced here because "rape"
and "adultery" were capital crimes, while "fornication" was not.) Morgan's comment on the commonness of executions for sodomy, and his implicit comparison
of such penalties with the punishments for what we now call "sex crimes," was
based on his impressionistic summary of the many original records with which he
was familiar, but no sources were cited.

In 1979, in an essay on "Sodomy and Buggery in Seventeenth-Century New
England," Robert F. Oaks claimed that Edmund Morgan was wrong, that sodomy
in the colonies was not usually punished by death.[44] Oaks's conclusion was based
on his own impression of colonial documents, and his survey of Plymouth Colony
records in particular. He cited three "definite homosexual offenses" in Plymouth
in which the capital sodomy law was not enforced, those found guilty not punished by death. Oaks pointed to the infrequency with which the death penalty for
sodomy was enforced, relative to the frequency of prosecutions for what he
termed "homosexuality"—cases that the records indicate involved sexual activity
between men or between women. Were the capital colonial sodomy laws "usually" enforced, or were they not? And how are we to interpret the evidence? The

question of sodomy law-enforcement is linked to the question of what acts were considered "sodomy."

Although colonial reports of prosecutions for "sodomy" are often vague about the specific acts constituting the crime, those reports, and several legal and theological commentaries on "sodomy," do provide evidence revealing the rationales for prosecutions and punishments. A "sodomy" charge may have sometimes been made simply to justify an official murder, implying no specific concept of the act. But most "sodomy" prosecutions and punishments did, at least, imply a particular idea of the crime. Early colonial "sodomy" and "sodomy"-related case records and commentaries indicate that the legal charges and verdicts implied one of three distinct, alternate concepts, which I call the *penetrative, penetrative-emissive,* and *emissive.* Analysis of the records of prosecutions and legal decisions makes explicit and systematic a patriarchal logic of penetration and emission which in the colonies was usually implicit and unsystematic.

According to the first concept, "sodomy" was that non-procreative act in which a penis "penetrated" an anus or the "unripe vessel" of a prepubescent girl. "Sodomy," according to this concept, referred to a male-female, or male-male act. The social dominance of a "penetrative" idea of sodomy meant that acts not involving "penetration" by a penis were not thought of as "sodomy." Such non-penetrative acts were therefore not punished as "sodomy," and their existence might not be discussed.

For example, the word "sodomy" was not mentioned in the case in which the Plymouth court, in 1637, found John Allexander and Thomas Roberts guilty of "often spending their seed one upon another." Allexander was also found to have been previously guilty of the act, as well as of "seeking to allure others" to it. Allexander was "severely whipped," "burnt in the shoulder with a hot iron," and "perpetually banished." Roberts was also "severely whipped," and disqualified from land ownership—unless he behaved better. These two men's "often spending their seed one upon another" did not include "penetration," the usual minimal definition of "sodomy." Even their repeated mutual emissions did not, in the reasoning of Plymouth judges, qualify as "sodomy." And if these acts were not then classified as "sodomy," the failure to impose the death penalty in this case provides only ambiguous evidence concerning colonial "sodomy" law-enforcement. At most, the lack of a death penalty in this case demonstrates that a penetrative or penetrative-emissive concept of sodomy was in effect, that the colonists did not execute all persons who committed acts which, in the 1980s, are called "homosexual."

The penetrative idea of sodomy was explicit in the legal commentary published in 1644 by the influential English jurist Edward Coke. He concluded that "Buggery" or "Sodomy" referred only to "penetrative" acts of males with males, and of male or female humans with beasts (apparently, of the "other" sex than their human partners, though no reference was made to the beasts' sex).

No reference was made by Coke to sexual relations between women. Within a strict definition of "sodomy" as penetration by a male organ the sexual relations of women with women were literally unthinkable. (The idea of women using a penis-substitute was not mentioned by colonial males, as it was by later males whose thought proceeded in terms of penetrative acts.)

A strict penetrative concept did, curiously, allow colonial lawmakers to imagine intercourse between women and animals (male animals were apparently inferred). It is ironic that colonial legislators, who hardly ever prohibited carnal relations between women (and never explicitly), did often explicitly penalize copulation of women with beasts. That the intercourse of women and (male) animals received much explicit statutory recognition indicates the social dominance of a strict penetrative concept. When illicit intercourse was defined primarily by reference to a male organ it was of only secondary import whether that virile member was attached to man or beast. The colonists' concern about the inter-penetration of humans and beasts was no doubt linked to their belief that interspecies intercourse could result in the birth of part-human, part-bestial creatures. And their concern about human-animal contacts was also no doubt linked to the temptations and probable prevalence of bestiality in an agricultural economy commonly utilizing animals for many other services.

According to the second concept of sodomy, both penetration and emission were required to constitute the crime. In 1642, the Reverend Partridge at first suggested that mere emission, a "voluntary effusion of seed," was sufficient to establish the crime committed when man lay with man. But Partridge then added that he was not confident of his opinion, that the prohibited act might also require "penetration." Such discussions were not just academic, but occurred in the process of deciding whether an individual was or was not executed. According to a penetrative-emissive concept, penetration without emission was not "sodomy," and so was not punished by death.

According to the less common emissive concept, "sodomy" was any act of male ejaculation without penetration, therefore without procreative possibility. Only according to this idea was a man's "spilling his own seed" (masturbation) included in the pantheon of "sodomitical" acts, as it was in the unusually broad New Haven law of 1656. It was perhaps under the influence of an emissive concept that William Plaine was seen as corrupting the youth of Guilford by "masturbations . . . above a hundred times," and was executed in 1646. (John Winthrop's comment on this case suggests that Plaine was punished solely for the youths' emissions, and the quantity of them induced, though Winthrop is ambiguous; Plaine was also accused of "sodomy" with "two persons in England," at least seven years earlier, and it is not clear if he was punished retroactively for those acts.) Usually colonial magistrates did not consider mere emission to be "sodomy."

Those three penetrative and emissive concepts defined sodomy and, by implication, licit copulation, from a specifically male viewpoint which did not include the "lewd" acts of one woman with another. In 1656, the Plymouth Court found Sara Norman guilty of "lewd behavior with Mary Hammon upon a bed," and punished Norman with a warning, Hammon not at all. "Sodomy" was not mentioned, and this case also has only ambiguous implications for the question of "sodomy" law enforcement.

A fourth, broad definition of sodomy was also formulated, specifically by colonial ministers. The existence of this concept—which I will call the inclusive —is documented in commentaries by Puritan clergymen in 1641–42. According to this definition sodomy included not just penetration and emission, but any genital "contact" or "rubbing," and even a variety of more vaguely alluded to acts. It was only this inclusive concept which defined (unspecified) acts of women with women as "sodomy."

This inclusive concept of sodomy existed primarily as a theoretical construct. Only the broad and somewhat ambiguous New Haven law of 1656 seems to have enacted the inclusive concept of sodomy, but this law was never, apparently, enforced. The magistrates' actual working definition of "sodomy" included only penetrative, penetrative-emissive, or emissive acts of men.

Paradoxically, the ministers' inclusive concept of sodomy, which transcended the magistrates' patriarchal focus on penetration and emission to include the acts of women with women, did so in the name of adherence to patriarchal Old Testament tradition—as interpreted in St. Paul's New Testament Epistle to the Romans (1:26), which prohibited women from changing the "natural use" into that "against nature." This was interpreted by colonial ministers to refer explicitly to women with women (as St. Paul did not).[45] The conflict between the ministers' inclusive definition of sodomy and the magistrates' narrower notions indicates an early divergence between secular and religious authorities. Even under the theologically justified government of the early colonies this conflict over the definition of sodomy was resolved in favor of the narrow, male-specific terms advocated by secular magistrates.

The known legal case records indicate that when the colonists charged a man with "sodomy" (or "buggery") the individual so charged was likely to be executed. Only in the Sension case of 1677 and the Georgia colony case of 1734 were men actually charged with "sodomy" not executed. (No information is available about the sentence in the Hillebrant case, of 1658.) The evidence indicates that to be charged with "sodomy" in the colonies usually meant death.[46]

In seven known cases the crime charged was described as "tending to sodomy" (including attempted sodomy), as "sodomitical" (meaning sodomy-like), or as merely "lewd" and "filthy" (with no reference to "sodomy," although involving two males or two females). The crimes described as "tending to sodomy" and "sodomitical" were usually punished by whipping, and sometimes also branding with a hot iron, banishment, disqualification from future property ownership, fine, or bond. "Lewd" and "filthy" acts were punished, in one case with a warning, in another by a public whipping.[47]

A major distinction was thus made in practice between the punishment for

(1) "sodomy" proper, (2) attempted sodomy, (3) "sodomitical" (sodomy-like) acts, and (4) acts between males, or between females, which were not, apparently, considered to be sodomy-related, but only "lewd" and illicit. These categories suggest that in analyzing the records of colonial legal prosecutions and punishments we need to distinguish carefully between acts then categorized as "sodomy" or "sodomy"-related, and acts that seem so related to us. Colonial sodomy law enforcement implied several historically specific concepts of the crime, concepts not identical to the modern "homosexuality."

Four colonial executions for "sodomy" now documented occurred quite early in the settlement process, between 1624 and 1712, with one more execution for sodomy in Georgia in 1743.[48] Almost all prosecutions for sodomy seem to have occurred during the early colonial period, when the existence of each colony was most precarious, the necessity of population increase the most pressing. (The execution for sodomy in Georgia, in 1743, took place early in that colony's existence; Georgia was chartered in 1732.) The number of executions and prosecutions for sodomy seem to have diminished as the colonists became more secure, population increase less important, and the movement toward an organized, independent commercial society more assured. By 1674, the Reverend Danforth's justifying the death penalty for sodomy and bestiality was apparently a defensive reaction to those Massachusetts citizens who thought capital punishment for such crimes too harsh. In 1677, Nicholas Sension of Connecticut was hardly penalized at all for more than thirty years of sodomy attempts, though his perseverance was sworn to by numbers of his fellow townsmen.

All the colonial sodomy statutes were passed by the early 1700s, the last new one being passed by Georgia legislators in 1732. The active period of capital sodomy law enactments, prosecutions, and executions, appears to coincide with the earliest period of settlement—in the English and Dutch colonies during the one hundred and eight years between 1624 and 1732. Although the statutory death penalty for sodomy did not generally begin to be abolished until after the American Revolution, long before that, apparently, it had ceased to be enforced.[49]

### Woman with Woman

The *Confessional* written in 1613 by the Spanish missionary Pareja asked Native American female converts to Christianity: "Woman with woman, have you had intercourse as if you were a man?" It is not known if Pareja's question was suggested by his actual knowledge of such relationships among native women, by some special interest of this era's Spaniards in female-female lust, or by Pareja's own idiosyncratic curiosity.[50] Such early explicit references to eroticism among women were quite rare among English settlers. Their rarity does not, however, diminish their importance as clues to early colonial modes of thought.

The "sodomy" provision of the Reverend John Cotton's proposed legal code of 1636 explicitly suggested punishing by death the "carnal fellowship" of "woman with woman," as well as "man with man." When Cotton's proposal to punish carnal acts between women was actually incorporated in the New Haven statute of 1656, the wording was changed to the more ambiguous prohibition against women changing the "natural use, into that which is against nature." That wording derived directly from the New Testament—St. Paul's Epistle to the Romans, 1:26–27, which said:

> For this cause God gave them up unto vile affections: for even their women did change the natural use into that which is against nature: And likewise, also the men, leaving the natural use of the woman, burned in their lust one toward another; men with men working that which is unseemly, and receiving in themselves that recompense of their error which was meet. [King James translation][51]

Here, the relevant point is how American Puritan ministers interpreted this biblical passage, not its internal logic or the original intended meaning of its author (or authors).

First, it should be noted, John Cotton's original proposal of 1636 explicitly demonstrated his intention to punish as "sodomy" the "carnal fellowship" of "woman with woman."

Second, although the wording of the 1656 law referred ambiguously to any woman changing the "natural use" into a use "against nature," a direct, explicit analogy was made to "any man" lying with "mankind" as a man lay with a woman. The intention of the colonial lawmakers was clearly to punish contacts between women paralleling those between men.

Third, separate, explicit prohibitions in the 1656 law against male-female anal intercourse suggest that that act was not thought of as identical to and included in the prohibition against women changing the "natural use."

No legal prosecution is known to have been instituted under that law of 1656, and no other colonial statute referred to the possibility of carnal connection between women.

Besides John Cotton's legal proposal of 1636, the written commentaries of five other New England ministers are now known to have included at least passing references to acts of women with women, as well as men with men.

In 1641, the Reverend Thomas Shepard linked "sodomy" with the sins of "men with men" and of "women with women." The Reverend John Rayner, in 1642, argued that non-penetrative genital contacts of men were capital crimes; he derived this from an interpretation of St. Paul's Epistle to the Romans as decreeing that women "guilty of this unnatural sin" should be put to death. Also in 1642, the Reverend Charles Chauncy referred, in passing, to the tradition of "unnatural lusts of men with men, or woman with woman being punished by death" (see 1641–42, Mass. Bay). The Reverend Samuel Danforth, in 1674, declared that sodomy was that activity in which "Males with Males and Females with Females work wickedness." A female-female crime, identical or analogous to male-male "sodomy," was thus occasionally referred to by colonial clerics.

There is no known case of a woman actually being charged with "sodomy" or "sodomitical" acts in the early colonies. There were two instances, however, of "unseemly practices," "unchaste," "wild," and "lewd behavior," and of "lascivious speeches" of women with women—the case of Elizabeth Johnson in 1642, and that of Sara Norman and Mary Hammon in 1649. But the language of the charges against these women, and the relatively light penalties imposed, suggest that the magistrates made no analogy to the much more severely punished "sodomy" of men with men. Activities which, in America of the 1980s, would be thought of and treated as "female homosexuality" (thus equated with "male homosexuality"), in the early colonies were not equated with "sodomy"; they were treated by magistrates as a relatively minor sin.

Early records referring to erotic relations between women represent a small part of the documents so far discovered. And all this evidence is the product of those males who controlled the means of legal or religious power, commenting on, or attempting to control and punish women. No known documents of this period record the voices of women themselves, speaking of their intimacies with women. But the very scarcity of references to female-female eroticism itself constitutes a significant kind of evidence—of women's subordinate position within the legal and religious spheres.

The legal dominance of male-centered concepts of "sodomy" seem to have left all erotic acts and intimate relationships of women with women relatively free from sodomitical taint. The "lewd behavior" of women with women apparently existed only at the margin of the colonists' minds, the "sodomitical" behavior of men with men existed nearer the center of their consciousness. Such conditions as the relative scarcity of women, and the need for population increase and new laborers no doubt pressured women to marry and procreate. But other conditions—the lack of competition between women for men, and male-specific concepts of sodomy—may have allowed some women to draw together in ways that in the twentieth century became more difficult. The relative infrequency of colonial statutory prohibitions, prosecutions, and discourse about erotic relations between women indicates either a real absence of such relations, or just less male interest in them—in which case intimacies of female with female may have been freer to develop than those of male with male, threatened as they were by sodomitical stigma.

### Blacks

Two sodomy case reports and two sodomy statutes are the only relevant early colonial documents known to refer to the presence of Blacks, though, by about 1680, Africans constituted the second largest occupational group after yeoman farmers.[52]

In 1629, the Dutch West India Company had promised to supply the large proprietors of the New Netherland Colony with as many Black laborers as were needed. (Whether these Blacks were low-status servants or slaves is now unknown.) Seventeen years later, a New Netherland Black was executed for sodomy. In 1646, Jan Creoli, identified as "a negro," was sentenced to be "choked to death, and then burned to ashes" for a second sodomy offense. The name of the ten-year-old party to the crime, Manuel Congo, suggests that he, also, was Black. Though Creoli's punishment was severe, it was apparently not more severe than the punishment allotted white men accused of the same crime in that colony, at about the same time. Fourteen years later, in 1660, Jan Quisthout, a white man convicted in New Netherland of (forcible) sodomy with a "boy," was sentenced to be drowned.

In the English colonies the slave status of Blacks was fairly well established by 1680. Twenty years later Quaker legislators of Pennsylvania, in revising their criminal code (including its sodomy provision), for the first time carefully distinguished between Black and white offenders, the only colonial sodomy legislation to do so. The Quaker laws of 1700 and 1706, the first in the colonies to abolish the death penalty for sodomy, provided life imprisonment for whites convicted of sodomy or bestiality. And both, in a separate "Act for the Trial of Negros," innovatively provided death for Blacks convicted of "buggery" (probably bestiality and sodomy), burglary, murder, or the rape of a white woman. As is common in women's history, a silence is revealing. The rape of Black women was not mentioned, an indication it was not considered serious enough to be singled out for the death penalty; a double standard concerning the sexual virtue of white and Black women seems to have been on its way to formulation. It is also a matter of some irony that the most lenient colonial sodomy laws, the first to abolish the death penalty (for whites), should also be the first to formalize the inferior status of Blacks guilty of sodomy. Here, also, it seems, is an early sign of that double standard which judged Black men more sexually threatening than white.

In 1712, "Mingo alias Cocke Negro," a slave, apparently, of a high Massachusetts magistrate, was said to have been executed for "forcible Buggery" (a phrase suggesting a male-male act, rather than bestiality). The evidence of that execution's occurrence is inconclusive, and the case is the last-known early colonial reference to Blacks among the documents of same sex eroticism.

## Intimacy: The Historical Experience

Though the proscriptive literature of the early colonies referred to sodomy as inner feeling, as well as overt act, the actual feelings historically associated with sodomy were not often recorded. In the known documents the specific historical

quality of emotion particular to sodomy (and other intimate same sex relationships) is hinted at only rarely and briefly.

In 1566, in Spanish-held Florida, a Native American male, a chief's son, was
said to live with and "love" a French "sodomite" "very much." In 1653, in New
England, the Reverend Wigglesworth felt guilty about the "filthy lust flowing
from my fond affection for my [male] pupils." That "fond affection" was the
source of Wigglesworth's "filthy" flow is evidence that this obsession with such
lust corrupted the experience of what might otherwise have been a lovely, though
intense emotion. That transformation of Wigglesworth's "fond affection" into
"filthy lust" is also the earliest evidence available of a link between "affection"
and an emotion we now call "homosexual."

The testimony at the 1677 Connecticut sodomy trial of Nicholas Sension
suggested that colonial New Englanders associated overt sodomitical activity with
affection. Sension had spoken, said one witness, of his "foolish" though "fond
affection" for his servant Nathanial Pond, the chief object of Sension's sodomy
attempts. Pond was also once asked "if his master used any Loving Expressions"
to persuade him to participate in sodomy. (Pond said his master had not.) Pond,
we learn, refused to leave his master's service and home, even though troubled
by Sension's sodomy attempts; his master, Pond explained to a witness, "had
brought him up from a child in his orphan state." Pond's feeling for Sension may
have been influenced by the servant's interest in receiving an inheritance from
his wealthy, childless master. Both economic and emotional factors may have
played a role in Pond's decision not to leave the home and employ of the
sodomitical Sension. The testimony hints at a close, complex relationship between the young servant Pond, and the man a witness derisively reported Pond
called his "Uncle Sension." That use of the word "Uncle" to denote a tie between
individuals unrelated by blood, is an early example of a fictitious kinship term
signifying a felt emotional bond. The terms uncle, nephew, aunt, niece, mother,
daughter, father, son, brother, and sister, were later used as ways of naming
intimate relationships between otherwise unrelated persons. The terminology, of
course, derives from the relations of family life, and the different, changing
historical forms of intimacy associated with it.

Since almost all the known documents of this early period record only
allegations of physical acts, not the character of the emotions that accompanied
them, it is difficult to know much about the quality of the subjective sodomitical
experience in this era. It would seem that, with a biblically derived stigma and
universal death penalty hanging over them, sodomitical activity and impulse were
usually associated with an enormous and particular quality of fear, guilt, and
shame. This is hinted at in the testimony concerning Nicholas Sension's praying
to God to save him from his sodomitical temptation. Wigglesworth's diary was
written in an attempt to assuage a similar guilt. Only by rejecting completely the
dominant religious morality could any early colonist, it seems, possibly resist the
emotional consequences of the orthodox condemnation of sodomy. Two reports

of unrepentant resisters (discussed below) suggest just such an atheistical stance.

Though the little available evidence makes any generalization tentative, it would seem that the executions for sodomy between males, and the very existence of a colony-wide death penalty, had a profound effect on the quality of intimate relationships between males. We may now speculate that executions for sodomy, the many well-known statutory death penalties for intercourse between men, and the honored biblical prescription, dirtied and deterred not only erotic activity, but also the deep affection of male for male. The social construction of sodomy as one of the most monstrous, frightful, death-deserving crimes seemingly created a universe in which the intimate, profound friendship of man with man was suspect. Lafitau's report of the Jesuits' suppression of intimacies among Native American men documents these Christians' suspicions of male-male friendship. The metamorphosis of Wigglesworth's "fond affection" for his male pupils into "filthy lust" documents intimacy sullied and made guilty by sodomitical association. It would seem that executions for sodomy, and that universal death penalty, cast a pall of death over the love of male for male, from the first days of American settlement.

## Resistance

All were resisters who in the colonies participated in sodomy, or other erotic acts with members of their own sex, or any non-procreative acts. Their behavior violated the sacrosanct rules of the established authorities. In two known instances, however, individuals, even under threat of harsh punishment, did explicitly resist repressive rulers. In both instances this resistance seemingly involved, not a defense of particular sexual acts, but explicit opposition to that religion which was the main justication of "proper" human intercourse.

In December 1642, Elizabeth Johnson, a servant in Essex County, Massachusetts, was sentenced to be fined and "severely whipped" for "unseemly practices" with "another maid," for "stubbornness to her mistress, answering [her] rudely and unmannerly," and for "stopping her ears with her hands when the Word of God was read." Though the "unseemly practices" between maids were unspecified, Johnson had apparently developed her own answer to the biblical injunctions concerning women changing the "natural use" and servants obeying their masters. Acting in defiance of theologically defined sexual propriety, the state religion, and her legally established subordination to her mistress, Elizabeth Johnson managed to violate three of the ruling group's major institutions—law, religion, and class.

In 1646, in New Haven, the resistant William Plaine was awarded the colony's most severe punishment—death—after he had admitted to sodomy with two persons in England, and (in John Winthrop's words) "corrupted a great part of the youth of Guilford by masturbations . . . above a hundred times." The very quantity of Plaine's masturbations suggest the great popularity of his practice with Guilford's youth, and that no coercive "molestation" was involved; Plaine seems to have been America's earliest, practical sex educator. Examined about his conduct, Plaine reportedly "did insinuate seeds of atheism, questioning whether there was a God." Winthrop condemned Plaine for challenging not only religion, but the sacred, legal institutions of marriage and procreation.

Elizabeth Johnson's and William Plaine's resistance did not reportedly include a defense of particular erotic acts. Both did reportedly reject that religion in the name of which they were condemned. In the early colonies it was unlikely that Johnson's and Plaine's resistance would take the form of defending specific erotic practices, or sexual relations between persons of the same sex. In a society in which women's erotic acts with women were not usually the subject of legal prohibition—in which there was little or no perception of a person called a "sodomite," little or no perception of specifically sodomitical feelings, and little emphasis upon "same" and "different" sexes—there was also little likelihood of a specifically sodomitical defense, or a sodomitical consciousness, comparable to a modern "homosexual," "gay," or "lesbian" awareness. In the early colonies, there was little possibility that those legally charged with sodomy or other erotic acts with members of their own sex would see themselves as members of a collectively persecuted group. Resistance, when it occurred at all, was likely to take the form of individual acts of opposition to that religion condemning all erotic acts and feelings not linked to male-female procreative acts in marriage.

Elizabeth Johnson and William Plaine evidently paid for their resistance—she with pain, he with death—and their defiance seems to have been calculated not to avoid punishment, but to affirm their own behavior and feelings. That any such defiance was recorded in the early colonies seems remarkable, given the institutionalized power of religious and civil authorities.

### The Present Usefulness of the Early Colonial Past

In America in the 1980s, a Bible-based morality is often invoked as the right-wing rationale for a mean-spirited anti-homosexuality. Yet that present anti-homosexuality is determined, I think, not by an old text or value system, but by those objective economic changes transforming traditional relationships between women and men, parents and children. Concern about the effect on "the family" and children of a more "tolerant" social response to "homosexuality" informs present legal decisions and expressions of anxiety. But those modern consumers, "children," and that modern consumer unit, "the family," are qualitatively different from their early colonial counterparts. Present concern about "the family" has different social origins and implications than the early colonists' concern to preserve their "family." The "sodomy" laws remaining on the books in the 1980s, and the harassment, arrests, trials, and imprisonments based upon them, may have a certain ambiguous continuity with the earliest colonial American sodomy laws and cases. Yet those colonial statutes and prosecutions do not explain the present existence of sodomy laws and prosecutions. Today's legislators who allow old sodomy laws to exist, and those officials who prosecute homosexuals, reproduce a version of the past in the present. Unless we believe that past conditions act to reproduce themselves, unless we in the present are mechanically determined by the past, we need to explain present conditions by the group interests now served by the selective reproduction of the past.

The early colonists' response to sodomy as mortal sin and high crime differs greatly from twentieth-century Americans' response to "homosexuality" as either an individual "disease" to be "cured," a "problem" to be "pitied," a "life-style" to be "purchased," or as simply one way of feeling, acting, and being human. To be sure, homosexuals are still sometimes physically beaten, even put to death (murdered, not executed). Homosexuals are now sometimes provoked to murderous hate, the destruction of self, or others. Homosexuals are still encouraged to acts of public self-denial, each a little death. Fear and hatred of homosexuals, active, institutionalized anti-homosexuality are, of course, still with us. But present historical forms of anti-homosexuality are not explained by early colonial anti-sodomy. Present anti-homosexuality is not causally linked to that colonial call for death.

Despite the much-touted, greatly exaggerated "sexual revolution," many of us today still struggle against a lingering "puritanism." But our contemporary "puritanism" differs basically from that original "Puritanism" documented here. It seems doubtful if any direct connections can be discovered between the early Puritan era and our own. Why then research and analyze that old, essentially superseded historical form of sex? If each form of sexuality is historically specific, what can the old forms tell us about our own society and lives?

One lesson of this history, I think, is precisely that the distant past has only a negative, contrasting relation to the present; our own contemporary social organization of sex is as historically specific as past social-sexual forms. Studying the past, seeing the essential differences between past and present social forms of sex, we may gain a fresh perspective on our own sex as socially made, not naturally given. Comparing past and present, we are usefully distanced from that sexuality whose specific social forms many of us, until recently, took for granted as "psychological," "biological," "natural," or "unnatural." Perceiving our own sex and affection as a historical, socially constructed form we better understand the possibility of reconstructing it. Understanding the different ways sodomy and other forms of sex were socially organized in the early colonies can help us question our own quite different historical organization of eroticism and intimacy.

# Documents

## 1607, June
### John Smith and others: *"Money, saxefras, furs, or love"*

A book titled *A Map of Virginia,* describing the early history of that colony through the eyes of one group of its settlers, was published in Oxford, England, under the editorship of John Smith, with contributions by himself and other eyewitnesses.[1]

Chapter two relates that within ten days after June 15, 1607, when the ships which had brought the colonists departed back to England, the remaining settlers were "oppressed" by "extreme weakness and sickness." The "cause" was said to be that while the ships had remained the settlers'

> allowance was somewhat bettered, by a daily proportion of biscuit which the sailors would pilfer to sell, give or exchange with us, for money, saxefras, furs, or love. [A printed marginal note identifies this passage as "The sailors' abuses."]*

After the sailors departed, inadequate food and housing, and "extreme toil," seriously weakened the remaining Virginia settlers.

The above narrative indicates that "love," seemingly meaning sexual favors, was one of those items which the first American settlers exchanged, along with money, sassafras, and furs, to keep themselves alive. That term "love" apparently referred to what are now usually called "homosexual" contacts; it was unlikely that seventeenth-century English sailors would have traded stolen biscuit for the settlers' affection, or given biscuit away because of their "love" for the settlers.

---

*In the old documents spelling and punctuation have usually been modernized and regularized for ease in reading, quotation marks have been added; nothing of substance has been changed. Occasionally, an original spelling or capitalization ("saxefras," for example) has been retained where it seemed to enhance the period "feel" of the text without distracting from its meaning.

Though a few of these early colonial texts were reprinted in *Gay American History,* for the sake of completeness I include brief versions of them here, often with some new details, and in a chronology in which they take on new resonances.

The marginal reference to the sailors' "abuses" lends credence to this interpretation. "Love" *was* used at this time to refer to "The animal instinct between the sexes, and its gratification"; the *Oxford English Dictionary* cites the King James Bible (1611): "Come let us take our fill of love until the morning" (Proverbs vii, 18). Since there were no women among the Virginia colonists in 1607, the "gratification" of the "animal instinct" cited above appears to be the first documented instance of carnal relations between Englishmen in the New World.[2]

The existence of this casual reference to a sexual exchange between males, in an account published and publicly distributed in England, begins to be explained by its historical context.

The *Map of Virginia* did not, according to its modern editor, "tell the side of the Virginia Company, with which [John] Smith was so often at odds." Smith and his close associates wrote their version of events "against the wishes of the Virginia Company," and together had it printed with the help of a group of sympathetic clergymen.[322]

The subtitle of the book promised that it unfolded the "fundamental causes from whence have sprang so many miseries to the undertakers, and scandals to the businesses." An opening note "To the reader" stressed the narrative's truth, and that it was written by "those that have lived residents in the land: not sailors, or passengers, nor . . . mercenary contemplators." The manuscript "was thought fit to publish" in its "rude" original form, since such an honest, unadorned account would best help to "purge that famous action" of colonization from "infamous scandal." The "discourse," it was said, "is no Judge of men's manners," and was "only a reporter of their actions in Virginia, not [intended] to disgrace any, accuse any, excuse any, nor flatter any." The narrative "can detract from none that intendeth there to adventure their fortunes." To "speak truly of the first planters, howsoever many difficulties obscured their endevours," is said to be a way of showing gratefulness and memorializing them.[376–77]

The reference to the "love"/"biscuit" exchange appears in chapter two of *A Map of Virginia*. Chapters one and two, apparently written by Thomas Studley, Robert Fenton, Edward Harrington, and John Smith, were intended to explain why "there was no better speed and success" in the early colonizing of Virginia.[377] The chapters relate a tale of sickness, storms at sea, "discontents," "envy," "dissention," "malice," and political intrigue among the first settlers, as well as assaults by hostile Indians. The casualness of the reference to the exchange of "love" for biscuit suggests that such life and death barters were common knowledge among some seventeenth-century Englishmen.

STATUTE

# 1610, May 24
## Virginia: "Sodomy" law

From the founding of the Virginia Colony at Jamestown in 1607 until 1610 apparently no law of that colony dealt specifically with "sodomy" or "buggery."[3] But the English statute making "buggery" a felony punishable by death was implicitly regarded as in force. In 1610, Sir Thomas Gates, governor of the Virginia Colony, first issued the "Articles, Laws, and Orders, Divine, Politique, and Martial," a code placing Virginia under martial law—a law including the earliest-known English–American penalty for "sodomy." The code, later elaborated upon by Governors De La Warr and Thomas Dale, remained in effect until 1618.

Some background explains the genesis of this sodomy law. By 1609, the heads of the London Company, the corporate owners of the Virginia Colony, felt the need for strict discipline in the settlement because they did not think the colonists were willingly channeling their full energies into work. On the London Company's initiative, Governor Gates proclaimed, and Governors de la Warre and Dale later maintained that martial law, including a long list of capital crimes. Among other offenses, death was provided for impious or treasonous speech, blasphemy, sacrilege, theft, illegal trade with the Indians, and the "sins of Sodomie." The plural "sins" probably referred to bestiality as well as male-male contacts. A series of lesser crimes were penalized by physical mutilation or other brutal retribution. The laws were enforced with a vengeance by the governor's personal decree, without trial by jury. These "ruthless policies," said historian Alden T. Vaughan, "rested on the assumption that the colony's plight necessitated stringent discipline." In England, Vaughan said, "Family, church, community, and government guided personal and group behavior. Virginia [at this time] had few such controls: almost no families, few clergymen, scattered and unstable communities, and an unpredictable government that took orders from a commercial organization." During its first decade "Virginia was essentially a military post serving a trading company." The colony's rulers were soldiers, recruited to defend the American outpost and impose order on its inhabitants. The London Company, sure that the colony had become a place for "Parents to disburden themselves of lascivious sons, masters of bad servants, and wives of ill husbands," initiated martial law as of "most dispatch and terror and fittest for this government." The Company heads decided that dissolute Virginians required "severe discipline . . . , sharp laws . . . , a hard life and much labor."

The ninth provision of the Virginia legal code of 1610 read:

No man shall commit the horrible, detestable sins of Sodomie upon pain of death; & he or she that can be lawfully convict[ed] of Adultery shall be punished with death. No man shall ravish or force any woman, maid or Indian, or other, upon pain of death. . . .

Fornication was also penalized—by a whipping for the first and second offense, and, for a third offense, by a whipping three times a week for a month, and a public apology in church.

Martial law remained in force in Virginia until 1618. From that year until 1661, the laws of England were apparently informally adopted by the Virginia settlers.

STATUTE

# 1613
# New Netherland: Sodomy law

The area now known as New York was under Dutch rule from this year until 1664, when the English took control. The law of Holland, which descended from the Roman Emperor Justinian, punished sodomy with death.[4] Sodomy cases in Dutch-held New Amsterdam were recorded on June 25, 1646; August 26, 1658; and May 13, 1660 (see).

LEGAL CASE

# 1624, November 30
# Virginia: Richard Cornish executed

The Virginia Colony's legislative and judicial body tried and executed Richard Cornish, a ship's captain, for an alleged sexual attack on William Cowse, his indentured servant and steward.

The detailed, explicit testimony in the Cornish case is reported in the records of the Virginia Council and General Court, in meetings from November 30, 1624 through February 6, 1626.[5]*

The twenty-nine-year-old William Cowse (or Couse) testified that on August 27, 1624, on board the ship *Ambrose,* anchored in the James River, Captain Richard Cornish "went into bed" and "would have" Cowse "come into the bed to him." When Cowse refused, Cornish allegedly "went out of the bed and did cut" Cowse's codpiece (the flap concealing the opening in the front of his breeches). Cowse stated that Cornish "made him go into the bed, and . . . there lay upon him, and kissed him and hugged him." Cornish allegedly said "he would

*The brief account below adds a few details to the fuller testimony reprinted in *GAH,* pp. 16–19.

love [Cowse] if he would now and then come and lay with him." And "so by force," said Cowse, Cornish turned him "upon his belly, and so did put [him] to pain in the fundament, and did wet him." Later, said Cowse, Cornish "would put his hands in [Cowse's] codpiece and played [with him] and kissed him." When Cowse refused Cornish's advances, Cornish allegedly "forbade all the ship's company to eat with him," and made Cowse "cook for all the rest."[34]

Walter Mathew, the "boatswain's mate" aboard the vessel, testified that he overheard Cornish calling Cowse "into his bed cabin." Mathew said he then heard Cowse reply to Cornish that "he would not"—saying that "if he did so, it would be an overthrow to him both in soul and body." Cowse reportedly "alleged the scripture" to Cornish. Later, Mathew said, Cowse told him that Cornish "would have buggered him," but did not confess that Cornish had actually performed the act.[42]

Richard Cornish was found guilty of buggery and executed. After Cornish's execution a number of persons objected strongly to the Virginia Court's punishment in this case—objections that, considering the possibility of losing one's ears for criticizing the colony's rulers, it took some courage to voice.

For declaring that Cornish was "put to death through a scurvy boy's means," and that Cornish "was hanged for a rascally boy wrongfully," one Edward Nevell was sentenced to stand on the pillory and there lose both his ears, to serve the colony for a year, and to forever be incapable of becoming a free man (he was, evidently, an indentured servant).[78, 81, 83, 85]

Thomas Hatch was an indentured servant who had arrived in Virginia on the ship *Duty,* in 1619, when he was seventeen. Hatch and other so-called "dissolute" persons were probably gathered up in the streets of London. His seven-year service to George Yeardley was to be over in 1626. Hatch, like Edward Nevell, also reportedly declared that "in his conscience" he thought Cornish was put to death "wrongfully." Warned that he too could lose his ears for such criticism, Hatch allegedly said, "I care not for my ears, let them hang me if they will." For this talk Hatch was, in 1626, ordered by the Court to be publicly whipped, to be set upon the pillory, and there to lose one ear. In addition, Hatch's service to George Yeardley was extended seven additional years, from the day of sentencing.[93]

Also following Richard Cornish's execution, his brother Jeffrey, while in Canada, upon hearing reports of what he allegedly called his relative's "wrongful" execution, was said to have sworn revenge against the governor and others. Jeffrey Cornish, however, remained out of reach of the Virginia Court's retribution.

William Cowse, Cornish's alleged victim, did not win his freedom by his master's execution. Though no one had legal claim to Cowse's service, the court ordered him to choose another master, who would then help compensate the government for the costs of prosecuting and executing Cornish. In effect, then, Cowse's labor helped defray the cost of his master's execution.

CROSSING PERSON/LEGAL CASE

# 1629, March 25
## Virginia: Thomas/Thomasine Hall

The records of the Virginia Court reveal the history of a servant, Thomas or Thomasine Hall, who claimed to be "both a man and a woman," but who was alleged by neighbors to be a man.[6] This document is valuable for the study of the historically specific reaction to sexual ambiguity (in this case, perhaps a physical ambiguity, certainly a mental one). The recorded testimony leaves it unclear whether Hall was actually physically hermaphroditic, or was a biological male who had long dressed and worked as a female and had come to consider him/herself male and female.

Whatever Hall's physiological character, the documents reveal a three-way competition to define Hall's sexuality: by Hall him/herself; by the general populace; and by the governor. These documents reveal Hall's neighbors trying to fit this sexually ambiguous individual into the existing category, "man." In contrast, the governor, in resolving this case, officially pronounced Hall "a man and a woman," and required him/her to wear items of each sex's clothing—thereby accepting "man" and "woman" as non-exclusive categories. This resolution was congruent with the relative lack of official stress placed on sexual differentiation in this era (discussed in the introductory essay to this section). Later, in the 1800s, the rigidification of and absolute opposition between the categories "male" and "female" would make such a resolution unlikely: Sexual ambiguity (physical or mental) would then be resolved by categorizing an individual as either "male" or "female" (as in two reports of "hermaphrodites" in 1836 and 1839; see backnote 37, p. 676.).

In testimony before the Virginia Court in 1629, Hall told of being "born at or near Newcastle Upon Tyne." Hall was often told of being christened "by the name of Thomasine," by which name he/she was called. Hall had dressed "in woman's apparel . . . until the age of twelve." At that age Thomasine Hall was sent to an aunt in London, where Hall lived for ten years. At that time Thomasine Hall's brother was pressed into military service. Hall, now twenty-two years old, "cut off his hair and changed his [woman's] apparel into the fashion of a man" —and joined the army. Returning from military duty to Plymouth, England, Hall again "changed himself into woman's apparel and made bone lace and did other work with his needle." Shortly afterward, Hall once more changed "his apparel into the habit of a man and so came over into this country."

After Hall's arrival as a male in America, he once again changed his social-sexual character, dressing and working as a woman. But rumors spread that Hall was actually a man—and that "he" had committed fornication.

Francis England told the Virginia Court of a "rumor" that "Hall did lie with a [serving] maid . . . called Great Bess." England also testified that, when questioned by a certain Captain Basse, Hall "answered . . . that he was both man and woman." Asked why he dressed as a woman, Hall reportedly answered, "I go in woman's apparel to get a bit for my cat" (apparently, a seventeenth-century working-class women's expression for sexual intercourse; the phrase seems akin to the modern heterosexual male [derogatory] expression "To get a piece of pussy.") But it is unclear why Hall would dress as a woman in order to obtain sexual access to a woman.

Hall's response to Captain Basse did not satisfy Virginians. Francis England further testified that he and Roger Rodes were alone with Hall after hearing the rumors that Hall was a man. Rodes then told Hall "I will see what thou carriest," whereupon Rodes and England "laid hands upon" Hall, "threw" Hall "on his back," and England "pulled out his members"—which convinced England that Hall "was a perfect man."

John Atkins testified that Alice Longe, Dorothye Rodes, and Barbara Hall, after hearing the rumors that Hall was "a man and a woman," physically searched Hall, afterward reporting that "he was a man." It was then that Captain Basse had asked if Hall was a "man or woman," and (according to this testimony) "Hall replied he was both, only he had not the use of the man's Ptc."[?] The original document, which is mutilated here, suggests that Basse inspected Hall and discovered "a piece of flesh growing at the [section missing] belly as big as the top of his little finger [an] inch long." After this, Captain Basse "commanded [Hall] to be put in woman's apparel," apparently deciding to accept Hall as female.

But those who had earlier searched Hall were still not convinced of Hall's female sex. About February 12, 1629, Hall was living at John Atkins's house. A group of searchers, finding Hall asleep, inspected Hall again, and once more found Hall "to be a man."

The following Sunday, a group of searchers assembled once more, and two women inspected Hall in John Atkins's presence. Atkins testified that he asked Hall "if that were all he had, to which he [Hall] answered 'I have a piece of a hole.'" Atkins, Hall's master, commanded Hall "to lie on his back and show the same." The women, searching Hall, "did again find him to be a man." Atkins then commanded Hall "to be put in man's apparel." The next day Atkins went to Captain Basse's, told him that Hall "was found to be a man," and asked that Hall "be punished for his abuse" (probably his fornication with Great Bess, and possibly his cross-dressing, and claim to be both man and woman).

The Virginia Court, accepting Hall's own self-definition, finally ordered it to "be published in the plantation" where Hall lived, "that he is a man and a woman." Hall was ordered by the court to "go clothed in man's apparel, only his head to be attired in a coyse[?] and crosscloth [a linen cloth worn across the forehead, especially by women] with an apron before him." Hall was also ordered to "find sureties" [leave bond] "for his good behavior . . . until the Court shall discharge him. . . ."

LEGAL CASE

# 1629, June 29
## Francis Higgeson: *"5 beastly Sodomitical boys"*

The Reverend Francis Higgeson's journal of his trip to New England on board the ship *Talbot* reported: "This day we examined 5 beastly Sodomitical boys, which confessed their wickedness not to be named." "The fact was so foul," said Higgeson, "we reserved them to be punished by the governor when we came to new England." The governor, he said, afterwards sent the boys "back to the company to be punished in old England as the crime deserved."[7]

On September 29 the General Court of the Massachusetts Bay Colony assigned two members to acquaint a director of the Massachusetts Bay Company in England with the boys' misdemeanor,

> and advise what punishment may be inflicted upon them, and how the Company may be legally discharged of them.

In England, sodomy was at this time a crime for which males over fourteen could be hanged. The boys' fate is unknown.

STATUTE

# 1632
## Maryland: "Buggery" law

Lord Baltimore was granted a charter making him the proprietor of Maryland. The English "buggery" law was considered in force, and apparently remained so in Maryland until 1793.[8]

LEGAL CASE

# 1635, February 14
## New Hampshire: *"Two men . . . committed sodomy"*

The papers of the Province of New Hampshire, settled in 1623, include a report[9]:

> Capt. Wiggin, Governor of Pascutaquack, under Lord Say and Brook wrote to our governor, desiring to have two men tried here, who had committed sodomy with each other and that on the Lord's day in time of public exercise. The governor and divers of the assistants met and conferred about it but did not think fit to try them here.

♀  STATUTE

# 1636, October
# John Cotton: "Sodomy" law proposal

The Reverend John Cotton, who had been asked to draw up a legal code for Massachusetts Bay, submitted his proposal to the General Court.[10]

Cotton proposed the death penalty for sixteen crimes: false worship, sabbath breaking, reviling the magistrates, cursing or smiting parents, blasphemy, idolatry, witchcraft, murder, adultery, incest, sodomy, bestiality, man stealing, false witness, wilful perjury, and treason.

The famous minister innovatively suggested that women, as well as men, be put to death for "sodomy," proposing:

> Unnatural filthiness, to be punished with death, whether sodomy, which is carnal fellowship of man with man, or woman with woman, or buggery, which is carnal fellowship of man or woman with beasts or fowls.

Cotton's code was not adopted in Massachusetts; instead, Nathaniel Ward's code was enacted in 1641 (see). But in 1656 (see) Cotton's sodomy law was adopted in the New Haven Colony, with a significant amendation: the explicit reference to "woman with woman" was replaced by the more ambiguous prohibition against women changing the "natural use" into that which "is against nature."

STATUTE

# 1636, November 15
# Plymouth: "Sodomy" law

In the earliest codification of laws in colonial America, Plymouth, founded sixteen years earlier, included eight offenses punishable by death[11]:

> Treason or rebellion against the person of the King, State, or Common Wealth, either of England or these Colonies.
>     Willfull Murder.
>     Solemn compaction or conversing with the devil by way of witchcraft, conjuration or the like.
>     Willfull and purposed burning of ships houses.
>     Sodomy, rapes, buggery.
>     Adultery to be punished.

This Plymouth law was next revised in 1671 (see).

LEGAL CASE

# 1637, August 6
## Plymouth: John Allexander and Thomas Roberts,
### *"Lewd behavior and unclean carriage"*

The Plymouth court found Allexander and Roberts guilty of "often spending their seed one upon the other."[12] The Plymouth crime of "sodomy" was not mentioned in connection with the case, for "sodomy," then, required "penetration," not mere emission, even if this emission was mutual, and "often." The class difference of the parties was also suggested; Allexander, presented as the instigator, was apparently a free man, Roberts an indentured servant. Whether this intermingling of social orders, as well as of seed, lent gravity to the crime in the eyes of the judges was not disclosed. The record states:

> John Allexander & Thomas Roberts were both examined and found guilty of lewd behavior and unclean carriage one with another, by often spending their seed one upon another, which was proved both by witness & their own confession; the said Allexander [was] found to have been formerly notoriously guilty that way, and seeking to allure others thereunto. The said John Allexander was therefore censured [sentenced] by the Court to be severely whipped, and burnt in the shoulder with a hot iron, and to be perpetually banished [from] the government [territory] of New Plymouth, and if he be at any time found within the same, to be whipped out again by the appointment [order] of the next justice, etc., and so as oft as he shall be found within this government. Which penalty was accordingly inflicted.
>
> Thomas Roberts was censured to be severely whipped, and to return to his master, Mr. Atwood, and serve out his time with him, but to be disabled hereby to enjoy any lands within this government, except he manifest better desert

The last five qualifying words were added, as an afterthought, in the margin.

On October 2, 1637, Thomas Roberts was one of four men charged by the Plymouth Court with "disorderly living, & therefore to be required to give an account how they live."

Four years later, on January 5, 1642, a "Thomas Roberts," possibly the same individual cited above, was mentioned in the Plymouth Court records:

> Thomas Roberts, of Duxborrow, is ordered by the Court that he shall lodge no more with George Morrey, a diseased person, and betwixt this and the next Court of Assistants provide himself of lodging; and then make report to the Court how it may be probable he may live without being chargeable.

STATUTE

# 1641, November
## Massachusetts Bay: Sodomy law

Massachusetts Bay legislators adopted (but did not yet print) their Body of Laws and Liberties, welcoming refugees from famines, wars, or "the Tyranny or oppression of their persecutors."[13]* This code, written by the Reverend Nathaniel Ward, included the death penalty for sodomy (refered to only as "man lying with mankind as he lies with a woman"). A list of those particular crimes punished by death was printed as a broadside, purportedly first in Massachusetts in 1641–42, then, with some additions, in London in 1643. The original Massachusetts broadside of 1641–42 (no copies of which now exist) was the first publication of any laws in colonial America.

Most of the fifteen capital crimes listed in the London broadside of 1643 were based on Old Testament references actually cited in the text. The capital laws of Massachusetts Bay provided death for

(1) "any man" who worshiped any God "but the Lord God";

(2) "any man or woman" who "be a Witch";

(3) "any person" who shall "blaspheme the Name of God";

(4) "any person" who commited "willful [premeditated] murder" (or "manslaughter");

(5) "any person" who "slayeth another suddenly," in anger;

(6) "any person" who slew another "through guile";

(7) "a man or woman" who shall "lie with any beast, or brute creature, by carnal copulation" (the beast also was to be "slain, and buried");

(8) "a man [who] lyeth with mankind, as he lyeth with a woman" (both parties were to be executed);

(9) "any person" who committed "adultery with a married, or espoused [engaged] wife" (both "the Adulterer, and the Adulteress" were to be executed);

(10) "any man" who had "carnal copulation with any woman-child under ten years old, either with, or without her consent";

(11) "any man" who "forcibly," without consent, "shall ravish any maid or woman that is lawfully married or contracted";

---

*The passage of this law, and the cluster of sodomy, bestiality, and related cases, 1641–42, coincided with an "economic depression which befell the [Massachusetts Bay] colony, in 1639, as a result of the drift toward civil war in England. Immigration came virtually to a halt." The "onset of war in 1642, together with the colony's growing reputation for intolerance, not only discouraged new settlers but even caused many of the colonists to return to England or settle elsewhere. These developments had a profound effect on the economy of the colony." With the "rapid growth of a debtor class" came "an attendant increase in crime"; see George Lee Haskins, *Law and Authority in Early Massachusetts; A Study in Tradition and Design* (N. Y.: Macmillan, 1960), pp. 107–09; also see pp. 60, 171, 177, 215. We may speculate that the temporary halt in immigration as a means of population increase was associated with a greater stress on procreation, a greater concern about non-procreative sexual acts.

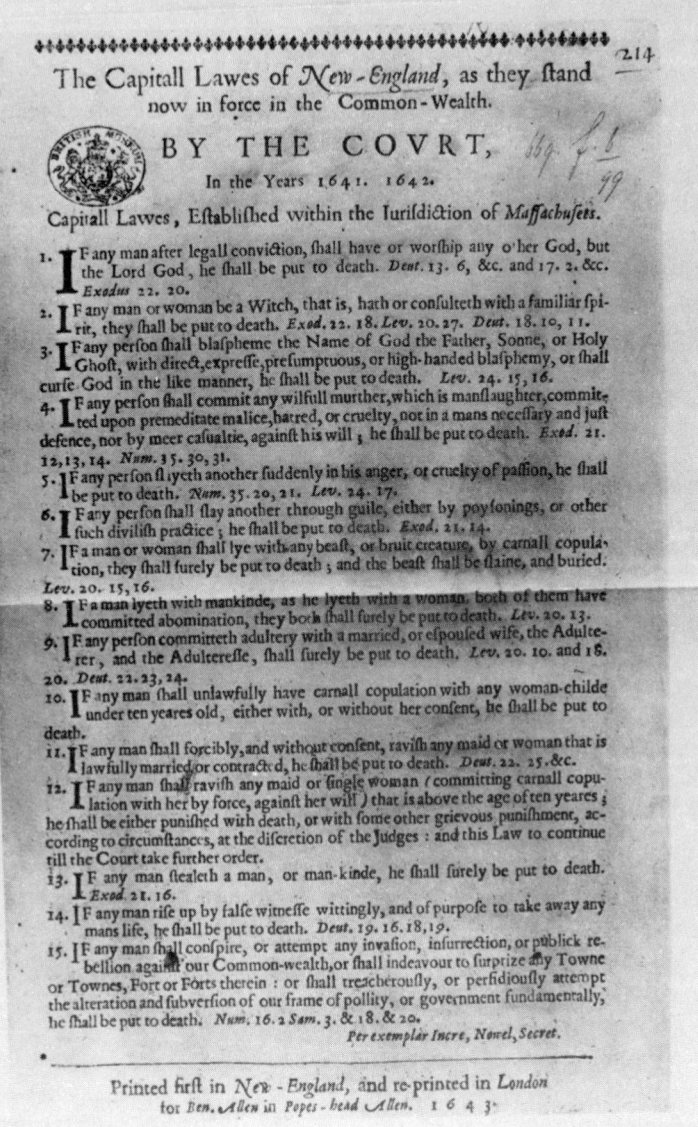

This broadside, published in London in 1643, was a reprint of one first published in New England.
The New England broadside listed the capital laws, passed in 1641 and 1642, of the Massachusetts
Bay Colony (in *Publications of the Colonial Society of Massachusetts,* vol. 17, *Transactions 1913–1914*
[Boston: published by the Society, 1915], p. 116).

(12) "any man" who shall "ravish any maid or single woman" above the age of ten "(committing carnal copulation with her by force, against her will)"—the penalty was either death or "some other grievous punishment, according to the circumstances";

(13) "any man" who "stealeth a man, or man-kind" (the latter term was no doubt intended to include women);

(14) "any man" who "by false witness" (perjury) intended "to take away any man's life";

(15) "any man" who shall "conspire, or attempt any invasion, insurrection, or public rebellion against our Common-wealth," or who shall "attempt the alteration and subversion of our frame of polity, or government fundamentally" (treason). (Crimes 10, 11, and 12 were added to the original list on June 14, 1642, after the case of male-female child abuse described in the next entry.)

The sodomy provision (number 8), quoted from the Old Testament, read:

If a man lyeth with mankind, as he lyeth with a woman, both of them have committed abomination, they both shall surely be put to death. Lev. 20:13.

The whole Body of Laws and Liberties was first printed in 1648.

♀ LEGAL CASE/COMMENTARY

# 1641–42
## Massachusetts Bay: "Sodomy"?

In 1641, in the Massachusetts Bay Colony, three men were discovered to have had carnal relations with two young girls when the eldest girl was between seven and nine years old.[14] The Massachusetts judges' need to decide the exact legal nature of the crime, and its punishment, resulted in a two-colony-wide discussion of "sodomy" and "sodomitical acts," the most detailed, lengthy, and revealing of such commentaries documented in American colonial records. That this discussion of "sodomy" was motivated by a crime of male against female illustrates the colonists' relative lack of preoccupation with gender in their categorizing of sexual acts and their relative emphasis on other characteristics of those acts.

Three Puritan ministers were asked "What sodomitical acts are to be punished by death . . . ?" Although these theologians' answers are long and their reasoning minutely detailed, this very detail clarifies the character of their ideas about sodomy and its punishment.

In resolving this case Massachusetts magistrates, contrary to the ministers' advice, finally charged the men, not with "sodomy," or even "sodomitical acts," but with "carnal knowledge . . . in a most vile & abominal manner," and with "abusing" the girls in an "unclean & wicked manner." The magistrates did *not* order the guilty men to be executed, but imposed a series of whippings, fines, and public humiliations.

John Winthrop, in his history of New England, reported that the sexual contacts in question had occurred over a period of two years, when John Humfry, one of the assistants to the governor of the Massachusetts Bay Colony, had gone back to England, leaving his daughters, Dorcas and Sara, at Lynn, with Daniel Fairfield. Fairfield was described as a former indentured servant, and a married man, who had been a "member of the church . . . in good esteem for piety and sobriety."

Winthrop's history related that the two girls had visited Fairfield's house,

> and were by him abused very often, especially upon the Lord's days and lecture days, by agitation and effusion of seed, and after by entering the body of the elder, as it seemed; for upon search she was found to have been forced. . . .

Another man, Jenkin Davis, was said to have

> abuse[d] the elder of these girls . . . but constantly denied any entrance to her body. . . .

Of the third man accused, John Hudson, Winthrop reported:

> he did abuse her [Dorcas] many times, so as she was grown capable of man's fellowship, and took pleasure in it.

Unlike Winthrop's account, the court records describing the case, and reporting the verdict, did not specify the exact nature of the crime, and did not mention either penetration or emission.

The Body of Laws of the Massachusetts Bay Colony was not adopted until November 1641, and the sexual acts in question were discovered before that time. The judges of the colony had, therefore, to decide, not only the exact nature of the crime, but the appropriate punishment. To this end the governor of the Massachusetts Bay Colony, Richard Bellingham, on March 28, 1642, wrote to the governor of Plymouth, William Bradford. The Massachusetts governor asked the Plymouth governor, his magistrates, and the colony's church elders for their advice "concerning heinous offenses in point of uncleaness." The Massachusetts governor was trying to ascertain if the case in question involved a "sodomitical act" punishable by death. (As there was at this time no law against rape in Massachusetts, and "no express law" in the Bible concerning rape, the magistrates did not consider whether the crime in this case might be so categorized.)

On May 17, 1642, Governor Bradford of Plymouth answered Bellingham of Massachusetts, apologizing for the two-month delay. Bradford said he had discussed the legal questions with his assistants, and referred them to the Reverend Elders of Plymouth, three of whose written opinions he enclosed. Bradford himself offered no conclusions concerning the specific case in question, but suggested that "if there be not penetration," the death penalty not be applied in cases of sodomy, bestiality, and adultery. But he added that "foulness of circumstances," and the "frequency" of the crime might also determine its degree of punishment.

The Reverend John Rayner of Plymouth answered the questions "What sodomitical acts are to be punished with death?" and what circumstances made sodomitical acts capital?[404–06]

"In judicial law," according to Rayner, (the "morality" of which was his concern) it was clear "that carnal knowledge of man or lying with man as with woman," with "penetration," was "sodomy," to be punished by death. His authorities were Leviticus and Genesis.

Rayner added "that this foul sin [sodomy] might be capital" though there was no "penetration," but only contact and rubbing leading to seminal emission. Such non-penetrative, emissive contact was capital, he argued, because Leviticus decreed that the man who was lain with, as well as he who lay with him, should be put to death. Non-penetrative (and even non-emissive) contact was also capital because St. Paul's letter to the Romans decreed that women, like men, "guilty of this unnatural sin" should be put to death. If such non-penetrative, non-emissive copulation of woman with woman was to receive death, so might other forms of non-penetrative, non-emissive contact, argued Rayner.

Non-penetrative contacts were also capital, said Rayner, by analogy with bestiality—for if a woman even attempted connection with an animal, whether there was penetration or not, Leviticus decreed that she should be put to death.

Non-penetrative acts were also capital, Rayner added, because certain characteristics of acts might make them equal to "penetration" in moral gravity. As examples he cited the "frequency" of acts—also their "long continence with a high hand, utterly extinguishing all light of nature." He added that sometimes even the determined intention to commit, and the "bold attempting of, the foulest acts" might be capital. He cited a biblical decree for attempted premeditated murder.

"Sodomy and bestiality" should also be punishable by death, continued Rayner, because these acts were "more against the light of nature than some other capital crimes of uncleanness." It was the greater foulness of sodomy and bestiality which made them capital, argued Rayner (with quite circular logic).

Sodomy should also be capital, he said, because "it might be committed with more secrecy and less suspician" than other crimes, and therefore needed to be more "restrained and suppressed by the law."

And finally, in a particularly obscure passage, Rayner concluded that sodomy should be capital even though this sin might not involve the same "degree of sinning against the family and posterity" as some other "capital sins of uncleanness." The idea seems to be that even if sodomy was less sinful than some other capital offenses against the family and procreation, sodomy was still sinful enough to merit death.

The Reverend Ralph Partridge of Duxbury also answered the question "What is that sodomitical act which is to be punished with death?"[407–08]

Partridge thought it probable that "a voluntary effusion of seed" produced by the intercourse of man with man (as of man with woman) was the sin forbidden by Leviticus, and punished by death. He thought such intercourse was capital even if there was no "penetration"—because other acts may be analogous to "penetration." But Partridge then admitted he was not confident of his opinion concerning the propriety of death for non-penetrative copulation, for the following reasons. First, Genesis described "the intended act of the Sodomites" on the analogy of "carnal copulation of man with woman" (that is, as including penetration). Second, "among the nations where this unnatural uncleanness was committed," it did include "penetration." And third, Partridge was informed that in the legal proceedings of English judges the indictment for sodomy defined the act as including "penetration."

The Reverend Charles Chauncy was the third minister to answer.[408–13] "The same question may be asked," he said, "of rape, incest, bestiality, unnatural sins, presumptuous sins."

Chauncy argued, first, that those laws of Moses which constituted the essential "moral law," were grounded on the "law of nature," and "are immutable and perpetual." He cited Luther and Calvin among his authorities.

Second, sodomy, adultery, incest, bestiality, and rape were punished with death in Mosaic law, said Chauncy.

Third, Chauncy listed the reasons why biblical authorities prescribed death as the perpetual punishment for the "foul sins" in question: Such sins represented "Infamy" to the whole of human nature"; even before Mosaic law such sins were punished by death ("even by the heathen"). He added: "The land is defiled by such sins, and spews out" its inhabitants. And, finally, all theological commentators agreed that not only was illicit "carnal copulation" itself to be punished by death, but all "attempts" to commit such copulation were also to be capital. For example, death was provided for persons who uncovered the "shameful parts" of the body (the sex organs) for the purpose of illicit copulation. By analogy, it was plain that non-penetrative sodomitical acts, such as "contact" and "rubbing" were to receive death.

Fourth, Chauncy argued that the common phrase "lying with," did not mean only "carnal copulation" (penetration), but "other obscure acts preceding" penetration (including, it would appear, acts in the 1980s commonly called "foreplay").

Fifth, punishments derived from Mosaic law were often arrived at by analogy, for there were always cases not specified in Holy Writ. For example, though the Bible did not expressly prohibit "destroying conception in the womb" (abortion), "yet by analogy . . . we may reason that a life is given for a life"—abortion was a capital offense. As to whether sexual "contact" and "rubbing" (without penetration) were capital crimes, analogy might be made to "Onan's sin" which was equal, Chauncy said, to patricide for to spill one's seed "is equivalent to killing the man who could have been born out of it." Chauncy also cited the Old Testament passage in which God commanded that if a wife, acting in defense of her husband, touched the genitals of a man who was attacking her spouse, her hand was to be cut off. Her punishment "is moral," said Chauncy. If even a woman motivated by such good intentions, who merely touched a man's genitals, was to receive death, it was reasonable for those to receive death who, "instigated by burning lusts, set on fire of hell," proceeded from "contact and rubbing" to "the spilling of seed," acting "against nature."

Chauncy also said that if the "unnatural lusts of men with men, or woman with woman, or either with beasts" were to "be punished with death," then, arguing from its equal gravity, the "natural lusts of men towards children under age are so to be punished." (This was a reference to the Humfry case.)

Chauncy concluded. Circumstances, he said, could affect the relative gravity of the sin, and its appropriate punishment. It was one thing to commit sodomy "by sudden temptation, and another to lie in wait for it, yea to make a common practice of it." Premeditation and frequency made the sin worse. When sodomy, the emission of seed, and adultery went together in the same act "this is capital, double and tripple." Sodomy and adultery were also worse if committed by professors or church members," or "committed with those whose chastity they are bound to preserve."

Each of the ministers also answered two additional questions. The first concerned the legally permissible means of extracting a confession from the accused in a capital case (such as sodomy). Responding to this question all three were sensitive to the fact that Puritans, as religious dissenters, were protected in England by a legal tradition providing that those accused of capital crimes were not required to testify against themselves. These New England Puritans were aware, however, that in prosecuting sodomy, or other crimes which usually took place in private, it was difficult to establish a conviction without those accused admitting their participation. In such instances, all three ministers conceded the necessity of obtaining a confession by "due means," rather than by legal trickery, threat, or torture. (Chauncy did think torture might be used to extract a confession in those cases concerning "the safety of states and countries." But he did not state whether he thought sodomy constituted such a case.)

The last question concerned the number of witnesses needed to convict in a capital case (such as sodomy). The three basically agreed that the Bible required two witnesses. They added, however, that in such cases, one witness and clear evidence might legally constitute a second witness, and thus be sufficient to convict.

♀ COMMENTARY

# 1641
## Thomas Shepard: "Heart sodomy"

The famous Puritan minister Thomas Shepard, pastor of a church at Newtown (now Cambridge), Massachusetts, first published "The Sincere Convert," a religious tract on the difficult way to a "saving conversion."[15] The obstacle in the path to salvation was original sin, a major theme of Shepard's works. Only by experiencing a deep desire for salvation, and a true belief in God, said Shepard, could the Puritan assure him or herself of salvation.

In this tract the preacher emphasized that "Every natural man and woman," even he or she who appeared to have "lived civilly," might still be guilty of "heart sodomy," and a whole range of other "sins of the heart." "Sodomy," for this Puritan divine, was inner feeling and outer act. That such concepts were not peculiar to this minister alone is suggested by the popularity of "The Sincere Convert." It went through twenty-one editions between 1641 and 1812, and was one of the most famous and well-read doctrinal essays of the early Congregational religion.

That the Reverend Shepard's public comments on the sodomitical stirrings of the heart had roots in his own heart-experience is indicated by his memory of youthful indiscretions at Cambridge college, in England. This was an era, he recalled, in which he "fell from God to loose and lewd company, to lust and pride." He had, he wrote in his private journal,

> lived in unnatural uncleanness not to be named and in speculative wantonness and filthiness with all sorts of persons which pleased my eye (yet still restrained from the gross act of whoredom which some of my own familiars were to their horror and shame overtaken with).

The phrase "unnatural uncleanness not to be named" suggests, specifically, sodomy, although Shepard's restraint "from the gross act of whoredom" indicates he may have indulged only in mutually emissive, not penetrative acts. "Speculative wantonness" was also one of Shepard's concerns in the following tract of 1641. "Every natural man and woman," argued Shepard (citing Romans 1:29),

> is born full of all sin . . . as full as a toad is of poison, as full as even his skin can hold; mind, will, eyes, mouth, every limb of his body, and every piece of his soul, is full of sin; their hearts are bundles of sin. . . .

Shepard told his reader:

> thy mind is a nest of all the foul opinions, heresies, that ever were vented by any man; thy heart is a foul sink of all atheism, sodomy, blasphemy, murder, whoredom, adultery, witchcraft, buggery; so that, if thou hast any good thing in thee, it is but as a drop of rosewater in a bowl of poison. . . .
>     It is true thou feelest not all these things stirring in thee at one time . . . but they are in thee like a nest of snakes in an old hedge. Although they break not out into thy life, they lie lurking in thy heart. . . .[28]

Shepard said that the governor of Plymouth, William Bradford, "would never have looked upon any one's lewd life" without reflecting on the lewdness within himself, and exclaiming, "In this my vile breast remains that sin" which I could have committed "as well as he." (A sodomitical tendency was not the exclusive possession of a particular group, as a "homosexual" tendency would later be considered.) Such self-scrutiny "might pull down men's proud conceits of themselves," especially the conceits of such men as "comfort themselves in their smooth, honest, civil life," men who think they were "never tainted with whoredom, swearing, drunkenness, or profaneness." Shepard added:

> O, consider of this point, which may make thee pull thine hair from thine head . . . , and run up and down with amazement and paleness in thy face, and horror in thy conscience, and tears in thine eyes. What though thy life be smooth, what though thy outside, thy sepulcher, be painted? O, thou art full of rottenness, of sin, within. Guilty . . . before God, of all the sins that swarm and roar in the whole world at this day, for God looks to the heart; guilty thou art therefore of heart whoredom, heart sodomy, heart blasphemy, heart drunkenness, heart buggery, heart oppression, heart idolatry; and these are the sins that terribly provoke the wrath of Almighty God against thee.[29]

As "fair a face" as a man wears in the world, said Shepard, he had

> some time or other, committed some such secret villainy, that he would be ready to hang himself for shame if others did know of it; as secret whoredom, self-pollution, speculative wantonness, men with men, women with women, as the apostle [Paul] speaks. (Rom. i.)

On the day of judgment, warned Shepard,

> all the world shall see and hear these privy pranks, then the books shall be opened. . . . there shall be a day of public hearing . . . that all the world may see the secret sins of wicked men. . . .[41]

LEGAL CASE

# 1642, March 1
# Plymouth: Edward Michell and Edward Preston,
## *"Lewd & sodomitical practices"*

The Plymouth court cited Edward Michell and Edward Preston for "lewd & sodomitical practices tending to sodomy" with each other.[16] Conviction under the Plymouth sodomy law of 1636 meant death, but these guilty parties were only whipped. The court, then, made a major distinction between "sodomy" proper, punished by death, and "sodomitical" (or sodomy-like) practices—those "tending toward sodomy"—punished by a whipping. The record states:

> Edward Michell, for his lewd & sodomitical practices tending to sodomy with Edward Preston, and other lewd carriages with Lydia Hatch, is censured to be presently whipped at Plymouth, at the public place, and once more at

Barnestable, in convenient time, in the presence of Mr. Freeman and the committees of the said town.

Edward Preston, for his lewd practices tending to sodomy with Edward Michell, and pressing John Keene thereunto (if he would have yielded), is also censured [sentenced] to be forthwith whipped at Plymouth, and once more at Barnestable (when Edward Michell is whipped), in the presence of Mr. Freeman & the committees of the same town.

John Keene, because he resisted the temptation, & used means to discover it, is appointed to stand by whilst Michell and Preston are whipped, though in some thing he was faulty.

The same court proceeding also cited

Lydia Hatch, for suffering Edward Michell to attempt to abuse her body by uncleanness, & did not discover [report] it, & [for] lying in the same bed with her brother, Jonathan, is censured to be publicly whipped; was accordingly done.

STATUTE

## 1642, December 1
## Connecticut: Sodomy law

The General Court of Connecticut adopted a list of twelve capital crimes, all but the rape law based on the Massachusetts Bay Colony's Liberties of 1641.[17]

The capital crimes in Connecticut were (1) idolatry, (2) witchcraft, (3) blasphemy, (4) murder with malice aforethought, (5) murder through poisoning, (6) bestiality, (7) sodomy, here referred to only as "man lying with man," (8) adultery, (9) rape, (10) kidnapping, (11) perjury with intent to cause a man to lose his life, and (12) treason.

This law was readopted in a codification of 1650, May (see).

♀ LEGAL CASE

## 1642, December 5
## Essex County, Massachusetts Bay:
## Elizabeth Johnson, *"Unseemly practices"*

The Essex County Court, meeting at Salem in Massachusetts Bay, reported the sentencing of a servant, Elizabeth Johnson, for a series of insubordinate and illegal acts[18]:

Elizabeth Johnson, servant to Mr. Jos. Yonge, [is] to be severely whipped and fined 5 li. [pounds] for unseemly practices betwixt her and another maid; also, for stubbornness to her mistress answering rudely and unmannerly; and also for stopping her ears with her hands when the Word of God was read. . . .

The record adds that Johnson was also punished "for 'spurning an ewe goat till both [mother and offspring?] died'; also for killing a pig and burying it."


COMMENTARY

# 1642
## William Bradford: *"Things fearful to name"*

In his history of the Plymouth Colony (unpublished in his lifetime), Bradford commented on an outbreak in 1642 of sodomy, bestiality, fornication, adultery, and rape.[19] After discussing the Humfry case (see 1641–42, Mass. Bay). Bradford marveled that "wickedness did grow and break forth" in New England, a land where wickedness was so much spoken against, investigated, and severely punished, "as in no place more." Even "moderate and good men" had censured New Englanders for their "severity in punishments." But all the orations against wickedness, and the strict punishments accorded it, "could not suppress the breaking out," that year and others, of various "notorious sins . . . , especially drunkenness and uncleanness." Bradford referred not only to "incontinency" between married persons, but to "that which is worse"—even "sodomy and buggery (things fearful to name)" had "broke forth in this land oftener than once."

Bradford suggested that such crimes might originate in "our corrupt natures, which are so hardly bridled, subdued and mortified." A more specific reason for such outbreaks might be that "the Devil" was more spiteful against New England churches because they tried harder than others to preserve holiness and purity, and punish sin. Perhaps the Devil was trying to "cast a blemish and stain" upon New Englanders for their virtues; Bradford would rather think that than believe that "Satan" had "more power in these heathen lands" than in more thoroughly Christian nations.

Bradford also suggested that in New England "wickedness being more stopped by strict laws," and so closely looked into, was like "waters when their streams are . . . dammed up." When such dams broke, the waters previously held back "flow with more violence and make more noise and disturbance than when they are suffered to run quietly in their own channels."[316] Bradford thus speculated that the strict suppression of sin caused it to break out in especially violent forms, that repression caused violent sexual expressions—a suggestion surprising to find in the words of an early Puritan.*

---

*Bradford's positing a hydraulic theory of lust—that its damming up (or repression) causes it to break out in even stronger waves—indicates that this idea is by no means new, radical, or an

Bradford did not think the discovery of wickedness in New England indicated the presence of more sin there than elsewhere. He did think that evils were more likely to be made public in New England by strict magistrates and by churches which "look narrowly to their members." In other places, with larger populations, "many horrible evils" were never discovered, whereas in relatively little populated New England, they were "brought into the light," and "made conspicuous to all."

Bradford described the case of Thomas Granger, a teen-ager executed, in September 1642, for buggery with "a mare, a cow, two goats, five sheep, two calves and a turkey." Granger, and an individual who "had made some sodomitical attempts upon another,"* were questioned about "how they came first to the knowledge and practice of such wickedness." The sodomitical individual "confessed he had long used it [the practice] in Old England." Granger "said he was taught it [bestiality] by another that had heard of such things from some in England when he was there, and they kept cattle together." This indicated, Bradford said, "how one wicked person may infect the many." He therefore advised masters to take great care about "what servants they bring into their families."[321]

It might be asked, said Bradford, how "so many wicked persons and profane people should so quickly come over into this land and mix themselves among us" —"us" being those "religious men that began the work," who "came for religion's sake."

Bradford answered that wherever the Lord sowed good seed the "envious man" will try to sow bad. Second, in the American wilderness "much labor and service," much "building and planting" was necessary, and "many untoward servants . . . were thus brought over, both men and womenkind"; these eventually founded their own families and multiplied (presumably increasing the numbers of "untoward" children). Third, and "a main reason," said Bradford, "some began to make a trade" of shipping passengers to America; these traders, to "advance their profit," did not care whom they transported as long as their passengers "had money to pay them." And "by this means the country became pestered with many unworthy persons."[321]

Finally, a "mixed multitude" came into the American wilderness, some being sent with the "hope that they would be made better," others so that they would be "kept from shame at home." Such persons "would necessarily follow their dissolute courses" in the New World. Thus, Bradford concluded, in the twenty years since the first truly pious settlers had arrived, the colonial population had perhaps grown "the worser."[322]

invention of Freud's, but is an old, middle-class ideology of eros. For a discussion of the "hydraulic theory of sexuality" see Jeffrey Weeks, "Discourse, Desire and Sexual Deviance: Some Problems in a History of Homosexuality," in Kenneth Plummer, ed., *The Making of the Modern Homosexual* (London: Hutchinson, 1981), p. 97.

*Probably Edward Michell or Edward Preston; see 1642, March 1.

COMMENTARY

# 1644
## Edward Coke: *"Buggery, or Sodomy"*

Coke, a prominent English judge, state prosecutor, and early systematizer of statute, discussed "Buggery, or Sodomy" in a section on "High Treason" in the third part of his famous commentary on the *Laws of England,* first published there in 1644.[20] Because this work greatly influenced the colonists' interpretation of statute, Coke's work is quoted here in some detail.

Coke's opening lines on "Buggery, or Sodomy" stated:

> If any person shall commit buggery with mankind, or beast; by authority of Parliament this offense is adjudged felony without benefit of Clergy. . . .

"Buggery," Coke continued,

> is a detestable, and abominable sin, amongst Christians not to be named, committed by carnal knowledge against the ordinance of the Creator, and order of nature, by mankind with mankind, or with brute beast, or by womankind with brute beast.

Coke distinguished between "Bugeria" (which he claimed was "an Italian word" for sodomy) and "Paederastes or Paiderastes" (which he called "a Greek word" meaning "Amator puerum," lover of pubescent boys). Boy love, he said was "but a Species of Buggery," and added: it was complained of in the English Parliament "that the Lumbards [Italians from Lombardy] had brought into the Realm the shameful sin of Sodomy, that is not to be named."

Contrary to Coke's suggestion (says historian Robert Oaks) the term buggery did not derive from an Italian word "Bugeria." That Italians from Lobardy introduced sodomy into England was folklore reflecting an economic conflict; Coke cited as his source a Parliamentary debate in which representatives of English traders attributed sodomy to a rival group of Lombard moneylenders.

The suggested punishments for buggery or sodomy were Coke's next subject:

> Our ancient Authors do conclude that it deserveth death . . . , though they differ in the manner of punishment.

One author said those guilty of sodomy should be burnt, "and so," added Coke, "were the Sodomites by Almighty God." Other authors said that "Those who commit unchaste acts with animals and sodomites are to be buried alive." In "ancient times," said Coke, males convicted of buggery were hanged, females were drowned (the reference here was apparently to female bestiality). In England of his own day, said Coke, as felons, those convicted of buggery were hanged by the neck.

Coke next considered the language used in English references to buggery.

"Detestable and Abominable," he said, were "just attributes" of the crime. The phrase "amongst Christians not to be named" was used in the "usual Indictment of this offence." The phrase "carnall knowledge" appeared in the indictment passage referring (in Latin) to "sexual relations," specifically, "penetration," or "the thing in the thing, either with mankind, or with beast." The "least penetration maketh it carnall knowledge," said Coke. A mere "ejaculation of seed," he said, did not constitute buggery; analogy was made to rape, in which ejaculation without penetration did not constitute the crime.

In buggery, Coke stated, both the "agent" and "consentient" (consenting party) were felons. That accorded with God's law as expressed in Leviticus, which said that, if a man lay with a man as with a woman, both had committed abomination, both must die. This also accorded with "the ancient rule of law" which said (in Latin) that "those who do it and those who consent to it were punished with like penalty." "The Sodomites came to this abomination by four means," said Coke,

> by pride, excess of diet [gluttony], idleness, and contempt of the poor.

Coke added:

> If the party buggered be within the age of discretion [under fourteen], it is no felony in him, but in the agent only.

In buggery, as in other felonies, said Coke, all accessories to the crime were also considered parties to the act.

Discussing the application of the buggery law to women, Coke claimed (falsely) that the English statute prohibited any "person" (male or female) from committing the crime with "mankind or beast." (The English law simply prohibited "Buggery . . . with mankind or beast," without specifying the sex of the parties.) The reference to females in the English buggery law was explained, said Coke, by the fact that

> somewhat before the making of this Act a great Lady committed buggery with a Baboon, and conceived by it. . . .

Thus did a curious bit of English folklore enter an influential commentary on the capital buggery law.

Coke concluded that "buggery" was one of four "crying sins" mentioned in the Bible—sins crying out for punishment. The "crying sin" of the "Sodomites" referred to Genesis 18:20–21. There God said that because "the outcry against Sodom & Gomorrah" was great he would visit those cities to see if the outcry was true. The last "crying sin" cited by Coke was "the voice of the oppressed and the unpaid wages of labor," a reference to several biblical passages condemning the economic oppression of workers by employers (passages now not often cited). The sins of the Sodomites, Coke thought, included not only sodomy, but the exploitation of labor.

LEGAL CASE/EXECUTION

# 1646, June 25
## New Netherland: Jan Creoli executed

The New Netherland Colony court sentenced "Jan Creoli, a negro," for a second "sodomy" offense.[21] The record stated: "this crime being condemned of God . . . as an abomination, the prisoner is sentenced to be conveyed to the place of public execution, and there choked to death, and then burnt to ashes. . . ."

Manuel Congo, a ten-year-old, "on whom the above abominable crime was committed," was also sentenced "to be carried to the place where Creoli is to be executed, tied to a stake, and faggots piled around him, for justice sake, and to be flogged; sentence executed."

LEGAL CASE

# 1646
## New Haven: William Plaine executed

The New Haven court executed William Plaine (or Plane), one of the original settlers of the town of Guilford.[22] In 1639, Plaine had been a signer of the Covenant in which the first Guilford settlers, while still aboard ship bound for New England, promised, "the Lord assisting," to be helpful to each other "in every common work, according to every man's ability and as need shall require." They had also promised "not to desert . . . each other," without the consent of the majority of the signers. The organization and membership of the church was left until actual settlement. Plaine was assigned a home lot of two acres, and, in 1645, was appointed by the Town Council to build the dam for the Town Mill, and to inspect chimneys as a fire precaution—responsibilities suggesting he was a trusted resident of Guilford. But the following year various charges were brought against him.

According to John Winthrop, the charges were that Plaine, though "a married man . . . had committed sodomy with two persons in England," and "had corrupted a great part of the youth of Guilford by masturbations . . . above a hundred times." When asked about such "filthy practice," Plaine "did insinuate seeds of atheism, questioning whether there was a God."

Winthrop reported in his journal that Governor Eaton of the New Haven Colony had written to the governor of the Massachusetts Colony seeking the magistrates' and church elders' advice about Plaine's punishment. All agreed that he "ought to die," giving different reasons "from the word of God." Winthrop added: "indeed it was *horrendum facinus* [a dreadful crime], and he a monster in human shape . . . , and it tended to the frustrating of the ordinance of marriage and the hindering the generation of mankind." Winthrop's reasons for considering Plaine's activities so wicked, their alleged anti-marriage, anti-procreative effects, summarized two main Puritan objections to sodomy.

Plaine's alleged "questioning whether there was a God," and his unrepentant sexual activity, suggests an active defiance of basic Puritan beliefs and laws. (See discussion of Plaine, Introduction to Part I, p. 56.)

STATUTE

# 1647, May 19
## Rhode Island: "Sodomy" law

Representatives of four towns met at Portsmouth, formed the government of the Rhode Island Colony, and drew up a body of laws, one of the earliest governmental codes passed by American colonists.[23] These laws, unlike those of the Puritan colonies, were not generally modeled upon biblical texts, but on the statutes of the English parliament.

Rhode Island's capital crimes of 1647 were: (1) treason, (2) murder, (3) manslaughter, (4) witchcraft, (5) robbery, (6) arson, (7) rape, (8) buggery, and (9) sodomy.

Treason was apparently considered the most serious offense, since for it alone the punishment was death by torture: the guilty insurrectionist was to be hanged, cut down alive, drawn and quartered, "his entrails and privie members cut from him and burned in his view." He was then to be beheaded.

Sodomy, buggery, rape, adultery, fornication, "and their accessaries" were listed together in this legal code, under the category of laws "touching Whoremongers." The sodomy provision, uncharacteristic of other Rhode Island laws, referred to biblical text as well English statute for its authority. This colonial statute was also unique among American sodomy laws in finding its religious warrant in the New Testament (St. Paul), rather than in the Old.

The Rhode Island statute of 1647 stated:

Touching Whoremongers.
 First of sodomy, which is forbidden by this present Assembly throughout the whole colony, and by sundry statutes of England 25 Hen. 8, 6; 5 Eliz 17. It is a vile affection, whereby men given up thereto leave the natural use of women and burn in their lusts toward another, and so men with men work that which is unseemly, as that Doctor of the Gentiles [St. Paul] in his letter to the Romans once spake, i. 27. The penalty con-

cluded by that state under whose authority we are is felony of death without remedy. See 5 Eliz 17.*

Rhode Island law was next revised in 1663 (see).


STATUTE

# 1648
## Massachusetts Bay: "Sodomy" law

The publication of the whole Massachusetts Body of Laws and Liberties, passed in 1641 (see) but not before printed, constituted the first collection of statutes published in the American colonies.[24]

The origins of these Massachusetts statutes were partly Mosaic, partly English common law, and partly an original colonial invention. The sodomy provision was identical to the Massachusetts law of 1641, except for the addition that boys under fourteen, or the party who was forced, were to be "severely punished," but not put to death.

This Massachusetts law was next revised in 1697 (see).


♀ LEGAL CASE

# 1649, March 6
## Plymouth: Sara Norman and Mary Hammon,
### *"Lewd behavior . . . upon a bed"*

Plymouth Court records included the accusation against two women, Sara Norman and Mary Hammon (or Hammond)[25]:

> We present [charge] the wife of Hugh Norman, and Mary Hammon, both of Yarmouth, for lewd behavior each with [the] other upon a bed. . . .

Recent research by J. R. Roberts in the Plymouth manuscript records provides background information on Norman and Hammon. At the time of the above charges Mary Hammon was fifteen years old, and recently married. Sara Norman's age is unknown, but she was apparently somewhat older, as she had been married in 1639. About the time of the court's first charge, 1649, Hugh Norman, Sara's husband, deserted his wife and children.

A marginal note in the Plymouth court record of March 6, 1649 reported

---

*The English statute known as 5 Elizabeth 17 was the 1563 reenactment of the 1533 "buggery" statute known as 25 Henry 8, 6, originally passed under Henry VIII, see p. 36. For St. Paul's letter to the Romans see p. 59.

that Mary Hammon was "cleared with admonition"—perhaps because of her youth. Sara Norman's case was evidently held over for later judgment.

A year after the first charge, on March 6, 1650, Sara Norman was cited again in the Plymouth court records, this time accused of "unclean practices" with a male, Teage Joanes. This charge was subsequently dropped, when her accusor pleaded guilty of perjury (see 1649, Oct. 29).

On October 2, 1650, the records report the outcome of the original charge against Sara Norman. The court punished her with a warning, and asked her to acknowledge publicly her "unchaste behavior" with Mary Hammon. This punishment, though publicly humiliating, was lenient compared to the death penalty imposed for male-male "sodomy."

Patriarchal custom was evident in the fact that court records in this case referred to the "wife of Hugh Norman"; although Sara Norman was publicly charged with a serious crime, her whole name was used only once in the documents.

The court record of 1650 said:

> Whereas the wife of Hugh Norman, of Yarmouth, hath stood presented [in] divers Courts for misdemeanor and lewd behavior with Mary Hammon upon a bed, with divers lascivious speeches by her also spoken, but she could not appear by reason of some hindrances unto this Court, the said Court have therefore sentenced her, the said wife of Hugh Norman, for her wild behavior in the aforesaid particulars, to make a public acknowledgment, so far as conveniently may be, of her unchaste behavior, and have also warned her to take heed of such carriages for the future, lest her former carriage come in remembrance against her to make her punishment the greater.

LEGAL CASE

# 1649, October 29
## Plymouth: Richard Berry and Teage Joanes, "Sodomy" charge

The Plymouth Court records reported a "sodomy" charge by Richard Berry against Teage Joanes.[26] After hearing "what can be said in the case for present" the court held the case over for a further hearing at the next session, five months away, taking money bonds to insure that the accuser, the accused, and their witnesses would then appear.

On March 6, 1650, the Plymouth court records reported the outcome of Richard Berry's charge:

> Whereas . . . Richard Berry accused Teage Joanes of sodomy, & other unclean practices also with Sara, the wife of Hugh Norman, & for that cause the said parties were both bound over to answer to this Court, & accordingly

appeared; the said Richard Berry acknowledged before the Court that he did wrong the aforesaid Teage Joanes in both the aforesaid particulars, & had born false witness against him upon oath; and for the same the said Richard Berry was sentenced to be whipped at the post, which accordingly was performed.

False witness for the purpose of taking a man's life was not yet a capital crime under Plymouth law or Berry might have received a death sentence.

Three years after the above hearing, on June 9, 1653, the Plymouth Colony court records reported:

An order was . . . passed from the Court requiring that Teag Joanes and Richard Berry, and others with them, be caused to part their uncivil living together, as they will answer for it.

Six years later, on October 6, 1659, a "Richard Beare" (probably the same "Richard Berry"), of Marshfield, was cited in the Plymouth Colony court records as

being a grossly scandalous person, debauched, having been formerly convicted of filthy, obscene practices, and for the same by the Court sentenced.

The records stated that "Beare," who had fallen afoul of the law, was summoned by the court to receive personally the sentence of "disfranchisement" from Plymouth, but he had not appeared. The court ordered that Beare "be disfranchised of his freedom" in the colony (banished and deprived of rights).

STATUTE

# 1650, May
## Connecticut: Sodomy law

Connecticut Colony legislators adopted Robert Ludlow's codification of existing law, known as "Ludlow's Code."[27] This code included the Connecticut law of 1642, which provided death for sodomy (here called "men lying with men"). Ludlow's Code was next revised in October 1672 (see).

INTIMACY

# 1653, February
## Michael Wigglesworth, *"Too much doting affection"*

The extraordinary diary of the Reverend Wigglesworth documents the inner life of this Puritan divine, famous as the author of the poem "Day of Doom," a popular classic in the New England hellfire and brimstone tradition.[28] His diary reveals that while Wigglesworth was a tutor at Harvard he was tormented by sexual feelings for his male students—feelings experienced as deeply sinful.

Edmund Morgan's introduction to the published edition of Wigglesworth's diary admits that "We should scarcely exaggerate . . . if we described Michael Wigglesworth as a morbid, humorless, selfish busybody," an "ugly," "absurd," "pathetic" cartoon caricature of a Puritan.[viii] As a striking example of the strict Puritan of popular imagination, Wigglesworth is a problem for those historians who, led by Edmund Morgan, have criticized the popular view of the early Puritans as "grossly overdrawn." The Puritans, Morgan stressed, did not exclude "enjoyment"; they "read books, wrote verse," "had their pictures painted," were "unashamedly fond" of beer, wine, and harder liquors, liked to eat well, "made no pretensions to asceticism," were "not prudish," and made "no attempt to stiffle natural passions in celibacy."

Morgan then admitted that "the mark of the Puritan" was "his zeal, his suspicion of pleasure, his sense of guilt." Those characteristics in Wigglesworth are not evidence of any purely individual eccentricity, but were "simply the qualities demanded of a good Puritan."

Many of Wigglesworth's contemporaries were probably not quite so distressed by their inability to live up to the demands of a religious ideal. Philip Greven's differentiation of colonial Protestants as strict "Evangelical," "Moderate," and "Genteel" usefully suggests a wider, and probably more realistic range of colonial personalities. Greven does view Wigglesworth's extreme sense of sin as typical of the Evangelical personality, however. And it was this strict Puritanism that was institutionalized in early statutes and in many prosecutions. Wigglesworth's writing for New England "the most popular book of his time," his teaching at Harvard, and his ministerial service to a Puritan congregation all suggest that his views were not unique, and appealed to a common chord in the early colonists.

Of special interest here are Wigglesworth's intimate, problematic relationships with males, worldly and otherworldly, in particular with his father, his Harvard students, with God his "father," and with Christ. Wigglesworth's loving these, and being loved by them, either not enough or (in some cases) too much, was a central and continuing preoccupation. His feeling that his earthly loves detracted from his love for God indicates a concept of love as a scarce and limited good. Wigglesworth's thinking of himself as a Bride of Christ (as did other Evangelicals, male and female) sometimes led him to speak of kissing and embracing his "husband," a metaphor with distinctly erotic overtones. Such ideas, together with his entries on marriage, make Wigglesworth's diary quite a complete and amazing account of early Puritan sexual and affectional life.

Throughout his diary, Wigglesworth often referred to an earthly "creature" who kept stealing his affection away from God. That "creature" was usually earthly comfort in general. But in the early entries especially, that seductive "creature" often turns out to be Wigglesworth's male students. It seems that one of the sins that made the Day of Judgment a "Day of Doom" for Wigglesworth was his "too much doting affection" for young Harvard males.

The most explicit, compromising sexual passages in the diary were written in a special shorthand code (decoded and printed in italics as in Morgan's edition). While Wigglesworth reported his sins quite frankly to God, his code suggests he wanted to keep them hidden from his fellow humans.

In the first entry, dating to February 1653, Wigglesworth asked:

> If the unloving carriages of my pupils can go so to my heart as they do; how then do my vain thoughts, my detestable pride, my *unnatural filthy lust that are so oft and even this day in some measure stirring in me . . . ?*[3]

On February 7, Wigglesworth feared

> there is much sensuality and doting upon the creature in my pursuit of the good of others. . . .[3]

On February 15, Wigglesworth declared:

> Lord I am vile, I desire to abhor my self (o that I could!). . . . *I find such unresistable torments of carnal lusts or provocation unto the ejection of seed that I find my self unable to read anything to inform me about my distemper because of the prevailing or rising of my lusts. . . .*[4]

On February 17, 1653, Wigglesworth wrote:

> *The last night a filthy dream and so pollution escaped me in my sleep for which I desire to hang down my head with shame and beseech the Lord not to make me possess the sin of my youth and give me into the hands of my abomination.*[5]

On February 26, he noted: "*Some filthiness escaped me in a filthy dream. The Lord notwithstanding.*" He fretted that when his affections were taken up with doing good, "it is very hard for me to set my heart upon God himself and not to rest in the creature."[6]

On March 5, 1653, Wigglesworth recorded:

> much distracted thoughts I find arising from too much doting affection *to some of my pupils one of whom went to Boston with me today.*

He felt no power to love God, he said, "my spirit is so leavened with love to the creature. This frame I am afraid of."[9]

On April 1, Wigglesworth asked the Lord, his "father," to "witness my daily sensual glutting my heart with creature comforts."[10]

And, on April 5, Wigglesworth found

> vain distracting thoughts molested me in holy duties. *I find my spirit so exceedingly carried with love to my pupils that I can't tell how to take up my rest in God. Lord for this cause I am afraid of my wicked heart. Fear takes hold of me.*[11]

One morning in April, Wigglesworth wondered "will the Lord now again return and embrace me in the arms of his dearest love? Will he fall upon my neck and kiss me?" He then lamented that his love for God had grown cold; he was also "afraid" of his "want of natural affection" for his parents.[13]

At the end of April, Wigglesworth begged God to "give me some sweet soul ravishing communion with thy self."[15] He also recorded *"whorish desertions of my heart from God to the creature."* Wigglesworth noted his "cooling affections" for God, and his "whorish outgoings of heart after other things. I fear my pupils formerly, and now my ease and sloth and pleasure are getting oft between christ and me." Despite such "backslidings" Wigglesworth thought that God did not "upbraid me of my other lovers." As a Bride of Christ he begged the Lord to restore "the love of my espousals thine to me and mine to thee."[17]

On April 27, Wigglesworth told the Lord: "I seek at the hands of a father pardon and power over my still prevailing lusts, principally pride and sensuality, want of love to thee and fervent desires after communion with thee."[19] Unable to savor communion with God "above communion with men," Wigglesworth felt unworthy.[20]

On June 24, Wigglesworth warned a rebellious Harvard student of "the dangers of pleasure"; the minister was later distraught to find that same student "at play" and making music "with ill company."[27]

On July 4 and 5, Wigglesworth reported:

> *such filthy lust also flowing from my fond affection to my pupils whiles in their presence . . . that I confess myself an object of God's loathing. . . .*[30–31]

On July 7, Wigglesworth complained that he was so involved in his own business, and in "my pupils' good," that he had lost his love for God, and feared his "own spirit of whoredoms." He prayed: "O give me a new heart a circumcized heart," so he could again love "harking to God's covenant."[31]

On October 14, Wigglesworth thought of "my want of love and dutifulness to my parents," and "the very next morning news is brought me of my father's death."

On October 18, he prayed for grace, wondering whether *"I might not be secretly glad that my father was gone."* He added:

> *The last night some filthiness in a vile dream escaped me for which I loath myself and desire to abase myself before my God.*[50]

On November 9, Wigglesworth told the Lord:

> when thou showest me my face I abhor myself. Who can bring a clean thing out of filthiness. I was conceived bred brought up in sin.

He reported "too much savoring of the creature."[53]

On November 30, Wigglesworth told the Lord that he knew he deserved "to be kicked out of this world because I have not had natural affections to my natural father," because he had thought evil of all his "governors," and because he had "rebell'd against . . . my heavenly father." He asked the Lord not to punish and destroy others for his sins, mentioning one of his pupils who had been "taken away for my sin in too eager seeking their good."[57]

On December 4, Wigglesworth wondered if he should get married, and hoped the Lord would guide him "in the weighty business that troubles me."[78]

On February 15, 1655, Wigglesworth referred to "my weakness," an "affliction" which exposed him to "sin and temptations by day," and caused him *dreams and self-pollution by night.*" Wigglesworth's "weakness" (which he distinguished from "wantonness") was apparently gonorrhea—with which he imagined himself to be diseased, and which he apparently thought of as provoking his sexual sins.[86 n. 42] He also mused that

> To continue in a single estate, Is both uncomfortable many ways, and dangerous (as I conceive) to my life, and exposeth to sin, and contrary to engagement of affections, and Friends' expectations, and liable to the harsh censure of the world that expecteth the quite contrary.

Yet he also believed that to get married and

> change my condition endangers to bring me into a pining and loathsome disease, to a wretched life and miserable death . . . and consequently I fear it would be injurious to another besides my self. . . .[79]

Wigglesworth seems to have thought that the availability of marital intercourse would increase both his lust and his bodily infirmity. He admitted that no one knew of his infirmities, that he had not talked to anybody about them, and had "even been afraid to pray for myself," since he feared to think much of his "sad condition." But with "spring approaching" he had written for advice to John Winthrop, Jr., son of the governor, to John Alcock, a doctor (with an ironically relevant name), and to John Rogers, a minister. He had also written and proposed to his cousin, Mary Reyner, "dealing plainly with her in the business, what danger I apprehended," so that she would "know with whom she matches."

On February 18, he reported preaching in public on the "sins of these times and places."[80]

On February 22, Wigglesworth declared himself

> *much overborn with carnal concupiscence nature being suppressed for I had not had my afflux [emission] in 12 nights. Friday night it came again without any dream that I know of. Yet after it I am still inclined to lust. The Lord help me against it and against discouragement by it and against temptations of another nature and disquietments.* [80–81]

On March 7, Wigglesworth wrote:

> I begin to think marriage will be necessary for me (as an ordinance of God appointed to maintain purity . . . ).[81]

On March 12 and 13, Wigglesworth reported that "fleshly lusts" were "sometimes too strong in me." He was ashamed

> that I wrong and grieve [Christ] my head and husband so by not loving and delighting in his presence; by my liking other loves more than him. Ah Lord! I pull down evils upon others as well as myself. Sickness, death of godly ones, wants, divisions, have not my sins a hand in these miseries?[82]

On March 18, Wigglesworth remarked that "sabbaths are blessed seasons wherein poor wandering harlots, may return to their husband again." (The harlot of the metaphor was Wigglesworth himself, the husband, Christ.)[82]

At the beginning of April, Wigglesworth, despite a fever, hastened to Massachusetts Bay "To redeem the spring time for marrying or taking physic, or both." There, Dr. Alcock advised him "to proceed with the business of marriage." The Reverend Rogers, however, advised "physick" first, marriage later. But after "a little reasoning," and a "fuller declaration of my illness," The Reverend Rogers also advised the "consumation" of Wigglesworth's planned marriage.[85–86]

Wigglesworth was ready to be "contracted" in marriage when the return of his "weakness" made him consult Dr. Alcock again. The doctor thought it would be a longer, more tedious, difficult cure by "physick" than "he hoped it would be by marriage." Alcock told Wigglesworth that many other men had taken the marriage cure "with good success." The doctor also told Wigglesworth "that mine was not vera Gon" (gonorrhea), but a condition caused by "a little acrimony" gathering in the mouth, which caused "humours to flow." Marriage "would take away the cause of that distemper."

Because of the inconvenience of "physick," the "great charge and expense," and Wigglesworth's inability to live "with comfort and honesty" as long as he was single, he decided that "god calleth to a speedy change of my condition, which I therefore desire to attend as a duty." Resolving further doubts about "the lawfulness of marrying with a Kinswoman," Wigglesworth was "contracted" with his cousin.[86–87]

"At the time appointed," he reported, "with fear and trembling I came to Rowley to be married." Because of "Physicians' counsel," and because "the institution of marriage" had been created by God "for the preservation of purity and chastity," Wigglesworth "went about the business which god call'd me to attend. And consumated it . . . by the will of god May 18, 1655."[87] The day following he noted:

> *I feel stirrings and strongly of my former distemper even after the use of marriage the next day which makes me exceeding afraid.* [87–88]

On July 28, he thanked the Lord for "so much comfort in a married estate contrary to my fears."[88–89]

On September 10, he recorded, of himself and his wife,

> *we can't lay severally [apart] without obloquy and reproach neither can we lay together without exposing me to the return of grievous disease.* [92]

On September 16, Wigglesworth reported:

*some night pollution escaped me notwithstanding my earnest prayer to the contrary which brought to mind my old sins now too much forgotten . . . together with my later sins.* [93]

In 1657 Wigglesworth still found his heart "as carnal as some years since," and begged: "mortify Lord these earthly members." He prayed: "let curiousness die this day for the Lord sake. I feel and I fear it."[98]

In an undated section in the back of his diary Wigglesworth wrote a list of "Considerations against Pride." This sin, he noted, "was the ringleader of Sodom's sins, and pull'd down streams of fire and brimstone upon their heads." Wigglesworth thought he retained "a Sodom [of pride] within the temple of the holy-ghost [his body]." He reiterated: "Sodom's ringleading sin" was that its citizens "were proud and haughty and they must fry in the flame of fire for it."[104]

LEGAL CASE

# 1653, March 23
## New Haven: *"Sundry youths";*
### *"much wickedness in a filthy corrupting way"*

The court records of the town of New Haven reported the sentencing of six young males, and a servant, John Clarke, who was returned to his master for punishment.[29]

Upon a complaint made to the Governor of sundrie youths in the Town that had committed much wickedness in a filthy corrupting way one with another, they were called before the Governor and Magistrates. . . . [Those charged were] Benjamin Bunill, Joshua Bradly, Joseph Benham, William Trobridg, Thomas Tuttill & Thomas Kimberly. They were examined in a private way, and their examinations taken in writing, which were of such a filthy nature as is not fit to be made known in a public way; after which the Court were called together, and the youths before them. Their examinations were read and, upon their several confessions, the Court . . . sentenced the youths above named to be whipped publicly. And whereas John Clarke, servant to Jeremiah Whitnell, was questioned and charged by one of them for some filthy carriage, he denied it, and another of the company in some measure cleared him from that the other charged him with, whereupon he was not sentenced to be corrected publicly, but the Court left it with his master to give him that correction in the family which he should see meet [proper], warning John Clarke that if ever any such carriage came forth against him hereafter, the Court would call these miscarriages charged upon him to mind again.

♀ STATUTE

# 1656, March 1
## New Haven: "Sodomy" law

The New Haven law of 1656 was based largely on a code drawn up by John Cotton but not earlier enacted (see 1636).[30] The New Haven "sodomy" statute is unique among American colonial legislation in extending the death penalty to acts of women "against nature," male-female anal intercourse, and, in certain circumstances, masturbation.

This New Haven law listed fourteen capital offenses in the following order: (1) idolatry, (2) witchcraft, (3) blasphemy, (4) willfull (premeditated) murder, (5) murder in a state of sudden anger, (6) murder "with guile," (7) bestiality (men or women), (8) men lying with men as with women (and under the same provision), acts of women "against nature," and some kinds of masturbation, (9) adultery, (10) man-stealing, (11) false witness (perjury) for the purpose of taking a man's life, (12) invasion, insurrection, or public rebellion (treason), (13) children over sixteen smiting or cursing their parents, and (14) rebellious sons over sixteen.

The sodomy provision prohibited, but did not specifically define, what was meant by women changing the "natural use into that which is against nature." Anal intercourse of males and females was separately and explicitly prohibited. Public masturbation and incitement to masturbation were explicitly prohibited; solitary masturbation seems to have been prohibited in the injunctions against a man defiling or corrupting himself. The explicit stress on public masturbation and masturbatory incitement seems indicative of the Puritans' concern about social corruption, and individual corruption as it effected the polity. The law's reference to masturbation in the presence of others as a kind of "sodomy" was an early expression of a link between self-stimulation and illicit same-sex relations which became more common in the 1800s.

Although this statute text is rather lengthy, and its language difficult, it does well convey a sense of the early Puritans' response to sex. The New Haven statute of 1656 read:

> If any man lyeth with mankind, as a man lyeth with a woman, both of them have committed abomination, they both shall surely be put to death. Lev. 20:13. And if any woman change the natural use, into that which is against nature, as Rom. 1:26 she shall be liable to the same sentence, and punishment. . . .

The act also prohibited

> any other kind of unnatural and shamefull filthiness, called in Scripture the going after strange flesh, or other flesh than God alloweth. . . .

Specifically prohibited was

> carnal knowledge of another vessel than God in nature hath appointed to become one flesh. . . .

This was further specified as "abusing the contrary part of a grown woman, or child of either sex." It also included carnal knowledge of the "unripe vessel of a girl," an act which involved leaving

> the natural use of the woman . . . which God hath ordained for the propagation of posterity. . . .

When nature was so "forced, though the will were enticed,"

> Sodomitical filthiness (tending to the destruction of the race of mankind) is committed by a kind of rape, [and] every such person shall be put to death.

The law also prohibited "any man" to

> act upon himself, and in the sight of others spill his own seed, by example, or counsel, or both, corrupting or tempting others to do the like, which tends to the sin of Sodomy, if it be not one kind of it. . . .

Or, added the law, if a man

> shall defile, or corrupt himself and others, by any other kind of sinful filthiness, he shall be punished according to the nature of the offense.

Finally, if in any of the above cases, a man's acts,

> considered with the aggravating circumstances, shall according to the mind of God revealed in his word require it, he shall be put to death, as the court of magistrates shall determine. . . .

The statute also provided that if, in any of the above cases

> one of the parties were forced, and so abused against his or her will, the innocent person (crying out, or in due season complaining) shall not be punished. . . .

Or, said the law,

> if any of the offending parties were under fourteen year[s] old, when the sin was committed, such person shall be severely corrected, as the court of magistrates considering the age, and other circumstances shall judge meet.

This law remained in force ten years, until January 1665, when Connecticut annexed the colony; then New Haven presumably came under the Connecticut law of May 1650 (see).

LEGAL CASE

## 1658, August 26
## New Netherland: Nicolas Hillebrant, "Sodomy" charge

The Fort Orange Records of the Dutch New Netherland Court reported the examination of Nicolas Gregory Hillebrant, from Prague, "on a charge of attempting to commit sodomy. . . ."[31] The case was referred to the director-general and council of the colony.

On October 2, 1658 the minutes of the New Netherland council noted the petition of Nicolas Gregorius Hillebrantsen of Fort Orange (apparently the same person) to be allowed "to defend himself from an accusation of sodomy. . . ." The case was referred to the local court. No additional information is available.

LEGAL CASE

## 1660, May 13
## New Netherland: Jan Quisthout, Death sentence for "sodomy"

The council of the New Netherland Colony recorded the first proceedings in a sodomy case of an indentured servant and a soldier.[32] The council ordered that:

> the indentures of Hendrick Harmsen, an orphan from Amsterdam, bound to Jan Quisthout [the soldier], be canceled, and that he be bound to another person.

On May 21, 1660, the council minutes recorded the "Indictment of said Quisthout, a native of Brussels."

And on June 17, the council minutes recorded a "Plea of guilty entered against Jan Quisthout van der Linde, a soldier accused of sodomy."

The soldier's sentence was recorded on the same date:

> Jan Quisthout van der Linde to be taken to the place of execution and there stripped of his arms, his sword to be broken at his feet, and he to be then tied in a sack and cast into the river and drowned until dead."

The council also sentenced Hendrick Harmensen,

> the boy on whom Quisthout committed by force the above crime, to be privately whipped, and sent to some other place by the first opportunity.

Three years later on August 16, 1663, the "widow of Jan van der Linden" (apparently the same "van der Linde"), named Jannken Barents, petitioned the New Netherland Council "to surrender all claim to her late husband's estate in favor of his creditors," and to be "discharged from such liabilities."

STATUTE

# 1661
## Virginia: Buggery law

Since 1618 (see) the laws of England had apparently been informally enforced in Virginia. In 1661 the laws of England were expressly adopted by the Virginia assembly (making the English "buggery" law official in the colony).[33] The death penalty for the crime was abolished (for free persons) in 1800.

STATUTE

# 1663, March
## North and South Carolina: "Buggery" law

From the first major settlement, in the 1660s, of the area which became North and South Carolina, the English "buggery" law was apparently regarded as in force, although neither colony's law made explicit reference to this crime.[34] South Carolina first passed its own "buggery" law by enacting the text of the English statute in 1712 (see). North Carolina's first explicit statutory reference to "buggery" was its law of 1792. The death penalty for the crime was abolished in North Carolina in 1869.

LEGAL CASE

# 1663, July 4
## New Hampshire: Mathew Giles, *"Buggered her servant boy"*

The New Hampshire Court, sitting in Dover, gave its verdict in one of the earliest cases involving a certifiably false charge of male-male "buggery"—in an acrimonious squabble between wife and husband.[35]

On an earlier occasion, the record indicates, "The wife of Mathew Giles" (her first name is never stated) had been bound in bond of twenty pounds "to be of good behavior" and had agreed if not able to pay it that she would submit to "this Court's Censure." The record continues: her promise of "good behavior"

> this Court finds to be often broken Since that time by her Cursing & Swearing & abusing her husband . . . , in saying he had buggered her Servant boy, & Laen [laid] with her daughter . . . in law, & saying her daughter was her husband's whore, & that she did hope to see her husband hanged ere long

& wished she might be damned in hell if she did not—This court having Considered the heinousness of these crimes, Sentence her to be forthwith whipped to the number of 20 stripes, & to be Imprisoned during the Court's pleasure, Provided that in case of dangerous sickness or any other Exegent [exigency] as shall be Judged by Captain Wiggin, Captain Waldren & Captain Pendleton she may have such enlargement & Liberty as they shall see meet, & [the] fees [of the] Court [shall be paid by her].

Wm. Penney Servant boy to Mathew Giles for accusing his master of buggering him, & afterwards says his dame had hired him so to say, & confessed in Court that it was not true that his master had done any such thing to him, Sentence him to be whipped to the number of 10 stripes forthwith.

It appearing to this Court that Mathew Giles hath not carried himself so towards his wife as was meet for him to do but hath used uncomly & Provoking speeches . . . in saying he had taken his daughter as his wife which is provoking. This court sentence him to have an admonition, which was forthwith Performed: & fees [of the] Court [to be paid by Giles].

Jnº Meader, Constable, is allowed 5 s[hillings] for whipping Goodwife Giles & her servant boy[;] to be allowed by the treasurer of Dover.

STATUTE

# 1663
## Rhode Island: "Sodomy" law

The Rhode Island Colony revised its sodomy law of 1647.[36] The new statute dropped the earlier law's New Testament citations, adopting a wording more like that of the English buggery law.

The law of 1663 read:

. . . whosoever shall perpetuate and commit the Detestable and Abominable Crimes of Sodomy, or Buggery, and be thereof Lawfully Convicted, shall suffer the Pains of Death, as in Cases of Felony, with benefit of Clergy.

This Rhode Island law was next revised in 1798 when the death penalty for sodomy was abolished.

STATUTE

# 1665, March 1
## The Duke of York's Laws: Sodomy law

In 1664 the English conquered the Dutch New Netherland Colony and it became a proprietary colony of the Duke of York.[37] On March 1, 1665, at Hempstead,

Long Island, representatives from several towns approved the code of laws drawn up by the duke's agent. These laws, which closely followed New England precedent in their wording, went into effect in what became the New York and New Jersey colonies, and in the Pennsylvania Colony (in 1676, see).

Eleven capital crimes were listed in the Duke of York's laws of 1665. These included: (1) blasphemy, (2) premeditated murder, (3) murder of a defenseless victim, (4) conspiracy to murder, (5) bestiality, (6) sodomy, (7) man-stealing, (8) perjury to take a life, (9) treason, (10) insurrection, and (11) children over sixteen smiting their parents.

The sodomy provision read:

> If any man lyeth with mankind as he lyeth with a woman, they shall be put to Death, unless the one party were Forced or be under fourteen Years of age, in which Case he shall be punished at the Discretion of the Court of Assizes.

This law was next revised when New York became a royal province in 1711 (see).

STATUTE

# 1668, May 30
# New Jersey: "Sodomy" law

The representative assembly of New Jersey, meeting for the first time, made "sodomy" and "buggery" capital offenses.[38]

The wording of the New Jersey sodomy statute was almost identical to the "Duke's Laws" of New York. As in New England at this time, children under fourteen and the victims of force were exempted from the death penalty, and were to be punished according to the court's discretion.

The New Jersey sodomy law was next revised in 1681 (see).

STATUTE

# 1671, June 6
# Plymouth: "Sodomy" law

The General Court of Plymouth added several capital crimes to those specified in 1636.[39] The new laws also qualified the "sodomy" statute, making persons under fourteen and the party to forcible sodomy exempt from death. The further qualification, that "all other sodomitical filthiness" shall be punished according to its nature, may have meant that anal penetration was necessary for the death penalty, and that other types of non-penetrative, "sodomitical" (sodomy-like) acts, such as mutual or public masturbation, were not to be punished so severely.

The sixteen crimes punishable by death in the Plymouth law of 1671 were listed as: (1) "Idolatry," (2) "Blasphemy," (3) "Treason," (4) "Conspiring against this Juristiction" (attempted invasion, insurrection, or rebellion), (5) "Willful murder," (6) "Sudden Murder in Passion," (7) "Murder by Guile or Poisoning," (8) "Witchcraft," (9) "Bestiality," (10) "Sodomy," (11) "False-witness," (12) "Man-stealing," (13) "Cursing or Smiting Father or Mother," (14) "The Rebellious Son," (15) "Rape," (16) "Willful burning of Houses, Ships, etc."

The provision, whose margin referred to "sodomy," reads:

If any Man lyeth with Mankind, as he lyeth with a Woman, both of them have committed Abomination; they both shall surely be put to Death, unless the one party were forced, or be under fourteen years of Age: And all other Sodomitical filthiness, shall be surely punished according to the nature of it.

This Plymouth law was revised when Plymouth was united with Massachusetts, in 1697 (see).

STATUTE

# 1672, October
## Connecticut: "Sodomy" law

Connecticut legislators passed a statute amending their laws of 1642 and 1650, May (see).[40] The new "sodomy" provision eliminated the death penalty for the party who was forced, or under fifteen. Age had not been mentioned in the earlier law. The bestiality clause remained the same. Two new capital crimes were added to the 1673 law, incest and the striking of parents by children over fifteen.

The capital crimes of 1672, listed in the following order, were: (1) idolatry, (2) blasphemy, (3) witchcraft, (4) murder, (5) murder through gile, (6) bestiality, (7) "sodomy," (8) incest, (9) rape, (10) man-stealing, (11) false witness, (12) conspiracy against the colony, (13) arson, and (14) children over fifteen cursing or smiting parents.

The law whose margin referred to "sodomy" read:

If any man lyeth with Man-kind as he lyeth with a Woman, both of them have committed abomination, they both shall surely be put to death, except it appear that one of the parties were forced, or under *fifteen* years of age. Levit. 20:13.

This Connecticut law was next revised with minor changes in 1750, 1796, and 1808. The death penalty for sodomy was abolished in Connecticut in 1821.

♀ COMMENTARY

# 1674

## Samuel Danforth: "The Cry of Sodom Enquired Into"

A classic hellfire and brimstone sermon on the "sins of Sodom," published anonymously in Cambridge, Massachusetts, is attributed to the Reverend Samuel Danforth of Duxbury.[41] The diatribe was issued after a youth, Benjamin Goad, was executed for bestiality. This punishment's harshness apparently caused criticism in Massachusetts of the late 1600s, dissension which this sermon seems designed to answer.

"The sins of *Sodom* were many and great," said Danforth, but that which was "most grievous of all" was the Sodomites' "abominable *filthiness* in all manner of Uncleanness." Their specific uncleannesses were said to be "pride, fullness of bread [gluttony], and abundance of Idleness [sloth]." Also, the Sodomites did not attend to the needs of "the poor and needy, and they were haughty and committed abominations." Such "wickedness" "*cried* unto Heaven for vengeance."[1]

The Lord, said Danforth, did not have to travel to Sodom to know its sins, for he saw "the most secret wickedness, and knoweth our thoughts." But to "set an Example" for magistrates of careful criminal prosecution, the Lord decided to go down to earth in the shape of a man, accompanied by two holy Angels.[2-3] The Sodomites' "Beastly incivility and rage against those Heavenly Guests, the two holy Angels," revealed the city's wickedness. For this wickedness the Lord destroyed Sodom "with Fire and Brimstone."[3]

So that no one could claim the ministry did not acquaint him or her with the "heinousness" of the Sodomites' transgressions, Danforth inquired into the exact nature of their "Abominable Uncleanness." What were the sins which brought divine vengeance? They were "Fornication, and going after strange flesh." Fornication included, "not only *whoredom* and Self-pollution, but also Adultery." "Going after strange flesh" included "Sodomy and Bestiality."

"Self-pollution" was that which occurred when a man practiced "filthiness with his own body alone." This was the "sin of Onan," who "abhorred the lawful use of the Marriage-bed, and most impurely defiled himself." This sin was "so detestable in the sight of God" that he slew Onan. "Some learned Interpreters" of the Bible, Danforth said, also believed self-pollution to include defiling one's body by "nocturnal Pollutions," a "hateful" and "odious sin."[3]

"*Whoredom*" Danforth defined as "the violating of a single woman." "*Adultery*" was "the violating of the Marriage bed." "*Incest*" was "uncleanness committed by parties that are near of Kin." "*Sodomy*" was

filthiness committed between parties of the same Sex—when Males with Males, and Females with Females work wickedness. *If a man lieth with mankind, as he lieth with a woman, both of them have committed an abomination: they shall surely be put to death, their blood shall be upon them,* Lev. 20:13. This sin raged amongst the *Sodomites,* and to their perpetual Infamy, it is called *Sodomy.* Against this wickedness, no indignation is sufficient. The *Athenians* put such to death. *Theodosius* [the Roman general and emperor] and Arcadius adjudged such to be Burnt.[42] Amongst the Romans, it was lawful for a man to kill him that made such an assault upon him.[4]

"Bestiality, or Buggery" was "when any prostitute themselves to a Beast."[5]

Danforth's discourse was intended, he declared, to vindicate God's "severity toward this vile and wicked Youth," Benjamin Goad. (That an execution for bestiality needed vindication seems a sign of a popular desire for the less harsh punishment of such crimes.) "Some among us," said Danforth, may "stand astonished" that God should make "such a Youth," a "Child of Religious Parents," a "Dreadful Example of Divine Vengeance." Such doubters were told: "You pity his Youth and tender years," but, "I pray, pity the holy Law of God, which is shamefully violated . . . , pity the Land, which is fearfully polluted and defiled."

In defense of "God's" severe punishment of Goad, Danforth argued that the youth

> lived in Disobedience to his Parents, in Lying, Stealing, Sabbath-breaking, and was wont to flee away from Catechism. . . . He was extremely addicted to Sloth and Idleness. . . . He gave himself to Self-pollution, and other Sodomitical wickedness. He often attempted Buggery with several Beasts. . . . he grew so impudent in his wickedness, as to commit this horrid Villainy in the sight of the Sun, and in the open field, even at Noon-day. . . . Though he be a Youth in respect of years, yet he is grown old in wickedness, and ripe for Vengeance. . . . If we will not pronounce such a Villain Accursed, we must be content to bear the Curse ourselves. The Land cannot be cleansed, until it hath spued out this Unclean Beast. The execution of Justice upon such a notorious Malefactor, is the only way to turn away the wrath of God from us. . . .[9]

The execution of Goad reminded New Englanders of God's "Divine Wrath," and would "strike a holy fear and dread" into all hearts, preventing further evil, argued Danforth.[9–10]

The harsh punishment of the wicked was said to impress all persons because "Our cursed Natures" inclined us all to every kind of sin; the "holiest man hath as vile and filthy a Nature, as the Sodomites." The Lord's "severity" to Goad showed that "Whoredom, Adultery, Self-pollution and Sodomy, are as odious . . . now, as ever."[11–12] The destruction of the Sodomites demonstrated the propriety of the execution of Goad, swept away "as dung and filth from the face of the earth." God had "Hanged up" Goad "before the Sun" as "an Instruction and Astonishment to all *New England.*"[13]

Was there anyone who, knowing of Goad's fate, was "not afraid to go on impenitently in the same sins," who did not repent of "Self-pollution, Fornication . . . Sodomy and Bestiality"? Such non-repenters were sarcastically exhorted:

> Go to now, ye wanton and lascivious persons, go on in your Frolicks and mad Pranks. . . . He that is a Sodomite, let him be a Sodomite still; he that is a Beast, let him be a Beast still. . . . Justify this poor Condemned Wretch in all his Villainy. . . .[14]

Those who did "justify Sodom in all her Abomination" willed themselves to be condemned.[13]

The "Wrath of God" which had lighted upon Goad will "restrain the rest of our Youth, and all others," argued Danforth. God "hath cut off this rotten and putrid Member" to "prevent the spreading of the "Infection."[15]

The preacher commanded his readers: "Detest and abominate the sin of Sodomy," and those who "abuse themselves with man-kind."[16] To be preserved from "Uncleanness," Danforth ordered, "Beware of *Pride,*" a sin which "makes men despise the Ordinance of Marriage," a "remedy" for "boiling and burning lusts." Beware of "Gluttony and Drunkenness," Danforth also warned.

And "Beware of *Sloth* and *Idleness,* added this exponent of the Protestant work ethic, for when "men are sluggish" in the labor which God called them to, the "Devil" will set them about his own work. Do not roll upon your bed when you should be "in the Field," commanded the minister. As the old maxims said: "Laziness breeds Lewdness. *No business, debauchery.* By doing nothing, men learn to do evil."[18–19]

Danforth also warned, "Beware of *Disobedience* to Parents and Masters in Families, and of casting off the Yoke of Government"; such rules "restrain the Enormities of Youth." And "Beware evil Company," "Irreligion and Profaneness." The profane Gentiles represented God "by images of Men and Beasts, wherefore God gave them over to vile affections . . . , so that they ran mad into Sodomitical wickedness."[19–20]

God's punishment of Goad might move those guilty of Uncleanness to "Repent." The guilty person might well ask, if God did not spare this "lewd Youth," why should he spare any other "old practitioner in Sodomitical wickedness"? Danforth instructed the wicked to repent "unclean Speculations, vile affections, unchaste fire," so that God's heart would not be broken by "thy whorish heart." The "only Sacrifice" God required was a "contrite heart."[20] (Repentance might save even an "old practioncer in Sodomitical wickedness.") The sinner was urged to labor through the

> help of Christ to mortify thy lusts and crucify the flesh. . . . Take the Sword of the Spirit, and thrust it into the bowels of thy lusts. . . . If once thou has escaped out of *Sodom,* tremble to think of returning. . . .[22]

"Let the fear of God" excite all hearts to "purity" and "love of holiness," exhorted Danforth. The impure of heart were warned to watch all their "thoughts and affections," to "Stop thine Ears at filthy Jests, amorous Songs," and to "Abhor all lascivious Touches, unchaste Embracings."[23]

Finally, Danforth urged, "let us carefully *Watch over our Children,* Servants, and all that are under our Care and Charge, lest they be stained and defiled."[23]

Such prevention of sin might prevent future destruction. The Lord had fore-
warned Abraham of the Sodomites' impending destruction so that Abraham
could "charge his Children and Family to beware of like wickedness."

"Arise," concluded Danforth, "and depart out of *Sodom*."[25]


STATUTE

## 1676, September 25
## The Duke of York's Laws: Sodomy law

The Duke of York's Laws, including a capital sodomy provision (see 1665), were
by an executive order of Governor Edmund Andros made operative in the area
later to become Pennsylvania.[43] This law was next revised in 1682 (see).


LEGAL CASE

## 1677, May 22
## Connecticut: Nicholas Sension, Attempted "sodomy"

Nicholas Sension, a wealthy, respected, married citizen of Windsor, Connecticut,
was brought to trial under that colony's sodomy law of 1672.[44] The testimony
against Sension is the most detailed known to exist in any colonial sodomy case.
Extensive excerpts from the original manuscripts are published here for the first
time.

Daniel Saxton, a servant of Sension's, was his primary accuser, testifying
that he saw Sension commit sodomy with another servant, Nathaniel Pond. Saxton also claimed that Sension attempted sodomy with him. Numerous other
townsmen testified to Sension's repeated attempts at sodomy with them or other
young men (most of whom were in their late teens or early twenties). Sension
apparently pleaded guilty to attempted sodomy, asserting his innocence of any
completed act.

"Goodman" Sension arrived from England on the ship *Elizabeth and Ann*
and settled in Windsor about 1640. The only reference to Sension in Windsor
court records before 1677, is a report of his refusal to testify, in 1640, against
Aaron Starke, accused and convicted of "buggery" with a heifer—a refusal significant in terms of Sension's own illegal sexual proclivity. In 1643, Sension bought
a lot and built on Silver Street, opposite Pigeon Hill Road. He married his wife
Isabell on June 12, 1645. In 1648, he received a bequest from Edward Chalkwell
of a gun, sword, bandoliers, vest, hat, and forty shillings. Isabell Sension was
admitted to the Windsor Church on January 22, 1649. A tax list of 1675 divided
the Windsor population into five classes: Nicholas Sension was in the first—those
with "a family, a horse [and] four oxen." Sension became prosperous: Of five

Testimony of John Moses, trial of Nicholas Sension, 1677, illustrating the quality of the manuscripts (see backnotes for source).

income groups in Windsor in 1676 he was in the second richest. In June 1676, Sension was listed among those voluntary contributors who gave to "the poor in want in other colonies"—his donation was two shillings, six pence. In 1680, after thirty-five years of marriage, the Sensions were reported to have had no children. Nicholas Sension died on September 18, 1689.

In 1677, the testimony at Sension's trial revealed that his sodomy attempts had begun over thirty years before, about 1646–47. George Griswold testified that thirty-one or thirty-two years earlier

I was in the mill house . . . and Nicholas Sension was with me, and he took me and threw me on the chest and took hold on my privy parts.[88a]

William Phelps testified that about thirty years earlier (about 1647) because of the "abuse" which Sension had offered to Phelps's brothers and many others, Phelps and "my friends were exceedingly troubled," fearing how God might punish such abuse. The "hazard" of Sension "infecting the rising generation," said Phelps, made him complain to a member of the court about Sension's "Sodomitical actings towards my brethren." Phelps said that when he confronted Sension about his activity, Sension had "acknowledged he took [it] up at the school where he was educated," admitting to Phelps "how long" he had pursued "this trade."[98]

Although Phelps indicated that court members discussed the matter in the late 1640s, Sension was not brought to trial at that time; he was instead privately confronted by individual court members. But even after this private confrontation Sension continued his "sodomitical" ways.

Jacob Gibs testified that about 1648 Sension had made overtures to him. Gibs said that "many times, if not all times," when he and Nicholas Sension were alone, Sension had made advances. Once Sension had tried "hugging" Gibs "in his arms & fell a trembling with his body"—reaching "his hands within my breeches, laboring to handle the low part of my body in an uncomely manner." Another time when they were working in a marsh, Gibs said that Sension suggested

> to keep our clothes clean let us roll off our stockings and breeches, and so we both did. . . .

Later, "when we sat down to drink and smoke," Sension

> came to me and . . . untied my shirt and uncovered me, being uncovered himself, [and] strove to close his body with mine. After much striving I told him that if he would not let me alone, I would cry for help. . . .[94]

Josiah Holcombe testified that about 1658 Sension made three separate overtures to him. One night Holcombe and Sension were on the watch together, and Holcombe suggested that they go to a house, apparently to sleep. Sension instead suggested that they go to his "haymow" (or haystack). "Thither we went," testified Holcombe,

> and when we were there, when I was almost asleep, ye said Sension did endeavor to untie my breeches and I, perceiving what he was about, wondered what he meant; and I was quiet and let him alone till he had unloosed my breeches and heaved them down over my breech [behind], and with his mouth and nose rubs about my breech, and being about to get upon me, I shoved him off and he promised me to be quiet.

"Another time the same year," says Holcombe, "I was mowing for my father," and

> Sension came to me and lighted his pipe and smoked by me, and I having an open pair of drawers, the said Sension thrust up his hand into them and at last went to untie my drawers.

And on another occasion, while Holcombe was bathing in the river, he recalled that

I went out upon the bank to dry myself, and the said Sension came to me with his yard or member erected in his hands, and desired me to lie on my belly, and strove with me, but I went away from him.[87a]

About 1667, twenty years after his first warning, Sension was privately confronted a second time about his behavior. At this time, Sension's indentured servant, the seventeen-year-old Nathaniel Pond, complained to his brother, Isaac Pond, about Sension's advances. Isaac Pond brought the complaint to John Griffen, asking for his advice and counsel. Griffen testified that Nathaniel Pond had "made known his grievance," telling his brother

what temptations he was liable unto by reason of his master Sension's grossly lascivious carriages towards him, who did often in an unseemly manner make attempts tending to sodomy, so that [Nathaniel] was forced by violence to throw [Sension] off from him, and yet his said master did often, and at the same times when he was resisted, reiterate his attempts of that nature so that, though Nathaniel was grown, and somewhat stronger than his master, yet [Sension's] attempts were so violent and constant that [Nathaniel] found it difficult work to keep [Sension] off. I advised [Isaac Pond] to use all means to procure his brother's release from Goodman Sension, and that if he and some friends could not attain it . . . , then to make his application to authority.[89]

Isaac Pond went immediately to Timothy Phelps for advice. Phelps, one of Windsor's wealthiest citizens, went with Isaac Pond to see Sension, and spoke with him in Nathaniel Pond's presence. John Griffen related the surprising result. Sension agreed

to let the said Nathaniel Pond at liberty, but the young man, after his way was made for him, out of his ingenuity (as I did judge when I heard of it), said that his Uncle Sension (as he styled him), having been the man that had brought him up from a child in his orphan state, and now being grown up, he was loath to leave him who had the trouble of his education in his minority, now he was fit to do him service. . . .

After Nathaniel Pond refused to leave his master, Sension offered to give Pond a year off his service, and forty shillings, "for his abuse."[89]

Nathaniel Pond's refusal to leave Sension, even though troubled by his master's sodomy attempts, suggests the emotional and economic complexity of these relationships. John Griffen referred to Nathaniel Pond's "ingenuity" in refusing to leave his "Uncle" Sension, suggesting, perhaps, that Pond stayed on in hopes of an inheritance from Sension's sizeable estate. Sension, though married, was childless, and Pond having been raised in the household may have hoped to receive some tangible benefit from his master's interest. Pond may have also truly felt gratitude and affection for Sension, in spite of his troubling "sodomitical" overtures.

Robert Renwert was apparently one of those who investigated the matter, questioning Nathaniel Pond about his master. Renwert later recalled that Pond "spoke very low the first time so that I could hardly understand him." Pond finally said that Sension "would have committed that Sin of Sodomy with me." Then Pond "Expressed the same words again, somewhat Louder." Renwert asked Pond

> if his master used any Loving Expressions to him to persuade him to it. He said "no, not any." I asked him if his master's clothes were on or no. He said his master's clothes were on.

Renwert also recalled one of the Enno family asking Pond if his master spoke with him "to persuade him to his wish." Pond answered no. Renwert recalled that Sension's wife "complained much how stubborn and disobedient" Pond was, how he would not obey lawful commands.[88b] (Renwert's testimony is among the most illegible.) Interestingly, in the late 1600s Windsor townspeople permitted Nathaniel Pond to remain in the Sension household, though both master and servant were subject to sodomitical "temptation." The matter of Sension's sodomitical advances was apparently resolved by a reduction in Nathaniel Pond's term of service, and Sension's payment to him of forty shillings.

Samuel Willson testified that about 1671 he had slept overnight with Nathaniel Pond and that, in the morning, Sension had "come up to the bedside and did put his hands into that bed. Nathaniel Pond and I lay back to back." When Sension put his hand "to Nathaniel Pond's breech," Willson "turned about" and Sension "pushed his hand out of the bed, and said he'd come for some tobacco."[91]

At the trial, in May, 1677, Daniel Saxton, the major witness against his master Nicholas Sension, testified that "he saw Nicholas Sension come to bed to Nathaniel Pond and make the bed shake." Saxton concluded that Sension "had committed the Sin of Sodomy with Nathaniel Pond."

Saxton also testified that, in April, the month before the trial, Sension had come up to his (Saxton's) room early in the morning. Saxton says he had resolved

> to see what [Sension's] intention was, thinking with myself whether he would commit the same wickedness with me as I had seen him commit with Nathaniel Pond.

Saxton said that Sension "turned me on my belly and took up my shirt, and with his lips kissed my tail[?] twice: and then got on me with his body, with that [end] of persuing his tricks[?]." Saxton violently "thrust him off," warning his master "that he would not leave this Devilish sin till he was hanged."[93] Another witness, Josiah Gilbert, testified that "in the chamber overhead" he "overheard" the words, "You'll never leave this Devilish sin till you are hanged."[87a] Gilbert's brother also testified that Josiah often said he had heard Daniel Saxton tell "his Uncle Sension that he would never leave his old trade till he was brought to the gallows."[95]

Other instances of attempted sodomy by Sension, some of more recent date, were testified to in 1677 by a series of witnesses.

John Parsons testified that Sension suddenly "clapped his hands about me and unbuttoned or unclaspted my breeches." Parsons told Sension to leave him alone, but "accidentally [Sension] got me down" and tried "to get upon me with his Yard in his hands."[88a]

Samuel Barboe testified that Sension "proferred me a bushel of corn if I would put down my breeches." Another time, said Barboe, Sension "put his hands in my breeches to my bare skin."

Peter Buoll testified that once, in Sension's barn, Sension

> told me if I would let him have one bloo [blow?] at my breech he would give me a charge of powder. And when my breeches was down he threw me upon my belly and would have committed the Sin of Sodom with me; but when I perceived what he was about I resisted him out of shame, not knowing the use of the thing. . . .[101]

At the trial of 1677 Nathaniel Pond's own testimony was unavailable; he had been killed a year or so before in King Philip's War (1675–76; fought by the English against several tribes of Indians led by Philip, chief of the Wampanoags). Joshua Holcombe testified that, "a little after the news came of Nathaniel Pond's death," Sension

> told me that he was afraid that it fared the worse to him for his foolish and fond [and Sinful] affections which he had toward him.[95b] [The words "and Sinful" were crossed out in the manuscript.]

Twenty-two year-old John Moses testified that when he lodged at Sension's he (Moses) slept in the same bed with Nathaniel Pond. Moses said that toward morning Sension came

> to the bedside where I lay and put his hands to my Secret parts, aggravating all about those parts, so making me ought [?] of love. . . .

Then Sension stopped, and Moses thought he had left, "but he Returned back again to the other side of the bed where Nathaniel Pond lay, and called softly to the said Nathaniel Pond. . . ."[97]

Thomas Barber's testimony indicates that Sension's behavior was widely known in the community, at least among the young men. Barber said that, while working as a servant, he made a trip to Hartford during which he and Sension "were appointed to lie together in a trundel bed." In the room there was also

> a standing high bed wherein lay two members of the General Court at that time. And [Barber] saith that he was unwilling and afraid to lodge with [Sension] because of some reports he had heard formerly concerning him, but being that the gentlemen lay in the chamber, and they were in a foreign place, he hoped no hurt would come of it, and therefore submitted and

yielded to lodge with [Sension] without making disturbance in a strange house. But not long after, [Barber] being in bed with [Sension] and turning his back parts toward Goodman Sension, the said Goodman Sension soon after strove to turn [Barber's] back parts upwards and attempted with his yard to enter his body. . . . [Barber], being awakened, and feeling what [Sension] was about, was in a great strait, fearing to disturb the courtiers in the other bed, and more, fearing he should be wronged. And [Barber] further saith that . . . to hinder [Sension] from prosecution of his devilish design, he turned his elbow back to Sension's belly with several blows which caused him to desist for that time. And so [Barber] slept in fear all night, and in [the] morning told his master . . . that he would lie no more with Goodman Sension. . . .[99]

Barber apparently felt some conflict about his incriminating testimony against Sension; he testified that he was "much beholden" to Sension for "entertainment in his house" during an earlier "time of troubles," when Barber and his wife were first married. Barber was "therefore . . . much troubled" that his testimony should "in the least measure" weigh against Sension. "But," added Barber, during the "time he and his wife [were] lodging in the middle room between Goodman Sension and his wife," Sension, "early in the morning, used to come out of his bed chamber with his shoes on, and so passed through [Barber's] room." Afterward, Barber said, "he heard a noise" of a bed "creaking"

as he suspected and thought—but never saw any such thing—only he knows that the said Sension was very familiar with Nathaniel Pond.[99]

Sension, it seems, was considered a good neighbor by Barber, and a kind master by Nathaniel Pond, even though both were troubled by his "sodomitical" attempts.

The testimony of twenty-two-year-old John Enno indicates that Sension felt remorse about his behavior, and worried about its public disclosure. Enno said that when he lodged one night with Daniel Saxton, Nicholas Sension came into the room, took the bed clothes off the sleeping Saxton, lay down in the bed by him, "and caused the bed to rock much." Sension "then rose up . . . , wiped something off from Daniel," and "went into the next room . . . and prayed to God to save him from this wicked sin that he had lived in a long time."[45]

Arthur Henberry testified that John Enno had told him that, after Sension had lain in Daniel Saxton's bed, Enno had seen what Sension "left behind him on the thighs of Daniel Saxton." Enno and Saxton had also told Henberry of "Sension's proffering to give Nathaniel Pond his black horse," apparently as an enticement for sexual favors.[90]

Another time, John Enno testified, he was sleeping with Nathaniel Pond. Toward morning Sension "came to the bedside and uncovered me, and seeing that it was me, he went to the other side of the bed and . . . lay down by Nathaniel Pond." Enno had many times found Sension lying by Pond's side of the bed.

Enno swore that Sension "desired me to say nothing of these things for one thousand pounds. . . ."[96a] Another witness, Arthur Hennerick, also once heard Sension plead with John Enno:

> Oh John, do not speak anything to my prejudice; I would not have thee speak of it for a thousand pounds. I love you and your mother and all the family.[88a]

According to colonial custom, proof of completed sodomy legally required two witnesses (or, possibly, one witness and evidence equaling a second witness), and Daniel Saxton alone testified to have "seen" Sension commit sodomy with Nathaniel Pond. The court, therefore, had legal grounds for finding Sension guilty of only attempted sodomy. As punishment, Sension's entire estate, his "lodging and land in Windsor, and all his cattle and swine and household stuff of all sorts," worth 300 pounds, were held in bond for his good behavior during his lifetime. If Sension behaved, he received no material punishment. Sension lived for twelve years after the trial, and there are no further records of legal proceedings against him.

Sension's relatively lenient sentence, despite the abundant evidence of his sodomy attempts, may be due to his wealth, high status, and personal favor in the community, as much as to the colonists' apparent reluctance after the 1660s to enforce the harsh penalty provided by their capital sodomy law. The fact that Sension's attempted sodomy was known in the community, and continued for over thirty years before any legal charge was brought, indicates that American colonists, by the late 1600s at least, were sometimes more tolerant of sodomy (and attempted sodomy) than their still harsh legal codes implied.

Historian Linda Bissell, who discussed the Sension case in her thesis on seventeenth-century Windsor, Connecticut, suggested that before Sension was finally prosecuted under the sodomy law, the community tried other social means to control his conduct. The community, concluded Bissell, used the law "to enforce obedience only when other means had failed and violations of norms were flagrant."

STATUTE

# 1680, March 16
## New Hampshire: Sodomy law

Legislators of New Hampshire passed the colony's first capital laws, copied almost word for word from the Plymouth laws of 1671[46]:

> If any man lie with mankind as he lies with a woman; both of them have committed abomination; They both shall surely be put to death: unless one party were forced, or were under fourteen years of age. And all other

Sodomitical filthiness shall be severely punished according to the nature of it.

This law was next revised in 1718 (see).

STATUTE

# 1681
## West New Jersey: Buggery law

The Quaker colony of West New Jersey, whose assembly met yearly starting in 1681, did not pass a sodomy law. Only treason and murder were explicitly made capital offenses, though the English "buggery" statute may have been formally in effect.[47] This colony's status changed when West and East New Jersey were united as a single royal colony in 1702 (see).

STATUTE

# 1682, December 7
## Pennsylvania: "Sodomy" law

The first assembly held in the Province of Pennsylvania under the proprietorship of William Penn, reflected Quaker leniency in a significant law reform.[48] The capital sodomy law of 1676 was repealed and a new Pennsylvania code (William Penn's "Great Law") limited the death penalty to murder, thereby abolishing it for sodomy, bestiality, etc. Since the earlier Quaker code of West New Jersey (1681) was silent about sodomy, this new Pennsylvania law was apparently the first in America to make sodomy a non-capital offense. The new punishment for sodomy and bestiality consisted of a whipping, forfeiting one-third of one's estate, and six months at hard labor for a first offense. A second offense was punished by life imprisonment. (This six months at hard labor for first offense sodomy was, according to Louis Crompton, the briefest incarceration provided by any American sodomy statute for two-hundred and seventy-nine years, until 1961.)

Although the Quaker law of 1682 abolished death for sodomy, the code's longest list of crimes were those against public morality, which were still punished severely. Adulterers received a whipping and one year's imprisonment for a first offense, life imprisonment for a second. For incest one forfeited half one's estate, and was imprisoned for a year for a first offense; a second offense received life. A rapist forfeited one third of his estate and was imprisoned one year for a first offense; a second rape received life. Bigamy, first offense, received life imprisonment. Other additions to Pennsylvania law provided that fornication was penalized by marriage (!), or fine, or corporal punishment, or by all or any of these, at the court's discretion. Penalties were also provided for profanity, drunkenness, gambling, dueling, and for presenting and attending stage plays, masques, card and dice games, lotteries, etc.

The Pennsylvania sodomy provision of 1682 read:

> . . . if any person shall be Legally Convicted of the unnatural sin of Sodomy or joining with beasts, Such person shall be whipped, and forfeit one third of his or her estate, and work six months in the house of Correction, at hard labour, and for the Second offence, imprisonment, as aforesaid, during life. [The reference to females was probably construed as applying only to the bestiality provision.]

No death penalty for sodomy (for white males), or for any other crime but murder, was specifically provided in Pennsylvania for thirty-six years, 1682–1718. (For a brief period, after June 1693 [see], sodomy and some other crimes may have implicitly been considered capital, according to English law. And in 1700 [see] Pennsylvania legislators provided the death penalty for Blacks guilty of buggery [bestiality and sodomy], murder, burglary, and the rape of a white woman.)

The Pennsylvania law of 1682 was next revised in June 1693 (see).

STATUTE

# 1683, March
## East New Jersey: "Sodomy" law

After East New Jersey was sold to a group of proprietors most of whom were Quakers, its general assembly drew up a new legal code significantly differing from the earlier law of 1668.[49] "Sodomy" was now grouped with many other crimes, ranging from swearing to murder and treason, all to be punished according to their "nature." Since sodomy, like murder and treason, was traditionally capital, the death penalty may have been assumed, although this was not specifically stated. The law may have reflected a positive desire to punish sodomy less strictly, or it may have expressed some ambivalence about penalizing it by death.

A separate provision of this law specified bestiality as a capital crime, indicating that human-animal contacts were considered worse than sodomy.

The sodomy provision read:

> all Offenses against God, as Cursing, Swearing, Lying, Profane talking, Drunkenness, Drinking of Healths, obscene Words, Incest, Sodomy, Rapes, Adultery, Fornication and other uncleanness (not to be repeated), all Treasons, Misprisons, Murders, Duels, Felonies, Seditions, Mayhems, forceable Entries, and other Villainies to the Persons and Estates of the Inhabitants

of this Province, and all Prizes, Stage-Plays, Games, Masques, Revels, Bull-baitings, Cock-fightings, which excite People to Rudeness, Cruelty, Looseness, and Irreligion shall be respectively discouraged and punished by the Judges and Courts of Justice in this Province, according to the nature and kind of the said respective Offenses.

This East New Jersey law remained in effect until East and West New Jersey were united as a single royal colony in 1702 (see).

STATUTE

# 1691
## New York: "Buggery" law

After the Glorious Revolution in England, in 1691, New York became a royal province.[50] From that time until 1787, the English "buggery" law (providing death) was apparently regarded as in effect. The death penalty for the crime was abolished in New York in 1796.

STATUTE

# 1693, June
## Pennsylvania: Sodomy law

While William Penn, temporarily in disfavor with William and Mary, was suspended from power for two years, the Royal governor appointed to replace him repealed most prior legislation, including the non-capital Pennsylvania sodomy law of 1682 (see Dec. 7).[51] No new sodomy law was passed during the Royal governor's less-than-two-year reign, and the English sodomy law was perhaps considered in force. When William Penn returned to Royal favor, the governor he appointed ruled according to the non-capital sodomy statute of 1682.

The next revision of Pennsylvania sodomy law was in 1700 (see).

STATUTE

# 1697, May 26
## Massachusetts: "Buggery" law

After the Massachusetts Bay and the Plymouth colonies were joined as the Massachusetts Colony, a revision of the old Massachusetts Bay law, of 1672, made a terminological change in the new sodomy statute.[52] The crime was now called "buggery" with men or beast; it was still "detestable and abominable" but it was now also "contrary to the very Light of Nature" (hinting that "Nature" was playing a new, prominent role in legal philosophy). Unlike most earlier laws in which sodomy was distinguished from bestiality, the term "buggery" here applied to both kinds of contacts. And both still remained capital crimes.

This Massachusetts "buggery" law, requiring death for the human participants and, in the case of bestiality, the execution and burning of the beast, was one of a series of provisions which also included acts against murder, rape, and "Atheism and Blasphemie" (the latter punished by "boring through the tongue with a red hot iron").

"An Act for the Punishment of Buggery" read:

> For avoiding of the detestable and abominable Sin of Buggery with Mankind or Beast, which is contrary to the very Light of Nature; Be it Enacted and Declared . . . That the same Offence be adjudged Felony. . . . And that every Man, being duly convicted of lying with Mankind, as he lieth with a Woman; and every Man or Woman that shall have carnal Copulation with any Beast or Brute Creature, the Offender and Offenders, in either of the Cases before mentioned, shall suffer the Pains of Death, and the Beast shall be slain and burnt.

This law remained in force until its revision in 1785. A law of 1805 abolished the death penalty for "Sodomy and Bestiality."

STATUTE

# 1700, November 27
# Pennsylvania: "Sodomy" law

The Pennsylvania assembly passed a new sodomy law to replace the statute abrogated in 1693.[53] Under the new Pennsylvania statute (as in the earlier Pennsylvania law of 1682), sodomy, committed by whites, was still not capital. The new law called for life imprisonment for a first offense and, at the discretion of the magistrates, a whipping once every three months during the first year. If the guilty man was married the punishment was castration, and his wife was granted a divorce. If a woman was guilty of bestiality her husband was granted a divorce.

A separate act, passed the same day, dealt with "negros." (The law of 1682 had not distinguished between Blacks and whites.) The new act imposed the death penalty on Blacks guilty of "buggery," burglary, the rape of a white woman, and murder. Though the text is ambiguous, "buggery" here probably meant both "sodomy" and "bestiality."

The Pennsylvania sodomy and bestiality provision read:

> . . . whoever shall be legally convicted of sodomy or bestiality, shall suffer imprisonment during life, and be whipped at the discretion of the magis-

trates, once every three months during the first year after conviction. And if he be a married man, he shall also suffer castration, and the injured wife shall have a divorce if required. And if a married woman be legally convicted of bestiality her husband may have a divorce if requested.

"An Act for the Trial of Negroes" read:

> if any negro or negroes within this government shall commit a rape or ravishment upon any white woman or maid, or shall commit murder, buggery or burglary, they shall be . . . punished by death. . . .

These laws were next revised in 1706 (see).

COMMENTARY

# 1701, June
## Cotton Mather: *"The Sins of* Sodom"

A sermon by the Reverend Cotton Mather, "A Christian in his Personal Calling," a classic Puritan statement, nicely demonstrates the connection between the Puritan work ethic appropriate to this period of primitive capital accumulation, and the Puritan attitude toward sin, specifically, "the Sins of *Sodom."* [54] Although the passing reference to Sodom's sins is brief, Mather's remarks indicate intimate associations between religious ideology, morals, sex, the value of work, family, neighborhood, and commonwealth. A Christian's "General Calling," said Mather, was "to Serve the Lord Jesus Christ, and Save his own *Soul.* . . ." A Christian's "Personal Calling," was

> a Certain *Particular Employment,* by which his *Usefulness* in his Neighborhood is distinguished. God has made man a *Sociable* Creature. We expect Benefits from *Human Society.* It is but equal, that *Human Society* should Receive Benefits from *Us.* We are Beneficial to *Human Society* by the *Works* of that *Special Occupation* in which we are to be employ'd, according to the Order of God.

A Christian in his Personal and his General Calling, was said to be "a man in a Boat, Rowing for Heaven." If he mind but one calling and not the other he "will make but a poor dispatch to the Shore of Eternal Blessedness." [37–38]

So that a man may give a "Good Account" of himself, said Mather, there should be some

> *Settled Business,* wherein a Christian should . . . spend the most of his *Time;* and this, that so he may Glorify God, by doing *Good* for *others,* and getting *Good* for *himself.* It is enjoined upon Christians . . . *Do your own Business. . . .*
>      Indeed, a man cannot live without the *Help* of *other* men. But how can a man Reasonably look for the *Help* of *other men,* if he be not in some *Calling* Helpful to *other* men?

For example, God put Adam into the Garden of Eden to tend it. One of Adam's sons was a "Husbandman," another a shepherd.[38-39] Jesus in his "private Life" was a carpenter, in his "public life" a minister.[40] There was a law among the Corinthians, said Mather, that if a "man could not prove that he lived by some good Labour, such a man should suffer as a *Thief.*" To be without a calling was unlawful. A man

> is Impious towards God, if he be without a Calling, for he is Unrighteous towards his *Family,* towards his *Neighborhood,* towards the *Commonwealth.* . . .[41]

"Yea, A Calling is not only our *Duty,*" exclaimed Mather,

> but also our *Safety.* Men will ordinarily fall into horrible *Snares,* and infinite *Sins,* if they have not a *Calling,* to be their *preservative.* . . . They who *Learn to be Idle,* (a thing soon Learnt!) will soon Learn the *things* which they *ought not.* Tho' it were part of the *Curse* brought in by *Sin, In the Sweat of thy Face thou shall eat Bread,* the *Curse* is become a Blessing, and our Sweat has a tendency to keep us from abundance of *Sin.* . . . The Temptations of the *Devil,* are best Resisted, by those that are least at *Leisure* to Receive them. An *Occupation* is an *Ordinance* of God for our safeguard against the Temptations of the Devil. A Bird on the Wing is not so soon catch'd by the *Hellish Fowler.* A man is upon the *Wing,* when he is at the *Work,* which God hath set him to do.[41-42]

"There are Gentlemen, 'tis true," admitted Mather, "who Live upon their Means." But the "Best Gentlemen" will find "some way of living Serviceable in the world." He added:

> *Idle Gentlemen* have done as much Hurt in the world, as *Idle Beggars.* And pardon me, if I say, any *Honest Mechanicks* really are more Honourable than Idle and Useless *men of Honour.*[42]

Mather concluded:

> God hath placed us, as in a common Hive; Let there be no *Drone* in the *Hive.* . . . The Sin of *Sodom was, Abundance of Idleness.* All the Sins of *Sodom* will abound, where Idleness is countenanced. . . .[42-43]

STATUTE

# 1702
## New Jersey: Buggery law

East and West New Jersey were united as one royal colony, and their proprietors surrendered all claims to govern to the crown.[55] No sodomy law was passed before the revolution, although since New Jersey was a royal colony, the English buggery act was formally in effect. In 1796, the state of New Jersey removed the death penalty for sodomy, punishing the crime with a fine and imprisonment for up to twenty-one years.

STATUTE

# 1706, January 12
## Pennsylvania: "Sodomy" and "buggery" law

The Pennsylvania assembly passed a new sodomy and buggery law removing the castration penalty for the crime, imposed in 1700.[56] Anyone above an undefined "age of discretion" consenting to either sodomy or buggery was to be imprisoned at hard labor for life. During the first year, at the magistrates' discretion, the guilty party was to be whipped every three months (not exceeding thirty-nine lashes per whipping). Distinction was no longer made (as in the Pennsylvania law of 1700) between married and unmarried men guilty of sodomy or buggery.

For bestiality men and women suffered the same punishment, and their spouses were granted a divorce disallowing remarriage.

A provision of the new law referring to "negroes" maintained the earlier death penalty for "buggery" (apparently, sodomy and bestiality).

The Pennsylvania "Act Against Sodomy and Buggery" read:

> . . . if any person or persons shall be convicted of sodomy and buggery, provided he or they be at the age of discretion, and consenting thereunto [he or they] shall suffer imprisonment at hard labor during life, and shall be whipped at the discretion of the magistrates (not exceeding thirty-nine lashes at one time) every three months during the first year after conviction.

The provision referring to "negroes" read:

> . . . if any negro or negroes within this province shall commit a rape or ravishment upon any white woman or maid, or shall commit murder, buggery or burglary, they shall be . . . punished by death. . . .

This law was next revised on May 31, 1718 (see).

CROSSING MAN

# 1707, February 9
## Lewis Morris: Lord Cornbury, Governor of New York and New Jersey

Lewis Morris, a bitter political foe of Edward Hyde, Lord Cornbury, governor of New York and New Jersey, wrote to New York's secretary of state.[57] Morris noted

Edward Hyde, Lord Cornbury, Governor of New Jersey 1703–1708. Oil painting, painter unknown (in Arthur D. Pierce, "A Governor in Skirts," *New Jersey Historical Society Proceedings,* vol. 83, no. 1 [January 1965], opposite p. 1; reprinted by permission of The New York Historical Society, owner of the portrait).

that Governor Cornbury had acquired the habit of dressing in women's clothes, and testified to the good character of a suggested replacement.

Morris, significantly, made no mention of sodomy or any other sexual practice in his accusation against Cornbury. There is no known document suggesting that American colonists associated cross-dressing, effeminacy, and male-male sodomy, though in some English cities at the time such a link was beginning to be made. The earliest document now known to associate Cornbury's cross-dressing directly with "sexual perversion" and "contrary sexual sensation" dates to 1881. Since Cornbury was one of the most corrupt and hated English colonial officials it would seem that, given his cross-dressing, a hint of sodomy would have soon clouded his name—if such an association had occurred to his many American enemies.

In 1707, Lewis Morris wrote of Cornbury's suggested replacement:

> He is an honest man and the reverse of my Lord Cornbury; of whom I must say something which perhaps nobody will think worth their while to tell, and that is, his dressing publicly in woman's clothes every day, and putting a stop to all public business while he is pleasing himself with that peculiar but detestable magot [caprice].

The next known reference to Lord Cornbury's cross-dressing appeared in 1829.

NATIVE AMERICANS

# 1709
## John Lawson: *"Sodomy is never heard of"*

Lawson, a British gentleman, surveyor and traveler, published a narrative of his voyage to Carolina.[58] This earliest-known mention of native sodomy by an Englishman denied its existence. Lawson reported that although the Indians he observed "are called Savages, yet Sodomy is never heard of amongst them." The Indians "are so far from the Practice of that beastly and loathsome Sin that they have no Name for it in their Language."

LEGAL CASE

# 1712, January 29
## Massachusetts: Mingo, alias Cocke Negro, executed

The diary of Samuel Sewall recorded that a grand jury, meeting at Charlestown, Massachusetts, found reason to arraign "Mingo, alias Cocke Negro, for forcible Buggery."[59] The following day, January 30, Sewall's diary added tersely:

Try'd the Negro, GOD furnish'd the Court with such a series and Frame of evidence that he was brought in Guilty. Not one word spoken on his behalf. Condemn'd.

On Friday, February 15, Sewall's diary included an entry seemingly referring to Mingo:

Went to Charlestown, and heard Mr. [Simon] Bradstreet [preach] from Prov. 24:32 ["Then I saw, *and* considered *it* well: I looked upon *it, and* received instruction"]. He brought it [the meaning of the proverb] down to the [unnamed] Condemned Malefactor then present; [Bradstreet?] had prayed excellently for him before: executed presently after Lecture. Mr. [William] Brattle Pray'd at the place of Execution.

Mingo, or Cocke Negro, a slave of Wait Winthrop, a chief justice of Massachusetts and major-general of the colony's militia, seems to have been executed under the Massachusetts law, of 1697, which provided death for "buggery," meaning both bestiality and sodomy. Sewall's statement that Mingo was guilty of "forcible Buggery" suggests that the crime in this case was sodomy (the issue of force versus an implicit consent would probably not have been cited if the case involved bestiality). However, no additional information has been found concerning this charge in the Winthrop Papers, existing newspapers, or Cotton Mather's diary. (Though "Mingo" may have been a common name for Blacks, the fact that a "Mingo" was mentioned as a mourner at Wait Winthrop's funeral in 1717 casts some doubt on the execution of "Mingo" in 1712.)

STATUTE

# 1712
## South Carolina: "Buggery" law

South Carolina legislators included the text of the English "buggery" law (and its death penalty) in the South Carolina statute, an explicit incorporation rare in the Southern colonies.[60] Usually the English buggery law was simply assumed to be operative. This South Carolina buggery law of 1712 remained in effect for one hundred and sixty-one years, until 1873, when the death penalty was repealed.

LEGAL CASE

# 1718, March
## North Carolina: Clark versus Winn

In an early case involving an accusation of attempted sodomy, John Clark charged William and Edward Winn with so libeling him.[61] In his formal charge against

William Winn (or Wynn), in the North Carolina General Court, John Clark, Esquire, declared that he (Clark) was "a good, honest, Chaste, and faithful Subject of our Sovereign Lord the King." Clark had "always from his Nativity . . . behaved himself with a good Fame, Character and Gesture." He had "been of a Good and Chaste life . . . among his Neighbors." He had "always lived unsuspected, unstain'd and without blemish of any matter of Incontinence, unchastity, Sodomy, Buggery, or any Such Nauseous, Scandalous or Notorious crime."[164]

Behaving himself so well, he had not only long enjoyed the "Esteem" of his neighbors, but had "got much benefit and advantage by Trading and Merchandizing with them." And by "living an honest, Chaste and Vertuous Life for many years past" he had "been thought worthy" by the Governor, Chief Officers, and Magistrates to be employed in "Posts of very Considerable Trust and Credit," Captain of a militia company and justice of the peace in Bath County. Clark still acted as an officer of justice. His neighbors had also chosen him as their representative in the colonial Assembly. But Winn's "long continued" and premeditated "Wicked malice" had been intended to injure Clark in his "good Name, Fame, Credit, Trade, Reputation, and Esteem among his Neighbors," the governor and other officers, and to bring Clark "into utter disgrace, Shame, and Infamy among them, and all other good, honest and lawful people."[165]

Clark charged, specifically, that Winn, on March 20, 1716, had "falsely and Maliciously, in the presence and hearing of divers good and honest Subjects," uttered "Scandalous, malicious, wicked and most injurious words" against him. Winn had followed Clark, "with a loud voice," saying that he, Clark, "would have Buggered me, and use[d] divers ways to seduce and persuade me to it." Winn had also said "divers other times, without any Provocation," that Clark was a "nasty fellow, and used his Endeavor [tried] to Bugger me," several times for many months past. Winn had also publicly declared that Clark "wanted to bugger my brother and I, and often persuaded me to let him do it."

Winn's malicious words had not only brought Clark into "great Disgrace, Trouble, Shame, Scandal, Injury, Scorn, [and] hatred amongst his Neighbors," the governor, chief officers, magistrates, and others, but had "Damnify'd" and hurt Clark "in his Trade and Commerce." Winn's charges had also brought Clark

> into very Great and apparent Dangers of Prosecution . . . for that most Notorious abominable, Odious, Shameful, and most hated Sins of Buggery and Sodomy, whereby he may undergo the disgrace and trouble of . . . Imprisonment, Trial for his Life, and the Danger of losing all his Estate."

Clark had also been forced, he said, to "Expend great Sums of money" to defend "his Reputation and Credit." Clark repeated that he was "much Damnify'd" and had sustained damages of "Two hundred pounds Sterling," for which he was bringing suit against Winn.[165]

William Winn's brother, Edward, was also charged by Clark, according to the same form, with having said on March 20, 1716, that Clark "had Buggered me," and that Clark "would have Buggered me," and had used "divers ways and means to Seduce and persuade me to it."

Clark also charged Edward Winn with having publicly declared that he (Clark) "wanted to Bugger my Brother and I," had often tried to persuade Edward Winn "to let him do it," and had "endeavored [tried] Several others (meaning young men in the neighborhood)." Clark also claimed two hundred pounds damages from Edward Winn.

A lawyer for the Winn brothers asked that his clients be allowed to answer the charges at the next court session, in July. No further records of this case are known to exist.[166]

STATUTE

# 1718, May 31
# Pennsylvania: "Sodomy" law

The death penalty for "sodomy and buggery" was reinstated in Pennsylvania, revising the colony's law of 1706.[62] This revision brought Pennsylvania law into conformity with English statute and common law.

The new statute's reference to "any person or persons" who committed "sodomy or buggery" theoretically allowed female-female relations to be included, though, in practice, "sodomy" probably meant intercourse between men, or possibly, between a man and woman.

The law of 1718 provided death for thirteen crimes: (1) treason, (2) murder, (3) manslaughter by stabbing, (4) serious maiming, (5) highway robbery, (6) burglary, (7) arson, (8) sodomy, (9) buggery, (10) rape, (11) concealing the death of a bastard child, (12) advising the killing of a bastard child, and (13) witchcraft.

The sodomy provision read:

> . . . if any person or persons shall commit sodomy or buggery, or rape, or robbery . . . he or they . . . shall suffer as felons, according to the tenor, direction, form and effect of the several statutes in such cases respectively made and practiced in Great Britain, any act or law of this province to the contrary in anywise notwithstanding.

This law remained in effect until 1786 when, after the Revolution, Pennsylvania legislators were the first to revoke the death penalty for sodomy.

STATUTE

# 1718
## New Hampshire: "Buggery" law

New Hampshire legislators revised its "buggery" law of 1680, adopting the Massachusetts law of 1697 with only minor changes.[63] However, the New Hampshire law, unlike that of Massachusetts, used the term "buggery" to refer to both "sodomy" and "bestiality."

The statute read:

> for avoiding of the Detestable and Abominable Sin of Buggery with Mankind or Beast, which is contrary to the very light of Nature:
>     Be it Enacted . . . that the same offense be adjudged Felony.
>     . . . And that every Man being duly convicted of Lying with Man-kind as he lyeth with a Woman; And every Man or Woman that shall have Carnal Copulation with any Beast or brute Creature, the offender and offenders in either the cases before mentioned, shall suffer the pains of Death, and the Beast shall be slain and burned.

This law was next revised in 1812, when New Hampshire legislators revoked the death penalty for this crime.

STATUTE

# 1719
## Delaware: "Sodomy" law

The Delaware Assembly passed a "sodomy" law reproducing the Pennsylvania law of 1718 (instituting the death penalty for the crime).[64] This Delaware law apparently remained in effect until 1826 when the death penalty for this crime was revoked.

COMMENTARY

# 1724
## Anonymous: *Onania; or, The Heinous Sin of Self-Pollution*

An anonymous book, *Onania; or, The Heinous Sin of Self-Pollution, And All its Frightful Consequences, in both Sexes,* was published in London in 1723, and reprinted in Boston in 1724.[65] This first warning against masturbation published in the American colonies, and one of the earliest such diatribes published in England, contains scattered references to Sodom and sodomy.

Although much of the book's rhetoric is religious, the author (a doctor, apparently) framed the argument against "Self-Pollution" primarily in terms of "disease" and other dire physical effects on the individual polluter. This illustrates a move away from earlier arguments against non-procreative sex, formulated in religious and social terms, toward a new secular ideology referring to individuals' "health."

By 1700 the busily trading American colonies were already qualitatively different from those tenuous outposts that had passed the early sodomy laws and tried the early sodomy cases. References in *Onania* to women as "the different Sex," "the contrary Sex," and "the other Sex" are the earliest such usages I have noted in colonial-era documents. Those phrases suggest that in England and America the sexes were being more insistently differentiated; the early colonists' relative lack of stress on sexual difference was on its way out.

*Onania* declared: Wherever it was said in the Old or New Testament, "Uncleanness, the Lusts of the Flesh, or the Abominations of *Sodom* are condemned" the sin of "Self-Pollution" was "hinted at among others."[7] Whether "we commit Abomination with those of our own Sex, as the Scripture says, Men with Men; or with Beasts; or that we defile our own Bodies ourselves with this shameful Action," it "destroys conjugal Affection, perverts natural Inclination, and tends to extinguish the Hopes of Posterity."[9]

Various punishments and sanctions kept people from fornication and adultery; and the "Punishment for unnatural Impurities committed with others is Capital." But, the author complained, in "Self-Pollution" many imagined they had nothing to fear.[11–12]

A letter from an anonymous female argued that after a woman had conceived or was past child-bearing, any sexual intercourse of husband and wife "centers in the Pleasure of Sense, and is a Frustraneous Abuse of their Bodies, the same . . . with Self-Pollution and Sodomy."[86] The author of *Onania* disagreed. It was inconsistent with the goodness and justice of God that any act "should be so heinous a Sin as Sodomy" and that he would not "have warned us against it."[93] If such intercourse as the letter writer condemned "was so heinous a Sin as Sodomy, and by every Body believed to be such, Procreation itself would suffer very much. The Danger of committing so capital a Crime, would render good People cautious beyond Necessity." The "Fear of having conceived already, would in many Cases hinder them from conceiving at all."[96]

Another letter writer, a male, said that self-pollution "has always appeared to me very Criminal," but much less so than "several Crimes that Mankind is too much adicted to; such as Sodomy, Whoredom, Profane-Swearing, Murder, and the like."[127]

A letter from "Nathaniel Pedagogus" hoped that most of "our Masturbators . . . are not so Wicked as to desire Persons of their own Sex, much less any of the Contrary, to be their Accomplices in gratifying their innate Corruption."[141] But the same writer admitted that "seldom do I evacuate [ejaculate] myself at any time of the Night, but that except I have some Bed-fellow, from whose warmth and Company I find my Desires and Inclinations almost insuperably heightened."[143] The writer denied the sinfulness of "a voluntary Emission of the Semen," if it was not accompanied by "impure" thoughts or desires. He had for "many Years followed this practice," and had never offended his maker "by having Carnally to do with any Woman."

The author of *Onania* answered that the letter writer was obviously not a good judge of his own morals:

> A Man who is so Lascivious in his Temper, that his Desires and Inclinations are almost insuperably heightened by a Bed-fellow of his own Sex, is in a dangerous Condition, and ought, far from pampering his Flesh by several Meals in a day [as the letter writer had admitted], to make use of the most effectual means to mortify it, before he can without Folly or Impudence hope for the assistance of Divine Grace.[155]

STATUTE

## 1732, June 20
## Georgia: Buggery law

The Georgia Colony was chartered as a private "trusteeship," with the English buggery statute apparently regarded as in force.[66] In 1777 Georgia legislators affirmed that the statutes of England (implicitly including its buggery law) were *still* in force, suggesting that this law was earlier considered operative.

LEGAL CASE

## 1734, March 25
## Georgia: *Three hundred lashes for "sodomy" in Savannah*

The diary of Johann Boltzius and Israel Gronau, Lutheran pastors who ministered to German settlers in the Georgia colony, reported a sodomy case:[67]

> Today an execution of judgment was held here in Savannah. A man from this place had been accused and convicted of sodomy and inciting others, for which he was to receive three hundred lashes under the gallows. . . .

# PART II
## The Modern United States:
## The Invention of the Homosexual,
## 1880–1950

# Introduction

   This analysis of the modern period, 1880 to 1950, focuses first on those medical journal articles produced in the forty years between 1880 and 1920. It was during those years, and in this literature, that the idea of the "homosexual" and "heterosexual" was first constructed by doctors. Here the terms, concepts, and responses still dominant today are recorded in their original process of formulation.

   The later part of this section, from 1920 to 1950, focuses on the movement of those medical terms and notions out of the narrow world of physicians into that larger world reflected in *New York Times* news reports, book, film, and play reviews, editorials, and obituaries. I make no claim that this *New York Times* coverage represents the response of the entire country, of all the inhabitants of major cities, or even of all members of the respectable middle class. The responses recorded in *The Times* do document the distribution of the doctors' notion of a "normal" and "abnormal" sexuality into an influential, national, commoditized culture of entertainment and information. A survey of *Book Review Digest* from the 1920s on, suggests the national scope of the critical response to works with increasingly explicit homosexual themes. In a place as far outside the major cultural centers as Salt Lake City, Utah, a group of lesbians privately condemned *The Well of Loneliness* for publicizing their existence, thus depriving them of the protective cover accorded by the earlier sexual reticence.[1] Some Broadway plays, whose homosexual themes were touched on in *New York Times* reviews, were also produced elsewhere in the country; a 1934 stage version of *Mädchen in Uniform* is said to have been "produced by high-grade amateur groups in more than one large American city and played to crowded houses."[2] Film representations of the "sissy" and the "mannish" woman were nationally distributed images. The subtle and not-so-subtle responses to sexual "normality" and "abnormality" in the popular culture of the working class, and in the high arts of the elite, among the various cultures of different American racial, regional, ethnic, and age groups, of women and men, is a subject for future research. A few excerpts included here from book and film reviews in such liberal periodicals as *The New Republic, The Nation,* and *The International Journal of Ethics,* suggest the character and limits of the most "modern," "advanced" sexual views.

In the early twentieth century, only the American medical literature referred directly and in any detail to sexual inverts; in *The New York Times* euphemism reigned. But by January 8, 1928, *The New York Times Book Review* was on such familiar terms with inverts and the current slang that a punning headline over the review of Proust's *Cities of the Plain* could refer to "Dead Sea Fruit." By September 16, 1928, references in *The Times Book Review* to female inverts had grown so common that a critic could claim the subject of "Sapphic women" had "grown hackneyed in recent years." On November 10, 1935, *The Times* reviewer of André Gide's autobiography thought "the public is no longer so horrified by disclosures of homosexuality"—people would no longer regard Gide's book "as it might have been regarded ten years ago—as something sensational." On August 1, 1941, a *Times* reviewer could claim that the theme of "Lesbianism" had been "done to death a decade or so ago."

*Times* reviews of books, films, and plays are of historical interest, reminding us of the presence and influence of those cultural artifacts. But the reviews themselves are also valuable as one measure of changes over time in middle-class responses to homosexuality. In a number of reviews, critics comment explicitly on a change they perceive to have taken place in the response to same-sex intimacy, sometimes even specifying an approximate date at which they think the change occurred. Such comments help us begin to locate different periods of American homosexual history. A number of medical journal articles also contain such explicit historical comments, or implicit historical perspectives on homosexuality. (For a list of all such references see "historical perspective" in the index.)

Although *Times* reviews were probably by New Yorkers and directed to New Yorkers, the books and films reviewed and, to some extent, the plays, constituted a national and even international culture of the normal and perverse erotic. Many representations of the homosexual in the media were distributed worldwide: Edouard Bourdet's *The Captive* was imported to America from France; Lillian Hellman's *The Children's Hour* traveled from America to Europe in multiple theatrical and screen versions, later shown on television. Even the news stories in *The Times* often reflected a national and international culture of "knowledge."

On the most obvious level, these reviews of books, films, and plays record a bit of heterosexual history—the often censorious and superior, sometimes anxious response to homosexuality. For example, *Times* theater critic Brooks Atkinson's problem in accepting a relatively sympathetic dramatic portrayal of Oscar Wilde's persecution is clear in one of his reviews (see 1938, October 11).

On a more subtle level, the images of the homosexual projected in the media and distributed throughout the culture deeply affected heterosexuals' and homosexuals' perceptions of their own feelings and selves. Reviews of books, films, and plays are, of course, reflections of reflections. But they point, I believe, to basic and influential changes in language, ideas, feelings, and active responses, to a new "modern" stress on a perverse and a normal eros, and even a new, historically specific "heterosexual" and "homosexual" experience. Future research in diaries, letters, and other personal papers will, I think, begin to establish the precise qualities of that temporally situated experience.

## From the Cult of True Love to the Theory of Normal Love

The "sexual pervert" was the late Victorian descendant, the degenerate cousin, of the early Victorian "true woman" and "true man." That true woman or man, described in early Victorian magazines, gift and advice books, and religious literature, was she or he who possessed the qualities and feelings deemed proper to either females or males. As described by historian Barbara Welter, the prophets of "The Cult of True Womanhood: 1820–1860" posited a "true woman" with four cardinal virtues: piety, purity, submissiveness, and domesticity.[3] Those ideal "female" characteristics translated into a feminine temperament whose emotional components were love of God and devotion to morality, a controlled, procreation-focused sexuality, a family-centered love, nurturing desires, and feelings of dependency. (Historians are now debating whether the "purity" of the Victorian true woman signified asexuality or a channeled procreation-linked eroticism. Here I have interpreted female "purity" as the latter, differing with Welter's more traditional interpretation. The place of eros in the dominant Victorian ideology of manhood is now also being debated by historians. In any case, as we shall see, the early Victorian true woman's and true man's true love was thought of as quite distinct from whatever lust either possessed.)

A parallel early Victorian cult of true manhood can also be discerned. The characteristic virtues of the true man were devotion to hard work and material success, a "pure," controlled (though insistent) sexuality, assertiveness, and the attributes of the benevolent, patriarchal ruler. These translated into a "male" temperament comprising love of this-worldly rewards and the struggle to obtain them, an ideally sublimated, procreative-focused lust, a desire for independence, and an authoritarian, protective feeling for wife and family.[4]

Those ideal female and male types originated in a social structure which strictly divided the activities of women and men, a society organizing those activities in essentially different ways. As child-rearer, the true woman was a moral mother, a major agent of values in a domestic sphere economically dependent on the activity of a true man—the wages of a workman or the profits of a businessman.

The concept of the true woman and true man equated biological femaleness and maleness with those constellations of qualities collectively called "femininity" and "masculinity." No basic distinction was made in this era between biological sex and culturally constructed womanhood and manhood. Ministers, doctors, and other ideologists of gender identified physiological sex with what may now be distinguished as socially determined, historically relative, gender-specific personality traits and temperaments.

According to this Victorian mode of thought, moral, intellectual, and emotional attributes were considered identical with the biological, linked irrevocably with the physiology of females or males. Anatomy equaled mentality. A woman who did not display the alleged mental, moral, and emotional qualities of her sex was a non-woman: Because she was godless, Frances Wright was said to be "no woman, mother though she be."[5] The cult of the true woman and man was the cult of a true-sexed being whose opposite was a false-sexed creature. The true woman and man gave birth to a false-sexed mutant, called by a variety of names.

For criticizing the traditional female role, in 1838, Mary Wollstonecraft, Frances Wright, and Harriet Martineau were condemned by a minister as "only semi-women, mental hermaphrodites." In 1873, Dr. Edward Clarke, in an influential volume attacking higher education for females, spoke of women's rights' advocates as manifesting a "hermaphroditic condition" of mind. (Such women were also said to display an "Amazonian coarseness and force" which made them "analogous to the sexless class of termites."[6])

The idea of mentally and physically true-sexed women and men made it possible to imagine those "unsexed." In 1853, an anti-feminist male called feminist agitators "unsexed females," and references to "unsexed women" continued to be a typical anti-feminist ephithet in the early twentieth century. In the 1880s, doctors began using the term "unsexed" to refer to female "sexual perverts." In 1883, for example, the woman-loving, cross-dressing, and cross-working Lucy Ann Lobdell was called an "unsexed woman." In 1895, in a diatribe against female suffrage, a doctor referred to "unsexed individuals" or "viragints," women whose "object is the establishment of a matriarchate" (a female-run government).[7]

The early Victorian cult of true womanhood and true manhood was also a cult of true love. This romantic love was considered both "chaste" (non-sexual) and "passionate"; the cult of true love was an ideal of "pure" passion. And this passion was not thought to have any inherent sexual "object"; true love had no gender. The true woman could truly love man *or woman;* the true man could love woman *or man*—with no fear of impropriety—because these true loves were thought to include no nasty lust. The passionate love of woman for woman and the intense love of man for man were thought of as completely distinct from "sapphism" or "sodomy," acts and relations conceived (if considered at all) as specifically lustful and genital. According to this Victorian sexual world-view, lust was cordoned off from love, segregated in the separate spheres of procreation or prostitution, or the even more rarefied realms of sapphism or sodomy. That conceptual separation of love and lust reflected a structure in which the social mode of procreation, of intimate relationships, and of eroticism were organized as distinct and separate spheres.

Among middle-class Victorian males, as well as females, chastity was the ideal. In 1878, the twenty-year-old Theodore Roosevelt wrote in his diary: "Thank Heaven, I am at least perfectly pure."[8] That "purity" denoted an erotic banished from the ordinary universe of even male-female relationships. Marriage did not give license to unreserved lust; the dominant middle-class ideal was chaste marriage, involving a moderate, restrained intercourse, undertaken only for pro-creation. Although by 1880 that Victorian cult of pure, passionate, romantic love was being attacked by doctors it lasted in the United States, in middle-class culture, until about 1920.

From about 1880 on, The Theory of Normal Love was offered by doctors in place of The Cult of True Love. In the late 1880s, a new medical idea of "normal" and "abnormal" love began to be formulated by physicians. This new normal love included the erotic. Lust was no longer ghettoized, isolated in a separate sphere of procreation or illicit pleasure, apart from love and passion. This new "sex-love" was thought of as all-pervasive—as underlying, for example, religious feeling. Even the most "spiritual" emotions were now thought of as touched by lust, as was all intense feeling. However, doctors now referred, not to a biblically named "lust," but to a new, secularly named "sexuality" to distin-guish their formulation clearly from theologians'.

As the idea of an all-pervasive eroticism was distributed throughout the culture it eroticized the language: Words and phrases which had earlier had no specific libidinous connotations took on a new lubricity. "Lesbian," which through the teens in the dominant culture meant, simply, one from Lesbos, by the 1930s referred specifically to woman-to-woman eroticism. The eroticization of that word may be traced from medical reports into *New York Times* book reviews (see especially 1914, June; and 1932, September 11.) Similarly, the name "Sap-pho" and the adjective "Sapphic," which first connoted female-female eroticism in medical discourse, were by the late 1920s being used in the same sense in *The New York Times Book Review* (see 1928, January 8 and September 16; 1935, August 18).

The phrase "to make love to," which had meant to court, and which had been used in the most respectable of company, came to mean "to have sexual intercourse with." A "lover" changed from one who loved spiritually to one who loved erotically. The word "orgy," which had meant an uninhibited gathering, came to refer to specifically sexual intermingling. The word "sex" itself, which early Victorians had used in polite discourse to refer to "the sexes" (males and females) or "The Sex" (females), now commonly came to have specifically erotic reference, as in the phrases "to have sex" or "sex appeal." "Sexology," by 1904 named the study of male-female marital and erotic relations. "Sexuality," an erotic entity, alleged to be of central influence in human life, began to be gener-ally recognized and discussed. The new "sex-love" was distinguished by sex radicals and by doctors from the old, allegedly "pure" romantic love. Whereas "purity" and "chastity" had once been defined as absolute values, doctors now began to call *lack* of erotic feeling and "extreme continence" (as well as sexual "excess") an "aberration" of the "procreative sense." (See, for example, 1884, July.) The idea of "pure passion" came to seem a contradiction in terms, as "passion" seemed necessarily to embody the erotic. The doctors' new sex-love was thought of as "congenital," part of the female or male constitution. And this new love was thought of as linked biologically to erotic feelings. The new sex-love was eroticized and engendered.

According to this new medical idea, feelings, especially erotic emotions, had a sex; emotions were considered male or female in the same sense as clitoris or penis. The "normal" woman or man was thought to feel "normal" emotions unique to her or his sex. Women's "normal" love was exclusively for men, men's "normal" love was only for women. A female's sexual attraction to a female was then thought of as the "wrong" feeling for her sex; a male's erotic interest in a male was then thought of as a feeling "inappropriate" to his sex. And since any intense emotion was now considered to be erotically endowed, all intense feeling for the "same sex" became suspect. Late Victorian doctors redefined the old pure, true love as a new normal love in which the urge to procreate, erotic desire, and romantic feelings for an "opposite" sex mingled promiscuously. The obverse of this "normal" love was "abnormal love," a perverse desire in which procreation was not primary, and erotic and romantic feelings had turned away from a "normal," other-sex "object." True womanhood and manhood were replaced by normal femininity and masculinity, the true woman and man by the normal female and male, and true love by normal love.

### "Normal"/"Abnormal"

In the 1880s and '90s, the dominant medical meaning of the sexually "normal" and "abnormal" was the procreative and non-procreative. Those emotions and acts contributing to baby-making were "normal," those not so contributing were "abnormal." But when that procreative norm was spoken of overtly by late Victorian doctors it was not usually said, as in the early colonies, to derive directly from a command of God to "Go out and multiply." Neither were the sexually "normal" and "perverse," the "natural" and "unnatural" of the late Victorians usually spoken of by doctors as emanating from some abstract, universal "Nature." The "normal" and "abnormal" sexual were both alleged to arise from the physical and mental natures of males and females. If pushed, some doctors might maintain that behind this alleged sexual-biological determinism God and God's Nature went about their mysterious ways. But usually late Victorian medical theorists of "sexual perversion" pointed to normal, procreative male and female natures against which the perverse had turned. That procreative norm was presented in late Victorian medical literature as an innate, biologically determined imperative, a "purpose" inherent in the structure and function of female or male bodies and organs.

The new concern of American doctors, in the 1880s and '90s, with "sexual perversion" indicates a late Victorian interest in specifying sexual "normality." The sharper definition of the non-procreative perverse served, finally, to help shore up a procreative norm, already beginning to be challenged by birth-control advocates and by the adoption of contraceptive measures by large numbers of people. The invention of the "pervert" provided a non-procreative monster whom the good could abhor, and implied an ideal procreator to whom the good could aspire. The concern of American doctors with "sexual perversion" and "normality" emerged as a specifically late Victorian preoccupation, a project involving the medical containment of an erotic beginning to escape its former fixity, its identity with the procreative.

In the American medical articles on "sexual perversion" dating from 1880 to 1895, the procreative definition of the "normal" was more often smugly assumed than overtly stated or argued. The procreative norm was not yet self-consciously defensive, not yet subject to that serious challenge it would receive in the teens and 1920s. In the 1880s and '90s, only a few sex radicals explicitly contested a primarily procreative definition of the sexual and were castigated as "free lovers." Even the early advocates of contraception argued in terms of controlling births, not in terms of realizing genital, orgasmic pleasures completely apart from insemination.[9] And yet by about 1895, the old, absolute procreative standard was already in a state of transition; the procreative norm was on its way out, a pleasure ethic was on its way in. By 1895, the pursuit of happiness in the arena of sex was already being spoken of by some as a human and civil right.

By the mid-1890s, the traditional, popular idea of the sexually normal as the procreative—a qualitatively defined concept—was beginning to be opposed by a new definition of the sexually normal as those acts and emotions most frequently performed and experienced by most people—a quantitative definition. It was according to that quantitative concept that the "normal" began to be spoken of as "ordinary sexual love," "ordinary sexual indulgence," or as the "average," "majority" sexuality—not as the essentially procreative.

That adoption of quantity as the criterion of the "normal" was linked to the new, social dominance of commodity production, the social death of the old domestic agricultural production for use. The institution of quantity as the standard of the sexually normal, and the use of a statistical norm as the standard of the "good" and "natural," was linked to the spread of a capitalist ethic ("the more the better") into the previously uncapitalized realm of "private" sexual life. The influence of democratic political ideology on sexual ideology may also be recognized in a new identification, in the sphere of the erotic, of the normal, natural, good, and the many. That bourgeois quantifying of the erotic would have its most sophisticated development and profound impact in the publication of the Kinsey reports in 1948 and 1953. By way of contrast, it may be noted that the historical association of the normal, natural, good, and the many was completely foreign to the early colonists who, making no pretense to majority rule, were concerned about the many damned for lust, the elite few saved from it.

The definition of the normal as what most people were most accustomed to do and feel left the way open for a new definition of the statistically "abnormal" as "normal" for one particular individual, or a small group of individuals. That was just the argument adopted, in 1895, by the lesbian heroine of the novel *Norma Trist*. The concept of a mode of sexual feeling and acting "normal" for an individual or for a "minority," though not for a "majority," would become one of the cornerstones in the historical development of a "minority group" consciousness among some homosexuals in the late 1940s and '50s.

### *"Perversion" as Feeling*

In late Victorian America that "sexual perversion" newly invented by doctors was thought of as essentially subjective, a perverse emotion. As Lillian Faderman has pointed out in her history of love between women, "abnormal" sexuality was defined by doctors quite apart from act. It was not overt genital expression that defined sexual perversity; emotions were considered "perverted" by doctors whether or not they ever issued in genital or other acts. "Sexual perversion" could lurk "latently" in the brain, even if never "overtly" expressed by the body; in the head it might be "conscious" or "unconscious." "Perversion" referred fundamentally to feeling; "inversion" was typically a "psycho-sexual condition," a matter, in Krafft-Ebing's famous title, of *Psychopathia Sexualis.* In the late Victorian medical view, merely feeling "perverted" or "inverted" emotions made one a "pervert" or "invert." "Perverted" emotions determined "perverted" being.

The notion that inborn "inverted" feelings defined the "congenital invert" led to what now seems a most curious mode of perception. Quite often in the early medical literature the "feminine" member of a female couple was spoken of as if she was not also a "pervert"; even her sexual activity with a "pervert" did not affect essentially her own "normal" status. In 1883, for example, Dr. Kiernan distinguished "the sexual pervert" from the "young girl" she married and was thought to have had sex with: the "young girl" was not perceived as "tainted" even by such active, intimate association. In 1895, Havelock Ellis referred to the "spurious imitation" of "sexual perversion" that existed when "normal" women copied the "congenital" invert. The idea was that "pervert" status was not conferred by a woman's relations with other women, however actively genital, orgasmic, or erotic. "Perversion" was inborn, "congenital," measured by the "pervert's" inherent distance from the "normal" woman or man. The "passive," "feminine" partner was a "normal" woman, not a "pervert." That now-peculiar idea would find classic statement in *The Well of Loneliness* (1929), where the congenital female invert Stephen appeared with her normal lover Mary.

American medical journals of the 1880s and '90s referred often to a perverted person. That variously named late Victorian "pervert" (also tagged an "erotopath," "neuro-erotic," and "neuropath") was the outcast offspring of the late Victorian Great Man or Notable Woman; the "pervert" was the Victorian good woman or good man gone wrong. (The "homosexual" as epitome of the "neurotic" was a creature found typically in American documents of the 1940s and '50s.) The late Victorian stress on the pervert was linked to that era's ideology of "individualism," an ideology linked to the social existence of an autonomous (usually male) wage laborer and his capitalist counterpart, "the captain of industry," and the development of an economy in which the individual, not the family, was the main unit of production. The Pervert, the Invert, and the Masturbator were cult figures in an erotic mythology of perverse individuals, the contrary counterparts of the individual of achievement.

The late Victorian medical concept of a "sexual perversion" defined by feeling was different from the early colonial idea of "sodomy." Though an early colonist could commit sodomy in the heart as well as in the commonwealth, that early sodomy was not defined essentially as feeling; it was equally subjective and objective (though the law left the punishment of "heart sodomy" to the puritanical conscience). Both late Victorian "sexuality" and early colonial "lust" were all-pervasive, but early colonial lust was free-floating: It had no inborn, inherent, or particular object, and no particular gender. Early colonial lust was sexless. In contrast, late Victorian erotic emotions were considered sex-specific; lust had a gender.

In the 1880s and '90s, doctors spoke of "sexual perverts" as individuals who felt the erotic emotion of the "other" sex. And they reported numbers of individuals who wished, believed, or claimed themselves to be, the "other" sex— because their feelings were perceived as female or male, the feelings proper and exclusive to either women or men. According to this logic, feeling determined being; as such persons felt, so they were. If a male felt the alleged emotions of a female, he must be a female or, at least, a "mental hermaphrodite." The belief or claim that one was "really" the other sex was a way for one to justify to others and to oneself, within the premises of the time, erotic attraction to the "same" sex. The often reported "desire [of a woman] to be a man" expressed a wish for that sexual nature which would permit a female to feel legitimately those emotions and perform that work prohibited to women. A male's desire to be female expressed a similar wish to legitimize feelings and acts prohibited to men.

### Crossing Persons

The actual social existence of persons whose mind-sets and behaviors corresponded closely to the ideal Victorian normal woman or man had its historical corollary in the existence of those I here call "crossing persons," those who performed acts or felt emotions established by custom as proper exclusively to the "other" sex.[10]

From 1880 on, American medical journal articles on "sexual perversion" described numbers of females and males who were said to have done one or more of the following: wore the clothes and hairstyle, undertook the work, played the games, gestured, walked, talked, drank the drinks, acted the political role, performed the sexual acts, and felt the emotions of the "other" sex. Such reports and persons reflected a society in which certain clothes, hairstyles, work, sports, manners, body movements, language, liquids, political and sexual acts, erotic and other feelings, were established by custom as specific and exclusive to either females or males. By constant association with one sex, for example, pants were "male" in the same sense as the penis was.

In the early twentieth century a particular kind of sexual crossing, wearing the clothes of the "other" sex, began to be newly named, studied, and analyzed (rather than merely reported). What newspapers had earlier called "masquerading" or "impersonating" was, in 1910, given the name "transvestism" by Dr. Magnus Hirschfeld (in a large German volume, *Die Transvestiten*). In an article first published in English in an American journal, in 1911, Edward Carpenter spoke of "cross-dressing." In 1913, in an American medical journal, Dr. Havelock Ellis called the same phenomenon "sexo-aesthetic inversion," and in an American medical journal article, of 1920, Ellis called it "D'Eonism."[11]

All those terms assumed the peculiarity of "cross-dressing." And all assumed without question the existence of clothes proper, exclusive to, and customary for each sex. But if no inherent link is assumed between particular clothes and a particular sex, a question arises about a phenomenon which can be called "homovestism"—the wearing of the clothes customary for the same sex to which the wearer belongs.[12] If the link between clothes and gender is social, historical, and relative, dressing in the apparel of one's own sex is seen to be quite as "peculiar," "obsessive," and problematic as "transvestism." What is equally at issue in transvestism and homovestism is the social use of clothes as visual signifiers of the difference or sameness of the sexes, and the profound emotional impact of such signifiers on the individual. The serious, analytical interest in cross-dressing occurred about the same time, and was linked to that same interest in gender that led to the same-sex/different-sex categorization of the erotic, the new homo/hetero opposition.

Though dressing in the clothes of the "other" sex has received prominent attention, other forms of sexual crossing (cross-working, cross-playing, and cross-feeling, for example) were equally prominent in the lives of many persons reported in the medical journals of the late 1800s. All of those crossings have meaning only in terms of an original social identification of certain work, play, and feeling with one sex or the other. In particular, in late Victorian medical journals, numbers of persons who felt "love" for, or erotic attraction to, the "same sex" reported themselves, or were reported, to be feeling the emotion of the "other" sex.

The theory of a female "soul" in a male body had first been formulated in Germany, in 1864, by Karl Heinrich Ulrichs, to explain and justify the erotic desire of males for males. American medical journal writers of the 1880s and '90s expropriated Ulrichs's word for their own purposes, referring to persons called "Urnings," and occasionally to a mental state called "Uranism," terms derived from the German *Uranier* and *Urning*, invented by Ulrichs, and expressing his theory.[13]

American doctors of the 1880s and '90s also commonly spoke of "contrary sexual sensation," "Contrary Sexual Instincts," "contrary sexual feeling," "contrary sexual impulse," and "Contrary Sexuality." Those terms were adopted from the German *"konträre Sexualempfindung"* (contrary sexual feeling), first used by Dr. Carl von Westphal in a medical journal article in 1869.[14] The feeling in question was "contrary" to that erotic emotion considered proper and exclusive to males or females.

American doctors also referred to "sexual inversion" and "sexual inverts," terms denoting feelings, a temperament, and beings turned upside down or inside out, improperly reversed.

All of those terms referred to feelings or the persons feeling. None of those early American terms yet focused explicitly on the gender of the persons party to an erotic act or feeling. Those terms reflect concepts in transition from an essentially procreative to a gender-based criterion. The explicit emphasis on a "same sex" versus an "opposite" or "different sex" eroticism, and the use of the terms "homosexual" and "heterosexual," would develop only gradually in the American medical journal literature after 1892, reflecting an increasing stress by doctors on the differentiation of females and males.

### *"Homosexual"/"Heterosexual"*

Because the homosexual/heterosexual distinction became the socially dominant usage, and is still so, it is useful to note in some detail that opposition in the process of its earliest American formulation. The homosexual/heterosexual distinction is now so deeply ingrained that it is difficult for us to think in other terms. An historical view helps us to situate the homo/hetero dualism in time, and distance ourselves from it.

The earliest American medical usage of "homosexual" and "heterosexual" did not yet signify two opposed, symmetrical eroticisms, defined by the "same-sex" or "different-sex" genders of their parties. In one of the earliest American uses of the term "homosexual," in May 1892, Dr. Kiernan (citing Krafft-Ebing) defined "Pure homosexuals" as persons whose "general mental state is that of the opposite sex." In the same article, "heterosexuals" were defined as those with a mental condition, "Psychical hermaphroditism," in which "Traces of the normal sexual appetite are discoverable"—those with "inclinations to both sexes" (now called "bisexuals"). "Heterosexuals" were also defined as those with inclinations "to abnormal methods of gratification" ("abnormal" here meaning methods unrelated to procreation, regardless of the actors' gender). "Normal" inclinations were implicitly those confined to one sex, and, presumably, only penile-vaginal acts of procreative intent and possibility.

In a medical journal article of July 1893 (a review of Krafft-Ebing's *Psy-*

*chopathia Sexualis*), the term "homo-sexualism" was associated with a vaguely defined "mental abnormality," with various "deviations of the sexual appetite" and "erotic feelings," with "sexual perversions," and with the "wrong exercise of the sexual passion." The implicit norm was procreative. No version of the term "heterosexual" appeared.

An article of October 1893, by Dr. Hughes, referred to "perverted homo-sexual instincts" (erotic feelings for the same sex). Hughes also referred to "homosexuality" (a mental state defined by erotic feelings for the same sex) and "homo-prostitution" (a same-sex commercial transaction of an erotic character). Two kinds of persons, the "homo and hetero sexual," also appeared. The "homo sexual" person possessed an "abnormal" erotic feeling for the same sex. The "hetero sexual" person possessed an "abnormal" feeling for *both* sexes. The "homo"/"hetero" distinction still did not signify two symmetrical, opposite eroticisms.

In an article surveying "The Study of Sexual Inversion" published in a U. S. medical journal in April 1894, Havelock Ellis referred to "homosexual love" and "homosexuality," distinguishing this feeling and condition from "sexual perversion" and "vice." A person, "the homosexual lover" was counterposed to "the normal heterosexual lover."[150] Ellis described Krafft-Ebing's categorization of "psychosexual hermaphroditism" or "bisexuality" in which the "homosexual instinct" predominated, but "traces of the normal heterosexual instinct" existed, and a "homosexuality" in which "the instinct goes out only toward the same sex."[154] (No parallel, exclusive "heterosexuality" was mentioned.)[15]

In 1894, in an article in a textbook on legal medicine, Dr. Chaddock referred to a psychological state involving a "predominating homosexual feeling" (erotic attraction to the same sex) and "a trace of feeling (heterosexual) for the opposite sex." Here, "homosexual" and "heterosexual" did signify two kinds of feeling, differentiated by the genders of "subject" and "object." But the terms still did not refer clearly to two symmetrical "same sex"/"different sex" eroticisms.

In March 1895, in the U. S. translation from the French of a medical journal article by Raffalovich, the terms "homosexuality" and "heterosexuality" were, for the first time in an American periodical, used consistently to refer to two polarized erotic emotions, temperaments, and persons (the present dominant usage). But it was some years before "homo-" and "heterosexual" were established as the dominant terminology and concepts, even in medical sources.

In the late 1890s, in the U. S., "homosexual" had just been launched on its way to becoming the dominant term of reference, with "heterosexual" still trailing somewhat behind as signifier of a parallel, opposed sexuality. In 1908, the anthropologist Westermarck gave prominence and greater respectability to the phrase "Homosexual Love" by using it as a chapter title in his book on *The Origin and Development of Moral Ideas.*[16] On October 24, 1926, the use of the word "homosexuality" in *The New York Times Book Review,* and on April 20, 1930, the use of "homosexual" and "heterosexual," indicated the movement of those terms from the rarefied discourse of doctors to the common speech of the respectable press.

The invention of a creature whose feelings were legitimately "hetero" and "sexual" was something new in the late Victorian night, a creature quite as unique as the "homosexual" under the late Victorian moon. The elaborating and detailing of the hetero's character was one epochal, historically specific mission of the Dr. Frankensteins of early twentieth century sexology. The medical manufacture of "the heterosexual" as name, concept, feeling, act, and relation, was quite as profound in effect as the invention of "the homosexual." That newly invented "heterosexual" was no more "natural" than the "homosexual" was "unnatural." To paraphrase Mae West, nature had nothing to do with it.

The historical construction and use of the terms "homo-" and "heterosexual" from the 1890s on, indicates an increasing stress on two eroticisms distinguished essentially by the genders of their parties. The distinguishing of a "same-sex" from an "opposite-sex" eroticism reflected an increasing social emphasis in the late-nineteenth and early-twentieth centuries on the differentiation of females and males. That stress on sexual differentiation is documented, for example, in 1897, in *The New York Times*'s publication of the Reverend Parkhurst's diatribe against female "andromaniacs," women who imitated "everything mannish," who tried "to minimize distinctions by which manhood and womanhood are differentiated." Similarly, J. Lionel Taylor, the biologist-author of a book on *The Nature of Woman*, reviewed in *The Times* in 1913, maintained that the movement for the female vote was a plot by "certain women" to make woman into a "female man," a campaign said to contradict the mental and bodily "unlikeness of woman to man." The stress on gender difference was a conservative response to that changing social-sexual division of activity and feeling which gave rise to the independent "New Woman" of the 1890s, and the ideally boyish-looking, bobbed, flat-chested flapper of the 1920s.

The invention of "homosexuality" and "heterosexuality" register an increasing stress by doctors of the 1890s and early twentieth century on the supposedly innate differences between females and males. In terms of social function, that stress on sexual differentiation was clearly an effort to contain the contemporary movement of women out of the traditional women's sphere and into the world of wage work, social reform, and electoral politics. The stress on a "same sex"/"different sex" eroticism both reflected actual, socially constructed differences between the sexes, and was itself one of the intellectual means of warfare used by anti-feminists against women's rights advocates. That containment attempt often involved a critique of the "New Woman," the relatively independent, autonomous female, active in the world outside the home. That maneuver on the battlefield of gender attempted to hold back a shift in the traditional concept of "woman" toward relative parity with the concept "man." When feminists themselves took up the theory of an innate female "purity" as a defense against excessive, unregulated procreation, and as an expedient argument for the female vote, the stress on female-male differentiation was even more firmly established.[17]

In historical perspective both "homosexuality" and "heterosexuality" are culturally relative constructions. Neither is natural or unnatural; neither is a biological or a social universal. The term and concept "heterosexual" reflected the existence of new emotional interactions between men and women in which the "sexual" was central and legitimate, and consolidated this ideal type as norm. The term "heterosexual" was both descriptive, a verbal and conceptual mirror, and normative, a tool of social-sexual control. However, if "heterosexuality" and "homosexuality," the "straight," "gay," and "lesbian," are not taken for granted as unchanging things, but understood as culturally specific inventions, their mode of social construction and functioning becomes problematic, a subject of historical research and inquiry.

Evidence from the period 1880–1950 documents the production of an erotic orthodoxy, The Heterosexual Mystique, the peculiar notion that heterosexuality is biologically or socially universal, that a particular historical relationship of American women and men originating in the late nineteenth and early twentieth centuries is physiologically necessary, socially ubiquitous, and historically omnipresent. In these years a similarly contingent Homosexual Mystique may also be observed in its original process of contruction.[18] The doctors' homosexual/heterosexual hypothesis was a self-fulfilling prophecy which helped to create those very creatures, emotions, mental states, and behaviors which medical men had first defined.

### The Medical Critique of "Pure" Passionate Friendship

Late Victorian medical journal articles on "sexual perversion" were one of the means used to discredit and abnormalize that "pure," "spiritual passion," those "passionate friendships" between women and between men which had flourished without duress in the early 1800s. Doctors' discussions of "sexual perversion" referred often to same-sex "friendship," "intimacy," "affection," "attachment," and to a "Platonic love," all newly suspected of harboring illicit erotic attraction, however "latent" or "repressed." The old concept of "pure," non-erotic same-sex passion was challenged by the new medical concept of "sexual perversion." Newspaper reports from the 1880s on into the early twentieth century also reveal the traditional, "pure" same-sex intimacy being challenged by the new idea of an all-pervasive erotic.

Dr. Blumer's discussion, in 1882, of the "perverted sexual instinct" of a male conscious of the "morbid" nature of his love for an "ideal [male] friend," is one of the earliest medical sources to cast suspicion on the old "pure" friendship of males. In May 1889, *The Aspen Times* reported the "Mad Infatuation" of one Colorado woman for another, calling her grand "passion" a "morbid" and "monstrous, unnatural affection." A new consciousness of an illicit erotic in the intimacies of women with women was appearing then, even outside the major coastal cities.

In 1889, Frances Willard, long-time head of the Women's Christian Temperance Union, included a chapter on "Companionships" in her autobiography. She spoke of her own "heart affair," "affinity," "attachments," and "friendships" with numbers of "beloved objects" of the female sex. She added: "The loves of women for each other grow more numerous each day." Willard's concept of "pure," passionate friendship was, among doctors, well on its way to being challenged by a new consciousness suspicious of an illicit erotic inherent in any intense intimacy.

In 1889, Willard wondered why the loves of women for women were not more talked about, since they were so common: "These days, when any capable and careful woman can honorably earn her own support, there is not a village that has not its examples of 'two hearts in counsel,' both of which are feminine." Lillian Faderman argues that close female-female relationships started to be spoken of as a threat at the time when economic conditions made it possible for significant numbers of women to act on their feelings and set up homes together, independent of men and the traditional family. This certainly begins to explain the medical morbidifying of romantic friendships between females. The doctors' discrediting of romantic intimacy between males functioned similarly to channel men into a new kind of companionate family, a family operating less often as a productive unit, more often as a mode of mutual personal consumption of material goods and pleasure. Among the pleasures of this new family life the "normal" erotic began to be offered as one legitimate satisfaction. The legitimation of this new companionate family involved the discrediting of the old same-sex companionate intimacy, the exposure by doctors of its "abnormal" erotic.

A conservative male response to the increasing economic independence of women, and an explicit anti-feminism were major sources of the special attention paid by doctors to the task of distinguishing a female "sexual perversion" from the male. In 1895, in the first American medical journal article to survey "Sexual Inversion in Women," even the relatively liberal Havelock Ellis warned that the women's emancipation movement "involved an increase in feminine criminality," "insanity," and "homosexuality." He stressed that women moving out of the domestic sphere were beginning to find love with other women "where they find work." Various (tactfully unspecified) "modern movements," Ellis said, might indirectly cause "sexual inversion," by promoting the overt development of inborn tendencies, and by causing a "spurious imitation" when "normal" women copied the "congenital anomaly" they saw frequently in "women of high intelligence."

Although American medical experts on "perversion" and "inversion" commented less frequently on females, these late Victorian doctors by no means denied the existence of eroticism in women. The existence of a female erotic, "normal" and "abnormal," was in fact assumed. The absence of eroticism, in either females or males, was now defined as pathology. Though references to men

predominated in medical reports of "sexual perversion" from 1880 on, brief
references to erotic "abnormality" in women were rather frequent—surprisingly
so if one starts from the assumption of a general Victorian denial of female lust.

A number of early medical writers noted and tried to explain the predominance of references to male "perversion." In 1884, Dr. Kiernan assumed the
reality of female eroticism, attributing the fewer reports of female "perversion"
to the fact that "a history of female sexual desire is much less easily obtained."
In his summary essay, in 1895, on "Sexual Inversion in Women," Dr. Ellis declared that "homo-sexuality" in females was almost or just as common as it was
in men, although less noticed. A "slight degree of homosexuality is commoner
in women than in men," Ellis said. But the customary "much greater . . . intimacy
between women" made "abnormal passion" less visible. Also, the "extreme
ignorance" and "reticence of women" about even "normal" female eroticism
helped make "abnormal" manifestations invisible. Women might feel strong
"sexual attraction" to women without understanding its "sexual" character. And
when the "sexual" nature of their feeling for women was understood, women
were less willing than men to talk about it.

Ellis's article stressed the existence of eroticism in the "passionate friendships" of females. In 1897, in Ellis's influential book *Sexual Inversion,* friendships
between women were spoken of by an American woman doctor as having a
"sexual basis," whether conscious or unconscious, and irrespective of how that
sexual feeling was expressed in action.[19] In 1917, when Clemence Dane's novel
*Regiment of Women* was reviewed in *The New York Times,* the "friendship" between
two school mistresses was explicitly associated with the "abnormal" temperament
of one teacher, and "crushes" between schoolgirls were spoken of as "abnormal
psychological manifestations." The erotically "innocent," passionate same-sex
friendships of the Victorians were well on their way to being discredited, not only
in medical journals, but also in the sphere of public discussion represented by
*The New York Times.*

Mid-Victorian sexual ideology had differentiated between the degree of
control true women and men were supposed to have over their erotic urges. If
that double standard did not completely deny female eroticism, it did assume
women's greater "purity," their greater control than men over their "animal
instincts." Because of that alleged greater control, intimate relationships between
women were probably less subject to any suspicion of eroticism than those between men. The new consciousness of "sexual perversion" in the 1880s and '90s
then had a different impact on the perception of female-female and of male-male
intimacies, casting relatively greater suspicion of eroticism on the alleged
"spirituality" of passionate female friendships.

In the early twentieth century, the increasing legitimacy of female eroticism
as an aspect of companionate heterosexuality also seems to have had a negative
effect on traditional female-female intimacies—a different effect than the "sexual
revolution" of the time had on traditional male-male intimacies.

In 1912, Catherine Wells's "The Beautiful House," the story of an intense, passionate, loving "communion" between two women, destroyed by the younger woman's specifically sexual love for a male, was published in *Harper's Magazine*. The portrayal of such female-female intimacy in a popular periodical suggests that such relationships were still not generally perceived as embodying any latent and "improper" eroticism (although the passion pictured now seems suffused with eroticism). The story also suggests that such passionate, but non-genital female-female relationships were, by 1912, being challenged by the more openly expressed and legitimate female-male eroticism of the period. When the younger woman, speaking of a male suitor, says: " 'We want to kiss!' " her older female friend knows that her own intimacy with the young woman is doomed.[20] If this story was any indication of a general trend in actual relationships (and I think it was), the greater heterosexual freedom of the teens, and the new value placed on female eroticism, had a negative impact on traditional woman-to-woman intimacies, making their lack of overt, explicit erotic expression seem limiting. The outmoding of the traditional "spiritual passion" by the new idea of a legitimate and all-pervasive erotic, probably had a greater impact on the "passionate friendships" of women than of men.

In summary then, the early Victorian concept of the erotic had stressed the need to control it, and the possibility of restricting it to the realms of procreation or prostitution, or the rarefied underworlds of sodomy or sapphism. The new medical notion of "normal" and "abnormal" sexuality posited an all-pervasive erotic, the too great repression or expression of which was dangerous to health. Between 1880 and 1920, the early Victorian idea of a non-sexual, spiritual passion was being challenged by the new idea of an eroticism pervading all human acts, relationships, and feelings, so that the concept of a non-erotic passion came to seem a contradiction in terms. In light of this late nineteenth and early twentieth century recognition and legitimation of a normal eroticism of everyday life, the sexual focus and concerns of Sigmund Freud are seen, not as unique, but as an aspect of a more general manufacture and distribution of "heterosexuality."[21]

Since the late 1960s, the affirmation of female eroticism has been associated with one branch of feminism. It is, therefore, important to be clear that in the 1880s and '90s, and well into the twentieth century, many feminists were proclaiming a special female "purity," while anti-feminist doctors were asserting the existence of both female and male eroticism in the interest of a conservative medical politics of sexual control.

### *Medical Colonization*

In 1869, the German word *"Homosexualität"* was used for the first time, in a public appeal for sodomy law reform issued by a homosexual doctor, Károly Mária Benkert.[22] When American doctors began to use the term "homosexual" in the early 1890s for the purpose of distinguishing a particular, medically defined "perversion," they were then appropriating for their own professional use a word coined by a homosexual in an early civil rights struggle of his group. But American doctors' expropriation of that term was more profound than mere word-stealing—it indicated the medical colonization of a people.

The American doctors who formulated the concepts of "inversion" and "homosexuality" from 1880 on, were concerned to assert their proprietary rights over a particular population group, and to assert the superiority of their medical expertise over that of legislators, lawyers, and judges. American doctors' production and distribution of the terminology and concepts referring to "sexual perversion" constituted medical imperialism, a successful attempt by the profession to expand the social and human territory of its legitimate authority into an area previously presided over by legislative and juridical professionals.

Late Victorian doctors distinguished essentially between "congenital sexual inversion" and "acquired sexual vice." They stressed that "inborn inversion" was a physical condition for which the individual was not "responsible," a condition therefore requiring medical treatment, not legal punishment. In contrast, the individual was responsible for "acquired sexual vice," and criminal prosecution was appropriate.

The doctors' distinction between "inborn inversion" and "acquired vice," and their discussion of moral and legal "responsiblity," are best understood in terms of American medical professionals' interest in asserting their right to the private ownership and control of "sexual perversion," the management of "perverts." The differentiation of a medically defined and treated "perversion" from a legally defined and punished "vice" was one manifestation of a late Victorian intra-class conflict between two groups of American professionals—doctors and legal authorities (primarily, lawyers and judges). In this conflict, medical and legal professionals were renegotiating their respective positions in relation to the state.

The struggle between these medical and legal classes is explicit in a number of doctors' comments. On July 19, 1884, Dr. Shrady declared that mental conditions "once considered criminal are really pathological, and come within the province of the physician." In August 1893, Dr. Daniel warned: The law ignored psychiatry, punishing the sexual criminal, then letting him or her "return and pollute society." Psychiatry, said Daniel, advocated sexual criminals' "perpetual sequestration from society and a radical asexualizing surgical procedure" (castration). Dr. Daniel thought it was a "peculiar political organization" which entrusted law making "to men who know nothing about the laws of health." Those who do "know better than any other class—physicians—are rarely ever called in counsel in framing laws." This political-philosopher of sex pleaded for a more "unreserved intercourse" between "physicians" and "jurists" to secure the enactment of laws "consonant with a more advanced state of medico-legal knowledge." In October 1893, Dr. Hughes asserted: "Medical science must . . . determine for society and for the State, what is restrainable and vicious [ a vice], and what are the morbid and resistless organic impulsions" causing "bizarre eroto-sexual states [perversions]."

The American medical literature on "sexual perversion" produced from 1880 on also reflected the development, since before the Civil War, of mental "asylums." Numbers of early medical reports on "sexual perversion" are based on doctors' observations of persons consigned to asylums. In an earlier age, the mental disturbance and threatening behavior of an individual like Lucy Ann Lobdell might have been ignored, or managed by local religious or legal authorities. In 1880, Lobdell was certified by two doctors as "insane" and dispatched to an asylum where her erotic attraction to other females caused her story to be published, in 1883, as one of the earliest American medical case histories of "Lesbian love."[23]

In another instance, in November 1886, an asylum doctor reported that a mentally disturbed working-class male, born in 1864, had been "effeminate from childhood, but this never attracted much attention." Doctors would seek to abolish such popular, pre-medical toleration of effeminacy. In 1902, a doctor reported indignantly on the case of a woman in rural New York State who had "married" a female and adopted four children. To the doctor's dismay the first woman's family "do not seem to have looked upon her relationships as abnormal."[24] In a number of documents the term "eccentric" was used as the popular pre-medical way of characterizing persons recognized as appreciably different from others. "Eccentric" as label expressed a degree of popular toleration for a different way of life; "pervert" expressed strong disapproval, however disguised as objective medical diagnosis.

The development of mental asylums as institutions for the control of social misfits caused an expansion of the category "insanity" and the numbers of those labeled "insane" or "pathological." Sexual activities like "sodomy," which had earlier been considered a "sin," "vice," and "crime," began, in the 1880s and '90s, to be reconceptualized and renamed "sexual perversions"—forms of "mental disease" to be "treated" by medicine and perhaps by incarceration in doctor-run institutions. Only recently have women and men associated with the feminist, lesbian, gay, and anti-psychiatry movements begun to organize against that medical colonization of love and lust.

## The Medical Construction of Self-hate

According to the doctors' theory of "congenital sexual inversion," such feelings might be weakened by medical treatment or stimulated by irresponsible, immoral indulgence. Just as doctors might treat "excessive" sexual feeling for the "other" sex with anaphrodisiacs, so they might treat "perverted" feelings for the "same sex." Although, to the consternation of doctors like George Beard (in 1884), a whole "class" of "sexual perverts" did "not wish to get well," others agreed to various desexualizing medical treatments. Some were apparently "helped" to deny their feelings.

The medical naming of the "sexual pervert," "invert," and "homosexual" was ambiguous in its social implications for the persons so described. On the one hand, the doctors' own reports inadvertently reveal these supposed alleviators of pain as inculcators of anguish. Medical journal articles from the 1880s on suggest how, with a blithe unawareness of their own role in the social construction of self-hate, doctors' derogatory terminology and judgmental comments on "inverts" served to induce in "invert" patients the dominant anti-invert morality. However "liberalizing" it may have been historically to move from "vice" and "crime" to "disease," the medicalization of "sexual inversion" meant that many individuals internalized a new "scientific" negation, becoming the social agents of their own self-denial.

From the extreme of male castration and female clitoridectomy to less extreme erotically calming sedatives, medical treatment meant an attempted asexualization. It also usually involved the social production by doctors of shame, guilt, and a long tradition of self-punishing activities. Medical journal reports provide evidence of the ways in which "inverts" were often made the immediate agents of their own and others' pain, even destruction. To cite just one example from a long list: In 1883, Dr. Hammond's repeated searing with a hot iron or chemical of his "pervert" patient's loins was a treatment in which this patient collaborated. The history of heterosexuality includes famous examples of poisoned, self-destructive, and murderous emotions. The history of female and male homosexuality also includes striking examples of pain-seeking and pain-causing, of murderous rage turned on the self and others. Paying in pain could be a way to atone for a religion-induced guilt, a way to come to terms with a medically structured shame. Often doctors, for a fee, played torturer to a homosexual patient's victim, collaborating in a "treatment" indistinguishable from punishment.

On the other hand, a medically defined "perversion," "sexual pathology," or "disease" could be (and was) used by individuals to justify their erotic feelings for, and sometimes their acts with, others of their own sex. If such feelings were inborn they were permanent; one couldn't help them. One might act on them or not, depending on one's ethical judgment of such acts, and one's estimate of the possible social consequences. A number of individuals reported that *not* acting on their feelings led to various emotional and physical ailments; the idea of sexual repression causing mental and somatic ills was quite common in the 1880s and '90s, as comments in American medical journals indicate. Acting out one's sexually "perverted" feelings was, then, one way of maintaining one's emotional and physical "health"—given such allegedly "congenital," ineradicable emotions, and the negative effects of repression.

The doctors giving a name and congenital status to "inversion" and "inverts" also contributed to a new form of self and group recognition, probably even helping to foster the early self-conscious formation of "invert" betterment associations.

### "Perverts" as a Group

American doctors' writings on "sexual perversion" constitute one response to the grouping of "sexual perverts" in the cities, and in urban commercial establishments providing a social place for the bartering or selling of illicit erotic favors. The literature on "sexual perversion" reflects the new visibility of "perverts" as a group or "type" of person, of "perversion" as a mode of erotic emotion and activity shared by a collectivity.

A book first published in Philadelphia in 1871 is the earliest known United States source to refer to congregations of those later called male "homosexual transvestites" or "sexual perverts." The volume titled *The Transmission of Life*, subtitled *Counsels on the Nature and Hygiene of the Masculine Function*, a sexual advice manual for males by Dr. George Napheys, declared that

> every unnatural lust recorded in the mordant satires of Juvenal, the cynical epigrams of Martial, or the licentious stories of Petronius, is practised, not in rare or exceptional cases, but deliberately and habitually in the great cities of our country. Did we choose to draw the veil from those abominable scenes with which our professional life has brought us into contact, we could tell of the vice which called vengeance from heaven on Sodom practiced notoriously; we could speak of restaurants frequented by men in women's attire, yielding themselves to indescribable lewdness; we could point out literature so inconceivably devilish as to advocate and extoll this utter depravity. But it is enough for us to hint at these abysses of iniquity. We cannot bring ourselves to do more; and we can only hope that the fiery cautery of public denunciation will soon destroy this most malignant of ulcers.[25]

In the 1880s, American medical journal articles recorded a new perception of "inverts" as a "class," rather than as singular sodomitical anomalies. In a letter written from America in 1882 (published in 1888), a sexual "pervert" referred to "our unfortunate class."[26] An article of 1889 referred to a "class of sexual perverts," and a "colony of male sexual perverts." An article of 1892 referred to "a class of sexual debauchees." By the 1880s, in the United States, sexually "abnormal" individuals were beginning to perceive themselves, and to be seen, as members of a group. The mutual association and new visibility of such persons in American cities, and their naming by the medical profession, made their group existence manifest in a way it had not been earlier. By way of contrast, in the early colonies, isolated enactors of sodomy did not perceive themselves, and were not seen, as members of a sodomitical collective.

The late Victorian development of "restaurants" and other commercial "resorts" catering to various illicit sexual groups and activities provided an established, institutionalized place for their mutual association and made this erotic underworld visible. The appearance in American cities of businesses catering to members of the sexual underworld, and their mutual association in urban centers of business, gave rise to a group consciousness. And that collective consciousness gave rise to a perception of mutual social persecution.

By about January 1895, according to Earl Lind, the effeminate male homosexual cross-dressers who frequented the New York City club known as "Paresis Hall" had formed the *Cercle Hermaphroditos,* "to unite for defense against the world's bitter persecution"—an informal grouping which, if not apocryphal, was the earliest American prototype of the later homosexual rights organization.[27]

## Resistance

From 1880 to 1950, the resistance to persecution by homosexuals and their supporters manifested a number of different historical forms, from the earliest, most spontaneous, "private" assertion of self-worth, to a first "public" letter to a doctor-author affirming the value of same-sex love, to a speech defending the humanity and rights of homosexuals, to the writing and publication of a poem or story affirming love between women or men, to an article or book in defense of homosexuality.

Some have argued that all homosexual emotions and acts constitute "resistance" (even "revolution") in a society organized to maintain heterosexuality as the dominant form of human relationship.[28] Opposing that argument is the view that distinguishes essentially between acts of illicit love and acts of "resistance." The latter view implies a basic distinction between essentially "private" acts of erotic affirmation and "political" acts of "resistance"—the private is not necessarily political. However, if we think of "resistance" only as conscious, organized, collective, political effort to initiate social change, we maintain a traditional and problematic distinction between the "political" and "personal." We may thus ignore the social import of those same-sex support networks in which individuals affirmed their worth and gained strength apart from "political" formations. Yet it seems unwise to ignore the fact that some personal acts of assertion are meaningful primarily in relation to one individual's career, while other acts have a meaning and impact wider than the self. In analyzing the history of the American homosexual "resistance," it seems important, then, to recognize a major, qualitative difference between sporadic, self-affirming acts of isolated individuals, and those acts taken with the support of, or as part of, a group, and having some extra-personal meaning and, sometimes, effect. It is important to recognize the existence of self-affirming acts of individual homosexuals whatever their social significance and effect. But it is also important to recognize the difference between that self-assertion benefiting only the individual and that affirmation taking shared, "public" forms.

In 1882, an emigrant, "obliged to reside in America" after his imprison-ment in his own country for sexual acts with another male, wrote to Krafft-Ebing in Austria. Because the writer believed his attraction to men to be an inborn "disease," he felt strongly that he had been unjustly jailed as criminally responsi-ble. He was conscious of himself, and many others like himself, being "derided, execrated, and persecuted," and hoped that "science" would "educate the peo-ple" to "rightly judge our unfortunate class."[29] Sending one's case history, and describing one's thoughts to a doctor who publicized the idea that "perversion" was an inborn "disease," not a "crime" or "vice," was an early active form of resistance. Later reports from America to Havelock Ellis in England and Magnus Hirschfeld in Germany were a way that lovers of their own sex encouraged the more liberal or emancipationist medical authorities of their time in their advocacy of legal *laissez-faire* in regard to "sexual inverts."[30]

An American medical journal report of July 1882 was one of the earliest of several describing the writings in defense of male "Urnings" by Karl Heinrich Ulrichs in Germany. In that report, Ulrichs was said to assert that a "great many" males, "as a result of their inborn nature, felt themselves drawn by sexual desire to male individuals exclusively." The brief but fairly common mentions of Ul-richs's work in these journals may have suggested to a few Americans the possibil-ity of a defense of "Urnings." The American emigrant who protested his "perse-cution" to Krafft-Ebing knew of Ulrichs's work, and some evidence exists of the circulation of Ulrichs's writings in the United States in the 1860s and early '70s.[31]

Occasionally, early medical articles mentioned persons who, despite their doctors' disapproval, refused to feel bad about their erotic emotions and sexual activity. An article of April 1883 mentioned a case of Krafft-Ebing's "Count Z," who "had many male lovers, was filled with ecstasy when having sexual inter-course with them," who "did not recognize his condition as abnormal," and who "felt himself morally elevated and happy after intercourse with men; regretted that social limits stood in his way." Another individual, a "literary man" men-tioned in the same article, cited the "poetically gifted natures" of his "fellow-Urnings," an early example of what may be called The Great Man and Woman defense (artistic creativity "excused" non-procreative "perversion"). Whatever we now think of such claims, this rationale for same-sex love was a form of defense in the face of oppression. American translations, in the 1880s and '90s, of early European medical articles on "inversion" may now be seen as a kind of mythic literature introducing U. S. doctors (and perhaps a few "inverts") to a large cast of erotic types, among them a few early fighters in the "Uranian" resistance.

On September 26, 1895, Dr. John Wesley Carhart copyrighted his novel *Norma Trist, or Pure Carbon, A Story of the Inversion of the Sexes,* published that year in Austin, Texas—one of the earliest American novelistic defenses of what the author called "sexual and affectional abnormalities" in relationships between women. Indicating that its heroine's erotic attraction to another woman had been given full, active expression, the novel defended her love as "normal" for her, though not for the "majority." (A majority/minority analysis of sex was in an early stage of formulation.)

In 1897, the first English edition of Havelock Ellis's *Sexual Inversion* reported the views of an American woman physician, Dr. K, who argued that "Current views" of "homosexuality" in women were "cruelly unjust." Ellis also cited a "Miss S" who used her "gift of loving" other women as a means to "high . . . spiritual attainments." Remarkable also was the statement Ellis quoted from "Professor X" (probably James Mills Peirce), an American who defended "homosexual love" as one pole of a "normal" and "natural" bisexuality. Ellis's book itself was intended to distinguish "sexual inversion" from the more nasty-sounding "sexual perversion" (discussed by Krafft-Ebing), and Ellis included a liberal plea for decriminalization of "inversion" on the basis of its congenital origin and harmlessness (if controlled).[32]

The private publication, in about 1908, of Edward Stevenson's *The Intersexes*, a 641-page "popular" survey and defense, was the earliest book-length apologia by an American. In 1911, the publication of a chapter in defense of "The Intermediate Sex" in the U. S. edition of Edward Carpenter's *Love's Coming of Age* gave wider distribution to the ideas of this English socialist-feminist advocate of "Uranians," although Carpenter's articles and pamphlets had been circulating in America since the late 1890s.[33] The profound personal impact of Carpenter's writings is illustrated by letters of appreciation written by two Detroit homosexuals in 1921.

On February 4, 1915, Edith Lees Ellis, a lesbian, writer, and the wife of sexologist Havelock Ellis, lectured in Chicago on "Sex and Eugenics," an historic, tactful public defense of the sexually "abnormal." Edith Ellis was publicly criticized for the vagueness and timidity of her comments by the more militant Margaret Anderson, also a lesbian. Edith Ellis's talk and Margaret Anderson's critique are the earliest public defense of homosexuality by lesbians documented in the United States. That same year Emma Goldman said she pleaded for the homosexual victims of "moral prejudice" in a public lecture in Portland, Oregon, and in June 1915, Goldman's anarchist associate, Alexander Berkman, is reported to have spoken on homosexuality in San Francisco.[34]

Margaret Anderson's militancy was in part attributable to her knowledge of Edward Carpenter's work, and his citation of "a community" of sexual "intermediates" in Germany, grateful "for every single voice that speaks in our favor." The international homosexual resistance was already having some effect. Among other early international acts of resistance are the efforts of an unnamed officer of the Chicago Society for Human Rights (probably Henry Gerber), to establish supportive contact with the British Society for the Study of Sex Psychology and other foreign sex reform groups (see 1925, June 4). An indignant report from New York, sent to a German homosexual emancipation journal, describing a police raid on a homosexual bath, was another international communication of resistant character (see 1929, April ?). The attempt of the English homosexual emancipationist George Ives to reach out to and influence an American psychiatrist who Ives thought might help better the social condition of inverts was another early international resistance effort (see 1934, May).

*New York Times* reports of the censorship of Radclyffe Hall's *The Well of Loneliness* in England, and later *Times* reports of the attempt to censor that novel in the United States, helped make the book an international cause célèbre and best seller. The complex, contradictory impact of Hall's novel, intended as a defense of the female congenital invert, is only now beginning to be understood; this impact is apparent in scattered references in several documents (see 1928, August 30; 1929, January 2; and the index under *Well*). The translation by Una Troubridge (Radclyffe Hall's lover) of a relatively sympathetic French homosexual novel may also be seen as an international act of resistance (see 1930, July 30). Dorothy Bussy's translations of Gide may be seen as similar resistance work (though of a somewhat ambiguous character; see 1935, November 10; and 1948, July 11). Bussy's introduction to her own anonymous memoir, *Olivia*, makes clear that it was intended as a humanizing portrayal of female inversion (though it was not so taken in *The New York Times Book Review;* see 1949, March 27). A similarly humanizing intention is apparent behind Gale Wilhelm's low-key stories of female-female love affairs (see 1935, August 18; and 1938, August 14). Ma Rainey's "Prove It On Me Blues" is almost unique as an unabashed lesbian apologetic in song and music; "Diana Frederics'" autobiographic *Diana* (see 1939) is a more traditional lesbian defense. Somewhat more ambiguous as lesbian defenses are Katharine Davis's sociological study (see 1929) and "Elizabeth Craigin's" probably autobiographical *Either Is Love* (see 1937, August 15). Alberta/Alan Hart's novel *The Undaunted* includes a homosexual defense in its portrait of a tragic male character (see 1936, April 12).

Three works of the 1940s stand out as major documents of homosexual resistance: poet Robert Duncan's essay "The Homosexual in Society" (see 1944, August), Jo Sinclair's novel *Wasteland* (see 1946, February 17), and James Baldwin's prophetic critique "Studies for a New Morality" (see 1949, Summer). All three affirm the humanity of homosexuals within the terms of an integrationist ideology. All raise interesting questions about our present and future responses to "heterosexuals" and "homosexuals" (see my comments below and my introductions to each of these documents). All three texts reflect a basic uneasiness about "difference"—those historically formed qualities of homosexuals which set them apart from an ideal, general humanity. That a group's discredited humanity might be reclaimed through the affirmation of that very "difference" denigrated was not generally perceived until the late 1960s. Both liberals and radicals of the 1940s and '50s advocated the "assimilation" of the "different," the "integration" of various "minorities" into the "majority" culture.

Baldwin's discussing homosexuality (and heterosexuality) in the context of a necessary "New Morality" moved such discourse from the realm of medicine and doctors, placing it squarely in the realm of values and public issues. His argument both reflected an old Puritan concern with qualities and values, and revised the old puritanical morality, anticipating and challenging today's new mean moralists, those recent puritans who deny the homosexual's humanity in the name of an old religious text. Thus, I am pleased to place near the end of this section of "modern" documents a resistant sermon by that secular Black preacher James Baldwin—a sermon contrasting nicely with those of the Reverend Shepard in 1641 and the Reverend Danforth in 1674. It is a final irony that Baldwin's speculations of 1949 should also raise questions about that negative label "homosexual," the positive reversal of which has led to and made possible this book on "lesbian and gay history."*

## Speech and Silence

At least since the last two decades of the nineteenth century "Conspiracy of Silence" is not an accurate overall characterization of the social response to those now called "homosexuals."

The phrase "Conspiracy of Silence" was first used in England, in 1870, in a public protest against the lack of press coverage of a feminist campaign against state inspection of prostitutes.[35] Since then the notion of a Victorian silence about sex has been publicized to such an extent it has become one of the best-known clichés about that period.

When, in December 1894, Lord Alfred Douglas published (in an Oxford University magazine!) his poem "Two Loves," referring to the "true Love" (of girl and boy) and the other love " 'that dare not speak its name,' " that second silent love was not only beginning to be publicly named, but was stirring to a new volubility.[36] The prosecution of Oscar Wilde in 1895, and the suppression of Havelock Ellis's *Sexual Inversion* in 1897, put the fear of the law and of public humiliation into the hearts of British homosexuals, the fear of prosecution and guilt by association into their supporters. Yet, from the mid-1890s on, Ellis was publishing articles on "sexual inversion" in U. S. medical journals, and in 1901, the volume *Sexual Inversion* and his other *Studies in the Psychology of Sex* were printed by a Philadelphia medical publisher. Bibliographies on homosexuality indicate a significant quantitative increase in discussion since the 1880s. Even when the critique of silence was launched, the erotic was on its way to certain forms of public expression. The dominant trend of this society has been toward an ever-increasing volume, and ever more explicit public discourse on those lusts which proved profitable within an expanding, capitalized mode of pleasure.

There have been silences: Overt censorship and self-suppression, writers' own strategic and patterned omissions, distortions, indirections, euphemisms, coding (by allegory, metaphor, symbol, and even color), and a psychological,

*For further comment on Baldwin's essay see pp. 171, 647.

subjective focus of discussion that has left the social and historical organization of sex, the political economy of lust, a mystery, even as "same-sex" and "different-sex" intimacies were more widely and openly debated. But, at least since the 1880s in the United States, speech and silence about the erotic have existed in uneasy tension, as two poles of a dialectic in which various social and economic groups have had particular and pressing vested interests. Among these groups were inverts themselves, newspaper owners, editors, and writers, book publishers and authors, film and play producers, legislators, lawyers, judges, and the police, feminists, birth control and social "purity" advocates, divorce and marriage reformers, ministers, penologists and prison officials, social workers, psychiatrists, psychologists, and evangelical moralists. All had ideological, economic, and personal investments in the public discussion, definition, and social management of sex.

Yes, there were and are silences, the blatant destruction and suppression of intimate letters, diaries, and manuscripts, book burnings and bannings, play and film censorship. But these have occurred in the context of a long-run increase in the talk in the commercial mass media on sex in general and the same-sex erotic in particular. In view of this increasing commercial loquacity, it is more accurate to inquire into the various historical forms of speech and silence about sex than to assume a predominant and total "repression." We usefully inquire: Who has been silenced, who permitted access to the means of public discussion? What has been the content of that discussion, and who and what interests have controlled its distribution to a mass audience? The interdiction, suppression, prohibition, and taboo—the silences about the same-sex erotic—are not accidental absences, but are produced, like speech. It is more realistic, then, to enquire into the historical production of sex-talk, sex-silence, and sex itself, than it is to posit an eternal battle between censorship and free speech, libidinal repression and expression.

In the medical journals surveyed, and in *The New York Times,* a number of silences may be noted. A passing, derogatory reference in the *Times* may allude to a Black lesbian (see the review of the play *A Florida Enchantment,* 1896, October 13). Black male homosexuals appear mostly in the guise of caricature. Between 1880 and 1920, no hint of a female erotic appeared in *Times* reports of cross-dressing women who lived on intimate terms with other women. When, in the 1920s, references to a female-female erotic began to appear in *The Times* it was to a "warped infatuation." In the writings of doctors, same-sex eroticism and intimacy was presented as a medical problem; in *The Times* it was presented as scandal or crime. Homosexuals themselves were rarely heard speaking in their own voices, directly about their own experience.

In *The New York Times Book Review* a particular pattern of silence is discernible. A *Times* review, in 1919, of Sherwood Anderson's *Winesburg, Ohio,* praised the volume, and mentioned the "poetry and pathos of the opening story," titled "Hands." The review did not mention that "Hands" is the tale of a teacher who had once almost been lynched in a small Pennsylvania town, due to his simply touching his male pupils, in an effort to reach out to them with a vision of the world's possibilities. The teacher's subsequent horror at his impulse to reach out was Anderson's theme.

That *Times* review was an early example of a pattern of omissions that emerges when we survey many reviews over a long time period. In a number of cases, when a book's portrayal empathized with the humanity or victimization of a character, homosexuality was not mentioned in the review. In 1929 *The Times*'s failure to review the American edition of the much publicized *Well of Loneliness* indicates a conscious decision that such sympathetic literature of inversion was not fit to review in print. *The Times*'s failure to review Blair Niles's *Strange Brother* (see 1931)—though it reviewed fourteen of her other works—indicates the same patterned omission. A *Times* review of Alan Hart's novel *The Undaunted* (see 1936, April 12) did not hint that one central, sympathetically portrayed male character was homosexual. Among the most striking later examples of this silence was the *Times* review of Jo Sinclair's novel *Wasteland* (see 1946, February 17), which did not mention that the book's second major character was a lesbian (one of the most human, complex, deeply developed portraits of a lesbian to appear in American fiction until the 1960s or '70s). As recently as 1961, a *Times* review of Constantine Cavafy's poems praised them highly without mentioning that many of these lyrics evoked the author's past sex-love affairs with men.[37]

The historical contest of silence and speech is understood if we realize that the documents we possess are the artifactual remains of several quite different social modes of discourse, the products of several distinct organizations of intellectual production. First, there is that private dialogue with the self represented by diary-keeping and the writing (for oneself) of poems and fiction (unpublished by choice, or lack of supportive patronage). Second, there is that "private" correspondence with another by letter, made possible by a certain education and leisure and the existence of a public postal system. Third, there is that discussion of doctors with each other, via a national and international organization of the means of medical publishing. Fourth, there is that public speech appearing in newspapers, magazines, books, plays, and films, organized as profit-making enterprises. Any discussion of the "discourse" on sex apart from its social-economic organization omits an element shaping, in essential ways, the form and content of that discussion.

American medical journal articles represent one mode of verbal intercourse about sex, *The New York Times* another, each organized on a substantially different economic basis. Medical journals, sold to doctor-professionals, dealt in frank detail with sex as an aspect of "disease" and "health," the doctors' stock in trade. *The Times*, sold to a general audience of middle-class respectables, dealt more reticently with sex as an element of scandal or crime. More explicit sex talk did not, until the 1920s, become a staple of respectable newspaper sales. Only then would overt, explicit recognition of a same-sex (and different-sex) erotic by *Times* writers become a legitimate aspect of this commodity's commercial function.

In May 1892, *The Times* report of Alice Mitchell's murder of her once-beloved Freda Ward referred to nothing more scandalous than Mitchell's statement that she "loved Freda desperately" and had wanted to marry her. In striking contrast were those medical journal reports of the same case which headlined it "Lesbian Love and Murder," and referred to "perverted sexuality." But even *The Times'* decorous language probably made readers newly aware of something "demented" about intense love relations between women. The national newspaper publicity in the Mitchell–Ward case probably marked a major shift in the public awareness of a suspect potential in the love relations of women, just as news reports of the Oscar Wilde trials, in 1895, probably heralded a greater consciousness of sex-love between men.

In May 1892, after much newspaper coverage of the Alice Mitchell case, Dr. Kiernan warned in a medical journal that "sexual pervert crimes of all types are likely to increase, because of newspaper agitation on the subject," and the desire of "hysterical females" to "secure notoriety." Kiernan did not like the press broadcasting information doctors discussed among themselves. In 1916, Kiernan declared (with, perhaps, some exaggeration) that: "Since the dramatic sex-invert homicide of Hattie Deuel" in 1878, and that of Alice Mitchell in 1892, "female sex invert manifestations of all kinds have been much exploited by the press. As a result sex invert friendships not hitherto viewed with alarm have been suspected by mothers."[38] The commercial newspaper publishing industry distributed to a wide public the idea of an abnormal same-sex erotic first discussed among a small group of medical professionals.

When, on August 20, 1916, a *New York Times* review of Edward Carpenter's autobiography reported that that Englishman "tells of his own mental and physical state, and develops those unpleasant theories as to the 'Uranian temperament' which are the subject of several of his books and pamphlets," the newspaper was moving toward that more explicit public naming characteristic of the 1920s. The knowing reference to "those unpleasant theories" suggests the reviewer's assumption of readers' familiarity with Carpenter's writings on sexual intermediates.

From 1880 to 1920, *The New York Times'* coverage of various scandals was conducted via euphemism and a high level of abstraction. In contrast, it is surprising to note that medical journal articles constituted a late Victorian literary genre in which erotic detail was graphically explicit. In the same years that books on birth control were being denounced as "obscene" and banned from the U. S. mails, American doctors were composing and reading a literature that vividly detailed far worse "perversions of the procreative sense." There is, occasionally, a suspiciously aroused, passionate tone to the doctors' denunciations of "perversion." Dr. Hughes's "lecherous gang of [Black!] phallic fornicators" trips just a little too sensuously over the tongue. In the same month, October 1893, Dr. Hughes both denounced "Sapphic literature" as pornography, called for its ban, and detailed examples of oral-genital and anal-genital acts not ordinarily staples of genteel Victorian literature.[39] The suspicion arises that early medical writings on "perversion" provided a stimulating outrage not found in other respectable literary genres. In any case, that medical accounts of "sexual perversion" constituted a break with an earlier silence was recognized by a number of doctors, who were at some pains to justify their sex talk in the name of "Science" and the social benefit of controlling the "perversions" discussed.

The euphemism of *The Times,* and the warnings of doctors, reflected the idea of solid citizens that to speak openly about "sexual perversion" might act as incitement. The middle class worried about its own and the "lower order's" control over their "animal instincts." Though "sexual perversion" was supposedly inborn, knowledge of its details was considered dangerously suggestive; "perversion" held a strange attraction. So provocative were the details of "perversion" that doctors often wrote them in Latin, thus limiting their accessibility to the college-educated few. An American medical journal review of Krafft-Ebing's *Psychopathia Sexualis,* in July 1893, praised that author's translation into Latin of those parts "where modesty would be offended by the bold revolting detail of scientific fact."

From Krafft-Ebing's Latin rendering, in 1892, of the details of *Psychopathia Sexualis* and *Contrary Sexual Instinct,* to Kinsey's graphing, charting, and statistical accountings, in 1948 and '53, of the comings and goings among *The Human Male* and *The Human Female,* to Masters and Johnson's ponderous prose rendering, in 1966, of *Human Sexual Response* (guaranteed not to rouse the slightest sexual response), to Foucault's difficult "discourse," in 1978, on *The History of Sexuality,* the language of the major tomes on the erotic has been notable for its somber seriousness, its striking distance from the rutty delights of its own subject. The form and language of those books was shaped fundamentally by the interest of a professional elite in speaking to and impressing others of their class, a group distanced and distinct from the general public—you and me.

The language of "serious" writing about sex has been designed, first of all, to give a bastard subject legitimacy among fellow professionals. An association with "Science," "Medicine," "Biology," or the higher abstractions of French Philosophy has been invoked in the effort to legitimize sex as "serious" among academic brain workers. If ordinary folk have occasionally made these books best sellers, this was an indication of their deep dissatisfaction with their sexual status quo, and their poignant hunger to know it and change it, not mere "prurience," and not their ability to penetrate the daunting discourse they discovered upon opening those tomes.[40]

In the 1880s, American doctors were first tentatively describing to other physicians a strange new creature, the "sexual pervert." By 1915, a "well-informed American correspondent" of Havelock Ellis's was referring (probably with some exaggeration) to "the wide knowledge" of "sexual inversion" in "American cities," claiming that "Ninety-nine normal men out of a hundred have been accosted on the streets by inverts," or had among their "acquaintances" men they knew were "inverted." "Everyone," it was said, "has seen inverts and knows what they are."[41] The review in 1916, of Edward Carpenter's autobiography in *The New York Times* is the first occasion that paper is known to have used a specific name (" 'Uranian' ") for that before unnamed temperament. When on October 24, 1926, explicit reference to "homosexuality" appeared in *The Times Book Review,* it announced the public debut of that erotic condition in middle-class society. In the late 1920s and early 1930s, "the homosexual" emerged into the sphere of the speakable.

The formulation of the homo/hetero polarity posited the homosexual as bad twin of the good sex normal, as heretical relation of the pious hetero, as all the monstrous things the good hetero was not. As a major term in a new ideology of gender and the erotic, the homo/hetero opposition asserted a new heterosexual separatism. It hypothesized the homosexual as absolute antithesis of the newly invented heterosexual. The construction of the homosexual required the invention of the heterosexual; the naming of the monstrous sex pervert made it imperative to name the ideal sex normal; the names "homosexual" and "heterosexual" established a new, clear, reassuring boundary between sex evil and sex good, between a "them" and an "us."

From the early twentieth century on, the monotonous, mindless repetition of the words "abnormal" and "normal" document the new homo/hetero politic in the process of production and reproduction, revealing a society in which the superiority of the numerical "majority," the sexually "average," the "adjusted," the "conforming," and the "same" became a smug assumption—a dictatorship of the "normal" in which the repeated incantation of that word demeaned and differentiated the now quite visible exemplars of abnormality. In modern times, hetero was set against homo, and norm replaced nature as the dominant term in the ideology of social-sexual control. As city replaced country, industry replaced agriculture, factory work replaced handicrafts, and production for sale replaced production for use, quantitative norm replaced a qualitative nature as the universal standard of moral judgment in the dominant sexual ethic. Though in the legal world the old "crime against nature" remained on the books, psychiatrists and psychologists were now called into court and before legislative committee as expert witnesses on "sex crime." The homo/hetero, abnormal/normal hypothesis reigned with absolute, unquestioned authority.

## Sex and Economics

Though some scholars dismiss it as a "vulgar" determinism, the economic, productive organization of society had (and has) a dominant (though subtle, complex, and contradictory) influence on the historical forms of and responses to the erotic.

The late-nineteenth-century concept of "sexual perversion" implied a procreative ethic which made child-bearing the end-all of sex. That reproductive morality was analogous, in the realm of sex, to the work ethic in the realm of production. The procreative ethic condemned non-procreative sexual spending and upheld sexual saving in the service of child production. The old work ethic condemned wasted energy and sloth, and extolled labor in the service of capital accumulation.[42]

But by the late nineteenth century, the old work ethic was challenged by a new consumption ethic, the old procreation ethic was in conflict with a "New Hedonism." The "three decades of triumphant business enterprise," 1865–95, were called by historians Charles and Mary Beard "the grand era of acquisition and enjoyment."[43] In 1899, Thorstein Veblen bemoaned the passing of the old "workmanship" ideal, criticizing its replacement by an ideal of "conspicuous consumption" (see his *Theory of the Leisure Class*). Starting after the Civil War, and reaching full development by about 1920, an economy devoted to consumer goods production led to the replacement of the old work ethic by a new consumption ethic. That transvaluation of work and consumption involved a positive reevaluation of pleasure under all its names, and in all its forms—"happiness," "fun," "gratification," "satisfaction," and "play"—erotic and otherwise.

By October 1893, Dr. Hughes was warning that when religion stopped regulating "moral conduct," when "self-gratification" and the unrestrained "pursuit of pleasure" were the goals of many, a person was in danger of developing into "an erotic pervert," an "erratic lover of his own sex." The doctor warned: "Freedom—physical, political, moral, mental is the Shibboleth of the people, and hordes of neuropaths now come to the surface."

By March 1895, when Marc-André Raffalovich's essay on "sexual inversion" was translated in a U. S. medical journal, he was already warning that the old procreative ethos was being challenged by a new pleasure ethos which claimed that everyone had a right to sexual satisfaction. And if men and women had a right to sexual pleasure with each other, Raffalovich warned that "sexual inverts" could logically claim such a right. He advocated the repression of both the "homosexual" and the "heterosexual." But the trend of the times was toward erotic desublimation. "This is an era of luxury," warned Dr. Weir in September 1895, in his anti-female suffrage, anti-"homosexual" tract—and luxury, he said, produced "degeneration," evident in "plays, books, and newspapers."

In 1915, Margaret Anderson quoted Otto Weininger's comment on that heterosexual double standard which condemned homosexuals for the same sexual pleasure-seeking males and females were more and more mutually engaged in: In the midst of the "present-day clamor about . . . different rights for different individualities," Weininger said, "we forbid the homosexualist to carry on his practice whilst we allow the heterosexualist full play," as long as open scandal was avoided.

In its early Victorian formulation, male-female intercourse was a kind of production in which any pleasure suffered was a "necessary evil," an incidental and illicit adjunct to serious procreative work. Judged according to the new pleasure ethic, both recreative heterosexuality and homosexuality were distressingly similar as forms of pleasure. Though the heterosexual individual was ambiguously procreative or recreative, the homosexual was the unambiguous epitome of the sexual pleasure-seeker, the erotic consumer. Like "The Flapper" of the 1920s (the new female consumer of dance, drink, and fun), the homosexual was an archetypal Consumer of Pleasure—the lesbian a paradigmatic Woman of Pleasure, the invert male a mythic Pleasure Man.[44]

As recreative heterosexuality became more legitimate, as some form of birth limitation was almost universally adopted, homosexuality could no longer logically be condemned simply as non-procreative and hedonistic. Erotic "abnormality" had to be made inherently tragic or evil. The lesbian had to appear as Vampire Woman or as Erotic Victim, the male homosexual as Immoral Indulger in Acquired Vice or as Tragic Object of Congenital Inversion. The Lesbian Vampire was a defective Woman of Pleasure, a Female Parasite, a Monster of Consumption, who cannibalized her female victim. That victim was also a Defective Consumer, one eaten up by her own irresistible impulse, her too intimate alliance with another woman, a relation in which same devoured same. In such grotesque guises, in the 1920s, did the homosexual step out from the narrow realm of medical discourse into the wider world of the mass media.[45]

In 1896, a *New York Times* review of Archibald Gunter's play *A Florida Enchantment* declared that the comedy, involving the transformation of a woman into a man (acted by a female) and her ensuing misadventures in love with women, demonstrated the "lowest depth" to which the stage could be sunk by "tasteless speculators." The reviewer thought that "Financiers always feel relieved when 'bed-rock' has been reached."

*The New York Times Index* first listed "Sex Crimes. See Lynchings" in 1910, and "Sex Hygiene" in 1912. That year, "Sex" first became an indexed category in *Book Review Digest.* By 1915, in Chicago, Edith Ellis referred to the "mass of books thrown upon the market today, which are supposed to enlighten us on sex problems." A "market" for the discussion of sex had developed by the mid-teens, and probably earlier. Pioneering tradesmen had begun to reveal the old dark secret, sex, in the light of day.

In the late nineteenth and early twentieth centuries, while some American businessmen, with military escorts, moved outward to other lands in search of markets and raw materials, others followed the trail of profit inward, exploring the previously uncharted sphere of the "libido." In their pursuit of new materials for exploitation, new markets for sales, these daring entrepreneurs of desire established the social conditions for new emotions. The production of "consumer demand" meant the capitalized construction of desire, erotic and other. The stimulation of consumer wants meant the arousal of new appetites, the creation and catering to of new needs. A new lust was invented, one whose satisfaction was congruent with the demands of profit. It was not simply that an old Victorian erotic was integrated into a new economy. New historical forms of desire were manufactured. The social organization of the erotic was separated from the social mode of procreation. The erotic was integrated into a new capitalist organization of commoditized mass consumption. "Sex," the explicit erotic, became the raw material, the subject of commercial communication. Newspapers, books, plays, and films touching on sex, "normal" and "abnormal," became available for a price. Restaurants, bars, and baths were opened, catering to sexual outcasts with money. Sexual acts and emotions were brought into the noisy nexus of cash and commerce which had formerly existed, if at all, in the silent sphere of "private" life, or in an isolated sphere of prostitution, outside the dominant mode of production and profit. Men of business lifted the veil off the blushing face of sex, bringing a previously unspeakable, unknown, and a newly invented lust into the realm of trade.[46]

In 1955, in *Eros and Civilization,* Herbert Marcuse criticized the ways in which the stimulation of certain eroticisms in the interest of a "profitable conformity" kept people unfree, refering to a repressive desublimation of lust. In 1978, the French historian Michel Foucault argued against the prevalent notion that "repression" had constituted the dominant social response to the erotic in modern society. He noted the vast "deployment" of forces promoting public discussion of certain historical forms of eroticism in the interest of "power" and "control."[47]

In the twentieth century, lust entered the marketplace; intimacy and alienation contended in the workplace and home. In the 1980s, we confront an eroticism and an intimacy brought into question by the opposite pulls of capital, the frustration and anxiety of the populace, and the organized, collective efforts of feminists, lesbians, and gay men to control their lives. We confront now new and paradoxical questions about love and lust.

### The Present Usefulness of the Recent Past

The recent redefinition of the old "sexual perversion" as one "life-style" among many is unquestionably "progress" for those so styled. But defining human life as "style" connotes a dedication to appearances, images, show, to surfaces and purchases, a trivialization unto death.

The redefinition of sex as play rather than performance, as consumption rather than production, frees it from the old bourgeois spirit of seriousness which condemned it to be heavy, never light-hearted. But the reduction of sex only to "fun" insulates life equally from profound ecstasy and deep pain.

The commercial separation of the erotic from the affectional makes it possible for us to value lust for itself, with no justification needed from love. But that same separation may leave us frustrated in lust as well as love.

The old "congenital sexual inversion" no doubt denied our responsibility for our own ways of being in the world. But the idea of homosexuality and heterosexuality as matters of sexual "preference" or "object choice" defines eroticism and intimacy as things plucked from a supermarket shelf, one brand of canned goods chosen over some other. The concept of "sexual object choice" suggests that one of us must inevitably be "object" to the other's "subject"—we cannot both simultaneously be subjects.

The old, allegedly "inborn" attraction of "opposite sexes" credited God or Nature for desire socially structured and internalized. But the recent idea of "variant sexualities" as "socially scripted roles" extends to human life a theatrical metaphor in which, on the world's stage, we are all forever playacting parts, not fully and deeply living our loves and lusts.[48]

The phrase "making love" suggests our active shaping of a desire once perceived as biologically given. But "making love" also suggests an alienated affection manufactured without feeling.

When we "have sex" today we no doubt do so with less anxiety than many of our forebears; but that having suggests a human intercourse become possession, a thing one owns and expropriates for private pleasures, regardless of the "other."

To the extent that our current, self-chosen terms "gay" and "lesbian" are simply positive, mechanical reversals of the old, negative homosexuality, our words, concepts, responses, and lives are determined by our adversaries. In response, for example, to the old psychiatric judgment that homosexual is "sick," we should reject that inane medical metaphor "the healthy homosexual." Confronting the moral judgment that homosexual is "bad," we should press beyond the simpleminded reversal "gay is good." To the contention that homosexual is essentially tragic and pitiful (proposed in a hundred novels), we should forgo pollyana-ish assertions about "happy homosexuals." Called disreputable, we should not demonstrate our respectability. Condemned as different, we should not prove our similarity. Set apart from the human, we should not assert our oneness with the species at the expense of our historical particularity. Against the old definition of our essence as "sexual," we should not deny the presence and value of our lust. Denounced as traitors to our sexes, gay men and lesbians should not deny our gender heresy, but affirm it as a public service—the subversion of the social links between biology and destiny. Pitied as victims, we should rediscover our various survival tactics and resistances.[49]

In the 1940s James Baldwin, Robert Duncan, and Jo Sinclair published pioneering works affirming the homosexual's humanity.* In the 1980s it is possible to see in those affirmations of the homosexual as human a denial of the homosexual as "different"—a denial of an identity which many of us have, since 1969, found it life-saving to openly affirm. But in the 1980s, it is also possible to read with a new thoughtfulness Baldwin's sermon against labels. A new inkling

*See discussion on pp. 161–62.

of the historical contingency of "heterosexual" and "homosexual" suggests (to me, at least) that those categories—yes, and even "lesbian" and "gay"—were either imposed by them on us, or taken up by us as a defensive response to them. That history suggests that even while we fight the necessary battles in the current war of sexualities we consider what it would mean to transcend a sexual world-view which posits them and us—thinking our way beyond distinctions based on the biological sex of our erotic or affectional partners.

Speaking for myself, in a way I did not anticipate a decade ago, the self-acceptance and public proclamation of "gay" has in some ways, in some contexts, made that category less important, less all-defining than it was when they still held it over me and us as an essential dirty secret of the soul.

What I am suggesting is that the very act of naming and categorizing the homosexual and heterosexual, the lesbian, gay, and straight, is in some ways limiting and oppressive, sexist. For example, many psychologists once assumed automatically that homosexuality was "the problem" of a homosexual patient. This labeling began by assuming that homosexuality was necessarily the central, essential dynamic in any mental conflict or disturbance. The dream of moving beyond such assumptions, beyond the heterosexual and homosexual, the lesbian, gay, and straight on a society-wide basis remains, in the present historical context, a utopian vision. But even today, on an individual basis, on limited occasions, in some parts of our lives, some of us are beginning to experience an inkling of what it means to move beyond gay and straight. In discussions with close friends, we sometimes find ourselves referring to our wage work, or dreams, or the qualities of our relationships—our friendly, amatory, or erotic feelings, our securities and insecurities, our contentments and anxieties—irrespective of the sex-biology of the persons involved. In a limited way we have begun to move beyond heterosexual and homosexual.

For some of us over the last ten years the focus on, and affirmation of, our lesbian and gay feelings and relationships has, in certain contexts, paradoxically and unexpectedly allowed us to put these aspects of ourselves in a new perspective, one in which the lesbian and gay may sometimes be peripheral to other, more central and important identities, interests, and concerns. Some of us recall a past experience of a closeted gay and lesbian existence in which our homosexuality was our one terrible, essential secret. One surprising result of coming out, for some of us, has been the discovery that we now have the option of considering our lesbian and gay feelings as essential or peripheral, according to the different social contexts in which we find ourselves. Obviously, face to face with a bigot, I am still going to affirm my gay feelings and behavior. But when discussing with a friend how to make a living, or how to express a new social vision, I may find the reference to the heterosexual or homosexual, the lesbian, gay, or straight, is irrelevant, limiting rather than expansive. One aspect of heterosexual oppression is to make a negatively defined homosexuality central in our lives. Our recent progressive response to that negation has been to make a positively defined lesbian and gay identity essential. But some of us are now beginning to think about more radically transcendent responses, those which both affirm our feelings and acts, and begin to go beyond the old hetero/homo polarity.

Today, however much we revise the valuations homo, bad, hetero, good, and however much we expand the continuum of homosexes and heterosexes—to refer to variations of act, behavior, career, category, concept, cognition, desire, emotion, experience, identity, life-style, person, role, term, or type—we continue to assume and maintain the old homo/hetero polarity. What should be at issue, I suggest, are not particular forms of the homo/hetero opposition, but that dichotomy itself. Taken for granted as essential and universal, that polarity and all its forms distort our understanding of the past and limit our vision of the future. To understand past pleasures of the flesh, past intimate conjunctions of souls, and to envision a new lust and friendliness in the future, we need new analytical terms and concepts. We need new tools of thought, which will allow us to imagine and create a world without homos and heteros, a world in which women could love women and men love men with as little remark as women and men love now.

To the extent that homosexual and heterosexual represent a limiting imposition on humanity, a labeling created for the purpose, and functioning in the interest of social control, we should consider how to transcend that polarity in theory and practice. To the extent that "lesbian" and "gay" represent, simply, reverse affirmations of the old homosexuality, thereby reproducing it, we need to ask how we might transcend any categorization of the human referring to the erotic and to sex-biology. I wish to be clear. I do not advocate "bisexuality" or "androgyny." I do not want us to claim: "We are human beings, not lesbian, not gay." There exists today a pressing political need for more of us to name ourselves publicly as "gay" and "lesbian" (the names by which we have been and are denied). There exists today a pressing personal need for us to reclaim that which is life-enhancing and lovely within the "lesbian" and "gay." Yet we have, I think, a simultaneous need to dive down deep, to risk, to question, to continually challenge the old terms, assumptions, and institutions, to radically remake the meaning of our lives and restructure the social organization of our bodies.

If naming the homosexual and heterosexual was one epochal invention achieved under the reign of capital, 1880–1950, the most advanced, radical, and humane sexual politic I know of now envisions an erotic and affectionate utopia in which those two sexualities would not be named. This far-reaching ideal envisions, not the liberal reform of masculinity and femininity, heterosexuality and homosexuality, but the revolutionary dissolution of all links between sex-biology and particular feelings and acts. There would then no longer be emotions or work inappropriate to either females or males. This sexual revolution would, in effect, abolish female and male as we now know them.[50]

Providing the conditions for the complete separation of the procreative and erotic, and demystifying both as matters, not of God, Nature, Biology, or Medicine, but of choice, taste, aesthetics, morality, and values—of politics and power —the present economy of sex allows us to perceive more clearly than ever before the social and human structuring of desire—freeing both heterosexuals and homosexuals to begin to cast off those confining names, to rethink, remake, rename, and unname themselves along radically new lines. But by fostering a mean, angry, vengeful spirit in numbers of traditional moralists, the same system provides the political setting for a new crusade against perverts, a new sexual inquisition, a new hunting of the witches. If, in the face of this new puritanism, we tailor our responses completely to immediate political exigencies the inquisitors will have won; we will cease to dream a revolutionary new world of love and lust.

We usefully explore together, in word, act, and organization, the possibilities of an intimacy and ecstasy conditioned in their depths by this economy of profit, desire, and the flesh.

# Documents

♀ INTIMACY

## 1880, October 10
## Alice Stone Blackwell to Kitty Barry Blackwell: *"Smashing"*

In an essay titled "Smashing: Women's Relationships Before the Fall" (1979), Nancy Sahli argued that after about 1875 in the United States intense, passionate, loving intimacies between women were increasingly discredited.[1]* Sahli attributed this discrediting to two causes: a new feminist ideology which placed more value on the intellect than on emotion and sensibility, and the rise of "professional scientific, medical, psychiatric, and social scientific communities" which redefined intimate relationships between women as sexual, therefore as abnormal. Sahli quoted from the letters of feminist Alice Stone Blackwell, longer excerpts from which are presented below.

In 1880 and 1881, Alice Stone Blackwell's ambivalent encounter with an affectionate "tom-boy" reminded her of "those wild unreasonable fancies which I used to take for older girls." A a year later, in 1882, Blackwell made no explicit reference to her own personal brushes with women-loving as she recounted a discussion of "smashes" (crushes) at women's colleges. Blackwell's account of those female-female intimacies contrasts with her comments, in 1877 and 1878, on ancient Greek "paederasty," which her professor, Augustus Howe Buck, had explained to his Boston University class. In Blackwell's letters she made no link between the intimate relations of ancient Greek males and what she later called "unnatural" intimacies between "girl and girl" in American women's colleges of her day. No such association occurred to Blackwell, since no term such as "homosexuality" yet linked the sexual intimacies of men and the passionate intimacies of women.

In a letter of December 24–25, 1877, Alice Stone Blackwell referred to an earlier letter in which she had recounted Professor Buck's explanation of Greek pederasty. Blackwell wrote to Kitty Barry Blackwell:

*In Part II, backnotes are numbered consecutively from 1, beginning with each new decade.

Paederasty is a word derived from *pais* a boy, & *erao* to love. It seems that men used to love each other impurely in old times, and keep boys as their mistresses. I believe it is sometimes called Sodomy. You must have read about it in Scripture. Now that you know what it is, reread what Prof. Buck said and see if you don't think I had reason to be shocked. I've no doubt Prof. Buck thought he was doing his duty by us, and giving useful explanation; but it did & does seem to me injudicious.

Alice Blackwell continued this discussion in a letter of December 31, 1877, to "My Dear Kitty":

I think you are entirely wrong about Prof. Buck, and I feel guilty and disgusted with myself for giving such an impression. What he said seemed to me unwise and shocking, and I was enraged at the time, and came home and told Mamma, who thought as I did. But neither of us believed that he spoke with intent to corrupt the class. He seems to be a shrewd, erratic, blunt, but kindly professor, and neither a villain nor a beast. He is very much liked, in spite of his sharpness, and is generally considered, I think, the backbone of the college. It is quite true that Greek literature—what I have seen of it, at least, except Homer—is so full of references to that particular vice, that an understanding of what it was is absolutely necessary, to understand what you read. You would otherwise be in continual bewilderment, and be exercising your imagination anything but beneficially. If Prof. Buck had confined himself to referring them to some book which would give them a brief explanation, as decent as the nature of the subject would allow, and there dropped it, I should have thought it enough. I suppose his palliations of the enormity of the practice were to save some of his beloved old heathens from too utter reprobation on our part. As for recommending such a vice to the class, he didn't, and you must be cracked to suppose it. Do you think any man in his senses, if he were so much of a rascal, would venture on such a thing before a whole class in B. U. [Boston University]? It would be tolerably sure to get to the ears of the Faculty, and the Faculty would be after him with a sharp stick. Why Bishop Foster's son is a member of our class; and Prof. Buck knows that anything he says is liable to be reported to our fathers and mothers. Aunt Elizabeth [Blackwell] has put in quotation marks "it had much to recommend it" [evidently, a quote from Alice Blackwell's earlier description of Professor Buck's comment on pederasty]. Please let me know whether I said that. He certainly didn't; but he did say the system "had its good side to it," or [words] to that effect; which was certainly bad enough. Mamma, while she thought it bad to get boys to investigating such a subject, supposed, of course, that he wanted them to know about it for its historical significance, and not with a view to demoralizing the class. Good gracious! I am astonished at you; and yet it struck Emma in much the same light. I have never heard a breath of suspicion against Prof. Buck's moral character, though he is blunt, and not particularly refined at times. He has a nice wife, is a convert to coeducation, and, as I said, is much liked by the students. I like him myself, although he sometimes exasperates me;

and I could almost box my own ears for having sent abroad such an impression against him.

Blackwell reiterated that she didn't think Professor Buck was trying "to demoralize his classes. Though, as I said, I object to what he said to us on that occasion."

"Do I suppose any of the Cambridge Profs would say such things before a class?" Indeed I do, and much worse, if by Cambridge you mean Harvard, where there are no girls to restrain them. Not all the Profs probably, but some of them, I've no doubt.

Two-and-a-half years later, on October 10, 1880, Alice Stone Blackwell wrote to Kitty Blackwell about her visit to the Boston studio of the Norwegian feminist painter Aasta Hansteen, and "her pretty daughter," Theodora. "I have not seen them since that memorable ride when the daughter squeezed me so distressingly; & I went with some secret dread." Aasta Hansteen had told Blackwell that in Norway

all the women stay at home like mice in their holes; & she, being the only woman who did anything in public, was regarded as a sort of monstrosity. Hence she could not go out without being stared at, & it went to such lengths & annoyed her so much that she determined to come to America.

The daughter

did not squeeze me much this time, but held my hand & kissed it occasionally, which was much less objectionable. She told me how the children she played with at home used to call her "boy-face," which I take to be equivalent to tom-boy: & how when she was little she begged her father for a suit of boy's clothes. She always delighted in climbing and swimming, & such boyish sports. When I came away she stood on the steps with the sun making her fair hair bright, & watched me away up the street. They are an odd couple, she & her mother.

The daughter's "queer ways make her doubtful" as a friend, added Blackwell.

Four months later, on February 20, 1881, Alice Blackwell wrote to Kitty Blackwell:

You remember that queer Norwegian lady, Miss Hansteen, & her handsome, masculine-looking adopted daughter? I have been in from time to time to call upon them. . . . Their broken English is very funny, & they tell amusing stories of Norway. The daughter I felt very sorry for. It must be hard for a young vigorous girl, who at home used to skate four or five hours daily, to be shut up in a city room, with no occupation & no companions. I didn't wonder that she suffered from migrains & poor health. But she is going to the Art School now. . . . She enjoys it greatly. The poor child has taken a liking to me—one of those wild unreasonable fancies which I used to take for older girls—and she comes to Dr. Clarke's on Sunday & sits by me, &

walks to the station with me afterward. I am sometimes a little at a loss how to deal with her, for she is uncouth in her ways—a sort of white bear's cub. As we walked up & down the platform waiting for the train one Sunday I tried to make conversation by saying that it was a beautiful sunshiny day. In reply to this highly original observation, she summoned up her English & answered—"You are the first sunshine in my heart." And she dreams about me at night, & tells me her dreams in extraordinary broken English. Her health has suffered from confinement & her mother & I are trying to make her take daily walks. . . . The mother is a bright woman, but odd. She is an artist. Papa does not like them; I fancy he has never quite got over his suspicion that that girl is a boy. But mother feels sorry for them, because they are strangers. . . .

The following year, on March 12, 1882, Alice Blackwell reported to Kitty Blackwell the findings of a committee of women's college graduates which had investigated the institution of "smashing." The committee

gave it as their strong opinion that one thing which damaged the health of the girls seriously was "smashes"—an extraordinary habit which they have of falling violently in love with each other, and suffering all the pangs of unrequited attachment, desperate jealousy etc. etc., with as much energy as if one of them were a man. I could hardly have believed that the things they told were not exaggerations, if Maria Mitchell hadn't told me, when I was visiting at Vassar, what a pest the "smashing" was to the teachers there— how it kept the girls from studying, & sometimes made a girl drop behind her class year after year. Miss [S. Alice] Brown, of our committee, told us her own experience, evidently not without some embarrassment, but for the general good; how she, at Smith, though not at all given to that sort of thing, had been a victim. "A veteran smasher" attacked her, & captured her, & soon deserted her for someone else; & she used to cry herself to sleep night after night, & wake up with a headache in the morning. And they write each other the wildest love-letters, & send presents, confectionery, all sorts of things, like a real courting of the Shakesperian style. If the "smash" is mutual, they monopolize each other & "spoon" continually, & sleep together & lie awake all night talking instead of going to sleep; & if it isn't mutual the unrequited one cries herself sick & endures pangs unspeakable. I listened with undisguised curiosity & amazement, for we had very little of that sort of thing at B. U. My theory is that it comes from massing hundreds of nervous young girls together, & shutting them up from the outside world. They are just at the romantic age, they see only each other, & so their sentimentality has no other outlet. The coeducational colleges don't suffer much from "smashes." The natural attraction between young men & young women is pretty sure to be stronger than this unnatural & fantastic one between girl & girl; but it [male-female attraction] can't go to such lengths, among respectable young people. There will be more or less mild flirtation, talking after class, & perhaps going to concerts & theatres together, as in the case of Miss Sanford & Mr Hunter; but the two can't be together continually, day & night, as when they are both girls. . . . Moral—the university system is better than the dormitory one, & coeducation than the contrary. Of course, in coeducational institutions the girls generally "pair off" together, as Gadge & I did, but without these violent & hysterical manifestations. There are plenty of cases of "particular friends," but few or none of "smashes."

MEDICAL

# 1881, February
# Dr. William Dickinson:
# "A Case of Sodomy," Hannibal, Missouri

The act called "sodomy" in this early medical journal report was a case of forcible male-male anal intercourse (but no distinction was made between this coerced act and a consensual one).[2] "This is a crime," said Dr. Dickinson, "which however frequently committed, is rarely brought to the knowledge of the police."

James Smith, eighteen, was "known to the police as an abandoned character." "Partly by persuasion and partly by constraint," Smith had conducted John Jones, "a street gamin" of thirteen to a deserted building in a remote part of Hannibal, Missouri. There Smith "compelled" Jones

> to submit to the perpetration of the crime of sodomy. John [Jones] states, that suspecitng the intention of foul play, he attempted to escape, but was prevented by the greater strength of his companion.

The physical injury caused Jones was discovered by a policeman who took the boy to a doctor. When Smith was arrested and charged with sodomy "he denied nothing," and later "confessed his guilt." He was awaiting trial at the time of the report.

♀ MEDICAL/CROSSING MAN

# 1881, August 20
# Dr. E. C. Spitzka: Lord Cornbury,
# "A Historical Case of Sexual Perversion"

In a Chicago medical journal Dr. Spitzka, of New York, presented his version of the history of Lord Cornbury, the colonial governor of New York and New Jersey (1702–08).[3] (See 1707, February 9.) Spitzka's is the earliest-known account to associate Cornbury's cross-dressing with what the doctor called "contrary sexual sensation." The new association of male cross-dressing, gender role violation, and erotic reversal is illustrated.

Describing Cornbury as "a degraded, hypocritical and utterly immoral being," Dr. Spitzka said:

> Unfortunately, only the most notable feature of his insanity has been pre-
> served in the records. But that single feature demonstrates the character of
> his mental disease. His greatest pleasure was to dress himself as a woman,
> and New York frequently saw its Governor, the commander of the colonial
> troops, and a scion of the royal stock, promenading the walls of the little
> fort, in female attire, with all the coquetry of a woman, and all the gestures
> of a courtezan. His picture . . . shows him to have had a narrow forehead,
> an unsymmetrical face, highly arched eyebrows, a very sensual mouth, and
> a very feminine expression. . . .

Spitzka explained that Cornbury evidently manifested

> "contrary sexual sensation." Here a male feels himself drawn to males, the
> female to females, and either feels himself or herself as if a person of the
> opposite sex. [A footnote referred to an article by Krafft-Ebing in German.]

> The doctor further explained that "Sexual perversion" (a "symptom" of
> "hereditary and degenerative mental states") was divided into "four groups." In
> the first "sexual feeling is altogether absent"; in the second it is "greatly exalted";
> in the third it appears at an abnormal time of life; and in the fourth "it is simply
> perverted, that is, not of such a character as to lead to the preservation and
> increase of the species."

The last group included lust murder, and cannibalism, "necrophilism," and "contrary sexual sensation."


MEDICAL/CROSSING MEN/NATIVE AMERICANS

# 1882, June 23
# Dr. William A. Hammond: "The Disease of the Scythians"

In a paper delivered to the American Neurological Association, Dr. Hammond, former surgeon-general of the U. S. Army, traced the history of the ancient idea of a "disease" which caused the "loss of the physiological and moral attributes of man," "impotence," the "disappearance of the beard," "atrophy" of penis and testicles, and the subjects even "believing themselves to be women." The subjects also clothed themselves like women, adopting "the manners, customs, and occu-pations of the female sex."[4] Herodotus and Hippocrates had claimed this "dis-ease" prevailed among the Scythians (the inhabitants of an area now in the U.S.S.R.).[339–41]

Lord Cornbury was cited as one who "would now probably be called a 'reasoning maniac' " (Hammond did not say if he thought Cornbury was subject to the Scythian "disease"). Dr. Hammond said Cornbury had appeared in female attire to show his respect for Queen Anne, an "insane motive." Hammond thought it "would be interesting to know" whether Cornbury "was addicted to pederasty, and whether or not he eventually became impotent."[353–55] (See 1707, February 9; and 1881, August 20.)

In 1851, while on duty as a U. S. Army medical officer at Laguna, New Mexico, a Pueblo village, Dr. Hammond had been informed of a native toward whom "the Indians observed a great deal of reserve and mystery." The "sex of this person" had allegedly "become changed from male to female," and

> he had assumed the garb of a woman, lived with women, and followed their occupations. He was called a *mujerado*. Literally the meaning is "womaned," . . . probably a corruption of [the Spanish] mujeriego, which signifies "feminine" or "womanish."[343]

Because Hammond had alleviated the rheumatism of "the old chief," he was permitted to see the *mujerado*. Taken to a secluded place "where the public corn was being ground by the women," Hammond was introduced to the *mujerado*, who appeared to the doctor to be indistinguishable from the women.[344] A private physical inspection revealed an "extraordinary development of the mammary glands," and the atrophy of the normal male genitals, a process which this individual claimed had begun seven years earlier.[345]

In the autumn of 1851, Hammond visited the pueblo of Acoma, New Mexico, in which he had heard there lived another *mujerado*. A physical inspection of this individual also showed the genitals to be atrophied.[346]

Hammond was told that "every pueblo" had one or more *mujerados*. He was informed by "several authentic sources" and by "the subjects themselves," that

> A *mujerado* is an essential person in the saturnalia or orgies, in which these Indians . . . indulge. He is the chief passive agent in the pederastic ceremonies, which form so important a part in the performances. These take place in the Spring of every year, and are conducted with the utmost secrecy, as regards the non-Indian part of the population. For the making of a *mujerado*, one of the most virile men is selected, and the act of masturbation is performed upon him many times every day. At the same time he is made to ride almost continuously on horseback. The genital organs are thus brought at first into a state of extreme erethism [irritability], so that the motion of the horse is sufficient to produce a discharge of seminal fluid, while at the same time the pressure of the body on the animal's back—for the riding is done without a saddle—interferes with their proper nutrition. It eventually happens that though an orgasm may be caused, emissions can no longer be effected, even upon the most intense degree of excitation. Finally the accomplishment of an orgasm becomes impossible. In the meantime the penis

and testicles begin to shrink, and in time reach their lowest plane of degradation. Erections then altogether cease.

But the most decided changes are at the same time going on little by little in the instincts and proclivities of the subject. He loses his taste for those sports and occupations in which he formerly indulged, his courage disappears, and he becomes timid to such an extent that if he is a man occupying a prominent place in the councils of the pueblo he is at once relieved of all power and responsibility, and his influence is at and end. If he is married, his wife and children pass from under his control, whether, however, through his wishes or theirs, or by the orders of the council, I could not ascertain. They certainly became no more to him than other women and children of the pueblo.

At the same time no disgrace attaches to the condition of the *mujerado*. He is protected and supported by the pueblo, is held in some sort of honor, and need not work unless he chooses. Men, however, do not associate with him, but this is more in accordance with his wishes and inclinations than from any desire on their part to avoid him.

Indeed, his endeavor seems to be to assimilate himself as much as possible to the female sex, and to get rid as far as may be of all the attributes, mental and physical, of manhood. Nevertheless, the condition is one which is, I believe, forced upon him by the power of tradition, custom and public opinion, and which—recognizing the impossibility of escape—he assumes probably with reluctance in the first instance, but eventually with entire complaisance and assent.

I could not ascertain, with any degree of certainty, whether the *mujerados* were public property for pederastic purposes at any other times than at the annual orgies, but I am inclinded to think that the chiefs or some of them have the right so to employ them, and that they do avail themselves of the privilege. They avoided all reference to the subject, and professed the most complete ignorance of the matter when I questioned them directly thereon. The old chief, however, who acted as my escort, while not disposed to be communicative, was not altogether reticent on this point, and admitted, by unmistakable signs and with perfect equanimity, that he himself, in his younger days, had made use of the *mujerado* of his pueblo in the manner referred to.[347–49]

Hammond remarked on "the fact that the deprivation of virility is intentionally produced [by the Pueblos] for a specific purpose," anal intercourse.[349, 351]

"The essential point in the 'Disease of the Scythians'" and in the related condition of the *mujerados* was that the "mental alienation" influencing men to dress and act like women originated in "sexual impotence."

Hammond hoped that he had succeeded in decorously "considering a subject revolting in some of its details." "Science," he ventured, "purified" everything.

# 1882, July
## Dr. G. Alder Blumer: *"A painful realization of the anomaly"*

In a medical journal article, Dr. Blumer of the New York State Lunatic Asylum, Utica, New York, discussed "perverted sexual instinct." He began by reviewing the writings on the subject up to that time.[5]

Blumer said that physicians were "first directed to the existence of perverted sexual instincts" by Professor Westphal of Berlin, in 1869. Westphal, the "first to consider the subject scientifically," described "the affection under the name of 'konträre [sic] Sexual-empfindung' [contrary sexual feeling]. He defined the anomaly as a 'congenital perversion of the sexual instinct,'" in which individuals were "'conscious of the morbid character of the condition.'" (For Westphal, see 1883, April.)

Other reports of the "anomaly," said Blumer, had brought the total number of recorded "cases" to seventeen.

Blumer then presented a "typical example" of the anomaly "out of his own practice," a long case history of "Mr. X," age about twenty-seven, "of high social status," whose physical characteristics included below average height, dark hair, eyes "brilliant and swimming," "long eyelashes," "expression womanly," "strides, quick and short," "voice and intonation, like a woman's," and an occasional lisp.[22–23] Mr. X also suffered from fainting, vertigo, and "nightmares."

As a child X had had no disposition for boys' pastimes, but had developed an early interest in reading, writing, and music, becoming a "brilliant pianist and composer of weird-like impromptus." His "Occupations and tastes" were "essentially womanly."

> Conscious of his youthful, unmanlike appearance, [X] is very sensitive on the subject, and resents imputations of womanliness. Admires manly men. . . .[24]

"Marital relations" were said to be "repugnant" to X. The subject admitted

> that he has on several occasions been approached by men of unnatural desire, and declares his unspeakable horror of paederastia. Has in conversation said that these latter individuals are able to recognize each other.[25]

Mr. X was reportedly successful in literature (fiction, apparently). He wrote about "eccentric persons" and was courted by "leading publishers." The doctor reported that Mr. X ate "in a nibbling, mincing manner like many women."

Then followed a long, abstract (and boring) history, dating to the 1870s, of Mr. X's relationship with an "ideal friend" who, "unable to comprehend or reciprocate" X's feelings, permitted his frequent visits and voluble expressions of affection. A strange episode in which X became "the apparent recipient of anonymous defamatory letters concerning his friend" ended with the revelation that X had himself written the letters.[25–33]

In summary, Blumer thought that X suffered from, among other things, a "neuro-psychopathic taint," and "the wickedness of the epileptic." The doctor suggested: the anonymous letters seemed intended to elicit sympathy and, by indicating Mr. X's devotion, to raise him in his friend's eyes. The case included "a painful realization of the anomaly on the part of the patient." Blumer was

> convinced that in this case there was nothing more than a vague, platonic, transcendental longing.[35]

♀ MEDICAL

# 1882
## Dr. Henry N. Guernsey:
### *"Young ladies . . . play with one another"*

In a book titled *Plain Talks On Avoided Subjects* Dr. Guernsey warned of "a variety of morbid conditions to which the female is liable, so that sexual desires arise in spite of every effort to keep aloof from them."[6] "Many a time" Guernsey "had pure-minded young ladies apply to me for medical aid, . . . confessing that they had impure thoughts which they knew were wrong, but of which they could not rid themselves." The doctor assured his readers that "proper medical . . . treatment always restores order in such functional derangements and the sexual disturbances of the mind disappear." He had "repeatedly cured nymphomania" by "curing" its physical cause.

"Too often" young women resorted "to *self-abuse*" or to "the caresses of the opposite sex," and were "ruined forever." He warned: "Every digression . . . paves the way for others." Whenever "a morbid condition" excited "immoral thoughts and sensations," a "judicious physician" should be consulted at once."[80–82]

The doctor asked:

> And is it true that some young ladies, the sweetest and fairest of our race, play with one another in an immodest and indecent way, teaching immorality to the pure and innocent? I fear it is, I *know* it is. Such things need not, must not, and will not be tolerated. This little book will go about in all classes of society confirming and strengthening the pure in heart in their purity and enlightening the ignorant who will joyfully hail the good news; all will join hands in one popular cry against indecencies . . . of an impure nature; and the vilest man even will be taught to fear . . . the combined world of chaste female influence . . . . Woman, naturally pure and lovely woman! the greatest part of this work must be done by you.[82–83]

# 1883, March
## Dr. William Hammond: *Two types of "pederasts"*

In his book *Sexual Impotence in the Male,* Dr. Hammond, then Professor of Diseases of the Mind and Nervous System at the New York Post-Graduate Medical School, said he had treated "several cases of sexual inversion," cases in which the subjects formed "amatory attachments to other men."[7] Such cases were "even more distressing and disgusting" than that in which a male had subjected himself to masochistic acts with a female.[55]

One of Hammond's cases was that of a man of twenty-three or -four, a cigar dealer, who at the age of about seven had "contracted the habit of introducing substances into the anus for the purpose of having sexual pleasure." At about the age of ten he had been sent to a boarding school, and "was initiated into mastur-bation and pederasty by the boys"—the "rôle of the passive" giving him the most pleasure. "Every night . . . he took part in these shameful performances," fre-quently half a dozen times or more. At the age of fifteen he left the school, his "health shattered, his nervous system irritable, with almost constant headaches," and various anal problems.[56]

He then "formed an association for pederastic purposes" with a young man who was to take the active part:

> Articles of agreement were drawn up between them in which each swore eternal fidelity to the other, and in which they were called, respectively, husband and wife. They took a room together and at night slept in one bed. There were two beds in the room and both were occupied for a few minutes so as not to excite suspicion. . . .
>
> Frequently the passive agent would array himself in female attire and would sit up at night waiting for the other to return home. . . .

Sometimes, the "husband," a liquor dealer, "was kept out late by his business," and the "wife" would "then receive him with every demonstration of affection."

This relationship continued for three years, until the liquor dealer had "to leave the city, in consequence of a difficulty with the police" concerning "a gambling operation in which he was engaged." Much "regret" and "grief" was manifested by both parties.

Hammond's patient had then looked for a new "man with whom he could establish *rapports*":

> He frequently fell in love at first sight, but was afraid to make advances, lest he should be refused, and perhaps exposed. All this time he had a very lively sense of the impropriety and illegality of his procedures. He knew that if detected disgrace and severe punishment would be the result. He endeav-ored, however, to reconcile his mind to his conduct, by endeavoring to

persuade himself that he could not help doing what he did; that the tendency was born in him, and, that though his body was that of a man, his soul was a woman's. He gave himself a woman's name, calling himself "Lida" whenever he was operating on himself [masturbating], and insisting on being called so by his acquaintances, telling them some story about its being an abbreviation of his real name.[58]

He then "formed a pederastic association with a man of about fifty," who proved "to be very salacious, and sometimes had relations with him three or four times in the course of the day and night." The patient then developed an anal fissure, began to suffer epileptic fits during intercourse, and went to Hammond for treatment.

> As soon as he entered my consulting room, I was sure, from his appearance and manner, that there was some derangement of the genital system, but I was not prepared for the horrible instance of depravity the details of which, after some difficulty, I succeeded in eliciting from him. Here was a man . . . who for nearly twenty years had had sexual orgasm in the strangely unnatural way mentioned, more times than an average of once daily. He informed me that he had made a calculation, and was sure that he had either acted upon himself or been acted upon by others, at least ten thousand times! He was exceedingly thin; his eyes, black, were deep sunken in their sockets, his hair was black, thin, and dry; he had no beard, and but a slight mustache; his skin was sallow, and the expression of his face that of a person who has committed a crime, and is fearful of being discovered. While speaking, he kept his eyes cast towards the floor. . . .
>
> He informed me that at times his inclination towards being a woman was so great that he had been repeatedly strongly tempted to amputate the genital organs. He had been told by his paramours, however, that if he did so he would no longer be capable of experiencing pleasure in the pederastic act, and this had restrained him.[60–62]

Hammond treated him with bromides (sedatives) for several months. "Finally in the winter of 1880–1881, he died of some lung trouble, in Cuba, whither he had gone for his health."[63]

Hammond's second case of "sexual inversion" was wealthy, well educated, and his "family was of the highest respectability"—all of which "increased the deep sorrow he felt" at his "tendencies." These impulses had started soon after he had been "severely flogged at school for some boyish offense." At this school he had taken part in pederasty, generally as the "active agent." At college he had "never once yielded to his inclinations" for anal intercourse, but masturbated almost every night with "pederastic" fantasies. "All this injured his mind and weakened his generative organs. He cursed himself . . . for the unnatural course which his sexual desires took." Attempts "to provoke a natural desire" with female prostitutes and "indecent" literature were all in vain:

He was fast becoming morbid and full of eccentric notions relating to sexuality. For instance, he spent the whole of one evening drawing the gluteal regions [buttocks] of the great men of the world, and imagining that he was having pederastic relations with them.[66]

Soon after leaving college, one night at a hotel, he had paid a bell-boy to stay with him, had experienced the most "intense venereal excitement" of his life, and had "committed pederasty eleven times before morning. His remorse over this was very great and his physical suffering intensive"; he contemplated suicide.

This patient was "seriously desirous of being cured." His behavior had apparently made "no serious inroads" on his health,

> except as regarded his mind. He was subject to severe fits of depression, during which he suffered the keenest feelings of remorse, and had thoughts of suicide. . . .

As treatment, Hammond "advised continuous association with virtuous women," and "severe study" of "abstract subjects," like math. He "recommended cold baths every morning," and "plenty of outdoor exercise." Hammond "cauterized the nape of the neck and the lower dorsal [back] and lumbar [loin] regions," and administered a sedative. "The cauterization [searing with a hot iron or chemical] was repeated every ten days." After three months of this "there had been a very decided improvement." After another three months there had been "still greater" improvement:

> Sleep had become regular and sound; his melancholic disposition had almost disappeared; his abnormal sexual tendencies no longer existed. In fact, there was no venereal excitement of any kind.[68–69]

After further treatment the

> images, which formerly excited him now disgusted him, for he associated them with some of the most remorseful feelings a man could have, and he had begun to take pleasure in the society of respectable women. He had not, however, experienced any but the faintest evidences of sexual excitement, though occasionally he had felt slight normal desires.

In March 1883, after a year of treatment, Hammond said the patient was "free from all pederastic tendencies" and was "thinking seriously of marriage."

> He had had, several times, natural sexual desires, accompanied by erections, but a high sense of morality . . . has prevented any yielding. He has nerve to keep himself perfectly chaste till his marriage, and then to use with discretion whatever power he may have.

Hammond concluded that the above cases typified two kinds of "pederasts." Other types were "not essentially different from those that have been described, and the pen wearies of writing of such moral, physical and hygienic iniquities."[69–70]

# 1883, April
## Drs. J. C. Shaw and G. N. Ferris:
## "Perverted Sexual Instinct"

A patient with "abnormal desires," who had "recently" presented himself to Dr. Shaw for "treatment" had called the doctor's attention to this "pathological sexual phenomenon."[8] In a medical journal article Shaw of Brooklyn and Ferris of Kings County Asylum reviewed case histories reported up to that time— German, French, Italian, and English reports dating from 1852 to 1882, of what the American doctors called "Perverted Sexual Instinct."

One of the cases abstracted was that of a female reported by Dr. Westphal in 1869, in one of the most famous early European medical journal articles on "contrary sexual feeling."[9] Translated into English and published in the United States, such European cases became part of American sexual-medical mythology. Dr. Westphal reported:

> Miss N., thirty-five years old, housekeeper in a young ladies' boarding school, which was conducted by her sister. . . . Many of [Miss N.'s] peculiarities had been overlooked on account of her physical defect, a cleft palate. Latterly her condition had changed. She became more melancholy and apathetic, grew quite passionate, threw things about, and used improper language. . . . Six days before her removal to Berlin Charité, was found by her sister weeping violently. Said she was dreadfully in love with a young girl, was very unhappy, and could no longer remain in the school . . . became so excited and threatening that she was sent to the Charité.
>
> . . . As a child she was particularly fond of boys' games, and liked to dress as a boy. Since her eighth year had a liking for young girls—not all, but certain ones. Made love to them, kissed them, embraced them, at times succeeded in touching their genitals. From her eighteenth to her twenty-third year had frequent opportunity to gratify her desire, and although she felt of the girls' private parts, she would never allow herself to be touched. When these opportunities were denied her, she would masturbate, especially just before and after the menses, while picturing to her imagination some beloved maiden. She had tried to conquer the habit, but when she forcibly suppressed the desire, she declared that she experienced at once a disgusting smell and taste, arising from her external genitals. Had never felt at all interested in men. . . . In her voluptuous dreams she appeared to herself to be a man. This desire for her own sex appeared frightful to her, and she wished to be free from it.
>
> . . . Was found several times embracing a weak-minded patient, and when the latter left the Charité, was very much grieved. . . .
>
> Five years later, Dr. Westphal looked patient up. Found she had been doing well, had had no further affairs with girls, admitted that she still often

masturbated . . . while thinking of the loved girl. Still had a great desire to be a man. Also told the doctor that since she was grown she had at times felt compelled to look fixedly at a certain object or place until her eyes hurt her. Could not control this impulse. Was at such times very much depressed, following a condition of periodical excitement at the menstrual epoch.[187–88]

Westphal reportedly remarked that the "girl seemed quite analogous to the [male] Urnings" described by others. He said that "these unfortunates claim to be bound together by a sort of magnetism, recognize one another, are worried about their perverted instinct." This doctor did "not consider all individuals given to unnatural lusts as pathological."[189]

Westphal's second case of 1869 was a man of twenty-seven, imprisoned several times for dressing as a female; he had never had sexual intercourse with men.[188]

Dr. Schmincke's case of 1872 reported

he was damned for all eternity; wished for death, but feared it . . . told the doctor the cause of his despair. He . . . had looked at handsome young men with pleasure. . . . On account of this affection for men, he considered himself a complete reprobate.[190]

In Dr. Scholz's case of 1873, "morbid sexual desire" was "less pronounced, but the character, occupation, and mode of thinking womanly." He "thinks that perhaps both natures are latent in man, and that the woman's in him was especially developed through his early education by his aunts."[190–91]

In 1875, Dr. Gock reported:

A Jewish servant-girl, twenty-eight years old, went of her own free will to an asylum; said she felt sick and miserable and wished to die. She had a great passion for a female friend; recognized the same as abnormal, but could not repress it; wished to be helped. . . . As a child was careless, mischievous; did not learn readily; played almost exclusively with boys; menstruated at twelve and a half years. . . . About this time experienced a preference for girls, particular ones who attracted her by the expression of their eyes; . . . when she kissed them, experienced a voluptuous sensation in her genital organs . . . when masturbating, thought of the loved girl. As she grew older, was shown some attention by men; had offers of marriage, but she would have nothing to do with them; was not interested in men, and at times experienced a real disgust for them. But her love for girls increased in intensity; was not content to kiss and hug them, but wished to sleep with them and handle their sexual organs. When resisted by them she became very much excited; finally recognized the fact that they did not feel as she did, and began to think that she was sick; neglected her work; . . . became very unhappy; attempted to drown herself. The suppression of her desire made her finally so unhappy that medical advice was sought. . . . In the institution was restless, depressed, worked but little; fell in love with a nurse and a childish patient; wished to embrace them and sleep with them; . . . improved very much; went home; did fairly well after another short exacerbation during which she attempted to drown herself.[191–92]

Dr. Servaes's case of 1876 (a male), had a face with

a peculiar, sly, lustful expression. . . . Invited the doctor to sleep with him, and when taken to task defended his position. Said sexual intercourse with men was the highest happiness on earth to him. Semen was the true food of life, of which he could never get enough. Misinterpreted Scripture to sustain his position. . . .[92–93]

Another case of Westphal's, reported in 1876, was subjected to "moral torture" by his consciousness of his "perverted" sexual desire. He had "never made any sexual advances toward men."[193]

One of Dr. Stark's cases of 1876, was an "elderly gentleman" with a "liking for beautiful boys and men, whom, however, he has never known sexually. Has a sweet, womanly presence."[195]

Krafft-Ebing's case of 1877 was "gloomy" and had an "ardent, although platonic love for his comrades and little boys."[196]

"Count Z," a Krafft-Ebing case of 1881, had as a child "played with dolls, did not like boys' games." At eleven was "fascinated by a man in church"; at thirteen "fell in love with an old man, who did not return his love."

Later had many male lovers, was filled with ecstasy when having sexual intercourse with them, thought other men must have similar thoughts when embracing a woman. . . . Did not recognize his condition as abnormal; felt himself morally elevated and happy after intercourse with men; regretted that social limits stood in his way. . . .[199–200]

"Dr. G.," a "literary man," reported by Krafft-Ebing in 1881,

thinks men of his character [have] poetically gifted natures; considers as such Voltaire, Frederick the Great, Eugene of Savoy, [August von] Platen, and many others of the present day. Recognized his sexual relations as abnormal, but not pathological or unjustifiable. For himself and fellow-Urnings there was nothing left but this unnatural love, which was higher and more ideal than abstract love. It was no vice, since they were driven to it by a natural power. Many of his peculiar views, his false philosophy, his ethical defects, his Bohemian life, his eccentric manner, led Krafft-Ebing to consider him partially insane. . . .[200]

Another Krafft-Ebing case of 1881, "Herr von N," did not, reportedly, "appreciate the value of money; wasted it. . . ."[200]

Shaw and Ferris's own "case" had been observed twice in the Spring of 1880, but "was so reserved" about his name and identity the doctors had found it "impossible to find him again." He was a thirty-five-year-old German merchant who "had almost uncontrollable desire to embrace men," and feared that "this horrible morbid desire may overcome him and he will really embrace some of his fellow clerks." He was "tormented by constant erections" when among men. He regarded "his desire as abnormal, and laments his condition." He was "ashamed to tell the doctor of his condition," since he thought the doctor "must consider him a horrible creature, and look upon him with disgust. Has never given way to his desires." Shaw and Ferris concluded:

> Patient is an intelligent man, and perfectly natural in his appearance and manner, except that he is distressed by his abnormal state, and wishes medicine to overcome it. Would disclose neither his name, residence, or family history.[202–03]

♀ NEWS FEATURE/CROSSING WOMAN

## 1883, May 27
### *Detroit Post and Tribune:* Sarah Edmonds Seelye, "The Story of a Remarkable Life"

Most of an interview in the *Detroit Post and Tribune* with Sarah Emma Edmonds Seelye was based, "word for word," on an account written by Seelye to a female reporter, but not intended for publication.[10] Sarah Edmonds Seelye, a native of New Brunswick, Nova Scotia, had masqueraded as a male, sold books, and fought in the Civil War, passing as Frank Thompson. She published a version of her life, *Nurse and Spy in the Union Army . . .* (1866). The present newspaper account documents a popular view of the sexes in which a female's dressing and passing as a male for the sake of independent action in the world was curious, but not yet "morbid," not yet a medical issue.

The reporter, who interviewed Seelye in 1882, began:

> I found Mrs. S. E. Seeley [sic], formerly Miss Sarah Edmonds, alias Frank Thompson, to be a woman between 40 and 50 years of age.

She had "black hair and eyes, a quick intelligent expression," and appeared to have "made her toilette with scrupulous care . . . , but possibly without a mirror."

> Her manner is direct, earnest and free from any trace of self-consciousness. With the exception of an occasional phrase, more current in the church of which she is still an active member, than elsewhere, her diction is as clear and graphic as her manner is unpretentious. She spoke freely of the past and when I expressed a desire to learn something of her early life and the causes which had led her into such exceptional circumstances, she gave an account of her girlhood which I shall reproduce as nearly as possible in her own words:
>> "You have expressed a desire to know what led me to assume male attire, I will try to tell you. I think I was born into this world with some dormant antagonism toward man. I hope I have outgrown it measurably, but my infant soul was impressed with a sense of my mother's wrongs, before

Sarah Emma Seelye as herself and as Franklin Thompson. Page from a scrapbook (from Sylvia G. L. Dannett, *She Rode with the Generals*… [New York: Thomas Nelson, 1960], opposite p. 160).

I ever saw the light, and I probably drew from her breast with my daily food my love of independence and hatred of male tyranny.

"Youth generalizes hastily. In our family the women were not sheltered, but enslaved; hence I naturally grew up to think of man as the implacable foe of my sex. I had not an atom of faith in any one of you. [The address to a male reporter indicates, evidently, a change in Seelye's text.] If occasionly I met one who seemed a little better than others, I set him down in my mind as a 'wolf in sheep's clothing,' and probably less worthy of trust than the rest. . . .

"Very early in life I was forced to the conclusion, from close observation and bitter experience, that matrimony was not the safe investment for me. Although I was favored with more than one touching declaration of undying love, I greatly preferred the privilege of earning my own bread and butter. When I was about 13 years old, one of those peculiar little incidents occurred which seems like God's own finger pointing out the way to a struggling soul.

"Late one evening an old peddlar came along, weary with his burden. My mother invited him in, gave him supper and made him comfortable for the night. . . .

"Next morning the old man seemed very grateful, and by way of appreciation of the kindness received, he presented me with a book entitled 'Fanny Campbell, the Female Sailor.'* It was the first novel I had ever seen.

[That day, young Sarah read the novel:]

"That was the most wonderful day in all my life. The battle of Bull Run wasn't a circumstance to it. Surely I must have been inspired! I felt as if an angel had touched me with a live coal from off the altar. All the latent energy of my nature was aroused, and each exploit of the heroine thrilled me to my fingertips. I went home that night with the problem of my life solved. I felt equal to any emergency. I was emancipated! and could never again be a *slave*.

"When I read where 'Fanny' cut off her brown curls, and donned the blue jacket, and stepped into the freedom and glorious independence of masculinity, I threw up my old straw hat and shouted. . . .

"The only drawback in my mind in regard to the book, was this: The heroine went to rescue an imprisoned [male] lover, and I pitied her that she was only a poor love-sick girl, after all, like so many I had known, and I regretted that she had no higher ambition than running after a man. Perhaps, later on in life I had more charity, and gave her a credit mark, for rescuing anybody—even a lover. From that time forth I never ceased planning my escape, although it was years before I accomplished it.

"A few weeks before I left home [at age fifteen] my father took it

*[Maturin Murray Ballou], *Fanny Campbell, The Female Pirate Captain. A Tale of the Revolution by Lieutenant Murray* [pseud.] (N.Y.: E. D. Long, 1844); also later editions and publishers.

into his head to marry me off, and get rid of me. In obedience to orders I became engaged, but while the preparations were going on for the wedding, one starless night, I most unceremoniously left for parts unknown.

Among the accomplishments narrated by Seelye was her becoming, while passing as a male, a "famous" book salesman (possibly in rural New Brunswick, Canada):

> I made money, dressed well, owned and drove a fine horse and buggy— silver mounted harness and all the paraphernalia of a nice turnout—took my lady friends out riding occasionally, and had a nice time generally.

Later, in Nova Scotia, still passing as a male book seller, Seelye said she "stopped at first-class houses, lived well, dressed well," and gave money "to benevolent societies"—"and came near marrying a pretty little girl who found that I should not leave Nova Scotia without her.

Referring to her "unusual career" as a Civil War soldier, Seelye explained that it was

> only in the light of later experience that it seems so very strange to me. I was so conscious of being led, so certain of my own self-respect that I never viewed it from a conventional standpoint. And then I was so busy. . . .

As to her later life, Seelye added that she had attended Oberlin College— in "feminine attire"—

> and then—well, you know how the census takers sum up all our employments with the too easily written words, "married woman." That is what I became. . . .

She and her husband had lived "for a goodly number of years very happy together."

♀ CROSSING WOMAN

# 1883
# Dr. James G. Kiernan:
## Marriage between women, Belvidere, Illinois

A medical journal reported that a woman of Belvidere, Illinois, had

> deserted her husband (with whom sexual incompatibility existed) and abandoned her children.[11] She donned masculine attire and obtained masculine work. While thus employed she won the affections of a young girl whom she married with the consent of [the "girl's"] parents. Six months later the woman's husband discovered that his wife and her "wife" were living at Waupun, Wis., in the apparent enjoyment of "matrimonial felicity." The

husband separated his wife from her "wife." The sexual pervert [the "woman"] had an enlarged clitoris two and one-half inches when erect. The girl's parents took her back but she frequently visited her late matrimonial companion, apparently with the full consent of the husband.

♀ MEDICAL

# 1884, January
## Dr. James G. Kiernan: "Perverted Sexual Instinct"

At a meeting of the Chicago Medical Society Dr. Kiernan read a paper on "Perverted Sexual Instinct," reviewing the history of physicians' interest in the subject (also see Kiernan, 1884, May).[12] In reference to two female "victims" of "perversion" (Lucy Ann Lobdell and her wife) the report explained: this involved "Lesbian loves (from Lesbos, an old Greek city)."[264]

In discussion following the paper, Dr. E. Andrews said that in cities of southern Europe "sexual perversion" was not regarded as "insanity" and that "in Italy many boys open vicious trade to travelers." Ancient literature documented "vicious habits" among Romans and Greeks.

Dr. R. E. Starkweather asked if Kiernan considered a Wisconsin case about which "the newspapers had published so much recently" a "mutual or mental disease?" The case was said to involve two females, one of whom was pregnant. (See backnote to 1883, Kiernan.)

Kiernan answered that there was "scarcely a civilized nation in which the vice" of "sexual perversion" was not practiced; but he thought a distinction should be made between "vicious" acts and "perverted ones." Referring to the last question, he doubted if both parties were really women.[265]

MEDICAL/CROSSING PERSONS

# 1884, April
## E. J. H.: *"Why should it be a crime to dress as you please?"*

A letter writer to *The Alienist and Neurologist,* a prominent St. Louis medical journal, differed with an author who had earlier declared that the issue of "Sexual Perversion" had "little forensic [legal] interest" in the United States.[13]

Part of the letter concerned cross-dressing, then being defined by doctors as one of the "sexual perversions." The correspondent argued that if the object was pleasure, and harmless to others, it should not be punished as criminal:

> Quite a large number of cases are occurring in all large cities, of persons arrested for dressing like the opposite sex. But few are criminals; many are highly respectable and honorable.

"No sane man," it was argued would submit "voluntarily to the tortures of tight corsets and high-heeled boots and false hair, hoops, pull-backs and frizzes," unless impelled to it by a motive stronger than "mischief." Such a "miserable being deserves pity rather than punishment."

The writer asked: "Why should it be a *crime* to dress as you please?" Those who cross-dressed for pleasure should be allowed this "comfort," under "proper conditions." An "asylum or retreat might be provided where they could resort when these paroxysms came on, and there enjoy (?) in seclusion . . . such indulgences as might be deemed proper." The writer knew of a "case" that "would be benefited, perhaps cured, by suitable treatment of this sort."

♀ MEDICAL

## 1884, May
## Dr. James G. Kiernan: "Sexual perversion"
## in a twenty-two-year-old girl

While the subject of "sexual perversion" might seem to touch "on the prurient," said Dr. Kiernan of Chicago, "in medicine the prurient does not exist."[14] Reviewing the history of doctors' interest in such "perversion" Kiernan distinguished between "pure" cases of "sexual perversion" and those manifesting "insane tendencies independently of the perverse sexual feeling."

Of three cases which Kiernan had himself observed, one was that of a "twenty-two-year-old girl" (see *GAH*, p. 134). She had liked to play "boys' games," to dress in "male attire," and sometimes felt "sexually attracted" by female friends with whom she "indulged in mutual masturbation." Conscious that "her lascivious dreams" were of females, and those of other females were of males, she looked upon her feelings as "morbid." Kiernan treated the "case" as if it were "nymphomania," aiding the patient's will by anaphrodisiacs, cold sitz baths, and a "course of intellectual training." These had helped her control her feelings, "so far." (For the later history of this patient, see 1894, June, and *GAH*, p. 135.)

To remove such a "condition" was "out of the question," since it was inborn. Kiernan recommended control. Another doctor recommended that "these patients be sent to asylums"; Krafft-Ebing proposed that they be "excepted from legal penalties and allowed to follow their inclinations when harmless and not violating public decency."

Although more male than female cases of "sexual perversion" had been reported, this did not indicate the full extent of female "perversion," since "a history of female sexual desire is much less easily obtained."[483–84]

♀  MEDICAL/RESISTANCE

## 1884, July 19
### Dr. George Shrady: *"Conditions once considered criminal are really pathological"*

An editorial in a New York weekly medical journal was evidently by its editor, Dr. Shrady.[15] The physician found "far down beneath the surface of ordinary social life" passions and actions "that would shock and sicken" the mind not used to considering everything about living creatures worthy of study:

> Science has indeed discovered . . . , amid the lowest forms of bestiality and sensuousness exhibited by debased men . . . , phenomena which are truly pathological and which deserve the considerate attention and help of the physician.

Some "Urnings" (as Ulrichs called them) were probably "victims of vicious lust" rather than "pathological perversion." "Urnings" were

> persons whose sexual feelings can only be aroused by intimacy with their own sex; they have an irrepressible desire to act the part of the opposite sex. . . . They attach themselves to some other man, and form sometimes purely platonic friendships with him. . . . They often masturbate while having lascivious images of the male beloved before their imagination.

"Congenital perversion" or "abnormal instinct" in males often began as early as eight or nine, showing itself in an "inclination to adopt the manners and practices of girls or women." These "'Urnings' have a mincing gait and sometimes the hips are broad like those of a woman." Their "perverted feelings" sometimes led to "melancholia," "insanity and suicide."

These "unfortunates" had common "mental peculiarities":

> They are of the artistic, poetical, and imaginative temperament, often exhibiting a tendency to rather weak philosophizing. Sometimes they are of a vigorous understanding. In most cases there is a great mental distress felt through a consciousness of their unnatural instincts. Two or three have, like Ulrichs, boldly defended their practices.

"Medical jurists" had devised "technical terms" for the acts following from these "sexual aberrations."

> The intercourse between woman and woman (Lesbian love) is known as tribadism. That between man and man, or unnatural intercourse between man and woman, is known as sodomy. When the victim is a boy it is known as paederasty.[70]

The "instinct" might be "cultivated and intensified by bad surroundings in childhood," such as "the exclusive society of women and immoral nurses."

The editorial concluded:

> we believe it to be demonstrated that conditions once considered criminal are really pathological, and come within the province of the physician. . . . The profession can be trusted to sift the degrading and vicious from what is truly morbid.[71]

♀ MEDICAL

# 1884, July
## Dr. B. Salemi Pace: Dr. P. Moreau's
## "Aberrations of the [Procreative] sense"

This translation of an Italian review by Dr. Pace of Dr. Moreau's work on "Aberrations of the Genesic [Procreative] Sense," was published in a prominent American medical journal.[16]

Surveying "Antiquity," "The Middle Ages," and "Modern Times," Moreau presented a "historic study of the aberrations of the genesic sense," as manifested in rape and other kinds of sexual violence, "Onanism," "Sexual relations abusively practised, illicit movements," various "forms of gratification" (solitary or associate), and "extreme continence."[370–75]

"Treatment" of "Genesic insanity" should vary with each case, although Moreau recommended douches, baths, and bromides. He counseled against clitoridectomy, for if "some surgeons have numbered a few successes," it was not certain that "all cases of nymphomania are connected with explosive hyperaesthesia of the clitoris or the labia minora."[382–83]

Moreau reportedly thought that it was "above all, important for the public morality and safety, that these individuals of defective organization, . . . these mental and moral mongrels . . . should be eliminated from social consort, by confinement in appropriate asylums." Moreau warned, however, that the law did not give "any man the right of depriving his fellow of liberty . . . merely for having an eccentric, abnormal character," even if that character might draw an otherwise law-abiding man "into blamable acts."[384]

It was added that the law did, however, protect "the honor and peace of families," and provide "complete security of property and persons."[384–85]

♀ MEDICAL/CROSSING PERSONS

# 1884
## Dr. George M. Beard: *"This class of people do not wish to get well"*

In a book on *Sexual Neurasthenia* or *Nervous Exhaustion, Its Hygiene, Causes, Symptoms, and Treatment,* published after his death, the renowned Dr. Beard included a section on "Sexual Perversion," summarizing earlier writers, and focusing primarily on men who cross-dressed, cross-worked, and sometimes took on the physical and mental characteristics attributed to women.[17]

"Cases of sexual perversion,"

> are very much more frequent than is supposed; but they are very rarely studied by scientific men, and only in exceptional cases do they consult scientific men. This class of people do not wish to get well. They are content with their lot, like the majority of opium-eaters and inebriates, and have no occasion to go to a physician; they enjoy their abnormal life, or, if they do not enjoy it, are at least not sufficiently annoyed by it, or are too ashamed of it to attempt any treatment. There are, as I have recently learned on inquiry, great numbers of such cases in the city of New York.[101–02]

Beard had been "consulted by a man whose constant desire was to attain sexual gratification . . . by performing the masturbating act on some other person" (whose gender Beard did not mention—the focus on "same-sex" versus "opposite-sex" partners in the categorization of sex acts was not yet as dominant as it later became). Beard did not know if his suggested treatment had helped this victim of "nervous trouble."[102]

Those who lived indoors, declared Beard, and used "mind much and muscle little" were more bothered by "sexual desire" than were their country cousins —and "savages."[102–03]

Some persons manifesting "sexual perversions" were "insane," as were those possessed by the "delusion that they are women"; these assumed the manners, dress, and customs of women, and could not be "corrected by the direct evidence of the senses." Such persons were essentially different from Native American *mujerados* and those "described by Ulrichs, whose sexual instincts are perverted, but who understand their perversion perfectly." They were not delusional or insane, but diseased.[104]

Beard claimed:

> exhaustion of the sexual organs, through excess or masturbation, brings on at first indifference to the opposite sex, then positive . . . dread of normal intercourse; confirmed, long-standing masturbators of either sex care little or not at all for the opposite sex; are more likely to fear than to enjoy

their presence, and are especially terrified by the thought of sexual connection.

Those who indulged in sexual "excess in a normal way" eventually became indifferent, then fearful of their partners, with the final result that

> they hate the opposite sex, and love their own; men become women, and women men, in their tastes, conduct, character, feelings, and behavior. Such, as appears to me, is the psychology of sexual perversion. . . .[106–07]

♀ MEDICAL

# 1885, April 18
## Dr. Charles Mills: "Nymphomania" and "erotomania"

"A Case of Nymphomania, with Hystereo-Epilepsy and Peculiar Mental Perversions—The Results of Clitoridectomy and Oophorectomy," was discussed before other physicians by Dr. Mills of Philadelphia, and reported in a medical journal of that city.[18] (Although there is only passing reference to "love" for her "own sex," this text is included because it documents an extreme case of sexual attitudes common to many Victorian women.)

A twenty-nine-year-old woman had written her own history. Her "sexual feelings" had been aroused before she was six "by intercourse with other children" (whose sex was not stated; gender was not yet the major basis of sexual categorization). About the age of twelve she had been taught "to do wrong" (participate in intercourse) and was told that

> if any man knew of it he wouldn't marry me. I did not know what it meant, and was ashamed to ask any one. . . . I was guilty of immorality when I did not know what it meant. My girlhood was spent in brooding over what I could not understand. I shrank away from men, and hid my impurity from everyone. I did not know that an orgasm could be produced by masturbation. I handled myself to quiet the excitement. . . . Gradually my nervous system became affected.

Various hysterical symptoms and depression followed. Medicine was taken to "strengthen my nerves," but then "orgasms would take place without my volition."

"The next thing tried was cutting the clitoris—extirpation it was called, "but the "relief from this lasted only six weeks."

She begged for another operation, "took an overdose of medicine, hoping it would kill me," and was tempted "to seek the company of men to gratify my passion, but was too modest. . . . I held myself above anything that looked 'fast,' and never soiled my lips with unclean conversation."[535]

In passing she declared:

I had not been educated as I wanted. I had earned my living by labor that occupied my hands, while my mind ambitiously dreamed of work that I would have to climb to. When I entered the hospital I decided that my vocation was to study the care of the sick. When I was given work to do I put my heart in it. In the seven months that I spent there, happy and living up to my highest intelligence, I was not once troubled with the nymphomania; but when I had to give it up and go away, crushed with disappointment, with weakness and poverty shutting out hope of attaining what I desired—when I had again to spend my days in work that held no interest for me—the old morbid depression came back, and with it the disease. I have also noticed that when my affections are aroused it counteracts animal passion. I could never love a man because he was a man. My tendency is to worship the good I find in friends. I feel just the same towards those of my own sex. If they show any regard for me, the touch of a hand has power to take away all morbid feeling.

When her "ovaries were found to be enlarged" they were operated on and removed. Peritonitis followed. For her pain morphia was administered, then discontinued. Her "nervous excitement" then returned. "I had to be drugged to keep me quiet." Later her clitoris

was so sensitive it made me twist all about. Another consultation was held, and it was thought it would be best to cut it away. This was done seven or eight weeks after the öophorectomy [ovary removal].[536]

After this operation she could control her sexual desire when awake, but in her sleep felt "something like an orgasm taking place." She thought she experienced "no diminution of sexual feeling," and said "If my will gave way I would be as bad as ever."[536] Her physical symptoms worsened.

Commenting on this case, Dr. Mills stressed that the patient's "sexual inclinations" were early "gratified in a morbid way by allowing other children to handle her," the source, he suggested, of her problem.

Summing up, Mills distinguished between "nymphomania ("extreme and abnormal excitement of the sexual passion") and "erotomania." The latter

is found in both men and women. Patients with this condition may have no sexual feeling whatever. The individual has some real or imaginary person to love. This is a platonic, sentimental, or affected love, and it may be for a person of the same or of the opposite sex. It is rather the emotion of love which is affected, not the sexual appetite as in the present case. It is shown rather by watching or following the footsteps of the individual, by writing letters and seeking interviews.[539]

IMAGE

## 1885, November 18
*Harper's New Monthly Magazine:*
"Christmas Carnival
In The New York Stock Exchange"

In 1885 male dancing with male was not associated with eroticism. But the invention of the "sexual pervert" as an erotic type, and the new stress on the existence of a "normal" male-female "heterosexuality," would eventually make male-male dancing taboo within the courts of commerce.[19] By 1946 an illustration in John Dos Passos's novel *The Big Money* (see 1936) would associate male-male dancing with sexual perversion.

MEDICAL

## 1886, August 14
Dr. Randolph Winslow: An "epidemic"
of gonorrhea at a Baltimore reform school

An "Epidemic of Gonorrhea Contracted from Rectal Coition" had occurred in a "certain institution near Baltimore" in which "a large number of boys" (aged nine to twenty-one) were "collected" and closely watched by "officers" (the institution was evidently a reform school).[20] The epidemic dated from 1883 to January 1885. Dr. Winslow reported:

> For a long time sodomy had been practised to some extent in the institution, but without any especially ill results in regard to health. The younger boys were generally selected to take the part of a female, usually for some substantial benefit, as a piece of tobacco, candy, or other delicacy, or a reciprocity of the favor.[180–81]

One boy had evidently contracted gonorrhea while on a leave of absence, and upon his return he transmitted it to others. Another, when questioned, admitted "active and passive paederasty." Asked if "he submitted to the approaches of his friends from any gratification which the act gave him," he "denied having any pleasure in acting the part of the female," and "only allowed it for reciprocal purposes."[181] Other "boys confessed to buggery and attributed the disease to it." One "attributed the disease to wearing the shirt of another boy." Another case of gonorrhea was "attributed by the boy to masturbation."

This "outbreak" was reported because of its "unusual mode of origin." The

Original caption: "Christmas Carnival In The New York Stock Exchange" (see backnotes for source).

epidemic ceased when a "strict watch was kept upon suspected boys," and "severe corporeal punishment inflicted upon those detected in the act of sodomy."* A few medical books were said to mention the possibility of "urethral inflamation" arising from "this unnatural and filthy practice" (anal intercourse between males, or between males and females).

MEDICAL/CROSSING MAN

## 1886, November
### Drs. Philip Leidy and Charles K. Mills:
*"He says his name is Jane, and that he is a girl"*

In a report of "cases" from the "Insane Department of the Philadelphia Hospital," Drs. Leidy and Mills described J. M., a male, admitted March 17, 1886, twenty-two years old, born in Philadelphia, white, with an elementary school education, who worked as a "comber of wool"—a case of "Sexual Perversion."[21]

The patient's father and paternal uncle "were both hard drinkers, and most probably died from the effects of alcohol." J. M.

> was effeminate from childhood, but this never attracted much attention.
> Prior to 1875 [at age eleven] he would leave home and keep his family in
> ignorance of his whereabouts.

He had lost several jobs because of "inattentive and foolish actions." The week before his commitment "he had returned home from one of his wanderings, and acted in a more than usually foolish manner," had "talked strangely and excitedly," and was "arrested at his mother's request." He was examined and found "insane."

He had talked constantly of "religious subjects," finally "imagined that he was a priest," and "also became very much excited over the Knights of Labor question."

He had hallucinations of "people strangely dressed," and heard them talking to him. He once "secured a knife and said 'he was going to kill a nigger.' " He defaced furniture and walls with sharp instruments.

> He practices masturbation, but his great propensity is to fondle men, both
> with his hands and mouth. He has been detected† in this loathsome practice
> a number of times, both in the airing court and at night. This, it appears,

---

*See Michel Foucault's historical analysis of surveillance in such institutions, *Discipline and Punish: The Birth of the Prison*, trans. by Alan Sherida (N.Y.: Vintage Books, 1979). The original title was *Surveiller et Punir: Naissance de la prison*.

†His overtures appear to be most gladly received by some epileptics who are known to be masturbators [note in original].

was a common practice with him before his admission to the hospital. He is very bold with it, and has ventured to try to make engagements with visitors for such purposes.

     . . . He says his name is Jane, and that he is a girl. He is fond of looking in the mirror. He talks in a squeaking, effeminate voice.

♀ MEDICAL

# 1888, October
# Dr. Richard von Krafft-Ebing:
## A "strange freak of nature"

A translation of an article by Krafft-Ebing on "Perversion of the Sexual Instinct" was published in *The Alienist and Neurologist* of St. Louis, one of the nation's influential psychiatric journals.[22] The English translation and American publication of Krafft-Ebing's case reports in his large volume on "psychopathic" sexuality (1892) would make this expert's erotic eccentrics among the most famous in the early U.S. pantheon of "perverts."

The "sexual predilections of an individual for those of his or her own sex, with an aversion for sexual intimacy with those of the opposite sex," was a "strange freak of nature," raising "wide-reaching social and legal questions" concerning the response to such an individual's "sexual conduct."

As "abnormal and diseased" sexual natures were studied the "horror and criminality" associated with the "malady" disappeared. "What at first sight seems so repulsive" could be distinguished as two different kinds of phenomena, "a perversion of natural instincts" resulting from "disease," and the "criminal offences of a perverted mind against the laws of morality and social decency." By such a distinction "science" rescued the "honor" and "social position of many unfortunates whom unthinking prejudice and ignorance would class among depraved criminals." Science served "justice" and "society" by "teaching that what seem to be immoral conditions and actions are but the results of disease."[564–66]

Five case histories were offered for "scientific" study. Among these was a German count of thirty-four whose passions were aroused by masochistic practices with female prostitutes. "His genuine sexual feeling, however, attracts him" to "handsome gentle boys with feminine features." For the count, "Masturbation and mistreatment by women is only a substitute for masculine indulgences." But he had "never been able to bring himself" to kiss, embrace, and make love to boys, "being restrained by moral and legal considerations." If male prostitution were legal, and he "could make use of a boy already prostituted, he would be happy."[572]

The patient had not felt unhappy in his perverted sexual instinct, but that social customs should deny what to him is the highest sexual enjoyment, makes him feel melancholy, dissatisfied and embittered, and increases his neuropathic symptoms. His practices with woman are but unsatisfactory make-shifts. . . .

The count had recently married, describing this as a "form to satisfy society."[572–73]

Another case was that of "Mr. Z," a "bachelor of high social standing," one of whose sisters was also "psychologically abnormal"; two others "dislike men and love women."[573]

As a child Mr. Z had been "weak-limbed" and "was fond of feminine work and play." He fondly remembered dressing as a woman at a party. "He had no fondness for boys' games or for hunting and was often laughed at and scolded for his feminine ways." At age thirteen, "he formed a burning attachment for an elderly officer"; from then on he only "cared for" males of "riper years and robust form." He "recognizes . . . that he can only find happiness by associating with men," and ascribed various physical symptoms from which he suffered "to the fact that he had been unable to satisfy his sexual desires," and to masturbation. When he did "gratify his passions he felt relieved and temporarily free from all neurasthenic symptoms." The "gratification" of such ejaculation "seemed to pervade his whole body like a magnetic current."[573–74]

> Through recent publications the patient became aware of the indications of disease which his perverted sexual instincts show. It troubled him, but at the same time gave him comfort, as heretofore his supposed dereliction from a moral stand-point had given him much disquietude. . . . the most painful feature of his situation is that he must not only repress his desires and thereby suffer deeply in mind and body, but that he dare not give expression to his feelings and desires or live in the manner in which they lead him. This throws a shadow over his whole life. The constant fear that his secret will be discovered and his social position thereby destroyed makes his whole life miserable.[575]

"Herr Von Z., a Pole, age 51," had at twenty-six developed a "fondness" for his own sex. "Compromised in a treasonous plot," he was sentenced to five years in Siberia, where his "perverted sexual instincts were aggravated" by masturbation. Released at thirty-five he suffered various physical complaints. His "fondness" for his own sex

> was entirely Platonic. He was satisfied with their friendship and with hearty kisses and embraces.[576]

His "refined qualities of mind withheld him with horror from the vice of pederasty." His appearance "did not give the slightest indication that he felt himself to be of abnormal sexual qualities and considered himself as a woman toward men."[577]

"Herr Y. Z., 29 years old, a real estate owner in Russian Poland," recognized the "evil effects of masturbation and did his best to refrain from it." Occasional "yieldings to the vice brought increased nervous troubles." In recent years "hypochondriacal symptoms" had appeared, "which led the way to delusions of persecutions but stopped short of masturbatory insanity." Since the age of nine he "had frequently been in love" with males. "His fondness for men was entirely Platonic until the age of twenty, when he began to feel a longing for sexual connection with them," especially with "old men of about sixty." He "found his pleasure in intimacy with men," a kiss or embrace was sufficient to produce ejaculation, "whereby he felt strengthened and refreshed."[578–79] He once "formed an attachment for a student and a bath attendant, but of a purely Platonic nature." Late in the fall of 1881

> the patient went to Venice. There he fell into the company of those of his own class (Urninger). He fell in love with a nineteen-year-old youth and made him his mistress. Their sexual intimacy consisted in kisses, embraces and the handling of the other's genitals. He never went so far as pederasty. He formed other similar attachments, caused a scandal in the hotel and was obliged to leave Italy. I saw him in the spring of 1882 and was surprised at the excellent mental and physical appearance of the patient. So long as he could satisfy his sexual desires the neurasthenic symptoms disappeared entirely and the delusions regarding persecutions remained dormant. When he returned home where he could not satisfy his sexual desires there was a recurrence of neurasthenia and delusions, which finally obliged his removal to an insane asylum.

Krafft-Ebing described Herr Y. A.'s "demeanor" as "shy, but in no way offensive." He did "not consider his perverted sexual instinct in the light of a disease."[578–79]

"Miss X, 38 years old," had consulted Krafft-Ebing in 1881, for "severe spinal irritation and chronic insomnia," for which she had taken morphine and chloral, another narcotic. Several months at Krafft-Ebing's clinic "removed" her symptoms of drug addiction and alleviated her nervous condition.

> At her first appearance the patient attracted attention by her clothing, features, man's hat, short hair, spectacles, gentleman's cravat and a sort of coat of male cut covering her woman's dress. She had coarse male features, a rough and rather deep voice, and with the exception of the bosom and female contour of the pelvis, looked more like a man in woman's clothing than like a woman. During all the time I had her under observation there were no signs of eroticism. When I spoke about her clothing she said she wore it because it was more convenient.
>
> I incidentally discovered that as a child she had a fondness for horses and masculine pastimes, but never took any interest in feminine occupations. She later developed a taste for literature and sought to fit herself for a teacher. She never enjoyed dancing, and the ballet had no interest for her. Her highest enjoyment was to go to the circus. Up to the time of her sickness

in 1872 she had no particular fondness for persons of either sex. After this there developed in her an attachment toward women, especially young women. She was never passionately aroused in her intimacy with them, but her friendship and self-sacrifices towards those she loved was boundless, while from that time on she had an abhorrence for men and male society. Her relatives informed me that the patient had an offer of marriage in 1872 but refused it. She took a trip to a watering place and returned entirely changed sexually, and made use of expressions which implied that she did not consider herself to be a woman. Since then she would only associate with women, had love affairs with them and let fall insinuations that she was a man. Her passion for women showed itself in tears, fits of jealousy, etc. While she was at the baths in 1874 a young woman fell in love with her, thinking she was a man in woman's clothing. When this young lady afterwards married Miss X became very melancholy and complained of faithlessness. Her friends noticed that after her sickness she evinced a decided preference for male clothing and a masculine appearance, while before her illness she had been in no wise other than a womanly character, at least as regards her sexual feelings.

Further investigations showed that the patient was carrying on a purely Platonic love affair with a young woman and wrote her tender love-letters.[579–81]

♀ MEDICAL

# 1888, November
## Dr. James G. Kiernan:
### *Removal of "inhibitions produces . . . sexual perversions"*

In a medical journal essay on various forms of "sexual perversion," Dr. Kiernan referred to the "morbid congenital type" (first recognized by the Germans, Casper and Ulrichs), "men who, as a result of their inborn nature, were attracted by sexual desire to males exclusively."[23]

Another form of "sexual perversion" was "sodomy," which "often is but simple vice," although sometimes also caused by "an imperative conception" and/or "congenital defect." Such "defect" was "the case with the amours of the paranoic Ludwig of Bavaria, and Wagner."

The essay also mentioned "experiments by females with the large clitoris of the pseudo-hermaphroditic female." Kiernan warned against physicians "prudishly" ignoring "sexual perversions."

The doctor theorized that the "original bisexuality" of the human race caused occasional "reversions," when "inhibitions" acquired through centuries of evolution were removed. Then "the animal in man springs to the surface." Removal of "inhibitions produces . . . sexual perversions," said Kiernan.

MEDICAL

## 1888, December
## Dr. E. C. Spitzka:
### *"Two men who were . . . cases of sexual perversion"*

In a paper presented to the New York Society of Medical Jurisprudence on the London "Whitechapel Murders" (the "Jack the Ripper" cases), Dr. Spitzka detailed past and present examples of the most violent lust murders.[24] Among these cases of "sexual perversion" he referred in passing to sexual "inversion." Spitzka added that at the previous meeting of the Society in New York, at which he had also presented a paper on the Whitechapel murders, "I noticed among the audience two men who were undoubtedly cases of sexual perversion." Spitzka suggested: the Whitechapel murderer might be "sitting among us at this very moment."[777]

♀ NEWS REPORT/LEGAL CASE/INTIMACY

## 1889, May 11
### *Aspen* [Colorado] *Times:* "Mad Infatuation"

A story headed "Mad Infatuation" suggests that a suspect, passionate love of one woman for another was becoming a subject of public discourse in the West as well as East:[25]

> One of the most peculiar cases that has ever engaged the attention of a court in any part of the world is about to come up for adjudication in Aspen.
> Strange to say, it grows out of the apparently insane infatuation of one woman for another. . . . One is a maiden lady some 28 years old, and the other is a girl of 17. The older lady insists that she is in love with the younger one, not as one lady usually loves another, but ["Beyond all manner of such loves"—a sentimental poem was quoted].
> The ladies are relatives, by marriage, and have been rooming together until recently, when the younger lady, who for the purposes of this article will be called "Belle," said to her father that she would not have anything to do with her cousin Blanche.
> "Why?" asked her father.
> "Because she hugs and kisses and squeezes me nearly to death. She won't let me out of her arms after we go to bed and presses me so close to her I can hardly breathe. She says if I don't marry her she will kill me, and talks so strange I have grown afraid of her. Papa, she is killing me by inches."
> When Miss Blanche was told all this she did not deny it, but, on the contrary, claimed she loved the young lady so much that life without her

was worse than death, and she proposed to marry her at all hazards.

"What nonsense you talk," said Miss Belle's father. "I, nor anyone else, would never have expected to hear such trash from a woman as sensible as you are. You will really persuade me soon that you are becoming insane."

"Not a bit of it," said Miss Blanche. "I am in the full possession of my reasoning faculties and never was more sincere in my life. I tell you I love your daughter as she never was loved and never will be loved again. I know it is out of the usual order of things for one woman to have the passion grand for another, but in all coolness and candor let me assure you that with me it is no ephemeral dream of fancy, but my being's destiny. You can't understand it; of course you can't, and I don't expect you to. The fact that my love for your daughter exists, however, just as strong as the love of man ever was for woman is beyond question, and I am ready to prove it with my heart's blood."

Nearly all of the above re-appears in the letters that have been written by the older lady since she has been separated from the younger one, for the father of Miss Belle fearing lest her cousin would do her great bodily harm, sent Miss Blanche back home, since which time she has written to her lady love every day. These letters are full of the strongest and apparently most heartfelt and ardent expressions of affection.

In one of them she asks Belle to meet her "on horse back at Woody," that they will ride to Aspen and get married before a justice of the peace. She adds "I will dress as a man and as I am somewhat masculine in appearance and figure, I think we can carry out the plan to perfection."

A *Times* reporter gleaned what facts he could in regard to the matter from a prominent citizen of Aspen. . . . This gentleman said the facts were about as the reporter had stated them to him, and as far as he was informed, and the case is one of the strangest he had ever heard.

Said he: "The ladies both live on farms below this city on the Roaring Fork river, and the oldest one has always been considered a practical, well-informed and extremely sensible woman. More than that, she holds a responsible position, and is far above the ordinary woman in point of education, business training and the position she has made for herself in the world. She never was even accused of morbid sentimentality before, and while not strong minded in the least, she is clear headed, clever and undemonstrative. What this mad infatuation is or why it has arisen in her mind to the exclusion of everything else, not the slightest explanation can be given. That it exists in a degree beyond that ordinarily shown by man for woman there is no room for a doubt after reading her letters and hearing Miss Belle tell how her cousin cuddled her up, hugged her and even bit her. The girl is actually afraid of her professed love, and only asked never to see her again. Opinion among the friends of both ladies seems to be undividedly in favor of the younger, all of them seeming to think that there is not the slightest excuse for such monstrous, unnatural affection. One lady suggested a dose of cowhide as the most practical method of curing such thoughts in Miss Blanche."

What the outcome of it will be nobody can tell, but as it is likely to come up in the court in Aspen soon judgment should be suspended until the witnesses are heard.

Two months later, on July 6, 1889, the *Denver Times* ran a front-page story identifying the two women, and reporting the most recent development in the case. The headlines read:

Lovelorn Girls

Strange Infatuation of a Pair of Female Cousins

Vain Efforts to Check It

A Beautiful Aspen Girl Passionately in Love With Her Cousin, Who Reciprocates Her Affection with Masculine Ardor

The Younger Falls the Victim to Nervous Prostration

They Refuse to Live Apart

Sensational Elopement of the Two Girls Who Came to Denver—Character of Their Many Love Letters.

SPECIAL TO THE TIMES.
    Emma, Pitkin Co., Colo. July 6.—Society in this section of the country has been rent from center to circumference during the past six weeks over the sensational love affair between Miss Clara Dietrich, postmistress and general storekeeper at Emma, and Miss Ora Chatfield, both nieces of the Hon. I. W. Chatfield, which culminated on Tuesday in the elopement of the two ladies who are now supposed to be stopping at a hotel in Denver.
    Miss Dietrich is a strong-minded lady of some twenty-eight summers and her cousin, who is the daughter of C. S. Chatfield, is not yet eighteen and a beautiful, accomplished and charming girl.
    A month or more ago Ora Chatfield was suffering so from nervous prostration that the matter was investigated, and it was ascertained that she was madly in love with Miss Dietrich, with whom she was living. The two were born apart [separated] and a warrant was procured in Aspen for the arrest of the older with the intention to have an investigation made as to her sanity. She promised the sheriff with tears trickling down her cheeks and her voice choking with suppressed emotion to give up her child wife.

Their Strong Affection.
    Ora called and delivered to Sheriff White the correspondence between them. The letters showed that the love that existed between the parties was of no ephemeral nature, but as strong as that of a strong man for his sweetheart, and it developed certain other extraordinary features in a manner that became the subject of newspaper correspondence. . . .* If the case ever comes into court, from a scientific standpoint alone it will attract

*Additional newspaper accounts of this case, including some of the women's love letters, were evidently published.

widespread attention and if elucidated it will perhaps explain some of the so-called occult sciences.

### Their Elopement.

Last Tuesday the lady lovers went to Aspen, Miss Dietrich with the avowed intention of marrying a gentleman who lives not far from this place (Emma), and Miss Chatfield to visit relatives. From here they went to Denver, and as soon as they were missed and their elopmeent suspected Hon. I. W. Chatfield was communicated with and requested to bring Miss Ora back from Denver.

At the time Miss Dietrich was arrested by the sheriff the matter appeared in the Aspen *Times*, with extracts from the correspondence that passed between the parties, but no names were given. This will be the first time that it has appeared in print with the names of the parties given.

### The Story Verified. . . .

A reporter for The Times this afternoon secured an interview with a prominent and influential citizen of Aspen who is in Denver for a few days. [He said:] "I had supposed . . . that the matter was all settled and that nothing more would be heard of it. Both girls appear to be perfectly rational in everything but their unnatural affection for each other, and had promised to give up their insane idea. What can have happened to cause them to run away from home in this manner I can hardly imagine."

### Description of the Girls.

"Their reputations have always been above reproach, and their family connections are of the best. In all matters outside of this Miss Deitrich [or Dietrich] appears to be a very sensible girl. She is a medium blonde, about 28 years old, tall and with a good figure and commanding presence.

"Miss Chatfield is but about fifteen years of age, rather slender of a delicate physique. She is, however, a remarkably handsome girl, and would attract attention anywhere. She appears to fully reciprocate the affection of her older companion, and her letters to the latter are usually signed 'Hubby,' and filled with the most maudlin kind of sentimentality. In this respect those of Miss Deitrich are fully their equal."

### A Fruitless Search.

Since the first telegram regarding the case was received at The Times office about 6 o'clock yesterday afternoon, reporters for this paper have searched the city in all directions, but without finding any trace of the missing couple. If they are in any of the hotels of the city, they are there under assumed names.

The gentleman referred to in the above interview is of the opinion that they would not stop in Denver, even if they camp here, as they are too well known and have too manny friends in the city.

## 1889, September 7
## Dr. G. Frank Lydston: "Sexual Perversion,
## Satyriasis, and Nymphomania"

In a lecture at the Chicago College of Physicians and Surgeons, Dr. Lydston of that city declared that "sexual perversion" was of great social, legal, and medical importance.[26] But "until a recent date" it had been "studied solely from the standpoint of the moralist." Due to the failure of the

> scientific physician to study the subject the unfortunate class of individuals . . . characterized by perverted sexuality have been viewed in the light of their moral responsibility rather than as victims of a physical and . . . mental defect.

That a "large class of sexual perverts are physically abnormal rather than morally leprous" should give satisfaction "even to moralists."

The "line of demarcation between physical and moral perversion" was often difficult to draw. And the two forms of "perversion" were "so often dependent" upon each other it was not always wise to attempt the distinction.[253]

The doctor declared:

> There is in every community of any size a colony of male sexual perverts; they are usually known to each other, and are likely to congregate together. At times they operate in accordance with some definite and concerted plan in quest of subjects wherewith to gratify their abnormal sexual impulses. Often they are characterized by effeminacy of voice, dress, and manner. . . . Their physique is apt to be inferior—a defective physical make-up being general among them, although exceptions to this rule are numerous.
>
> Sexual perversion is more frequent in the male; women usually fall into perverted sexual habits for the purpose of pandering to the depraved tastes of their patrons rather than from instinctive impulses. Exceptions to this rule are occasionally seen. . . . I know of . . . a woman of perfect physique, who is not a professional prostitute, but moves in good society, who has a fondness for women, being never attracted to men for the purpose of ordinary sexual indulgence, but for perverted methods. The physician rarely has his attention called to these things. . . .

And many doctors ignored such matters as "unholy."

"Sexual perverts" were of three types: those having "a predilection (affinity) for their own sex"; those having "a predilection for abnormal methods of gratification with the opposite sex"; and "those affected with bestiality."[254]

Referring to reproductive activity Lydston said:

were the act of procreation divested of its pleasurable features, the species would speedily become extinct; for the act of procreation *per se* is possessed of no features of attractiveness, but of many that are repulsive and in themselves productive of discomfort.

It is puzzling to the healthy man and woman to understand how the practices of the sexual pervert can afford gratification.[255]

The doctor again returned to urban life:

There exists in every great city so large a number of sexual perverts, that seemingly their depraved tastes have been commercially appreciated by the *demi-monde*.

Lydston referred, as his following comments indicate, to the "depraved tastes" of males for female prostitutes who performed oral sex, as well as other "sexual perversions." The cashing in on depravity had

resulted in the formation of establishments whose principal business is to cater to the perverted sexual tastes of a numerous class of patrons. Were the names and social positions of these patrons made public in the case of our own city [Chicago], society would be regaled with something fully as disgusting, and coming much nearer home, than the *Pall Mall Gazette* exposures [probably a reference to the Cleveland Street Scandal in London; see 1889, November 17.]

The individuals alluded to would undoubtedly resent the appellation of "sexual pervert"; but, nevertheless, in many instances they present the disease in its most inexcusable form: that from vicious impulse. Personally, I fail to see any difference, from a moral standpoint, between the individual who is gratified sexually only by oral masturbation performed [on him or her] by the opposite sex, and those unfortunate mortals whose passions can be gratified only by performing the active role in the same disgusting performance [on a member of the same sex].

The latter performer of oral sex was "only to be pitied for his constitutional fault"; the former (who had oral sex performed on him or her by female prostitutes) was "to be despised for his deliberately acquired debasement." The female prostitute who "panders" to males' "depraved tastes" for oral sex had the "excuse of commercial instinct," and in some cases "the more valid" excuse of "essential sexual perversion." The "majority of her patrons" did not have such excuses.[256]

The German, Dr. Casper, had reportedly "read the correspondence of known pederasts" and had "found them applying to each other, under the forms of the most passionate language, idealistic names which legitimately belong to the diction of the truest and most ardent love."[258]

NEWS REPORT

# 1889, November 17
## *N. Y. Times:* The London Scandal on Cleveland Street

*The Times* carried a report of what was called "The London Scandal" (and variously termed "The West End Scandal" and "the Cleveland Street Scandal," a court case involving a house of male prostitution and members of the British nobility).[27]

"Ten days ago," reported an anonymous *New York Times* correspondent from London, it looked as if "official pressure was going to succeed in hushing up the tremendous aristocratic scandal to which I referred last week."

> Everybody was talking about it. . . . But there was a general feeling that it would never get into the courts. Now the prospect is different.

Newspaper reports of the affair assured that it would be discussed in Parliament. The press had publicized the fact that Albert Victor "was mixed up in the scandal"; this "stupid, perverse boy," the public now realized, had "finally become a man and has only two highly-precarious lives between him and the English throne":

> the suppression of the scandal in which he, with some dozens of young and middle-aged samples of the nobility and gentry of England, is involved has become impossible, and . . . every day the attempt is further persisted in will do enormous damage, not only to the Government, but to the aristocratic social structure generally. . . .
>
> There is more indignation and ruffling of the equanimity of the English mind just now than I have ever seen before.

*The Pall Mall Gazette* had demanded to know how the British government had "prevented prosecution" of those involved in the scandal. The Paris press had carried

> sensational accounts of the thing, *Le Matin* leading the way with an outspoken onslaught on London society under the suggestive caption "La Sodome Moderne." The effects of this terrible revelation, when sooner or later it is forced into daylight, cannot but be prodigious upon the whole political and social edifice of contemporary England.

Although "a full exposure will seem most lamentable" for many reasons, the compensation would be had "if an effective blow is dealt to the wretched little class of titled young loafers and scoundrels who have brought the name of English gentlemen down into the mud."

The Earl of Euston, it was rumored, had been arrested, and the names of

Lords Henry, Somerset, Beaumont, Seaton, and Dudley were mentioned in connection with the case.[1:1]

On November 24, *The New York Times* reported that "the great scandal which
for ten weeks has furnished all Britain with a furtive sensation has been at last
brought into the courts" and "all other topics of talk fall into insignificance."

Lord Euston, whose position as "heir to one of the great Dukedoms" and
"an intimate friend of the Prince of Wales made him the most distinguished of
the men outside the royal family, charged with complicity in the crime," was
known to have been pressured to "fight the charge when his name was printed
in the North London Press."[1:2]

On November 27, a *Times* dispatch reported that the Earl of Euston had
charged the editor of the *North London Press* with criminal libel. The Earl had
"admitted that he had visited the house in Cleveland-street, but claimed that he
visited there for a lawful purpose." As soon as he was told "its character," he said
"he threatened to knock down the keeper and hastened away."[2:6]

And on January 10, 1890, *The Times* reported that in the trial of

> the persons charged with conspiring to defeat justice in connection with the
> West End scandal a boy witness referred to two aristocrats who frequently
> visited the house in Cleveland-street. The court ordered that their names
> be suppressed for the present, and that they be indicted as "Lord C." and
> "Lord L."[2:6]

*The New York Times Index* lists no further stories on the case in 1890.

♀  INTIMACY

# 1889
## Frances E. Willard: "Companionships"

In a chapter titled "Companionships" in her autobiography, Frances Willard, the
famous feminist and head of the National Woman's Christian Temperance Union,
enumerated those who had "entered the inner circle of my confidence" during
fifty years of life—a classic statement of passionate, romantic (mostly) same-sex
love.[28]

Willard "was hardly six" (1845) when "the flame of the ideal burned in my
breast for a sweet girl of sixteen, Maria Hill." Hill's coming to Oberlin, Ohio,
"meant a new world, her going shrouded my little life in gloom." Maria Hill

> was my first "heart affair," and I have had fifty since as surely as I had that
> one. I have had the subtle sense of an affinity for persons of all ages and
> conditions, for man and woman, youth and maiden, boy and girl. The solar
> system has for a season seemed to revolve around each one of these beloved

objects and for each of them I have endured all stages of the divine disease that was meant . . . to acclimate us to heaven.[639]

In Willard's fifteenth year "came the vision of my cousin Mary G," who little dreamed of "the commotion that her presence stirred in the wayward heart of her Western cousin." For Mary, Willard "felt nothing less than worship," and Mary's "soft, white hand on mine seemed to complete the circuit that brought me into harmony with the electric tides of God's great universe."

"Next came the sweet-faced blind girl, Carrie . . . ; then Anna C . . . , but she liked my sister Mary best and my budding hopes were swiftly nipped; then my blind music teacher, a young married man of beautiful nature. . . ."[639]

When he went away "the next enshrined ideal of my life was Marion, . . . the high-bred girl with whom in 1857 I contested the palm for scholarship in Milwaukee Female College; then Susie B . . . , who was a very Saint Cecilia to my ardent fancy; and then Maggie H., . . . the 'wild girl' of the school." For the "affront" of arranging a tryst with two males, Willard "refrained from speaking to my *inamorata* for three weeks, but finally made up."

In Evanston, Illinois, Willard "met Mary B., for whom my attachment was so great that when she very properly preferred my brother, although I had devotedly desired their union, the loss of her was nothing less than a bereavement, a piteous sorrow for a year and more, as my journals testify, one of the keenest of my life. . . ."[640]

> Other attachments followed, so much less restful than friendships, that I cannot fairly call them by that consoling name. Their objects were good women all, thank God! and the only trouble was not that we loved unwisely, but too well. . . . One of them, dating from 1864, led to my trip abroad.

That "attachment" was with Kate A. Jackson, who later accompanied Willard to Genesee Wesleyan Seminary as a teacher, and taught with her at Northwestern University, leaving with Willard in 1874.

Another of Willard's "inner circle of affection" was Anna A. Gordon, "a lovely Boston girl," whom Willard

> found the rarest of intimate friends. For twelve years she has been at once a solace and support in all my undertakings. I call her 'Little Heart's-ease'.
> . . .

As Willard was much Gordon's senior, "she seems quite sure to be my loved and *last.* "[641]

Willard then generalized:

> The loves of women for each other grow more numerous each day, and I have pondered much why these things were. That so little should be said about them surprises me, for they are everywhere. Perhaps the "Maids of Llangollen," (in Wales) afford the most conspicuous example; two women,

young and fair, with money and position, who ran away together, refusing all offers to return, and spent their happy days in each other's calm companionship within the home they there proceeded to establish. Tourists visit the spot . . . to praise their constancy and sigh for the peace that they enjoyed.* In these days, when any capable and careful woman can honorably earn her own support, there is no village that has not its examples of "two hearts in counsel," both of which are feminine. Oftentimes these jointproprietors have been unfortunately married, and so have failed to "better their condition" until, thus clasping hands, they have taken each other "for better or for worse." These are the tokens of a transition age. Drink and tobacco are to-day the great separatists between women and men. Once they used these things together, but woman's evolution has carried her beyond them; man will climb to the same level some day, but meanwhile . . . the fact that he permits himself fleshly indulgences that he would depreciate in her, makes their planes different, giving him a sense of larger liberty and her an instinct of revulsion . . . . Among the leading advocates of woman's advancement, and of an equal standard of chastity for both sexes, we do not find tobacco users or drinkers of beer and wine.

The friendships of women are beautiful and blessed; the loves of women [for men] ought not to be, and will not be, when the sacred purposes of the temperance, the labor, and the woman movements are wrought out into the customs of society and the laws of the land.[641–42]

♀  MEDICAL/PERSONAL TESTIMONY

## c. 1890
## Dr. Charles Torrence Nesbitt: "Sexual perverts"

In a previously unpublished autobiographical account (written in 1938), Dr. Nesbitt describes five encounters with "sexual perverts" during his years in medical school, and just after.[1] Nesbitt, who was twenty years old in 1890, went on to a career in public health, mostly in North Carolina. Most striking, perhaps, is Nesbitt's description of a witty, intelligent female "pervert," a member of the New York City "detective group," in the early 1890s. But Nesbitt's lighthearted descriptions of his own and another's physical attacks against effeminate male "perverts" also provides arresting evidence of the long history of such violence. Nesbitt first describes his exploration, with a male friend, of New York's sexual underworld:

As late as the eighties and early nineties I can testify that perverts of both sexes maintained a sort of social set-up in New York City, had their places

*For a modern study of this famous female pair see Elizabeth Mavor, *The Ladies of Llangolen: A Study in Romantic Friendship* (Harmondsworth, Eng.: Penguin Books, 1973).

of meeting, and advantage of the police protection for which they could pay. There were several resorts called beer gardens in those days on the Bowery and lower east side in which male perverts, dressed in elaborate feminine evening costumes, "sat for company" and received a commission on all the drinks served by the house to them and their customers. The only place of assemblage that I remember for male perverts was a place called "The Slide."* Here a great number of these queer creatures assembled each night, dressed in male costume and sitting for company on the same basis as the others [the feminine perverts]. . . . It was here that we met and had a long conversation with the "Princess Toto," who was at that time the social queen of this group. This chap was unusually intelligent, he had pretty clear cut ideas about his own mental state and that of his fellows. What he had to say about it all can be boiled down to a very few words which I will use here . . . as direct quotation.

. . . "My kind finds out early in life that he desires above all things sexual gratification and that he cannot secure satisfaction with the opposite sex in the normal way. It is but a short step to the adoption of our kind of life. We, quite naturally, consider ourselves superior to the perverts in artistic, professional and other circles who practice perversion surreptitiously. Believe me there are plenty of them and they are good customers of ours."

There was a place of rendezvous called Walhalla Hall somewhere in that section . . . where these folks meet with their friends for the enjoyment of dancing and other types of social diversion. Through Toto we obtained a note of invitation to attend one of these balls. We did not fail to go and found an orderly crowd of about five hundred couples waltzing sedately to the music of a good band. There was no confusion. One could quite easily imagine oneself in a formal evening ball room among respectable people. Toto sought us out and very kindly introduced us to quite a number of especial friends, quite a few of them were masculine looking women in male evening dress. There were quite a lot of young fellows of the male persuasion present, also dressed in male evening costume. We both noticed that many of them wore a little tuft mustache, close-cropped just beneath their nostrils, the rest of the face being cleanly shaven. I asked Toto what vagary they represented, and why they wore that little moustache tuft. He explained that they belonged to a fraternity of perverts who provided sexual gratification to both men and women. The latter used them as the active participants

*In November 1892, Dr. Rosse reported that "Only a short time ago a notorious place" of male and female prostitution in New York, "known as the 'Slide,' was broken up by the authorities, mainly through the publicity given to it by the *New York Herald*"; see backnote 1892, November, p. 803 in original document. *The New York Times Index* for 1892, under "New York City. Excise 'Dives' Raided" (p. 620) lists a news report, of February 16, about the trial of Thomas Stevenson "for keeping a disorderly house known as 'The Slide,' at 157 Bleecker Street"; see 6:1. Prostitution was not mentioned explicitly. A *Times* story, of February 17, reported "The 'Slide' Man Found Guilty"; see 8:7.

in that form of perversion which is scientifically known as cunnilingus, and that this little tuft of moustache was really important in producing satisfactory results. He further explained that this little moustache was, and had been, so far as he knew, for many years a visible advertisement of the profession of the wearer.*

The masculine females who dressed in male attire were especially interesting. The most intelligent one of these I met that night was a big, not especially good looking, red-headed girl, who was presented as an important member of the city detective group. I made up my mind to get further information from this source and dated her up for dinner at one of the numerous so called French table d'hôte restaurants which flourished in those days. She seemed as much interested in me as I was in her, in a non-professional way, of course, because she dwelt among the denizens of the well of loneliness and had no use sexually for a man.

Nesbitt and his male friend

stayed at the dance a comparatively short time, made our devoirs [goodbyes] with due politeness and consideration, convinced that here was something that should be recognized as basically a biological problem as well as a social problem. There were, of course, all degrees of this type, many of them indescribably debased. We were not interested especially in those who were ardently destroying themselves with neglected disease and the peculiar type of savage violence to which they were subjected by the non-sympathetic in their own social stratum. Even the better sort could be dangerous when several of them could wreak their displeasure on a single unprotected individual. I shall later tell you of an incident of this sort.

I met the red-headed girl detective as per arrangement and we sat down to one of those queer, coarse dinners, each provided with a bottle of cheap claret which we commonly called red ink. She was quite plainly and as mannishly dressed as the styles of that time would permit. Her conversation was ready, full of wit and quite well worth listening to. There was but brief reference to her vagary and friends, but quite enough to inform me that there were many of her kind in the city and not all of them, by any means, were so masculine as she. Her sort occupied a relatively higher social plane than the male prototypes. Not many of them [the females] commercialized their peculiarities as such. They were usually occupied in some gainful way otherwise, while many of them were married and lived in homes of their own, to all outward appearances with perfect respectability. . . . Somewhat to my surprise this woman was deeply interested in her detective work. Of course she was operating with and in the interest of Tammany Hall. Her particular field of activity lay among the constitutional feminine thieves. Many of the department stores of that day suffered severely from shoplifting by women. They paid Tammany for protection just as the thieves paid

*About the use of those little moustaches dear Princess Toto may have been "putting on the researcher" and having a good laugh. But in 1941 "to have a mustache" is reported as "a jocular euphemism for cunnilinctus"; see 1941, Legman.

for protection, and her conversation about the interplay of these interests was not only interesting but vastly amusing. This woman had brains plus. I saw her several times afterwards and enjoyed every minute of our conversations. She was a born and bred New Yorker and like a host of others of the same type had little knowledge or appreciation of the country and its inhabitants which existed west of the Hudson.

Several years before this time in Philadelphia I went out to dinner with a fraternity brother who was a student at Jefferson Medical College. He was entertaining an acquaintance from his home town in western Pennsylvania. This guest was a big broad-shouldered farm lad of about twenty, who was enjoying his first visit outside his habitat. . . . Sexual perversion was just as rife in Philadelphia as in any city of the east. These creatures solicited on the streets on very much the same terms as elsewhere. Between Chestnut and Walnut Streets [late that night] we were accosted by an over dressed male pervert who began his solicitation in the usual way which was more or less inferential. His mannerisms and speech were, of course, exaggeratedly feminine and his face was clean shaven and highly decorated with cosmetics. The big farm boy looked at him in utter amazement. It had probably never occurred to him that such a creature could exist. He turned to George for an explanation.

"Is this a woman dressed up in man's clothes?"

"No."

"Then what the hell does he want?"

George explained to his friend in language more lucid than printable. The pervert was standing close by with an expectant smirk on his face. Without a word the farm boy delivered a straight liner to the chin with his big right fist which landed the fairy on the back of his neck in the middle of the street completely out for several times the pugilistic count. I remember with some pricks of conscience that the three of us walked away without the slightest concern for the immediate or future well-being of the victim, George and I highly amused and the grim-faced farm boy muttering profane and obscene observations on the encounter.

As an instance of my own reaction to the group cat-like ferocity of male perverts I will relate a personal experience of which I'm not particularly proud.

My [female] singing friend . . . who lived in the house on Murray Hill [in New York City] that I inhabited, asked to be taken to one of these French table d'hôte places for dinner so I obliged, carrying her mother along as chaperone. I took them to a place of comparatively good repute . . . located on one of the cross streets below twenty-third.

Nesbitt took a seat with his back to the rest of the dining room.

During the course of the dinner I noticed that the younger lady was blushing furiously and was obviously seriously annoyed. Turning about to look for the source of the annoyance I found seated at one of the round tables immediately adjacent, two middle-sized and one big fairy who were evidently enjoying the discomfiture of my friend and guest. I excused myself for a moment and being quite thoroughly enraged I went over to their table and spoke to them in the sort of language they could readily comprehend, alluding to the three of them individually and collectively as having un-doubted immediate canine ancestry ["sons of bitches" seems to be the phrase alluded to]. In a few minutes they were gone and I had dismissed them from my mind.

Upon leaving, Nesbitt was told by one of the "waiter captains" that someone wanted to see him—he pointed up the staircase to a bedroom.

. . . like a damn fool, seeing red, I went up those steps two at a time and into the far end of that hall bedroom. The door was slammed to behind me and I found myself facing the three perverts. . . . The big fellow had his back against the door and the other two stood behind me and him. I wasted no time in comment but swung on the two nearest with both fists and feet and met the on-coming big chap with the ice-water pitcher full in the face. The pitcher was smashed and so was his face and I have often wondered if he was ever able there-after to cover up his gashes with cosmetics. The whole thing happened in about ten seconds. I walked over their prostrate forms and quietly closed the door behind me. I took stock of myself and found that not even my detachable collar and cuffs had been mussed.

Nesbitt concluded, philosophically, that everyone was born "either a criminal or a saint, most times both."[110]

He continued:

Before we leave the subject of sex perversion I want to tell you of the most striking instance in which I found this defect displayed. Not long after my graduation in medicine [1893] . . . I went to a mountain resort where . . . there was held a cultural assemblage. . . .

    On the morning of the Sunday during my vacation I went with my mother to hear the pulpit orator [of national repute]. . . . He spoke for more than an hour and never before or since have I heard many who were more gifted. His English was perfect, his reasoning thoroughly balanced, and his oratory flowed with the smooth rythmn of the Iliad as rendered by Pope. He gave one the impression of being a great intellectual personality without a flaw.

When the orator later became ill, Nesbitt was called to attend to him, soon calming his stomach trouble.

He asked me to stay for a while and converse with him. . . .

    He did the talking and selection of subjects for discussion. It did not take me long to discover that he was more interested in my young and healthy body than what I thought about or wanted to know. The conversation soon led to where it was unmistakably his purpose to obtain through me the perverted gratification of his sexual desires. Having an aversion to such practices I left him rather abruptly.

MEDICAL

## 1891, August 15
## Dr. Charles L. Dana:
### *"Sexual Perversions—as rare as they are disgusting"*

A paper on "Certain Sexual Neuroses," delivered by Dr. Dana at the New York Post-Graduate School of Medicine, focused mostly on masturbation.[2] But Dana's "Classification of Functional Sexual Disorders" or "Psychoses" distinguished between (1) "Vicious Habits" ("such as masturbation"); (2) "Sexual Perversions" (including "masturbation, sexual murder and anthropophagy [cannibalism], flaggelation, exhibitionism") (3) "Contrary Sexual Instincts" (including "pederasty" and "bestiality"); and (4) "Excessive Sexuality."

"Sexual Perversions" were "as rare as they are disgusting." Sometimes they were "evidence of mental deterioration." And sometimes they were "acquired vices," resulting from "a continual search for a new sexual stimuli on the part of voluptuaries."[242]

♀ NEWS REPORT/LEGAL CASE/MEDICAL

## 1892, January 26
### *N. Y. Times*, etc.: Alice Mitchell murders Freda Ward

A front-page story in *The Times* was headed: "A Most Shocking Crime/A Memphis Society Girl/Cuts A Former Friend's Throat."[3] A subhead read: "Alice Mitchell, Daughter Of A Wealthy Retired Merchant, Jumps From A Carriage, Seizes Freda Ward, And Kills Her."*

The story reported a "sensational tragedy" the previous day in which "The victim was a young woman, and her slayer is of the same sex." Both Alice Mitchell and Freda Ward were "familiar figures in society." Mitchell was nineteen, Ward seventeen, and the daughter of "a planter and wealthy merchant" of Gold Dust, Arkansas.

The story ended:

> To-night the murderess made a singular statement . . . that she loved Freda desperately, better than any one in the world; that she could not live without her, and that long ago they made a compact that if they should ever be separated they should kill each other.

Having been "forbidden" to speak to Freda Ward, Mitchell "knew of nothing else to do but to kill her." The "girl is regarded as demented."[1:3]

*Compare the medical journal account of this case by Dr. F. L. Sim in *GAH*, pp. 53–58.

A *Times* account, of January 29, was headed "Jealousy The Motive. A Strange Story Told By The Memphis Girl Murderer." Mitchell's lawyers claimed "insanity" as her defense, stressing that her mother had a history of being "mentally unbalanced." Supporting Mitchell's insanity plea was her claim:

> "I killed Freda because I loved her, and she refused to marry me. I asked her three times to marry me, and at last she consented. We were to marry here and go to St. Louis to live. I sent her an engagement ring and she wore it for a time. When she returned it I resolved to kill her. I would rather she were dead than separated from me living."

Letters between the two indicated "that Freda had willingly consented to the proposed marriage."[1:3]

On January 31, *The Times* cited "the theory of the State that malice was the inspiring cause of the crime, and not mental unsoundness, as the defense claim."[1:4]

On February 2, *The Times* reported that Mitchell's counsel would petition for a "lunacy" hearing "as soon as they can arrange for . . . medical experts to testify as to her mental condition."[1:3]

A *Times* report, of February 16, said Mitchell's lawyers had asked to inspect her and Freda Ward's letters, held by the attorney general. Mitchell's defense wished to submit these letters to various "experts in mental diseases."[3:2]

On February 28, *The Times* reported that the Memphis judge in the case had called the "crime" the "most shocking and malignant ever perpetrated by woman."[9:7]

And on July 31, *The Times* reported the verdict in the case: "Alice Mitchell Insane. The Murderess Of Freda Ward To Be Placed In An Asylum." A jury had decided that Mitchell was at present insane. If ever released as sane she could then be tried for murder; only her present mental unsoundness had been at issue.[1:4]

Medical journal accounts referring to the Mitchell–Ward case were much more specific than *The Times* in discussing the alleged sexual character of the two women's relationship. This medical literature, and the nationwide newspaper reports of the case, made it one of the major incidents in the public history of lesbianism in the United States, comparable to the publication in 1929 of *The Well of Loneliness.*

On July 23, 1892, before the verdict, the New York *Medical Record* headlined a brief report of the case "Lesbian Love and Murder." The "Lesbian relations" and "perverted sexuality" of the pair were discussed. Though "victims of sexual perversion" might be "insane," the writer doubted the law would find Alice Mitchell "irresponsible."

On August 13, 1892, after the trial, Dr. Shrady, in the *New York Medical*

*Standard,* criticized the alienists who had helped to have Alice Mitchell declared insane and irresponsible. Mitchell was allegedly "afflicted with an affection which Science, with a big S, calls Psychopathia Sexualis." But it was doubtful if this "pervert," who had "attached herself to a Sapphic friend," was really insane:

> if this alleged lunatic had been treated for worms, leukorrhea [vaginal discharge], constipation, or some other of the frequent mechanical excitements of unhealthy sexual desire, or if she had been taken in hand early by those in authority and received a course of bread and water and, perhaps, some strong corporeal applications, she would not have become a Lesbian lover or a murderess.*

In August 1892, the *Memphis Medical Monthly* published a long summary of the case, including a detailed account of the women's relationship and the murder, Mitchell's testimony, and the reported "expert testimony" of doctors at the trial.†

The doctors all testified that Mitchell was insane, and had inherited her condition from her mother, whose history of mental disturbance was stressed. The Tennessee doctors' testimony also linked the violence, the intense love of Mitchell and Ward, and "perverted love" in general. A number of doctors, however, did not think Mitchell and Ward had indulged in "perverted" acts.

Dr. F. L. Sim, of Memphis, testified that "No evidence of sexual depravity" had been submitted; sexual "excesses" had "nothing to do with" Alice Mitchell's "condition." He could judge such things, since no doctor who had practiced medicine "for any length of time could have failed to observe a class of sexual debauchees."[392] Sim regarded the feeling between Mitchell and Ward as "purely platonic love," just like that existing "between the opposite sexes before marriage." (No "heterosexual" attraction was yet assumed to precede matrimony.) "Sexual instinct," dominated by an "insane temperament" and "Imperative Conception," had "led Alice Mitchell to place her affections upon her own sex." He did not view Mitchell "as a purely *sexual* pervert."[393]

Dr. B. F. Turner, of Memphis, looked upon "Alice's perverted love" as a manifestation of a "derangement" existing in her mother.[395] Having interviewed Mitchell, Turner did not think "the relations between her and her companion . . . could compromise either of them."[396] He did not think it proof of insanity if "one girl passionately loves another." However, if one of the "girls" wanted to marry the other, he did consider this "indicative of an insane tendency."[397] If "perverted affections" were "extremely passionate" he thought "they might be indicative of insanity."[398]

Dr. E. P. Sale, of Memphis, called the feelings between Mitchell and Ward "an insane or pathological love."[402]

*For source of quote see backnote 1893, October, p. 556 in original document.
†The main text of this article in *GAH*, pp. 53–58, excluded the "expert testimony" printed here.

Dr. J. H. Callender, a specialist in "mental unsoundness," referred to "perverted passion" as "more ardent, intense and all-engrossing than the normal passions," as "morbid," and evidence of "insanity."[405] He spoke of Mitchell's "morbid passionate attachments," her "unnatural disposition," and her "unnatural and perverted passion."[406] In his interview with Alice Mitchell, it appeared her sole motive for killing Ward "was that she loved her and could not bear . . . losing her, or having any other person share her affection."[408] She had no idea of "the preposterous character of the marriage she looked for" with Ward. The "sincerity of her manner" suggested either "delusion," imbecility, or a child's lack of knowledge of "the purpose of the organs of generation in the sexes."[409]

Dr. Michael Campbell, of Knoxville, was asked if he thought "a girl loving another passionately" was "an indication of insanity." He answered:

It would depend on the intensity of the passion. If it went so far as to cause a murder I would say it was indicative of mental trouble. [So much for the wisdom of experts.]

Campbell did not think the victim, Freda Ward, had been insane because she "was not the active agent," but "was dominated" by Mitchell.[413]

In September 1892, an article by Dr. T. Griswold Comstock, of St. Louis, in the *New York Medical Times*, referred to Alice Mitchell as "A Case of Sexual Perversion or 'Urning' (A Paranoiac)." Dr. Comstock had attended Mitchell's mother during a period of deep mental disturbance more than thirty years earlier, and linked the violence particular to Mitchell's murder of Ward with "sexual perversion" in general.

"The facts" about Mitchell, said Comstock, "will long be treasured in medical works on insanity, and mental and moral perversion." The public would recall that she "cut the throat of her dearest companion and friend." A few people in Memphis had been "so horrified" by Mitchell's crime that they had "suggested violence" (lynching, apparently).

It was of great importance "that such a case" be "thoroughly analyzed by the medical profession," especially by the most "reliable medical experts." There "must be something radically abnormal in the mental and physical development of such a murderess."

There had been an "unnatural affection" between Mitchell and Ward. Their "love," to the public, seemed difficult to explain, "but to experts in insanity it is nothing unusual."[170] "Scientific experts recognised it "as insanity of a peculiar kind." Mitchell's desire for "marriage with one of her own sex" indicated she was that type known in legal medicine as "a *sexual pervert.*"

The subject of "sexual perverts" was "revolting" to the "laity," who "have no toleration for anything of that kind." To the "medical expert," however, the subject was "strictly a scientific matter of professional interest and of great importance." Comstock added: "Until recently, little has been said upon this subject in text-books of insanity." Krafft-Ebing's book on "psychopathic" sexuality was described.

The German term "Urnings" referred to those who were sexually stimulated only by their own sex. It applied to those

> who indulge in unnatural sexual practices. But it especially includes sensuality and sexual desire of one female for another, and a disgust for a male. The same may be said for males. . . .

Krafft-Ebing, it was said, describes the "Lesbian Love"—(tribadism), saphismus, cunnilingus, fellators, paedicatio mulierum [anal intercourse with women], sadismus, masochismus and fetischismus.[171]

(Comstock cited one example of "cruelty" in which a male decapitated a "live chicken, a duck, a rabbit or a dog" in the presence of a female lover. He also mentioned "Jack the Ripper.")[172]

"There exists a mysterious bond of psychological sympathy" between "sexual perverts," declared Comstock.

> Instances have been authenticated to me where such perverts when meeting another of the same sex, have at once recognized each other, and mutually become acquainted and have left in company with each other to practice together their unnatural vices. I am informed by an expert in nervous diseases, that in New York, upon the elevated railroad, these perverts travel and frequently meet others of the same sex, and leave the cars in order to be in each other's private company.[172]

"The sexual function and passion," said Comstock, "are not to be trifled with." For "it is nothing less than the keystone of society." The particular "practices of sexual perverts" could not be described, and were "fit to be studied only by competent medical men." Although "perverts" were "naturally objects of disgust" to the general public, to

> a professional man they excite the deepest sympathy. We have known many cases, sad to say, among the ministers of the Gospel—in high places—who were perverts, and one case not long since in the medical profession.[172]

"Among sexual perverts jealousy is always a prominent passion" (as in the Mitchell case). And among "perverts" "paedicatio," "saphism," "intense violence and the killing of their victims . . . are frequently practiced." The doctor explained: when sexual relations were "practiced in any unnatural manner,"

> Nature will certainly avenge herself upon the offender. Mental disturbance and insanity will often follow.[172]

Comstock concluded: the Alice Mitchell case "must cast its dark shadows far and wide."

MEDICAL

# 1892, January
## Dr. Graeme M. Hammond: "The Bicycle in the Treatment of Nervous Diseases"

A paper in the *Journal of Nervous and Mental Disease,* reported Dr. Hammond's having prescribed bicycle riding as a treatment in four cases of paralysis due to physical diseases, one case of "hysterical paralysis," six cases of "neurasthenia," one case of "abnormally developed sexual appetite," and one case of "sexual perversion."[4][38] (Dr. Hammond, incidentally, was the inventor of "masturbation drawers," which fastened about the waist with steel bands, and into which the tempted patient padlocked himself for the night and hid the key.)

"Case XII," wrote Dr. Hammond,

> a young man, twenty-four years of age, had observed for the past year a gradually increasing desire for members of his own sex. He had been able to control his appetite so far, but was fearful lest it should finally overcome him and lead him to perpetrate acts which were naturally abhorrent to him.[43–44]

For that patient, and for another "whose naturally vigorous sexual appetite had been fed by indulgence, till it seemed as if the gratification of his desires was his only object in life," Dr. Hammond tried the bicycle cure, along with "medicinal treatment."

"Both of these patients,"

> have repeatedly told me that a hard ride would invariably abolish all sexual desire, even if the appetite was at its strongest just before the ride was taken.[44]

MEDICAL

# 1892, February
## Dr. C. H. Hughes: Suicide in St. Louis, Missouri

A suicide in February 1892 was reported in a medical journal essay on "Morbid Eroticism."[5] Besides guilt, the dead man's letters to his unresponsive loved one reveal half-concealed murderous impulses; suicide was evidently perceived as retaliation against the friend for unrequited love. Conscious self-destructive impulses are also evident; a desire for punishment is clear in this document, as it is in many reports of persons who considered themselves "sinners." Dr. Hughes reported:

a quiet, cultured and gentlemanly appearing young man committed suicide by shooting himself at his room in a hotel in St. Louis. A combination of causes probably led to the despondency which ended in the rash act. Pecuniary embarrassment may have been one of them, but the chief cause, as elicited at the Coroner's inquest, as testified by the male friend of whom he was enamored, was that he had a morbid attachment for that friend. He wrote long letters to him teeming with endearing words. They had roomed together, but at the time of the tragedy they were rooming apart. This was his second attempt at suicide. At the time of his death he carried a locket about his neck containing the picture of the man he loved. He was an educated professional man, kind-hearted and of good address.[541-42]

Letters written by the suicide to his beloved were reprinted to illustrate the "erotopathic condition" of his "mind," and to reveal "the ardent feeling of the . . . disappointed lover." This emotion, said Dr. Hughes, was

much the same feeling as one madly in love normally might have for his heart's idol of the other sex, but never but unnaturally and abnormally for one's own sex, with homicidal and suicidal impulses of maddened desperation added.[542]

The letters revealed that, upon returning from a Cathedral where a Bishop preached, the future suicide thought about his move toward "eternity." The suicide wrote to his beloved, "It is cruel of me to do this act for it will blight your life." He wrote: "I won't wish you happiness";

you will never have that again and you will follow in my footsteps sometime. Men of our natures and sins must have their punishment, and ours comes in a terrible shape.[543]

The suicide wrote: "I have loved you better than you have ever loved or will ever be loved again." Dr. Hughes explained: "Much more than a sentiment of warm friendship" was expressed in these "epistles of passion," with no

remorse for, or full appreciation of, the unnatural character of this perverted love. Though his Christian training had taught him to regard his unnatural passion as a sin.[544]


OBITUARY

# 1892, March 27
## N. Y. Times: The death of Walt Whitman

Whitman's death in Camden, New Jersey, on March 26, occasioned a long evaluation of the poet who had "had the courage to speak out" on "the sexual function and the human body in all its parts."[6] (Although excerpting sections from this long obituary gives them greater prominence and impact than they have in the original, still, these sections were present in *The Times* for those who chose to read them.)

The obituary rather daringly quoted Whitman:

> And I will show of male and female that either is but the equal of the other;
> And sexual organs and acts! do you concentrate in me—for I am determined
> to tell, with courageous clear voice, to prove you illustrious. . . .

"In his intercourse with men and women," Whitman had "impressed his own personality at all times, often rousing great affection, and in many cases lifelong friendships. . . ."

Of those who enjoyed the "oddities" of Whitman's verse, many "fell away when they came to . . . passages in which Whitman contends like an inspired physiologist for the beauty and dignity, nay, the poetry, of functions and organs not mentioned save in medical works."

"The love of man for man, as well as for woman, forms a striking element" in Whitman's "chaotic creed"—and with Whitman "love reaches out beyond humanity and embraces the cosmos with the same passionate affection with which he regards a blade of grass."*

♀  INTIMACY

# 1892, April 27
# Mary Grew to Isabel Howland:
## *"A closer union than . . . most marriages"*

Abolitionist and feminist, Mary Grew (1813–96) wrote to thank a friend, Isabel Howland, for her letter of condolence upon the death of Grew's "beloved friend" and lifelong companion Margaret Burleigh.[7] A note of defensiveness may be explained by the newspaper publicity then being given the Alice Mitchell–Freda Ward relationship (see 1892, January 26). Although Grew's "love" for her friend was traditionally Victorian her idea of "passion" as "sexual" was new. Grew wrote:

> Your words respecting my beloved friend touch me deeply. Evidently you understood her fine character; & you comprehend & appreciate, as few persons do, the nature of the relation which existed, which exists, between her & myself. Her only surviving niece, Miss Ella Jones, also does. To me it seems to have been a closer union than that of most marriages. We know there have been other such between two men, & also between two women. And why should there not be. Love is spiritual; only passion is sexual. . . .

*For later references to Whitman in *The Times* see 1920, November; 1921, August 28; and 1946, February 24. For other Whitman references see the index.

Why do we speak of those who have "gone up higher" as though they were of the past? They live more really, more fully, than ever before; & they love us with a firmer, tenderer, nobler love. . . .

And I have the comfort & confident hope that my time on earth is nearing its end; for I am seventy-eight years old. I try to wait patiently. I do not feel wholly separated from her who was so large a part of my life.

♀ MEDICAL/LEGAL CASES

## 1892, May
## Dr. James G. Kiernan:
## "Responsibility in Sexual Perversion"

In one of his wide-ranging articles on "sexual perversion," Dr. Kiernan focused on the question of legal responsibility.[8] "Most American physicians and lawyers" regarded perversion as a "purely morbid" phenomenon, as a disease causing actions for which there could be no legal responsibility, since the will was impaired.[185] Kiernan stressed that questions of responsibility were not settled.

Referring to a case in which a married woman (passing as male) had married a "young girl," Kiernan wondered if the first woman's husband could have sued the "girl" for alienating his wife's affections; "such suits" had been brought, "but always settled [out of court] to avoid scandal."[208–09] (See 1883, Kiernan.)

About 1872, "a divorce was granted in Chicago" in a case in which one female had married a male in order to be near her female "friend." Such "friendships" had also resulted in legal separations in Indiana.[209]

Two legal cases in which women had murdered their female lovers were described. In one of these the murderer was said to have been "found guilty of 'manslaughter in the heat of passion.' "* Kiernan declared:

> sexual pervert crimes of all types are likely to increase, because of newspaper agitation of the subject, among hysterical females, from a desire to secure the notoriety dear to the hysteric heart. All such cases should be carefully scrutinized, and the mere existence of an alleged perversion should never be admitted as proof of irresponsibility. . . . Each case should be tried on its own merits, and the exact mental state of the accused determined.[210]

Included in this article was a chart of Krafft-Ebing's classification of "abnormal . . . sexual appetite" (from the first English translation of *Psychopathia Sexualis* [Phila.: F. A. Davis, 1892]). Under "Sexual Perversion proper" were listed:

"Psychical hermaphroditism or heterosexuals." Psychical hermaphrodites

---

*See references to the Hattie Deuel case of 1878, at Pokomoke City, Md., p. 165, and to the Mitchell-Ward case, 1892, January 26.

were those in whom "Traces of the normal sexual appetite are discoverable." "Heterosexuals" were those with "inclinations to both sexes," as well as "to abnormal methods of gratification."

"Pure homosexuals" were those whose "general mental state is that of the opposite sex."*

"Effemination or viraginity." In these "the mental state of one sex coexists with the physical attributes of the other."

"Gynandry and androgyny." (These were not defined; apparently the terms' meanings were assumed to be common knowledge.)[198–99]

♀ MEDICAL

## 1892, November
## Dr. Irving C. Rosse: "Perversion of the [Procreative] Instinct"

Rosse, a Professor of Nervous Diseases at Georgetown University, a Catholic institution in Washington, D.C., published a long medical journal article on "genital abuse," or "perversion" of the "genesic" (procreative) "instinct," that is, any orgasm produced by either sex apart from "normal coitus."9[795] (Although Rosse's essay now reads like a sometimes ghoulish, sometimes humorous satire on the most extreme Victorian racism, sexism, and erotic myth-making, its author was, apparently, perfectly serious.†)

"The uncleanness forbidden by God and despised by man" calls "at the present time for more earnest attention from the physician"; it concerned, not only "personal and public hygiene," but also legal medicine, and the "welfare of the family and posterity." While the "moral point of view does not concern us as physicians," claimed Rosse, "bodily and intellectual welfare" was very much "within our province." "Medical men are clearly the only persons qualified to give trustworthy information in regard to sexual matters." There was no other subject about which "people are more anxious to be correctly informed."[798]

"Crimes of sexuality" or "vices" in animals was discussed. "Unnatural crime" existed among prehistoric "troglodytes." Rosse himself had "observed common instances of sexual perversion in dogs and turkeys." A friend of his, having heard that a celebrated stallion ("the favorite on whom the largest bets were made"), had masturbated the day before a big race, "risked his pile on another horse, who by the way came in ahead" (proving, it would seem, that virtue

---

*This use of "heterosexuals" and "homosexuals" is the earliest known to have appeared in an American medical journal. According to this usage "heterosexuals" included those now known as "bisexuals." In 1892, "heterosexuals" and "homosexuals" were not yet thought of as diametrically opposed groups.

†Parts of Rosse's article excerpted in GAH, pp. 40–42, are only briefly cited here, with sections not previously reprinted.

literally paid). Rosse had, in the Washington Zoological Gardens, watched two male elephants, " 'Dunk' and 'Gold Dust,' " entwining their probosces caressingly—with "simultaneous erection of the penis." This kind of osculation, Rosse pointed out, was "prohibited by the rules of at least one Christian denomination."[799]

"*Bestiality,*" or "sodomitical intercourse with animals," was Rosse's next subject.

Rosse then discussed a "band of negro men" of "androgynous" character, raided by the Washington police. "Phallic worship" among Blacks had been described to the doctor by an informant who had studied such "rites" among "lower races." In one such rite, "a big buck" had "allowed his comrades to caress," and even kiss his penis, "decorated with gaily colored ribbons."[802]

"Having spent two seasons among the Eskimo of Bering Strait," Rosse had reason to believe the "sodomitical habit" of "*pederasty*" existed among these people."[802]

"Rectal coitus" between males and female prostitutes, as well as between males and male prostitutes, was common. A "notorious" place of such prostitution, "the Slide," had only recently been broken up by the New York police, following the publicity given to it by the *New York Herald.* (See p. 219 and footnote.)

Rosse also mentioned a "religious hypocrite" living in a small village who had "ruined a number of boys"; three had died, one had committed suicide. In Washington, D.C., a "man with a very pallid complexion" had "enticed messenger boys to a hotel," got them drunk, and "accomplished his fell purpose."[803] A "noted pederast," tried in Philadelphia, had given syphilis to "a dozen or more of his victims." Rosse had observed anal syphilis in a "ward-room boy" who had worked on ships.[804]

Syphilis of the mouth called for the discussion "of a hideous act that marks the last abjection of vice" (oral-genital sex). "So squeamish" were some English-speaking people that they had "no terms to designate the 'nameless crime' that moves in the dark." But Continental writers spoke of the matter; a "quotation from Erasmus shows that *lesbianism* had a place in his thought." (Rosse used "lesbianism" to refer to oral-genital contacts, whether between men and women, or between women.)[804]

Rosse mentioned "the French lesbian novels" *Mademoiselle Giraud ma Femme,* by Adolph Bêlot and *Mademoiselle de Maupin* by Théophile Gautier, and other novels whose subject was "tribadism" and male "perversion." The sale of such literature in the United States was so great "the Post Office Department yearly destroys tons of pornographic literature." He added that "degrading acts tend to spread more and more in the great centres of population."[805]

In Washington, D.C., a doctor friend had told Rosse of treating an "old soldier" with oral syphilis. This "patient with unblushing effrontery did not hesitate to say how it was contracted."

A judge and the police informed Rosse that men indulging in oral sex were frequently arrested in Washington; recently the police had made,

> under the very shadow of the White House, eighteen arrests in Lafayette Square. . . . Both white and black were represented among these moral hermaphrodites, but the majority of them were negroes.[806]

"Years ago," from "a neurotic" female patient "whose conversation showed an extremely erotic turn of mind," Rosse had learned "some particulars" as to the "spread of sapphism."
Cited was "the case of a prostitute,"

> who from curiosity visited several women that make a speciality of the vice, and on submitting herself by way of experiment to the lingual and oral manoeuvers of the performance, had a violent hystereo-cataleptic attack from which she was a long time in recovering.[807]

The doctor also knew of a "woman who practices the orgies of tribadism with other women" after getting them drunk.[807] A professor of obstetrics at Columbia College had told Rosse of "a case of tribadism" in which "a young, unmarried woman became pregnant through her married sister," who simulated "the male act on her just after copulating with her husband."

But why publicize "details of such a repugnant subject"? Physicians and lawyers needed to be able to "pass upon" an individual's "responsibility," to decide if "a certain act is the result of an unsound mind or merely one of a libidinous nature." If "We fight against anarchy, nihilism and cholera," why not "root out acts" that attack "general health" and destroy "moral essence"?

"There is at the present time" a "powerful influence" in "immoral publications, indecent advertisements, and newspaper articles," as well as printed pictures, which tend to concentrate "the thoughts on the lower portions of the genital tract," and "to bring about much sexual depravity." Such publications cause "great anxiety," disseminate "immorality," and teach "crime." Rosse mentioned the "Sapphic literature that is yearly vomited forth by the Continental printers," causing railway bookstalls in Belgium to be closed. He also cited the action in England against Charles Bradlaw and Annie Besant for publishing a book on birth control, and the "recent" prosecution of Zola's *Nana* (which referred to lesbianism).

A U. S. Post Office official had told Rosse that "so much obscene matter comes through the Dead Letter Office that he is obliged to prohibit women clerks from opening the mail."[809]

Rosse was opposed to any laws interfering with liberty. How then were those guilty of "unnatural and immoral practices" to be treated? He advocated "judicious education with the employment of appropriate medical and surgical measures."[809–10]

Self-control during puberty was especially important. Since most "insanity" was linked to "defective inhibition" Rosse believed young people "of all classes" should be taught "self-restraint." To this end "manly exercises" and athletics were useful.

To be sure, we do not want to make record breakers of our boys, but who would not rather have his son contract a bad heart or hernia than to see him a sexual pervert?

Rosse concluded with a line of poetry warning: "Ill fares the land . . . Where wealth accumulates and men decay."[810]

PERSONAL TESTIMONY

## c. 1892
## Lincoln Steffens: Jacob Riis and "fairies"

In his autobiography (1931), journalist and social critic Lincoln Steffens recalled a scene between newspaper man and reformer Jacob Riis of the New York *Evening Sun,* and Riis's assistant, Max Fischel[10]:

Crime was a business and criminals had "position" in the world, a place that was revealing itself to me. I soon knew more about it than Riis did, who had been a police reporter for years; I knew more than Max could tell Riis, who hated and would not believe or even hear some of the "awful things" he was told. Riis was interested not at all in vice and crime, only in the stories of people and the conditions in which they lived. I remember one morning hearing Riis roaring, as he could roar, at Max, who was reporting a police raid on a resort of fairies.

"Fairies!" Riis shouted, suspicious. "What are fairies?" And when Max began to define the word Riis rose up in a rage. "Not so," he cried. "There are no such creatures in this world." He threw down his pencil and rushed out of the office. He would not report that raid, and Max had to telephone enough to his paper to protect his chief.

There were fairies; there were all sorts of perverts; and they had a recognized standing in the demi-world; they had their saloons, where they were "protected" by the police for a price. That raid Riis would not report was due to a failure of some one to come through with the regular bit of blackmail overdue.[223–24]

PERSONAL TESTIMONY

## 1893, May 8
## Frederik Hammerich: Danish emigrant to the United States

Among those who emigrated to the United States as forced or voluntary exiles from their own lands, the "homosexual" has not often been mentioned.

A "scandal" involving Frederik Hammerich began in 1893, in Copenhagen, Denmark, when a seventeen-year-old working-class male, Anders Andersen, was arrested and charged with having had sexual relations with an eleven-year-old boy.[11] During interrogation Andersen said that he himself had been "immorally treated" (though "not unwillingly") for the first time the previous summer by two men, Martin Kok and Frederik Hammerich.

Martin Kok, an impoverished author of patriotic poetry and plays, was soon arrested. The sensationalistic Danish press strongly hinted that, as a boy, Kok had himself been seduced by Hans Christian Andersen, the author (who had died in 1875). This allegation was denied by Kok.

Frederik Hammerich, twenty-five years old, the other accused, fled from Denmark to Sweden two weeks before news of the scandal appeared in the press. A museum curator, and member of a well-known and respected family of civil servants (his father was a judge), Hammerich was able to raise money to emigrate to America. On February 4, 1893, from a temporary hide-out in Helsingborg, Sweden, Hammerich wrote to his elder brother Kaj, a junior civil servant in the Danish Ministry of Justice. Hammerich said he had booked passage to the U. S. and would leave in a few days.

For some reason, Hammerich's departure was postponed and he went back to Copenhagen. On February 18, he appeared, apparently voluntarily, before a

Frederik Hammerich, 1893. This photograph was taken while he stayed in Helsinborg, Sweden, just before he emigrated to the United States (Collection of Charts and Pictures, The Royal Library, Copenhagen).

judge in the city's criminal court. He confessed to having been masturbated by Anders Andersen, but denied having reciprocated. Hammerich was not detained, probably because of his family connections. On March 1, Hammerich's brother Kaj appeared in court and said that Frederik had left Denmark and was on his way to the United States.

That same day, Frederik Hammerich wrote to his brother from Sweden: "My nerves have been very bad and I still could not get any sleep." It would be best not to see his parents before leaving for the United States: "I am not heartless, but you will understand how hard it is for me to see any of my family." Hammerich thanked his brother for his help.

Frederik Hammerich's next extant letter was written to his brother Kaj, and Kaj's wife, Louise, from Taylorville, Illinois, on May 8, 1893. Frederik thanked them for their "dear letters," and said "I am now well and strong." His "courage with regard to the future" was "unweakened." He had "unfortunately not yet found work," but, because of language problems, he had only started to look for employment a few days earlier. He planned to teach French and German when his own English improved. "If I can stay as interesting as I am now," he wrote,

> I shall get a lot of pupils. You must remember that Taylorville is only a small town. And small towns are in many ways very much alike, even if they are located thousands of miles apart. My arrival here has been a big event, and so far the young ladies have been desperately wooing me in a very energetic American way. . . . They are very much like provincial girls at home regarding bad taste in dress and manners.

Both Danish and American young women were "excessively splendid," but the Americans "seem to be more able, fresher and stronger." He would not stay in Taylorville more than a year, as he could not utilize his knowledge of language,

> and I shall never really be at ease in this place. The town is too small, people are too inquisitive and prying and—there is too much religion. Twice every Sunday I go to church. . . .

He also attended other religious meetings at least three times a week. "I don't drink liquor any more," he said, "but as long as I smoke and do not join any of the 8 halfwitted or totally crazy religious communities (can you believe it, 8 churches for 4000 people)," he would remain an outsider. "One of the good qualities that I believe I possess is tolerance and deference for the convictions of others. But I demand peace in my own territory. That I shall never get here."

Hammerich referred to one "exceptionally good and honest fellow, of whom he was fond, though the man had "never heard of anything but Temperance and Free Methodism." The Dane also described a Free Methodist clergyman with a face like a knife and a will of iron. He is determined to have me converted. But I will not be converted into his faith, which is hard and cold, and only ardent in intolerance and fanaticism, which kills all life and joy on earth, considers everything not directly connected to Faith as sin and danger, rejects art, science, knowledge, love of parents, love of brothers and sisters, etc.

Hammerich said that "Mama writes to me today" that religion in Illinois must be like one of the Danish fundamentalist movements. Hammerich disagreed. Danish fundamentalism, he declared, was "pure fun and games compared with Free Methodism." But he told his brother and sister-in-law:

Don't think I am crushed by this. I won't let myself become bothered, and I keep as much to myself as possible, but sometimes it is undeniable that I feel a little closed in.

Hammerich asked his brother to collect his royalties for a play and some articles, and requested a picture of his brother's son, "my beloved Little Boy. . . . I often long for him, Louise will understand better than anybody. Next to our parents he is the one that I miss the most." The exile thought of his brother and sister-in-law with both sorrow and

comfort and joy, because I know that you have forgiven me, and that you think of me with forbearance and love. . . . I have no Little Boy here but a little Frank, with whom I have made friends, only in reality he is an atrocious child. . . . Just now he is howling and screaming: Freeeederik, and kicking his mother because she won't let him disturb me. When he is well-behaved —which he seldom is—he is irresistible, especially when he discovers that there is a common word that I don't understand and screams: Oh, Goodness gracious!

Hammerich ended: "Good by for now, dear Louise and Kaj. We shall always stick together."

Frederik Hammerich's letters to his family in Denmark continued until 1917. For about five years he worked as a clerk in the Pullman Car Company in Portland, Oregon. From about 1900, he lived in San Francisco, where his main social contacts seem to have been with that city's colony of Danish immigrants. Other letters to his brother do not tell much about the exile's life, but it appears to have been lonely and difficult. When Hammerich's father died in 1916, the obituary in a Copenhagen newspaper mentioned all his sons who held important positions in Danish society. Frederik Hammerich, the outcast, was not mentioned.

On January 11, 1919, an item in a Danish newspaper reported "The Death Of A Copenhagener In San Francisco." The fifty-one-year-old Frederik Hammerich had committed suicide by gassing himself. The story said "The life of Frederik Hammerich was storm tossed and troubled," but nothing about the scandal that had exiled Hammerich was mentioned. The obituary quoted a brief autobiographical account of Hammerich's life in the United States which he had written, in 1911, for the twenty-fifth reunion publication of his high school:

As happens to everybody coming to this country I have been tossed about to a degree that would dizzy every Dane who stayed at home, but have usually landed on my feet. I am and have been one thing today, another yesterday, and something different a year later. . . . I have been cast from the Atlantic to the Pacific, from the Mexican Gulf to the border of Canada, but have now reached the city that I love, San Francisco, where I have lived through joy and sorrow, from earthquake to reconstruction. Life in America is hard, for many crushing, but it is extremely interesting, and I am glad that I have been given the opportunity to live it.

Hammerich's Danish obituary concluded: "Apparently this unsettled life had become too difficult for the aging man, since he chose to end it himself." A final line declared: "Frederik Hammerich was unmarried."

♀ MEDICAL

# 1893, June 27
## Dr. C. H. Hughes: Delia Perkins and Ida Preston, Indianapolis, Indiana

An essay on "Morbid Eroticism" reported that two "girls" had been arrested in Indianapolis on June 27, 1893:[12]

Their names are given as Delia Perkins and Ida Preston. They had run away from home together because of their love for each other. Delia had cut off her hair and offered it for sale in order that she might obtain money on which to help defray the joint expenses of herself and the loved Ida. When Delia's step-father was summoned by the Chief of Police to come for his run-away daughter, she threatened to kill him, and when he came treated him coldly. To her step-father's importunities to go back home with him she only finally agreed on promise of being permitted to see Ida whenever she should desire to, imprinting burning kisses upon the cheeks and lips of the paramour of her own sex on parting. These two devoted girls had been together almost constantly since their departure from home and they had not been in the company of gentlemen. The intense and active passion seemed to be on the part of Delia, Ida being reported as regarding the matter "as a huge joke." When Delia was returned home the following colloquy took place with her mother (now Mrs. Mendenhall):
MOTHER: "You will not run away again, will you?"
DELIA: "Not if you let me go with Ida."
MOTHER: "That I will not do."
DELIA: "Then I will kill myself and you will be responsible."
MOTHER: "Don't say that. We will try to make you happy and you must try to forget all about Ida. I can't understand why you do not forget this foolish fancy and fall in love with a man and marry him."
DELIA: "I do not care for the best man that ever walked, and never will.

Ida is the only one I ever loved and I will continue to love her until I die, and if we are not allowed to go together *I will kill myself and her, too.*"

The other young woman, Ida Preston, told reporters:

"I didn't want to leave home, . . . but Delia told me she loved me so dearly that if I did not consent to go with her she would kill herself and me, too. I like the girl, but don't believe I care as much for her as she does for me."

♀ MEDICAL

## 1893, July
## Dr. Edward C. Mann: *"Morbid attachments for persons of the same sex"*

In a discussion of "Morbid Sexual Perversions As Related To Insanity," Dr. Mann spoke of an "aberration of the moral faculties" in which "perverted feeling and conduct" was "never absent," and the "wishes, inclinations, attachments . . . are morbidly changed."[13] He continued:

I have known of this morbid sexual love for a person of the same sex, starting, probably, with some one girl, of a faulty nervous organization, in a young ladies' seminary—almost assumed the form of an epidemic (genesic erethism)—and several young ladies were brought up before the faculty, and were told that summary dismissal would follow if this were not at once dropped. The terrible mischief which was thus arrested, and doubtless originated with an insane girl, in this case evidently assumed an hysterical tendency in others not insane, but who might have easily become so if they were neuropathically endowed, as they doubtless were. Sometimes, in cases of masturbation, perverted sexual feelings, such as forming morbid attachments for persons of the same sex are quite marked. Dementia and death is generally the end of these cases. . . .[474–75]

MEDICAL/RESISTANCE

## 1893, July
## T.: Dr. Krafft-Ebing's *Psychopathia Sexualis*

Brief reviews of the first American edition of Krafft-Ebing's *Psychopathia Sexualis, with Special Reference to Contrary Sexual Instinct* (1892) and the German edition (1893) appeared in a St. Louis medical journal.[14]

The reviewer gently chastised Krafft-Ebing for

criticising the case of Dr. G. (pages 301–303 [German ed.]), who defended his homo-sexualism before the police magistrate of Graz, Austria, and claimed protection, or at least tolerance for his mental abnormality.

Krafft-Ebing hesitated "to openly defy public opinion." (The point was that Krafft-Ebing did not fully defend the decriminalization of that "homo-sexualism" he had defined as an inborn mental condition rather than as crime.)

The reviewer otherwise praised Krafft-Ebing's volume for "delicately" treating the "multiform deviations of the sexual appetite" and "erotic feelings," and for translating into Latin those sections "where modesty would be offended by the bold revolting detail of scientific fact." The "wrong exercise of the sexual passion" was a legitimate matter "of medical and juridical study."

The reviewer endorsed the book even though Krafft-Ebing was said not to distinguish clearly enough between "sexual perversions" resulting from "repression of the normal exercise of the natural sexual instinct," and those caused by the "tyrannical impulsions of a diseased organism."

This book, warned the critic, was "to be read by the sexually mature and psychically balanced." Its "examples and personal histories would prove psychopathic poison" to the "prurient curiosity of that morbid sexual element, which too extensively abounds in modern social life." The "alienist" could not refrain from studying "the foulest phases of psychical life," just as the general practitioner could not fail to examine "excrement and other unwholesome excretions." "Revolting details" had to be recognized as part of the "perverted psychical symptomology of [the] morbid organism, as vice and crime are necessarily subjects of study to the moral economist."

Krafft-Ebing's work would "bring light into spheres of life that many of us scarcely dared to speak of heretofore," providing understanding of facts "whose existence was denied." The autobiographies of "sexual psychopathics" collected by Krafft-Ebing referred to realities

> found within the reach of every practising physician. Some recent occurrences in the States . . . are the best proof of this, and show the necessity for the medical man, as well as for the lawyer, to study works like this.

♀ MEDICAL

## 1893, August 16
## Dr. F. E. Daniel: Castration of "sexual perverts"

"Should Insane Criminals or Sexual Perverts be Permitted to Procreate?" was the title of a paper read by Dr. Daniel at a medical-legal congress, and reprinted in several medical journals.[15]*

Dr. Daniel, of Austin, editor of the *Texas Medical Journal*, argued that in fifty years it would cost too much "to provide asylum and medical treatment" for the many offspring of those in whom insanity was latent, and those of "the lower

*Excerpts from this document in *GAH*, pp. 135–37, omitted details of political significance included here.

classes, particularly negroes," known for their "extremely common" illicit intercourse.[370]

"All medical men" recognized that the "healthy" "sexual sense" was a "great incentive to action, to the acquisition of property, the struggle for social eminence, and the foundation of a home." But few understood that sexual "anomalies or perversions" were expressed in "unnatural acts"—like masturbation—acts affecting future generations.[370–71] The committer of such "sexual sins"

> should be rendered incapable of a repetition of the offense, and the propagation of his kind should be inhibited in the interest of civilization and the well-being of future generations.

"Hanging, electrocution, or burning at the stake" did not prevent sexual crimes, said Dr. Daniel, arguing against capital punishment for such acts. Instead of execution, "castration is proposed." The doctor (including women as well as men in his proposal) added: "In light of the Alice Mitchell case, it might be well enough to . . . asexualize all criminals of whatever class."[376–77]

Castration to prevent "the hereditary transmission of either disease or vices of the constitution" had "recently" been advocated by doctors William A. Hammond, G. Frank Lydston, and Orpheus Everts. Doctors Blummer, Gardner, and White are also said to have advocated or used castration to "cure" epilepsy.[378]

Because of the insanity and irresponsibility of those who committed sexual crimes, Dr. Daniel, "would substitute castration as a penalty for all sexual crimes or misdemeanors, including confirmed masturbation."[378]

If ovary removal cured hysteria in women, "castration will, by obliterating the [sexual] sense, relieve some . . . of the disturbances of the mind [in men]." Castration "would be an advisable hygienic measure in habitual masturbation . . . by arresting the wasting of vital force by seminal losses."[379]

Daniel argued: "We are warranted" in "making the experiment on a scale large enough to test the operation as a therapeutic measure." He criticized the "outcry" that had recently forced Dr. Joseph Price to stop the "experiment" of removing the ovaries of women in a Pennsylvania hospital on the grounds that "being presumably insane, these women could not give their consent." The "scheme of our government, and the tendency of our civilization" was "to foster the criminal and mentally defective classes." He referred to that class which, in all large cities, propagated a large number of idiots, lunatics, and criminals.[379]

Those who "outraged society, and forfeited all other rights, civil, religious and political," should not have a right to procreate. "Is it not a remarkable civilization," asked Daniel, "that will break a criminal's neck, but will respect his testicles?"[380]

It was a "peculiar political organization" that entrusted lawmaking "to men who know nothing about the laws of health." Those who do "know better than any other class—physicians—are rarely ever called in counsel in framing laws."[380]

The doctor had recently discussed with Governor J. S. Hogg, of Texas the "legality of castrating a patient as a therapeutic measure." Hogg had assured the doctor of the "legal right" of an insane asylum superintendent "to castrate a patient for mental trouble." The superintendent had "the same right to castrate a patient as he would have to bleed him in the arm, or to amputate a limb, or do any other operation."

"But it is not alone in [insane] asylums that castration should be done." Castration should also be done in prisons, "as a penalty for sexual crimes," or "misdemeanors." Castration "will have a more powerful restraining effect on the rapist than does hanging, burning at the stake, or electrocution."[381]

To create a "Sanitary Utopia," said the Texas doctor, "Preventive Medicine" should bring to "the breeding of people the principles recognized . . . by every intelligent stock raiser in the improvement of cattle." In Daniel's "humble judgment the substitution of castration" for the "cruel execution of criminals" was the "first step" in such a "reformation."

Dr. Daniel declared:

> Rape, sodomy, bestiality, pederasty and habitual masturbation should be made crimes or misdemeanors, punishable by forfeiture of all rights, including that of procreation; in short, by castration, or castration *plus* other penalties, according to the gravity of the offense.[381]

He closed with a plea for a more "unreserved intercourse" between "physicians" and "jurists" to secure the enactment of laws "consonant with a more advanced state of medico-legal knowledge."[381–82]

♀ NEWS REPORT

# 1893, October 21
## *The* [New Orleans] *Mascot:* "Sodom and Gomorrah Discounted"

Under the heading: "Good God! The Crimes of Sodom and Gomorrah Discounted," a New Orleans periodical linked the Alice Mitchell–Freda Ward case and "A Shocking State of Sin in Our Midst."[16]

"For several years past, disgusting stories have been hinted at, in which men were the participants." But when the "full story" of the Mitchell–Ward case "became known to the public"

> indignation and astonishment filled the land. Medical men and others wrote several works on what they were pleased to term a feminine mania. Many persons read the mildly written newspaper reports, . . . others read the medical stories. . . .

PRICE 5 CENTS

THE MASCOT.

"AS SOON AS SHE WILL BE WITH YOU BAD LUCK WILL DISAPPEAR."
ACT 1ST. SCENE 2nd.

TWELFTH YEAR.    NEW ORLEANS    Oct. 21, '93    NUMBER 609

# GOOD GOD!

## The Crimes of Sodom and Gomorrah Discounted.

*The Mascot*'s editors reported a local "story of the love of two women—licentious, horrible love." One of the "girls" attracted

all eyes as she walks Canal street. She is one of the most beautiful girls in the city. She is virtuous—so far as repelling the advances of men, but she is viler than the most lost harlot on Basin or Burgundy street.

The "orgies she and her chosen friend indulge in" had been described in *The Mascot* office, but "modesty" prevented publication of the "disgusting practices."

... One of the girls, not the one in the photographic establishment, recently called on a friend of hers, a grass widow [a woman separated from her husband], and told her of the fine time she had with the photograph girl.

The widow submitted "to the vile passions of her friends."

Then—oh what pen could describe what took place. We have the story from an eye witness. ... The young girl approached the widow and said "Oh! what a beautiful form you have." She then said "I wish you would let me see you without your clothes." Well, the widow consented—and—

The picture on *The Mascot*'s front page "but feebly tells the tale of what we wish to describe."

♀ MEDICAL

# 1893, October
# Dr. C. H. Hughes: "Erotopathia—Morbid Eroticism"

In a paper read before the Pan-American Medical Congress's section on "Mental and Nervous Disease," Dr. Hughes, editor of the influential *Alienist and Neurologist,* recommended the life incarceration and castration of "sexual perverts."[17] Focusing on what he called, variously, "homo-sexuality," "homo-prostitution," and persons called the "lesbian lover," and the "homo and hetero sexual," Hughes discussed the alleged social causes and effects of "Erotopathia."[532, 535, 557, 563]

"Within the past few years" the "neurologist" and "alienist" had "become familiar with many strange morbid perversions" of the "erotic sentiments" which need to be "classified" by "Science" according to their relation to society, morals and law.[531]

Dr. Hughes distinguished "erotomania" ("perversion of the proper and natural human passions") from those "ardent affections of the heart" which were "chaste and honorable."[531–32] "Normal and natural love" was linked with "reproduction," physically and psychically.[533] "Normal love cherishes the loved one. Abnormal passion ... considers not the welfare of its object so much as the wishes of self," and "destroys" both body and mind, if necessary.[535] The Alice Mitchell case was cited.[537, 544–53]

There were many "neuro-erotics" whose "mental derangement" was marked enough to be "classed as insane." But these individuals could perceive their "perverted erotic feeling" was "wrong," and could understand the "propriety" of "resisting it." These "erotics feel abnormally but still act rightly." If their "malady" progressed they might "need from without the restraint they cannot exert from within." Because of their "erratic, perverse and destructive erotic inclinations" they might need the "seclusion from the world which a properly organized asylum for the insane affords."[539]

The "tendency of the age" was to lessen,

> if not abolish, moral restraint. Freedom—physical, political, moral, mental, is the shibboleth of the people, and hordes of neuropaths now come to the surface, that in other ages when laws were more rigid, were suppressed.[539–40]

The "sentiment of moral non-restraint or relaxation of self-control" was producing much insanity. "Sexual sensualism" in those "congenitally predisposed" brought on "perversion of the genital instinct." When religion stopped regulating "moral conduct," when "self-gratification" and the "pursuit of pleasure, without prudent restraint," were the aim of many, people became

> startlingly deformed in mental feeling. . . . He or she develops into an erotic pervert or an erratic lover of his own sex—an *"erninger"* [*Urning*], a *"maedchen schmecker"* [literally—girl-taster], a *sadist, fetichist, tribadist,* etc.—an unnatural libidinous lover of a fellow-being organized like himself or herself, an erotopath. . . .[540–41]

Two suicides "personally" known to Dr. Hughes were reported:

> A lawyer of my acquaintance, of ability, but of lowly heritage, he never cared to disclose, acknowledged to perverted homo-sexual instincts and impulsions, and finally, under mortification and chagrin, and fear of disclosure of his perverted instincts, committed suicide. Cases like these are common.[541]

The second suicide had occurred in St. Louis, in February 1892 (see).

Every inquiry into "morbid eroticism" should distinguish between a "perversion of pure Platonic love without genesiac [genital] concomitants" and "perverted lusts or . . . unregulated licentiousness, dissociated from love."

> Medical science must . . . determine for society and for the State, what is restrainable and vicious, and what are the morbid and resistless organic impulses of these *bizarre* eroto-sexual states.[561]

"Every study of morbid eroticism" should distinguish between "love and lust," between "healthy" and "perverted . . . sexual passion." Such distinctions were "necessary to a proper understanding of those historical and every-day recorded instances of pure but perverted Platonic affection and those oft recurring . . . reversions of sexual love into murderous hate, . . . so often chronicled in the public press." Examples included the "excesses of Heliogabalus" and "the Lesbian love" (unspecified).[562]

Much could be done for the "victims of *libido morbosus* by treatment." The "mind and feelings" could be "turned back into normal channels, the homo and hetero sexual changed into beings of natural erotic inclination." ("Hetero sexual" here meant persons now called "bisexual.") Hughes added:

> medical, hypnotic and in some cases surgical remedial treatment is hopeful of curative results in acquired sexual perversion, but only of repressive results in hereditary sexual perverts.
>
> Society, organized into government, for the better security of person and property and personal and collective happiness, is specially concerned in the maintenance of chastity and morals. . . . The State . . . cannot be too careful as a protector of morality . . . for sexual crimes are on the increase in our modern civilization. . . . Considerations of psychical sanitation demand alert attention to this subject from physicist [physician], moralist and jurist. The moral pestilence is in our midst, Sodom and Gomorrah are revived and surpassed.[563]

The "law ignored psychiatry," "dealing violently" with "sexual vice," punishing the sexual criminal, then allowing him "to return and pollute society." "Psychiatric science," knowing how deep rooted "sexual perversions" might be,

> asks for their victim's perpetual sequestration from society and a radical asexualizing surgical procedure, such as the father of Heloise visited on Abelard [castration].
>
> Inspired only by the spirit of vengeance, Law protects society by punishing the criminal, while Medicine would mercifully protect both society and the maimed victim of a sexually and mentally degenerate organism.[563]

Hughes's "Appendix" reprinted several Krafft-Ebing cases of female and male same-sex love, and concluded with a

> record of a mild form of intermediate sexual perversion in the person of one of my servants, a colored male creole, who has more womanly than manly attributes.

This individual delighted in "wearing his hair as long as it will grow," and wore "a woman's high-heeled gaiter button shoe." In his "household work, waiting on table, etc., he prefers a woman's long white apron." He had "a special fondness for ribbons, flowers, and kid gloves," admired women's dresses, "keeps a picture of himself and a male friend in his room," and "keeps his wife's clothing." He had been married, "but says women are frauds, yet in strange incongruity shows plainly . . . that he would have been a woman if he could."[577]

# 1894, April
## Dr. Havelock Ellis: "The Study of Sexual Inversion"

In his earliest-known article on sex published in an American medical journal Dr. Ellis summarized the history of the discourse on what he called "sexual inversion," "homosexuality," and "homosexual love."[18][150, 155]*Ellis clearly stood in this article for a less negative view of "sexual inversion" than that expounded by Krafft-Ebing.

Focusing on the doctors who had put the study of "sexual inversion" on a "scientific basis," Ellis called Krafft-Ebing's "the best-known book on the subject of sexual perversion." Ellis gently criticized the Austrian doctor; although Krafft-Ebing's "rather fine spun classification has doubtless contributed to give precision to the subject and to advance its scientific study," it was doubtful if that classification could be maintained in the future. Krafft-Ebing was praised for his "enthusiasm" in "conquering a great neglected field of morbid psychology, which rightly belongs to the physician."[152–53]

The book (in German) by Dr. Albert Moll on "contrary sexual feeling" (1891) was praised by Ellis as "beyond doubt the most important discussion of sexual inversion which has yet appeared." Moll "For the first time . . . entirely clears away the ancient prejudices and superstitions surrounding sexual inversion." Not all sexual inverts possessed a "hereditary neurotic trait," Moll suggested. That doctor did not stress "the morbid character of sexual inversion," and excluded "insanity." He "shows excellent judgment . . . in rejecting any minute classification of sexual inverts." Moll emphasized the congenital origins of "psycho-sexual hermaphroditism and homosexuality," and ridiculed "the supposed influence of 'vice.' "[154–55]

This "psychological anomaly," Ellis concluded, must be studied "among the general population" (not just in special populations, like criminals). "Inversion" may "sometimes be found" in persons with a

> high degree of intellectual and artistic ability, and where it does not easily fall under the physician's observation.[157]

*For additional discussion of this article by Ellis see p. 148.

♀ MEDICAL/RESISTANCE

## 1894, June
## Dr. James G. Kiernan:
## "Psychical Treatment of Congenital Sexual Inversion"

An essay on the treatment of "sexual inversion" indicates that inverts were adapting the doctors' sickness theory to their own purposes of ego enhancement.[19] And non-inverts, reading the new medical works on inversion, were suffering the first recorded "perversion" panics, fearing their own latent inversion.

Speaking of inverts, Dr. Kiernan warned his fellow doctors of a

prevalent tendency on the part of these anomalies to regard themselves as "interesting invalids" to whom sympathy is a duty.

"This notion is decidedly opposed to proper management of the abnormal symptoms."

"Certain sexual neurasthenics," who studied the literature on "the sexual organs" had come to believe themselves "victims of sexual perversion." Two males cases of Kiernan's, "during the past year," were "sexual hypochondriacs, who had formed the notion that they were incipient sexual inverts despite normal coitus and excitation by female images."[293]

Successful treatment of even "congenital sexual inversion" was possible. This was indicated by an update of a female case history first reported by Kiernan ten years earlier (see 1884, May, and *GAH*, pp. 134–35). This woman, attracted to other females, and treated with anaphrodisiacs and "intellectual training," had married the brother of her female lover. After this female lover had died the woman had borne a child, and had now transferred her love to her daughter and her husband. Her history indicated that "there is entirely too much sympathy wasted on these patients, since sympathy to them is as poisonous as to the hysteric." (Sympathy might encourage inverts to find positive meaning in their condition.) "Insistence on the morbidity of the pervert ideas," "prohibition of sexual literature," and "anaphrodisiac methods cannot but benefit." These patients "will not 'will' to be cured while they are subjects of sympathy."[294–95]

RESISTANCE/INTIMACY

1894, September 16
## Robert Allan Nicol to Edward Carpenter:
*"My loves, men & women, come and want me,*
*and I give gladly"*

The letters of Robert Nicol, from Weimar, Placer County, California, to Edward Carpenter, in Sheffield, England, provide a glimpse into the American life of a mystically inclined, socially conscious English immigrant between 1894 and 1896.[20]*

Although more a spiritualist than a practical reformer, Nicol had been friends with a group of independent socialists in Bristol, England, when they were struggling to reconcile the conflicting claims of personal, sexual, economic, and political issues. Nicol was interested in men and women reconstructing their relationships to their bodies, as well as to their social world. He expressed a vague, romantic ideal of a social transformation making the world congenial to beauty, love, eroticism, and other "spiritual" values.[21]

Although Nicol's letters are ambiguous as to his exact relationships, his eroticism clearly included attraction to both men and women. Whether or not his love and affection for men—such as that expressed for his artist friend, Harris Osborn, and for Carpenter—was ever genitally expressed, male-male intimacy is a recurring theme in Nicol's letters. This correspondence also suggests that Nicol had been close to the recently deceased Miriam Daniell, a radical socialist and feminist from Bristol, who had immigrated to the United States with her friend and political comrade, Helena Born.[22]

Nicol's distribution of Carpenter's *Homogenic Love* in the canyons of California, in the 1890s, is an unexpected discovery—reminding us that the influence in the United States of Carpenter's socialism, feminism, and homogenic emancipationism remains to be explored.

Nicol's confused struggle to define and affirm new, positive feelings about the body and eroticism, and his inability to transcend a procreative concept, indicates the difficulties facing even sex radicals in freeing themselves from Victorian standards.

On September 14, 1894, Robert Nicol suggested to Carpenter that he (Nicol) might get a U. S. publisher to reprint Carpenter's three pamphlets, *Marriage, Sex-Love,* and *Woman* (the fourth pamphlet in the series, *Homogenic Love,* was not yet printed). Nicol reported that sale of an American edition of Carpenter's

---

*For other letters from America to Carpenter see excerpts dated 1914, March 27; and 1921, April 4. For U. S. reviews of Carpenter's books see 1899, January; 1902, July 5; 1911, July; 1914, October; and 1916, August 20. For other references to Carpenter see the index.

*Civilization: Its Cause and Cure* had "boomed during the Homestead Strike" (1892), and that it and Geddes and Thomson's *Evolution of Sex* "*have had the largest sale of any* [books] *in the Humboldt Library series.*"[1–2]*

On December 28, 1894, Nicol thanked Carpenter for sending Kipling's "wonderful" *Jungle Book* to Nicol's daughter, Sunrise. Nicol also thanked Carpenter

> for the sandal patterns and directions. Of course I have made a pair for myself and they are a success far beyond my expectations. I took off the sleeves of my shirt but bare arms have not nearly the same radical effect on mind and body that emancipated feet have. One begins to own one's own body at last. Farewell to tailors and shoemakers and the unclean fears emanating from Mrs. Grundy. My ankles are skinned a little with the unusual friction, but I am speedily becoming hardened. Last night, when I was coming down the trail in the dark with Sunrise on my shoulder, I got into a gulch and wrenched my ankle; but that was no fault of the sandals. I have an order from a woman neighbor for a pair, and expect some others soon.

Nicol wrote: "3 women have settled in the Little Codfish Canyon," nearby.

> They are students of the occult and are remarkable women. We go down once a week or so to help them clear and burn brush, and it is very pleasant. They have all come through the marriage ordeal and I guess have learned its lesson.

One of the women "has a wonderful fund of knowledge about the use and control of bodily forces."[6]

Nicol hoped that those in Holmesfield, England, were enjoying Christmas. He added:

> I remember Fox Lane and the road to Chesterfield, for did not Edward C. come home in the dusk with me from Chesterfield one summer evening his arm in mine, And it was sweet?[8]

On July 2, 1895, Nicol asked Carpenter to forward to "Dr. Hawver, Placer County, California," a copy of Carpenter's four pamphlets, *Woman, Sex-Love, Marriage,* and *Homogenic Love.*[2]Dr. Hawver wanted Carpenter's writings after Nicol lent him *Woman.*[6]

Reading in a new edition of *Towards Democracy,* Nicol said he found Carpenter's poems "strong meat," and had to proceed slowly:

> But after all I care for you, dear one, before anything you've written. You contain all; though I am so glad you can write so well for the people.

*Patrick Geddes and J. Arthur Thomson, *Evolution of Sex* (N. Y.: Humboldt Publishing Co., 1890), Humboldt Library of Popular Science, nos. 132, 133, two parts.

Later in his letter Nicol reported:

> Had Harris Osborn, my artist boy, up for a week and had a lovely time. Up
> and down canyons bathing—sun-baths—lots of laughter. He is a quiet great-
> eyed chap—paints and paints away silently: quite a boy and yet *knows.* He
> has been taught much by an old Boston artist who is also a Spiritualist. Some
> day Harris will live here. . . .[6]

In November 1895 Nicol wrote to Carpenter:

> Dear one, I received your lovely letter. . . . How dear you are. Why should
> I love you so much? It is so sweet to have you. Ah! I cannot express my
> feeling to you.

Nicol continued:

> I am beginning to feel the descent to the earth of wonderful forces—of
> all-powerful Love, and I am eager, willing, to let it pour thro' me so that I
> may heal the sick, the nations. It is tremendous. I feel the older order
> doomed to pass away, and right here and now man is going to rise supreme,
> master and lord of Creation. Would that I could take the wretched, sick
> [and] poor to my heart and give them what has come to me. But Love, and
> all their chains, terrors, pains would fall away.[1]

Nicol added: "My loves, men and women, come and want me, and I give gladly
so that they in turn may give also."

Nicol told Carpenter he would like to hear from Gertrude Disc:

> You know I like women as much as men. Can you send me 2 copies of
> *Towards Democracy.* I'll pay you when I've sold them. Every book of yours I
> have is out on loan now. Have you any photos of yourself for Yankee
> comrades, and can I have 2 copies of H. L. [*Homogenic Love*]?

Nicol added: his daughter Sunrise, and Harris Osborn, "my young Yankee Artist
comrade, are here now, and we roam over the mountains day after day."[3]

When will England "cease this mean grab," asked Nicol (in reference to
moves of British imperialists in South Africa or Venezuela). "What a despicable
part she plays everywhere."[4]

In March 1896, Nicol wrote that

> for the first time in my life I could distinguish myself as something apart
> from and superior to my brain and intellect. There swept thro' me a power
> of mastery over my body—not an attitude of rejection, but self-realization.
> . . . I want to realize my body and all its faculties. . . .[1]

Nicol also told Carpenter:

> I long for glorious comradeship—a band of brothers, men and women—
> each with their art, who would co-operate and picture and utter for the race
> —sing the glad day which dawns and lead the people to the reconstruction

of society—and humanity. Of myself I can do so little—as you once said to me—and with my comrades I could do so much.

"Slowly but surely," said Nicol, "the nucleus of the new society . . . is gathering in Young America." He added:

> we young fellows are coming together, tho' we have not met one another yet . . . we are frank and open with each other—as Walt [Whitman] says, no "venereal taint, rum-drinker" or untrue man or woman can come—and tho' we present "no stainless perfections," yet we must be *honest* even in our seeming animalism, weaknesses . . . impurity simply consists in knowingly abandoning reality for illusion. . . .

He who embraced illusion Nicol could but watch from afar: "Then when he is thro' with it—done with the sad and bitter suffering, I take him to my arms again and kiss his tears away forever."[3]

"My dear lover," Nicol told Carpenter, "I am blessed far beyond ordinary mortals for I have the dearest comrades who love me and stand by me firm as rocks."

> I wish you knew Harris Osborn, my Yankee artist (24), great grandfather captain in army of the Revolution, poisoned by the British—you would love him. We shall have our photo taken soon and send you one. Another of my comrades who has been much to me is Edmund Russell, of New York. . . . He is coming to England this summer and wants me to ask if you will receive him. He is . . . a wonderful chap—with a great heart—so great I fear few people will understand him. Gladstone called him the "American Ruskin." I hope someday to work with him, for he understands materials, being an artist, musician, poet, etc. . . .[4]23

Nicol had recently had a mystical insight: Through "marriage" to a woman, a man became aware "of the Soul or Intuition in himself." The woman became "aware of the Intellect or male principle in herself." Their child represented "the union of intellect and intuition." A "married couple might have many children before they saw the significance of their child production, but when they did then the purpose of marriage, sexualism, child-breeding is fulfilled. . . . there is a rank animalism possible, but give me decently trained (unfolded) children, and with sane normal instincts, not damned by Civilization, and we shall quickly ascend . . . to *mastery*. . . ."

> No longer can *priest* or *anyone* cast obloquy on the sexual act, or on woman —on the testes or vagina—or womb, or the sweetness of coition. It also has its place—so long denied. . . .

Nicol added: "Harris and I are wearing sandals and are entering into partnership as 'makers for America.' Nicol, Harris, and Sunrise "hope to take a trip to San Francisco soon on foot. We shall haul Sunrise in a little wagon."[6]

Nicol asked Carpenter to send copies of *Towards Democracy* and the pamphlets *Sex-Love, Marriage, Woman,* and *Homogenic Love* to Edmund Russell and to J. W. A. Scott, a Boston artist. Russell was an "unusual" person, and wielded "a wide influence." He was "writing a series of books and I am very anxious he should know your works."

Nicol ended: "My dear love to you, and a kiss to you my love."[8]

In April 1896, Nicol reported that Edmund Russell had written from New York to say he was " 'deeply moved' " by Carpenter's *Towards Democracy.* Nicol said: "Edmund is one of the strongest men I have ever come across. He was a great friend of Mme. Blavatsky's" (the founder of Theosophy). Edmund Russell "tells me he has 12 books under way just now." Nicol said of Russell: "I love him very much, tho' I have never seen him physically."[1–3]

Nicol and Harris had just returned from San Francisco, where they were introduced to an impressive group of "splendid women" occultists, led by a "Madame Beaumont" (author of "She of the Holy Light"), who was "working out the great Sex question" along Carpenter's lines.[3] Nicol perceived Madame Beaumont,

> not so much as a woman as a sexless unity. When I look at her I am not conscious of sex—rather I feel to be in the presence of one who includes man and woman. It is such a joy to meet such folk.[8]

"How these Yankees like your books!" Nicol told Carpenter. In San Francisco, Nicol "was always introduced as 'the gentleman who knows Ed. Carpenter.' " Nicol heard stories there about people who had taken up Carpenter's ideas —"really you have quite a following in San Francisco alone."[9–10]

Nicol also

> looked up the Socialists in S. F. but did not see much of them. Everybody seems to be expecting a break-up in the U. S. in a year or so. Certainly things seem tending that way. But I'm not afraid.[10]

♀ MEDICAL

# 1894, October ?
## Sarah Stein to Gertrude Stein:
### *"An aversion to the opposite sex"*

A letter to Gertrude Stein from her sister-in-law, Sarah, in San Francisco, discussed Sarah Stein's recent talk with her doctor, Oscar Mayer.[24] Subjects included unmarried women who had sexual intercourse (presumably, with men), masturbation, "abnormal" sex practices that caused an "aversion to the opposite sex," and castration of women and men as a "cure" for such "immoral" practices. Gertrude Stein, who was in Boston studying psychology at Radcliffe, had evidently earlier discussed such matters with her sister-in-law. The casual frankness about sexual matters contradicts the notion of an all-pervasive late-Victorian silence on the subject, especially among women. Sarah Stein wrote:

> Dearest Girl
>     Oh! I have just had such a splendid talk with my dear doctor. . . . Somehow we drifted to the question of self-abuse, and he let forth. How you two would agree! He feels just as you do towards girls and old maids, and says he has every bit as much respect for the unmarried women *he knows* have intercourse and maintain appearances as for the maimed.

The doctor spoke "with great feeling," said Sarah Stein. She added that Dr. Mayer

> has two young girls now under treatment; one of whom he feels convinced he can cure, the other he knows to be hopeless. Both are of fine family. He gives them moral! . . . lectures and *very* strong medicine to dissipate the sensations, and finds the medicine effective in most cases.

Sometimes the lectures failed, and in

> certain cases when the habit is particularly abnormal in its method and by very long practice there follows an aversion to the opposite sex, and marriage itself is of no avail. Then there is but one recourse left, and to that neither male nor female will submit, . . . the removal of either ovaries or testicles.

(A half-sentence, crossed out, began "The cases that have [submitted to castration] are so rare as to.")
    Dr. Mayer had "made a particular study of these physiological phenomena," said Sarah Stein:

> I wish you had spoken to him more freely when you were here, for I am sure he could have told you of many interesting cases that might have helped you in time to come, for, my dear girl, I feel more and more every day that it is the *duty* of such women as you to fortify the weak [unclear word] even before the necessity actually arises.
>     Oscar Mayer is constantly doing missionary work among boys, but finds that he can counsel "purity" only where he is *sure* of the "moral stand point," as he expressed it, otherwise that in itself leads them to the very other extreme.

(A doctor's anti-masturbation counsel might provoke an "immoral" boy to the very act warned against.) "In most cases," reported Sarah Stein, Dr. Mayer counseled " 'healthy intercourse' and early marriage."
    She concluded: "I don't dare to re-read this letter for fear I will tear it up." She hoped that Gertrude would realize "that I am only telling you the things . . . I would naturally talk over with you. . . ."
    On October 11, 1894, in another letter to Gertrude Stein, Sarah Stein

reported that Gertrude's friend Adele had visited that morning, and "We spoke of the subjects that Dr. Mayer and I discussed." Sarah Stein added that a friend

> whose chum is a student at the Art School told me that she had recently met a Miss Hall whom her chum considered the most original member of the class, and admired immensely.

Sarah Stein's friend had

> found Miss Hall repulsive instead of attractive, and was most surprised to find that all the girls there were more or less in love with her, particularly a Miss McCormick. . . .

"Naturally I appeared to be very indifferent" to the gossip about Miss McCormick, said Sarah Stein; "but secretly" she had been "very glad" that Miss McCormick was "not a victim" to the charms of Miss Hall. The hint is that Sarah Stein, herself, was a little in love with Miss McCormick. In any case, Stein made no conscious connection between these "love" relations of females, and the "immoral" and "abnormal" sex practices discussed earlier.


♀ MEDICAL

# 1894
# Dr. Charles G. Chaddock: "Sexual Crimes"

A chapter by Dr. Chaddock on "Sexual Crimes," in a textbook on legal medicine, contained sections on "Rape," "Sexual Abuse of Children," "Sodomy" (including "Pederasty," "Bestiality," and "Tribadism"), "Incest," "Exhibition—Indecent Exposure," and "Sexual Perversion."[25]

The section on "Sexual Perversion" included parts on "Psychosexual Development," "Sexual Paradoxia" (manifestations of sexual desire at ages when "sexual inclination is normally absent"—youth and old age), "Dress-fetichism," "Contrary Sexuality or Sexual Inversion," and "Responsibility." "All manifestations" of the "sexual instinct" not in accord, "directly or indirectly," with "propagation" were "perversions." But some "deviations" were due to "disease," some to "vice."[550]

Since the "majority" of males and females felt "sexually attracted by the other sex" that kind of desire was "normal." Desire for the "other sex" was also "inherent," "conditioned by the anatomical peculiarities which determine sex." And distinctive organs were linked to "corresponding psychosexual characteristics." Any "deviation from the normal relation of [the] anatomical and psychical" was either "congenital" or "acquired."

A detailed evolutionary theory of physical and psychical sex differences followed, with Dr. Chaddock concluding that "the psychical part of sexuality is profoundly influenced" by education "in harmony with the anatomical sex."

In a high state of civilization sex distinctions were, to a child, "less obvious physically," more obvious "in dress and occupation." Under such circumstances "the child learns only comparatively late to classify himself sexually; and . . . the possibility of sexual perversion is increased." The "modesty of cultivated society" also prevented the early recognition of "sexual perversion in the child." This "modesty" was unfortunate since early acquired perversion was less subject to change than a later manifested perversion.[553–54]

"All observers agree," Dr. Chaddock said, that a "neuropathic nervous system" was prerequisite to the "development of sexual instinct for the same sex (homosexuality)." But some other "cause" was also necessary, such as "excessive masturbation, fear of pregnancy, and venereal infection."

Types of "inversion" included that in which "predominating homosexual feeling" was accompanied by "a trace of feeling (heterosexual) for the opposite sex."[570] (That is the earliest known reference in an American medical source to "homosexual" and "heterosexual" feeling—although "heterosexual" does not here yet mean exclusive sexual feeling for an "opposite" sex.)

An "unpublished autobiography" illustrated "a case of sexual inversion of early development." The male writer had "never experienced a trace of sexual feeling for a woman," and did not associate with women because, "knowing my condition I feel so inexpressibly unhappy by reason of it." "My desires are for men exclusively," but he had always been able to control those feelings. As a child he had been "fond of dolls and sewing and other feminine things," even "prior to forming the habit of masturbation." The

> knowledge that I am so unlike others makes me very miserable. I form no acquaintances outside of business, keep mostly to myself, and . . . do not indulge my sexual feelings. . . . I do not want to create the impression that my feelings for my own sex are weak, for they are strong; but I have heretofore had sufficient will-power to restrain them. . . . My desire . . . has always been to handle the genitals of those for whom I feel affection and to have them do the same to me. I am therefore somewhat uncertain as to whether I should consider myself in an active or passive role, but probably passive. This, with embraces, seems to be the extent of my desire.[570–72]

An individual's "perversion of the sexual instinct is not sufficient to establish personal responsibility" for a criminal act, Dr. Chaddock concluded. The majority of such persons controlled their "abnormal sexual impulses." A judgment of irresponsibility for a crime committed by a "sexual pervert," required that it be shown that the crime resulted from a "neuropsychical constitution" which made the individual incapable of acquiring "ideas and feelings which act in opposition to animal impulses," or that disease had overcome such restraints.[572]

♀ MEDICAL

## 1894
## Dr. Allan McLane Hamilton:
### *"A class by themselves . . . recognized by the police"*

An essay on "Insanity in its Medico-Legal Bearings," in the textbook *A System of Legal Medicine,* included a section on "Disturbances of . . . Emotion."[26]

"Unusual" sexual impulses indicated "mental degeneration," found in the "victim of evolutionary insanity." The behavior of the "sexual pervert need not be conspicuous." The "pervert" was generally "fairly strong intellectually," despite a "complete transposal of his normal appetites."

"Many individuals entertain sexual longings only for their own sex"; but Hamilton refused to specify their "form of gratification." He added:

> In many large cities the subjects of the contrary sexual impulse form a class by themselves and are recognized by the police. The men have their balls, where they dress as women even to the details of dainty underwear.
>
> They adopt the names of women, and affect a feminine speech and manner, "falling in love" with each other, and writing amatory and obscene letters. In New York City alone there are not less than one hundred of these, who make a profession of male prostitution, soliciting upon the streets and in parks when they get the opportunity. Physically, many of these men whom I have examined present the stigmata of degenerative insanity, or else physically approach the female type, and hypo- and epispadias [malformations of the penis] are common. The female pervert or *Lesbian* rarely differs from others of her sex, except that the active agent is gross, wears mannish attire, and cultivates masculine habits.

Other "perverts" were masochists, sadists, and fetishists; other related conditions were "mania hysteria," nymphomania, and satyriasis.

NEWS REPORTS/RESISTANCE

## 1895, March 3
### *N. Y. Tribune* and *N. Y. Times:* The trials of Oscar Wilde

Reports in two New York newspapers provide a mini-history of Wilde's downfall, as it was considered fit to print.[27] These stories trace Wilde's libel suit against the Marquis of Queensberry; the Marquis's acquittal and Wilde's arrest for "gross indecency"; Wilde's first trial and the jury's disagreement; Wilde's second trial, imprisonment, release, and death.

These papers' accounts are notable for their reticence concerning Wilde's

Original caption: "Male Sexual Pervert"
(photograph accompanying Hamilton's
article, p. 50; see backnotes).

exact crime, and even the exact charge against him (neither the crime nor the charge was ever spelled out). Curiously, this ambiguity either left readers quite in the dark about Wilde's transgression, or forced them to use their imaginations to make sense of the reports.

Wilde's refusal to escape from England to the Continent (thereby saving the state the embarrassment of trying him, and publicizing sexual matters usually left unspoken) may now be seen as an early, individual form of resistance—resistance by martyrdom. Wilde's insistence on being tried did force into print, however euphemistically, the love that earlier had not dared to speak its name. There appears in *The New York Times,* in 1895, a version of Wilde's "eloquent" (though equivocating) defense of intense "spiritual" relationships between older and younger males. That speech (however ambiguous as to love's body) amounted to a public advertisement for a male-male intimacy then under siege—an endorsement paid for by Wilde's imprisonment, humiliation, and eventual death.

In Wilde's prosecution, the opprobrium accorded his consorting with males of the "lower orders" is clear in the newspaper reports.

On March 3, 1895, the *Tribune* reported the conflict between Wilde and the Marquis of Queensberry. Wilde had charged that Queensberry had "persecuted" him "with the utmost cruelty," and the Marquis had been arraigned. Queensberry's "last act of persecution" was leaving at Wilde's club a card "upon the back of which was written a vile and disgraceful epithet." (The *Tribune* did not report that the Marquis, in a rage over Wilde's intimate relationship with his son, Alfred Douglas, had written: "To Oscar Wilde Posing as a somdomite" [sic]. (The spelling mistake is intriguing. Was sodomy so terrible a word it could not be written? Or was the Marquis simply so angry he couldn't spell?)

The porter at Wilde's club had put the card in an envelope, so "it might not be seen by other persons than Mr. Wilde." The Marquis, his lawyer claimed, had been "acting under the influence of great indignation, based upon abundant provocation."

Wilde's lawyer, charging the Marquis, mentioned that Wilde "was living upon the most affectionate terms with his wife and two sons."[2:3]

On March 10, a *New York Times* story from London said: "It is impossible not to mention" the Wilde–Queensberry affair, scheduled for trial later that month. "A thousand stories are afloat, hinting at various phases of the thing." A "diversion" of "Bohemian London" was listing "the young literary, artistic, and social celebrities whose engagements will probably take them to Brussels toward the end of the month." (The grim joke referred to those who would leave England fearful of being implicated with Wilde, when Queensberry defended himself against the charge of "persecution.")[1:2]

In March, Wilde defiantly visited Monte Carlo with Alfred Douglas. On April 3, Wilde's case against Queensberry for libel began in London.

On April 5, the *Tribune* reported: Wilde had been cross-examined about his relationships with a number of young, working-class males whom he had met at tea parties given by a man named Alfred Taylor. This Taylor had "burned perfumes in the room, but candles and gas were not lighted." Wilde admitted knowing that

Taylor had been arrested. Taylor had introduced him to five young men, none of whom had any trade, profession or employment, so far as [Wilde] knew. He had made them presents of money for the reason that they were poor.

Wilde said of two brothers: He "was not aware that one of them was a valet and the other a groom, both of them out of employment"; he "had given them money." Wilde admitted knowing that Atkins, another youth, was "employed by a bookmaker." Wilde had met Atkins through "a man whose name he declined to give, but handed it up to the Judge" (the name was not reported). Atkins had gone to Paris with Wilde, who "paid the fares." Wilde had also given Atkins presents and money. Another "youth" had stayed with Wilde "in a hotel in London"; Wilde had given him a cigarette case. Still another "youth" known to Wilde was "a servant" to Alfred Douglas.

Though Wilde had at first "succeeded remarkably" in "maintaining composure under the severe cross-examination," he later began "to lose his temper," claiming Queensberry's lawyer had "insulted him." Wilde said: "All the young men who visited him at his rooms called as his guests."

"Before leaving the witness-stand," Wilde had

> explained his liking for the society of young men by saying that he disliked the old and sensible, while the company of the young, happy, careless and original had a wonderful charm. The mere fact of their youth was amazing.

Queensberry's lawyer said his client's sole object in castigating Wilde had been "to save his son" from the writer's "influence."

The management of a newspaper, the *St. James Gazette,* had announced: "Owing to the nature of the testimony" in the Wilde–Queensberry libel suit, the paper would no longer report the case.[3:3]

On April 6, *The New York Times* reported that Wilde's libel case against Queensberry had ended in the Marquis's acquittal. The jury had found: "Queensberry's charges were true and had been made for the public good." Wilde had been arrested and taken to a cell.

Earlier in the day, while the case was still at trial, Queensberry's lawyer had said he would put on the witness stand

> men who would speak freely of their acquaintance with the plaintiff, Wilde. The ages of these men varied from eighteen to twenty-three years. They were of the class of servants and valets, not of Mr. Wilde's station in life, not interested in literature or art, yet they addressed this distinguished dramatist by his first name.

"Overwelming evidence" of Wilde's "immorality" would be produced. After some legal maneuvering by Wilde's lawyer the jury had retired, without the introduction of further witnesses.

When Queensberry's acquittal was announced, he "left the dock amid loud cheers." Wilde was ordered to pay the costs of Queensberry's defense.

Queensberry had told United Press:

> I have sent this message to Wilde: "If the country allows you to leave, all the better for the country; but if you take my son with you I will follow you wherever you go and shoot you."

After the verdict, Wilde (out on bail), Alfred Douglas, and several companions, had gone to a hotel room. Later, Wilde had withdrawn his funds from a bank.

A London evening paper printed a letter written by Wilde. He could not have proved his case, he said, unless Alfred Douglas had testified against his father. But rather than putting Douglas in that "painful" position, Wilde had determined "to bear upon my own shoulders whatever ignominy and shame might result from my prosecution of the Marquis."

Managers of London theaters running Wilde's plays were asked how the case "would affect future business." The closing of *The Importance of Being Earnest*, said one, would put 150 people out of work.

The London *Daily Telegraph* had claimed: The verdict against Wilde also indicted "all the shallow . . . arts by which he attempted to establish a cult and even set up new schools of literature and social thought."

Daniel Frohman, manager of a New York theater where Wilde's *An Ideal Husband* was playing, had defended that play as a "moral one," but had "ordered Wilde's name erased from programmes and advertisements." In Detroit, the actress Rose Coghlan had dropped Wilde's *A Woman of No Importance* from her repetoire.[5:1]

On April 7, *The New York Times* correspondent in London reported:

> It would be impossible to convey to American readers the faintest idea of the terrible fascination with which the Oscar Wilde tragedy has dominated London attention this week. However much might have been one's wishes otherwise, the episode irresistibly forced itself upon people's thoughts and talk, and, like the [American] Beecher–Tilton trial [involving adultery], it broke down a great number of conversational barriers ordinarily maintained in social intercourse. . . . Another week of it would have spread incalculable murrain [plague] throughout society. For this reason alone, there is a good deal of regret among calm-minded folk that the arrest was not postponed till to-day, so as to give [Wilde] a chance to fly from the country last night, as he intended.

Wilde had allegedly been warned of his impending arrest before it occurred.

The reporter concluded:

> Wilde will probably get seven years of penal servitude and die before the first year is finished, unless he finds some way of killing himself before. . . . scores of rival stories are afloat about other men incriminated, including some names known throughout the English-speaking world.[1:2]

On April 7, the *Tribune* reported that bail had been refused Wilde and Alfred Taylor (who had arranged Wilde's meetings with young men). At a pre-trial hearing Charles Parker, nineteen, had testified: Taylor "had told him Wilde was 'good for money.' "

Alfred Wood also testified. He had met Wilde at the Café Royal in 1893:

> He went to Wilde's house. . . . He was drunk at the time. . . . Wilde, he said, had often given money to him, and had visited him at his lodgings, but he strenuously denied any wrong doing. In regard to this point the witness was strongly pressed by the magistrate. . . . Wilde had given £35 to him altogether, on the receipt of which sum he had handed over to Wilde a number of letters written by [Wilde]. Subsequently he went to America, remaining abroad fourteen months.

Wilde had paid for Wood's passage to America.[4:3]

On April 8, a *Times* feature story on "Oscar Wilde's Disgrace" referred to "the depravity" Wilde's "downfall" had made public (but did not further specify that character of that "depravity").

On April 10, the *Tribune* reported that, in St. Louis, Missouri, the librarian had ordered the works of Oscar Wilde—poems, stories and plays—"withdrawn from the Public Library."[3:6]

On April 12, *The Times* reported further testimony in pre-trial hearings. Charles Parker had said he "committed offenses with many persons." The owners of a "private hotel" testified that Wilde "was visited there by a number of young men." One, Atkins, who had gone to Paris with Wilde, was said to have "acted as Wilde's secretary for about half an hour."[5:2]

The *Tribune* of April 20 said that, as further pre-trial hearings continued, "Wilde appeared ill and fatigued." His "hair was ruffled and his general appearance indicated carelessness." Bail had again been denied Wilde and Alfred Taylor.[3:6]

*The Times* of April 24 reported the official indictment of Wilde and Taylor (though no specific charge was mentioned). Wilde's "valuable collection of prints" and art "will be sold at auction tomorrow."[5:2]

On April 27, *The Times* reported that Wilde's and Taylor's trial had begun. Both had pleaded not guilty. "Wilde looked careworn and anxious."[5:1]

On April 28, *The Times* said the cross-examination of Atkins had shown this witness against Wilde to be "a blackmailer."[5:1]

On May 1, *Times* headlines reported "The Defense of Oscar Wilde" and added: "Eloquence of the Accused Man Provokes A Burst of Applause." The judge had threatened "to clear the court unless silence was observed."[5:2]

On May 2, *The Times* reported that Wilde and Taylor had been found not guilty of "conspiracy." But the jury had been unable to agree on the other charges; Wilde could be tried again on those remaining accusations.

Before the verdict the judge had "begged the jury to dismiss from their minds all press comments and other outside expressions of opinion upon the case." The judge agreed with Wilde's lawyer that the three main witnesses against Wilde "were blackmailers." The judge had advised the jury not to hold against Wilde his authorship of the novel *Dorian Gray.* But "The sonnets of Lord Alfred Douglas, which Wilde approved," were much more relevant evidence, as were Wilde's letters to Douglas.

After the verdict, Wilde and Taylor had been returned to jail. *The New York Times* added: "Several newspapers" had said that Wilde's eloquent speech to the court (mentioned earlier, in passing) "may have saved him from a verdict of guilty." These papers "quote as the most eloquent part of his plea the following phrases":

> "It is such a great affection of the elder for the younger man as existed between David and Jonathan; such as Plato made the very basis of his philosophy; such as we find in the sonnets of Michael Angelo and Shakespeare. It is that deep spiritual affection which is as pure as it is perfect, and

dictates great works of art like those of Shakespeare and Angelo and these two letters of mine, such as they are.

"This love is misunderstood in the present century—so misunderstood that on account of it I am placed where I now am. It is beautiful; it is fine; it is the noblest form of affection. It is intellectual and has existed repeatedly between an elder and a younger man when the elder has the intellect and the younger has all the joy and hope and glamour of life. That it should be so the world does not understand. The world mocks at it and sometimes puts one in the pillory for it."[5:3]

On May 7, *The Times* said that Wilde would pay bail and be released. The government had not yet decided if he would be retried:

the heads of the Church and many other eminent persons urge . . . that much harm would be done to the public morals by the adoption of such a course, referring to the reprinting of details of the case.

The police had been "ordered not to maintain too close a watch upon Wilde's movements and not to prevent him from going to the Continent if he wishes to go there."[5:2]

*The Times's* London correspondent wrote in a report published on May 12:

There is genuine regret at the understanding that Oscar Wilde is to remain in the country and stand a fresh trial. . . . the chances are felt to be in favor of conviction. There has come a feeling that the man has been punished enough already and that a sentence to eighteen months or a year of the English prison terrors can only make a martyr of him in the minds of many impressionable young men, hence do more harm than good. Moreover, the whole hateful episode lasted too long, and people are anxious to be done with it and forget it.[1:3]

The government did decide to prosecute; Wilde and Taylor's second trial opened on May 20. On May 26, *The Times* reported: "The jury returned a verdict of guilty and the Judge sentenced Wilde and Taylor . . . to two years at hard labor each."

The judge's charge to the jury had been "strong against" Wilde. In regard to Wilde's letters to Alfred Douglas, the judge said:

"they might be 'prose poems' and none the less poison to a young man's mind. Their writer was clearly not a desirable companion for the young."

The report ended:

When the sentence was pronounced, Wilde appeared to be stunned. As the last word of the sentence was uttered he was hurried to his cell.[5:1]

On the same day, a front-page feature in *The Times* reported from London:

The impression that high influences were at work to protect Oscar Wilde has been so prevalent that his conviction has taken everybody by surprise. It was supposed that, at the most, the jury would again disagree.

The police were said to have "a list of 400 gentlemen of England"; following the maximum sentence given Wilde, these gentlemen would be ordered to "abandon all possible suggestion of offense, including association with people known to the police, or leave the country within three months."[1:3]

An item in *The Times* on June 5, reported that "Wilde's mental condition is seriously affected," and he was being "carefully watched by a medical staff of the prison."[5:2] On June 30, a *Times* story said that Wilde was "in good health, but the doctors have prohibited his being put on the treadmill [a form of prison discipline]. Consequently he is kept picking oakum [fiber from old hemp ropes], but it is understood that he will soon be making matches." Wilde's plays were about to reappear in London theaters.[16:2]

On November 13, 1895, the *Tribune* reported Wilde's being brought from prison to bankruptcy court. He was found to owe more than three thousand pounds, and had "no available assets." Wilde "looked ill." His "answers to questions were almost entirely monosyllable and given in a low voice."[4:2]

On October 10, 1896, the *Times Book Review* reported that Wilde's "physical state is very distressing." He was kept in prison under "the silent system, and this is rigidly enforced." It was believed "Wilde will lose either his life or his reason as a result of his imprisonment."[1]

And on December 1, 1900, *The Times* reported Wilde's death in an "obscure hotel" in Paris, Alfred Douglas by his side. The "great scandal" of 1895 had arisen from the desire of the Marquis of Queensberry to protect his son, "over whom Wilde exercised an evil influence."

> The evidence at Wilde's trial shocked the civilized world and covered him with disgrace which it was not possible for him to outlive. . . . From a pet of society he had become the most despised of social outcasts.

Wilde had died in "abject poverty."[1:5]*

♀  MEDICAL/COMMENTARY

# 1895, March
## Marc-André Raffalovich:
## "Uranism, Congenital Sexual Inversion"

Although published in medical journals in France and the United States, a wide-ranging essay by Raffalovich did not pretend to be anything other than a moral diatribe against the active expression of "congenital sexual inversion."[28]† But Raffalovich, of Russian-Jewish origin, with a deep interest in Catholicism (he later

---

*See 1902, April 5, for *The New York Times* review of Wilde's *The Importance of Being Earnest*.
†Parts of this essay reprinted in *GAH*, pp. 137–38, focused on "treatment," omitting important details included here.

converted), was also against the active expression of "heterosexual" desire. The "superior homosexual" and "heterosexual," he argued, was "chaste."*

Raffalovich's critique of the autobiographies of sexually active "inverts" as self-justifying, and of Krafft-Ebing as a supporter of invert rights, suggests that such accounts could have, for homosexuals of the late 1800s, a relatively positive, legitimizing function.

Raffalovich argued that a "homosexual," "heterosexual," or "indifferent" sexual impulse was inborn, but that its "form" of expression was determined by education and circumstances.[159] He stressed the importance of discovering the alleged signs of inborn homosexuality in the child, and regulating early influences, in order to encourage later "continence" and "chastity." Raffalovich's essay is one of the earliest in American medical journals to discuss "homosexuality in children." His reference to the child's "carnal attraction" denied the earlier Victorian notion of the pure, innocent, angelic, non-sexual child.[33–34; 39–42]

Signs of "infantile uranism" or "homosexuality" in the male child were "exaggerated modesty" in the presence of adult males, "vanity" and a "taste for finery." Raffalovich thought: "All masquerading should be avoided." Little girls should not be dressed like boys. (Although focusing on males, Raffalovich referred occasionally to female inverts.) Everything which "tends to confuse the notion of sex for the child is to be feared"; an early stress on sexual differentiation was advocated. Brothers and sisters might influence each other: "The delicate and feminine brother would bring out all that was masculine and energetic in the sister." A precocious "Love of pretty things," of dress, and of art, in boys, should make parents "watchful."[61]

Physicians' attempts "to cure inverts" exposed these patients to "dangers." Raffalovich did not believe in "permanent cures of the sexual sense." Attempts at cures might make an "invert" into a "pervert." (By "pervert" Raffalovich apparently meant anyone, heterosexual or homosexual, who acted freely on his or her sexual impulses, without procreative intent.) And "if the invert is dangerous and contagious," the "pervert is much more so." For the "superior invert" who wished to reform (and only a "superior invert" desired strongly to change "his condition"), Raffalovich recommended chastity.[36–37]

Raffalovich's critique of inverts was based on their active carnality, despite any theoretical agreement they might give to the proposition that sexuality was bad. The invert thought he could judge "the baseness of sexuality,"

> but he has not the courage to . . . aspire to chastity; he invents arguments in favor of his own propensities. If he were the superior being that he imagines himself to be and if he had any religion, he would shake off the bonds of the flesh and make himself useful to humanity.

*On this use of "homosexual" and "heterosexual" see introduction, p. 148.

When "the invert ceases to call for the indulgence of society, he will begin to justify himself in the eyes of truly superior men."[42]

If "heterosexuality is not suppressed," Raffalovich argued, logically, "homosexuality ought to be equally favored." The "repression of heterosexuality," he stressed, "is one of the problems of the future."[42] The value placed on sexual control led Raffalovich to "assert the superiority of the invert who *restrains himself* over the heterosexual man who abandons himself."[43]

As "an observer and living much in the world," Raffalovich had "known many inverts and noted others."[34] He could, therefore, generalize: "Inverts . . . are either very reticent or very boastful." Many of them "have a craze for seeing their kind everywhere."[45] Inverts "are liars." By "speaking of their childhood," inverts sought to excuse themselves, or "make themselves interesting by virtue of their passion and ignominy."

The "licentious, vaunting or diseased inverts have had the honor of so much publicity," that other, quieter inverts "are as yet little known." The latter attained "moral maturity without considering sex the pivot of the universe. They have nothing to complain of in their lot."[46]

The "young invert"

knows that his conduct would be execrated, but he does not consider himself any worse than the men or the women who are attractive to each other and love each other. He justifies himself with the thought that these are the sexual pleasures which are called by the name of love. . . . Being naturally homosexual, he does not see any difference between his vice and that of the heterosexual. . . .

Finding heterosexuality treated with too much "indulgence and enthusiasm," the invert's

conscience does not trouble him. It is only in learning to . . . despise or to surmount sexuality and sensuality that the congenital invert can turn away from homosexuality.[49]

"The superior [chaste] invert has equal chances with the heterosexual and analogous dangers." "Sexuality cannot be the goal of existence for a superior person whether homosexual or heterosexual." The "great men claimed for homosexuality have been great because they have not allowed themselves to be overmastered by their sexuality. The grand inverts have been grand in spite of their inversion." Walt Whitman was cited as one of the "grand inverts,"[50] (one of the earliest references to Whitman's "inversion" published in the United States).

"When we speak of the injustice of fate and society" in its treatment of the invert, why do we not also think of other "admitted injustices"? The "poor, hard worked," young heterosexual man who could not marry had, from the sexual standpoint, "as much to complain of as the invert." Both should tell themselves "that the sexual act should not be the pivot of their existence."[51–52]

Krafft-Ebing was called "the representative of those who claim justice for the invert." That "demand"

> has as its basis the theory that every man has a right to sexual satisfaction. If one grants the right to heterosexual, I do not see how it can be refused to the inverts. . . . But in my opinion every man has not the right to lay claim to the sexual satisfaction of his desires.

The moral law that forbids the heterosexual with a "transmissible disease" from procreating "forbids the invert from yielding to his propensities."[52]

Autobiographies of inverts were receiving too much attention in studies of inversion. The autobiographies of "adulterous women" showed the "same fierce egotism," "remorse," and "apologies," yet scholars did not excuse and pity those adulterers because of their adultery.[53]

The "enthusiastic uranists do not wish to change." Neither did "abject or enthusiastic inverts" think they should be "pitied." The "superior inverts are no more to be pitied than superior heterosexuals." The "inverts who moan and lament and who beset writers with their stories" would probably have carried on the same way "if they had been heterosexual." No heterosexual easily found a person who simultaneously satisfied "sex, the soul and society and the family."

> Why should the invert have that which the heterosexual finds with so great difficulty? How many heterosexuals are unhappy by reason of their sexual life?[53]

*"There is no line of demarcation between the heterosexual and the homosexual."* The "man who allows himself to be dominated by his sexuality . . . is sexual before he is uranistic or heterosexual. The man who is above his sexuality can . . . be either homosexual or heterosexual."[56]

A backnote by Raffalovich's American translator, C. Judson Herrick, concluded:

> The American reader will note that the social conditions upon which this paper is based are those of Europe and differ widely from those of this country.

The relatively "sparse population and different social organization" existing in the United States made European "forms of vice" unfamiliar to "native-born" Americans. The "dangers to be guarded against in this country at present" were not "the preventive education of possible uranistic children," but the "prevention of those social conditions which encourage" inversion and "other vices."

> With the massing of our population, especially the foreign element, in great cities, these [social] changes will assume greater and greater importance.[65]

♀ MEDICAL/RESISTANCE

# 1895, April
## Dr. Havelock Ellis: "Sexual Inversion in Women"

A survey of "sexual inversion in women" was the most detailed, wide-ranging, and sympathetic to have appeared in a U.S. medical journal up to that time.[29]* But here, Ellis's pose of scientific impartiality sometimes gave way to quite overt moral judgment, as when, toward the end, his comment on the "disadvantages" of the women's movement clearly taxed all semblance of objectivity.

Two executions of women for sexual acts with females were cited, that of a weaver reported in Montaigne's journal of a trip to Italy in 1580, and that of Catharine Linck, "condemned to death for sodomy," in Germany, in 1721.[141]30

"Homo-sexuality is little if at all less common in woman than in man," although the chief works on "sexual inversion" devoted "little space to women." This was because men had rarely criminalized it. "Inversion" was also "less easy to detect in women" than in men, since "we are accustomed to a much greater familiarity and intimacy between women," and are "less apt to suspect the existence of any abnormal passion."[142] Also cited was the "extreme ignorance" and

> reticence of women regarding any abnormal or even normal manifestation of their sexual life. A woman may feel a high degree of sexual attraction for another woman without realizing that her affection is sexual, and when she does realize it she is nearly always very unwilling to reveal the nature of her intimate experience, even with the adoption of precautions, and although the fact may be presented to her that by helping to reveal the nature of her abnormality she may be helping to lighten the burden of it on other women.[142–43]

Also, while "a slight degree of homosexuality is commoner in women than in men, and is favored by the conditions under which women live," "fully developed" inversion was rarer in women than men.

Cross-cultural examples of "Lesbianism" in "lower races" were mentioned, as were female "homosexual practices" in prisons and lunatic asylums."[144]

"Ardent attachments" at puberty, of girls at school, were discussed, as was "affection and devotion" between a female student and a schoolmistress. The "devotion" of a school girl was "surcharged with emotion," though she was "often unconscious . . . of the sexual impulse," and sought "no form of sexual satisfaction." However, "kissing and . . . sleeping with the friend" were sought. "Often" even the "unresponsive friend" felt "sexual emotion," though this might not be understood as such.[145] "This rudimentary . . . homosexual relationship

*Part of this essay, reprinted in *GAH*, p. 139, included only a small section on treatment.

is more common" among girls than boys, who found intimacy with other males "unmanly." Also, "the girl has a stronger need of affection and self-devotion to another person." Under "existing social conditions" young women were compelled to "hold the opposite sex at arm's length," while "propriety" allowed "a considerable degree of physical intimacy between girls"—at once "encouraging and cloaking" manifestations of "homosexuality."[146]

"Passionate friendships, of a more or less unconscious sexual character, are certainly common" among females. A young woman's "love at a distance" for a man might alternate with "intimate attachment" to a female friend, though "No congenital inversion is usually involved" in such intimacies. Either the relationship with a man developed, or "knowledge of the real [sexual] nature" of the feelings for women led to a "distaste for them," or the female-female intimacy became "permanent." In such cases the "specific sexual phenomena" vary greatly. The "emotion" might be "unconscious," or "all on one side," or was "often . . . recognised and shared." Such "cases are on the borderland of true sexual inversion." In these relationships "sex" was not "essential." Such relationships were termed "hypertrophied friendships," the "excessive development" being "due to unemployed sexual instinct." (In other words, friendships remaining non-genital might be more intense than genitally enacted relationships.)[146–47]

A "class" of women existed "in which homosexuality, while fairly distinct, is only slightly marked." These were the women to whom the "actively inverted woman is most attracted." The "sexual impulses" of this class of women were slight, but they were of a "strongly affectionate nature." They "possess a genuine, though not precisely sexual preference for women over men."[147–48]

The "actively inverted woman" possessed an essential "trace of masculinity," although she was frequently not "a 'mannish' woman."[148]

Two female cases were detailed, the second of which, "Miss X," was the disguised history of Edith Lees, Havelock Ellis's wife (who would later lecture in the United States; see 1915, February 4.)* "Miss X" believed

> homosexual love is morally right when it is really part of a person's nature and provided that the nature of homosexual love is always made plain to the object of such affection. She does not approve of it as a mere makeshift, or expression of sensuality, in normal women. She has sometimes resisted the sexual expression of her feelings, once for years at a time, but always in vain. The effect on her of loving women is distinctly good, she asserts, both spiritually and physically, while repression leads to morbidity and hysteria. She has suffered much from neurasthenia at various periods but under appropriate treatment it has slowly diminished. The inverted instinct is too deeply rooted to eradicate but it is now well under control.[152]

*Edith Ellis's sexual history is included here as one of the rare instances in which such a detailed erotic account of a female subject is known to exist, and because of the importance of recovering, when possible, the history of the specifically erotic and genital, especially in female-female intimacies.

Edith Lees's somewhat altered case history reported that her first "sex feelings" at age eight or nine "were associated with dreams of whipping and being whipped." Her "earliest affection" at age thirteen was for "a graceful coquetish girl with long golden hair and blue eyes."[149] Falling in love with a cousin in her teens was "full of delicious sensations; if the cousin touched her neck a thrill went through her body." She later regarded this thrill as "sexual."

After leaving school at nineteen she met a "womanly" female of about the same age who "sought to gain her love." Miss X was also attracted, partly by the "sense of power" this love gave her. An "intimate relationship grew up," and became physical. They "used to touch each other's parts and kiss each other tenderly (especially on the *mons veneris*) with equal ardor." Both "experienced a strong pleasurable feeling in doing this," but "no orgasm." They were "lovers," but tried "to hide this fact from the world." This intimacy lasted "several years," until Miss X's friend,

> from religious and moral scruples, put an end to the physical relationship. Miss X had been very well and happy during this relationship; this interference with it seems to have exerted a demoralizing influence and also to have aroused her sexual desires.[150]

Soon afterward, Miss X "yielded recklessly" to her "sexual feelings" with "another girl of a very fleshy and voluptuous type," who "made violent love" to her. Miss X was "much ashamed" of this episode "ever afterwards." When her previous friend "implored" for a resumption of their old intimacy, Miss X "resisted every effort to restore the physical relation." Another "intimate relationship" with a "congenial friend lasted for several years."[150–51]

Miss X's "feeling toward men is not in the slightest degree sexual." She "much enjoys the society of men," but this was an "intellectual attraction." For marriage she had always had an "absolute repugnance," but could "imagine a man whom she could love or marry."[151] (Much is suggested here about Lees's and Ellis's marriage.)

Miss X was attracted to women "sincere, reserved, pure, but courageous in character." While "not attracted to intellectual women," she could "not endure silly women." Women "somewhat younger than herself" attracted her, and she liked to take a "protecting role with them."[151]

Miss X

> finds sexual satisfaction in tenderly touching, caressing and kissing the loved one's body, especially the pudenda [the external sexual organs, the vulva]. (There is no *cunnilingus*, which she regards with abhorrence.) She feels more tenderness than passion. There is a high degree of sexual erethism [arousal] when kissing, . . . but orgasm is rare and is produced by lying on the friend or by the friend lying on her, without any special contact.

She liked being kissed better than kissing.

Continuing his survey, Havelock Ellis pointed out that women who dressed and acted like men were "by no means necessarily inverted."[152] It was "note-worthy that women seem with special frequency to fall in love with disguised persons of their own sex." Sexually inverted women did have a "pronounced tendency to adopt male attire," chiefly "because the wearer feels more at home in them."[152–53] A "pronounced taste for smoking (sometimes found in quite feminine women)," was "frequently found in the sexually inverted." A "dislike and sometimes incapacity for needlework and other domestic occupations" was also mentioned as characteristic of female inverts, as well as a "capacity for athletics." Indifferent to males, the female invert showed "nothing of that sexual shyness and engaging air of weakness and dependence which are an invitation to men."[154]

The "inverted woman" might be "full of tender ardor for the woman whom she loves." This "passion finds expression in sleeping together, kissing and close embraces, with more or less sexual excitement, the orgasm sometimes occur-ring." The "extreme gratification is *cunnilingus, in lambendo lingua genitalia alterius* [literally, consisting in licking with the tongue the partner's genitals], sometimes called sapphism." Ellis denied that inverted women had an enlarged clitoris, "as was once supposed." The "sexual habits" of the inverted woman "rarely" in-cluded "the degree of promiscuity" common among inverted men. "Homosexual women love more faithfully and lastingly than homosexual men."[154–55]

Many expert observers had stated that "homosexuality is increasing among women," in America, France, Germany, and England. Ellis agreed. "Civilization to-day" encouraged "such manifestations."

> The modern movement of emancipation—the movement to obtain the same rights and duties, the same freedom and responsibility, the same education and the same work—must be regarded as on the whole a wholesome and inevitable movement. But it carried with it certain disadvantages. It has involved an increase in feminine criminality and in feminine insanity, which are being elevated towards the masculine standard. In connection with these we can scarcely be surprised to find an increase in homosexuality which has always been regarded as belonging to an allied, if not the same, group of phenomena. Women are, very justly, coming to look upon knowledge and experience generally as their right as much as their brother's right. But when this doctrine is applied to the sexual sphere it finds certain fixed limitations. . . . The sexual field of women is usually restricted to trivial flirtation with the opposite sex and to intimacy with their own sex; having been taught independence of men and disdain for the old theory which placed women in the moated grange of the home to sigh for a man who never comes, a tendency develops for women to carry this independence still further and to find love where they find work.

The "influences of modern movements" did not "directly cause sexual inversion, though they may indirectly, in so far as they promote hereditary neuro-sis; but they develop the germs of [sexual inversion], and they probably cause a spurious imitation." Such imitative inversion was "due to the fact that the congenital anomaly occurs with special frequency in women of high intelligence who . . . influence others."[155–56]

A closing section on the treatment of congenitally inverted women recommended the "ideal of sexual abstinence in so far as indulgence may be doing injury to others." (If indulgence did not do injury abstinence was not necessary, but this point remained, carefully, implicit.) For the "nervous disorders" associated with sexual inversion Ellis advocated "a wholesome . . . course of physical and mental hygiene." This would help the patient overcome "morbid fears and suspicions" sometimes "fostered by excessive sympathy and coddling," and establish a "tonic condition of self-control."

♀ NEWS FEATURE/INTIMACY

## 1895, June 24
## N.Y. Times: "Friendships of Women" and "Woman's Emancipation"

In "Some Most Terrible Statements" about women by an unnamed English author, reprinted in the *Times,* a problematic intimacy between females was said to cause their inability to combine to realize their sex's interests.[31] Although elitist, harshly critical of women, and repeating a number of clichés, these statements appear, finally, to be intended as a feminist critique. The essays also refer to a historic link between female-to-female intimacy and feminism.

The first statement, on "The Friendships of Women," claimed that "Such relations never become stable or sacred," since they "begin by chance, proceed with passion, and die at breath." A woman was at any moment

> ready to sacrifice her friend at the behest of any man in whom she is momentarily interested. For his entertainment she will betray any confidence without a scruple. . . .

If women

> are seldom true to men, their fidelity to their own sex is rarer far, for there are no Davids and Jonathans among women, no friendships founded on mutual faith and held in honor. Until woman learns to conduct her relations with her own sex on the same principle as that on which men act, the sisterhood of women will never come within measurable distance of the possible. She has learned so much from man in this decade that it is not unreasonable to hope she may yet learn the true character of friendship, as well as the policy of combination. When woman stands shoulder to shoulder with her sister in public and in private life she will stand at the very gates of her kingdom. . . .

The second statement argued (as the headline put it) that lack of fellowship between women "Has Deferred Woman's Emancipation." It began: "The bond of fellowship which exists between man and man simply by virtue of a common sex is entirely absent between woman and woman"; it was "replaced by a fundamental antagonism." This opposition was counteracted, in individual cases, "by affection or by sympathy," But apart from such "personal sentiment," enmity severed "every living woman from the rest of her sex." This antagonism "arises from woman's incapacity for impersonal feeling or abstract emotion." She "fights" for herself or, "more often, for some one man or woman whom she loves, but rarely for the welfare of her sex at large."

If not for "this strange lack of humanity" in woman's "nature," the "emancipation of woman would not have been so grievously retarded." If the "few women" who had suffered restrictions of liberty had

> been able to count on the sympathy and co-operation of all women, the time of their subjugation would have been enormously abbreviated. As it was, the first seekers after freedom met with more opposition from their own sex than they did from the other; nor, indeed, do they fare better to-day. Enormous changes in their social status were effected by an inconsiderable minority of women brave enough and logical enough to impress the male powers that be with the justice of their demands. But for their courage they received no sympathy, and for their success not one word of thanks—nothing, in fact, but execration from the huge inert feminine mass in whose service their strength was spent.

MEDICAL/CROSSING MAN

## 1895, Summer
### Dr. Austin Flint: *"He was sent to his home in the West"*

Dr. Flint's callous view of a crossing man is indicated by the physician's publishing this subject's nude photograph and case history with no reference to the ethics involved.[32] The working class and "feminine" character of the subject, and his status as curiosity, explains the doctor's objectification. That cross-sex "masquerading" was the province of a doctor and his medical "expertise" was taken for granted. And that lack of sexual feeling in a male was given a medical name, "anaesthesia," indicates that profession's appropriation of eroticism as its proper proprietary concern. (Eroticism, as Michel Foucault points out in his *History of Sexuality,* may alternately be considered the province of aesthetics, philosophy, ethics, or religion.) That the "feminine" or "masculine" character of the human speaking or singing voice is in part a product of social engendering, rather than anatomical destiny, did not occur to Dr. Flint.

In 1894, as a medical inspector at Elmira Reformatory, Flint had observed "a number of sexual perverts such as are usually found in penal institutions for males only."

In the summer of 1895, on a visit to Bellevue Hospital in New York City, Flint noticed a young man "affected with sexual abnormity." The man

> had been arrested in Central Park for masquerading in feminine dress and had been sent to the hospital for examination into his mental condition. When I saw him he was dressed as a boy; but in a hand bag belonging to him were found a woman's gown, corsets, a skirt, women's drawers, long stockings and garters, and women's shoes, in which clothing he was attired when arrested.
>
> I was then visiting at what is now [1911] called the Psychopathic Ward, and I directed that he be sent there for examination. The general appearance of this individual, in his woman's dress, is shown in Fig. I [apparently taken in the summer of 1895].
>
> The facial expression is certainly somewhat peculiar. He had a very scanty beard and it seemed that the hairs had been habitually plucked out. His manner was that of a silly girl, with certain assumed "airs and graces" more or less characteristic. His voice was high pitched and feminine in quality.
>
> He gave the following account of himself, but this, of course, must

Original caption: "General appearance of the individual in his woman's dress."

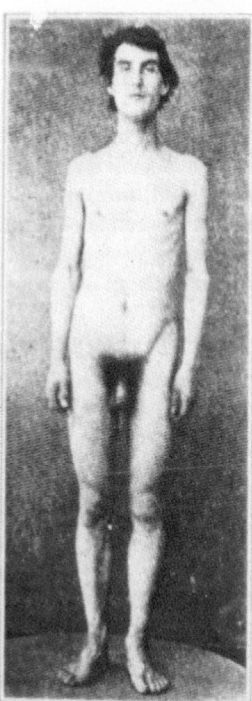

Original caption: "Showing actively masculine conformation of the individual."

be taken with due allowance for mendacity, as it was not confirmed.

He said that he was twenty-one years old, which probably was true: that he always had preferred women's dress and occupations and usually dressed as a woman; that he had acted for a long time as a domestic servant, and that his last place was as ladies' maid in a family in Boston. While acting in this capacity he attended his mistress in her bath and slept in a bed with the other girls, by whom his sex was not suspected. On close questioning, he denied that he had any sexual feeling or inclination, either for men or women; denied lascivious dreams and nocturnal emissions and said he had never had an erection. Fig. 2 shows an entirely masculine conformation, with full developed external sexual organs. This information was about all that could be obtained from him that seemed trustworthy.

The peculiarity of his voice was very striking, and this point of interest in the case may serve as an excuse for its presentation. He said that he liked music and sometimes sang; but when he was requested to sing, said he "had a cold" and made various trivial excuses of rather a feminine character and in a decidedly feminine manner. However, he finally asked if he should sing "Annie Laurie," which he sang in a high key and a perfect woman's voice. One would say it was a high soprano; and he sang with correct intonation and fairly well. I think I am sufficiently familiar with the human voice to be able to say that his was not the voice of a boy or of an adult male soprano, but a pure woman's voice.

I intended to have made a laryngoscopic examination on the following day: but before I could do so he was sent to his home in the West.

It is chiefly the voice in this case that is interesting. All the physical characters of this individual were distinctly masculine, and his external genitals were even generously developed. It is also interesting—if true—that there was absolute sexual anaesthesia. . . .[1111–12]

In July 1896, a year after the subject's photos were taken, they were published in a medical journal ("Case I"), along with those of another crossing man who had earned his living as a female cook ("Case II").

Original caption: "Psychopathia Sexualis. Case I."

Original caption: "Psychopathia Sexualis. Case II."

♀ MEDICAL/RESISTANCE

## 1895, September 26
## Dr. John Wesley Carhart: *Norma Trist; or Pure Carbon:*
### *A Story of the Inversion of the Sexes*

Carhart's *Norma Trist* (published in Austin, Texas) is one of three fictional works known to have appeared in 1895, all seemingly inspired in part by the Alice Mitchell–Freda Ward intimacy and murder (see 1892, January 26).[33]* But unlike Mary Wilkins Freeman's short story "The Long Arm" and Mary R. P. Hatch's novel *The Strange Disappearance of Eugene Comstock* (both discussed by Lillian Faderman), Dr. Carhart's novel is emphatically pro-invert—until its final turnabout.[34]

As *Norma Trist* begins readers learn that the title character, daughter of a wealthy widow of La Grange, Texas, has a passionate fondness for books, learning, and "young ladies," but none for "young gentlemen." Her father, before he died, requested that she receive an education to suit her tastes, and to fit her for "usefulness in the world."[6–7]

Mrs. Marie LaMoreaux, Norma's music teacher, a young-beautiful-talented-educated-cultured widow, is the "one person" whom Norma says "I truly, dearly, passionately love," and in whom she has confided "one strange feature of her life."[11, 22]

Symptoms of Norma's strange condition are that she enjoys dancing with her young lady friends and Mrs. LaMoreaux, but opposes male-female dancing. She does not like those perfumes associated with males.[20, 21] Just before leaving to become a student at Maplewood Young Ladies Seminary in Pittsfield, Massachusetts, Norma, alone in her room with Mrs. LaMoreaux, throws her arms about her, and embraces her "most fondly and passionately"—jealous of Mrs. LaMoreaux's verbal interchange with a Spanish captain. Mrs. L. reassures Norma, "I love you better than any one else in this world," and Norma goes off to Seminary promising to write "love letters" to her friend.[36, 37]

*See comment on *Norma Trist* in the Introduction to this section, p. 159.

Cover illustration, *Norma Trist*.

At Maplewood, in the Berkshires, Norma, an outstanding student, writes to Mrs. LaMoreaux "as though to a lover, to whom she was devoted with all the powers of her mind, body and soul."[51]

Miss Elwell, a teacher of "uncertain age," accidentally intercepts one of Norma's love letters to Mrs. L. and, shocked, takes it to President Spencer of Maplewood. He calls a faculty meeting at which Norma's letter is read.

"My Dear Mrs. LaMoreaux," Norma's letter quite formally begins,

> I love you with all the powers and faculties of my nature. I am happy only when I think of you and fancy that I have you in my arms, hugging you to my bosom. You are . . . the inspiration of my thought, the only stimulus of my amorous feelings. How happy the hours in the past, when, unsuspected, I could yield myself in your embraces to the full sway of passion's convulsive joys. . . . I know that my absorbing passion for you is strange, and often troubles me; and I know not what the world would say could the half be known. But the laws and customs of human society are one thing. My love for you, in its peculiar form is my nature, which God gave me, and how can I help it? I do not want to help it. . . . Think of me as your "sweetheart." . . . Your dear presence was a magnetic stream; it was a peculiar power your being exercised over me. . . . In the night of sorrow I had but one star,— the star of your love![52–54]

Although President Spencer teaches "mental science," he and the faculty of Maplewood are mystified by Norma Trist's letter to a "lady friend." They cannot believe that such expressions of Norma's "mental and affectional nature" could have been "awakened by a woman, no matter how intense her friendship," or how deep her love. The existence of a "pathological psychical vita sexualis" never for a moment enters their minds.[55–56] They have not heard of such a thing, says Carhart, because American literature, whether philosophy, science, or fiction, is "entirely barren" of comment on the subject. And although religious literature (biographies and revival histories) contain relevant facts, "the ministry regarded every departure from a given standard, and every variation from their notions of normal affectional manifestations, as vice"—not fit for pulpit discourse.[56]French and German fiction on "sexual abnormalities" is so "gross" it is said not to have been translated for American readers.

The Maplewood faculty thus decides that Norma's letter must really be to a male—a form of prohibited correspondence.[57]Her letter is returned to her without comment (as if it had not been read), and a second letter of Norma's is intercepted. Fearing that her first letter has been read, Norma writes to Mrs. LaMoreaux:

> What if my feeling for you should become known? I feel no condemnation for aught I have done or for aught that I feel. But, oh! I dread the criticisms and scoffs of society who can not understand, and refuse to appreciate.

Norma has only lately realized "that I am not as other people. I have no love or desire for the opposite sex—indeed the thought of intimacy with them is abhorrent to all the finer, better feelings of my nature."

Norma can conceive, she says, a state of society in which "platonic love might exist between two of the opposite sex"—after Christ has reigned for a thousand years! Imagining such social conditions, Norma says: "I have given no special thought to the propagation of the species"; she thinks some "more pure method," involving "no suffering" might be instituted by the "Divine Father."

She writes of her "horror" at the thought that she is "not as others":

> From my earliest years my inclination has been for the female sex. In my thirteenth year, I first felt a trace of sexual feeling. At that time, and ever since, feminine forms have exclusively appeared in my dream-pictures.[60–62]

President Spencer, still not knowing what to make of Norma, contacts a Pittsfield pastor and five "alienists," none of whom provides any useful interpretations of the case. A third letter of Norma's is intercepted in which she describes her "erotic delight" in touching the furs given to her by Mrs. LaMoreaux, furs which she refers to as her "fetich." (The source of such details is Krafft-Ebing's *Psychopathia Sexualis.*) Norma also tells Mrs. LaMoreaux that their love inspires her to "great things." In this "exalted" state, says Norma, she "should be perfectly happy but for the fear of publicity, and the harrowing thought that at some time you may fail to reciprocate my love. . . . These thoughts at times, drive me almost to madness."[66–68]

The author comments: "The beautiful blending of the sensuous," the "sensual," and "the truly, sublimely religious and poetic in Norma's nature" remains an enigma to President Spencer, even after a discreet inquiry to Mrs. Trist in Texas brings the information that Norma is indeed corresponding with a Mrs. LaMoreaux. Without explanation by the author, Norma is allowed to continue on at Maplewood, where, before graduating, she is elected valedictorian by her fellow students, against the wishes of several female teachers who favor another young woman. At the instigation of these teachers the subject of Norma's strange love letters is again revived. It is said that the teachers cannot excuse

> one girl falling in love with another girl as though she were a man. They thought that if it did not betray an unmentionable depravity, it was altogether too mannish—a thing they utterly "hated, abominated" and were "utterly disgusted with. . . . A girl should be a girl until she becomes a woman, and then she should be a true woman." They did not hesitate to say that they were "utterly down on 'short-haired women and long-haired men,' " and it was their opinion that "there should be a law passed to prevent all such abnormal conduct. . . ." In their opinion, it had "become exceedingly difficult to control young ladies, anyway. . . ."[155–56]

President Spencer calls another faculty meeting to try to placate those female teachers who characterize Norma's "love affair with a woman" as "unnatural, inexplicable, disgraceful and abominable," warning that it is "impossible to tell to what it might all lead. . . ."

Another of Norma's intercepted letters to Mrs. LaMoreaux is read:

My Dearest Loved One:—How I long . . . to press you to my heart of hearts once more. . . . When I look at my white arms which feel so empty without your dear, sweet self in their embrace, I feel that half their mission is unfulfilled. . . . If I could stroke your silken hair, watch the heavings of your breasts and feel their fond pulsations it would be to me an Eden of love and delight. . . . how sweet it will be when we are united for life, as I hope to be, . . . not by the formalities that society imposes, but by the spiritual and fleshly bond that I feel must forever unite us.

Professor Gerster, the German teacher of calisthenics, with President Spencer the only other male at Maplewood, thinks little of the fuss made about Norma's "psychical and affectional abnormality," as "such things were not unusual in the older civilization of Europe," and Gerster says nothing.[163]

President Spencer surprisingly allows Norma to graduate as valedictorian, and she returns to Texas—to find that Mrs. LaMoreaux is engaged to be married to the Spanish captain introduced earlier. Norma's passionate love immediately turns to bitter gall; she attempts to murder Mrs. LaMoreaux by stabbing her in the breast.

Every daily newspaper in the nation headlines the case, some with the words:

A Girl Murders Her Female Lover
Sexual Perversion
A Girl in Love With a Woman, Kills Her in the Public Street[182]

Mrs. LaMoreaux does not die. She recovers rather quickly, marries her Spanish captain, and goes to live in Mexico.

Norma is tried, declared "insane," and sent to the Austin asylum. The publicity about her causes a "few investigators and original thinkers" to turn to the subject of "psychopathic conditions, mental abnormalities and affectional aberrations," and to discover reports of other such cases in the courts and "casebooks" of physicians.[186]

After observing Norma for some time the head of the Austin asylum decides that she is not insane, and remands her to the legal authorities. A second trial is held.

Norma's lawyer defends her by proposing to show

that there was in certain cases, what was known as a psycho-sexual condition manifest in one falling in love with another of the same sex, wherein affectional, social and sexual excitement, and so far as possible, relations exist as between those of the opposite sexes.

Such a state of psychopathia sexualis might exist, and frequently does exist between one man and another, and between one woman and another woman. It might be congenital or it might be induced or acquired.

The lawyer also proposes to show that between either "the opposite sexes," or between those of the "same sex," love may "be sadistic in character." Instead of "admiration" and "a desire to possess the one loved," it takes the form of "a desire to mutilate or destroy the one loved. . . ." He proposes to show that Norma is a subject of both these "abnormalities" (love for the same sex, and sadistic love) and that "such a condition did not imply an insane mind."[205–06]

Although not compelled to testify against herself, Norma is the first witness in her own defense, her manner, reportedly "frank, without equivocation, and apparently unembarrassed." She makes no "attempt to conceal facts, no matter how delicate they might seem. . . ."

Asked if the lady for whom she entertained such an "erotic passion" knew the character of her love, Norma answers that "no objections were ever made to her advances, or to the character of her passion. . . ."[208–09] (Mrs. LaMoreaux, we have been told, in passing, is a Roman Catholic, of French extraction.)

When her love is termed an "infatuation" Norma denies the negative implications of the term. Her feeling for her friend, she says,

is as pure as the deepest, purest, most God-given passion between two of the opposite sexes can possibly be, and I may modestly say, as intelligent. . . . The stronger the passion the happier I was; it was and is a stimulus to my ambition, prompting me to highest intellectual effort, inspiring me with delightful, unflinching courage. . . ."[209]

Describing what motivated her to try to kill her beloved, Norma, with tears streaming down her face, speaks of a "jealous frenzy" and "bewilderment" caused by love.

Asked whether she realizes that the love for the same sex is "not according to nature," Norma answers:

It is according to the profoundest and most irresistible instincts of my nature. . . .

She adds:

"I am painfully aware that I am not as the majority of people are; and also that I may be regarded as not in harmony with the common sentiments or wishes of society."

Asked if her conscience has ever bothered her, Norma says no.

The prosecuting attorney's last question, he says, is "a somewhat delicate one." At this we are told the spectators present in court display an "intense eagerness" to hear the question and the answer—especially the many "ladies."

The prosecutor asks Norma "if, in your relations with Marie, your love experienced perfect satisfaction?"

> Norma, apprehending the exact purport of the question, and wishing to relieve him from all embarrassment, said:
> "I understand you to mean satisfaction of the erotic desire?"
> "That is what I mean."
> "I have no hesitancy in answering frankly and freely, that my love for and relations with Marie afforded the highest and profoundest satisfaction of which the entire human being is capable in the realm of human love."[207–11]

(That statement constitutes probably the most explicit, unequivocating defense of genital-orgasmic relations between women published in English in the nineteenth century.)

The head of the Austin insane asylum testifies that "sexual and affectional abnormalities," while "freaks of nature," are not forms of insanity. Asked if "the light reading of the present time" might cause such abnormalities, he thinks it might, but not in Norma's case. Asked if Norma was "responsible" for her acts, he answers that she is just as responsible as one would be who, in "a transport of jealousy for the opposite sex, should commit overt acts."[215–17]

A Dr. Jasper, expert in "sexual abnormalities," makes the "startling statement" that "the numbers of those suffering from such abnormalities would reach into the thousands, possibly tens of thousands."[217] He also denies that such a condition is insane, adding that acquired, non-congenital cases can be cured by hypnotism.[218]

After arguing for forty-eight hours, the jury, eleven to one for conviction, can't agree. Norma's bail is paid by Frank Artman, who from their youth has loved her, even though his passion has been unreturned.

Frank Artman is assured by Dr. Jasper that he can "cure" Norma; Artman approaches her with the suggestion that she might "be placed under treatment for the abnormal condition of your mind and heart." She responds:

> "Oh, Frank! you surprise me. You shock me! I must correct you and inform you that my love for Marie is as natural to me as your love for me is natural to you."
> "I know, I know!" said Frank with evident embarrassment, "I meant abnormal, as people generally view such things."
> "Yes," said Norma, "it is abnormal in the eyes of the community."

As to treatment, Norma says: " I have no wish at present to cease to love [Marie], except to avoid bringing trouble to others." But then, apparently to

avoid bringing such trouble, Norma does decide to try hypnosis, for which Artman has offered to pay.

Interviewing Norma's mother, Dr. Jasper comments on the grief her daughter's abnormality has caused:

> one of the saddest features of her case, as well as of thousands more suffer-
> ing from similar sexual and psychical perversion, is the fact that there is little
> sympathy for her and for those of her class.

Mrs. Trist agrees:

> "Norma is as innocent as a child of any wrong purpose, as her strange love,
> and ever her jealousy is, to her as natural as love or jealousy between those
> of the opposite sexes."[239–40]

Attempting to understand how Norma's condition might have been encouraged by her situation, Dr. Jasper asks about her "early occupations and
sports."[242] Mrs. Trist answers that Norma, an only child, had been "capable of
almost unlimited physical exercise." Her father was "passionately fond of her.
She was his idol" and "He wanted her with him everywhere." Norma always
"rode man fashion" on her pony, wearing a male riding outfit, and often enjoyed
riding with her father:

> She became brown as a nut, athletic and courageous; and at times impressed
> me as having more the characteristics and disposition of a great, healthy,
> well developed, vigorous and fun-loving boy, than those of a girl. This just
> suited her father, as he often said, she was all the boy he had.

Dr. Jasper finds these facts of "utmost importance," indications that

> at the dawn of puberty, there was developed more of the masculine than
> of the feminine instincts, and it required but little so to impress the mas-
> culine feeling upon her that it soon became a habit of thought and feel-
> ing.[244]

Norma's treatment by Dr. Jasper consists of the hypnotic suggestion:

> I abhor the love of my own sex, and shall never again think women hand-
> some. I shall and will become well again, fall in love with Frank Artman, be
> happy and make him happy.

This treatment succeeding, Norma marries Frank Artman, has two "healthy"
children, and leads a "delightful life" of "bliss." The years testify to the genuine-
ness of her love. (With that turnabout, Dr. Carhart ends his story.)

## 1895, September
## Dr. James Weir, Jr.: "The Effect
## of Female Suffrage on Posterity"

Writing in *The American Naturalist* Dr. Weir produced a classic anti-feminist, anti-"homosexual" tract, touching on what he called "matriarchy," "communism," "homosexuality," "masculo-feminity," "the tom-boy," "viragints, gynanders, androgynes," "unsexed individuals," and "female psycho-sexual aberrants."[35]

"In the very beginning," said Weir, "woman was, by function, a mother; by virtue of her surroundings, a housewife." Man was then, "as now, the active, dominant factor" in affairs beyond the "fireside." Wives were "communal," and "collectivism" was a way of life. "Laxity in sexual relations was . . . common to all races of primitive men." Women's serving as wives to "all men of the tribe" led to a "matriarchate" in which women ran the government, directly or indirectly.[815–17]

"Matriarchy or female government" is "neither new nor advanced," and "the 'New Woman' was born many thousands of years ago." "A return to matriarchy at the present time," would be distinctly . . . retrograde." For if "women are granted the privilege of suffrage, they must be given the right to govern." Weir traced the "reason for this atavistic desire (for matriarchy) in the physical and psychical histories of its foremost advocates."[818]

"The doctrines of communism and of nihilism," he began, are products of "a reversion to the mental habitudes of our savage ancestors." The doctrines of "the matriarchate are likewise degenerate beliefs."[819]

> The woman of to-day, who believes in . . . the doctrines of matriarchy, . . . is as much the victim of psychic atavism as was Alice Mitchell who slew Freda Ward, . . . and who was justly declared a viragint by the court.[819]

"Every woman"

> who has been at all prominent in advancing the cause of equal rights in its entirety, has either given evidence of masculo-feminity (viraginity), or has shown, conclusively, that she was the victim of psycho-sexual aberrancy.

"Every viragint" in the "history of the world" was "either physically or psychically degenerate, or both." Joan of Arc, Catherine the Great, Messalina, and Queen Elizabeth were cited.[819]

Weir reiterated: The "chief promoters of equal rights are probably viragints —individuals who plainly show that they are psychically abnormal," a condition "occasioned by degeneration," acquired or inherent.[822]

A "mild form" of "viraginity" was visible in "the tom-boy who abandons her dolls and female companions for . . . marbles and masculine sports." In the "loud-talking," "slang-using young woman" another form of viraginity was visible. The "square-shouldered, stolid, cold, unemotional, unfeminine android" was another type of viragint. Weir then declared:

> The most aggravated form of viraginity is that known as homo-sexuality. . . .[820]

But with that form his paper was not concerned.

"Gynandry" was another form of viraginity in which the "victim" had "the feelings and desires of a man," as well as "the skeletal form, features, and voice" of the "opposite sex."

The case of Sarolta, Countess V., illustrated how "gynandry" was "acquired." Very early her father had "dressed her in boy's clothing, called her Sandor, and taught her boyish games."

> At thirteen she had a love relation with an English girl, to whom she represented herself as a boy, and ran away with her.[820–21]

Sandor/Sarolta frequented brothels, and "had many love affairs with women, always skillfully hiding the fact that she herself was a woman." She even married and lived with a female for some time before being discovered.

> Notwithstanding this woman's passion for those of her own sex, she distinctly states that in her thirteenth year she experienced normal sexual desire.

Her male "environments" had made her "a victim of complete gynandry."

"Many women of to-day who are in favor of female suffrage" did *not* also want women governors; "they do not belong to the class of viragints, unsexed individuals whose main object is the establishment of a matriarchate."[821] Nevertheless, "the final effect of female suffrage on posterity would be exceedingly harmful."[822]

If female suffrage came about physical and psychic changes in women would follow, and be passed on to posterity, causing "a social revolution, in which the present form of government will be overthrown and matriarchy established." Weir attributed "an alarming increase of suicide and insanity among women" to their already changed environment. Women "have already too much liberty." Influences had been removed which had "formerly made woman peculiarly a house-wife," and "woman mixes freely with the world." Women's suffrage would entail new "desires and emotions," exhausting to the female nervous system. Weir quoted Krafft-Ebing to the effect that increased nervousness meant "increase of sensuality"; this led to "excess among the masses," and "undermines the foundations of our society—the morality and purity of family life." If such conditions destroyed women's "ethical purity" morality would be lost.[823–24]

"This is an era of luxury," and luxury produced "degeneration," evident in plays, books, and newspapers:

> The greater portion of the *clientele* of the alienist is made up of women who are suffering with neurotic troubles. . . . The number of viragints, gynandrists, androgynes, and other female psycho-sexual aberrants is very large indeed.
>     . . . The New Woman glories in the fact that the era which she hopes to inaugurate will introduce her into a new world. Not satisfied with the liberty she now enjoys, . . . she longs for more freedom, a broader field of action. If nature provided men and women with inexhaustible supplies of nervous energy, they might set aside physical laws. . . .

But nature did not so provide; energy was limited.[824] The doctor concluded:

> The simple right to vote carries with it no immediate danger, the danger comes afterward, . . . when woman, owing to her increased degeneration, gives free rein to her atavistic tendencies, and hurries backward toward the savage state of her barbarian ancestors. I see, in the establishment of equal rights, the first step toward that abyss of immoral horrors so repugnant to our cultivated ethical tastes—the matriarchate.[825]

MEDICAL/RESISTANCE

## 1895, December
## Dr. Havelock Ellis: Thirty-three case histories

In a paper read before two medical-legal groups, and published in a New York medical journal, Ellis summarized thirty-three original case histories of male "sexual inversion."[36] Though presented as objective, scientific discourse, Ellis's implicit aim was clearly that of a sexual liberal, to reduce the negative element in the social response to inverts. The simple point had not before been made that cases of inversion observed by doctors or the police were bound to be weighted with negative attributes. Ellis's essay was also one of the few times a doctor distinguished clearly between society's and the invert's views, crediting the invert with some legitimacy. Ellis was at pains here to portray the invert as good, hard-working bourgeois. One reason for Ellis's opposition to the idea of acquired inversion appears here to be its unsettling implication that both inversion and "normal" male-female attraction are socially determined and mutable, not biologically given and unchangeable.

"My cases," said Ellis, "were not gathered from my medical practice, nor by the aid of police officials. In this respect they differ from the groups of inverts presented by previous observers who have consequently been led to overestimate the morbid or vicious elements in such cases."[255]

The families of inverts, Ellis stressed,

do not usually possess such profound signs of nervous degeneration as we were once led to suppose. What we vaguely call "eccentricity" is common among [these families]; insanity is much rarer.[256]

Sixteen, or nearly half of Ellis's inverts were said to possess "unimpaired" physical health, enabling them to do "at least their fair share of work in the world." That work was of "high intellectual value" in a "considerable proportion" of his cases.[257]

"Emotional tendencies to affection and self-sacrifice" were also present in a "considerable proportion" of Ellis's cases.[258] (Six of his subjects were "psychosexual hermaphrodites," those who "found sexual satisfaction with their own and the opposite sex"—now called "bisexuals.")[259]

Referring to "the invert's own attitudes towards his anomaly," Ellis noted that three of his cases "loathe themselves and have fought in vain against their perversion." Six others were ambivalent, and had "little to say in justification of their condition," which they tended to regard as "morbid." But the "majority" of Ellis's inverts,

> seventeen in number, are emphatic in their assertions that their moral position is precisely the same as that of the normally constituted individual; one or two even regard inverted love as nobler than ordinary sexual love; a few add the proviso that there should be consent and understanding on both sides and no attempt at seduction. The chief regret of one or two is the double life they are obliged to lead.[260]

Ellis rejected the idea that inversion was "acquired," since this "logically involves the assertion that the normal instinct is also acquired." (That the mutual attraction of females and males might be socially induced was a possibility rejected without thought as absurd.) Also, since "in nearly every country . . . men associate chiefly with men, women with women," inversion would be the rule "if this influence is the determining one." The theory of acquired inversion also meant that the "most fundamental human instinct had remained aimless," only accidentally linked to procreation. This Ellis did not accept.[261–62]

"What is sexual inversion?" Ellis asked. Was it an "acquired vice, to be stamped out by the prison"? Was it "a beneficial variety of human emotion, to be tolerated and even fostered"? Was it a "pathological state qualifying its victims for the lunatic asylum"? Was it a "natural monstrosity, a human 'sport,' the manifestations of which must be regulated when they become anti-social"? "More than one of these views" had some truth, said Ellis (equivocating, as usual, in the name of scientific objectivity). Sexual inversion, he argued, was not a "disease" or form of "degeneration," but a "congenital abnormality," which could remain "latent," or could be stimulated by environmental factors. It was comparable to "organic variations" seen throughout "nature, in plants and animals."[262–64]

♀  BLACK AMERICAN/INTIMACY

## 1896, February
## Angelina Weld Grimké: "Under the Days"

"The Buried Life and Poetry of Angelina Weld Grimké," a Black woman-loving writer who lived from 1880 to 1958, is the subject of a recent essay by Gloria T. Hull, summarized here.[37]

In February 1896, a young friend, Mamie Burrill, wrote to the sixteen-year-old Grimké, mixing school gossip and church news, and recalling good times together:

> Could I just come to meet thee once more, in the old sweet way, just coming at your calling, and like an angel bending o'er you breathe into your ear, "I love you."

In a letter to Burrill, written later in 1896, from Carleton Academy, Northfield, Minnesota, Angelina Grimké said:

> Oh Mamie if you only knew how my heart overflows with love for you and how it yearns and pants for one glimpse of your lovely face.

Grimké asked Mamie Burrill to be her "wife," and ended:

> "Now may the Almighty father bless thee little one and keep thee safe from all harm, your passionate lover."

It is not clear if Mamie Burrill was the partner in a disastrous love affair recorded in Angelina Grimké's diary of July 18 to September 10, 1903, when she was twenty-three. On September 6, Grimké wrote: "I am through with love and the like forever."[19] Although the gender of the lost lover was unspecified in the diary (indicative of a significant coding), poems written by Angelina Grimké at the same time suggest the lover was female.[20]

In "Rosabel" (or "Rosalie"), a poem written in the early 1900s, Angelina Grimké spoke of "Winds that breathe about, upon her / (Lines I do not dare) / Whisper, turtle, breathe upon her / That I find her fair."

In a love poem, "El Beso" (The Kiss), first published in 1909, Grimké spoke of "your provocative laughter, / The gloom of your hair; / Lure of you, eye and lip"; and then: "pain, regret—your sobbing."

In an unpublished poem about a female Grimké regretted: "I may never press / My lips on thine in mute caress."

Another unpublished poem, "Autumn," recalled a bygone "love, our first love, glorious, yielding." The final stanza recorded a present in which "the smile is not for me . . . [but] for the new life and dreams wherein I have no part."[21]

Other unpublished lines recorded the wish: "If I might taste but once, just once / The dew / Upon her lips."[22]

Angelina Weld Grimké (1880–1958).    From the Mooreland–Springarn Research Center, Howard University.

Another fragment mourned: "And oh! the crying want of you."[23]

In some of the unpublished poems carried furthest to completion, to type-script, Grimké substituted "he" for the original "she," where gender was unavoidable.[22]

Angelina Grimké died in 1958 at the age of seventy-eight. Her poem "Under the Days" spoke of her life buried under leaves that "cover me, / They crush, / They smother, / Who will ever find me / Under the days?"[24]

♀  PLAY REVIEW / CROSSING PERSONS

## 1896, October 13
### N. Y. Times: Archibald Gunter's A Florida Enchantment

A play by Archibald Clavering Gunter, A Florida Enchantment, was adapted from the novel of the same name, which Gunter had co-authored.[38]

"What is needed now at Hoyt's Theatre is not criticism, but chloride of lime" (a disinfectant), The Times reviwer began. This "was the worst play ever produced in New York"—"Theatricals have never before sunk quite so low in New York—on a decent stage."

The play was "not only vile stuff—it is unutterably stupid." If "the author fancies that his audacity is going to draw the paying public in large numbers he is sadly mistaken." If the theater owner did not close the play there was "danger that Mr. Anthony Comstock [head of the Society for the Suppression of Vice] may be stirred up . . . and start to advertise it."

"While there are a few of the most indecent ideas in the piece that mortal man has ever tried to communicate, the playwright is so bungling that none but very sophisticated persons catch his drift." Several theater pieces which had, up to then, been thought "the nastiest things ever inflicted on New York," were cited; Gunter had aimed "to outdo them."

> The story he tries to tell is of a fool of a woman who finds a magic seed that will transform her into a man and swallows it. Thereafter she says "damn," smokes a cigarette, and makes violent love to girls. [The phrase "to make love to" then meant "to court," rather than to have genital relations with.] A darky maid servant is similarly transformed, and some of the so-called men in the play are changed into women.

On October 18, reviewer Edward Dithmar commented in The Times that A Florida Enchantment

> shows us the lowest depth in which the theatrical stage can be sunk by tasteless speculators. Financiers always feel relieved when "bed-rock" has been reached.

He did not think newspaper denunciations of the play would "make the venture profitable." But the play was still running, he noted.

An unidentified newspaper clipping of October 1896 is headed: "Mr. Gunter Wrestles With A Question Of Sex." It was one thing "to print descriptions of animal feelings, sexual developings, . . . and another to speak of them." The "world recognizes lots of things it does not speak about." But Gunter had decided "that the only new thing left under the sun is to speak about them." (Those distinctions between printed discourse and verbal speech, verbal speech and "recognition" [conscious thought], are major ones in the history of sex.)

After eating the seed and changing her sex, the actress playing Gunter's heroine uttered "a burst of profanity." She then

> kisses everything feminine in sight. The physiological study increases, and she begins to assume swaggering, assertive attitudes, to discover a sudden and irrelevant mustache, and to want to vote. So far she is masking her changed sex in woman's clothes—and it is here that the plot thickens.
>      The ex-woman is seized with a sudden passion for her former girl friend. I say passion advisedly, since Mr. Gunter has carefully excluded anything so mawkish as sentiment from his playful little physiological study. This sudden mannish passion, palpitating under a tea gown, makes things difficult for the seed-swallowing freak. . . .*

The "sexual transformation of the maid" was said to be "even less subtle than that of the mistress."


♀  NEWS FEATURE

# 1897, May 23
## N. Y. Times: Rev. Charles Parkhurst on "andromaniacs"

Comments on "Woman" by the Reverend Parkhurst, a famous New York antivice crusader, were excerpted in The Times.[39] Though no reference was made to eroticism or intimacy, the reverend used the terminology of "disease," and coined a medical-sounding derogatory name for independent women, a strategy akin to that of doctors in naming "psycho-sexual aberrants" and "homosexuals." This minister's scientific naming is indicative of an increase in the power and status of the medical, relative to the theological profession. His stress on the difference between true woman and man was typical of gender conservatives of the late 1800s and 1900s. Parkhurst's comments had been published in The Ladies' Home Journal, and reprinted in a book.

Parkhurst declared: "An element in the feminine world is suffering from

---

*The term "freakish" is documented in 1930 as Black slang for "homosexual"; see backnote to 1928, June; and the index under "freak."

what I shall call 'andromania,' " a "passionate aping" of "everything mannish."
This imitating by "those affected with the disease" was an attempt "to minimize
distinctions by which manhood and womanhood are differentiated."

> I am not criticising any particular act of the "andromaniacs".... My criticism
> is only upon the disposition apparent in many quarters to narrow the dis-
> tinctive features of woman to the smallest possible area. The contention is
> that if she broadens out into new lines of employment or service, at the
> impulse of a conviction that activities that are suitable for men are suitable
> for women, and that the supreme distinction between the two is physiologi-
> cal, she is misconstruing her own nature. . . .

Parkhurst insisted on the "intrinsic superiority" of the female's "womanly fibre."

> Sex is not an accident of personality, but is an element that is constituent
> in every thread and fibre of it. If a man is a man, the flavor of manhood will
> permeate him in his entirety.

The same was true of woman and womanhood.

A civilization that transformed a woman "into the female duplicate of a man,
is a false civilization." To retain their "supremacy" women would have to make
"more and more of their womanliness," not try to be "mannish." "Woman's
proper destiny is on a distinct line from that of masculinity."

> Nature has so wrought its opinions into the tissue of woman's physical
> constitution and function that any feminine attempt to mutiny against wife-
> hood, motherhood, and domestic "limitations" is a hopeless and rather
> imbecile attempt to escape the inevitable.

"All the female congresses in the world might combine in colossal mass meetings" and vote that "woman's sphere" was coincident with the whole earth, "but
the very idiosyncrasy of her physical build and the limitations essentially bound
up in it," would counter that vote. "God and nature had very different intentions"
for woman than "for her brother."

Parkhurst was glad "increased attention is being given to the discipline of
the female mind." College training would not "unsex" woman if it was "dominated by the feminine instinct and mortgaged to maternal ends."


MEDICAL

## 1898, May
## Dr. Francis W. Anthony:
### *"A band of urnings," Massachusetts*

A paper on "Responsibility in Cases of Sexual Perversion" was read to the Essex
North Branch of the Massachusetts Medical Society by Dr. Anthony, surgeon at

a Haverhill, Massachusetts, hospital.[40] "The ordinary forms of perversion" spoken of were "sadism"; "fetichism"; "homosexuality, sexual leaning toward members of the same sex; bestiality; pederasty; sodomy; necrophilia and incest."[289]

Anthony reported one case of "homosexuality," and one of "perversion" involving a five-year-old boy, "addicted to the habit of masturbation," who had allegedly made his three-year-old brother "the active or passive agent of sexual gratification."[290]

Anyone who thinks such cases "rare," said Anthony,

> has little idea of the underground life of our cities. I have been told that there is in a community not far removed—and I am informed that the fact is true of nearly every centre of importance—a band of urnings, men of perverted tendencies, men known to each other as such, bound by ties of secrecy and fear and held together by mutual attraction. This band . . . embraces, not as you might think, the low and vile outcasts of the slums, but men of education and refinement, men gifted in music, in art and in literature, men of professional life and men of business and affairs. To themselves, by the attraction of their presence and surroundings, they draw boys and young men, over whom they have the same jealous bickerings and heart burnings that attend the triumphs of a local belle. Quarrels for preference are frequent; yet must, by the nature of things, be kept to themselves. The triumphant suitor carries to his house and his room his innocent victim, and then begins a course of sexual perversion, the teacher an adept, the pupil a novice, until a new star arises, or satiety compels a rest. The sexual propensities of the young is perverted, or may be inverted, and a life is ruined almost beyond hope of recovery. . . .

Such acts were "committed by men most, if not all, of whom are legally and morally responsible." Was it not important then, "that the subject be brought to the attention of the general practitioner, that he may be on the alert?"

> It may fall to the lot of one of you to be the active means of destroying such a school of vice and perversion. Nay, more than that, it may be your son or the son of your intimate friend whom you are called upon to rescue. If it comes in the line of your duty to take a hand in the overthrow of such a circle, I beg of you to let no dread of notoriety, no consideration of position, . . . come between you and the fulfilment of such a duty. Exercise all due charity, have the suspected and accused submitted to a most thorough examination to determine his responsibility, and then have him removed from the community in his proper place, be it asylum or be it prison.[290-91]

# 1898
## Dr. Mary Wood-Allen: *"A sex mania"*

In her book *What A Young Woman Ought To Know,* Dr. Wood-Allen, the "National Superindentent of the Purity Department of the Women's Christian Temperance Union," and author of *The Man Wonderful in the House Beautiful,* included chapters on "Solitary Vice" and on "Friendship Between Girls."[41]

In the chapter on "self-abuse," Dr. Wood-Allen warned:

> while in the human being the procreative act does not kill, it exhausts, and no doubt takes from the vital force of those exercising it. One can feel justified to lose a part of her own life if she is conferring life upon others, but to indulge in such a waste of vital force merely for pleasure is certainly never excusable, and least excusable of all is the arousing of pleasurable emotions by a direct violation of natural law.
>
> The only natural method of arousing a recognition of sexual feeling is as God has appointed in holy marriage. . . .[150]

She warned that girls might "revel in imaginary scenes of love-making . . . which arouse the spasmodic feeling of sexual pleasure, and yet be unaware that they are guilty of self-abuse."

"Sexual feeling in itself is not base," she said, "but it can be debased either in thought or in deed."[151]

In her comments on "Friendship Between Girls," Dr. Wood-Allen said:

> I believe in reserve even in girl friendships. Girls are apt at certain periods of their lives to be rather gushing creatures. They form most sentimental attachments for each other. They go about with their arms around each other, they loll against each other, and sit with clasped hands by the hour. They fondle and kiss until beholders are fairly nauseated, and in a few weeks, perhaps, they do not speak as they pass each other, and their caresses are lavished on others. Such friendships are not only silly, they are dangerous. They are a weakening of moral fibre, a waste of mawkish sentimentality. They may be even worse. Such friendship may degenerate even into a species of self-abuse that is most deplorable.
>
> When girls are so sentimentally fond of each other that they are like silly lovers when together, and weep over each other's absence in uncontrollable agony, the conditions are serious enough for the consultation of a physician. It is an abnormal state of affairs, and if probed thoroughly might be found to be a sort of perversion, a sex mania, needing immediate and perhaps severe measures.
>
> I wish the friendships of girls were less sentimental, more manly. Two young men who are friends do not lop on each other, and kiss and gush. They trust each other, they talk freely together, they would stand by each

other in any trouble or emergency, but their expressions of endearment are not more than the cordial handgrasp and the unsentimental appellation, "Dear old chap."

I admire these friendships in young men. They seem to mean so much, and yet to exact so little.[173–74]

BOOK REVIEWS/RESISTANCE

## 1899, January
### *International Journal of Ethics:*
### Dr. Ellis's *Sexual Inversion*
### and Carpenter's *An Unknown People*

Evidence suggests that *The International Journal of Ethics* (published in Philadelphia, later at the University of Chicago), served as a means of information exchange between sex radicals and liberals in the United States and England.[42]

Commenting on Edward Carpenter's *An Unknown People* (1897), reviewer H. Sturt called it "a popular account of sexual inversion." Carpenter "presents the main facts in an accurate and agreeable form, saying little, of course, about their darker side." His "chief point is that the class of inverts may have a useful function in society as reconcilers and interpreters between the two sexes."

Ellis's *Sexual Inversion* (1897) was described as "a solid and valuable contribution to the psychology" of that subject. He "gives the impression that he is a genuine scientific man doing his best to illustrate an obscure . . . province of human nature."

"At present, there are two main theories of sexual inversion." It was "congenital" or it was "the result of habit and suggestion," therefore "curable through counter-suggestion." Ellis "adopts the congenital theory with due allowance for the secondary influence of other factors."

Ellis's "practical conclusions" were "cautious." He condemned hypnotic treatment as "futile and repulsive." He did not think "inverts" should be encouraged to marry and "perpetuate an abnormal stock." Ellis was quoted: a " 'tendency to sexual inversion in eccentric and neurotic families' " seemed Nature's way " 'of winding up a concern which . . . has ceased to be profitable' " (the capitalistic metaphor suggests a relation between the political economy, language, and thought).

"It is useless," Ellis believed,

to try to change the invert's nature. It is better to influence him to a good life and to direct his homosexual sympathies into channels which will make him a useful and happy member of society.

Mr. Ellis further recommends a relaxation of the severe English law against unnatural vice. Here he is less convincing. Our present law is not very logical, but, from the general common sense of those who administer it, seems to work fairly well.

There are some who would raise the general question whether a subject like the present can fitly be made the matter of a published treatise. Many excellent persons have a horror of everything related to the homosexual tendency. Their feeling commands our respect, and yet it seems better to have the subject brought out into publicity. That all sorts of immature and half-educated people should read Mr. Ellis's book is, of course, most undesirable. But in view of the prevalence of sexual inversion it is necessary that every schoolmaster, every criminal lawyer, we had almost said every head of a family, should be acquainted with its phenomena. Were the subject better understood, mistakes would be avoided that have ruined thousands of lives.

PERSONAL TESTIMONY

# 1899, April 8
## New York State Report: "Male degenerates"

Testimony taken by a special New York State body, the Mazet Committee, mandated to investigate New York City public officials, included references to "resorts" where there gathered "male harlots," "Nancys," "fairies," and "degenerates."[43]* Among these New York resorts were Manilla Hall, Paresis (or Columbia) Hall, The Palm, The Black Rabbit, Little Bucks, The Artistic Club, and perhaps The Fifth Avenue Hotel. Apparent in this record is the conflict between upstate Republican committee members, and the Democratic officials of New York City's Tammany Hall, whom they were investigating.

In the first excerpt New York City Police Chief William S. Devery was questioned about conditions on the Bowery and in the Tenderloin district:

Q.  I wanted to show you a little advertisement that I had from the Manilla Hall to go down there and see the rag-time, and the Ki-ki. . . .† Do you know what they are? . . .

A.  [The rag-time] is a dance, I believe. . . .

Q.  Is it a good dance? I mean a moral dance?

A.  They say at times it becomes vulgar. . . .[I, 173]

Q.  What about those male degenerates that frequent the Manilla? Did you hear about that? . . . Do you know what a male degenerate is?

A.  I presume I understand what you mean. . . . I have heard about people of that class frequenting those places.

*For additional Mazet Committee testimony see *GAH*, pp. 44–47. The testimony below was not previously reprinted.

†For "rag-time" see footnote, p. 299. Here "Ki-ki" evidently named a "vulgar" dance; for later homosexual usages of the term see 1941, Legman; and entry of 1947, June, p. 626.

Q.  Have you heard, then, that there are male degenerates upon the Bow-ery in sufficient number to be noticeable?

A.  No; I have not heard that. . . .

Q.  What have you heard about Paresis Hall?

A.  Touching on the degenerates that you spoke about that frequent there.

Q.  That is a place that is noticed because it is frequented by those persons, is it not?

A.  That is presumably the reason it gets that name.*

Q.  And the men that go there are noted characters and are known by women's names, are they not?

A.  I believe they are. . . .[I, 174]

Q.  Why do you not, as chief of police, when you hear of a hall notable for these filthy and abominable practices which have no defender anywhere in human civilization, why do you not go to it and stamp it out?

A.  I have done so.

Q.  What have you done?

A.  Placed them under arrest. . . . The proprietors of those places.

Q.  Do you know that what they do [sodomy] is a felony (I mean the individuals) punishable by imprisonment for twenty years?

A.  . . . I don't know anything of that kind in it.

Q.  You have never heard of their giving circuses around that neighbor-hood?†

A.  No, sir. . . .

Q.  The Palm is another one?

A.  Yes, sir.

Q.  And the Black Rabbit is another?

A.  [The answer was positive.] It was closed. . . . I don't think those people frequent that place now.[I, 176]

In testimony on April 10, 1899, Police Chief Devery mentioned that the resort commonly called "Paresis Hall" was officially named Columbia Hall, add-ing: "It is rumored that the gentlemen [degenerates] . . . frequent there once in a while, as they do many other hotels in the city."[I, 278]

---

*"Paresis" was a medical term for a form of paralysis thought to be caused by venereal disease. The committee chairman, Mr. Mazet, was referred to as the originator of the name Paresis Hall; see I, p. 277 in document. That derogatory name was disliked by the inverts who visited the Hall; see *GAH*, p. 367.

†Re "circuses": In an article published in August 1914, Dr. S. A. Tannenbaum discussed the "unconscious homosexuality" behind the desire of males and females to watch other males and females in the sexual act. Tannenbaum added: "New Yorkers may be reminded of certain exclusive and expensive resorts known as 'circuses' where people were given the opportunity to satisfy these perverse cravings"; see backnote 1914, August (which includes Tannenbaum's comments, p. 533 in original document).

On November 3, 1899 an officer of the City Vigilance League, George P. Hammond, was asked by the committee about

> places that are well known as being resorts for male prostitutes. Has that unmentionable crime, so far as it is open to the people been on the increase?
> A.   It has increased wonderfully within the last six months.

Paresis Hall was mentioned, and Hammond was asked:

> Q.   Is it not a fact that there is not any of these resorts . . . for dissolute classes, which has not its male degenerates? . . . How many of those places do you know of that are open from the street, where boys go in freely, and where they have attached to it as a feature of the place, a male degenerate?
> A.   On the Bowery alone there is to my knowledge certainly six places. There are other places where they have them.[V, 5125]
> Q.   Do these poor, miserable creatures make themselves public? Do they show themselves?
> A.   They do. They exhibit themselves and solicit. I have seen them solicit openly, and they have solicited me.
> Q.   Do you remember an occasion recently when one of those persons, after exhibiting himself, walk[ed] through the audience and offered his photograph for sale?
> A.   Yes, sir. He just got through singing a song. I should not say he, I should say "it." "It" just got through singing a song . . . there were three or four gentlemen sitting there, he offered the photographs. Those are the photographs sold by him at that place that night. (Showing photographs.) I bought these from that party. That was a place called "Little Bucks," at the Bowery; . . . it is diagonally opposite from Paresis Hall. It is an off-shoot of that. It is the place . . . where they used to give what they called "the circus." He was not the only man of that kind that was present. . . . there were either three or four of them. There were two of them sang; sang a duet. There were men and women in that place. There was immoral solicitation and immoral conduct. They danced the rag time there. By the rag time I mean a decidedly immoral dance. That is one of the evils of this thing. You will find the word "rag time" used in high social circles. The people do not know what it means. They do not know where it emanated from. If they did they would blush for shame. It sometimes makes me boil over with indignation when I hear that phrase used.[V, 5126]*

---

*The scandalous meaning of "rag time" was not specified. My guess is that the phrase referred to that time at which a menstruating woman was "wearing the rag," thought not to be having intercourse, and therefore thought to be possessed of a particularly amorous, energetic nature. (For "rag," see Natalie F. Joffee, "The Vernacular of Menstruation," *Word*, vol. 4, no. 3 [December 1948], pp. 181–86.) The various dictionaries consulted indicated no "wicked" meaning to "rag time"; see examples from 1899 on in the *OED Supplement* (1933). *Webster's Unabridged*, 2nd ed., says "ragtime" derives from "ragged time, term first applied (c. 1890) to New Orleans music as played by Negro orchestras on Mississippi River boats." The word is defined as referring to "a type of American dance music popular from about 1890 to 1915. . . ." The document above suggests some illicit sexual connotation, and it would not be surprising if standard dictionaries were inept in the face of such carnal derivation.

♀ MEDICAL/NEWS REPORT

## 1899, April 30
### *N.Y. Times:* Dr. John D. Quackenbos on "moral perversions"

*The Times* headed a long story "Hypnotism The Cure-All."[44] A subhead added: "Prof. John D. Quackenbos Would Regenerate the Human Race." Another subhead spoke of "His Successful Experiments," and claimed that "Crime and Disease Succumb to the Treatment."

"Hypnotism as a means of reforming criminals," of "removing crime and moral obliquity," was "the latest theory which advanced science has to offer." Prof. Quackenbos, of Columbia University, had been "conducting experiments," and said that by means of hypnotism he had cured "stammering, drug and alcoholic addiction, moral perversions, and excessive cigarette smoking." (A medical journal report by Dr. Quackenbos later the same year was explicit about his curing "nymphomania, masturbation, gross impurity, [and] unnatural passion for persons of the same sex"; see *GAH*, pp. 144–45.)

The doctor suggested that his hypnotism cure be used in prisons and slums. His experiment at "the Newsboys Home" had been "entirely successful." He said: when the "hypnotist physician gets a patient under his control the patient is for the time being part of himself." The patient "lost his own will, and has to act and think as the hypnotist suggests." If "elevated ideals" were suggested, the patient was "elevated." Quackenbos had cured a thief by suggesting to him "that he lived in a country where honesty not only prevailed, but was rewarded." The doctor was arranging with the New York Juvenile Asylum "to get some boys and girls with whom to experiment."

♀ MEDICAL/NEWS REPORT

## 1899, June
### Chicago: Nettie Miller shoots Charles Seibert,
### A case of probable contrary sexual feeling

A recent issue of the *Chicago Daily News* had reported what a Detroit medical journal called "A Case of Probable Contrare Sexualempfinding" (sic—contrary sexual feeling) in a woman.[45]

Charles L. Seibert had been "shot by Mrs. Nettie A. Miller because he had married Hattie Leonard, a woman for whom Mrs. Miller possessed a strong affection."

The former Hattie Leonard, "the object of Mrs. Miller's affections," explained that she had lived with Miller "for fourteen years and claimed to have been held under hypnotic influence." Hattie Leonard had cared for Nettie Miller when Miller was ill. At this time Miller

> fell desperately in love with Hattie Leonard. This infatuation deepened more and more as time went by.

> Miller had forbidden Leonard's "going with any man." Hattie Leonard had left Miller four times, and was "each time forced back by . . . this hypnotic power." She "tried to resist and could not."

> Leonard claimed that Miller had "assaulted her for accepting the attentions of a drug clerk," and threatened the clerk, so that they had stopped "going together."

> The medical journal said that "Aberrations of the sexual instinct" were "inherited," but the question of responsibility in all such cases was not established. "Jealousy" had motivated many crimes. The responsibility for such crimes was "not altered because the object of the affection happens to belong to the same sex as the perpetrator."

MEDICAL

# 1899
## Dr. George J. Monroe: *"Habits . . . worse than beastly"*

"Sodomy" was defined by Dr. Monroe of Louisville, Kentucky, as "unnatural intercourse" between man and man; "pederasty" was anal intercourse between man and woman.[46] The introduction of the male organ into the mouth of either male or female "is commonly called mouth sucking."

> These habits are so abominable, so disgusting, so filthy, and worse than beastly, that the medical profession, from a sense of decency and respect, are loth to write about them, or even to discuss them with other physicians. Yet they are . . . so commonly practiced, that I believe it is the duty of the medical profession to direct more attention to them. . . .[431]

Speaking, apparently, of anal intercourse, Monroe said: "Bad as the practice is becoming in America," it was more common in other countries.

> The practice in the United States has been restricted to a great extent to soldiers, sailors, miners, loggers, campers, and others whose occupations separate them for the greater share of the time from women.*
>     It is however becoming quite common in our large cities, where this condition [of sexual separation] does not exist.

*This is the earliest known published expression of the idea that these archetypal male pioneers were particularly prone to sodomy and other erotic intercourse with each other, but evidence for this proposition is so far sadly lacking; also see *GAH*, pp. 511–12.

Males and females in every large city were said to devote themselves to oral/genital acts for profit.

> In my own city a number of instances have become public where young men, middle-aged men, and the aged even, have made a regular business of using their mouths for this purpose.[432]

> One result of male-female anal intercourse was "an excessive development of the buttocks—the hips enlarge." The penis of the active pederast was said to be small. But this "is not always the case, for sometimes the penis is very large."*

> There must be something extremely fascinating and satisfactory about this habit; for when once begun it is seldom ever given up.

Sodomy and pederasty were allegedly "practiced to a greater extent among the low and degraded than . . . among the better class."[433]


♀ MEDICAL

<h1 style="text-align:center">1900, May 5<br>Dr. William Lee Howard:<br>"Effeminate Men and Masculine Women"</h1>

"When a child demonstrates in its acts and tastes an indifference to the natural preference and inclination of its sex," said Dr. Howard of Baltimore, "it should be strictly confined" to the company of its own sex.[1]† Every encouragement should be

> given it to develop its normal attributes. An indifferent boy who grows up an effeminate man should be allowed to share the ridicule and contempt thrust upon him with his parents, the mother being given the major part.

Howard especially condemned a boy's association with embroidery, dolls, and make-believe tea parties with girl playmates. Such a boy "grows up psychically unsexed, detested by the vigorous male," and admonished by the "true father" for his "mincing manners."

> The female with masculine manners is always amusing and often pitiable; but the attenuated, weak-voiced neuter, the effeminate male: pity him, but blame his mother for the false training, and give scorn to the father for his indifference. . . .
> The female possessed of masculine ideas of independence; the viragint who would sit in the public highways and lift up her pseudo-virile voice, proclaiming her sole right to decide questions of war or religion, or the

---

*Past and present folklore concerning penis and clitoris size is an intriguing subject for study.
†For Howard's explicit equation of the effeminate male with the male "sexual invert" see his article of 1904, January.

value of celibacy and the curse of woman's impurity, and that disgusting antisocial being, the female sexual pervert, are simply different degrees of the same class—degenerates. These unsightly and subnormal beings are the victims of poor mating. When a woman neglects her maternal instincts, when her sentiment and dainty feminine characteristics are boldly and ostentatiously kept submerged, we can see an antisocial creature more amusing than dangerous. When such a woman marries, which she often does for the privileges derived from attaching Mrs. to her name, the husband is certain to be one she can rule. . . .

If this female becomes a mother

she ceases to be merely amusing, and is an antisocial being. She is then a menace to civilization, a producer of nonentities, the mother of mental and physical monstrosities who exist as a class of true degenerates until disgusted Nature, no longer tolerant of the woman who would be a man, or the man who would be a woman, allows them to shrink unto death.

"The female who prefers the laboratory to the nursery," and the woman "with child" who involves herself in social conditions "are true degenerates." The children of "such human misfits are perverts, moral or psychical," influenced by conditions opposite to those the "real woman" would choose. "The child born of the 'new woman' is to be pitied." Its brain cells

are twisted, distorted, and perverted psychic growth promoted by the false examples and teachings of a discontented mother.

Those were the conditions that had produced the "antisocial 'new woman' and the disgusting effeminate male."

It is this class that clamors for "higher education" for the woman; that crowds public halls, shouting for the freedom of woman and demanding all the prerogatives of the man.

"It is these female androids" who were the " 'ism'-ites, and mental roamers," who "form sects and societies regardless of sense or science." It was such women who "claim to know more about the science of medicine than the men who have devoted their lives to that science." It was these women who walked about "flaunting our health laws . . . in the faces of the assumed intelligent masses."[687]

♀ PERSONAL TESTIMONY/RESISTANCE

## c. 1900

### Mary Casal: *"At last . . . I was not a creature apart"*

Early in the twentieth century the pseudonymous Mary Casal and her lover, Juno, discovered that they were not the only women in the world dedicated to a sexual-love union with females.[2] Despite Casal's previous passionate affairs with a number of women she had continued to believe herself and Juno to be the only women committed to a female-female relationship.[*]

The autobiography of Mary Casal is one of the few early life histories of American lesbians. Born in 1864, into a poor farming family in rural New England, Casal was the youngest of nine children. From an early age she liked "boys' sports and out-of-doors life," hated dolls, and wanted a "jack-knife" and large handkerchief (boys' prerogatives).

At an early age Casal experienced the first of a number of sexual molestations by older boys and adult males.[†] Before meeting Juno she mentions passionate relationships with eight women, some involving genital contact.[‡] But her female partners were experienced as different from herself—apparently because of their lack of exclusive devotion to a woman-woman union. At about the age of twenty (around 1884), Casal says, "I felt that I was the only girl who had the sex desire for woman, rather than the accepted one for men."[92-93]

Casal graduated from a coeducational Midwestern university, taught in a small, rural, New England school, and then in Boston at a select girls' day school on Beacon Hill. Trying to be "normal," she married, and was later divorced. Trying to become a mother, she had two still-births.[§] In New York City she opened a successful private school in a "large studio apartment on Washington Square." She was secretary in an art gallery in which hung "four of Corot's most famous works." She invented, manufactured, and successfully marketed a paper toy. She ran a farm, and was a commercial artist. Despite this wide experience and seeming worldliness, Casal and Juno continued to believe that "we were the only ones in the world who cherished such a love." None of their friends "knew of the real union, of our bodies."[||]

Throughout her book (published in 1930) Casal argues for frank discussions with children about sex, and in defense of the "superior" type of female-female sex-love relationship she shared for a time with Juno. Casal also reveals her belief in a number of sexual myths—among them that masturbation is physically debilitating, and that male "inverts" are sex-obsessed child molesters. Her dislike of male "inverts" may be due, in part, to the fact of Juno's eventual marriage to a male with a history of inversion. Casal's autobiography, *The Stone Wall*, was published in Chicago when she was sixty-six, probably at her own expense.

In the following expisode, a friendship with an actress whom Casal calls "Little Ben" (a quick-change artist who sometimes played male roles) leads to a visit to the Brooklyn home of a woman here named the "Philosopher"—who informs Casal and Juno of the world of sexual "inverts."

*For Casal's description of her meeting with Juno see *GAH*, pp. 548–56.
†See pp. 23, 29–30, 34, 57, 71, 79–80.
‡See pp. 47, 50, 61, 68, 77, 82, 85, 97, 105.
§See pp. 47, 94–95, 99–102, 110–12.
||See pp. 112, 116, 135, 138–42, 164, 165, 167.

Upon arriving we were presented to a most astonishing personality—a little woman with short, black hair tinged with gray, wearing heavy white silk pajamas, smoking, and very hospitable. She had the most charming manners and beautiful but very piercing hazel eyes. She looked us through, and I knew at once that she too knew! I was impelled at first to seize my Juno and run, for I did not want to think that there was anyone else in the world who knew of love such as ours. Of course, I did no such foolish thing, and in a way I was held by a certain fascination which I could not analyse.

In one way we, both Juno and I, were glad of that night, for we stayed all night, which was nearly all given up to listening. We learned a great deal. I will call our hostess "Phil," short for Philosopher. We dined, of course, and all smoked, and Phil did most of the talking. She talked freely about herself. Early in the evening we learned from her lips that she was a bastard and that she had had many love affairs with women. She was well educated and spoke beautiful English with a British accent. We afterward knew that her father was a British nobleman, but she never divulged his name to anyone. He made her an allowance, and she visited him at intervals during his life. Her mother was an Italian for whom she had no love. She was a great student of philosophy, ever seeking, as she said, the Truth. At this time she was a Theosophist and a near friend of Madam Blavatsky.

We were fascinated by her as something unique in our lives. . . . Phil warned us against any further contact with Little Ben, as she was a very notorious character in all large cities and to be seen with her would condemn us at once. We always felt it was mighty fine of Little Ben, realizing as she must have done, and as did Phil, that we did not really belong in that class, to have protected us thus.

Phil did interest us more and more. We saw her frequently and we became warm friends. Her life had been spent largely in Europe, and her loves had all been women of great beauty and famous in the world of letters and on the stage. We had ample proof of the marvelous stories she told us, as there were many letters and autographed photographs which she showed us.

At last, and too late, did I find that I was not a creature apart as I had always felt. How much suffering would have been saved me and what a different life I would have led if I had known earlier that we are not all created after one pattern nor according to any set rules, but that each is as "normal" as any other!

In spite of all we learned at the feet of the Wise One, neither Juno nor I could reconcile ourselves to the thought that we were of that class who seemed to have little constancy. We knew we were not promiscuous as were Little Ben and Phil, who was much older than we and said she was through with love forever. We could not speak of our love. It was too sacred to us. We also knew that we had not entered that group because of any thought that they were of a class apart, but . . . because of curiosity about an actress [Little Ben] who acted the male so perfectly. We were not sexually attracted by her or by any whom we met by knowing her. We were sufficient unto ourselves, though we both thirsted for knowledge on the subject.

None of our other friends or family were ever introduced to any of this group. We were as children whose curiosity had been aroused, and we were also anxious to learn as much as possible of a love which was, and to me ever will be, of a beautiful type but which has carried a stigma in the minds of many who have never understood it in its perfection.

What wonder that I . . . had not much respect for the accepted form of marriage! There certainly was not much of sanctity in the marriages that came under my notice, and I have not changed my mind in the least from all I have since known. I do not say that there are no true unions in marriage, but with marriage as an institution today, I think many will agree with me, there is certainly something wrong. But as to Juno and me, I shall always feel that as long as our lives together lasted (Oh, yes, there came a break, but our union lasted much longer than most marriages do nowadays, not-withstanding), it was the purest and most ideal of any type of union known.

There was not a human impulse in my nature that Juno did not meet. She represented the highest type of any kin. She was my child, my sister, my sweetheart, my wife, my pal, my friend, each distinct in its character. She completely filled my life with joy as long as I was able to hold that love.

The one time that we were forced to make a trip with Phil, we were convinced that in some way she was a marked woman. An epithet was hurled at her which made the cold shivers run down our backs. While she was the only one addressed, we felt utterly degraded, and she was so angry we feared there might be murder then and there. We understood her aversion to going on the street. Yet there was nothing coarse about her appearance. Her hands were beautiful, and her features showed her to have been well born.

What a brilliant mind was there, powerless to be used for the benefit of mankind because of the conventions of society which made it impossible for her to find a place in the world! A convent as a child, where all her natural propensities were developed to the full. Then as a young woman, life in the European capitals, where she had entree to the best circles. Later to New York, where she was so shamefully treated.

Juno and I always felt out of place among the people who were "differ-ent," we felt so secure in our love for each other and so out of their class; yet we kept in touch with them in a degree ever curious. While we were with Phil one day there came to see her a youth about twenty years old—hand-some with a wonderful complexion, well-groomed, clever in music and an actor of sorts, though not a star. I noticed that Phil was watching Juno and me very quizzically, apparently for some reaction on our part. He sang and played for us and was very charming. After he had gone, Phil asked us how we liked him. We said we found him very attractive and talented. Upon further questioning we acknowledged that we had seen nothing strange about him.

She smiled and then proceeded to enlighten us on another phase of the great problem of sex. She said he was the perfect type of invert. She went on to explain the meaning of this term which we did not know. We were aghast! While we had been astonished to learn that there were other women who cared for each other, the surprise was even greater to discover that there existed a like propensity in men.

It seemed no less than a crime that we, grown women, should not have known these things. Other women, mothers of boys, there must have been thousands, did not know of conditions like that, we had all been "so carefully brought up!" Imagine sending our young boys to the great cities so ignorant of the menace of the male solicitor on the streets, even though they may have been warned about the women who might approach them!

Just at that time it was considered very smart to go slumming in New York. Of course we wanted to see everything and do as the rest of the people were doing, so we went slumming too.

With two men friends who knew the ropes, and one other woman we put in one night of frightful experiences. We knew many of our married and unmarried friends who were anxious to go again and again, but that one night was all we ever wanted of slumming. The ugliness of the displays we saw as we hurried from one horrid but famous resort to another in and about the Bowery has no place here; for many years I have tried to forget the sights I saw that night, so that I dislike even to try to recall them. However, as a matter of education I am glad I went that one time. In the study of types, it was a good school. Seeing hundreds of male inverts, for instance, gathered together in a group made it easy to recognize them on any occasion where we might meet or see them, and so avoid any contact.

Juno and I had had enough of that class of humans. For many years we kept to ourselves and let them all drift out of our lives. We had had our education along those lines and that was what we were after. . . .

Our lives were on a much higher plane than those of the real inverts. While we did indulge in our sexual intercourse, that was never the thought uppermost in our minds. That was but an outlet for emotions which too long had been pent up in both our lives for the good of our health. We found ourselves far more fit for good work after having been thus relieved. But we had seen evidences of overindulgence on the part of some of those with whom we came in contact, in loss of vitality and weakened health, ending in consumption.

PLAY REVIEW

# 1902, April 5
## *N. Y. Times:* Oscar Wilde's
### *The Importance of Being Earnest*

Wilde's comedy opened in New York in the first production since his trial.[3] *Earnest* was said by a *Times* reviewer to be

inextricably associated with the saddest and most revolting scandal in the history of the English drama—perhaps of all drama.

Every man of intelligence, no doubt, wishes to dissociate the man

Oscar Wilde from the playwright, to rejoice in the excellence of his quality, while not forgetting its defect. But those who assembled last night at the Empire Theatre must have suffered many a deep misgiving. It was while writing this play that the clouds of social retribution closed in about the author, and while reading it one clearly notes the flagging of wit in the last act. The simper of Bunthorne leers from the page; the prisoner of Reading Jail utters his unforgettable cry, "All men kill the things they love," and death mows [grimaces] from the page at one. It is impossible to forget the broken and almost abandoned man of genius who crept away to a by-street in the Latin Quarter [of Paris], to die like a rat with a broken back in an alley. The paradoxes somehow spell the awful name of truth, the inversions of common sense rebound upon their author.

It is the final triumph of the play and of the playwright that on the boards the sheer brilliancy and skill of the piece surmount all this. . . . The spirit of sheer gayety is, then, bubbling, effervescing, always absurd and unexpected, always refined in its way, always intellectual. . . . As a farce of manners, the play stands alone, as clearly . . . the best thing of its kind in the language.

BOOK REVIEW/RESISTANCE

## 1902, July 5
### N. Y. Times Book Review:
### Edward Carpenter's *Ioläus: An Anthology of Friendship*

The way in which a slightly disguised defense of same-sex love might be accepted innocently in the mass media is illustrated by a *Times* review of Edward Carpenter's *Anthology of Friendship*. [4] The book also documents the long-standing special interest male lovers of the male have had in the history, literature, and language of "friendship," as one of the few legitimate alternatives to male-female love. (Carpenter focused on male-male friendship, although a few examples of female friends were included.) Carpenter's was an early example of a cross-cultural and historical study used in the interest of demonstrating the variety of legitimate same-sex relationships.

Under the heading "The Literature of Friendship," Carpenter's anthology was reviewed as "a philosophical work of considerable ingenuity," in which quotations from documents were a way of illustrating how the customs of different times and peoples formed a "varied evolution on the subject of friendship and the language in which this sentiment was and is expressed." Carpenter included introductions to each historical period showing "the conditions under which" that era's documents of friendship "were produced."

Carpenter's comment on ancient Greek friendship was quoted:

The extent to which the idea of friendship (in a quite romantic sense) penetrated the Greek mind is a thing very difficult for us to realize; and some modern critics entirely miss this point. They laud the Greek culture to the skies, . . . and at the same time speak of the stress [the Greeks] laid on friendship as a little peculiarity of no particular importance—not seeing that the latter was the chief source of their bravery and independence, one of the main motives of their art, and so far an organic part of the whole polity it is difficult to imagine the one without the other. The Greeks themselves never made this mistake, and their literature abounds with references to the romantic attachment as the great inspiration of political and individual life. Plato himself may almost be said to have founded his philosophy on this sentiment.

Carpenter's anthology was called "an appropriate gift book," and a "convenient reference . . . for composers of 'polite' literature."

MEDICAL

## 1902, December 18
## Dr. William S. Barker:
## "A case of homosexuality"

Dr. Barker, of St. Louis, in a paper on "Sexual Contrariety" read to the Medical Society of City Hospital Alumni, cited "a case of homosexuality" between men.[5]

About two years earlier, "W" had been "treated for sexual hypochondriasis" (extreme concern over erotic ailments). He had for a year

shown unnatural fondness for the society of ["B"], a younger man aged 20, whose physical contour and bearing was rather feminine. These two seemed inseparable. The unsophisticated regarded it as a sort of Damon and Pythias affair; but an existing homo-sexuality, and not a beautiful friendship of the classic type, evidently was the bond.

When B married in mid-November, 1902, W's "intense jealousy" became a "frenzy," and he soon shot and killed B and himself.[271]

♀ MEDICAL

## 1903, February
## Dr. E. H. Smith: "Masturbation in the Female"

In a medical article on female masturbation Dr. Smith, a "country doctor," said that when "girls" at puberty were in school they heard "vice" discussed, and began "to ponder over the use and abuse of their genital organs."[6]

No thoughtful parent will, when this matter is thoroughly understood, permit a child of school age to go and sleep with another child. It is bad for their minds, their morals and their bodies. It is one of the most frequent beginnings of sexual vices. I have had mature women acknowledge to me, that as girls, they and their girl chums mutually manipulated each other while sleeping together. Often the vice is taught a child by an adult servant. In the farming communities the children frequently sleep with the employees of the house. This is a most fruitful source of all sorts of petty vice and sexual filth. Many a girl of respectable parents can trace her downfall to some depraved servant girl.[77]

A single woman, age twenty-eight, from a "respectable family in good circumstances," had consulted Dr. Smith for "pelvic trouble" and constipation. When examination revealed "hypertrophied [overdeveloped] labia minora," Dr. Smith persuaded the woman to confess that she had masturbated since age fifteen. One night she had been

> sent to sleep with a servant when the house was full of company. She was waked out of a sound sleep by the servant girl manipulating her. She said that the girl acted in such a way that she feared to cry out or resist for fear of violence. After a time she had an orgasm. The servant girl tried to persuade her to perform the same service for her. This she would not do, but afterward began to practice the vice herself, and did so sometimes three times in 24 hours until she was 26 years old, when she began to be sick at her stomach and vomit every time she had an orgasm. This frightened her and she quit for three months; afterward she occasionally practiced the vice.[82]

The patient's history after confessing to Dr. Smith was not revealed.

Another woman, married, age twenty-two, of "questionable parents," also had "hypertrophy" of the labia minora. She denied ever having an orgasm by self-manipulation,

> but said she "used to fool with it when in bed." She also said that she and a girl friend often slept together and that they "fooled with each other." I happened to know that the girl friend was a victim of nymphomania.[83]


MEDICAL

# 1904, January
## Dr. William Lee Howard:
### " 'My feelings are exactly those of a woman' "

In an article on "Sexual Perversions in America," Dr. Howard defined these "perversions" as "any deviation from the normal sexual instinct, such as paederastia, cunnilingus, sodomy (bestiality), etc."[7] The doctor's attack on "Puritan" values indicates that he considered himself a sexual "modern." He apparently concurred in one male patient's notion that he possessed the feelings "true" to the female sex. The presentation of a second case assumed sexuality to be a dangerous and explosive force.

The history of "Mr. B." was given. B. was a Princeton graduate and lawyer, whose father, also a lawyer, had been an alcoholic, and whose mother was "one of those New England women brought up to believe that every deviation from Puritan standards was due to viciousness and controlled by the 'evil one,' the remedy for which was prayer and the whining objurgations of the deacons."

B. had been taught at home by women, and learned to "sew, embroider, and read the nauseating stuff written for girls at that period." Dr. Howard presented B.'s history in the first person:

> I did want to play with the boys, . . . but they made fun of me. They would call me "Sissie" and other affectionate nicknames. Once when I tried to throw a ball, they all laughed at me and told me I was a girl, not a boy. I went home crying and asked my mother to put me in dresses. That I was not like a boy, I knew, for I could not play like boys. So I remained away from all boys, and soon began to go entirely with girls, entering into their games and social gatherings.[11–12]

At about age fourteen he saw another boy's penis, which put him into

> a feverish mood; thoughts of men and manly deeds, of strong boys ar. . brave young men, possessed me, and I went to bed that night a changed being. I never thought of my sexual organs as being the same as that boy's.

(Dr. Howard said that B.'s "sexual apparatus was undersized.") As to "sexual passions" for men, B. said "I have fought desire after desire."

> I have no desire for paederasty or any other abnormal act. My feelings are exactly those of a woman. I want to be caressed, loved, ordered about and feel dependent upon some powerful man. As near as I can explain it, I am a woman in every detail except external appearances. . . . I have never, never lost my virtue. I am virtuous as far as physical acts with another person are concerned; but psychically I am constantly reveling in erotic dreams which I know are fast ruining my health.

Dr. Howard said that "B.'s struggle against his impulses were heroic," but they finally caused him to secretly take morphine. "He was found early one summer morning dead in his office."[12]

Another case, "Mr. A.," a college student, had been brought up by three sisters "in all the artifices . . . belonging to the female sex." He had "a library dealing with sexual perversions," and had studied the subject on his own.

> Music is his pleasure and his curse. After attending an opera or recital of classical music it is impossible for him to resist the sexual impulse to enjoy the pleasure of a youth. Rushing from the opera house, trembling and rabidly impulsive, he surges on . . . until he finds the object of his desire.

A. had controlled his behavior for three months, with Dr. Howard's aid. Then "he went to New York to attend the opera." This was "the match to the powder magazine, and the sexual explosion took place."[13] Dr. Howard concluded:

> Every physician should understand the sexual side of life, for it is sexual activity that governs life, permits the continuation of the species and promotes crime and its causes. It is the basis of all society. . . .[14]

♀ BOOK REVIEW

## 1904, June 18
### *N. Y. Times Book Review:*
### Charles Godfrey Leland's *The Alternate Sex*

Leland's book, subtitled *The Female Intellect in Man, and the Masculine in Women,* was reviewed anonymously.[8] In this review, the idea of a female or male "nature," however androgynously distributed, reveals clearly its traditionalist aspect. However, Leland's argument for androgyny may have been a disguised defense of "inversion."

Leland's "contention is that the fundamental intelligence of the two sexes is radically different, but that certain of the characteristics of each remain in the other."

The reviewer summarized: "There is . . . a separate intellect in each human being, quite apart from . . . the intellect of waking reason," that

> thinks while he sleeps. This is the "alternate sex" in us—the female nature in the man, the male in the woman, asserting itself when it can. . . .

It is "as lucky" for a man to have "a lady in his head, as for every woman to have a man." Without

> the lady in his mind it is doubtful . . . whether man would ever feel or write poetry or yield to any aesthetic influence, or even invent anything. He would be a machine, a brute. . . . It was the feminine soul in Goethe, Shakespeare, Shelley, Byron, Darwin, that did their work. . . .
>
> Conversely, there is a male intellect in woman—less marked, less interesting. Man in woman "keeps a shop. . . ." This element usually manifests itself in such as are "come-outers." Thus Joan of Arc, and George Sand and George Eliot.

Leland maintained that "most" of George Sand's works were written by "the man in her brain."

The author's "theory of 'sensitivity' " referred to that "force in nature" whereby organisms "are led to attract or repel other objects." This "sensitivity" is a marvelous guide in all selection and affinity. . . . There often exists in man an intense attraction to others, men and women, quite apart from all amorous passion—this is sensitivity in action.

In discussing "sensitivity" the reviewer stressed the "tonic or salutary effect of one sex upon the other."

Leland's book was a "contribution to the literature of its kind."

CROSSING PERSONS/IMAGES

## c. 1905–20s
## Postcards: The mannish woman and the womanish man

Several American postcards present negative images of early twentieth-century women who wore "mannish" shoes, shirts, collars, ties, and coats, who smoked, went to bars, and who moved independently in the world.[9] Other cards portray effeminate men and, specifically, those then called "fairies." These popular images express the same feeling of threat to traditional "femininity" and "masculinity" expressed in contemporary medical journal articles and in *The New York Times Book Review* discussions of sexual differentiation and "abnormality."

Illustrated Post Card & Novelty Company, New York, 5004-7, Copyright 1905. All postcards not otherwise identified are from the collection of Marshall Weeks.

No date or publication data.

The Gibson Art Company, Cincinnati, published
1908–1920.

Artist: "Bishop"; postmark 1910.

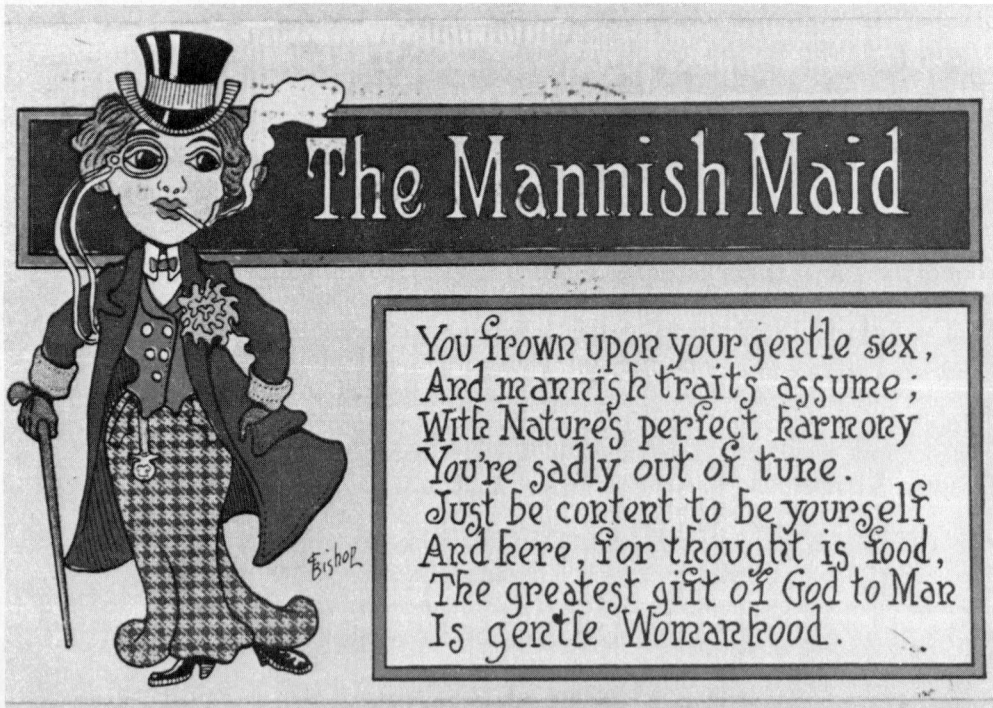

Published 1910; postmark July 29, 1911;
identification on back "S 116."

An effeminate clerk in a dry-goods store fixes his hair while customers go unattended; vanity and the needs of consumer capitalism are implicitly at odds. As early as 1860 a parody of Walt Whitman's "Song of Myself" attacked the poet by picturing him as a "weak and effeminate" dry-goods salesman or "Counter-jumper," an occupation thought suitable for only the most effete of males (see *GAH*, p. 655 n. 133.) A reference of 1868 refers to a song titled the "Gay Young Clerk in the Dry Goods Store," by Will S. Hays, a female impersonator (cited on the published sheet music of Hays's "Mistress Jinks of Madison Square," N.Y.: J. L. Peters, 1868, in the collection of Marshall Weeks).

Postmark August 10, 1911. In this postcard, part of a
set, a limp-wristed effeminate male is charmed by a
policeman.

Postmark July 1, 1910(?); year unclear. In this
ambiguous card, either a female recognizes an
effeminate male as "One of Us" (women), or an
effeminate male thinks he recognizes a lesbian, or a
male in female guise.

## Wnen We Dance, One of a Couple Has to Be the "Girl"

World War I, Newport, R.I., 1918, inscription: "This is really the way we dance" (from *Lesbian/Gay History Researchers Network Newsletter,* Number 2 [Summer 1980], p. 7).

Date unknown. On back: "Raphael Tuck & Sons' Post Card Series No. 2322, 'Life at West Point,' Art Publishers To Their Majesties The King And Queen. Dancing is a compulsory branch of instruction during two years of the four-year course. 'Hops' are held on Saturday evening every two weeks throughout the term, and there are also additional events in the way of dancing graduation week and other periods of special festivity."

Formal male-male dancing at the U.S. Military Academy at West Point was publicized as an innocent, if quaint custom, in this photographic card. At some point in the twentieth century such physical contact between males, and such ambiguity of role, would become suspect, especially in those sexually segregated military training institution designed to produce "men" and fighters. The subject requires further research. The *Autobiography* of Admiral George Dewey (N. Y.: Scribner's, 1913, p. 17) refers to a "stag hop." According to the early homosexual emancipationist Edward Stevenson, a book, *The Spirit of Old West Point, 1858–1862* (Boston: Houghton Mifflin, 1907) "presents the military souvenirs of General Morris Schaff, of the United States Army. . . . In its author's pen-portraits of early friends in the famous Military Academy . . . are to be noted many delicate suggestions of the uranian emotion in young and soldierly comrades. Indeed the accent of a manly similisexualism of psychic quality pervades the record. . . . Especially in its elegiac passages, it is eloquent of the homosexual thrill in young hearts that beneath uniforms can beat so passionally for each other"; see Xavier Mayne (pseud.), *The Intersexes* (c. 1908), pp. 209–10. For an image associating male-male dancing with sexual perversion see 1936, Dos Passos.

The 1920s; on back: "No. 739 Flappers.
12 Designs.  Made in U.S.A."

♀ MEDICAL

## 1906, June 4
## Dr. William Lee Howard:
## "The Sexual Pervert in Life Insurance"

In an essay read to the American Association of Medical Examiners in Boston,
Dr. Howard evaluated the risks to corporations which provided life insurance to
the male or female sexual "Invert."[10] Howard had had "a large number of these
unfortunate and misunderstood persons under personal care."

The doctor warned his fellow practitioners that the "invert or pervert will
never disclose his condition . . . unless he is certain that the physician will
recognize his true deformity and not consider him a person to . . . avoid as a moral
leper."

He explained:

> As the sexual inverts live a life apart from the rest of mankind they become
> morbid, introspective and suspicious. They read all the literature on sex
> matters possible to obtain and many are better informed on this subject than
> the average physician.[207]

Infrequently, it was said, a male invert met an "anatomical woman" with a "male
brain, and these two live together."

The invert's career "is usually shortened by early death, suicide being the
end of many." The "whole life of a congenital invert is one of fear and horror
of exposure and the agonizing dread that the sexual impulse will at some fatal
moment overpower them."

Since the "whole psychic life" of male inverts was "feminine, muscular
exercise is repugnant to them, hence at about forty years of age we find them with
fat, flabby bodies." The "invert who does not meet with violent assaults or
succumb to alcohol and other drugs develops some organic disease." There
was

also the danger that the abandonment of a business career for a life of leisure may favor dissipation with its attendant predisposition to excess and its increased liability to venereal infection.

Much benefit to the company is derived if the medical examiner knows the applicant and his surroundings. . . . [The examiner] cannot be a detective but he can and must realize the meaning of increased liability. He must know what the moral hazard means, . . . and he must appraise its value in his estimation of the risk.[206]

Dr. Howard added:

What I have said concerning the male invert does not always hold true of the female invert. In the female invert mentally and psychically we have a man with all the powerful desires of a man; hence, while anatomically and socially we have a woman, the physical development will be such as to make the individual a good risk, and also, being classed as a female, however much her masculine tendencies may be objectionable, she is usually free from personal assaults, and the alcohol that she drinks seems to have a better physiological absorbing surface.[207]


MEDICAL

# 1906, July 24
## Dr. R. W. Shufeldt:
### *"A typical example of contrary sexual instinct"*

Dr. Shufeldt, a major in the U. S. Army Medical Corps, photographed a twenty-three-year-old " 'fairy' from the slums of Brooklyn."[11] In 1917, the doctor published the photos and the subject's history in a medical journal article titled "Biography of a Passive Pederast." Known in Brooklyn and in Potsdam, Pennsylvania, as "Loop-the-loop," the subject believed his anus to be an "aborted vagina," and claimed to menstruate (he probably bled occasionally due to a hemorrhoid condition). His features were said by Dr. Shufeldt to have a "criminal cast." The subject was described as "a typical example of contrary sexual instinct."


♀ MEDICAL

# 1906, September 8
## Dr. T. H. Evans: "The Problem of Sexual Variants"

An essay by Dr. Evans of Philadelphia is an early, embryonic attempt to formulate a sociological and economic analysis of the "problem" of "homosexuality."[12] The use of the terms "Sexual Variants" and "variance" indicated a desire to develop a morally neutral sexual vocabulary.

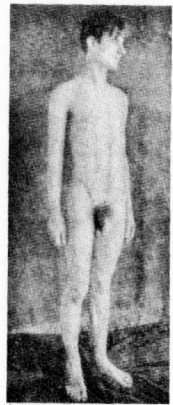 

(*Left*) Original caption: "A Passive Pederast. The subject of the present paper." Photograph taken July 24, 1906.
(*Right*) Original caption: "The same subject...in female attire." Photograph taken November 4, 1906.

In his article "The Problem of Sexual Variants," Dr. Evans declared that "The increase of homosexuality is due to two main factors." The first was the lessening need for "propagation," and the possibility of "leisure." A second cause was "the shifting economic relations of men and women; so that displacement of function brings about incertitude of characteristic." (That is, changes in the sexual division of labor caused changes in the characters of the sexes, including their erotic interests.) The "control of body" was "today" closely related to "the evolution of . . . our corporations, which stand as overhumans, sexless, passionless, insensitive and many-handed—great creatures of Frankenstein destiny."

> The sexual friendship of two young men, or young girls, follows the lines of economic cleavage when marriage is too expensive or the penalty of illicit intercourse too dear.[214]

> Dr. Evans said: "As economic values shift, the desirable characteristics are mutable, and in every general upheaval there is a greater or less increase in sexual variance plainly marked.[14]

♀ MEDICAL

# 1906, November
## Dr. Harold N. Moyer: "Is Sexual Perversion Insanity?"

"Is Sexual Perversion Insanity?" asked Dr. Moyer of Chicago, in a survey of opinion on the subject.[13] Moyer's cast included a number of erotic monsters.

A Doctor Sommers was cited to the effect that when a man was proven to be "perverse"—when he was sexually excited by another male—he should be punished for a corresponding act, just as in the case of an impulse "to possess the property of others." Moyer added:

> As long as the moral ideas of the majority of the people are opposed to homosexual acts and the laws give expression to these ideas, the so-called contrary sexual persons must control their impulses, as the man who, hungry, must control his impulse to possess himself of the property of others.[197]

After discussing a male's necrophilia with a recently buried girl, mate-devouring spiders, and "hermaphroditic snails," Moyer said:

> That these conditions should crop up in woman inverts, especially those in whom autoeroticism has dulled normal excitability, is not surprising. While woman is normally the least anti-social of the sexes, she naturally becomes more anti-social than man when she departs from her type.[199]

Moyer also discussed a married woman who, after intercourse with her husband, "had to arise, catch and caress a chicken, and finally wring its neck ere orgasm could occur." He then cited a case of Dr. Kiernan's in which an "Indiana girl" had "perverted another girl into tribadism and canine copulation."[204]

NEWS REPORTS/LEGAL CASES

# 1907, May 30
## *N. Y. Times:* The Moltke–Eulenburg scandal

A scandal in Germany involved Count Kano Moltke and Prince Philip Eulenburg. It began after a magazine editor, Maximilian Harden, published articles intimating an impropriety in the two men's friendship and lives.[14] Moltke, the military governor of Berlin, and Eulenburg were confidants of and advisors to the German Emperor, and the accusation against them arose out of personal, political, and class conflicts.

*New York Times* coverage of the Moltke–Eulenburg scandal, 1907 through 1909, was so veiled as to render superfluous any extensive reprinting of the news stories. Scattered here and there throughout these reports were references to "scandal," "scandalous" and "immoral practices," facts of "an extremely delicate nature," a "nest of degenerates," "secret vices," "secret misconduct," "orgies," "wild doings," "artistic leanings," "vicious inclinations," "wrongful actions," "sensational rumors," and "enthusiastic friendships." But a casual and sexually naive reader would have been hard-pressed to say exactly what all the fuss was about. As in *The Times* coverage of the Oscar Wilde trials in 1895, a most notable aspect of the news stories was their euphemism.

*New York Times* reports of the German scandal cast vague suspicions on the intimacy of Moltke and Eulenberg, and on that of Eulenburg and his valet.

Moltke's wife had told one witness that Moltke "loved Eulenburg more than he did her." Moltke testified that after a fight with his wife he had

> picked up a handkerchief belonging to Eulenburg and kissed it in an affectionate manner to see whether . . . this would provoke an outbreak of jealousy from the Countess.

Moltke denied that he "habitually used cosmetics to beautify his appearance."

Another story reported Moltke being found free from "vicious inclinations." He and Eulenburg were simply "men of artistic tastes whose friendship, dating from their youth, had grown stronger with the passing years."

The case turned against Eulenburg after his valet, a former fisherman, confessed in court that "the worst charges made against the Prince were true." Eulenburg continued to deny any "immoral practices." The prince testified in court:

> I certainly am no angel . . . and I have many weaknesses. My best qualities have been expressed, I think, by enthusiastic friendships and generous acts, but unfortunately even these qualities are twisted by the world into vileness.

The case ended in 1909 after editor Harden agreed not to appeal a fine for libeling Moltke, and after Eulenburg "had an attack of heart failure in court."

♀ NEWS REPORT/CROSSING WOMAN

## 1907, November 11
### *The Trinidad* [Colorado] *Advertiser:* Katherine Vosbaugh

A Colorado newspaper headline read: "Woman Who Posed As Man 60 Years, Dead, . . . / Only Reason Was to Secure Man's Work."[15] The story said:

> Katherine Vosbaugh, who for sixty years posed as a man, wearing male garb, living the rough life of the pioneers in the Southwest and who even "married" another woman, died yesterday morning at the San Raphael Hospital in this city, where she had been a county charge since the secret of her life was discovered by Dr. T. J. Forham, of this city over two years ago.
>
> Born nearly four-score years ago [1847?] in France of a good family, this remarkable woman donned male garb when but a slip of a girl, came to America and worked as a bank clerk, bookkeeper, restauranteur, cook, and sheep herder for over half a century without her sex being known.
>
> In July, two years ago, "Frenchy," a cook and sheep herder on the Sam Brown ranch, near this city, was taken with pneumonia and brought to the hospital where her secret was revealed. Even then, this strange woman refused to wear skirts. Clad in regulation man's attire, she has since worked about the hospital and was known by the nickname of "Grandpa."
>
> Katherine Vosbaugh was left an orphan at the age of twenty years. Her

father, a well educated man of considerable means, gave her an excellent business education. At his death she was an expert accountant and spoke her native tongue, English, German, and Hungarian. Her only motive in assuming the disguise at first seems to have been to enable her more easily to secure employment.

She worked in several cities all over the country before settling at Joplin, Mo., where she worked for fifteen years as a bank clerk, and it was in this city where she married. The name of her "wife" was never learned, but the ceremony seems to have taken place for the purpose of saving the woman's good name. A few months after the marriage a child was born to the wife, which died after a few months.

Shortly after the death of the child the two women came to this city and opened a restaurant on Commercial street. Here she was known as "Frenchy" and the establishment was one of the most popular restaurants in the Southwest.

What became of "Frenchy's" wife is not known. She drifted away and her "husband" refused until the time of her death to reveal the woman's name.

After leaving here the woman [Vosbaugh] secured a position as cook on a big sheep ranch near Trinche ranch. The eccentricities of youth became more pronounced as she grew older and more and more she came to look like a man. For years she lived with men on the ranch, cooking for them, assisting them in the ranch work and sleeping in the same rooms, but her secret was never suspected.

Two years and four months ago she was stricken with pneumonia, and it was then her secret was discovered. Since then she failed rapidly in body and mind and her death was due to a general breakdown. . . .


NEWS REPORTS/LEGAL CASE

# 1908, April 2
## N. Y. Times: Fischer-Hansen tried for extortion

The Times reported a New York City legal case in which Carl Fischer-Hansen, a lawyer, was tried for extorting $15,000 from Joseph E. O'Brien, a "Philadelphia decorator."[16] A third major figure in the case was Antonio Macaluso, a nineteen-year-old.

Although Times reports were euphemistic, vague, and contradictory, O'Brien had evidently written " 'incriminating letters' " to Macaluso, with whom he'd probably had some sort of romance. Macaluso testified that lawyer Fischer-Hansen, hearing of those letters, had told him: " 'Man you ought to have a pile of money.' " On Fischer-Hansen's initiative, apparently, Macaluso had gone along with the lawyer's blackmail of O'Brien.

Fischer-Hansen was charged with having threatened to publish O'Brien's incriminating letters unless O'Brien paid up. The lawyer was also charged with threatening that Macaluso would sue for "damages" for O'Brien's having "ill-treated him." The assistant district attorney prosecuting Fischer-Hansen told the jury that O'Brien's relationship with Macaluso was not at issue—only Fischer-Hansen's alleged extortion.

On June 13, a *Times* headline declared that "Philadelphia Decorator" O'Brien had testified and described Fischer-Hansen's extortion. "O'Brien said he lived with his mother, and is unmarried."

A friend of O'Brien's, Francis Dowling, was subjected to a "savage cross-examination." He "was single" and had known O'Brien for thirty years.

> He was asked if he had not been known as "Miss Dowling," and answered, "That is a lie!"

Dowling denied he had "told O'Brien that he would have to give up his friendship either for him or the boy."

Dowling was asked if he had not been afraid of being indicted with O'Brien, if the money was not paid. Dowling said he had not been afraid:

> It wasn't nice to be mixed up in the case, but I was not influenced by fear of exposure, though I did think it might affect my social standing.[4:2]

On June 16, *The Times* said that under cross-examination Joseph O'Brien had "lost his composure and told how anxious he was to get the letters, though they were not incriminating." The "greatly agitated" O'Brien explained why he had paid $15,000 for the letters:

> I wanted to put an end to the whole thing; I was afraid of exposure; my social life, business, everything—and I thought it would kill my mother.

Antonio Macaluso had testified about his "friendship" with O'Brien. (*The Times* gave no scandalous details.) Macaluso revealed that a larceny charge against him had first led him to consult the lawyer, Fischer-Hansen.

On June 17, *The Times* reported one of the alleged threats made by Fischer-Hansen: the publication of O'Brien's letters would " 'create a terrible scandal' " —and "even if O'Brien was acquitted of a crime the stigma would always remain."[5:5]

On June 18, *The Times* said that Fischer-Hansen had denied any extortion. He said that he had only tried to collect money in settlement of a claim by Macaluso.[16:4]

The following day *The Times* reported that the Catholic and Protestant chaplains of "the Tombs" prison had both testified. Lawyer Fischer-Hansen's "reputation for truth was bad." One chaplain called it " 'Very bad.' "[6:6]

On June 20, *The Times* reported that Fischer-Hansen had been acquitted of extortion.[5:3]

A week after Fischer-Hansen's acquittal, Joakim Reinhardt, a Danish immigrant to the United States, discussed the lawyer's trial in a letter to a friend (Karl Larsen, author of a novel about inversion, *Daniel-Daniela,* 1908). Joakim Reinhardt had first "escaped" to the United States in 1877, at age eighteen, after he was accused of attempted sexual acts with a male. In 1889, Reinhardt had moved permanently to the United States, where rumors from Denmark about his past interfered with his securing adequately paid work.

Reinhardt wrote from Brooklyn on June 24, 1908, that Fischer-Hansen, a fellow-Dane, had been "acquitted by the *jury*" even though the press, the prosecutor, and the judge "considered him guilty" of involvement in extortion. Reinhardt explained: "Money had been extorted by a beautiful young Italian" from "a rich decorator who had a soprano voice and trembled like an aspen leaf in court."

Reinhardt attributed the jury's acquittal of Fischer-Hansen to "middle-class" bigotry:

> Although the more informed have now begun to see these matters more clearly, the ruling middle class is still as prejudiced as the church councils of the Middle Ages that burned "urnings" because their presence brought "flood, greedy mice and pestilence" into the country, or Emile Zola who hated the same class of people and persecuted them with his writings and speeches. . . .

♀ RESISTANCE

# c. 1908
## Edward Stevenson: *The Intersexes*

A privately published 641-page volume, *The Intersexes: A History of Similisexualism as a Problem in Social Life,* by Xavier Mayne (pseudonym of Edward Stevenson) is the earliest book by an American in defense of what the author called, variously, uranianism, uraniadism, feminosexualism, similisexualism, and homosexualism.[17] Stevenson's comments on the situation of male and female homosexuals in the United States in the first decade of the twentieth century constitute a rare, extended discussion of the subject by an American homosexual.

As did Edward Carpenter and John Addington Symonds, Stevenson in *The Intersexes* asserted:

> Happiest of all, surely, are those Uranians, ever numerous, who have no wish nor need to fly society—or themselves. Knowing what they are, understanding the natural, moral strength of their position as homosexuals; sure of right on their side, even if it be never accorded to them in the lands where they must live; fortunate in either due self-control or private freedom—day by day, they go through their lives, self-respecting and respected, in relative peace.[515]

Defending homosexuality as an inborn "instinct" that might be lived in different ways, but never eradicated, Stevenson's ideas reflect the biological, racial, sexual, and ethical theories of his time, now mostly discredited. His idea of inborn homosexuality is best understood in terms of its implications for the amelioration of persecution (homosexuals should not be oppressed for feelings they couldn't help and couldn't change if they wanted to). But Stevenson's concern, as a homosexual, with the social situation of oppression contrasts with the preoccupation of contemporary doctors with the cause, character, and cure of homosexuality.

Stevenson dedicated his book to Krafft-Ebing, and often reiterated his faith in doctors and "science" as emancipators of homosexuals. This view saw "social prejudice" as a matter of ignorance, social reform as a job for professional educators—deemphasising structural causes of oppression and the need for the political organization of the oppressed. His book is valuable now as a record of the ideas of one American homosexual in the early years of this century, and for the rare glimpses it provides into the little-known homosexual culture of that time. *The Intersexes* was, in part, an early survey and history of homosexual social life.

In his most extended comment on "Uranianism in the United States," Stevenson noted the "relatively little" material on the subject in English.

> As to popular literature in the vernacular, to aid the American Uranian to understand his own case, or to understand conditions of similisexualism in other countries, this is still eminently lacking. The topic of similisexualism is *tabu* in the United States and in Canada, except through observations by and for medical students and physicians.

Among the "intelligent laity," "Homosexualism is generally regarded as a 'diseased' and 'abnormal' state of the individual; as relatively a rare matter; as a moral, religious and anti-natural offense," as " 'degeneracy.' "[638]

In recent years, in "many printed 'disclosures' of similisexualism in London, New York and Paris, in club-life and other social fraternities, we have seen the word 'degenerate' in frequent employ." American and English newspapers, especially, had contributed to the misuse of "degenerate" as a common term, though psychiatrists taught that "the similisexual instincts" (including "feminosexualism and Uraniadism") did "not necessarily mean clear physical, intellectual or moral degeneracy."[409]*

Contradicting himself, Stevenson also said that in America and England the publication of legal proceedings that bear on " 'unnatural offences' is not encour-

---

*For a reference to a female "sexual pervert" as a "degenerate" see document of April 1896 in *GAH*, p. 61. For references in common speech to male "degenerates," and "degenerate men" see the testimony of 1899 in *GAH*, pp. 45–47. For a reference to a self-described "gentleman degenerate" (1904) see *GAH*, p. 145. For other uses of "degenerate" see listing for this term in the index. The terminology of "degeneracy" is associated with various eugenics theories.

aged by the press, nor [so] often detailed as in Continental Europe." This "squeamishness" about *"speaking* of homosexuality" kept such matters from print, or disguised its character.[469] In the United States,

> some useful German literature circulates hazardously and sparely: and not with any real currency in social life. Even in order to own works of a medico-psychiatric sort, as the "Psychopathia Sexualis" of Dr. von Krafft-Ebing, or Dr. Moll's "Conträre Sexualität," or Dr. Hirschfeld's studies, the volumes must be procured strictly on a physician's certificate![638]

The "enormous diffusion of Uranianism and of similisexual intercourse" in the United States and Canada was clear to an "intelligent observer" of the "larger cities." The numerous German population "has a special bearing on similisexualism in North America." The

> wide agricultural "West" . . . is pervaded with uranian tendencies. In the Southern States, the Creole type is not lacking the impulse, in spite of all its heterosexuality.

The male "American negro has ever been similisexual" (though the relatively free sexual relations of Black males and females was "counteractive" to the development of male homosexuality—Stevenson's racist, sexist, and moralistic phrasing is not necessary to reproduce). "The North American Indian has also always inclined to practical homosexualism."[638–39]

Large U. S. cities were "centers of uranianism," no matter "how suppressed is the homosexual topic."[639] In New York City "homosexual prostitution" was a veritable *"armée de vice."*[434] But in the United States there was "far less . . . open male prostitution" among the civilian population than in Berlin or Paris, and soldier-prostitution only in "certain centers" of America. The relatively little prostitution by American soldiers was due to the comparatively small military presence in American cities, the difficulty of finding places of rendezvous, and the better pay of the American soldier relative to the European.[639]

The American soldier expressed his affinity for males "more as a buyer of the foreign-born male prostitute" than as a seller of himself. An exception was "a garrison noted for its homosexual contingent" in San Francisco, "where especially during the time of the sudden Spanish–American War excitement (1898)," soldier-prostitution was so active that the "Presidio" quarter was a regular visiting place. "Amiable young soldiers were to be 'had' so plentifully" that their prices fell. And "This in a country where homosexual intimacies are severely punishable!"[221–22] In the United States the lack of any legal regulation of female prostitution also "increases the dread of diseases," thus increasing the "inclination to homosexuality" among males.[639]

The case history of an American male, B. R., a "designer for a firm of silversmiths," was furnished by an American doctor. Like many early medical reports it revealed a male at odds with his sexuality. A friend, however, whom he had met in art school abroad,

> was perfectly satisfied with his own psychic organization. He told R— that he was "foolish to worry," that "thousands of men were so," and that it was only a question of concealment and custom. R— was, however, morally more and more in unrest, believing himself vicious, criminal, and also dreading the reactions that came. . . .[92–93]

B. R. appealed to an American doctor who advised against marriage as a way of trying to change

> his inborn similisexual nature; against losing faith in himself as to being morally depraved; . . . urging him to as much intellectual and physical distraction, . . . to strong efforts toward self-control. . . .[96]

"A special observer of youthful homosexuality in America has stated that the practices of uranian boys in school are . . . 'nowhere quite so general' as in the United States."[640]

"Universities, the world around, are centers of similisexual attraction and of 'relations' between fine-natured young collegemen"; Harvard and Princeton were cited.[177] University theatricals in which males played female roles were mentioned as "homosexual influences."[177–80]

It was also said:

> The present tendency to educate young women in colleges for "girls only" promotes feminine similisexuality. American and English girl-colleges are famous cultivators of the passions that belong to the Uraniad [Stevenson's term for the female Uranian]. Often a mature Uraniad looks back over a long life, in which not for one moment since her first friendships, . . . has she been other than a woman-loving woman.[182] [That is the earliest known use of the phrase "woman-loving woman."]

"Certain smart clubs are well-known for their homosexual atmospheres" in New York, Boston, Washington, Chicago, New Orleans, and St. Louis.[640] Some homosexual resorts in New York City and elsewhere were "masked"—as a "literary-club," an "athletic society," a "dramatic-society," or a "chess-club"—so "No outsider easily suspects what really goes on."[432]*

"Steam-baths and restaurants are plentifully known—to the initiated." There was "no police interference" with "many such resorts," though their "proceedings and patronage . . . are perfectly plain." In "most baths each patron had a separate room, "usually with a couch," and what " 'goes on' is under the

---

*For a homosexual correspondence and "Friendship Club" of 1905 see *GAH*, p. 48; for Henry Gerber and the 1930s pen-pals club "Contacts," see p. 554; for his reference to a homosexual "rocket club" of the 1940s see p. 557.

guest's own lock and key.''[640] Elsewhere Stevenson contradicted himself; the several baths in New York

> cannot be utilized, then and there, for homosexual practicalities. They are merely establishments for—anatomic inspections; for making appointments to meet elsewhere—some near hotel, for example.[440]*

The "homosexual capitals" of the United States were listed as New York, Boston, Washington, Chicago, St. Louis, San Francisco, Milwaukee, New Orleans, and Philadelphia.[640]

> A distinguished European singer (homosexual) who has several times visited the United States, and is now familiar with every part of it, states that he "has never been in any country where the uranian element was so widely-distributed, and averaged such high-class moral and intellectual types as in North America." A homosexual actor of Continental fame, not only for talent but beauty, has declared that after an exceptionally large experience in "attentions," no other male public has ever so often written to him, or otherwise sought contact socially with him through homosexual passion for him as the American homosexuals.

> "The married Uranian is constantly encountered in America." But "scandals" involving "uranianism and marriage are not plentiful."

> In the United States the "proportion of Uranians" was allegedly one in eighty-five, compared with one in sixty in the most "male-loving" nations (Turkey, Persia, Arabia).[75]

> Physicians claimed that "the Uraniad" (woman-loving woman) was less frequent in the United States, "owing to the peculiar nervous organization of the American woman who seems, often almost wholly, without sexual desires."[641]

> The case history of "Miss A," a thirty-year-old American piano teacher had been provided by an American doctor "from his personal acquaintance." Nothing about Miss A "suggests masculinity, unless it be a certain rapid firmness of her walk, a long step, and her rather heavy timbre of voice." She had sought medical advice, being "much disturbed" at her sexual life. As a young girl, dancing with another girl, and being embraced by her, made Miss A " 'quiver all over with delight.' " She had had a number of sexual affairs with females, and "in the case of several discarded lovers she has continued to retain their friendship and even intimacy."[130–31]

> Miss A "slowly became aware of her abnormality but has never had any clear idea of the matter, and has thought only of hiding it from those not likely to understand it." She had "never any desire to wear male attire, her own beauty is a pleasure to her in so far as it attracts to her women whom she admires." She had recently become despairing of ever having a "normal" sexual

---

*This reference, of about 1908, to homosexual baths is the earliest known. For a police raid on such a bath see 1929, April?

life, and worried about becoming older and "less attractive" to women.[132]

While reading novels she "is frequently excited sexually by descriptions of female loveliness, by depictions of how a man feels in sexual excitement . . . as it offers 'just what she feels' when with a woman that she sexually loves."

The doctor-informant said:

Miss A— impresses me as having a fine moral nature, as a person who instinctively loves truth, unselfishness, modesty, refinement, dignity of character. . . . She does not know exactly how far she is wanting in domestic tastes, for . . . she has lived chiefly in boarding-houses and hotels, and has not much experience of routine feminine work. But she dislikes all sewing and fancywork, knows little of cookery, and does not like to make use of what little she knows."[133]*

Of women professionals Stevenson said: "The intellectual Uraniad . . . resorts to the great artistic and educational centers, for aesthetics and for a free life"—New York and various European cities "are familiar to her." She was present on "Wall Street." In "the bustling United States, many an Uraniad is 'the right hand *man*' of the private-office, counting room, shop, and factory."[403]†

"In New York, only a few years ago," a scandal (similar to the Cleveland Street affair of 1889 in London) in a popular club "cast the city into a quiver of nervous distress." This affair had been hushed up by the flight of many.[423] American homosexuals were among those *"emigrés"* who escaped from "social and legal perils" in their countries of origin.[425]

In the United States and elsewhere both "social prejudice" and the law encouraged the blackmail of homosexuals. In the United States the blackmail *victim* was a felon.[457–58] Stevenson nevertheless urged homosexuals to "courageously" denounce blackmailers to the police, since blackmailing itself was also a serious crime. But "often in America" homosexuals dealt with blackmail by suicide.[461]

The legal "punishment for homosexualism" was "severe" in all the United States. Long imprisonments were "typical" in New York State. And no dissenting view was presented.[71]

While the "scientific excuse for homosexualism" had led to an "improved sentiment" in Europe (especially in Germany and Austria), "old standards" still held in English and American courts.[483] A "scientific" view of homosexuals

---

*There followed several case histories "Of the 'amazonian' or 'viraginous' Uraniad, the really man-like type," as found among American women: Mr. Z (or Mrs. X), pp. 140–44; Johann Bürger and Anna Mattersteig, pp. 148–49 (*GAH*, p. 252); "Harry Gorman," pp. 149–50 (*GAH*, pp. 249–50).

†"Friendships of uraniad force and constancy are many among women of the intersexual type;" Stevenson cited *The Story of a Friendship; A Memoir* (N. Y.: Knickerbocker, 1901), by "Miss A[nnie] C. Wood," which sketched the "life of Miss Irene Leach, a Virginian lady with whom Miss Wood had been intimately associated for more than thirty years."[404] The actress Charlotte Cushman was cited as "strongly uraniadistic . . . (psychically)."[407] Cushman had died in 1876; see Joseph Leach, *Bright Particular Star; The Life and Times of Charlotte Cushman* (New Haven: Yale University Press, 1970), which documents her intimacies with women.

is largely unknown in Great Britain and in America. In those large domin-
ions, with their multitudes of homosexuals, the Uranian seems likely to
remain a social and a legal victim for an indefinite time to come.[520]

In a section on literature, Stevenson called Walt Whitman "one of the
prophets and priests of homosexuality." The "Calamus" poems in *Leaves of Grass*
were "the most openly homosexual" in their "idealizing (but sensuously idealizing) man-to-man love, psychic and physical." (This was one of the most explicit
statements in English up to that time on Whitman's "homosexuality.") Of Whitman's "own personal homosexualism there can be no question"; Whitman's Civil
War prose pieces were cited, as was his relationship with the "young Irish tram-
driver, Peter Doyle."[377] Whitman had stressed "the importance of masculine
ties" (like those of "the Sacred Band" in ancient Greece) "as vital to the State,
in the restoration of true democracy."[380] In Whitman "is to be heard a new
voice" affirming "the purity, the naturalness of true uranian love and its high
mission to the individual and toward nations."[381]

♀  BOOK REVIEW/INTIMACY

# 1909, March 13
## *N. Y. Times Book Review:* Clarissa Dixon's
## *Janet and Her Dear Phebe*

In the early twentieth century the "true love" of two little girls was described as
"innocent affection." But in a few years even the childhood intimacies of girls
would be suspected of harboring a dangerous eroticism.

An anonymous *Times* reviewer explained that *Janet and Her Dear Phebe* "is a
very intense sort of a love story in which the lovers are two little girls who are
devoted to each other with that fervency known only to feminine childhood."[18]

But the fates, with their usual malice toward true love, do not allow the
course of even their innocent affection to run smooth. A feud divides their
families, the children are torn apart and for many years are lost to each
other, until they meet again in their womanhood. In the talk and the letters
and verses of the children the author has kept very close to the child heart
and the child mind. . . . A sweeter, truer picture of childish philosophy and
childish feeling has not been made in a long time.

## 1910, August
## Dr. James G. Kiernan:
### *"Artificial consciousness of self-esteem"*

An essay by Dr. Kiernan on "A Medico-Legal Phase of Auto-Eroticism in Women," discussed the alleged effects of masturbation.[1] These included a disinclination to "normal coitus" with the "opposite sex," an "artificial consciousness of self-esteem" and "mental arrogance." The "habitual female masturbator" was "often abnormally deficient in feminine shyness." An acquired "sex inversion" was also possible.[329–31]

Female masturbators often exhibited "an affection of high moral tone aggressively urged, a tendency to denounce normal sexual indulgence and to suspect the sexual purity of others." These tendencies appeared "frequently in leaders of social purity movements and the spinster denouncers of 'that horrid man.'" These "women are a social danger," said Kiernan. They caused "marital incompatibility" and the "break up" of others' families.[335–36]

> Much of the so-called social purity movement is marred by the presence of auto-erotists of various forms ranging from masturbators and exhibitionists to inverts and perverts among its leaders. One such leader who consulted me, not for inversion which she regarded as normal and beautiful, but for occasional obsessions of psychic hermaphroditism which she regarded as disgusting and abnormal since they awakened desire for the normal relations between the sexes, could not, except with difficulty, be brought to see that her seduction of girls was as bad by her or even worse than it would have been by men. Of the consequences of the girl seduction by this class of women, Bêlot has drawn a rather nosologically [diagnostically] overstrained picture [in his novel *Mademoiselle Giraud, My Wife* (Chicago: 1891)].[337]

The female case history included "Manual masturbation at 16, followed by embraces by her girl friend," which "produced an intense orgasm initiated by contact with her friend's clitoris. . . . The imagery excited was alternately masculine and feminine."[331] After an engagement to a man was broken, "the female element tended to dominate in sexual imagery, produced by masturbatory procedure."[332] Recently her "imagery circled around plump women who appeared to be herself, but at the same time with whom as a male she copulated." She regarded her "sense of repugnance toward men" as "abnormal, believing herself to be what she called unsexed." She reportedly made a "good recovery" via "rest treatment" and "intellectual training in science, literature and sociology from the evolutionary viewpoint."[333]

♀ BOOK REVIEW/CROSSING WOMAN

## 1911, January 14
### N. Y. Times Book Review:
### Theodore Stanton's *Reminiscences of Rosa Bonheur*

"Woman Artist Rosa Bonheur Dressed Like a Man, but Didn't Want Other Women To," said the headline over an anonymous review of Theodore Stanton's biography of the French painter.[2]

The "frank and cordial self-revelation" with which Bonheur "was generous" revealed "nothing worse than a sturdy and courageous spirit seasoned with a hot temper."

> Love was an important element in her nature. She had for her friend Mlle. Nathalie Micas, with whom she lived, a passionate affection. Not until the death of this friend did she lose the magnificent joy in life that belonged to her temperament. Four years afterward she wrote: ". . . Since my dear Nathalie has gone from me, the world is an object of indifference and I look at everything as though I were seeing a play." In later years she admitted to her household and intimate friendship Miss Klumpke, the American artist, who became in due time her heir, to the exclusion of her own kin.
>
> She loved animals perhaps next to her friend, and surrounded herself with them. . . .

Calling Bonheur a "strongly idiosyncratic nature," the reviewer added: She "usually dressed like a man, but it would have been disagreeable and even difficult for her to visit the stockyards and other places to which her vocation took her, when she was a young women, if she had not done so; but she reproached the girl pupils who once cut off their hair to pay her the flattery involved in imitation."[14]

COMMENTARY

## 1911, April 5
### Chicago Vice Commission:
### *"Whole . . . colonies of these men"*

Between July 5, 1910 and April 5, 1911, a Vice Commission studied "The Social Evil in Chicago," and later issued a report.[3] Focusing on the prostitution of females with male customers, the report also included a description of "Sex Perversion" between men.

"At the very outset of the Commission's investigation, its attention was called . . . to sexual perversion which was said to be enormously prevalent and growing in Chicago." Two judges and several police officers "said that the most striking thing they had observed in the last year was the great increase of sex perversion." The Commission had put an investigator "in the field to find out the nature and extent of this form of vice," punishable by a maximum of ten years under a law of 1845 against " 'The infamous crime against nature.' "[295–96]

The Commission's investigator was, of course, unable to gain entrance into those circles of the very well-to-do, which are engaged in these practices, nor did he concern himself with the lowest stratum of society, which is the class most observable in our courts. Nor did he gain any information about the much more occasional cases among women, of which the Commission heard something from other sources. He most readily, however, became acquainted with whole groups and colonies of these men who are sex perverts, but who do not fall in the hands of the police on account of their practices, and who are not known in their true character to any extent by physicians because of the fact that their habits do not, as a rule, produce bodily disease. It is noteworthy that the details of information gained from a police officer, who was once detailed on this work, and from a young professional student, who himself, for a time, has been partially engaged in this practice, were completely substantiated by the Commission's investigator.

It appears that in this community there is a large number of men . . . who mostly affect the carriage, mannerisms, and speech of women; who are fond of many articles ordinarily dear to the feminine heart; who are often people of a good deal of talent; who lean to the fantastic in dress and other modes of expression, and who have a definite cult with regard to sexual life. They preach the value of non-association with women from various standpoints and yet with one another have practices which are nauseous and repulsive. Many of them speak of themselves or each other with the adoption of feminine terms, and go by girls' names or fantastic application of women's titles. They have a vocabulary and signs of recognition of their own, which serve as an introduction into their own society. The cult has produced some literature, much of which is uncomprehensible to one who cannot read between the lines, and there is considerable distribution among them of pernicious photographs.

In one of the large music halls recently, a much applauded act was that of a man who by facial expression and bodily contortion represented sex perversion, a most disgusting performance. It was evidently not at all understood by many of the audience, but others wildly applauded. Then, one of the songs recently ruled off the stage by the police department was inoffensive to innocent ears, but was really written by a member of the cult, and replete with suggestiveness to those who understood the language of this group.

Some of these men impersonate women on the cheap vaudeville stage, in connection with disorderly saloons. Their disguise is so perfect, they are enabled to sit at tables with men between the acts, and solicit for drinks the same as prostitutes.

Two of these "female impersonators" . . . afterwards invited the men to rooms over the saloon for pervert practices.[296–97]

As a "remedy," the Commission affirmed the "thoroughly practical ideal of a straight and pure sexual life both before and after marriage." The law of 1845 "should be altered . . . under the guidance of scientific men who understand these practices," to make it clear that "society regards these abhorrent deeds as crimes." But it was "very doubtful" if

any spread of actual knowledge of these practices is in any way desirable. Probably the purity and wholesomeness of the normal sexual relationship is all that is necessary to dwell on.[298]

♀  BOOK REVIEW/RESISTANCE

# 1911, July
## *International Journal of Ethics:*
## Edward Carpenter's *The Intermediate Sex*

An American journal of ethics that frequently published liberal discussions of sex included a review by J. Arthur Thomson, of Aberdeen, Scotland, of Carpenter's *The Intermediate Sex, A Study of Some Transitional Types of Men and Women,* an early defense of those later called "homosexuals."[4]*

Facts were said to support Carpenter's argument that there was no "sharp cleavage" between the "masculine" and "feminine." Carpenter showed that

there are many different degrees of feminine men and masculine women, and that a strong attraction between those of similar sex is not inconsistent with a high degree of intelligence and fine feeling. It does not necessarily imply sensual excess, and though it may sink to bestiality, so may a respectable marriage. A strong fondness between those of similar sex is a variety of the normal sex-attraction, but it is not necessarily morbid.

The reviewer rejected the:

assumption that the intermediate types discussed in this book are wholly undesirables. We mean in respect of their peculiarity, of course, for it is well known that some have been geniuses. It seems likely that an artificial mor-bididy is sometimes induced through lack of scientific knowledge and by the intolerance of impure minds. Mr. Carpenter pleads for a better-informed

*Thomson was co-author, with Patrick Geddes, of a popular book, *The Evolution of Sex* (N. Y.: Humboldt, 1890).

and broader consideration of these transitional types—which he shows a tendency to idealize—and every one must admit that the day of ignorant, wholesale branding of every departure from type is over.

Thompson then added two of his own qualifying "convictions": "there is some reason to suspect unwholesomeness (in the broad sense) in the constitution of the intermediate types"; and "the probable line of progress in the differentiation of man and woman is that which makes the most of the deeply rooted and old-established fundamental constitutional differences between them."[501–03]

MEDICAL

## 1911
### Dr. William Lee Howard: *"Never sleep with a man"*

Dr. Howard presented the sleeping etiquette of a newly eroticized and dangerous world, an etiquette opposing a common Victorian custom: persons of the same sex bedding down together for the night.[5]*

In a book of sexual and personal advice to boys, Dr. Howard warned that "to sleep with another person was unhealthful"; it "prevented your skin from breathing fresh air and . . . you could absorb the poisons from another's skin."

Sleeping with another "sends blood" to the "sex organs" and "causes a feeling of attraction towards these delicate organs." Many boys "will be tempted to talk and play with each other," acts ending in "self-abuse." "Thousands of boys have been started on the habit through sleeping one with another." He warned:

> Never trust yourself in bed with a boy or man. No matter if you are so situated that there is only one bed to be had. Sleep on the floor, anywhere; go without sleeping rather than have that "first time" happen to you. . . .[102]
>
> There are things in trousers called men, so vile that they wait in hiding for the innocent boy. These things are generally well dressed, well mannered—too well mannered in fact—and pass as gentlemen; but they are really human skunks hatched from rattlesnake's eggs. . . .
>
> Look out for these vermin, be suspicious of any man in trousers who avoids real men, who never enters or takes interest in manly sports, who tries to see you alone and prefers to go in bathing with boys instead of men. . . . They are only waiting to teach boys to help them in self-abuse or something far nastier.
>
> So never sleep with a man, except your father. If you should be so situated that you find yourself in bed with a man, keep awake with your eyes

---

*Though much of this was reprinted in a backnote to *GAH*, p. 642, it may have escaped the reader's attention, and its charm justifies its inclusion here. For a female companion piece see 1914, Steinhardt.

on something you can hit him with. At the slightest word or act out of the way, HIT him. . . .

It is to be hoped that you will never . . . know such beastly men. There are not many of them sneaking around, nevertheless I feel I should warn you against everything that might be the commencement of your ruin.[103–04]

♀  MEDICAL/RESISTANCE

# 1912, November 2
# Dr. Douglas C. McMurtrie: Homosexuality in women

Most "Cases of abnormal sexual development" concealed "the facts of their condition" from psychologists and physicians, and "are inclined to work out their own salvation," said Dr. McMurtrie of New York City.[6] "The great majority of the sexually abnormal live their lives without ever coming in contact with the medical profession."

"Homosexuality in women" was "one of the least known phases of sexual abnormality"; the many studies of "inversion" devoted "little attention to female manifestations." One reason for this was

> the difficulty of recognizing sexual inversion in women, due to the customs of the day which permit and even call for caresses and outward demonstrations between members of the female sex. In addition women are very generally ignorant of the details of sexual character, . . . not recognizing themselves the character of their tendencies. . . .

"Attraction of woman for woman" was referred to "rather fully" in creative literature. "The prototype of the woman invert has usually been regarded as Sappho, the Greek poetess of Lesbos, and from the name of her home city homosexual affection between females has taken the appellation of Lesbian love."[487]

McMurtrie described "some cases" (females and males) "which have come to my immediate notice."

"B.," a twenty-two-year-old female prostitute "confessed to being an invert." She "was in the constant company of two men, themselves pronounced inverts," and the case involved "attraction between inverts of opposite sexes." B. "played the masculine, while the feminine part was taken by the males." These males were "chorus men in a musical show." She would "call for them after the theater," and paid for their drinks and cigarettes. "In every way the relationship was active on her part rather than on the part of her consorts."

One of these males, twenty-six, "of a good family," had been "forced to leave his home city" after his homosexual practices became known, and he had been "completely cut off and ostracized by his family." In the musical comedy

company "he was not regarded with quite the same stigma as in other circles."
He had some liaisons with "masculine men" as well as with "inverted women."

> He was very busy in arraigning society for its attitude toward those of his
> type, and was prepared to ethically justify his characteristics and practices.

He was known "by the name of Rose."[488]
Another female "case," R., thirty-eight,

> proclaims her characteristics in the most flagrant way through her manner
> of dress which is always the most masculine, straight tailor hats and heavy
> shoes. She makes a living by prostituting herself homosexually to various
> women.

She had a "strong *liaison*" with a woman who took "the feminine part in their
relations."

> R. feels absolutely no shame or delicacy regarding her position. In the city
> . . . she frequents public places dressed in a manner to attract general notice.
> She is heaped with contempt and scorn by the normal and feminine women
> who see her. She seems, however, to rather glory in this attention and
> adverse criticism.

The partner in her liaison always played "the passive or feminine part."[488]
Another female "case," G., had as a girl taken part "almost exclusively in
boys' games and occupations." In later life she had "great ability in farming,
carpentry, machine work and other usually masculine pursuits." Her work had
"been of the highest standard and comprised valuable service to the community."
She "can see nothing wrong" in sexual and love relationships between women,
"except promiscuity, and regards the bond as being as holy as the conventional
marriage vow." She "is highly regarded by all who know her, and not even her
relatives and closest friends have the slightest idea of her sexual characteristics."[489]

♀  BOOK REVIEW

# 1913, March 30
## N. Y. Times Book Review:
## J. Lionel Taylor's *The Nature of Woman*

Professor Taylor's analysis of "woman's nature" was "a biologist's view, based
on careful scientific study," said an anonymous reviewer.[7] "The campaign for
woman suffrage" was regarded by Taylor as an "effort of certain women . . . to
give woman a status that would fit . . . their conception of her as nothing more
or less than a 'female man.'" Taylor was "impatient" with this concept. He was
quoted:

"though there are manly women, and womanly men, and men with female minds, and women with male minds, yet womanliness is a broad characteristic of woman and manliness of men."

He holds that this has been true always and that history and science flatly contradict those who say the unlikeness of woman to man has been forced on woman by circumstances in which she has lived. He believes, too, it is for the good of all concerned that the unlikeness between man and woman exists, and thinks any effort to change woman's nature to the end that she may become a female man will fail and should fail.

"I am convinced," he remarks, "that the question of woman's distinctive individuality, mental and bodily . . . , lies at the root of all fruitful investigation of the woman's question, as regards her education, her social position and representation, and her own and man's relationship in the house."

Prof. Taylor unreservedly admits he does not know precisely how to account for the discontent manifested by a small percentage of the great body of women. . . .

. . . Taylor finds no support whatever for the contention that woman would be a real female man if she had not been kept in subjection. . . .

Taylor referred to "a lack of inclination on the part of woman toward creative works," although he stressed the value of woman's "noblest function"—motherhood. Taylor demanded that economists provide for "the economic dependence of the married woman on the man" (which he alleged implied "domestic dependence of the man on the woman"). Taylor argued:

Nature . . . says, "Two types of body and mind I need," womanly and manly, a state of being for motherhood and . . . a state of doing for achievement.

Taylor claimed that "Nature . . . will prevail."[175]

♀ BOOK REVIEW

# 1913, October 19
## N. Y. Times Book Review: Walter Heape's Sex Antagonism

"Scientist" Heape's analysis of "feminine unrest" claimed that it was "primarily a biological question," specifically one of "generative physiology," said an anonymous reviewer.[8] Women's "present struggle" for "social change" expressed a conflict between a "masculine impulse" (toward the "roving" and "adventurous") and a "feminine impulse" (a "maternal instinct" seeking "to restrict the male").

Heape argued that "the present woman's movement has its origin in sex antagonism"; its "driving force is engendered by the desire to alter the [natural] laws which regulate the relations and therefore the relative powers of the sexes."

It followed, said the reviewer, that "the ascendant power in the community is soon to be a spinster, dubbed by Mr. Heape as a waste product only." Heape was quoted:

> The bulk of those who take an active part in the [women's] movement are undoubtedly spinsters, a dissatisfied and we may assume an unsatisfied class of women. . . . Should extended political power be granted to women it seems certain that those who will exercise that power most freely are women of this class—and they will exercise it chiefly for their own advantage. Thus extended power given to women threatens to result in legislation for the advantage of that relatively small class of spinsters who are in reality but a superfluous portion of the population; and since their interests are directly antagonistic to the interests of the woman who is concerned in the production of children, legislation enacted on their behalf will tend to be opposed to the interests of the mothers themselves.

The reviewer suspected that "quick-tongued feminists of either sex" could offer "telling objections" to Heape's refusal to treat "the feminist movement" as "anything other than biological." Many would argue that "considerations economic and social are of as primary importance as those biological."[561]

MEDICAL

# 1913

## Dr. Douglas C. McMurtrie: *"The situation and its dangers"*

McMurtrie's "Notes on Homosexuality" document the role of medical professionals in producing a new consciousness of male-male affection as "dangerous."[9]

"A homosexual infatuation of a young man 23 years of age for a boy aged 17," was reported by McMurtrie. The homosexual, J., "was abnormal in several ways." In school "he had been regarded as 'queer' by his mates." His "religious tendencies" became "almost an obsession." He "also had musical inclinations."

At college J. had met the seventeen-year-old M. The subject, J., had become "affectionate," had attempted to kiss M., and "wrote him impassioned love letters." M. remained indifferent.

"The circumstances" had come to Dr. McMurtrie's notice "through a chance remark by a family member of M.'s, "that J. wrote such remarkable letters." The "case" was "clearly one of infatuation by a sexual invert." Since M. was "entirely ignorant" of J.'s "condition," the doctor "most emphatically advised . . . the complete breaking off of the acquaintance. This was done."

> It is noteworthy, however, that though all the facts were in the possession of M.'s family, they had no recognition of the situation and its dangers.

Ignorance on such matters is very general among the laity and it would seem an urgent duty of physicians to offer advice in similar cases, even though it may not be specifically requested.[66–67]

The doctor also reported that in Germany the laws against "all homosexual acts," even those committed by two adults in private, resulted in trials, scandals, and suicides which gave "much publicity" to homosexuality. One recent result had been in Germany "a determined effort by intelligent physicians" to secure the repeal of the penal code criminalizing homosexual acts. (McMurtrie's sense of homosexuality as danger coexisted easily with a judgment favoring decriminalization.)

MEDICAL

# 1913
## Dr. Francis M. Shockley:
## "Homosexuality in the Genesis of Paranoid Conditions"

Freud's theory of the "role of homosexuality in paranoia" was discussed by Dr. Shockley of the Government Hospital for the Insane, Washington, D. C.[10]* Shockley presented several of his own case histories. As in almost all the essays in a series of Freudian speculations on homosexuality and paranoia no recognition was given to the existence of intense social condemnation as an important contributing factor. Shockley argued that the "paranoia" of homosexuals arose from a "failure" to suppress homosexual desires. That such desires should be suppressed was assumed. However, it is clear that in the history of "X," paranoia resulted from suppression; "happiness" and "contentment" followed homosexual acts. The contradiction between that Freudian theory assuming a need for suppression, and the actual history of X was not recognized by Shockley.

After marrying and failing to find "passionate enjoyment in his conjugal relations," X had become "despondent and had many suicidal ideas." He began to imagine that his wife tried to hurt him, and that "friends were acting peculiarly toward him."[433]

One night, shortly after this, a clergyman of considerable prominence was obliged to remain over night at his house.

As there were many guests the clergyman "was obliged to sleep with X."

During the night he attempted to hold perverted relations with X, and he being thus seduced found that this unexpected experience replaced the happiness he had expected to find with his wife. This clergyman gave him

*Shockley said: "Freud, in 1895, was the first to call attention to the role of homosexuality in paranoia." On homosexuality and paranoia also see 1933, May 31.

much information concerning the lives of homosexual individuals. After this X gave himself up to many relations with males. His interest in life returned and the depression rapidly gave place to contentment, which enabled him to progress rapidly with his work. At numerous times he became possessed with the idea that these relations were unethical and attempted to repress his inclinations. Each time however, this led to another attack of these paranoid ideas that every one was watching him and talking about him. No hallucinations were ever present, but . . . when someone would look at him a little too long, as he thought, he would feel sure that this person was thinking something derogatory to his character. . . . he had grown so used to this condition that whenever he began to have these ideas of persecution he immediately sought out his particular type of sexual experience and they soon disappeared.

There was absolutely no deterioration of intellect present in this man, a quiet well-dressed man of rather youthful and absolutely masculine appearance. . . . No one could find any evidence of a psychosis present, nor would one have considered him in any way effeminate, although he found sexual gratification only in the feminine role in fellatio.[434]*

MEDICAL

## 1914, January
## Dr. Douglas C. McMurtrie: "Pederastic Practices in Prison"

"Recent observations" at Sing Sing Prison in New York led Dr. McMurtrie to conclude that the majority of prisoners were either "active" or "passive pederasts," engaging in anal or oral sex acts while in jail.[11] McMurtrie reported:

Various acts of incredible atrocity were found to have been committed. The keepers had full knowledge of conditions and yet did nothing to improve them. There was one instance of the assault of a young new prisoner by seventeen men, the method employed being immissio membri virilis per anum [emission from the penis through the anus]. As a result of the mistreatment the boy went insane and had to be transferred to one of the state asylums.[16]

The system of assigning two inmates to a cell also led to the sexual use of the younger by the older prisoners, and this was tolerated by the guards.

McMurtrie continued:

---

*The "feminine role in fellatio" was apparently that act in the vernacular called "cocksucking." This act was evidently considered "feminine" because it was judged to be demeaning—thus the role of the female. This categorization, however, reversed the usual association of the "feminine" with "passivity," the "masculine" with "activity."

Some of the relationships formed in prison are not as animal or brutal as the instances already alluded to. In many cases the original attraction seems spiritual rather than physical and many of the manifestations of normal love may be observed. Thus we see an older man taking a younger as a protégé, acting as his protector and helping him in every possible way. The average person feels, I believe, the need of another human being upon whom to lavish and from whom to receive affection, and I believe it is this impulse, laudable in its character, which is responsible for the inception of some of the liaisons in prison. The impulse, however, under the absolutely abnormal conditions of our present penal methods, takes an abnormal mode of expression.

Such a relationship as I have just described will soon ripen into love. Often, of course, some form of physical gratification may eventually ensue. There are many instances, however, where the moral standards of the older man prevent such practices.[16–17]

MEDICAL/CROSSING MEN

# 1914, February 21
## Dr. Bernard S. Talmey: "Transvestism"

In a paper read before the Society of Medical Jurisprudence, Dr. Talmey discussed "One of the newest discovered anomalies" " 'cross-dressing' " the "abnormal desire" of a male to dress as a woman, of a female to dress as a man.[12]

This document raises questions about the desire to cross-dress, the wish to change sex, and the desire to love and/or be loved by one's "own" sex or the "other" sex. In the 1980s, these are usually distinguished as qualitatively distinct entities: "transvestism," "transsexualism," "homosexuality," "heterosexuality." A "normal" desire to wear the clothes customary for one's own sex, and a "normal" identification with one's own sex are usually assumed—not analysed as problematic. A "normal" attraction to the "other" sex has also received much less attention than desire for the "same" sex. This document is useful in helping us put aside modern differentiating labels. The phenomena at issue here are the precise emotions of those men whose histories are reported, and the prevailing social categorizing of clothing, persons, and feelings according to sex-biology. These male histories suggest that their subjects' wish to cross-dress or to be female involved a desire to legitimate certain feelings socially identified as proper only for women. Those feelings sometimes included love and erotic attraction for men. The subjects' several-times proclaimed hostility to homosexual feelings is indicative of that very non-acceptance which the acquisition of "female" clothes or a female body was intended to reverse.

The "first patient," Mr. S., was said to have a "marked feminine sensibility." He was "very sensitive to pain, still he is stoic enough not to complain." He was "of a yielding disposition," though sometimes "quite strongheaded."

The patient possesses normal love and admiration for the other sex and experiences some sex attraction for women. . . . Still his sexual feelings were and are very little pronounced for women and never for men. . . . He has no homosexual inclinations, but rather a profound repugnance to homosexual relationship. He never longed for a male instead of a female lover. Still he seems to want a man before whom he could expose the charms of his own person and who would kiss and caress him. . . .

Mr. S. desired "to be a complete woman," and from childhood had "had the wish to be a girl." His "desire now is to live as a woman absolutely." He never wished to experience having a baby, but "often wished to be castrated to be more like a woman." He "longs for the female form." Dressed as a woman, "he has all a woman's feelings and longings."[364] In his

Original caption: "First patient, as Queen Louise."

Original caption: "A characteristic symptom of patient No. 1; posing in imitation of a celebrated painting."

daydreams, when in female attire, he sometimes fancies being . . . led to bed, but by a woman and not by a man. In these fantasies he remains passive and is conquered, kissed and hugged by the woman.[365]

Mr. S. was married, had fathered three children, headed "a large business," was a writer and lecturer, and officer in social and literary societies.[365]

Dr. Talmey's fifth "case" (here presented out of order) was thirty-six, "an artist painter who is about to marry." In a letter to the first "patient" in December 1907, the artist said:

As far as I can judge from your letter, it looks as if you consider man's love for dressing in female clothing equal to homosexualism. . . . I can tell you that homosexualism has always been an abhorrence to me, and that the sole reason for my desire to wear gowns is purely a feminine love for what is beautiful and picturesque. In my relations to the other sex, I am just as normal as any other man.

Because of social pressures he hoped to abandon cross-dressing when he married.[367]

The second "case" was that of a sixty-two-year-old "gentleman" living in the western United States, who had dreamed as a child that he "was a girl," and had sometimes been dressed by his mother as one. He wrote:

My inclinations are always toward strongminded energetic women of the masculine type. I have also an uncontrollable admiration for other men of my type, when seeing them attired as women. Still I never had any homosexual inclinations. I always had an almost uncontrollable desire to wear woman's attire.

At age fifteen a "fanatic preacher," an uncle, had denounced him to his father for sometimes wearing girl's clothes; his father had said " 'he would cripple me' " if he was seen in girl's clothes again. He soon left for the far west,

landing at Grand Island, Neb., in the spring of 1867. I drove a team on construction work of a railroad and, in the fall of the same year, found myself hunting buffalo. In the five ensuing years I have done my part in the winning of the west, with the result that I carry two Indian bullets in my legs to this hour. But I cover them up with petticoats as often as opportunity permits. . . .

I have never dissipated at any time of my life. I have served as a detective in a United States marshal's office, as a sheriff, and as a justice of the peace. For five years I was publisher of a newspaper. I never failed to make good in any of my ventures. . . . I have been able to conquer most everything except my uncontrollable passion for female attire. . . .

Now, really why should I resist it? I am doing no one any harm. . . . I know that the majority of modern mankind regards such an inclination as a silly weakness in a normal man, but that does not make it so. . . .[365–66]

The third "case" was thirty-two, married, a printer, and living in London. His self-description was signed "Blanche," followed by his male name, "Harold I. J." He wrote that he had "a complete female mind with a normal male body." His "feminine instincts" had manifested themselves at age four, when he was first "put into knickers," and experienced a "horrid feeling." After some protest from his mother, he was allowed "to wear frocks" for his first eighteen years. Then, since he needed to earn a living, "and since that could not be done as a girl, I was forced to go out into the life of the world as a boy"—though he "never gave up feminine underwear." He exclaimed: "How different one feels in the two styles of clothing." He "never felt happy unless dressed as a lady." Referring to "sexual congress," he said, "the feeling that would lead to such behavior has never worried me." In "the company of young men, I seem to feel altogether out of place, and a shrinking, timid feeling takes possession of my mind." He was "perfectly at home in female company," and could "converse upon the subjects most dear to the female heart, dress, etc." His emotions when with men, said Dr. Talmey, "resemble greatly those of homosexual individuals," though the "patient does not manifest any homosexual inclinations."[366–67]

The fourth "patient," Professor M., sixty-two, was living in a "farmer town of 7,000 to 8,000 inhabitants," and wrote:

> I do not go down to the business section of the town, dressed up in female attire. Too many people here are just looking to cause trouble. . . . The past two years I lived in Dayton, Ohio, a city of 100,000 inhabitants. The people did not molest me, and I had police protection. While in this place the populace have persecuted me in all kinds of ways, even when dressed as a man. They made threats of mob violence and attempted to incarcerate me in a lunatic asylum. So you see I am up against it. God and my hypnotic

Original caption: "Third patient."

power were all that saved me. I am plucky and not afraid of any one, so long as I am in the right.

I was arrested in this city April 1, 1905, for appearing on the street dressed in female attire, although I have a State license to protect me in trying to make a living outside my pension from the government on account of my old army trouble. . . . A number of years ago I was strong sexually and fond of the opposite sex. . . . Nowadays I care more for my own sex. . . . I have thought for some time, I was possessed with a female spirit, or a female soul inhabited my body. If I am a man, why is it that some men wish to have sexual relations with me? Is it a chemical affinity or a mental attraction, or something else attracts them?

Dr. Talmey found "interesting" this patient's

wail and cry that the common herd does not understand him. It is the old feminine protest that men do not understand women. It is the familiar catch phrase which a flattering yellow journalism and mediocre literature are continually dishing out to their women readers. Men will never understand women, is preached in and out of season, insinuating a certain depth in and mystery about her psyche.[367]

"Neither does man understand," said Talmey, "the wonderful instinct of the hymenopter" (an insect). Yet that "insect seems to be less proud of its mystery than our patient of his." (Talmey's analogy between women, insects, and the "patient," and the doctor's outrage at the patient's pride, reveals this doctor's own "interesting" emotions.)

Original caption: "Fourth patient, dressed for the street."

PERSONAL TESTIMONY

## 1914, March 27
## Jack London and Edward Carpenter:
### *"Will keep an eye [out] for INTERMEDIATE TYPES"*

Novelist Jack London wrote from Glen Ellen, California, to Edward Carpenter in England.[13] The novelist said he had

> read you and followed you for years. Incidentally, I may mention that I have for years specialized on sex, but that, because of my wandering life, mostly off in the South Seas and in Alaska, . . . I have always been unable to get your book *The Intermediate Sex.*

London asked if Carpenter's publisher could send him a copy, for which he'd forward a check. "Any time you are out in California, please know that our home is open to you," he added.

On June 25, 1914, "Mrs. Jack London" wrote to Carpenter that her husband had been away, was just catching up on correspondence, and had asked her to acknowledge Carpenter's "good letter" and autographed photo. London had sent Carpenter his novel *Martin Eden,* and Mrs. London had selected some photos of her husband for Carpenter. "Also, I heard him chortle gleefully . . . that he had your *Intermediate Sex.*" She could envision London "settling down to enjoy your book; and he will keep an eye [out] for INTERMEDIATE TYPES."*

Edward Carpenter, 1905. The photograph sent to Jack London (from Carpenter's *My Days and Dreams* [London: George Allen & Unwin, 1916], opposite p. 208).

*For another reference to invert-spotting see July 1914.

♀  MEDICAL

## 1914, June
## Dr. Douglas C. McMurtrie: "Lesbian Love"

McMurtrie's regular column on "sexual psychology" included a section on "Lesbian Love and the Lexicographers."[14] This doctor's defining "love . . . between women" as "lesbian" and "erotic" discredited the old romantic love-friendship which supposedly had no such erotic component.

As early as January 1883, an American doctor had referred in a medical journal to the erotic relationship between Lucy Ann Lobdell and her wife as "Lesbian love" (see *GAH*, p. 222). But in the early twentieth century this medical definition of "Lesbian" as referring to a female-female eroticism had not yet reached that middle-class public represented by *The New York Times*. On May 4, 1913, *The Times Book Review* (p. 263) referred, without embarrassment and without illicit connotation, to Sappho as the "Lesbian poet." Similarly, *The Times Book Review* on May 10, 1914 (p. 228), reported the discovery of a " 'new Sappho poem' " (addressed to Anactoria); *The Times* called Sappho "the famous Lesbian singer," and even referred to those of her poems concerned with her "pupils and girl friends"—still with no illicit erotic connotation. By 1932, however, *The Times Book Review* was referring directly to the "homosexualism" associated with Sappho's name (and, presumably, with the word "lesbian"; see 1932, September 11).

In 1914, Dr. McMurtrie told his fellow doctors:

> Lesbian love as the designation of love relationships between women is widely used and its meaning is universally understood, at least by all persons at all versed in sexual science. Yet the standard dictionaries which list medical terms . . . take no notice of the terms relating to sexual inversion in women.
>
> The exact sexual characteristics of Sappho . . . are in some dispute among historical authorities, but the literary and scientific acception of the terms ["sapphism" and "lesbian"] is in no dispute whatever. There seems therefore to be little excuse for their omission by the lexicographers.

McMurtrie had looked up the above terms in several prominent lexicographical works, and reported:

> Under the adjective *lesbian*, Murray, in the *Oxford Dictionary*,[1] fails to note its association with the homosexual love of women. . . .
>
> The Century Dictionary, the most extensive American lexicographical work, omits any definition of *tribade* or *tribadism*. It also fails to especially identify the adjective *lesbian* with love relations between women.[2] In the course of the definition of the word "*Lesbian*, adjective and noun," it is remarked: "From the reputed character of the inhabitants and the tone of

their poetry, *Lesbian* is often used with the implied sense of 'amatory' or 'erotic'." . . .

[Pierre] Larousse[3] defines both *tribade* and *tribadism*. In translation his entries run as follows. *"Tribade* (Greek, *tribas,* from *tribo,* I rub), woman whose clitoris is developed to an exaggerated degree and who misuses those of her own sex." And of tribadism: *"Tribadism,* vicious practices of tribades." [Claude] Augé, in an edition of one the Larousse works,[4] notes among other meanings, the use of the adjective *lesbienne* substantively as a synonym for tribade.[296–97]

1. James A. H. Murray, *A new English dictionary on historical principles.* Oxford, 1908, vol. 6, p. 207.
2. *Century Dictionary.* New York [1911], vol. 5, p. 3417.
3. *Grand dictionnaire universel.* Paris, n.d., vol. 15, p. 482.
4. *Nouveau Larousse illustré.* Paris, n.d., vol. 5, p. 652.

♀ MEDICAL

# 1914, July
## Dr. Douglas C. McMurtrie: *"Sexually inverted infatuation"*

A new practice, invert-spotting, was recorded by Dr. McMurtrie, whose regular medical journal column on "sexual psychology" evidently put him in touch with a national network of such spotters.[15] (See 1914, March 17, for another reference to invert-spotting.) The column also indicates that a stereotype of the female invert couple was being circulated around the country.

A section of McMurtrie's column was headed "Homosexual Infatuation Between Women." A "recent report" had reached him (from an unnamed Midwestern city) which he "diagnosed," "on the basis of social relations alone," as "sexually inverted infatuation."

Two young women, aged approximately twenty-eight and thirty-one years respectively, of good family standing and education, lived together in a luxurious house, the property of one of them who is very well-to-do. They employed several servants but none of these latter slept in the house. . . . The two ladies were never known to attend any social functions, but whenever they were seen, were invariably in each other's company, either driving, walking, or shopping.

The aggressive member of the pair was the elder, the one who had the money. She dressed in masculine fashion, wearing stiff collars and plain fedora hats. The second young woman exhibited feminine characteristics. Her appearance was comparatively weak.[351]

♀ MEDICAL

## 1914, August
## Drs. Wilhelm Stekel and S. A. Tannenbaum:
## "Masked homosexuality"

An essay by Dr. Stekel of Vienna, a disciple of Freud, was translated and annotated by Dr. Tannenbaum of New York City.[16] Tannenbaum's introduction began: "It is almost unbelievable" that there were doctors, "even" in New York, "who have never heard of homosexuality, and who do not know that such a condition exists."[530]

"The best informed thinkers," said Tannenbaum,

> are now agreed that by nature all human beings are psychically bisexual—capable of loving a person of either sex; that as a result of various social forces the homosexual tendency is repressed as the individual attains adult age and the heterosexual tendency is . . . established as "normal."

The "repressed homosexual tendency," Tannenbaum said, "manifests itself in sociability, comradery, friendship, and humanitarianism." A "disturbance" in the development to heterosexuality resulted in a "fixed" homosexuality.[531]

Examples of "masked homosexuality" were discussed by Stekel. Among these were men going "into raptures over women with marked masculine traits." Men thus fell in love with "female bicyclists, women in riding habits," and "prostitutes whom they have seen in drawers." Masked homosexuality in women was manifested by their falling in love with "effeminate men," "men with long hair, or men wearing long cloaks." "Very dangerous to such women" were "a priest in his cassock," "a physician in his gown," and "artists with long curly hair." Male "neurotics" were also said to be "very powerfully affected by women who smoke, ride, shoot, climb mountains, or otherwise manifest mannish tendencies of an aggressive nature."[532]

Stekel said that "homosexuality betrays itself" in men who in the sex act preferred "to take the position 'normally' occupied by the woman," or who preferred to perform the act from behind or in the anus. Women showed homosexual "tendencies" when they "experience an orgasm only when they are on top." (Tannenbaum here added that one of his own patients "indicated her homosexuality and her 'masculine protest' in this indignant utterance: 'Everywhere, even in the Bible, woman is placed under the man!' ") Stekel said: "Some of the perversions, e.g. fellatorism, cunnilingus, are indicative of homosexuality."[534]

A "homosexual component" was revealed, said Stekel, when "A woman suddenly discovers that her long hair is a nuisance and has it cut off."

> She changes the fashions of her garments, loves to wear jackets, . . . derbies, . . . and begins to take an interest in the movement for women's rights. (In

a very large percentage of active suffragettes the driving force is the un-satisfied sexual desire. She wants what the man has. The woman craves to have the man's "right" to indulge in premarital or extramarital coitus. In others the driving force is the repressed homosexuality: the desire to associ-ate with women. Only very rarely, if ever, do women whose libido is satisfied take any interest in the suffragette movement. . . .)[534]

Stekel continued: among "onanists," many were "asocial and shun company."

But there are some among them who take an extremely active interest in social and fraternal organizations of all sorts. That female agitators are strongly homosexual is well known and furnishes themes for the humorists connected with the comic journals. Less well known perhaps is the fact that some of these agitators are rabid onanists and active homosexuals.[535]

Stekel concluded: "Only the careful study of the masked forms of homosex-uality will enable us to understand the tremendous significance of bisexuality in our psychic life." He was sure that the knowledge gained of masked homosexual-ity "will arouse violent opposition in many quarters." He suggested: "much of the general resistance to psychoanalysis has its origin in homosexuality. *What civilized humanity is least willing to acknowledge is its bisexual constitution.*"[537]

♀ MEDICAL/RESISTANCE

## 1914, September
## Dr. Douglas C. McMurtrie: "Hirschfeld, Champion of Homosexuality" and "Moral Conditions Among Seamen"

A medical journal column on "sexual psychology" included a section headed "Hirschfeld, Champion of Homosexuality."[17] This quoted from an article by R. Russell Herts about his visit with Dr. Magnus Hirschfeld in Berlin. In the doctor's office Herts had been "introduced to two young 'ladies.' " The younger, about nineteen, "was dressed in a somewhat mannish sailor suit," and was "exceedingly good looking." Hirschfeld explained in front of the two that the oldest was really a perfectly formed male whom the government had granted permission to wear female attire because "he was more conspicuous in the clothes of his own sex."

The other young lady herself explained that she had been trying to get permission to dress as a man. She felt as a man and loved only women, she told us quite simply. The pair had been to Dr. Hirschfeld in the first place to see if by an operation they could change places sexually.[432]

McMurtrie headed another section "Moral Conditions Among Seamen."

In a recent conversation with a gentleman exceptionally conversant with all phases of the seaman's life, I was told that homosexual practices among sailors had decreased in recent years to a notable extent. This he considered to be due to several causes, the most important being the passing of long voyages, such as used to be taken in the old sailing ships, not touching land, in some instances, for six months at a time. The majority of trips at the present time are in fast steam vessels having a maximum period of two weeks between ports. Another reason for the decrease of the practice . . . was the rise of public sentiment, condemning it, among the men. This would operate, of course, to put a check on the conduct of individuals.[436]

♀ BOOK REVIEW/RESISTANCE

# 1914, October
## *International Journal of Ethics:*
## Edward Carpenter's *Intermediate Types Among Primitive Folk*

Carpenter's cross-cultural study of "intermediate types" in "primitive" cultures, subtitled a *Study in Social Evolution,* was reviewed in the United States-based *International Journal of Ethics.*[18] T. Whittaker, of London, called Carpenter's book "a perfect example of the scientific and speculative discussion of a subject which only of late years has met with anything that can be called scientific treatment."[110]

"Intermediate types," the reviewer explained, were those who, "as regards psychology of sex, may be called intermediate between man and woman." This term and categorization Carpenter himself admitted to be inexact, as "intermediate types" included both the " 'ultra-virile' " and " 'ultra-feminine.' " Carpenter argued, said the reviewer:

> The more effeminate type of intermediate men . . . among primitive peoples turned from the ordinary male occupations to religion, being found especially apt for divination, clairvoyance, [and] ecstasy. . . . The more masculine type founded such institutions as those of military comradeship among the Dorian Greeks. In both cases, he suggests the type might possibly fulfil a positive and useful function. Simply to enter into a tirade against so widespread a human tendency, easy as it might be, would not be the method either of common sense or of science.[111]

After further reviewing Carpenter's theories of the positive social function of "intermediate types," the reviewer concluded by approving "the example set in the present book: neither to denounce nor to lament, but to try to understand."[113]

♀ MEDICAL

# 1914, November
## Dr. Douglas C. McMurtrie:
## "Sexually Inverted Infatuation in a Middle-Aged Woman"

Dr. McMurtrie reported an "extreme case of sexually inverted infatuation in a middle-aged woman."[19] The case had "recently come under my observation."

Very soon after her arrival in a hospital for the removal of her ovaries, "T," forty years old, married, with a twelve-year-old daughter, "fell violently in love with one of the nurses." When she recovered from her operation Mrs. T one day "hid in the bushes." As the nurse went by Mrs. T "passionately threw herself at the nurse with such force that the two fell to the ground and had to be extricated by attendants."

Dismissed from the hospital, Mrs. T sent the nurse "a stream of love letters" which McMurtrie called "excellent examples of homosexual declarations."

The nurse, he said, was a "typically feminine and attractive girl with a good figure. She had no trace of homosexual characteristics."

Mrs. T, apart from her infatuation, appeared to be "normal." She was not

particularly masculine in appearance, though she was not at all attractive, judged by feminine standards. She had no intimate relations with her husband, who came to the hospital from time to time to inquire formally regarding her condition. He did not, however, ever ask to see her. The daughter, who seemed a fine, healthy girl, came to see her mother regularly; as far as could be gathered the husband realized his wife's peculiarities and lived with her in a perfunctory manner, fulfilling his practical obligations for the sake of the daughter. There was no affection whatever between him and his wife.

"Infatuations" for women "were frequent with Mrs. T." "A considerable number of nurses" who tended her before her operation "had all been driven away by her homosexual importunities."

The "vigor and baldness" of these importunities made this case unusual. Dr. McMurtrie described it as "Lesbian nymphomania."

♀ RESISTANCE

# 1914
## George Ives's *Criminals, Witches, Lunatics*

The activities of George Ives as one of the major, early British defenders of "sexual inverts" are discussed in later entries (see 1934, May; also 1925, June 4).

Identifying himself publicly as a writer and criminologist, Ives's one book published in the U. S., *A History of Penal Methods: Criminals, Witches, Lunatics* (1914), was a study of the punishments legally accorded those three groups.[20]* Included was a brief essay on "sexual inversion"—a tactful defense. Ives's indirection in this book, on a subject about which his diaries show he felt passionately, indicates the constraint to which even a privately militant homosexual might feel subject in his public discourse. In this book, Ives presented "sexual inversion" as an essentially biological phenomenon, manifesting different historical forms. He stressed the psychic similarity of males and females, and the many varieties of emotional combinations, in order to present "inversion" as, simply, one kind of attraction, to divest it of its aura of sin, crime, or pathology.

Legislation referring to inversion, he said, made it impossible not to discuss publicly this "difficult" subject.[291] "Sexual inverts may be compared to the left-handed." "They are indeed always a minority in every population, but an *eternal* minority."† Inverts were a physiologically constituted, universal, unchanging group, according to Ives. But the "primordial homogenic instinct has had a most amazing history," ranging from "a religious cult" to "a crime." (The term "homogenic" was Edward Carpenter's coinage.) It "has been present in all ages and places," he claimed. This "innate," biological "homogenic instinct" took different social forms.[292–95] "Manifestations of passionate attraction, both of the homosexual instinct and of the venal, substitutional and acquired vices which have often gathered round it, have been visible from the beginning." But only in the late 1800s had "Science" take up this "melancholy subject," this "social problem," behind which, Ives suggested, lay "a social wrong." He hinted that "obstacles" were "placed in the way of new lines of research which criticise the treatment of a tabooed subject."[296]

In "periods of ignorance the mad were placed within the province of the priest; equally hopelessly, the unfortunate inverts have been left to the policeman."[296] When inversion became the province of "Science," Ives implied, it was on its way to more proper study. Havelock Ellis's were the "most important volumes" on the subject, for he did not use his medical knowledge to try "to 'explain' emotions which we do not understand in terms of pathology."[297]

Alluding to the "American seer" (Walt Whitman), Ives stressed: "A vast similitude underlies all," and that "recent scientific researches" emphasized the "unity" of males and females:

*A link between the social treatment of homosexuals, witches, and lunatics (and other heretics) has often been pointed out by defenders of homosexuals; see for example, Dr. Thomas Szasz, *The Manufacture of Madness: A Comparative Study of the Inquisition and the Mental Health Movement* (N. Y.: Harper and Row, 1970) and the letters of Henry Gerber, p. 553.

†This is one of the earliest known references in English to inverts as an omnipresent "minority." The same notion is found in John Boswell's *Christianity, Social Tolerance, and Homosexuality* (1980), and in my own earlier book. For homosexuals as a "minority" also see 1925, Robinson. Also see "minority" and "majority" in the index.

In the human race the similarity is far greater than we mostly realize. Custom, education, costume, and maternity have all tended to accentuate the difference and obliterate the likeness of the two sexes, but, in reality, . . . they stand extremely close together.

Between the male and female "poles" were "all varieties of temperament, from the ultra-masculine to the infra-feminine," spread out like a "spectrum, the colours (temperaments) blending into one another. For, psychically, there is no great gap between the sexes, which may indeed be said to overlap, on the emotional plane."[299–300] There were "infinite kinds" of emotional "attractions," among them the "homogenic." But it was not criminology's function "to *explain* the emotions."

Nor does it help us much to moralise and ask why such an instinct should have been created or to reflect what an amount of misery would have been saved if it had never been. We have, unhappily, a very present and practical problem to deal with, which it is useless to deny, and most immoral to ignore, since the first principles of *justice* are involved. It is that we may rightly understand the nature of the phenomena, and not continue to beat about the shuttlecocks of convention in an atmosphere of lies, that I have tried to show what the facts really are.[301]

♀ MEDICAL

# 1914
# Dr. William J. Robinson:
## "My Views on Homosexuality"

Dr. Robinson, editor of two medical journals dealing with sex, and chief of the Department of Genito-Urinary Diseases, Bronx Hospital, is mentioned as a sex reformer in various English and German sources.[21] The limited liberality of his views on homosexuality, apparent in the present excerpt, is striking when contrasted with the ideas expressed about the same time by Margaret Anderson (see 1915, June 4).

"Our brutal treatment of any man found guilty of homosexuality," said Dr. Robinson, had led some to dissent from "popular notions." Until a "short time ago" the prevailing idea had been that "homosexuals are a low degraded type of men, depraved mentally, morally and physically, and deserving of the severest punishment for their 'crime.' "

Some sexologists were now claiming "that homosexuality is not a crime, not a vice, not a sign of degeneracy, not even a sexual abnormality, merely a sexual variation." Robinson disagreed; homosexuality was "a sign of degeneracy"; it was

a sad, deplorable, pathological phenomenon. Every sexual deviation or disorder which has for its result an inability to perpetuate the race is *ipso facto* pathologic, *ipso facto* an abnormality, and this is pre-eminently true of true homosexuality.[550–51]

The fact that "homosexuals are not satisfied with their condition, and would give a good deal to get rid of it, is proof that they themselves are aware that . . . they are abnormal." All the homosexuals Robinson had ever met "considered their condition a great punishment, tho some of them were resigned to it."[551]

The tendency of "certain sexologists" to present the homosexual as "normal," and even as "superior to normal," must be opposed. Though some homosexuals were "sweet," and some "capable artists," Robinson had not seen "a great or even a capable thinker among them." And "all show one or more points of distinct inferiority to the normal man"; they were not doing "something of large permanent value."[551] The "world could get along very well without these step-children of nature." He concluded:

> Let us demand the abolition of all stupid laws against the homosexuals which do no good but only breed disgrace and foster blackmail. Let us work for a humane, intelligent attitude towards them, but let us not minimize their faults, let us not exaggerate their virtues, in short let us not falsely idealize them. . . .[552]*

♀ MEDICAL

# 1914
# Dr. Irving D. Steinhardt:
## *"Avoid girls who are too affectionate"*

In his book *Ten Sex Talks to Girls (14 Years and Older),* Dr. Steinhardt of New York warned of masturbation: "When practised by one girl it is harmful enough, but when practised between girls it is a most pernicious habit which should be vigorously fought against."[57]22

> Avoid girls who are too affectionate and demonstrative in their manner of talking and acting with you; who are inclined to admire your figure and breast development; who are inclined to be just a little too familiar in their actions toward you; who are inclined to be rather free and careless in the display of themselves in your presence; who press upon you too earnestly invitations to remain at their homes all night, and to occupy the same bed they do. When sleeping in the same bed with another girl, old or young, avoid "snuggling up" close together. Avoid the touching of sexual parts, including the breasts, and, in fact, I might say avoid contact of any parts of the body at all. Keep your night robe about you so that you are as well

---

*Robinson's anti-homosexual views were opposed by Dr. E. S. Shepherd; see 1918, June. For Robinson's 1925 revision of his ideas, see entry of that date.

protected from outside contact as its size will permit, and let your conversation be of other topics than sexuality. Do not lie in each other's arms when awake or falling asleep; and, after going to bed, if you are sleeping alone or with others, just bear in mind that beds are sleeping places. When you go to bed, go to sleep just as quickly as you can. If possible, avoid sleeping with anyone else. It is more healthful and sanitary to sleep in a separate bed. . . . certain diseases, both those affecting the genital organs and others, are often conveyed through contaminated bed clothes, body contact, the breath, etc. You can see for yourselves, therefore, that separate beds are good for more reasons than one.[60–61]

Those who became the "slaves" of masturbation lost their "normal sexual appetite." And even that "normal" appetite did not need to be acted upon: "Masturbation or actual sexual relations are absolutely unnecessary to either man or woman."[62]

"As many girls have learned bad habits . . . through females as through males." He added:

some girls are low enough to accept pay for bringing about the moral ruin of members of their sex; . . . they are to be found everywhere, in the smallest village as well as in the largest town. Girls who have become discontented with their lot are easily influenced by the sweet, honeyed lies of these vile creatures. Beware of strange women, as well as of strange men, who seek to shower favors and other things upon you for no apparent reason except that they are strangely attracted to you. If you do not, you will live to regret it. Thousands of your sex already have, and lie in nameless graves away from home, most likely in a pauper's burying-ground, because they had become so degraded in name and fact as to be lost to "the old folks at home."[63]

♀ RESISTANCE

# 1915, February 4
## Edith Lees Ellis's Chicago Lecture,
## and Margaret Anderson's response

On her second speaking tour of the United States, Edith Lees Ellis lectured in Chicago and Milwaukee, on such subjects as Edward Carpenter, "The Loves of Tomorrow," and "Sex and Eugenics," the latter, in part, a gingerly phrased, public defense of the sexually "abnormal."[23]

Published quotes and comment following Edith Ellis's Chicago lecture on "Sex and Eugenics" indicates that this talk was identical or similar to her essay "Eugenics and the Mystical Outlook," the more abstract, tame, and briefer of two essays referring to sexual "abnormals." (The other, bolder essay is "Eugenics and Spiritual Parenthood.") Both were printed in a collection of her writings titled

Edith Ellis, about 1914 (from Havelock Ellis, *My Life*
[Boston: Houghton Mifflin, 1939], opposite p. 578.)

*The New Horizon in Love and Life* (London, 1921). That, by 1915, Edith Ellis may have prepared the bolder, more extended talk on "inversion," but chose not to give it, suggests the courage it took in 1915 for a woman and a person without medical credentials to speak publicly on the subject at all.

Havelock Ellis's autobiography, published in 1939, twenty-three years after Edith's death, spoke publicly of his wife's lesbianism, and about their unconventional marriage. Subsequent biographies of Havelock Ellis have added a little to the available information about Edith Ellis, although, to my knowledge, no recent article or book has presented much new evidence about her life and work. Edith Ellis never, apparently, spoke publicly as a lesbian (an act unheard of in 1915). But her rather abstract public comments in Chicago on the "abnormal" are (with the lectures of Emma Goldman and Alexander Berkman) among the earliest public defenses of homosexuality known to have been delivered in the United States, and constituted an individual act of lesbian resistance.

On February 4, 1915, *The Chicago Daily Tribune* printed an ad announcing: "Mrs. Havelock Ellis will present a lecture on 'Sex and Eugenics' at Orchestra Hall,'" that night. Ticket prices ranged from fifty cents to $1. The lecture had been arranged by Dr. Effie Lobdell and a "Miss Cook," and sponsored by the Medical Women of Chicago. Ellis's talk was originally announced as for women only, but men were admitted, upon Edith Ellis's request; her explanation was that men needed education in sex as much as women.

At the time of Edith Ellis's talk, the reactionary implications of eugenics for race and class politics, and even its full anti-feminist implications, were not yet clear to liberal and leftist thinkers. Until the Nazis' advocacy of such racial, hereditary, and evolutionary theory discredited eugenics in the 1930s, analyses of sex and society were often formulated in its terms. (Eugenics was an early form of what is now called "sociobiology."*)

In the essay published as "Eugenics and the Mystical Outlook" (evidently that given in Chicago) Edith Ellis stated that men had "for generations" accentuated "masculinity"; "women have minimised or caricatured the sexual instinct which in normal womanhood is neither a frigidity nor an obsession." (A deemphasis of differences between the sexes was typical of "modern," liberal thinkers.) Ellis added:

> If sex relationships to-day are assuming different manifestations, both in so-called normal and abnormal relationships, it is time we faced the matter.

"The mass of books thrown upon the market to-day, which are supposed to enlighten us on sex problems," either confused through "sentimentality or puritanism," or by "exaggerating physiological needs."

"Think . . . of the ordinary sexual life of to-day!" she ordered. She referred to the "commercialism of prostitution, the parasitism of women," the "sexual gluttony of men and women," and the "stultifying narrowness and jealousy" of many "virtuous homes"—which made "legitimate mating . . . almost as dangerous as war." Only when "love is not complicated with property, slavery, or one-sided legislation" would "sex" cease to be regarded as "mere animalism" or only as procreation. The production of art "may be as fine a manifestation of love as a fat crowing baby." (That defense of artistic production as equal in value to baby production had radical implications for creative and childless women.) She urged a combination of "physiological sexuality and spirituality."[41]

Edith Ellis warned of the "dangers of interfering with Nature's purpose, which . . . may possibly include eccentricities." She added: "Only the scientist of limited vision and the doctor who pins his faith on mere knife and drug" dared approach the "vast problem" of sex "undismayed."

The object of eugenics,

> is not only to limit the production of the unfit, but to get the best results out of those in the community who are a bewilderment to the State and who seem unfitted from a eugenic standpoint to propagate. Consider the neurotic and the abnormal. . . . How can we secure that there shall be no waste or ruin of their special powers of work for the race? It is surely an accepted

*The euphemistical transformation of "eugenics" into "sociobiology" is documented in the genealogy of several periodicals and an organization. *Eugenical News,* published from 1916 to 1953 by the American Eugenics Society (which also published *Eugenics: A Journal of Race Betterment*), was superseded by *Eugenics Quar' .ly;* this was continued by the periodical *Social Biology,* published from 1969 to 1972 by the same Society which then changed its name to the Society for the Study of Social Biology.

fact that many of the most capable people are neurotic or abnormal. . . .

According to the severe code of some eugenists, not only an Oscar Wilde, but a Michael Angelo, a Nietzsche, a Chopin, a Tchaikovsky, a [Helena] Blavatsky, a Rosa Bonheur, a William Blake, and a Mrs. Eddy [founder of Christian Science] stand in the same class of the neurotic or the abnormal, to say nothing of a vast mass of less distinguished people. Is it not a part of Eugenics and a part of religion to indicate to these people how they can directly aid the improvement of the race . . . to turn them into allies instead of ostracising them into rebels? . . . It is our duty as advanced citizens to see to it that equality of opportunity for this end is given alike to the normal and abnormal men and women in our midst.* Often by a stupid, vindictive, or conventional attitudes toward what we do not understand we waste or ruin powers which could otherwise have helped the world. . . .

"Bigoted" attitudes produced "much personal suffering."

Ignorance and conventional theories, in and out of doctors' consulting-rooms, paralyse more creative force than we are prepared to admit. . . . Doctors and eugenists should not look upon people only from the point of view of aptness or inaptness for physical procreation, and praise or condemn them accordingly.

She urged the use of "any impulse or power in a human being which can . . . serve the whole community." To "the poet and the mystic, love, in every one of its manifestations, has all the possibilities of making earth into heaven here and now."

"In the near future," she said,

the average sexual relationship of men to women to-day will be looked upon with as great an aversion as that for which Oscar Wilde was crucified. For Oscar Wilde was a martyr to unscientific legislation. He was not responsible before heaven's tribunal as many normal men and women are to-day for their consciously gross sins against both Nature and Love. Wilde's mother had for nine long months, before he was born, prayed continually for a girl. Her imagination dwelt upon this during nearly all her pregnancy. That her prayer was partially granted in that perplexing mixture of artist, man, woman, and egotist the world knows as Oscar Wilde was perhaps one of Nature's satires in order to show what we do when we force, through our limited laws and barbaric persecutions, these peculiar people into becoming menaces to the State through lack of capacity either to understand them or to educate them. . . . Even in abnormality, in its congenital manifestations, Nature may have a meaning as definite . . . as the discord is in music. . . .

We curse and kill the so-called abnormals when they transgress what we are pleased to call the moral law, but what of the normal and self-righteous among us, who, within the law of wedlock, indulge to excess or

---

*This is the earliest known public plea for "equality of opportunity" for "abnormal men and women"—in context, men and women like Michaelangelo, Tchaikovsky, and Rosa Bonheur—inverts.

restrain to extinction? . . . Every man who takes a woman against her will, in wedlock or out, . . . is inverting the uses of humanised sex functions. Every woman who surrenders to physical passion for ulterior reasons, such as being supported economically, . . . is also inverting the . . . spiritual uses of sexual desire. . . . Often what we count as vicious, or even abnormal or insane, through the very fact of unusual suffering involved in it, or of some new courage born of a rare vision of love on a specialized plane, may be an aid to purity, rather than a degradation.

"We must learn to trust new spiritual intuitions, while organising a new love world," Edith Ellis declared.[51]

On February 5, a page-one headline in *The Chicago Daily Tribune* declared: "300 Brave Men Hear Mrs. Ellis / 1,200 Women Applaud English Lecturer. . . ." Starting her speech Edith Ellis had said:

"It is my first chance to say what has been in my heart ever since I was 18. I have studied woman and I have loved her. I have been afraid of man. I have tried to understand him and I have been married to a man for twenty-three years."

In her talk Edith Ellis reportedly "exhorted her sisters to get away from prudery" and "excoriated man for his inhumanity to woman."[1:2]

Another paper, *The Chicago Daily News,* stressed Edith Ellis's defense of the " 'neurotics and abnormal and insane' " including " 'many of the most capable' " in the arts (Oscar Wilde, Michaelangelo, Tchaikovsky and Rosa Bonheur were cited).[7:3]

In January 1915, before Edith Ellis's talk on "Sex and Eugenics," *The Little Review,* the avant garde cultural magazine edited and produced in Chicago by Margaret Anderson, a lesbian, commented that Ellis's lectures in that city had so far been "a little disappointing." The editorial (probably by Anderson) said that Edith Ellis did not "loom as large as some of her more 'destructive' contemporaries." Ellis had not gone "quite the whole distance," had not spoken with as much "thoroughness" as Margaret Sanger did about birth control. But one of Ellis's short stories ("The Idealist," which she had presented publicly), "should be read aloud by all those who draw their rigid distinctions between 'normal' and 'abnormal.' " Edith Ellis was praised for her charm, "simplicity," "humor," "frankness," "idealism, and her fine boyishness." She was "a personality one must not fail to know." Her future speech on sex and eugenics, to be given "exclusively to women," would "include a discussion of sex abnormalities."*

In March 1915, *The Little Review* printed "Two Points of View" on Edith Ellis's talk, "Sex and Eugenics"—one by Mary Adams Stearns praising it, one by Margaret Anderson criticizing it. Only Anderson's comments included an extended discussion of "homosexuality." Anderson's critique also constitutes the

*Little Review, v. 1, n. 10, p. 32.

earliest militant defense of homosexuality known to have been published by a lesbian in the United States.

"A few days" before her lecture, wrote Anderson, Edith Ellis had said she meant "to discuss love, spirituality, [and] sex abnormalities," even " 'if I am sent to jail or put out of Chicago for it.' " She had also said "she meant to talk of those people who, through perverted or inverted sexual tendencies, faced the problem of having to turn their abnormality—perhaps their gift of genius, if we understood these things better—into creative channels."[16]

But in her actual lecture Ellis read a paper, "beautifully written and charmingly delivered, . . . which said nothing at all."

> She said in brief that there should be no war between body and soul, and that Oscar Wilde should have been understood rather than sent to jail. These things are not ideas; they are common sense. They are all quite simply recognized by thinking people; and most of Mrs. Ellis's audience was composed of thinking people who wanted her individual philosophy on these matters. They were not asking her for art but for thought. . . .

Ellis should not have implied that she was "offering a completely new view of sex." If she considered herself a "poet" she "should have given a substantial vision of a future state when love in all its aspects is valued." Anderson thought that Ellis "*can* be blamed for that attitude which promises more than it has to give, and very seriously blamed for that spirit which hints that there may be cause for shame where there is no cause." That hint of "shame" was implied by Ellis's suggestion that her ideas were "shocking," when they were not.

> Nearly all the people in Orchestra Hall that night had read [Havelock] Ellis and [Edward] Carpenter and [Otto] Weininger and other scientists [who had written on sex], and they expected to hear how far Mrs. Ellis's personal views coincided or disagreed with these authorities.* But she had no intention of such elucidation . . . in her reference to intermediate types, she didn't mention homosexuality; she had nothing to say about the differences between perversion and inversion, nor did she even hint at Carpenter's social efforts in behalf of the homosexualist. What does Mrs. Ellis think about

---

*Havelock Ellis's articles on sexual inversion had appeared in U. S. medical journals since 1895. Ellis's (and John Addington Symonds's) *Sexual Inversion* had first been published in English in 1897; the first U. S. edition appeared in 1901; the last U.S. revision in 1915. Edward Carpenter's *Ioläus. An Anthology of Friendship* was first published in the United States in 1902 (Boston: C. E. Goodspeed). His *Love's Coming of Age,* the edition with a chapter on "The Intermediate Sex," was first published in the United States in 1911. Carpenter's book *The Intermediate Sex: A Study of Some Transitional Types of Men and Women,* was first published in the United States in 1912. His poems, *Towards Democracy,* with the fourth, most overtly homoerotic part, was first published in the United States in 1912. His book-length cross-cultural work, *Intermediate Types Among Primitive Folk; A Study in Social Evolution,* was first published in the United States in 1914 (all N. Y.: Mitchell Kennerley). Carpenter's relatively frank autobiography, *My Days and Dreams,* was published in the United States in 1916 (N.Y.: Scribner's). Otto Weininger's *Sex and Character* was published in New York in 1906. Margaret Anderson's extracting a defense of homosexuality from Weininger shows how a blatantly misogynistic work could be used selectively in the interests of inverts.

Weininger's statement that intermediate sexual forms are "normal, not pathological phenomena, . . . and their appearance is no proof of physical decadence"? Does she agree with him . . . that inversion is an acquired character. . . ?

Anderson quoted Weininger:

It might equally be sought to prove that the sexual inclination of a normal man for a normal woman was an unnatural, acquired habit. In the abstract there is no difference between the normal and the inverted type. In my view all organisms have both homosexuality and heterosexuality. . . . In spite of all present-day clamor about . . . different rights for different individualities, there is only one law that governs mankind. . . . It is in opposition to that law . . . that we forbid the homosexualist to carry on his practices whilst we allow the heterosexualist full play [as long as he avoids open scandal]. . . . from the standpoint of a . . . criminal law untainted by the pedagogic idea of punishment as a deterrent, the only logical . . . treatment for sexual inverts would be to allow them to seek and obtain what they require where they can, that is to say, among other inverts.

Anderson commented:

It is not enough to repeat that Shakespeare and Michael Angelo and Alexander The Great and Rosa Bonheur and Sappho were intermediates: how is this science of the future to meet these issues?

The issues in question moved "into the realm of the world's sublime tragedies when one reads the manifesto of a community of such people in Germany":

—"The rays of sunshine in the night of our existence are so rare that we are responsive and deeply grateful for the least movement, for every single voice that speaks in our favor in the forum of mankind."* Mrs. Ellis may have thought her audience entirely too unsophisticated . . . to admit of specific treatment. But that is all the greater reason to talk plainly. When you reflect how difficult it is for the mass to become educated about sex it becomes rather appalling. It is worth your life to get Havelock Ellis's six volumes [on sex psychology] from a bookstore or a library. You can only do it with a doctor's certificate or something of that sort. Even if you ask for Weininger you are taken behind locked doors, forced to swear that you want it out of no "morbid curiosity," that you will keep it only a week, and above all that you won't let anyone else read it.

Anderson thought it was "practically impossible" to do the work of sex education "under the auspices of women's medical leagues or similar organizations."

*Research indicates that Anderson quoted from Edward Carpenter's chapter "The Intermediate Sex" in his *Love's Coming of Age* (1906; in the 12th ed., London: George Allen and Unwin, 1923), p. 137; Carpenter translated and quoted from Otto De Joux, *Die Enterbten des Liebesglückes* (Leipzig, 1893), p. 21.

But Mrs. Ellis had dared the impossible. I can't help comparing her with another woman whose lecture on such a subject would be big, brave, beautiful. . . . Emma Goldman could never fail in this way.[18]

"It is not a question of what could or could not be said on a public platform; it is a question of what *should* be said." The "findings of science" should be made "accessible."

"A week ago, as I write," said Anderson, a young man had been hanged in Chicago for strangling a four-year-old girl, although he did not recollect the murder, and his father testified his son was epileptic. "Sixty people" had watched the youth's "murder" (his hanging) and "not a voice was raised in protest." She asked: "How far have we advanced when things like this can still happen? . . ." (Anderson evidently considered the youth irresponsible due to physiological disturbance, and opposed punishing him as retribution.) She also opposed retribution for illicit love:

> With us love is just as punishable as murder or robbery. Mrs. Ellis knows the workings of our courts; she knows of boys and girls, men and women, tortured or crucified every day *for their love*—because it is not expressed according to conventional morality. All this was part of her responsibility [to speak of] on February 4th; and that is why I say she failed.[19]

♀ MEDICAL

# 1916, February
## Dr. James G. Kiernan: "Androphobia"

In his regular medical journal column surveying recent writings on "Sexology," Dr. Kiernan referred to "Androphobia" (fear of males).[24] This name

> may well be applied to the married and unmarried hysteric "old maid" attitude toward the "horrid man." Often this is an expression of masturbatory excess or at times of inchoate homosexuality. . . .[104]

A book of the period, *Orange Blossom*, began by referring to man as "a combination of peacock, pig and goat," for he had "the vanity" of the peacock, the "love of comfort of the pig" and "the perversity of the goat."[103] Kiernan thought that "Sex advice" of that type was "an expression of the androphobia which lies behind much marital incompatibility and unhappiness."[104]

Discussing "Tomboyism and Inversion," Kiernan commented on a recent article by Woods Hutchinson that "points out the absurdity" of the fear of "tomboyism as a source of unlady-like conduct and mannishness."

> The athletic tendencies of the modern woman do not render her less womanly than the anemic ill-health poseur of the mid-fifties of the 19th century. Indeed the least suspected and most socially dangerous inverts are the madonna types, who from infantilism appear peculiarly feminine. . . . The

early conception that tomboyish meant mannishness made this madonna prominent in "social purity" advocacy which consists in pointing out the peculiar indecency of even marital coitus for maternity reasons.[104–05]

Discussing "Psychic Evolution and Sex Inversion," Kiernan argued that inverts were mentally and physically arrested, therefore "many" retained a "youthful appearance through life."

> Often these people are vain and egotistic. . . . The females are often sexually anesthetic prostitutes, prurient prudes, hysteric reformers, or gossip-mongers.

A male invert's "sexual instincts" might be "female," leading to "extreme modesty toward males" and "intense liking for female occupations and dress."[106]


MEDICAL/BLACK AMERICANS

## 1916, June
## Dr. James G. Kiernan: *"Chicago has not developed a euphemism yet"*

In his regular survey of "Sexology," Dr. Kiernan commented briefly:[25]

> The method of negro perverts who solicit men in certain Chicago cafés is usually fellatio, although paederasty by the customer is permitted. At one time a resort of these people existed under a Chicago dime museum. Lately, as shown by some recent arrests, certain cafés patronized by both negroes and whites, are the seat of male solicitation. Chicago has not developed a euphemism yet for these male perverts. In New York they are known as "fairies" and wear a red necktie (inverts are generally said to prefer green). In Philadelphia they are known as "Brownies."[350]


♀ RESISTANCE/BOOK REVIEWS

## 1916, August 20
## Edward Carpenter: *My Days and Dreams*

The autobiography of Edward Carpenter, published in the United States in 1916, is one of the few public self-revelations, and the only one by an "intermediate type" published in English under the author's own name in the early twentieth century.[26]* Carpenter's autobiography is also remarkable for his linking, however vaguely, the fate of the feminist movement and the emancipation of those he

---

*Another of the rare, explicit examples of public self-identification as homosexual published in the U. S. before 1950 is the autobiography of André Gide, *If It Die,* translated by Dorothy Bussy (N. Y.: Modern Library, 1935; see Nov. 10). Another self-revealing statement is that of the poet, Robert Duncan; see 1944, August 1.

called "intermediate types." (He focused here on male intermediates, though he elsewhere spoke more extensively of females.)

Carpenter introduced the discussion of his emotional character by speaking of the "need" of his "affectional nature, that hunger which had indeed hunted me down since I was a child." He could still "hardly bear" to think of the Victorian era's denial "of the obvious facts of the heart and of sex," a denial that had left the needs of his unmarried sisters "unspoken and unallowed," a society which "set up gold and gain in the high place of the human heart." The "non-recognition" of "sexual needs," he thought, "weighed terribly hard upon the women" of that era, creating a "disparity of the sexes."

He referred also to a "growing disinclination" of upper-class men to marry, arising, in part, "from an increase in the number of what may be called an intermediate type."

> There have of course been, in all ages, thousands and thousands of women who have not felt that particular sort of romance and attraction towards men, but only to their own kind; and in all ages there have been thousands and thousands of men similarly constituted in the reverse way; but they have been, by the majority, little understood and recognized. Now however it is coming to be seen that they also—both classes—have their part to play in the world.[96]

Though Carpenter had "always had excellent and enduring alliances among women," he said, the "romance of my life went elsewhere." Whether such a state was "desirable" and "moral" was sure to be asked—"in a land where *everything* is either moral or immoral"—but such questions did "not alter the fact" of his "emotional nature." A footnote here referred to "Many examples of this kind of temperament" in volume two of Havelock Ellis's *Studies in the Psychology of Sex* (the volume on *Sexual Inversion,* though the tactful Carpenter did not give the full title). He especially recommended cases VIII and XVII, the anonymous sexual histories (though he did so not identify them) of himself and his lover, George Merrill.[27]

Carpenter had been troubled by the absence from his life, until a relatively late age, of any equivalent of marriage:

> I realized in my own person some of the sufferings which are endured by an immense number of modern women, especially of the well-to-do classes, as well as by that large class of men of whom I have just spoken, and to whom the name of Uranians is often given.
>
> Certainly my isolation was in a sense my own fault—due partly to reserve and partly to ignorance. When at a later time I broke through this double veil, I soon discovered that others of like temperament to myself were abundant in all directions, and to be found in every class of society; and I need not say that from that time forward life was changed for me. I found sympathy, understanding, love, in a hundred unexpected forms, and my world of the heart became as rich in that which it needed as before it had seemed fruitless and barren.
>
> The Uranian temperament in Man closely resembles the normal tem-

perament of Women in this respect, that in both Love—in some form or other—is the main object of life. In the normal Man, ambition, moneymaking, business, adventure, etc., play their part—love is as a rule a secondary matter. The majority of men (for whom the physical side of sex, if needed, is easily accessible) do not for a moment realize the griefs endured by thousands of girls and women—in the drying up of the wellsprings of affection as well as in the crucifixion of their physical needs. But as these sufferings of women of one kind or another, have been the great inspiring cause and impetus of the Women's Movement—a movement which is already having a great influence in the reorganization of society; so I do not practically doubt that the similar sufferings of the Uranian class of men are destined in their turn to lead to another wide-reaching social organization and forward movement in the direction of Art and Human Compassion.[97–98]

On August 20, 1916, an anonymous *New York Times* review of Carpenter's autobiography noted that that Englishman "is now 72 years old," and that his "writings and speeches have had little effect upon the society of which he has been so loud a critic." Carpenter's reminiscences nevertheless had "a certain historical importance," as he had been "associated with radicals and 'advanced thinkers' of different sorts." This autobiography was also important

as a psychological study because of the extraordinary way in which Mr. Carpenter narrates events in his life which most men would gladly conceal. He tells of unusual propagandas in which he has taken a leading part, of strange speeches and strange acts, with what his friends call engaging frankness and others gross and shameless egotism.

"With one exception, Mr. Carpenter tells us, women have not influenced his life." (This is inadequate, and a distortion of a man who was a leading, early male feminist.) The exception was "a woman whom he calls 'Olivia,' " separated from her husband, artistic, " 'hating everything British and philistine and commercial; detesting the Bible and religion, she had fought her way through social odium.' "

"In the fourth chapter of his book," said *The Times* reviewer,

Mr. Carpenter tells of his own mental and physical state, and develops those unpleasant theories as to the "Uranian temperament" which are the subject of several of his books and pamphlets.*

---

*" 'Uranian temperament' " is the first such explicit naming found in *The Times*. For a chronology of the subsequent earliest, explicit *Times* usages see: *"abnormal psychological manifestations"* or *"crushes,"* 1917, February 4; *"Sexual inversion,"* 1925, July 5; *"the intermediate sex,"* 1926, October 10 (quoted in entry of 1920, November); *"homosexuality,"* 1926, October 24; *"psychopathic relationships,"* 1926, November 15 (see *GAH,* p. 83); *"The Invert"* (film), 1926, December 15; *"sex perversion,"* 1927, January 21 (see *GAH,* p. 85); *"abnormality,"* 1927, March 7 (see *GAH,* p. 89); *"sexual inversion"* and *"the vice of Sappho,"* 1928, January 8; *"Sapphic women,"* 1928, September 16; *"homosexual love"* (and the first known use of *"heterosexual liaison"*), 1930, April 20; *"homosexual"* and *"the invert,"* 1930, July 30; *"homosexuality"* and *"hetero-sexual,"* 1930, September 28; *"homosexualism,"* 1932, September 11; *"unnatural affection,"* 1932, September 21; *"latent homosexuality,"* 1933, November 19; *"Sapphic intimacy"* and *"the Lesbian relationship,"* 1935, August 18; *"lesbian,"* 1937, March 7.

Carpenter's vegetarianism, socialism, and sandal-making were also mentioned.[328]

Carpenter's autobiography was also reviewed in the *International Journal of Ethics,* by F. W. Stella Browne, of London, an early ardent feminist-socialist.

Browne said:

Written from the very heart of the liberating and constructive movement of our time, these reminiscences touch many sides of life, with extraordinary clarity, sympathy and humor. What a picture of the combined shallowness and repression of even a prosperous and high-principled early Victorian home. . . . There are illuminating glimpses of . . . endowed and privileged University humbug; and there is the crown of . . . absurdities, summarized in the simple sentence "No elder person *ever* spoke to me about sexual matters—no mother, father, brother, monitor or master ever said a word."[124]

"Most valuable" of Carpenter's messages, said Browne,

in a world which tends to grow more and more drilled and institutionalized is this "that people should endeavour (more than they do) to express and liberate their own real deep-rooted needs and feelings." Particular importance attaches to the equally explicit and delicate statement of a "most intimate and organic part" of Edward Carpenter's own nature, and the speculations as to the ultimate social outlet for the Uranian temperament "in the direction of Art and Human Compassion."[124–25]

MEDICAL

# 1916
# Dr. Emil Oberhoffer: "The Influence of Castration on the Libido"

The American publication of an essay by Dr. Oberhoffer, assistant director of an insane asylum in Germany, suggested that "castration" was a successful, beneficial treatment for a vaguely-defined "case" of pederasty.[28]*

*Oberhoffer's "castration" cure suggests it would be useful to consider Freud's stress on a "castration complex" in males and females in relation to the fact of actual or threatened castrations for illicit eroticism in late Victorian and early twentieth-century Austria and Germany. Oberhoffer's castration cure may also be considered in relation to early German experiments in surgical "sex change," and later Nazi experiments in sexual surgery; for "sex change" experiments see Dr. Ludwig L. Lenz, *The Memoirs of a Sexologist: Discretion and Indiscretion* (N. Y.: Cadilla Pub. Co., 1954), on his work at Magnus Hirschfeld's "Institute of Sexology" and Niels Hoyer, (pseud. of Ernst Ludwig Harthern Jacobson), ed., *Man Into Woman; An Authentic Record of a Change of Sex, The True Story of the Miraculous Transformation of the Danish Painter Einar Wegener (Andreas Sparre),* trans. from the German by H. J. Stenning, intro. by Norman Haire (N. Y.: Dutton, 1933); the operation was performed in Dresden by Dr. Warnecross. For Nazi sexual surgery see Joseph Wechsberg, ed., *The Murderers Among Us: The Simon Wiesenthal Memoirs* (N. Y.: McGraw Hill, 1967), p. 155. For the Nazis' persecution of homosexuals also see the index to *Almanac.* For a survey of castration of men and women as a medical treatment and punishment see Johan Bremer, *Asexualization: A Follow-up Study of 244 Cases* (N. Y.: Macmillan, 1959). For Thomas Jefferson on castration as penalty see *GAH,* p. 23–24.

Dr. Oberhoffer's "Case II" was an experienced handicraftsman, born in 1875, who "began to masturbate at an early age." He was sentenced at ages eighteen and twenty-one

> for obscene practices with boys. . . . Arrested again after his release and committed to insane asylum.
>
> Indifferent to feminine attractions and only aroused by the thought of boys. In 1904 and 1906, he was again arrested and he finally decided to have himself castrated. The operation was performed in July 1906. It was followed by deep depression and certain obsessions. He thought every one was talking of his case and that other patients were persecuting him. He was released in October. After that he was never aroused sexually by the sight or thought of boys and expressed himself very happy over the fact that his "abominable instincts" were dead. The patient, however, felt at times an anxiety he had never experienced previously.[59]

Of "Case II" it was said that after his castration his "homosexual tendencies"

> died out within five months. The patient is now a useful individual absolutely free from the tendencies that previously drove him to commit not only sexual delicts [offenses] but all kinds of other reprehensible acts.

Oberhoffer noted: "in the case of the homosexual the sexual instincts disappeared entirely."[60]


♀ BOOK REVIEW

# 1917, February 4
### N. Y. Times Book Review: Clemence Dane's Regiment of Women

An anonymous reviewer commented on the first novel by Dane, an Englishwoman (Winifred Ashton):[29]

> In schools exclusively for girls there are certain abnormal psychological manifestations among the young women known as "crushes." Miss Dane's novel is the story of a "crush," a story in which a sort of vampire woman in a girls' school has the temperament and character that enable her to produce a "crush" upon herself whenever she likes, and who deliberately feeds her vanity, selfishness, and egotism by inspiring these self-sacrificing devotions among the younger teachers and the pupils of the school in which she is one of the higher powers.

The author took "over 400 closely printed pages" to detail

> the devotion of one of the teachers to Clare Hartill,* the selfish and magnetic mistress, and of the growth of the friendship between her and Alwynne

*Hartill is a pun for "heart ill," as Jeannette Foster noted, Sex Variant, p. 257.

Durand, one of the younger mistresses; the tragedy that sends a dark shadow across the life of the school, the love affair that finally puts a rift between the two women, the efforts of Miss Hartill to regain her empire over the younger one.

. . . Within her teacup limits of action Clare Hartill is a Machiavelli whose chief purpose it is to make her puppets dance to the jerking of the strings which she controls. In only one respect does she fail, to the American reader, to be quite convincing. That is in the fascination which she exerts over her girl devotées and the young woman who is ready to lie for her, live for her, die for her if there should be such need. Possibly English young women and girls can be won over to such intensity of devotion by the cavalier attitude Miss Hartill seems so much of the time to adopt toward them. . . . Miss Dane does not make manifest to the American reader sufficient reason for the fascination which Miss Hartill is able to exercise over her associates in the school. Otherwise it is a noteworthy picture of a scheming, clever, selfish, vain woman who has become, temperately, more or less abnormal—a vampire woman who confines her preying to the minds and souls of other women and contemptuously casts mere men out of her world.

The book takes its title, in which "regiment" is used in its old English sense of "rule," from John Knox's "First Blast of the Trumpet Against the Monstrous Regiment of Women" [an early anti-feminist tract].[1558].

MEDICAL

# 1917, April
## Dr. Edward J. Kempf: *"Enlightened . . . sublimation of the abnormal"*

A paper by Dr. Kempf, a psychiatrist at St. Elizabeth's Hospital, Washington, D.C., compared the "social and sexual behavior" of human beings and of six caged monkeys (five males, one female).[30] Kempf's comments were based on eight months of observation (of the monkeys), and upon the tenets of behaviorial and Freudian psychology. His study "was made possible by a grant from the Carnegie Institution." His report was read to the American Psychoanalytic Association and published in its journal. The doctor's remarks on "deteriorating personalities" referred to "many young men" received at his hospital "from the army and navy." The focus in this excerpt is on Kempf's conclusions about homosexuality in humans.

"We can no longer hold that the individual is solely responsible for his tendencies to homosexuality, autoeroticism or perverseness in his sexual life," argued Kempf. "His progenitors developed . . . such interests and we must bring about an enlightened course of sublimation of the abnormal sexual tendencies which often cause so much suffering."[128]

"Much of the future work of psychiatry will be concerned with the reconstruction of the personality in the sense of shifting the values of undesirable forms of stimuli, which have become adequate for the primary sexual reflexes, to such forms and zones of receptors as meet with the approval of his race."[141] (Translated, this meant that persons finding erotic pleasure in socially disapproved ways were to be reeducated by psychiatrists into approved feelings and acts.)

A detailed description of sexual acts between monkeys noted that one animal "squinted his eyes and smacked his lips." A footnote added: "Strikingly similar squinting of the eyes and smacking of the lips (but of course more suppressed) were observed in the homosexual advances made by two American diners to several Hawaiian serenaders in a ship's dining saloon."[136] The monkey–man analogy continued:

> Like an isolated band of male monkeys who revert to homosexual relations, groups of isolated men also normally revert to forms of homosexual relations whenever esthetic, athletic and refined interests are not strongly and consistently encouraged. This frequently occurs in prisons, asylums, and among soldiers and sailors. Too severe moral restrictions of heterosexual interests in such men is an extremely serious innovation and one that must be given the gravest consideration before the misconceptions of certain types of well-intentioned moralists are applied.[142]

Referring to eroticism, Kempf said:

> Perhaps no other feature of the constitution of man has caused so much social turmoil and self-imposed distress as this phylogenetic predisposition of his affective-sensorimotor system. He . . . calls it the work of the devil, immorality, the result of the sins of Adam and Eve, the wickedness of the flesh, and threatens his unruly neurones with the pains of hell fire and even castration. Hatred, anxiety, divorces, insanity, suicides, murders and social ruination commonly result from the conflicts with his phylogenetic predisposition of erotogenesis.
>
> A sexually obsessed social system, as it is at present constituted, cannot be favorable to the biological welfare of our species. It certainly does not tolerate the biological sincerity of the individual. A new insight and more sensible methods of sublimation than persecutory and suppressive methods are necessary . . . [143–44]

Kempf warned: "Excessive sexual indulgence as well as excessive sexual suppression through subtle forms of fear, such as lie hidden in social censorship, disease, and impregnation, apparently blunts the individual's acquisitive faculties and social efficiency, whether married or single."[143–44]

In human beings, it was stated, "the universal precedence of overt or disguised homosexual interests during the growth of the individual is recognized as normal."[146] But "Fixation at the homosexual level in either sex is recognized as a biological failure and is the cause of, in many cases, the gravest states of anxiety, with perhaps complete wrecking of the personality or suicide."*

> Some of the most profound . . . tendencies to chronic dissociations of the personality are based upon the fearful anxiety caused by complete sexual inversion. Why it is universally considered to be more "effeminate," "weak," "unmanly" or "deficient" to be the homosexual object than to be the homosexual patron seems to have its foundation farther back in the phylogenetic scale than the influence of social culture."[147]

"Probably the irrepressible sexual craving to assume the female role in the sexual act causes so much distress because the individual's other wishes, namely to be 'manly,' 'strong,' biologically as potent as others, are so seriously conflicted with and belied." There was apparently a "biological root" to the "grave distress shown by men and women who cannot modify their tendencies to submit themselves as homosexual objects (biologically unproductive, hence perhaps censured by the species)."[148]

The "anxiety" of homosexuals "apparently permits two solutions: either resignation to the tendency and indifference to the censuring social demands," or "incessant . . . striving" for acknowledgment from society for "some valuable social service," imagined or real.[148]

> Man is greatly dependent for his uplift upon the effective sublimation of his homosexual and heterosexual erotogenic capacities, and many of his truly fine and valuable achievements in science, art, literature, religion and his social system are fruits of this sublimation of his sexual-affective motives. Upon the other hand much of the universal element of hatred, anxiety, persecution and distrust that largely determines the present constitution of our social system results from the discomforts caused by our unintelligent persecutions and suppression of our vital biologic needs.

"At present" one of the "most insistent problems of psychology and psychiatry is the acquirement of insight into the . . . possible, natural methods of sublimation . . . and the healthy suppression of perverse tendencies."[152–53]

♀ MEDICAL

# 1917, August
## Dr. Alfred Adler: "The Homosexual Problem"

"Like a spectre the condition of homosexuality rises up in society," declared Dr. Adler of Vienna, paraphrasing Karl Marx.[31] Adler's long essay on homosexuality

---

*Kempf's observations of World War I soldiers and sailors led him to name and analyze a "homosexual panic" (the fear that one might be homosexual), later called "Kempf's syndrome"; see 1920, Kempf.

was translated in a major American medical journal, *The Alienist and Neurologist* (St. Louis). As one of the early theorists of psychoanalysis, Adler, with Carl Jung and Freud formed a famous trinity. Adler's essay is especially revealing of the ploys adopted by some homosexuals to affirm their own feelings within the framework of a medical (and usually condemnatory) model. Adler's unabashed moralism raises a question: How was such a diatribe ever perceived as objective "science"?*

Adler declared:

In defiance of everything the number of perverts is on the increase. . . . Children, adults, the aged, men and women participate in the evil. It provides work for the pedagogist, the sociologist, the neurologist and the jurist.

No "means of conquest," neither "severe penalties," nor "the most considerate indulgence," had prevented "the spread of this anomaly." And "yet its advocates are not absent." The many different theories of "homosexuality" indicated "that a large part of the population are untrue to their sexual role."[268]

"The greatest concession" toward homosexuality that could be obtained from the public "is concealment and non-interference." Already,

many quashed prosecutions on the part of the police show a tendency to indulgence. *The barriers of society against the toleration of the perversion remain unshaken by every theory,* for they are formed of the safeguards and social disinclinations of normal feelings.[269]

Adler referred to an "adverse" attempt "to further increase the number of homosexualists in order to compel the toleration of the perversion." That "opinion which tries to justify the existence of the perversion and . . . ascribe a high value to it" was "devoid of reason." The

emancipation of Woman and the awakening of her self-consciousness are increasing. Man is forced to doubt his pre-eminence. *From his feeling of uncertainty and insecurity the conquest of Woman seems to him a venturesome undertaking.*

"Man" therefore sought "the restoration of his security and superiority" by depreciating or idealizing "Woman," and by creating a "*'distance'* between himself and Woman." The "homosexuality of our times" was "a symptom of the *'flight from Woman.'* "[269]

Homosexuality, and all the other "sexual perversions" ("sadism, masochism, masturbation, fetishism, etc.") could be understood only via "the school of individual psychology." This indicated that "Every perversion is an enlarged *spiritual distance* between Man and Woman," a "revolt against" the "normal sexual act." Perversion in men was compensation for feeling inferior to women. "Perversion in women is also . . . to overcome the feeling of inferiority against the greater power of the man."[270]

---

*That any such moralistic malarkey was ever taken seriously as "science" is evidence of the power achieved by medical professionals in the United States by 1917.

Homosexuality was "a denial" of the "popular will" and the "ideal of perpetuation." For that reason it was "stamped as a crime and a sin." But the "danger of punishment" was that such punishment might result in increasing the act punished.[273]

"The full-fledged homosexualist" always appealed to "the false thesis of an hereditary homosexuality" to "establish the *irresponsibility* of his conduct," and to justify his existence. This "shows an active hostility towards society," an aim "contrary to the requirements of social life," a lack of "public spirit" and "good-will towards others." The "homosexualist" does "not seek peaceful adaptability and harmony," but "hostile measures."[273–74]

The "low self-esteem" of the "homosexualist," said Adler, "robs him of all unconstraint." This "self-depreciation" was understood by the physician in light of the "tragic fate of the homosexualist and his cowardice against normal life."[274]

The chances of "successfully" treating homosexuality were "today as unfavorable as could be." For "What chances of success have we when we try to change a grown-up coward into a courageous man?" He stressed: the *"eradication of homosexuality is a question of the bringing up of the child."*[275]

Of one "homosexualist" who came to him for treatment Adler said:

> Just as soon as he became engaged he came to me with his "hereditary homosexuality," not so much for the purpose of cure as for a substantiation of the disease in order that he be justified in withdrawing from his betrothal.[277]

This patient "regarded homosexuality as unalterable" and quoted "a whole series of citations" demonstrating that unalterability. This led Adler to conclude:

> such authorative assertions—as of the incurability of the homosexuality—serve to sustain the patient in his misconception.[276]

Adler hoped physicians would "hold back somewhat the expression" of their views.

"The most important" insight Adler had come to from his study of "perversion" concerned "the sinister, often well concealed *obstinacy* of the patient" to persist in "perversion."

Among "homosexualists" Adler noted a "snake-like," "serpentine quality."[278] He criticized the boy who rebelled against his "father's demands of him for manliness." He criticized the boy who, "uncertain in his understanding as to his future sexual role, *renounced the masculine striving for power.*"[278; 281] In girls, "fighting and scuffling, climbing and running, excessive sport and dreams of such performances," pointed "to a discontent with the female character and to a 'male protest' against it."[281] Adler warned of the homosexual patient's tendency, "by the legitimation of the disease or by emphasizing its hereditary side," to deny "his responsibility" for it.[286]

Adler warned physicians of a type of homosexual patient who had come to him for treatment—not with a desire to rid himself of the homosexuality but as an attempt to become convinced of the fruitlessness of treatment so that he could justify a relapse to his perversive relations.

This patient,

> came to me in the full expectation that I would confirm his own opinion of the unalterability of the perversion about which he had read in the works of well-known authors.

Adler finally "succeeded in breaking him off from his homosexuality, but for two years I waited in vain for any change to the normal in his relations to women." The "whole progress that I was able to obtain" was that this patient turned to "masturbation and occasional masochistic practices with [female] prostitutes." The patient's studies were also "very much behind," because of "a paroxysmal somnolency [falling asleep] just as soon as he begins to study."[287]

♀ BOOK REVIEW

## 1917, September 2
### N. Y. Times Book Review:
### J. D. Beresford's *House-Mates*

Beresford's novel concerned Wilfrid Hornby, a boarder in "a house inhabited by all sorts and conditions of men—and women," said an anonymous reviewer.[32] Among his "House-Mates" was "the girl with whom he quickly falls . . . deeply in love."

> A certain touch of novelty is provided by the fact that his rival for the affection of Judith Carrington is not a man, but another woman, Helen Binstead, who adores Judith with a jealous exclusiveness and is willing to go to any lengths in order to keep Wilfrid Hornby away from her. To such extreme lengths . . . does she go that they constitute . . . [a] weak point in the book. Her conduct is not impossible . . . but it seems so highly improbable that it makes the reader skeptical. . . .[322]

♀ MEDICAL

## 1918, March
### Dr. Horace W. Frink: *Some "militant suffragists are . . . sublimating"*

A section in Dr. Frink's book *Morbid Fears and Compulsions; Their Psychoanalytic Treatment,* is a classic American-Freudian example of a doctor associating "neurosis" and "militant feminism."[33] The term "abnormal" also functions here as a form of name-calling, masking Frink's political disagreement with his patient. Underlying Frink's medical terminology is a value judgment that conformity and adjustment to one's society is good, dissatisfaction, anger, and militant action against it bad. That some radical reformers (and some conservators of the status quo) may harbor unconscious impulses in conflict with their conscious purposes only gives some apparent credence to Dr. Frink's analysis, making it more evil than it would have been if it contained no germ of truth.

Dr. Frink cited

the case of an unusually intelligent young woman who, from about the age of eighteen had been a most ardent and militant feminist. On all such questions as woman suffrage, equal pay for teachers, marital reform, etc., she had talked, written and fought with the enthusiasm of a fanatic. Her dream was of a time when woman should be on the same plane with man in all particulars, doing the same work, enjoying the same rights, having, in short, complete equality. Aside from problems such as these there was very little in life that seemed to interest her.

There were certain features in her case, however, which, even before she broke out with a definite neurosis, might well have indicated that her absorbtion in these matters was not entirely a normal one. In the first place, for any one possessed of such really unusual intelligence and knowledge of her subject, her methods were very ill-considered and her results surprisingly meager. Though a very industrious worker, she was an astonishingly inefficient one. In addition to this was the fact that her emotions on some of the questions of feminism were so markedly exaggerated as to be quite obviously abnormal. For instance, the slightest suggestion that women were in any way inferior to men, even in physical strength, would set her in a passion of the wildest anger and let loose a flood of vehement and for the most part unreasonable denials. For her to hear it mentioned that the first coitus is painful to the woman, or, for that matter, any statement that tended to associate the idea of pain with the performance of the sex functions, would have a similar maddening effect, as would a tale of a man's being brutal or domineering to a woman, compelling obedience from her, or treating her as an inferior.

Upon analysis this patient's violent warfare against all forms of subordination of women was revealed to be very largely a compensation for a strong but imperfectly repressed masochistic tendency. That is to say, the idea of a man's mastering, domineering over, and inflicting pain and violence upon a woman, particularly in an erotic way, strongly appealed to the patient's instincts and Unconscious, though in the main repellent to her conscious personality. Some of the very stories of brutality and suggestions of subordination which most excited her rage at the same time gave rise to intense sexual emotion and compelled her to masturbate. Her militance against the subordination of women was thus in essence an effort to do away with those sources of stimuli which, in her, inspired feelings she felt to be morbid and shameful.

I have reason to believe that this case of militant feminism is not entirely unique. A certain proportion of at least the most militant suffragists are neurotics who in some instances are compensating for masochistic trends, in others, are more or less successfully sublimating sadistic and homosexual ones (which usually are unconscious). I hope this statement may not be construed as an effort on my part to throw mud on woman suffrage, for on the whole I am very much in favor of it. As a matter of fact it is nothing to the discredit of any movement to say that perhaps many of its conspicuous supporters are neurotics, for as a matter of fact it is the neurotics that are pioneers in most reforms. The very normal people who have no trouble in adjusting themselves to their environment, are as a rule too sleek in their own contentment to fight hard for any radical changes, or even to take much interest in seeking such changes made. To lead and carry through successfully some new movement or reform, a person requires the constant stimulus of a chronic discontent (at least it often seems so) and this in a certain number of instances is surely of neurotic origin and signifies an imperfect adaptation of that individual to his environment. . . .[134–36]

MEDICAL/RESISTANCE

## 1918, June
## Dr. E. S. Shepherd: *"Our streets and beaches are overrun by male prostitutes"*

Dr. Shepherd answered an anti-homosexual statement made by sex reformer Dr. William Robinson.[34] (For a sample of Robinson's views see 1914.)

Though "One is frequently tempted to agree" with the proposition that homosexuals should be eliminated, Shepherd warned that "it might be well to first make sure that such wholesale elimination would not remove a number of valuable citizens." (If homosexuals were not socially contributive it was, presumably, legitimate to eradicate them.)

To sketch "a few intermediates who were of social value" was difficult, since "To call a man an intermediate is, in the popular conception . . . , equivalent to calling him a fellatrist and the mere accusation of such iniquity will ruin any man, even though he can prove his innocence." (How one would prove one's innocence of fellatrism was not specified.) It was therefore "impossible to vivisect one's acquaintances in a journal," since details of accomplishment and "perversity" were required. Because "our unsatisfied sexuality" motivated a "cruel and malignant persecution," one could not tell the truth about the achievements of intermediates.[241]

Doctors saw only the "lower classes of intermediates," ignoring "those boyantly healthy intermediates who frequently do not know that they are different." Doctors thus supposed that intermediacy "is synonymous with fellatio, sodomy, and the various sadistic-masochistic methods."[242]

"That our streets and beaches are overrun by male prostitutes (fairies) is obvious." (This reference to "beaches" as a gathering spot for male prostitutes is the earliest discovered.)[243] It was "usually assumed" that all such " 'fairies' " were "worthless degenerates who should be exterminated by the police."[245] But intermediates should not be judged by their "lowest manifestations," just as "womanhood" should not be judged "by the lowest class of [female] prostitutes." That biographies of men and women of achievement said nothing about their sexual lives was a kind of "tombstone mendacity," since many leaders were known to a few "to have been more or less perverse."[243]

Even if their preferred methods of coitus were with the other sex, "masculine women and effeminate men" were not "normal," and should be regarded as "members of the so-called third sex, the intermediates."[243] Shepherd defined "intermediates" as persons of "mixed psyche," possessing both "feminine" and "masculine" emotions and characters, whatever the gender of their sexual partners.[245] Male intermediates, for example, possessed a "quite feminine sympathy," a "collective motherliness," which turned many of them "towards social service." Reformers and "propagandists of the better sort belong to this class."[246]

Shepherd hoped that future theories would clarify the mystery of the intermediates, and "put us in a position to salvage many who are now socially worthless."[253]

MEDICAL

# 1918, November
# Dr. Lilburn Merrill:
## "Sexualism Among . . . One Hundred Delinquent Boys"

Dr. Merrill, a "Diagnostician" with the Seattle, Washington, Juvenile Court, reported his two-year study of "Sexualism," or "habitual pathological functioning of the sexual mechanism," among a group of one-hundred "delinquent boys."[35] Seventy-one of these boys were "habitual autoeroticists." Of these, thirty-one "presented a history of fallatio [sic] relations." All thirty-one reported nightly masturbation. And "practically all" cited the

> habitual recurrence of the imagery associated with one or another fallationous relation, the memory of which they held agreeably dominant. . . .
>
> The fallationous relations, excepting three cases where the subjects were seduced by men, occurred exclusively with boy companions. . . . Approximately sixty per cent of them were seduced by pubescent boys and the others consorted by mutual approach with prepubescents. Four of the seduced group stated that they were coerced by pubescents when they were

about six years old or younger. The others expressed no memory of having offered resistance. The usual statements indicated that there was more or less mutual interest in the acts which generally occurred in their play associations. In most cases other erotic acts and conversation led the novices to participate somewhat in the nature of an adventure. . . . The entire number subsequently made use of their memories as erotic stimuli. A fact of social significance was shown in the histories of five twelve to fourteen-year-old boys of the fallatio group who, after a year and more of association with playmates, voluntarily frequented low-grade amusement resorts and the water front to solicit men with whom they consorted for financial considerations.

Only in a few cases was a predonderant interest in heterosexual relations noted. This may be explained by the fact that fifty-seven of the seventy-one members of the sex group were of prepuberal age at the time of our inquiry. . . . It is gratifying to note that subjects who were physiologically at puberal imminence or beyond had, in addition to their interest in homosexual acts, normal amative desires and probably were limited in their heterosexual relations only by their environment. . . .[258–59]

Six of the boys had been arrested for "Sexual misconduct." Two of these

were complained against because of masturbation with younger boys and two were taken by the police for fallationous association with men. The latter [boys] had personally sought the adult companionship and their selection of consorts older than themselves was a choice based upon other experiences they had had with both boys and men.[261]

"One subject of fourteen years" traced his history of delinquency

back through five cleverly-planned thefts to an inceptive act of stealing from the hotel room of a man directly after they had mutually induced orgasms. Notwithstanding the fact that the subject stated he encouraged the sedulous interest of the man during more than an hour of erotic desire, he impulsively purloined his gold watch and did not fully comprehend the nature of the theft until he was on the way home. He had never theretofore . . . stolen anything. He expressed no consciousness of guilt nor dislike of the man during the analysis though he recalled some feeling of disgust at the close of his [own] orgasm which the man had coercively prolonged.[262–63]

MEDICAL

# 1918
## Dr. Albert Abrams: "Homosexuality—A Military Menace"

Dr. Abrams discussed an "electronic" test for homosexuality, based on the "radio-activity" of the ovary and testes.[36] The first world war gave birth to one of the earliest medical articles on how to recognize homosexuals in the U. S. armed forces.

"Recently, in San Francisco," began Abrams,

> a "vice club" was raided. The gruesome revelations pertaining to this club of homosexualists invited the attention of the military authorities, who saw the corruption that must necessarily ensue among the soldiery if it were not summarily suppressed.

To comment on the omnipresence of homosexuality was not necessary. Abrams warned:

> Although these unfortunate inverts are not criminals, but biological products of perverse heredity, they exert a baneful influence on their environment. . . .
>
> In recruiting the elements which make up our invincible army, we cannot ignore what is obvious and which will militate against the combative prowess of our forces in this war and the deterrent post-bellum influences
>
> From a military viewpoint, the homosexualist is not only dangerous, but ineffective as a fighter.

It was also a matter of "common knowledge" what "the impossibility of satisfying sexual desire in the natural way will do in encouraging perverse acts" (a reference to the hardly surprising tendency of those placed in institutions composed exclusively of their own sex to engage in various forms of intercourse with their own sex).

> It is imperative that homosexualists be recognized by the military authorities. Homosexuality is difficult of diagnosis when attempted in the conventional way.

"To all appearances" the homosexualist "may be like a normal individual," with no special distinguishing "secondary sex characters." And it might take "months of painstaking psychoanalysis before the inversion is discovered" by Freudian treatment. Dr. Abrams claimed: "By a simple method, based on the 'Electronic Reactions of Abrams,' one is able to make a biologico-physiological differentiation of sexuality."[528]

> By aid of the electronic reactions, it can be shown that every tissue possesses its own definite radioactivity which may be readily demonstrated. Specifically, the ovary yields a definite area of ventral dullness, and this is likewise true of the testicle.
>
> Six homosexuals (males?) thus far examined by the writer yielded from anatomically perfect testes an ovarian reaction in four instances, and in the other two subjects (bisexualists) an ovario-testicular reaction (ovarian predominating by measurement). These phenomenal facts are of stupendous importance.

"The electronic tests" were detailed elsewhere.[529]

MEDICAL/IMAGES

# 1919, April
# Dr. G. Sherman Peterkin: "Sex trees"

In a medical journal article Dr. Peterkin advocated the "Cultivation and Control," rather than the "Suppression of Sexual Instinct," in the name of "True Family Life and "pure patriotism."[37] This advocacy of "controlled" eroticism as an aid to male-female bonding was typical of the new theory of "normal" heterosexuality.

"Civilization to-day" was not recognizing in the physical sex act "the means given by the Almighty to express the finer sentiments"—those uniting "more closely husband and wife." This civilization was therefore growing "stunted, deformed and short-lived . . . sex trees." A deformed sex tree was pictured next to a "Tree of Sex (Cultivated and Cared for)," with "Normal," "Happy" leaves. The decaying sex tree included "Perverted" and "Abnormal" leaves. The doctor's "sex trees" gave visual expression to a new, wide-ranging ideology of marital, familial, and male-female relationships. (See sex trees, p. 384.)

BOOK REVIEW

# 1919, June 29
## N. Y. Times Book Review: Sherwood Anderson's Winesburg, Ohio

The stories in Anderson's *Winesburg, Ohio* "might have been written before the advent of the new psychology," said an anonymous *Times* reviewer.[38] "But if so they would have been misunderstood" because they were "actuated" by interior motives. "Freud and Jung have taught us how hopes and ideas crammed back into subcellars of consciousness emerge in grotesque masquerade when pressure slackens or becomes too taut." The "tragedies and comedies" in Anderson's book "have the support of scientific revelation."

Anderson's book had an "extraordinary quality of vividness, sincerity, and tenderness." The author "loves what he touches"—the reviewer referred to "the poetry and pathos of the opening story in the book, *Hands.*"

(*The Times* review gave no details, but "Hands" is the story of a school master who had once almost been lynched in a small Pennsylvania town. Rumors had been started by his touching his young pupils with his hands—in an effort to reach out to them with a vision of the world's possibilities. The teacher's horror, thereafter, at his impulse to reach out, is Anderson's theme.)

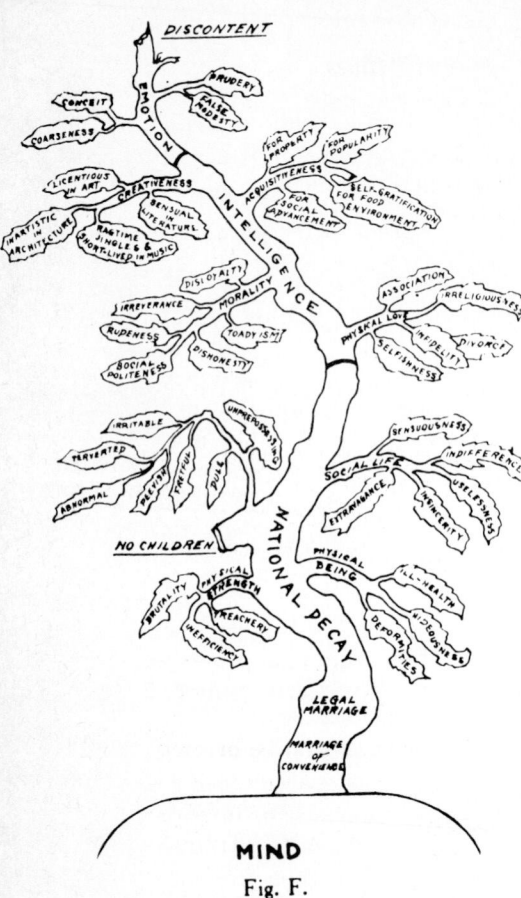

THE TREE OF SEX
(UNCULTIVATED-SUPPRESSED-NEGLECTED)

Fig. F.

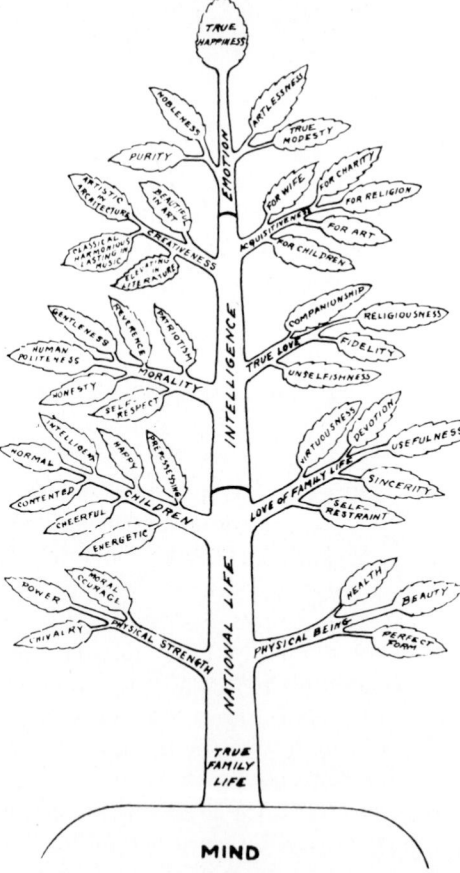

THE TREE OF SEX
(CULTIVATED AND CARED FOR)

Fig. G.

♀ MEDICAL

## 1919
## Dr. Constance Long: *"A sign of the times for those who can read portents"*

At the first International Conference of Women Physicians, held in New York, Dr. Long, an Englishwoman, presented a psychoanalytic view of "homosexuality."[39] Long's comments represented a relatively "liberal," "tolerant" view, perhaps all the more insidious for its unexamined negative value judgments. For example, Long assumed homosexuality to be a "problem" indicating a "block" in development to "mature" heterosexuality, caused by social conditions. Separating Long's moralism from her social observations, her comments do point to some historical changes in post-war Europe and the United States that may have led to an increase in homosexual relations.

The subject of homosexuality, said Long, "has been brought before us in England recently" by Clemence Dane's novel of a girls' boarding school, *Regiment of Women,* and Alec Waugh's novel of a boy's public school life, *The Loom of Youth.* * That these and similar books had appeared "is a sign of the times for those who can read portents."

> The European war has had the effect of separating men and women into masses of their own sex. It has produced tremendous emotional problems of every sort. It has torn youthful civilians from home and normal conditions of life and placed them under conditions where the ordinary moral notions are entirely reversed. Months of segregation in camps, barracks, on ships and on expeditions are . . . being experienced on such a huge scale. We have already a few obvious legacies from these cataclysmic times. There is a mass of venereal disease, a great outbreak of hysteria and other psychoneuroses among men and . . . there is a shortage of some ten million men in Europe. At such times homosexuality is bound to make its appearance as a problem for humanity.
>
> Something else has been happening. Women have been obliged willy-nilly to do men's work in engine yards, in munition factories, on the land —in every field . . . of industrial and professional life. Something so-called male in a woman's psychology has been called for, and . . . there is a latent sex-element which enables her to respond. . . . the regulation tasks of the sexes have been completely mixed, for in many camps and hospitals the women's work has been done exclusively by men.
>
> If homosexuality crops up at such a time . . . its existence is not new. Perhaps the necessity to accept and consider it as one of the problems of

---

*For *The New York Times* review of *Regiment of Women* see 1917, Feb. 4; the U. S. edition of Waugh's novel, reviewed in the *N. Y. Times Book Review,* May 2, 1920, p. 220, contained no reference to intimate relations.

our times is new. Franker discussion of all sex problems has made it possible to consider it here today.

Homosexuality then is love for members of the same sex. It begins at home among brothers and brothers, sisters and sisters, and has always united mothers and daughters, fathers and sons, in bonds of friendly love. This useful emotion is emphasized in school and college life. . . . It has great value in promoting esprit de corps. It can act against imposed discipline, for it sometimes unites and strengthens the class against the teacher. . . . It has been historically significant in times of slavery. It has a personal value. It is the beginning of lasting friendships. . . .[77–78]

But Long warned that this positive homosexual emotion was bad if acted out genitally:

Personal friendships which are fraught with so much fair promise have their dangers, too. The erotic element is capable of taking concrete and undesirable forms. Here, too, the heavy hand of conventional morality comes down with excessive tyranny, and boys particularly, and more rarely girls, are sometimes summarily expelled from school for an error they but half understood. Some promising careers have been wrecked this way, and love . . . has been tortured into a demon shape.

Such punishment either makes rebels, or it plunges the culprit into the abyss of self-depreciation. . . .[79]

In the novel *Regiment of Women* the teacher, Clare Hartill,

used the devotion she had the gift to inspire for the purpose of power. She could not live without a sensation, and obtained it from the erotic love of younger teachers and pupils. One of her pupils in an excess of emotionalism throws herself out of the window. . . . The love was not recognized for what it was either by Clare Hartill or by her admirers. She could not have faced the word homosexuality. . . .[79–80]

Long said that exclusively homosexual persons were so because their "libido" had become "fixed in this immature and regressive form." And a "fixed" homosexual tendency "is a very undesirable thing."

It arises . . . out of unnatural conditions such as the segregation of the sexes —or out of the economic difficulties in the way of marriage. Among women, whose numbers considerably surpass those of men, there is an arithmetical reason for it in the impossibility of marriage; much less excuse for it exists amongst adult men, since the whole of the sex life is more or less arranged for their convenience, except in the case of genuine homosexuals who are . . . very much fewer than those who indulge in homosexual practices. Justice demands that we must allow the genuine homosexual to express what is his normal sexuality in his own way. In many respects he is already heavily handicapped by nature. Instead of this we make homosexuality a penal offense in men. . . .

She advocated decriminalization, and "raising the age of consent considerably for both sexes."[81]

In the discussion following Long's paper, a Dr. Jackson of Pasadena, California, commented: "The subject of homosexuality is of vast importance."[82] She favored co-educational schools because a girl needed to become acquainted with the attractions of boys,

> in order not to get her likings too strongly fastened to the qualities and attractions of the other girls. I happen to be an old maid, and I will tell you part of the reason. I lived with my grandmother. . . . There were no men, no boys in the household. I have an adopted daughter. She has been mine since she was eight months old. There has been no man, no boy in the household. This daughter of mine since she was fifteen, sixteen, seventeen, began to get crushes on girls of her own age, and while she was at Stanford, she had a terrible crush on a girl of her own age. She said to me: "Why, you have so-and-so," my best friend, a woman. I said: "Yes, but don't you see I am an old maid?"
>
> I wanted that daughter of mine to see that to be an old maid is not a thing desirable, that it is not the end and aim of a woman's life; and that to care too much for these girl friends of hers, to show them all of the devotion that would normally express itself in other directions might inhibit the preferable development. She was not abnormal but simply passing through that phase of homosexuality, and I said just that to her. She went horseback riding with a young girl chum the day a lieutenant in the army came one hundred miles to see her, left him waiting while she went riding with a girl college chum, which was an awful mistake. (Laughter.)
>
> I had one school teacher under my care. She had a neurosis which expressed itself in all sorts of symptoms. She was a very decided homosexual. . . . She was a principal. She loved her pupils and she was splendid in the handling of her teachers; but she had one chum with whom her relations were more intimate than they should have been. This was the cause of the hyper-sex tension that revealed itself as asthma and anxiety and neurosis and a few more things.
>
> The subject of sex should never be approached as one requiring apology, for it does not. . . .
>
> As I discussed these things with the school teacher . . . , she would fear I was going to criticize her and be censorious, and she fairly screamed at me one day: "Don't make it nasty; I cannot stand it if you do."[83–84]

MEDICAL

# 1920, January
## Dr. W. C. Rivers: "A New Male Homosexual Trait(?)"

A prominent American medical journal, *The Alienist and Neurologist*, published an essay by Dr. Rivers, of Yorkshire, England.[1] Rivers announced his discovery of a "New Male Homosexual Trait," cat loving.

In 1913, Rivers had published *Walt Whitman's Anomaly,* the first work in English to trace "the inverted sexual disposition of that poet." The doctor had then been contacted by "an English public school 'coach,' " who "was an invert himself; and not only this, but a member of a homosexual coterie; and not only that, but one who physically indulged his abnormal appetite." Because Rivers, as a young doctor, found contact with this individual "too potentially compromising," he "declined further communication." But he noted that the man "kept a large cat of which he seemed very fond." The man also "remarked that many of his inverted friends had the same taste in pets." Further inquiry by Rivers indicated that another man recently convicted of "petty fraud" had been found "to have been previously convicted of attempted sodomy," and was also "an exhibitor of prize cats."[22]

Since Magnus Hirschfeld's large work on homosexuality did not mention the "trait" of cat loving, Rivers had begun his investigation. Starting with Hirschfeld's list of "eminent men who were of inverted disposition," Rivers had searched for "records of their affection for cats." He then took a list of "eminent men" who had been "cat lovers, and looked for evidence of inversion in them" (the men).

Rivers found that four out of thirty-one "eminent" male inverts listed by Hirschfeld were cat lovers. Among "eminent" cat loving men, Rivers found suggestions of inversion in several. For example, the life of "the artist-critic Wainewright, who murdered his friends for their insurance policies," suggested that he was possibly inverted. Wainewright had died of apoplexy, "his sole companion a cat."

Rivers ended: "If fondness for cats be entitled to a place among male homosexual traits, the reason will be that it is a woman's taste."[27]

INTIMACY

# 1920, November
## *The Dial:* Emory Holloway, "Walt Whitman's Love Affairs"

In a magazine article Holloway offered evidence to debunk the legend put forward by some Whitman biographers that the poet had had a romance with a woman in New Orleans in 1848.[2] The legend was based, in part, on Whitman's poem "Once I Pass'd Through a Populous City"—which in the version published by Whitman detailed a liaison between the speaker and a woman.

"A few years ago," revealed Holloway, "I discovered the original manuscript of this poem in a private library in New York," and found that, "historically," the piece belonged "among the Calamus poems, which glorify that intimate friendship of man for man which . . . Whitman preached as a sort of sentimental-religious democracy."

Holloway quoted the original manuscript poem, about a male-male intimacy:

> ". . . now of all that city I remember only the man who wandered with me there, for love of me, Day by day, and night by night, we were together. All else has long been forgotten by me—I remember, I say, only one rude and ignorant man, who, when I departed, long and long held me by the hand with silent lips, sad and tremulous."

Holloway supposed that Whitman's "reason for disguising the emotion which gave birth to this poem was the poet-prophet's desire to avoid a charge of effeminacy." The poem indicated that Whitman retained in adulthood an "ability" to direct his romantic sentiments toward man as well as toward woman." The "artist is expected to pass in his imagination from the man's point of view to the woman's and back against at will." But "Whitman is unique among the great poets of the world . . . in his power to do this with his heart." Holloway said that Whitman thought this "peculiarity"

> indicated his kinship with the great religious teachers of the world. But he also knew that such a nature as his would be misunderstood by most men, and that it might even prove dangerous to him. In an unpublished manuscript memorandum of 1868 he thus admonishes himself: "Depress the adhesive [manly love]* nature. It is in excess, making life a torment."

Later in this same article, Hollway discussed the alleged evidence in this manuscript diary for Whitman's possible "romance" with a female of Washington, D.C. Holloway concluded that the diary did record Whitman's unhappy, final affair with a woman.[480–82] (This diary evidence is now generally considered to refer to Whitman's friend-lover Peter Doyle.)

A year later, in 1921, Holloway reprinted the original male-male version of "Once I Pass'd Through" and relevant sections of Whitman's previously unpublished notebook-diaries in the two-volume *Uncollected Poetry and Prose of Walt Whitman.*[3] These volumes were evaluated in *The New York Times Book Review,* on December 25, 1921, by critic Bliss Perry, who said they included significant new materials about the poet:[8]

> Holloway prints (Vol. II., p. 102) what appears to be the original draft of "Once I passed through a populous city." "It is clear," to quote the editor's words, "that the poem originally inspired by a 'Calamus' friendship with a man, was altered [when published] to celebrate romantic love for a woman. . . . The history of the poem goes far, I think, toward showing that Whitman retained in manhood some of the characteristics of the sexually indiscriminate affection of a child." The point need not be elaborated here, but those

*The bracketed phrase is Holloway's. Whitman's diary entry beginning "Depress the adhesive nature" is now said to date to 1870, and to apply to his relationship with Peter Doyle; see Gay Wilson Allen, *The Solitary Singer* (N.Y.: New York University Press, 1967), pp. 421–23.

familiar with the controversies raised by the "Calamus" section of "Leaves of Grass" will perceive its bearing. That the "two-natured" Walt Whitman was, as late as 1870—fifteen years after the first edition of "Leaves of Grass" and four years after the close of his heroic service as an army nurse in Washington—in a pitiable moral and physical condition is seen with painful clearness in Notebook No. 9 (Vol. II., pp. 95, 96). Here surely, is no demi-god or superman, but rather what William James would have called a "sick soul," struggling lamentably for mastery over itself.

The Notebook pages last referred to reprint parts of Whitman's diary in which he recorded his emotional distress and "weakness," and admonished himself to "preserve a kind spirit . . . to 16. But PURSUE HER NO MORE." Holloway noted that the number, "16," had been substituted for "An initial, which might be P or V," and the initial had been erased. In another entry dated July 15, 1870, Whitman vowed: "TO GIVE UP ABSOLUTELY . . . this FEVERISH, FLUC-TUATING, useless, undignified pursuit of 164. . . ." Whitman also ordered himself to "Depress the adhesive nature/ It is in excess—making life a torment/ All this diseased, feverish disproportionate *adhesiveness.*" Holloway noted that "adhesiveness" was Whitman's term for the " 'intense and loving comradeship' " of man with man.

It is now established that "16" and "164" are references to the sixteenth and fourth letters of the alphabet, P and D, the initials of Whitman's Washington intimate, Peter Doyle. That Holloway failed, apparently, to decipher that simplest of codes seems evidence of his desire *not* to perceive the obvious: the cause of Whitman's perturbations was a male. (On the decoding of Whitman's diary see Allen, *Solitary Singer,* pp. 422–23.)

Holloway's desire to preserve the image of Whitman as woman-lover was documented in 1926, when he published his own biography of the poet.[4] Here he amazingly reiterated the legend of Whitman's New Orleans affair with a female, inferring this romance from the published (male-female) version of "Once I Pass'd Through"—ignoring his own earlier discovery of the original (male-male) version. This scholarly gaffe was so blatant it was discussed in *The Times Book Review.* There on October 10, 1926, reviewer Herbert S. Gorman began, "It is now more than thirty-four years since Walt Whitman died;" during those years the "huge" amount published about the poet had been "mainly controversial." Gorman added:

No true interpretation of Walt Whitman can be made without a due consideration of the man's curious nature as exemplified in the "Calamus" poems and here, it is to be suspected, Professor Holloway is unduly reticent. Frankly, there is a very strong supposition that Walt belonged, at least by a strong inclination, to what is carefully called "the intermediate sex."* It

---

*This reference of 1926 to " 'the intermediate sex' " is one of the earliest instances in which *The New York Times* gave an explicit name to that group. The "intermediate sex" was Edward Carpenter's favored appelation; its use in *The Times* indicates the spread of his influence.

is impossible to accept the reading of some of his poems as no more than moods clothed in a rather sexual imagery and not at all an expression of an inhibited (if it was inhibited, and neither Professor Holloway nor anybody else living knows) desire that was sometimes tragically strong. Professor Holloway seems to dismiss this side of Walt's nature to a great degree and he should not do so. Although, perhaps, distasteful it should be fairly considered. Professor Holloway will possibly assert that he has considered it in that he has given his own version of the reading of some of these poems and perhaps he is right. . . . But the doubts concerning Whitman are not quashed. The old problem remains as it will always remain and various critics must take one side or the other. This question and the question of Walt's mysterious affair in New Orleans still loom as the most perplexing portions of the poet's life.

So far as the New Orleans episode goes, Professor Holloway is not satisfactory. It is his theory that Walt had an affair with a [female] Creole prostitute and he infers this from a poem beginning "Once I Pass'd Through a Populous City" and two lines from the poem beginning "From Pent-up Aching Rivers." It is difficult to connect the two [poems]. . . . And anybody turning to Professor Holloway's compilation of the unpublished poems and prose of Walt Whitman [discussed earlier] may see there that "Once I Pass'd Through a Populous City" was originally written to a man and then changed to refer to a woman when it appeared in the 1860 volume [of Whitman's poems]. It was, perhaps, a feeling of fear on Walt's part that caused him to change this poem and, in itself, it might be taken to be as sound evidence as anything that Professor Holloway advances for the other side of the problem. But to consider the matter fairly even this is no actual proof. It is evident that Walt had strong leanings toward friendship with men, that a sort of Platonic ideal was in the back of his mind, and even the sexual imagery might have been induced from a kind of poetical trance. . . .[5]

♀  MEDICAL/IMAGES

# 1920
## Dr. Edward J. Kempf: "Homosexual panic"

Dr. Kempf was best known for coining the phrase "homosexual panic," an anxiety attack he said was "due to the pressure of uncontrollable perverse sexual cravings."[5] Kempf's and other doctors' definition of homosexual "cravings" as "perverse" obviously played a prominent role in that panic which sometimes developed in persons experiencing such "cravings"—yet Kempf and other physicians were insensitive to their own contribution to such disturbances.

Homosexual panics were frequent, said Kempf, "wherever men or women must be grouped alone for prolonged periods, as in army camps, aboard ships, on exploring expeditions, in prisons, monasteries, schools and asylums." Kempf was a psychiatrist at a U. S. government mental hospital in Washington, D.C., and many of his case histories are of soldiers and sailors who had suffered homosexual panics during or soon after World War I.

Kempf's textbook, *Psychopathology,* is replete with captioned photographs, supposedly illustrating various responses to homosexual feelings. Several of these photos and their original captions are reproduced below, providing images of the homosexual as mentally deranged.

"Tensions of facial muscles showing desperate striving as a defense against fear of becoming effeminate and homosexual. His final solution was suicide."[552]

"Masculine compensation in a woman. Following the mother's interference with her mating she developed a psychosis in which she solved her unhappiness by becoming male, the priest of an elaborate new religion and philosophy. Her attitude is that of aggressive homosexuality. She made the costume."[701]

"Terrific striving to become omnipotent as a defense against fear of homosexuality and impotence."[706]

"This biological result is typical of the chronic oral erotic dissociated personality."[708]

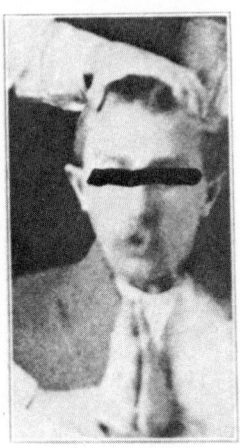

"Compulsion to prayer as a defense and purification against oral eroticism."[722]

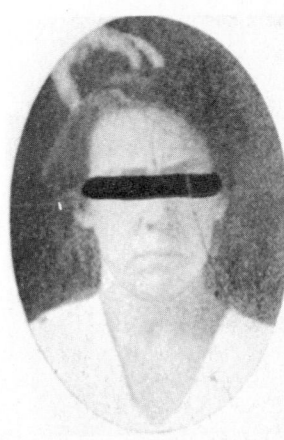

"The face shows intense hatred.
This individual is the victim
of intense anal erotic cravings."[723]

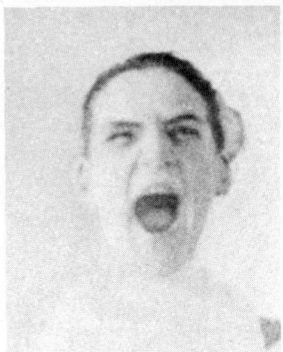

"Joyous abandonment to anal and
autoeroticism."[723]

NEWS REPORT

# 1921, January 24
## "Earl Lind" and the *N.Y. Times:*
## The death of Kermit Engelhart

In his autobiography *The Female Impersonators* "Earl Lind" reported reading on
January 24, 1921 of

> a girl-boy of eighteen [who] committed suicide in New York City by jumping
> from a thirty-five foot bridge upon railroad tracks.[6] Adolescent androgynes
> are continually putting an end to their lives because bitterly persecuted
> merely on account of their bisexuality and [because of being] most unfeel-
> ingly told by their closest associates that they are deeply depraved, and
> because prohibited by the leaders of thought from acquiring scientific
> knowledge of their idiosyncrasy.[208]*

Lind's reference points to the homosexual character of a victim about whom a
*New York Times* story said little. On the date cited by Lind, *The Times* reported:

> The body of Kermit Engelhart, 18 years old, choir singer in the Richmond
> Hill Baptist Church, was found early yesterday morning between the tracks
> of the Long Island Railroad beneath a bridge in Forest Park. . . .

Engelhart had been a "mechanic in the Cadillac Motor Company's Brooklyn
shop." The police theorized that Engelhart "drank some acid" and committed
suicide. Engelhart's father claimed his son had been murdered, and that

> his son had not the slightest reason for wishing to take his life and that he
> was as cheerful as usual Saturday evening when he left to take his accus-
> tomed evening walk in Forest Park. . . .
>       Kermit was rather shy, his father said, usually preferring to take long
> walks by himself at night to mixing much with other persons. He was espe-
> cially interested in the Sunday school and the choir.
>       "I had warned him repeatedly . . . that wandering in Forest Park at

*"Earl Lind" also used the name "Ralph Werther-Jennie June"; see 1921, August.

night was dangerous and that he might meet with hold-up men, but he always laughed. . . ."

It was first believed the boy had been robbed, . . . but later it was discovered that he had left his pocket-book at home. The father said the youth was in no sort of trouble, had no love affair, and no worries to cause depression.

RESISTANCE/INTIMACY

## 1921, April 4
## Anonymous Detroiters to Edward Carpenter:
### *"An oasis for the heart"*

Just several months apart in 1921 (by coincidence, apparently), two men-loving men living in Detroit wrote to Edward Carpenter, telling him how his writings had helped them reclaim their lives.[7] The first correspondent was twenty-one years old in 1921. In 1983, he would be eighty-three and, possibly, still living; because, if alive, his situation is unknown, his letter appears here anonymously (as does that of the second correspondent, whose age was not stated). Both letters document the importance of Carpenter's books to Americans struggling for self-affirmation in the early twentieth century.

On April 4, 1921, the first American wrote:

My dear Mr. Carpenter:
It is hard to begin a letter to you, because I love you so much. . . .
Several years ago I read "Love's Coming of Age" and "The Intermediate Sex" for the first time. . . . I am so glad that I read them when I was (and while I am) young. They have meant a great deal to me in my personal life, and in my own understanding of early passions and inclinations.

Besides Carpenter's books, "first honors" in the Detroiter's library went to Whitman, Wilde, H. G. Wells, "the Russians (especially that devil in cleverness, Artzibashef)," Louis Wilkinson, and "my friend Mr. Frank Harris" (an early sex radical whom the letter-writer had known when living in New York).* He imagined that Carpenter was like Harris in possessing "such youthful love and vigor."

One of the writer's "dearest friends" in New York ran a "little playhouse" and had in his rooms "many pictures" of Carpenter and Whitman.

---

*As to "Artzibashef," *The National Union Catalog, Pre-1956 Imprints,* lists no such author. It does list several similar names, and the writer referred to may be Mikhail P. Artybashev (1878–1927), a novelist, playwright, and essayist. Louis Wilkinson was probably the English author of novels and other works under the name Louis Marlow; he corresponded with Oscar Wilde; see Wilde's *Letters* p. 769. A story by Wilkinson is in *Calamus: Male Homosexuality in 20th Century Literature,* ed. by David Galloway and Christian Sabisch (N. Y.: Morrow Quill Press, 1982). Carpenter's correspondent also mentioned reading the authors Ernest Dowson, Arthur Symons, and G. B. Shaw.

The writer sent Carpenter several poems, asked for his opinion of them, and if Carpenter had a photo or verse he could send: "Anything you have touched . . . would be of great value to me." He concluded:

> If this great selfish world knew our lives and the peculiar mystery, which some contain, great sufferings would be averted. Perhaps, the silence and secrecy, which shelters certain loves and friendships but adds to their charm. There is a naively beautiful quality in anything beyond the sordid conceptions of the vulgar and common man.!?
>
> From early youth, I have known a few real and beautiful friendships. Once in a small "Christian" college, such a friendship resulted in a distressing misfortune. At that time, when my relationship with brutal orthodox mentalities was close and my companionship with suffering intimate, your books were as great candle-lights in the darkness. They brought to me a knowledge of my self, and as Shakespeare said so aptly: "To thine own self be true."
>
> Unless one has experienced this real suffering he can hardly know the strength and beauty which such a fine understanding as yours may give to him.
>
> It is as food in famine; it is an oasis for the heart. Now you may understand why I am so grateful to you, and why I write to you so frankly and intimately about my self. . . .

The writer hoped that his letter would find Carpenter and "the good friend who shares your home enjoying to the deepest measure the health and happiness of Life." (Carpenter's romance with George Merrill was evidently of international renown—the letter-writer had not yet read the autobiography in which Carpenter spoke of Merrill.) "Our friends are our Gods," said the writer, "so may our Gods be friends." He ended: "May this Spring of the year bring you new joys and beauty."

The second Detroiter wrote to Carpenter five months later, on September 1, 1921. He hoped that his "beloved Teacher" would understand "when my lips say, 'I love you.' "

> To you, Edward Carpenter, I owe my life and all that it may ever mean to me. You have come to me as a pure and radiant angel of light to roll away the stone from above my sepulcher, freeing me from the limitations of my hitherto paradoxical and inexplicable nature. When I think of the long cruel years, lived in the most rigid state of repression, doubting myself, desiring the unattainable in spite of myself, living, hoping, praying and, above all, fearing—when I think of all this, and of how beautifully and completely it has been removed through your glorious influence, how can I help but be grateful? How can I help but love you—you who have been my Savior.
>
> Only a short time ago I thought I had truly reached the Trail's End, but in that final moment, you, through the magic of your words, have brought me back from the grave—or from the mad-house—and have filled me with a greater determination to live, to live my own life just as God has given it to me in spite of the fact that so doing may mean the alienation of

both friends and family. Oh, surely you, who must know what I have suffered, you, who must realize the awful process of purgation through which
I am passing, can understand!

Oh what a sweet and sacred thing it is to love and to be loved!—to hold
within one's arms the visible representation of that beautiful spark which
daily seems to grow brighter and more wondrous, to remove one's thoughts
from the realm of self and let them dwell rapturously and selflessly upon
some beloved companion, to press his glorious body close to one's own, to
feel the warm, red blood pulsing deliciously through both, to feel his soft
arms lie caressingly about one's shoulders, to pillow one's head upon his
breast, to touch one's lips to his hair, his eyes, his lips! Is Paradise more
wonderful?

I would ask for nothing more in the world than just that. I have tasted
—only tasted—of its exquisite pleasure and of its necessary pain, but that
tiny morsel has filled my heart with rapture unspeakable, with joy ineffable
and even though that One stands somewhat apart from me, pitying my
suffering rather than understanding my affection, the memory of that One
Blissful Night will never, never leave me. I live it again and again, daily and
hourly—it has reconstructed much that has been torn down, it has broad-
ened and deepened my life, it has touched a chord that nothing else has ever
done and I am a bigger and better man for it.

Still, I am torn between two contending emotions—the desire to have
him completely understand, to have him with me always, always, and the
feeling that I want him to live his own life in exactly his own way without
thought or suggestion from me. I do not want to limit his life in any way,
I would not have him feel that he must return some degree of love or
affection just from a sense of duty. I would not have him sacrifice one bit
of happiness for my sake, yet I am selfish enough to hope that he may learn
to understand! I want him, but, equally, I want him to be happy. His unhappiness would be my unhappiness, and a knowledge that he was comparatively happy would help to atone for the terrible heartache which I should
suffer were he never to understand.

And so Edward Carpenter it is you who have given me the knowledge
which has made this love possible, it is you to whom I am thankful for this
beautiful experience—and I love you for it. I earnestly pray that the day is
not far distant when I can make the journey to England for no greater
purpose than to stand in the radiance of your Presence. . . .

A Mohammedan prayer was quoted, and the writer ended.

♀ INTIMACY

## 1921, Spring
## Gertrude Stein: "The song of Alice B."

Stein composed "A Sonatina Followed By Another," an affectionate, erotic prose-
poem about her intimacy with Alice B. Toklas, containing a section headed "The

song of Alice B.," a lilting love note.[8] This private declaration provides a sharp contrast with the bleak medical literature and newspaper reports, suggesting that fond world women might construct with each other out of and against the marriage patterns and roles of the dominant society.

Stein wrote of Toklas:

> I caught sight of a splendid Misses. She had handkerchiefs and kisses. She had eyes and yellow shoes she had everything to choose and she chose me. In passing through France she wore a Chinese hat and so did I. In looking at the sun she read a map. And so did I. In eating fish and pork she just grew fat. And so did I. In loving a blue sea she had a pain. And so did I. In loving me she of necessity thought first. And so did I. How prettily we swim. Not in water. Not on land. But in love. How often do we need trees and hills. Not often. And how often do we need birds. Not often. And how often do we need wishes. Not often. And how often do we need glasses not often. We drink wine and we make, well we have not made it yet. How often do we need a kiss. Very often and we add when tenderness overwelms us we speedily eat veal. And what else, ham and a little pork and raw artichokes and ripe olives and chester cheese and cakes and caramels and all the melon. We still have a great deal of it left. I wonder where it is. Conserved melon. Let me offer it to you.

NEWS REPORTS

# 1921, July 20
## N. Y. Times: Franklin D. Roosevelt
## and the scandal at Newport, R.I.

In the spring of 1919, Franklin D. Roosevelt, as acting secretary of the U. S. Navy, had established a vice squad to investigate alleged immoral conditions at the Naval Training Station at Newport, Rhode Island.[9] Roosevelt later claimed he had not known (in Frank Freidel's words) "that the investigators, while acting as decoys to trap perverts, had several times engaged in sodomy."* When Roosevelt learned of this in September 1919, he said he had immediately ordered the vice squad to alter its methods.

Later, a Navy Court of Inquiry had investigated the investigators, taking six thousand pages of testimony, comprising fifteen volumes.

In the summer of 1921, the Newport case became a public scandal when Roosevelt's Republican opponents accused him of having condoned the vice squad's engaging in immoral sexual acts (in order to entrap "perverts"). On July 19, 1921, a subcommittee of the Senate Naval Affairs Committee (composed of

*Frank Burt Freidel, *Franklin D. Roosevelt* (Boston: Little, Brown, 1952–54), 2 vols., v. 2, pp. 41, 46, 96–97; and notes.

two Republicans) released to the press their majority report on "Alleged Immoral Conditions at Newport."

The next day *The New York Times* reported that Roosevelt and Josephus Daniels, former secretary of the navy, had been "denounced for methods used in investigating wartime scandals among enlisted men." Most of the Newport scandal's details were "of an unprintable nature." Roosevelt and Daniels were charged with knowing that enlisted men "were used as participants in immoral practices for the purpose of obtaining evidence on which to dismiss offenders from the navy." Such a use of enlisted men, the committee report charged, violated "the rights of every American boy who enlisted in the navy to fight for his country."

The "unusual conditions of wartime" *The Times* continued, had given rise to the original situation in Newport, where 15,000 to 20,000 "boys and young men" who had enlisted in the navy were put up in "cheap lodging houses."

Referring to the vice squad's activities, *The Times* reported that the committee had charged:

> Conduct of a character at which seasoned veterans . . . would have shuddered was practically forced upon boys, who, because of their patriotism . . . had responded to the call of the country to defend their flag and their homes.

That Roosevelt and Daniels had, according to the committee, "allowed enlisted men to be placed in a position where such acts were ever liable to occur is . . . a most deplorable, disgraceful and unnatural proceeding." Roosevelt "must have known of the methods being used."

The "difficulty at Newport," said *The Times,* had originated with "a few men of bad character among the many thousands concentrated there under the emergency of war."

The committee commented:

> to send out into Newport young men, some of them mere boys, . . . to use their own "discretion and judgment" whether they should or should not actually permit to be performed upon them immoral acts, is in the opinion of the committee utterly shocking to the American standard of morality.

In response, Roosevelt said that the Republican committee members' report attacking him was politically motivated. He denied having had any direct supervision of the Newport vice squad.

Roosevelt had learned from two friends of a Newport minister, "who had been tried in a local court and acquitted," that "members of the investigating squad had used highly improper and revolting methods in getting evidence." Learning of these methods Roosevelt said he had immediately ordered them stopped.

## 1921, August 12
### N. Y. Times: Harry Gribble's March Hares

A "curiously effeminate comedy" for "the amusement of the over-civilized" was the way *Times* theater critic Alexander Woollcott described *March Hares,* which had opened the night before.[10]

To "impart the flavor" of the comedy required the same "innuendo and elliptical method" used by the playwright. This comedy was "just the opposite" of what was called " 'A Red-Blooded Hundred Per Cent American Play.' " Woollcott noted that the playwright "uses Oscar Wilde" as "background" for the piece. Its central character was "an odd young professor of elocution," the kind who would describe himself as an " 'artiste,' " who was pursued with such violence that he finally reached the point of "planning marriage with the lady elocutionist to whom he has been negligently engaged."

Commenting on *March Hares* in *The Times* of August 21, Woollcott again mentioned Oscar Wilde, adding that the play included "sultry moments when a casual reference to the Union Station at Gomorrah would not seem so fearfully incongrous." The comedy was "peopled with odd folk" who "talk a good deal about one another's sex appeal."

A comment on a 1928 London production of *March Hares* was published that year in *The New York Times.* Charles Morgan said that what kept the hero, Geoffrey, from marrying Janet was that "he has never 'mastered' her"; she "is forever quarreling with him." Calling the play a study in "sexual antagonism," Morgan reported:

> Janet, in order to infuriate Geoffrey, brings home a girl called Claudia Kitts, who, she declares, is her "affinity." Geoffrey retaliates by inviting to stay in the house a young man named Edgar Fuller. Claudia then falls in love with Geoffrey, Janet discovers them together, leading to further quarrels.

(Despite the play's flirtation with same-sex "affinity," male-female relationships apparently triumphed.)

INTIMACY

## 1921, August 28
### N. Y. Times Book Review: D. H. Lawrence on Walt Whitman

A dispatch from London reported that writer D. H. Lawrence had just published a long study of Walt Whitman in *The Nation.*[11] Here it was stressed that Whitman's idea of male-male comradeship as superior to male-female marriage was not subersive of that "sacred" institution. A relation between male-male intimacy, male-female marriage and democratic politics was mystically asserted. (Readers uneasy about the stability of the new "heterosexual" order of the twenties could rest assured of the basic compatibility of " 'manly love' " and marriage.)

> What Mr. Lawrence adores in Whitman is his gospel of comradeship—something higher than marriage, yet requiring and holding it sacred. . . . Comradeship is to be "the final cohering principle of the new world, the new democracy. . . . It is the soul's last and most vivid responsibility, the responsibility for the circuit of final friendship, comradeship, manly love."
>
> In the end, Mr. Lawrence hymns Whitman. "Great like a great Greek. . . . And what is the responsibility? It is for the new great era of mankind. And upon what is this new era established? On the perfect circuits of vital flow between human beings."

♀ MEDICAL/RESISTANCE

# 1921, August
# Dr. Perry M. Lichtenstein and Ralph Werther
# (Jennie June): "The 'Fairy' and the Lady Lover"

In the *Medical Review of Reviews*, Dr. Lichtenstein, physician to New York's City Prison (the Tombs) and to the House of Detention, asked:[12]

> Does the "fairy" or "fag" really exist? . . . There is no doubt but that this type of degenerate is a reality. . . . In my official capacity I have come in contact with several hundred of such individuals, and have in every instance felt sorry for the unfortunate being.

"Recently,"

> one of these individuals was arrested, charged with soliciting. . . . he was searched, and on him were found a set of artificial busts, a wig and a box containing powder and rouge. . . . He lisped and in speech closely approached a bashful female. When interviewed his answers were usually prefixed by "my dear."
>
> . . . He ran away from home and met some boys whom he considered good company. These young men were of the same type as he. It was not long before he began pervert practices, and in this way made enough money to live.
>
> . . . On one occasion ten such individuals were arrested in a raid by the police. . . . I had an opportunity to observe them closely. In every respect they resembled the female. . . . One was known as Fritzi Sheff, another as Mary Garden, a third as Dolores, a fourth as Agnes. They had a typical feminine walk. One of these prisoners was taken sick with indigestion, and when I questioned him as to the cause of his ailment, one of the others

suggested that he was probably having his period. They all wore bow ties, some of which were brightly colored. They . . . were not at all insulted when one of the trustees called them "fags."

The case was also cited of a syphilis-infected "pervert" who tried to commit "sodomy" upon a recently discharged soldier—which "serves to prove that the 'fairy' is just as great a menace as is the [female] prostitute."[371]

One finds many of these unfortunates among negroes. Several years ago a negro was shot and killed by a detective. This negro's practice was to dress up as a female, solicit men and then go thru their pockets while having intercourse in some hallway. He had . . . gotten possession of a rubber arrangement which in every way resembled the female external genitals.[371]

The doctor mentioned that "many of the so-called 'social elite' are . . . included among these people." He said: "All men who are homosexually inclined are to be placed in the same genus with the individuals already described."[371]

A letter was quoted from a " 'fag' " calling himself Ruth St. Denis to "My dear loving Princess."

I'll send you a few pennies, so you can buy a few eats, while you are in The Tombs. . . . After you come out, I do want you and I . . . to room together. . . . We, I am sure, can be very happy together, working in our jobs, and after we get thru, we stroll in the evening, but you must leave off sniffing that dangerous stuff, for instance, look at poor Dodo Regay. . . .* How terrible I felt when I saw Flora [a male], with a black eye. . . . I am putting her clothing in condition, and everything else in order, and everything with mothballs. I shall help her very much, and when you come out, the both of us can do a lot more for her. I just wrote her brother a long letter.[372]

Dr. Lichtenstein then discussed

that class of female who abhors the company of man and gains sexual satisfaction from association with other females. This is a common occurrence among prisoners. . . . Both white and colored women indulge in the practice. It is also quite common among actresses, more particularly of the chorus girl type. . . . They wear strictly tailor-made clothing, low shoes and they seldom wear corsets. The hair is usually bobbed. This is not, however, the rule; for many retain their feminine characteristics.

Almost all had an "abnormally prominent clitoris." Newspapers often reported the deaths of women who had passed as men and married other women—"just another case of 'lady lovers.' "[373]

Lichtenstein had examined a young woman who said "she had indulged in the practice of 'bull diking.' "† She was a prisoner in a reformatory, and there a

---

*"Dodo Regay" may be an early usage of the word "gay" in association with homosexuals; also see 1922, Stein.

†This is the earliest use of "bull diking" or "dike" I have discovered. "Bulldiker" is defined as a "lesbian" in the glossary to Carl Van Vechten's *Nigger Heaven* (N. Y.: Knopf, 1926). Also see "dike" in the index.

young woman, a waitress, "fell in love with her." One morning the waitress jumped into the other's bed and "had intercourse with her by friction of the clitoris." After that morning "the practice was continued with regularity." Such practices were often found among nurses.

> Such women seldom marry. Because of their dislike for men they are, as a rule, looked upon by the community as virtuous.[373]

The problem was how to "prevent such individuals from practicing pervert acts and thus becoming a menace to society."

> At present when such a person is arrested he receives a sentence of probably six months on The Island. . . . Most of the arrests are of those . . . who frequent the toilets in the subways. . . . My advice is that they be sent to an institution and kept there for an indefinite period, at the end of which time they may be released on parole.

A special institution should be founded to "house both mental and moral defectives," upon whom "endocrine therapy" might be tried.

But much depended on parents. "Where boys show . . . decided feminine traits, such as delight in crocheting, sewing, playing with dolls, it is the duty of the parent to correct them."[374]

The November 1921 *Medical Review of Reviews* carried a letter from "Ralph Werther (Jennie June)," who described himself as "perhaps the best authority in the United States on androgynism, having associated with fairies to a greater extent than any other writer."*

He was "deeply grateful to Dr. Lichtenstein for his words of sympathy for these most misunderstood and bitterest persecuted of human beings"—though Lichtenstein was corrected on some points.[539]

"Fairies" should not be prevented by society from acting on their sexual feelings, Werther argued. They were "impelled to those acts by the strongest of instincts"; the "acts are absolutely innocuous"; and the "number addicted is too great for a segregation of these sexual cripples." Segregation would mean isolating "some of our brightest minds and most useful members of society." Edith Ellis was quoted on genius and inversion.[540]

Werther argued that "The word 'perverted' as used by Dr. Lichtenstein" meant only " 'unusual.' " It was "only prejudice and bigotry" that considered "ultra-androgynes as a 'menace to society.' " Werther asked:

> Why deny to the ultra-androgyne the gratification of the strongest of human instincts, while permitting it to all who are sexually full-fledged? If it be maintained that the race is perpetuated by the latter's functioning, I answer that this consideration would only permit to wedded couples a sex-union

---

*Ralph Werther (Jennie June) also used the name "Earl Lind"; see 1921, Jan. 24; also see Earl Lind ("Ralph Werther"-"Jennie June"), *Autobiography of an Androgyne* (N. Y.: Medico-Legal Journal, 1918), and Ralph Werther-Jennie June ("Earl Lind"), *The Female Impersonators . . .* (N. Y.: Medico-Legal Journal, 1922; both, photo reprint N. Y.: Arno Press, 1975).

when offspring was the object—that is, for an American cultured couple, from one to three times thruout their married life.[541]

Werther-June signed himself: "Yours for the relief of the oppressed and the betterment of the race."[542]

♀ NEWS REPORT/CROSSING WOMAN

# 1921, December 16
## N. Y. Times: Ethel Kimball/John Hathaway

A special cable to *The Times* from Boston reported the arraignment of "Ethel Kimball, 29, who has lived as a man, doing a man's daily work, and married a Somerville girl after two years' courtship."[13]
   After her arrest

   policemen brought her woman's clothing, but she refused to put off her man's attire. An alienist who examined her declared she was sane but abnormal.

Using the name of John (or James) Hathaway, Kimball had posed as several different wealthy men. "Garbed as a man she lived opposite the girl she was courting for two years and completely deceived even the girl's relatives." The "disillusioned bride," Louise M. Aechtler, had disappeared. Kimball/Hathaway had been in trouble before on "charges of forgery." She had once studied to be a nurse.

   In her cell the woman talked freely. . . . Thin-faced, bespectacled, aquiline nosed, she presented the appearance of the "new woman" artists delighted to depict in male attire in the early days of the suffrage movement.
      "I wore men's clothes because I wanted to approach life's problems from a man's viewpoint, especially the problem of unemployment," she said.[5:3]

A follow-up story in *The Times* of December 21, reported that Ethel Kimball had told a court that her marriage to Aechtler "was a prank and that Miss Aechtler knew that she was a woman." Kimball pleaded guilty to "falsifying the record" when applying for a marriage license.
   The outcome of the case was not reported.

## 1922
## Gertrude Stein: "Miss Furr and Miss Skeene"

In a playful piece written between 1908 and 1912, first published in Boston in 1922, and then in July 1923, in *Vanity Fair* magazine, Gertrude Stein evoked the lives, intimacy, and break up of "Miss Furr and Miss Skeene"—and the subsequent triumphant perseverance of Miss Furr.[14] The two women, Stein reiterated, pursued self-expression by cultivating their voices, and by being "gay" and doing "gay" things—the word "gay" was repeated by Stein to reveal multiple meanings. It has not yet been discovered if "gay" was used as early as 1908–12 as an in-group code word for lesbian or homosexual, though by the 1920s there are hints that the word was so used.* The background of this piece suggests that Stein may well have used "gay" here in its sense of homosexual. She may also have played on that American slang usage meaning "Forward, impertinent, too free in conduct, 'fresh' " (1896–1915); see the *OED*. Even if the word did not yet refer specifically to same-sex erotic intimacy it did function in Stein's piece as a positive signifier of a female's escape from pleasant dullness, her affirmation of her identity, her self-chosen project, and her autonomy.

Stein's model for Miss Furr was Maud Hunt Squire, and for Miss Skeene, Ethel Mars. In his study of Stein's circle, James R. Mellow reports that Squire and Mars were

> midwesteners with cultural ambitions—they both dabbled in watercolors—who had arrived in Paris, early in the century, somewhat mousy, tailored, and prim. Within a year they were habitués of the local cafes, Miss Mars had dyed her hair flaming orange, and both appeared in public so heavily made up their faces had the appearance of masks. Alice [Toklas] had met Miss Mars at one of the Saturday evenings at the rue de Fleurus [the Stein–Toklas salon], and they had discussed make-up together—it was, then, a new fashion—classifying the women present according to types. . . .[133]

Miss Furr was portrayed by Stein as having left her father and mother's home to go off and live with Miss Skeene, but the extent to which the lives of Furr and Skeene parallel those of Squire and Mars is unknown. In the Fall of 1933,

*On "gay" see footnote referring to the song the "Gay Young Clerk in the Dry Goods Store" (1868); footnote referring to "Dodo Regay" (1921, Aug.); and the footnote on the song from *Bitter Sweet* (1929–1936). A three-act farce, "The Gay Young Bride" (1923), included a song of the same title sung by Tom Martelle, "America's Greatest Female Impersonator" (sheet music in collection of Marshall Weeks). Also see "gay" in the index. The earliest known documented use of "gay" to mean "homosexual" is that listed by Noel Ersine in *A Glossary of Prison Slang* (1933): "gay cat," a "homosexual boy" (quoted by Eric Partridge in *A Dictionary of the Underworld* [1950], p. 280). The earliest usage in the *OED Supplement* (1972) is "Geycat," a "homosexual boy" (1935; the source is N. Ersine's *Underworld and Prison Slang*). Also see 1938, March 4.

when Maud Hunt Squire wrote to Gertrude Stein, she and Mars were still living together. Squire reported that she and Mars liked living in Vence, near

> Nice & the shore—which is gay & sophisticated. You see Miss Furr still likes gay things & being gay & wanting everybody & everything else to be gay.

Squire ended: "With lots of love to you both—Miss Furr and Miss Skeene." [268–69] Whatever "gay" meant to her, Squire was still its enthusiastic advocate and proselytizer.

Read slowly, Stein's repetitious lines lose their obscurity, and Miss Furr emerges as the heroine of a primitively painted female folk-tale, an American woman's saga of independence, survival, and even social leadership in being "gay."

Stein's "Miss Furr and Miss Skeene" began:

> Helen Furr had quite a pleasant home. Mrs. Furr was quite a pleasant woman. Mr. Furr was quite a pleasant man. Helen Furr had quite a pleasant voice a voice quite worth cultivating. She did not mind working. She worked to cultivate her voice. She did not find it gay living in the same place where she had always been living. She went to a place where some were cultivating something, voices and other things needing cultivating. She met Georgine Skeene there who was cultivating her voice which some thought was quite a pleasant one. Helen Furr and Georgine Skeene lived together then. Georgine Skeene liked travelling. Helen Furr did not care about travelling, she liked to stay in one place and be gay there. They were together then and travelled to another place and stayed there and were gay there.

They were "not very gay there, just gay there."

Helen Furr, however, "was gayer and gayer there, that is to say she found ways of being gay there." "To be regularly gay was to do everyday the gay thing that they did every day." That was "to end every day at the same time." "They were gay every day."

"They did go back to where Helen Furr had a pleasant enough home and then Georgine Skeene went to a place where her brother had quite some distinction." Every few years they both went visiting "to where Helen Furr had quite a pleasant home." "Certainly Helen Furr would not find it gay to stay, she did not find it gay." She

> said she would not stay where she did not find it gay, she said she found it gay where she did stay and she did stay there where many were cultivating something. . . . She always did find it gay there.

Furr and Skeene lived where many were "cultivating in themselves something." They "did then learn many ways to be gay." They were "learning little things in ways of being gay." They were learning "gay little things, they were gay inside them the same amount they had been gay."

Then "Georgine Skeene went away to stay two months with her brother. Helen Furr "did not go then to stay with her father and her mother." She

> stayed there where they had been regularly living the two of them and she would then certainly not be lonesome, she would go on being gay. She did go on being gay. She was not any more gay but she was gay longer every day than they had been being gay when they were together being gay. . . . She learned a few more little ways of being gay. . . .
>
> She was not lonesome then, she was not at all feeling any need of having Georgine Skeene. She was not astonished at this thing. She would have been a little astonished by this thing but she knew she was not astonished at anything and so she was not astonished at this thing not astonished at not feeling any need of having Georgine Skeene.

Helen Furr "used her voice." And she "was never tired of being gay that way." She had "learned very many little ways to use in being gay." And "Very many were telling about using other ways in being gay."

> They did not live together then Helen Furr and Georgine Skeene. Helen Furr lived there the longer where they had been living. . . . Then neither of them were living there any longer. Helen Furr was living somewhere else then and telling some about being gay and she was gay then and she was living quite regularly then. . . . She remembered all the little ways of being gay. . . . She told many then the way of being gay, she taught very many then little ways they could use in being gay. She was living very well, she was gay then, she went on living then, she was regular in being gay, she always was living very well and was gay very well and was telling about little ways one could be learning to use in being gay, and later was telling them quite often, telling them again and again.

NEWS REPORT/CROSSING MAN

# 1923, June 20
## *N. Y. Times:* Fred G. Thompson/Mrs. Frances Carrick

*The Times* reported the arrest, June 19, in Chicago of Fred G. Thompson, who had lived for thirteen years as " 'Mrs.' Frances Carrick, legal wife of Frank Carrick."[15] Reports of men passing as women are rarer than stories of women passing as men. Perhaps fewer men tried to pass as women, for whom fewer employment opportunities existed. Also, a crossing man lost status, while a crossing woman gained it. Observers may have also been more reluctant to report crossing men.

"Mrs. Frances Carrick" had been accused by the widow of Richard Tesmer of being the " 'terrible woman who killed my husband.' " When Mrs. Carrick was brought to the police station, an examination by two doctors had "caused the police to change their plans for taking the 'slim girl' in the dark blue silk dress to the women's detention quarters." Beneath the silk blouse "the physicians found a device which gave feminine curves. Cheap silk stockings and pointed-toed slippers concealed masculine calves."

At the trial on October 3, 1923, *The Times* reported that Fred Thompson (alias Mrs. Frances Carrick) had testified

> in the low tones a woman might use, nervously clasped and unclasped his hands, and sobbed as he told of his double life.
>
> After his marriage to Carrick, he testified, he married Marie Clark, but did not live with her.
>
> When asked by his attorney if he killed Tesmer while garbed as a woman, Thompson answered:
>
> "No, gentlemen, I could not kill a cat or a dog."
>
> The witness then covered his face with his hands and sobbed.
>
> After a brief cross-examination Thompson was excused by Justice Caverly, who remarked: "That will be all, lady."

A jury found Thompson not guilty after deliberating about two hours. *The Times* added:

> Thompson has posed for twenty years as a woman, and for fourteen years as the wife of Frank Carrick.

During the trial the husband, Frank Carrick, had taken the stand to testify on behalf of Thompson. But "When he admitted that he had been married to Thompson," the presiding judge agreed with the State's objection that the husband could not testify in defense of his wife.


♀ BOOK REVIEW/RESISTANCE

# 1924, May 4
## *N.Y. Times Book Review:* Sylvia Stevenson's *Surplus*

"Self-Expression Again" was the heading over a *Times* review of *Surplus,* published in New York.[16] In the novel a "love" distinct, but not necessarily separate from, "sex" and "passion," characterized one woman's deep feeling for another. This review is interesting and useful as one of several explicitly setting a book in historical perspective.* The review opened:

> Fifty years ago [1874] such a novel . . . would have been impossible, for girls fashioned of such emotional timbre as Sally Wraith simply did not exist. Or if they did exist they never dared to express themselves. It is only in modern times and since Dr. Freud flung the gates open to many a chafing inhibition

---

*For other reviews presenting such a historical perspective see 1928, May 20, and "historical perspective" in the index.

that the Sally Wraiths began seriously "expressing" themselves. There are two types of modern young women and Sally Wraith belongs to the second category. The first includes the eugenic pioneers, the preachers of the equality of the sexes who believe that woman's primary function is the establishment of the home. . . . [For such women it] is the method that has changed and not the objective. The second type, to which Sally has been assigned, are still more revolutionary. For them the objective has changed. They no longer believe in the old household gods. Rather do they believe in complete self-expression as their individual natures may guide them, and if they are emotionally unfitted for the role of wife and mother (as in the case of Sally Wraith) they pursue other roads.

Sally Wraith is the independent type of modern young woman who is not particularly intrigued by the idea of marriage and who draws away from it. But she is lonely in spite of her restlessness and does not like the thought of being alone all her days. Therefore she goes to live with another independent young woman, Averil, and their days pass pleasantly enough, first in diggings in London, and later in a country cottage. The long expected and inevitable man makes his appearance and Averil falls in love with him, marries, and goes her way. But Sally, who has conceived a deep and vast affection for Averil, cannot dispose of her life so easily. Between her and the prospect of love and a home looms the shadow of Averil. Such a subject is difficult to handle with any seriousness, but . . . for the most part the book does what it sets out to do.

The whole core of the story, the lesson which the modern young Sally Wraith seems to imbibe from her experiences, is contained in a single paragraph which may be quoted as representative of the dominating motif of the book:

> It came upon Sally with the force of a new truth that love, and not the reproductive instinct, is the greatest force in the world—the only human attribute that is certain to survive time, if humanity itself survives. And it had nothing whatever to do with the question of sex. . . . love may exist alongside passion or without it—it is the same power, greater than any instinct, greater than the atoms and rays and currents of which the scientists are busy building them a new conception of the universe, immeasurably greater than the brains of those same scientists. And to limit the fullest manifestation of that power to beings between whom the physical tie of matehood or parenthood exists is like declaring that electricity can only be generated by one particular kind of dynamo.

What Miss Stevenson is saying here is that love between two women or two men may be just as great and intense and exalted as between man and woman. It is to be doubted that she actually proves this in her novel, for too many of her premises must be implicity accepted if the reader is to find any pleasure in her book. . . . In the particular case of Sally and Averil, however, it seems to be true that Sally, at least, has reached such a plane of mental love. Averil attempts no such thing and as a result she seems rather more natural and less wholly theoretical and speculative than Sally.

Sally's attitude after she has parted from Averil seems to be that second love is not worth while. . . . One must accept Sally as an individual case and let it go at that. . . .

A mixed review in the Greensboro, North Carolina *Daily News,* August 10, 1924, commented

Miss Stevenson . . . is mistaken in thinking that the mere characterization of a more or less perverted woman is sufficient content for a good novel.

Forrest Reid, in the *Literary Review of the New York Evening Post,* called *Surplus* "absolutely, almost fiercely, clean"—and "unique." As an "analysis of an emotion that, though not common, is doubtless commoner than we believe," the book deserved "high praise" for its "skill," "sanity," "courage," and "insight."*

The *Book Review Digest* of 1924 described *Surplus* as "the story of a girl who believed there was such a thing as perfect friendship." Sally Wraith and Averil Kennion were called "exponents of modernism and careers for girls." Sally, the "unusual" one, "feels marriage is not necessary for happiness," yet has an "insidious fear of being alone." She was said to shower "affection" upon the "more normal" Averil. The latter "is annoyed by her intensity of devotion and absorbing jealousy." At the end,

tho years have passed, a chance glimpse of Averil is enough to make Sally send away forever the man to whom she is betrothed. We leave her going up the empty road alone—surplus.

INTIMACY

# 1924, September
# F. O. Matthiessen to Russell Cheney:
### *"We must create everything for ourselves"*

A summary of the life of Francis Otto Matthiessen in the *Dictionary of American Biography* (1975) mentions "the extraordinary insights into the life of the working artist he received from the painter Russell Cheney."[17] Matthiessen had met Cheney while returning to college in England in 1924. "Their friendship was almost instantaneous; their attachment also proved to be deep and lifelong," lasting twenty-one years until Cheney's death in 1945. A book Matthiessen wrote about Cheney was, in part, his "tribute to the closest personal relationship of his life." Later, Matthiessen taught literature at Harvard.

*Forrest Reid's own novels with male homosexual content are cited by Ian Young, *Male Homosexual in Literature* (1975), pp. 110–11.

For most of his students and younger colleagues Matthiessen's homosexuality was suggested, if at all, only by the fact that his circle was more predominantly heterosexual than was usual in Harvard literary groups at the time and that he was unusually hostile to homosexual colleagues who mixed their academic and sexual relations.

Most of Matthiessen's

writings clearly reflect a life larger than the "academic"—a word which ... Matthiessen often used in a pejorative sense. He thought of himself as a socialist from the time he was at Oxford. ... He worked for or supported numbers of liberal, pacifist, or radical causes.

The death of Russell Cheney and other close friends, and the isolation Matthiessen felt during the Cold War era, were said to have caused a major depression, and he committed suicide in 1950, leaving a note which said, in part:

How much the state of the world has to do with my state of mind I do not know. But as a Christian and a socialist believing in international peace, I find myself terribly oppressed by the present tensions.

The first meeting of Matthiessen and Cheney on the ocean liner *Paris,* in September 1924, was described by Matthiessen in a letter to a friend written six months later. Here Matthiessen called Cheney "Rat," the nickname the two had adopted, as Cheney would call Matthiessen "Devil." (Most of the bracketed inserts were added by the editor of the published letters, to disguise Matthiessen's references to members of the Yale senior society, Skull and Bones, to honor its code of secrecy.)
Matthiessen recalled his meeting with Cheney:

I found Rat on board the "Paris." We fell into an easy intimacy from the start. There was little restraint on the part of either of us; in a day or two I was talking to him of my family and of my religion as freely as I would have to [my closest friends], and he had shown me probably his most sacred possession—a little leather case containing a picture of his mother. By morning of the fourth day I found that by laughing and kidding and being serious by turns we had [told each other about most of the important events of our lives]. There remained one signal omission: sex. I realized that in order to be on a basis of complete truth and freedom with him I must drag out the skeleton of my twisted psychology that I had [disclosed to a few intimate friend in New Haven several months before]. All that morning and afternoon I gulped for courage and the right opportunity without success. I steered the conversation to Havelock Ellis, but lost my nerve at the crucial moment. My unsuccessful artfulness was very amusing. That evening while we stood at the rail watching the stars, the formulated words were half a dozen times on my lips, but I put off and put off: Later, I said, Later. You see the crux of the situation was that I did not want to be emotional or alarmist. I wanted to treat of the matter seriously, but calmly. And being a kid I was nervous and excited.

Came two o-clock, and we went down to our cabins. Now, I said, steeled by desperation, now, now, I'll never get up courage enough if I don't do it now. So I sat Rat down in a chair in my cabin on the pretense of giving him some fruit before we went to bed. And while his mouth was stuffed with a pear, I said in a voice that attempted to maintain its usual pass the bread, please conversational tone, but which sounded queer and remote for all that:

"I know it won't make any difference to our friendship, but there's one thing I've got to tell you: before [my extraordinary senior year at Yale] I was sexually inverted. Of course I've controlled it since. . . ."

The munching of the pear died away. There followed perhaps half a minute of the most heavily freighted silence I have ever felt. Then, in a far away voice I had never heard came the answer: "My God, feller, you've turned me upside down. I'm that way too."

I was as amazed as he had been. For minutes we were speechless as the truth sank in upon us that here at last we had each found someone who could not only understand, but *feel* our sexual complexities and difficulties. Then the tension was broken, and our dammed up experience began to pour out. They were very similar, only that the knowledge of what he was had come to Rat much later in life than it had to me. By four o'clock we were exhausted and went to bed. As he left my Cabin, Rat lightly brushed my hair with his hand—a gesture of the pure essence of friendly gentleness, and turning said, "God, you're a slick feller to have had the nerve to tell me this. Of course our friendship was all formed before, but this can't help [but] strengthen it."

All through that night the sense of the other feller's being surged into and pervaded our hearts. But even then we had no comprehension of the magnitude of the transformation of our lives. If anyone had told me then that I was in love, I would probably have laughed. The last two days on the boat passed swiftly. The last night we sat on the couch in Rat's cabin talking, his head in my lap. There was tremendous joy in his nearness, nothing more. After a few hours my back began to be cramped, and I got up and stretched, and then lay down beside him. We were both fully dressed, but the subtle, electric quality that ran through my whole being as our knees and shoulders lightly brushed against each other is indescribable. I had attained complete harmony with another spirit for the first time in my life. Rat had shown me new visions of beauty. I had shown him fresh fountains of simplicity and peace. Many hours we lay there, saying little, but feeling the steady, warm throb of the body at our side. About dawn Rat turned and with full red lips kissed me fully on the lips. The very tips of my fingers tingled with the new dynamic electric force as I ran them lightly through his black hair.

That was all. The next morning we shook hands and I got off the boat at Plymouth. I knew I had a new, unbelievably rich friendship. I knew that I should write Rat often. I knew that I would be with him in Italy at Christmas. But it took absence and separation to make us realize the full sense of what had happened to us. I cannot hope to trace for you the progress of this gradual realization. I can only say that I wrote him five times in the first week, and every day after that. . . .[17–18]

On September 23, 1924, Matthiessen wrote to Cheney, trying to give a name and definition to their relationship:

. . . Little by little the largeness of what has happened sweeps over me. I thought I realized it all that last night together; but first the intellect sees, and then when it has created its imaginative symbolism it gives the whole man something to live by. I saw very clearly that night and called it a marriage. The imagination has since been working, and I live body and soul in this new relationship.

Marriage is a mere term; only as a dynamic vivid thing does it dominate life. That is: you can visualize marriage or you can live it. Now I am living it.

Marriage! What a strange word to be applied to two men! Can't you hear the hell-hounds of society baying full pursuit behind us? But that's just the point. We are beyond society. We've said thank you very much, and stepped outside and closed the door. In the eyes of the unknowing world we are a talented artist of wealth and position and a promising young graduate student. In the eyes of the knowing world we would be pariahs, outlaws, degenerates. This is indeed the price we pay for the unforgivable sin of being born different from the great run of mankind.

And so we have a marriage that was never seen on land or sea! . . . It is a marriage that demands nothing and gives everything. It does not limit the affections of the two parties, it gives their scope greater radiance and depth. Oh it is strange enough. It has no ring, and no vows, and no [wedding presents from your friends], and no children. And so of course it has none of the coldness of passion, but merely the serene joy of companionship. It has no three hundred and sixty-five breakfasts opposite each other at the same table; and yet it desires frequent companionship, devotion, laughter. Its bonds indeed form the service that is perfect freedom.

I have hesitated about writing this. I am always afraid that I will be thought too bold. But what I am now experiencing is what I have deeply known only once before—and that vicariously, [when from a good friend] I heard a story of unbelievable beauty. And now that story is my own.

How many, when reading this, would think so? Ah there's the mockery of it: those gates of society are of iron. And when you're outside, you've got to live in yourself alone, unless—o beatissimus—you are privileged to find another wanderer in the waste land.[29–30]

On November 4, 1924, Matthiessen wrote to Cheney:

As I read over your letters of yesterday I become more and more convinced that you are right on the question of "labels." "The splendid untrammeled freedom of love"—that's the essence of it all, right. Why give it a name that really doesn't belong to it? It isn't a marriage except in a very unusual mystical sense, and so don't adopt the conventional terms to speak of it. Our union has no name, no label; in the world it does not exist. It is simply the unpalpable, inexpressible fullness of our lives.[46]

The following day Matthiessen wrote:

Yesterday I bought and read through Edward Carpenter's "The Intermediate Sex." It doesn't tell us anything we don't know already, but presents the position of the Uranian in society in an appealing fashion. The idea that what we have is one of the divine gifts; that such as you and I are the advance guard of any hope for a spirit of brotherhood. I have marked and checked some passages that struck me particularly, and am sending it on. You can skim through it quickly.

Reading it brought back to me the last occasion when I had a book on the subject. That was last spring—here at Oxford I was reading Ellis's volume on inversion. Then for the first time it was completely brought home to me that I was what I was by *nature*. Before that, when I told [a few close friends] I thought . . . that it was entirely a question of early environment, having been led into the wrong sexual channels by older boys at school. Well [one friend] doubted, and [he] was right. How clearly I can now see every act and friendship of my boyhood interpreted from my proper sexual temperament. But reading Ellis last spring was something of a shock. I remember coming face to face with the fact that I could probably never marry, serious and wide-eyed. I told [the same friends last June] how matters seemed to be tending, but they refused to take it seriously. Oh, no, Devil, you'll get married all right. Great fellers, they didn't want to face the possibility of my being unhappy. But I wasn't satisfied. I wanted to be understood. So when I visited [Russell Davenport, or "Mitch"] at Colorado Springs, and we spent evening after evening when Harriet had gone to bed, sitting out in the car somewhere in the dark on Broadmoor, telling [about our lives], I outlined to him in rigid detail all my repression, how I sat reading Ellis, sexually aroused, seeing no hope of ever expressing it. I told Mitch that I didn't want to be alarmist—wasn't sure. But it seemed to me that I might very well likely be altogether homosexual; and in that case I didn't know whether I could keep from getting morbid without some expression. Two alternatives: self-abuse and the old business with men. Which? "I know which I'd do" said Mitch very seriously, leaning over toward me as I sat beside him in the car, "self-abuse." "I don't know," said I. "But let's not get depressed." And I changed the subject.

Two alternatives? I had never dreamed of the third. If I had read this Carpenter book last spring I would have been surprised at the beautiful pictures he gives of love between men. Was it possible? I had known only lust. I prided myself that it had never touched the purity of my friendships. Was it possible for love and friendship to be blended into one? But before I had time to even ask the question it was answered. What is this wistful yearning I feel on these grey foggy mornings? It's not fog in my throat but an inchoate surge from my heart. What makes this new sensitive tingling in the tips of my fingers and on my lips? It isn't the cold. It's love.[47–48]

On January 29, 1925, Matthiessen wrote to Cheney:

Of course this life of ours is entirely new—neither of us know of a parallel case. We stand in the middle of an uncharted, uninhabited country. That there have been other unions like ours is obvious, but we are unable to draw on their experience. We must create everything for ourselves. And creation is never easy.[71]

On January 31, Matthiessen wrote to Cheney that many of William Blake's poems

glorify the freedom and beauty of human love. Their implication is that the sexual act alone can stimulate and unite the highest and lowest functions of man. Before our life together this might have bewildered me. Now I believe it to be true. How many times when lying limply beside you an ineffable sense of serenity, security and confidence swept over me. I was part of you. You were part of me. Didn't we actually feel of the same flesh as we dropped off to sleep in each other's arms? No more loneliness, no more dark corners where the light of radiant sympathy could not penetrate. But a solid union of understanding, shoulder to shoulder—like our San Marco figures [sculpture seen in Italy]—with life before us.[72]

Matthiessen added:

Oh, the majesty and abundance of knowing what you are, of having faced life fully and of having admitted that you and I are born unlike the majority and yet have found a love more complete and sacred than any I had dreamed.[73]

NEWS REPORTS

## 1924, December 5
### N. Y. Times: Fritz Haarmann, the "vampire slayer"

A special cable from Germany reported the start of the trial, in Hanover, of Fritz Haarmann, "Accused of twenty-seven murders, which makes his case unparalleled in the history of Germany and possibly of all other countries."[18] The Times, in the 1920s, was circumspect in referring to the sexual aspect of the murders—simply stating that all the victims were males.

During the trial's proceedings, Times stories contained numbers of guarded references to Haarmann's relationships with males. Asked if "a certain youth was among the victims," Haarmann had replied, as reported on December 5: "No, I did not kill that chap, but let his name stand on the list—I don't mind."[3:5] Another report, of December 7, said: "Often with a smiling face," Haarmann confessed to murder after murder," telling "exactly how he had killed the unfortunate youths who had fallen into his power, showing a certain pride as he narrated the scenes."[30:2]

On December 12, *The Times* reported that "Every day of the trial" brought "new and revolting details of this vampire slayer's methods," his ways of killing "men and boys."* The Federation of German Women's Clubs had protested that "Inestimable harm accrues to our youth from the publication of the terrible details involved in this trial." A December 13 report said that one of the murdered youths had "disappeared after he met a man at the railway station who had promised him work."[17:7] The "alleged connivance of the railway station police in Haarmann's underworld activities" was discussed at the trial. As reported on December 14, "Evidence was given to show that the doubtful nature of the butcher's nocturnal goings-on was generally known about the station and that he was often seen to leave with men he had picked up there, some of whom are assumed to have been victims of his killing mania."[10:1] And on December 16, the police were reported as investigating "charges of police complicity in the underworld activities of Haarmann."[12:3]

Two days later, on December 18, three German "alienists" were reported to have found Haarmann responsible for his acts. Haarmann had earlier claimed that "in the perpetration of the crimes he was in a state of abnormal excitement." One psychiatrist also spoke of Haarmann's "inordinate vanity," and said the murderer wanted "a big monument erected over his grave with an inscription testifying to his breaking the world's record for wholesale murders."[24:1]

A *Times* story, of December 19, mentioned that most of Haarmann's victims were "young men," and added:

> Haarmann's efforts to play upon the sympathies of the jury by reference to his love for his mother and his loyalty as a soldier were cut short by the Judge, who asked whether he desired to rehearse the whole story of his life.
> "No," replied the prisoner, "but humanity should not think me worse than I am."[14:1]

On December 20, *The Times* reported that Haarmann and an accomplice, Hans Grans, had been found guilty of twenty-four murders and sentenced to death. The court had "excluded the presence of abnormal pathological traits," and found Haarmann "in full possession of his mental faculties."

Grans's lawyer denied charges that "such an affair was possible only in Germany." and declared a "long chain of cases leads from Gilles de Retz, via Landru, Loeb and Leopold, to Haarmann."[1:2] (All were murderers; Nathan Leopold and Richard Loeb had been tried and found guilty in the United States, in 1924, for the murder of a young male.)

---

*On the association of homosexual and vampire see p. 169 and backnote 45, p. 688; also see "Vampire" in index.

BOOK REVIEW

## 1925, February 22
### N. Y. Times Book Review: Thomas Mann's
### Death in Venice and Other Stories

In at least two of the three stories included in this collection, said an anonymous reviewer, "the protagonist is an author, middle-aged, over-refined and smitten in his gray hairs with a homesickness for the life of the senses which he has sacrificed to his art without finding peace or release."[19]

In the story "Death in Venice"

> Gustav von Aschenbach, a writer of international fame, suddenly tires of his hermit life in Munich and takes the old, old trail to the South. Crumbling, ill-famed Venice is the magnet to his morbidezza, and Venice, plague-smitten, raises esthetic anguish to an almost intolerable pitch. "The picture of the diseased and neglected city hovering desolately before him aroused vague hopes beyond the bounds of reason. . . ."
>
> On the sands of the Lido the forlorn beauty of the pagan world becomes incarnate for Gustav in the person of Tadzio, a beautiful Polish lad, marked for early death, who plays before his window daily. A strange metaphysical love for the boy grows up in the heart of the grizzling philosopher. "It seemed to him as though the pale and lovely lure out there were smiling to him, nodding to him . . . were signalling to him to come out, were vaguely guiding toward egregious promises." For Tadzio's sake the man disregards repeated warnings to depart, follows the boy from afar through one ill-smelling "calle" after anothe and dies on the day of his departure, less from the cholera than from an over-charged heart. Given the theme of the story, it should in fairness be added that it is written with exquisite tact and delicacy and that its implications will only be misunderstood by the coarse and literal mind.

BOOK REVIEW/RESISTANCE

## 1925, May 31
### N. Y. Times Book Review: Cyril Hume's Cruel Fellowship

This novel, said an anonymous reviewer, "concerns Claude Fisher and his unfortunate environment," starting with his "early childhood"[20] The influence of Freudian psychology was indicated by this stress on childhood and its influence on "sex." Various euphemisms were still given to a certain unspeakable erotic eccentricity. The author's concern with the salability of such themes is also notable, as is his apparent desire to justify his "eccentric" character.

Claude Fisher, said the reviewer,

was born in a New England village, and reared by his widowed mother, two maiden aunts, and an epicene uncle.* This, Mr. Hume seems to say, gave Fisher a false outlook on life, which, of course, means sex. A childhood and youth of "don't," of hush, hush, and of a morbidly induced self-consciousness is followed by an unhappy term of years at a college, and a wretchedly paid job in a New York bookshop. . . . The novel is essentially a character study of Claude Fisher, with didactic implications on the subject of sexual education, or what the young man ought to know.

Claude is himself slightly epicene. A girl in a dance hall, a blatant gold digger, for whom he conceives a fatuous infatuation, calls him an "old woman." He is persuaded to give up his charming, if sentimental, fiancée by the man he calls his only friend, whom others call "the Violet."

When the author's "mouthpiece," at the novel's end, called Claude Fisher

"a creature of dreams" who "had no defense against reality," it can but seem a peculiarly egregrious form of special pleading. It also seems a rather abortive attempt to clothe the eccentric figure of Claude with universal significance, in line with the previous inanity: "There is something of Claude in everybody."

Fisher's story was that of "a mal-adjusted man, who is, apparently, unable to win friendship or love. . . ."

The "fear that his chief character and the situation may be found 'unpleasant,' " was expressed by the author, who "anticipates a rejection of Fisher." One character remarks that readers won't " 'condemn an honest portrayal of anything.' " The author himself declared in the book that he wanted to make " 'as much money as I possibly can as soon as I possibly can, by writing stuff that readers will pay for.' " He wondered if the present book's " 'unpleasantness' " will " 'appeal.' "

RESISTANCE

# 1925, June 4
# The Society for Human Rights, Chicago:
*"Bettering the living conditions of the intermediate type"*

On December 24, 1924, the state of Illinois issued a charter to the Society for Human Rights, founded by Henry Gerber, and officially dedicated to "promote and protect the interests" of people who, because of "mental and physical abnormalities," were hindered in the "pursuit of happiness."[21]† The Society would also

---

*For "epicene" (having characteristics of the other sex; or, lacking characteristics of either sex), applied in *The Times* to the love of woman for woman, see 1926, May 9.
†For the charter of the Society for Human Rights see *GAH*, pp. 386–87.

"combat the public prejudices against" such people by the dissemination of "scientific" information.

Gerber and others in the group were arrested on trumped-up charges, jailed, and publicized in a scandal-mongering Chicago newspaper. Though the case was finally dismissed on the grounds that the arrests had occurred without a warrant, that prosecution put an end to the earliest documented homosexual rights organization in the United States.

In 1953, twenty-nine years after the incorporation of the Society for Human Rights, Henry Gerber briefly described the group's fate in a letter, published anonymously in the newly established homosexual emancipation magazine *ONE*.* Gerber wrote:

> In 1925 [*sic*—1924], I met several inverts in Chicago and conceived a society on the order of that existing in Germany at that time, Society for Human Rights and we published a few issues of a paper, called Friendship and Freedom and even had a charter from the State of Illinois.†
>
> But one of our members turned out to be a married man (bisexual) and his wife complained to a social worker that he carried on his trade in front of his children and the social worker found a copy of our paper and all of us (4) were arrested without a warrant and dragged to jail.
>
> I managed to get out on bail and hired a good lawyer but the first judge was prejudiced and threatened to give us the limit ($200 fine) but I got a better lawyer who was politically connected and we also got a new judge, who was rumored "to be queer himself" and he dismissed the case and fined the married member $10 and cost.
>
> I was then a postal clerk and a stupid and mean post office inspector brought the case before the Federal commission with an eye to have us indicted for publishing an "obscene paper" although of course, like your paper, no physical references were made. But the commissioner turned it down. However, the post office inspector, even in spite of us being acquitted, arranged my dismissal from the post office. The whole thing cost me all my savings of about $800 and no one helped us, not even the homosexuals of Chicago.
>
> Of course, I see now the faults we committed, we should have had prominent doctors on our side and money on hand for defense, and a good lawyer. . . .‡

Little is now known of the Society for Human Rights. But evidence indicates that some member, probably Henry Gerber, had sought affiliation with an English sexual reform group, the British Society for the Study of Sex Psychology.

The British Society had been established in 1914, with Edward Carpenter

---

*A longer description, omitting some details in this original letter, was published by Gerber in *ONE Magazine* in 1963, and reprinted in *GAH*, pp. 388–93.

†No copies of the paper, *Friendship and Freedom,* are now known to exist; if either of the two published copies could be found this would be a major discovery in American homosexual history.

‡*ONE Magazine* (Los Angeles), vol. 1, no. 7 (July 1953), p. 22.

as first president, Laurence Housman as chair, George Ives and Stella Browne among the active members, Havelock Ellis and others as backers.* The group was concerned with "sexual psychology" in its "medical, juridicial and sociological aspects," and with educating the public toward greater toleration on sexual matters. Several active members were, as they called themselves, "sexual inverts," or early supporters of invert rights. Ives was the founder of a secret invert emancipation organization of which the socialist-feminist Housman was a member. A special sub-committee of The British Society for the Study of Sex Psychology focused on sexual inversion. Members of the Society gave lectures, and the Society published seventeen pamphlets between 1915 and 1933.

On June 4, 1925, George Ives's handwritten minutes of the executive committee of the British Society for the Study of Sex Psychology report:

> A letter was read from the Society for Human Rights, Chicago, announcing their formation and suggesting cooperation. It was agreed to reply pointing out that the aspect of the subject which appeared to be their particular interest [the rights of "intermediate types"] was only one of the aspects covered by our society, and suggesting membership for any of their members who would care to receive publications as issued.

The executives of the British Society were afraid of any direct affiliation with the American group dedicated specifically to the rights of "intermediates."

On August 6, 1925, the minutes of the British Society record:

> Capt. Green read a letter he had received from the Society for Human Rights, Chicago, relating to the prosecution of their officers, to which he promised to reply.

(Neither the letter from Chicago nor Green's reply seems to have been preserved in George Ives's papers.)

In October 1925, the printed "Eleventh Annual Report" of the British Society declared that it had been "in correspondence with" Magnus Hirschfeld's Institute for Sexual Science, Berlin, with another such institute in The Hague, and with "the Society for Human Rights, U.S.A."

A rough draft of this annual report includes a paragraph deleted from the printed version, providing a few more details about the U. S. group, and even a quote from the group's correspondence:

> The Society for Human Rights was formed in Chicago at the beginning of the year with "the Ultimate aim of bettering the living conditions of the intermediate type of persons." They started with an ambitious programme

*For Carpenter and Ellis see index; for Housman see 1934, May; for Ives see 1914, and 1934, June 4; for Browne see p. 370, and Sheila Rowbotham, *A New World for Women: Stella Browne—Socialist Feminist* (London: Pluto Press, 1977); on the British Society for the Study of Sex Psychology see Weeks, *Coming Out.* For additional comment by Henry Gerber on the fate of the Chicago Society, and his feelings about it, see 1940, January 27.

which included the publication of a monthly paper entitled "Friendship and Freedom." Unfortunately their offices [sic—officers] did not scrutinise the qualifications of intending members with sufficient care, and the Society has been involved in legal proceedings from which it has emerged vindicated, but its resources have been severely strained by the cost of these proceedings.

The annual report of the British Society in October 1925, also mentioned that the group had three honorary members in the United States. Two of these were probably Margaret Sanger and Dr. William Robinson.[22] Whether Henry Gerber was a member of the British group is not known.

BOOK REVIEW

## 1925, July 5

### *N. Y. Times Book Review:* Marcel Proust's *The Guermantes Way*

A long analysis of Proust's "complex" work was by Rose Lee.[23] The reviewer mentioned that author Edith Wharton, writing in the *Yale Review* (January 1925), had

> found Proust's central theme to be "the hopeless incurable passion of a sensitive man for a stupid, uncomprehending woman." This does not seem entirely just to an author who is known, among other things, as an authority on sexual inversion.*

Proust's central theme, said *The Times* critic, was that "in a world of fluctuating stimuli 'man is the measure of all things.' "

♀ BOOK REVIEW

## 1925, July 19

### *N. Y. Times Book Review:*
### Marion Mills Miller and David Robinson's *The Songs of Sappho*

Referring to Sappho's one known complete poem, the "Hymn to Aphrodite," in a new translation, *Times* reviewer Percy A. Hutchinson, said:[24]

> Most previous translators, among whom were Sir Edwin Arnold, Thomas Wentworth Higginson, Moreton John Walhouse, and J. Addington Sy-

---

*The medical terminology had reached *The Times*—and was redistributed to the middle class. For the next *Times* reference to "sexual inversion" see 1928, January 8; for a *Times* reference to "The Invert" (a film) see 1926, December 15.

monds, took the unwarranted liberty of changing the sex of the object of
Sappho's love from feminine to masculine. Dr. Miller makes no such compromise with truth.

That Sappho's "majestic" and "passion"-filled poems "should have perished as
the result of deliberate human intention" made the loss especially "appalling."
The reviewer explained:

> The fanatical Christians who in 391 A.D. burned the library at Alexandria
> because the writings it contained were pagan, began the orgy of destruction.
> Some of Sappho's pages escaped, but the destruction was made complete
> when such as remained . . . were publicly burned in Rome and Constantino-
> ple in 1073, by order of Pope Gregory VII. The cause of the Church's
> antipathy to Sappho is only too clearly evident: but the pity of the immola-
> tion is not thereby lessened.*

♀ BOOK REVIEW

## 1925, December 23
### *New Republic:* Naomi Royde-Smith's *Tortoiseshell Cat*

A *New Republic* reviewer praised this English writer's first novel, calling it "modern"—

> also daring because among the threads of passion runs that of homo-sexual
> love. This is handled with a reserve made natural by the innocence of the
> altogether delightful heroine.[25]

A *New York Times* reviewer also liked the novel, but did *not* indicate it touched on
"homo-sexual love."

*Book Review Digest* for 1925 described the novel: Gillian, a teacher at a
"correct school for girls," in England, was led by her "enthusiasm" for literature
and the sound of words into an "indiscreet choice of lines for study." To the
school's head and "to the horrified parents" the lines "mean something quite
different," and Gillian is fired.† Later, Gillian, who is inexperienced in love,

> falls under the influence of an older woman who is all too tragically ex-
> perienced in affairs of the kind. There is a disastrous termination to the
> friendship and Gillian's awakening is sharp and complete.

---

*Though the alleged "cause of the Church's antipathy to Sappho is only to clearly evident"
(and was hinted to refer to the female subjects of her love poems), this love was still too touchy a
subject to be specified in *The Times*. Within a few years, however, the *Times* would be referring directly
to "the vice of Sappho" as "sexual inversion"; see review of Proust's *Cities of the Plain*, 1928, January
8.

†The sexual innocent confronted a new consciousness of a dangerous erotic contained in
language—and eroticism vanquished innocence, and, later, friendship.

## 1925
### Jessie Binford:
*"Little boys . . . soliciting men"*

A summary of "The Year's Work" of the Juvenile Protective Association of Chicago, by its director, provides a brief glimpse of various "homo-sexual practices" and of a little-known support network among destitute boys and men.[26] That young boys actively sought out erotic and remunerative relations with older men, and were not in any simple sense the older men's "victims," is clear from this report:

> The sex appeal made through our cheap magazines and post cards is equalled and excelled by that in certain *theaters,* where the performances are as vulgar and sensual as is found in houses of prostitution. The detailed description in our records of the performances given in a certain West Side theatre and witnessed every afternoon and every evening by a large audience of men and boys would, I am perfectly sure, be barred from our mails because of indecency. It would be interesting to have a psychologist attempt to estimate the effect of such performances on the boys who witness them.
>
> It was through the investigation of these performances that we found the almost unbelievable situation of little boys, as young even as ten years of age, frequenting certain theatres for the purpose of soliciting men for *homo-sexual practices;* and many of these boys have been brought to us by a volunteer worker. We found them to be truants, runaways, defectives—and thus they live. We have been able to be of great assistance to them.

The study of conditions in theaters had led to another study in the summer of 1925, by Nels Anderson,*

> of the *homo-sexual group of men and boys* who have their headquarters in Grant Park, publishing a paper of their own, using a vocabulary which no one outside the group could easily understand. These men and boys constitute a unique and puzzling phenomenon in our complex city life. Homo-sexual problems have extended to the boys' organizations.[12]

---

*Anderson was also the author of *The Hobo; The Sociology of the Homeless Man . . . A Study Prepared for the Chicago Council of Social Agencies Under the Direction of the Committee on Homeless Men* (Chicago: University of Chicago Press, 1923). He later authored (as "Dean Stiff") *The Milk and Honey Route, A Handbook for Hobos* (N. Y.: Vanguard, 1931); and *The Homeless in New York City; A Study* (N. Y.: Welfare Council of New York, 1934).

♀  MEDICAL/RESISTANCE

## 1925
## Dr. William J. Robinson: "Nature's Sex Stepchildren"

In this essay, sex reformer Robinson, influenced by his contacts with homosexuals
and homosexual emancipationists, updated his comments of 1914 (see), and
modified somewhat the condemnatory tone of his earlier article.[27] Robinson's
comments indicate the narrow limits of the toleration upheld by one of the liberal
sexologists of the 1920s. The homosexuals who told their stories to Robinson
may now be seen as engaging in resistance activities. The doctor declared:

> I have had occasion recently to converse with a number of homosexuals of
> both sexes. They told me their life histories, described to me their feelings,
> their aspirations. . . .
> I have met among them lovable, sympathetic types, some men and
> women of high intelligence. My attitude towards homosexuals of both sexes
> has undergone some change, has become broader, more tolerant, perhaps
> even sympathetic; but I am not yet ready to regard the homosexual with the
> same eyes that Dr. Hirschfeld or Edward Carpenter does.
> I still cannot help feeling that there is something "not quite right" with
> the male or female homo.
> The thing that struck me peculiarly in almost all homosexuals is their
> pathetic eagerness to claim . . . as homosexuals people whose homosexuality
> is extremely doubtful. . . . Thus they speak of Shakespeare, Byron and
> Whitman as belonging to their class, as if their homosexuality . . . were a
> well-established historical fact.
> I am afraid that the noble protagonists in the movement for the
> humane treatment of the homosexual are not altogether blameless for
> this. . . .
> The psychology of the eagerness to claim as homosexual as many great
> men and women as possible is a perfectly simple one. . . . Every oppressed
> or despised minority* tries to prove that many of the world's Great belong
> or belonged to it. The epileptic feels great satisfaction when he is told that
> Caesar and Napoleon were epileptics. . . . Even the Jews who really have a
> much larger proportion of both intellectual and moral geniuses than any
> other nation try occasionally to claim . . . great men whose Jewish origin is
> quite doubtful. . . .[475]
> But more than pathetic, absurdly grotesque is the peculiar claim put
> forward by some inverts, that they . . . stand on a higher level than those

---

*This is one of the earliest American conceptualizations of homosexuals as a "minority"—one
"oppressed or despised." It may be noted that Robinson's civil libertarian "minority" ideology was
consistent with his firm assumption of heterosexual superiority. For an earlier reference to "minority"
see 1914, Ives. For later references to homosexuals as a "minority" see that term in the index.

normally sexed, that they are the specially favored of the muses of poetry and the arts. . . .

In spite of the statements . . . of my good friend Dr. Magnus Hirschfeld, . . . I cannot help regarding the homosexuals as abnormal, even if not inferior. There are exceptions of course. But as a general thing, I insist, the homosexuals are mentally, morally and physically different from the normally sexed men and women. Let us agree with Hirschfeld to call homosexuality merely a "variation," an intersex or a third sex—this does not change the essence of the thing. A creature with male genitalia and a female psyche is an abnormality; and a creature with female genitals and a man's soul and desires is an abnormality. Calling it a "variation," a sport of Nature, does not . . . change the essence of the abnormality. No, the homosexuals are not superior, but with some glorious exceptions, *taken all in all,* rather inferior, human beings, and homosexuality . . . *is* a misfortune, and . . . it is quite proper to consider them . . . as Nature's stepchildren. And this will be the case even after all the cruel laws against the homosexual have been removed from the statute books of all countries.

A particularly obnoxious specimen—and I have met several of them —is the homosexual who boasts of his sexual exploits, . . . and what prominent men fought for his favors. One such man I met only this morning— a toothless ruin of seventy [born, then, about 1855], and up to recently a successful stage dancer. In the cause of science, and out of politeness I had to listen to his story, but I felt quite nauseated and had to ask him to "cut it short."

A normal Don Juan is disgusting, a homosexual specimen of this variety—ten times more so.

. . . Whenever I speak of homosexuality I speak of true congenital homosexuality. The venal or acquired variety, male prostitution, pederasty, etc., is not homosexuality. It is an acquired perversion and can . . . in the majority of instances be cured.[476]

As to laws against homosexuality, it goes without saying, that I am opposed to any. . . .[477]

♀ BOOK REVIEW

## 1926, May 9
### N. Y. Times Book Review:
### Dimitri S. Merezhkovsky's *The Birth of the Gods*

*The Times* indicated that *The Birth of the Gods* touched on an "epicene" affection between women.[28] The Cretan Empire, fourteen hundred years before Christ, was the setting of a novel whose protagonist was Dio, "virgin priestess of the Great Mother." Dio's "epicene loves" included her "romance with Eoia," another female. This romance was "less convincing than the late Pierre Louÿs's treatment of similar themes, although they were informed by no such lofty purpose" as the present author's.*

♀  BOOK REVIEW

# 1926, June 20
## N. Y. Times Book Review: Thomas Burke's "The Pash"

In a *Times* review of Burke's short stories the passionate feelings of a young woman for an older was defined as a naturally passing stage. An illicit, "secret desire" of an older female social worker for the young woman was shown emerging to consciousness as problematic.[29] This book of stories, said reviewer John W. Crawford,

> touches upon a peculiarly poignant situation in "The Pash," which is the variety of impassioned attachments of a young girl for an older woman that American college girls know as a "crush."† To Amy, Miss Englefield represents order, refinement, competence, vision, wider horizons, and everything else that her dingy, muddled home life and the inconceivable depression of her days in the factory have never given her. To the welfare worker, Amy is a belated answer to a repressed and denied secret desire. Miss Englefield lets down all her defenses before Amy and is, of course, betrayed to the first personable young man who stumbles into the life of Amy. The resolution of the tension which develops in Miss Englefield verges upon melodrama, and clouds with a slight dissatisfaction the reticent and dignified treatment Mr. Burke has given a difficult theme.

♀  PLAY REVIEW

# 1926, September 30
## N. Y. Times: Edouard Bourdet's *The Captive*

The *Times* theater critic, Brooks Atkinson, reviewed *The Captive,* a play translated from Edouard Bourdet's *La Prisonnière,* which had opened in New York City the night before.[30] The international publicity surrounding productions of *The Captive* probably marked a historical turning point in the middle-class public's aware-

---

*For "epicene" applied in *The Times* to males of ambiguous character see 1925, May 31. Pierre Louÿs was author of several pseudo-classical volumes of poems about female-female love, including *The Songs of Bilitis,* after which The Daughters of Bilitis, the early lesbian rights organization, was named in the 1950s.

†For a *Times* reference to "crushes" as "abnormal psychological manifestations among . . . young women," see 1917, February 4.

ness of woman-to-woman love as (in Atkinson's words) a "twisted relationship," and "warped infatuation," "loathsome" and doomed.*

The horror provoked in some males by *The Captive,* so clearly recorded by Atkinson, derived from the final triumph of the female captivator—her prey, the play's heroine, in the end left her man for that mysterious woman who never actually appeared on stage. This captivator thus retained the fearsomeness of a monster unnamed and unknown. Though the word "vampire" was not used in *The Times* in reference to *The Captive,* the play's title communicated the image of a ghoul preying on her helpless victim. The horror this captivator provoked derived from her power—an attraction so strong she could lure another female away from the formerly all-powerful male. The female captivator and her female captive were characters in a patriarchal nightmare of the 1920s. The fight of an embattled male against a woman-loving woman for "possession" of "his" woman was also the theme of D. H. Lawrence's *The Fox* and of Thomas Dickinson's play *Winter Bound* (see 1929, November 13). This war of heterosexual males to secure their traditional property in women through love and marriage, and by defeating the new threat to that property arrangement—the predatory other woman—was one archetypal response documented in the 1920s. That these male authors and reviewers could envision female-female intimates only as active predator and passive prey suggests much about these males' heterosexual relationships.

Brooks Atkinson began: "Most of the theatrical news from Europe for several months past" had "hung about this drama, . . . vastly popular, sensational in its theme, and the subject of pietistic rebukes." The playwright's sensitive handling saved a work which might otherwise "degenerate into commercial exploitation of a revolting theme."

Commenting again on "The Captive" in *The Times* of October 10, 1926, Atkinson wrote:

> The preoccupation of the current stage with diverse phases of eroticism seemed to indicate another salacious flourish in the direction of prurient theatergoers. For however noble such drama-lovers may be, . . . they pay good money at the box office; and producers are not above making a living when they can.

The American production of *The Captive* was praised for presenting its story of an "abnormal relationship" as "tragedy rather than a malodorous trucking to low curiosity. It would have been easy to spade up the muck." The production did not play up "sensual delights"; its heroine was "crushed by a frightful tyranny

---

*For Atkinson's review of September 30, 1926, see *GAH,* p. 82. For the response of Helen Carey Thomas to a play about lesbians (probably "The Captive") see p. 7.

In its 1926–27 reviews and news reports on *The Captive, The Times* never used the words "lesbian" or "homosexual." The paper did refer once or twice to "psychopathic relationships," "adult" and "advanced" subjects, "sex perversion," an "indecent theme," "certain persons" (to be "pitied" rather than "censured") and "abnormality"; see *GAH,* pp. 82–90.

beyond her control"— an "evil spell." The "aberration" was presented as a "malignant threat, an indefinite horror." Atkinson liked the author's portrayal of the "agony of a woman lost to herself," almost "crumpled from the pain of her affliction" and her "bondage."[viii, 1:1]

Between October and the end of 1926, numerous reports in *The Times* recorded conflicts among theater producers, Actors' Equity, individual actors, the mayor, district attorney, the police of New York City, and the public, concerning the presentation of *The Captive* and other sexually explicit and controversial plays. The controversy over sexual themes in plays continued in 1927, ending with the New York State Legislature outlawing "sexual perversion" as a theme on the state's stages, a law which remained on the books until 1967.*

♀ BOOK REVIEW/PERSONAL TESTIMONY

## 1926, October 24
*N. Y. Times Book Review:* Dr. Joseph Collins's
*The Doctor Looks at Love and Life*

John E. Lind ended his *Times* review of Dr. Collins's book with the comment that it discussed "certain problems which have always agitated the adolescent, the neurotic and the prurient, the problems of continence, of frigidity, incompatibility, homosexuality and promiscuity.[31]†

Collins's *The Doctor Looks at Love and Life* was one of the earliest erotically detailed, popular books on sex to receive much attention in the mass media. His discussion of homosexuality in females and males was probably read by many. Whatever the authenticity of the personal "letters" presented by Collins, their details ring true, providing indications of the various responses of homosexuals to the literature on the subject. In a chapter on "Homosexuality," one of the most extended in a popular book, Dr. Collins discussed the current discourse:

> The anomaly has been in existence as long as man has. It has been called by many names, some opprobrious, some laudatory. Now that the world dares say sex and sexuality aloud, it seems to be agreed that such individuals shall be called homosexuals, though they, if one may judge from their writings on the subject, prefer to be called "the intermediate sex." . . .
> It will probably be difficult to convince the generation succeeding ours

*For the controversy in 1926 and 1927 see *GAH*, pp. 82–91.
†This is the earliest use of the word "homosexuality" discovered in *The Times*. For earlier *Times* references to "the 'Uranian temperament' " see 1916, August 20. For "sexual inversion" see 1925, July 5. For " 'the intermediate sex' " see review of October 10, 1926, quoted in document entry of 1920, November. For the next known *Times* reference to "homosexual" and "heterosexual" liaisons see 1930, April 20, and the following references of the same year (the year in which the "homosexual" and "heterosexual" may be said to have made their official debut in *The Times*).

that, when this country was at its zenith of her commercial prosperity, it was improper to utter the word homosexuality, prurient to admit its existence and pornographic to discuss the subject. It was proper to read novels in which it was treated more or less openly if the setting was European: decadent people in decadent countries. Here, if it existed at all, it could not flourish; our soil is unfavorable, our climate prejudicial, our people too primitive, too pure.[64]

Collins maintained: "the majority of homosexuals, male and female, are not degenerates," and "Genuine homosexuality is not a vice, it is an endowment."

My experience does not agree with that of Forel and other European psychiatrists that homosexual love is pathological in nature and that all its victims are in a more or less marked degree psychopaths or neurotics.* Forel's opinion is a reflection of his enormous asylum experience. Mine is largely of private practice. I have known many well-balanced homosexuals of both sexes. Some of them have made distinctive positions for themselves in various fields of activity from arms to the pulpit. . . .

    . . . Some of them, possibly the majority, do not admit that they are abnormal; they contend that the heterosexual merit the designation more than they, that they [homosexuals] are vouchsafed us for the benefit of the world, and constitute perhaps nature's effort to create a race of superhumans. They admit the wisdom and necessity of conjugality, but for progeny only. Spiritual endowment, esthetic appeasement, emotional fellowship, sympathy, understanding and friendship they seek and obtain from their own sex. They plume themselves on their superior intellectuality and affectivity and point with pride to their membership list which includes such names as Michel Angelo, William Shakespeare and Walt Whitman. One of them says, ". . . if a severe distinction of elements were always maintained the two sexes would soon drift into far latitudes and absolutely cease to understand each other. As it is *there are some remarkable and indispensable types in whom there is such union or balance of feminine and masculine qualities* that these people become to a great extent the interpreters of men and women to each other."†

    . . . their claim has no justification. They are not nature's elect, but deviates who will one day disappear from the world when we shall have guessed the last riddle of the sympathetic nervous system and the ductless glands.

        There are many persons who indulge in unnatural sexual relations who are not homosexuals. They are the real degenerates. There are many

---

*Dr. August Forel's *The Sexual Question; A Scientific, Psychological, Hygienic and Sociological Study for the Cultured Classes* was first translated and published in English in 1906; its first United States publication, under the above title, was in an "English adaption" by Dr. C. F. Marshall (N. Y.: Rebman, 1908). It contains a section on "Sexual Inversion or Homosexual Love" in females and males, pp. 241–54, and other scattered references.

†Research indicates that the quote is from Edward Carpenter's chapter "The Intermediate Sex" in his *Love's Coming of Age* . . . (London: George Allen and Unwin, 1923), p. 131.

potential and actual homosexuals whose intercourse with persons of their own sex is confined to emotional and intellectual contact, to establishing romantic friendship. . . . There are others in which intercourse is physical as well. The rank and file considers them degenerates. . . .[65–66]

"We are shorter of tolerance in this country than of any other virtue," said Collins. A "more enlightened viewpoint" toward "the abnormality" would come through "understanding."[67]

There had grown up around homosexuality an "enormous literature,"

some of which may have been begotten in the interest of science, but most of which has been claimed by pornography. Strangely enough, this literature has come largely out of the country that precipitated the World War and that was decimated by the war [Germany]. Ulrichs, Krafft-Ebing, Freud, Stekel and dozens of their countrymen have flooded the Western world with it. Their writings were promptly translated and published in this country [not true of Ulrichs—J.K.], and though it has been claimed that their sale is restricted to clergymen, physicians, lawyers, social workers, etc., the books have been sold to high grade imbeciles, esthetes and flappers, pruriency mongers and potential perverts, to their great injury. . . .

I have but small hope that I shall be able to convince the majority of my readers that urnings are not monsters in human form. . . .[67]

They are the most to be pitied of all of nature's misfits. They live in a state of constant fear; fear that their secret will be guessed; fear that they will become the prey of blackmailers; fear that they will fall into the clutches of the law. . . . Small wonder that many of them essay a certain speciousness to conceal their self-consciousness and feeling of guilt. Others, intolerant of their endowment and ever conscious of the conflict that it imposes, take their own lives. They merit our prayers. Only those who contend that it is a patency of distinction and a badge of cultural efficiency deserve our contempt. . . .

Dr. Collins quoted four letters from homosexuals. One, a male, was a twenty-eight-year-old university instructor in Romance Languages who had written:

I am most desirous to continue my work as teacher. The success I have had counsels me to continue, and I have genuine pleasure in it; but I want the assurance that I shall be able to hold my particular views on the matter of love as of use . . . only to myself and to my kind, and I want above everything to be assured that I shall not become a corrupting influence among the young. The only assurance that I have had up to now is that given me by Edward Carpenter personally and by his writing.[69]

During college he had fallen in love with a "High School boy" who had finally left him for the "society of girls."

About this time I came across a review of Wilde's Essay on Shakespeare, *Mr. W. H.* * It opened my eyes on myself and I followed every clue that I could discover in books until finally I had a pretty clear theoretical notion of the subject.[71]

He had consulted two psychiatrists,

perhaps one would prefer to be called a psychoanalyst. He counselled me to lose my shame for my instinct and to seek the company of men where perhaps I might find love. But he was unable to suggest to me how I could overcome my shyness among them. . . .[71]

The other psychiatrist had advised him to pursue women. Then,

a few months ago, quite by chance, . . . I happened to meet a man many years older than myself who wanted to be friends. It was not long before I learned that he loved me. We are now living together. It is a congenial arrangement, for he is intelligent, artistic and experienced in the ways of the world and I find myself able to meet him on an intellectual plane. This experience has proved valuable to me in increasing my woeful lack of self-confidence, my burdening abundance of self-consciousness. Sometimes I think I am on the way to self-adjustment. . . .[72]

He again asked for Dr. Collins's assurance that he would not "corrupt" the youths he taught.
    Collins responded:

It requires no special perspicacity to detect the note of superiority, arrogance even, in this letter. The writer knows what he is and does not seek deliverance. What he is striving for is to shed self-consciousness and gain self-confidence that he may not be a marked figure in his community.[72]

Collins changed the subject. "Many people think"

that masculine homosexuals are invariably timid, shy, retiring, fastidious, dainty even, and what is popularly called effeminate. Some are, but many are not. I have known husky, articulate, self-opinionated and even domineering ones.[73]

He added:

The belief that a male homosexual is necessarily a misogynist and shuns or despises women has little foundation in fact. In a measure the contrary is

*Oscar Wilde, *The Portrait of Mr. W. H.* . . . (N. Y.: Mitchell Kennerley, 1921); review by Richard Le Gallienne, *N. Y. Times Book Review*, July 24, 1921, pp. 3, 22. Le Gallienne commented: "It is surely not unreasonable to suppose that Shakespeare may have been interested in a beautiful young actor, both as a medium for his art and as the object of that neo-Platonic friendship which was usual during the Renaissance, and the expression of which . . . was often absurdly and misleadingly ecstatic and high flown. Poets in those days, indeed, addressed mere patrons in all the hyperboles of amorous devotion, and Shakespeare's passion for his friend may have been merely a matter of business! And yet, one likes to think not. . . ." The debate about the relation between romantic friendship, an unnamed, illicit, male-male amour and the historical language of love had reached *The Times* by 1921.

true. . . . Women find him understanding, intuitive, sympathetic and are thus led into close friendship with him and what might be called spurious intimacy. . . .*

The other extreme—the man of broad hips and mincing gait, who vocalizes like a lady and articulates like a chatterbox, who likes to sew and knit, to ornament his clothing and decorate his face, and the woman who makes her garb approximate man's, who swaggers and swears, uses a cane and often a monocle, who goes in for horses and hunting, business and sports—everyone knows.[74]†

Collins presented a letter from a woman who no one would suspect was "one of the strange sisterhood," a teacher of music in a Southern college. She had written the doctor to inquire if there was any way to overcome the "aberration" of "homosexual attraction."[75]

At age thirteen, she said, she was reading

a "doctor book" and was jolted into a frightful state of self-contempt and remorse when I came upon certain information regarding my childish bad habit [masturbation]. The change in me had some of the features of conversion; it came suddenly; it took complete possession of me; it conditioned my conduct. I set up an ideal of purity which stayed with me through later years and resulted in a fastidiousness of mind which made me consider a story, even slightly suggestive, contemptible and insulting. I studied, practised the piano, worshiped God, admired nature and read omnivorously.[77]

After graduating from high school, she got a job as secretary with a New York publisher.

A girl in an adjacent office began making ardent love to me; her caresses often palled upon me but she seemed lonely and I was sorry for her. Gradually I became very fond of her and before long I was able to respond to her overtures with an ardor equal to her own. . . .

I longed to be with———, but her kisses and caresses (and I may say that our love-making never transcended those) had invariably thrown me into such a state that I refused to allow her to visit me though she begged me to do so. Moreover, I was tremendously chagrined because she, the aggressive one, had been able to maintain a normal attitude toward life.[78]

That relationship was broken off.

At age twenty-seven she returned to New York from the South and attended Columbia University.

---

*Now that true intimacy between women and men was defined as "heterosexual," as including a legitimate erotic, any female-male relationship which did not was "spurious," however close.
†See the postcard images of masculine women and feminine men, c. 1905–20s.

And then I met Rachel. She was a teacher who had come to Columbia to acquire a knowledge that would permit her to get a better position. I thought she was wonderful the first moment I saw her. Her looks and her temperament revealed her German–Jewish blood. She was selfish, aggressive, intelligent, full of pep and zest for life. She was quite handsome in a hard, glittering way. Although she attracted me tremendously I was determined, after the turbulent experience I had passed through a few years before, that I would not let myself be made love to by another girl, neither would I make the advances. There lingered in my own mind the idea that it was legitimate only to love a man and I hoped that by resisting the illegitimate the other [heterosexual love] would come to me. The desire for marriage, while purely idealistic, persisted.[81]

A close friendship developed between the two:

There were times when I felt that her personality, her very being was knit and bound to me. When we were together there was that warmth, that satisfaction in nearness which gives rise to luscious laughter, moist and sparkling eyes, and free and easy interflow of opinion which I have never been able to experience with any one else. At other times, jealousy and hurt pride caused antagonism and temporary separation which I know gave her pain as well as me.[82]

Rachel began to talk of marriage to a male:

Her family wanted her to marry. She told me if she ever married it would be for purely practical reasons as she had never loved and could never love any man. She said she had no desire to be kissed by a man and the idea of intercourse nauseated her. I never grew tired of hearing this. I could not bear the thought of her marrying.[83]

After Rachel finally became cold and distant the letter writer

began to look about me for some way to renew my interest in life. . . . I no longer hoped for marriage. Edward Carpenter's *Love's Coming of Age* had fallen into my hands and I knew that I belonged to the "intermediate sex." I took down the picture, "Young Mother," which had hung over my bed for so long. It mocked me.

 The only thing that had any interest for me was the phenomenon of homosexuality itself. I haunted the library of the University and the library of the Academy of Medicine in search of information regarding the subject that interested me. I read the lyrics of Sappho and endeavored to find all I could about her life. I came upon John Addington Symonds' remarkable book *A Problem in Greek Ethics* and I was literally bowled over by what I found there. I could not take in then, and I cannot take in now, how the Greeks were able to raise homosexual passion to the moral and spiritual efficiency it obtained in the camp, palaestra and the schools of the philosophers. I felt myself more of an outcast than ever when I learned that the Aeolian women had made a degeneracy out of that which the Dorian men had made a virtue. And then I read the *Amores* of Lucian which showed me that the Greeks felt an abhorrence for sexual inversion in women* similar to that which moderns feel for its manifestation in men. The more I learned the further I slipped into the mire. I hated myself and I hated all mankind save Rachel. . . . An indefinite gnawing unrest hindered me from concentration or application. Everybody around me seemed happy. Why? Because they were normal and I was a pariah, an outcast, a blot on creation. Why had nature made me an emotional hunchback?[83–84]

She asked Dr. Collins:

Am I a real homosexual, or am I a victim of autosuggestion and fright? How can I rid myself of this incubus? I heard a lecturer say recently that dwarfs could be made to grow up and giants down if the abnormality were detected early enough. If doctors can do that they should be able to lasso the sex instinct that has strayed and drag it back into the pasture lands that were prepared for it.[85]

Collins commented on the above letter:

I consider this an excellent example of what homosexual writers call the normal uranian woman: feminine, gracious, intelligent and intuitive, whose inner nature approximates the masculine.[86]

He added: "though genuine homosexuals are no more prone to nervous and mental disorders than heterosexuals," the above woman was "a good example of the psychoneurotic individual."[86–87]†

Collins presented a letter from a mother who wrote to him about her daughter. Cynthia had

never been quite like other girls. She has always been a little solitary, shy, self-contained, a little indisposed to share her enthusiasms or disappointments; more indifferent to dress and to society than the average girl and, I suppose I must say it, she has never been popular. She likes horses but not men. She is fond of outdoor sports and has plenty of ability. . . . She has not many friends but she has always had one; and a friendship formed in recent years goes so much further than any previous ones that I am really alarmed.

Cynthia is twenty-five; her friend is twenty-one and the relation between the two girls amounts . . . to an infatuation of no ordinary degree.

---

*The *Amores* (*Affairs of the Heart*) is no longer attributed to Lucian. It is available in what Boswell calls a "reasonably frank translation" in volume 8 of the Loeb Classical Library edition of Lucian; see Boswell, *Christianity*, p. 19. This dialog depicts, says Boswell, a Rome "in which tolerance of homosexuality is declining";[73] the dialog also "consistently juxtaposes love for 'women at their fairest and young men in the flower of manhood' as two sides of the same coin."[86] Boswell (pp. 126–27) further discusses and quotes from the *Amores*.

†The "homosexual" as "neurotic" would become a staple of the Freud-influenced discourse of the 1930s and 1940s; see, for example, 1932, May 29; 1941, February 23.

. . . [Cynthia] is as tender to her as a mother to her child, and so harsh with us. . . .

She is happy only when she is with that girl and for her she has forsaken all her other friends and withdrawn her sympathy and her presence from her family; and now she looks me straight in the eye and without a quiver in her voice says that she must live with her friend and can never live with me again.[88]

When the mother asked Cynthia

why she cannot live at home, she says that our points of view, our outlook on life are so different; that home is no longer tolerable. If I attempt to tell her what her parents have tried to do for her, she becomes violent and at the slightest suggestion of a separation from her friend or the smallest opposition to her plans and purposes, she goes wholly beyond control, frantic, violent and destructive.[89]

Dr. Collins asked this mother: " 'If a sane woman of twenty-five chooses to live in a way of which society does not approve, is it for me to say that she shall not?' " He suggested that someone beside the mother might make Cynthia realize " 'that she is a unit of a community which it is her duty neither to offend nor scandalize.' "

I might have added that most of those in my experience who were determined to live as Cynthia was determined to live went to Paris, London or Rome and lived there. . . . Or I might have pointed out to her [the mother] that women endowed or afflicted as was Cynthia often have peculiar qualities of domination and leadership which make them successful uplift workers for their sex in social, political and religious spheres, and that she should try to steer her daughter into some such activity.[90–91]

Dr. Collins stressed: "Homosexual tendency often shows itself in both sexes very early in life," and that was the time to try to "overcome it."

I do not mean to say that a boy who plays with dolls and clings to his mother's apronstrings, wants to learn to crochet instead of whittle, bawls when boys affront him instead of blackening their eyes, can be transformed by taking the doll away, or by giving him boxing lessons; but I am sure this method can do no harm and in conjunction with organotherapy [administration of animal organ extracts] it may work the miracle. . . . [The physician] will always have in mind that success appears to have followed testicular transplantations in a few of Steinach's cases. [Eugen Steinach was famous for his "monkey gland" experiments.][91]

The last letter Collins presented was that of a married, female sculptor, worried that something about her made her the repeated subject of romantic overtures from women.[92–100]

Dr. Collins's chapter on "Homosexuality" concluded with a discussion of biologists' experiments with plants: "When a plant with 60% feminine cells meets another with 80% feminine cells, the originally feminine subject turns masculine and the union of the two produces offspring." These experiments suggested

there is small difference between the two sexes. One produces spermatozoa and the other ova and one has more energy than the other. These constitute essential masculinity and essential feminity. . . .

The other distinctions between the sexes are negligible. The anatomical differences on first consideration seem tremendous but at the last analysis they are not. . . . There is apparently great psychological difference as evidenced by behavior but it is not an inherent one. If male and female children were brought up in exactly the same way . . . this behavioristic difference would diminish.

. . . In the vast majority of human beings there is preponderance of male or female elements. In the minority there is not. They are the homosexuals. They have been with us since time immemorial but they may not continue to be so. The experiments that have been made on the reproductive glands suggest that the time may come when the male who has a preponderance of female elements may have his deficit [of male elements] made up by transplantation—the female likewise.

. . . We may one day be able to supply male and female hormones. In these two resources [hormones and gland transplants] lies the hope of the homosexual.[103]

Collins ended with a "word of advice to homosexuals:"

so long as homosexuals maintain that by virtue of their "double nature" they have command of life in all its phases, and that they are not only the reconcilers and interpreters of the world but its pathfinders, they will have to tolerate their affliction.[103]

FILM REVIEW

## 1926, December 15
### N. Y. Times: Carl Dreyer's Chained

German producers delighted in filming stories set in France, England, or Russia, "with historical characters who were not exactly a credit to their respective countries," said Times movie critic Mordaunt Hall.[32] A film "now known as Chained" was "said to be based" on the life of Auguste Rodin, the French sculptor. "If the producers were bent on delivering such a theme to the screen" they might have more successfully adapted Oscar Wilde's The Picture of Dorian Gray or Robert

Hitchens's *The Green Carnation* which, "distasteful though they may be, at least possess real dramatic values."*

The film *Chained* had also been called *The Invert*, said *The Times*. † It told the story of a "youth" who was the sculptor's "protege and model" becoming fascinated by a princess, and absenting himself more and more from the artist's home.

♀ BOOK REVIEW

## 1927, September 4
### *N. Y. Times Book Review:*
### Rosamund Lehmann's *Dusty Answer*

In England, said an anonymous reviewer, the phrase " 'post-war' " signified "preciosity," "degeneracy," a "nasty and naive" disillusionment, a combination of "realism" and "self-pity."[33] Rosamund Lehman's first novel "analyses the effect of 'post-war' " on an "innocent" English "girl," Judith Earle, at Cambridge University.

"Judith is feminine, dependent, serious." She "feels emotionally." Her friends are "thrilling."

> Charlie was beautiful. Roddy could draw wonderfully. Julian could play the piano. . . . Judith fell in love with Roddy, but he was "post-war" with a young man named Anthony Baring. Judith had a friend, Jennifer, but she was "post-war" with a dark lady named Geraldine Manners and was quietly expelled from college. Roddy seduced Judith, more or less to get rid of her. She suffered.

One character declared: " 'If only the people with unwanted love could hand it on to the people who'd die for it and there were none of these ghastly gaps—everybody loving some one who loves another person.' "

*Wilde's novel *The Picture of Dorian Gray*, was first published in the United States, in *Lippincott's Monthly Magazine*, July 1890; it contains a scene cut from later editions, in which Basil Hallward tells Dorian that he loves him. Robert Hitchens's *The Green Carnation*, a satire on Wilde and Alfred Douglas, was first published in England on September 15, 1894, and in the United States the same year (N. Y.: Mitchell Kennerly); see Wilde, *Letters* (1962), pp. 257 n. 1, 372 n. 1. *Bitter Sweet*, a Broadway operetta adapted from *The Green Carnation*, was first reviewed in *The Times* on July 19, 1929, 14:2; the last of several productions was reviewed in 1936. In a song on one recording of *Bitter Sweet* a male chorus sang: "We are the reason for the nineties being gay"; I thank Rudy Grillo for the last information.

†For an earlier *Times* reference to "sexual inversion" see 1925, July 5; for a later *Times* reference to "sexual inversion" see 1928, January 8.

♀  BOOK REVIEW

## 1927, November 13
### N. Y. Times Book Review: Compton Mackenzie's
### Vestal Fire

Mackenzie's novel, said an anonymous reviewer, was "a study in the disintegration of a colony of Americans and Europeans on a pleasant island in the Bay of Naples," a disintegration "brought about by the intrusion of an exotic French nobleman with Hellenic ideas."[34] That phrase, and "androgynous propensities" (below), quite clearly served here as code words for homosexual. These rather transparent euphemisms indicate *The Times*'s old indirection moving toward more explicit reference, as in the review of Proust's *Cities of the Plain;* see 1928, January 8.

The island, Sirene, was dotted with mansions called Villa Decamerone, Villa Paradiso, Villa Amabile, Villa Hylas, Villa Parnasso, inhabited by English, French, Russians, Americans, and Italians. On Sunday everyone gathered at afternoon tea at Villa Amabile, home of the Pepworth-Nortons, "two kindly spinsters, Mrs. Virginia Norton and Miss Mamie Pepworth—or perhaps it is the other way around —who have bracketed their names and devoted the afternoon of their lives after a long morning in Idaho to dispensing hospitality in Sirene."

Count Marsac, the "villain of the piece," came to Sirene "accompanied by a handsome boy named Carlo—whose place in the story assumes a questionable aspect, soon enough." In a rented villa, Marsac gives "elaborate entertainments of the most exotic sort, while the Villa Hylas is being built for him." Then

> the poison begins to work. There are stories about Marsac's androgynous propensities. Sirene is tolerant, though, and nothing is done. But other forces of dissension are at work.

The discovery of Marsac's "past" resulted in bitter conflict.

MEDICAL/SLANG

## 1927
### Dr. Aaron J. Rosanoff: *"A clannishness among themselves"*

In a *Manual of Psychiatry,* Dr. Rosanoff of Los Angeles discussed "Sexual Psychopathies"—including "Frigidity," "Auto-eroticism," "Fetichism," "Exhibitionism," "Sadism," "Masochism," "Bestiality," "Necrophilia," and "Homosexuality" (in that order).[35] Rosanoff's comments also included one of the earliest published lists of male homosexual slang, a special vocabulary suggesting a subculture with a fairly developed system of private communication.

The conversation of (male) homosexuals was characterized by a "somewhat labored refinement" followed, upon "more intimate acquaintanceship," with "suggestive remarks" that "reveal a fondness for most obscene expressions, [and] salacious stories." They devoted care to "style of hair cut" and "decoration of living apartment." There was much "evidence of a special relationship" between "the schizoid or autistic element of personality and homosexual inclinations." "Exhibitionism and 'peeping' is a very common . . . feature" of the homosexual's behavior. A "passion for handling the partner's genitals is also common." A "relatively frequent incidence of masochism" was noted in homosexuals, "especially in passive pedarists" [sic].

Conventional society abhors homosexuals and these patients are in dread of detection, social ostracism, blackmail, economic ruin, and legal prosecution. Hence arises . . . an attitude of reserve, aloofness, and mistrust and . . . a clannishness among themselves. A heterosexual person cannot really break into their inner circles. They have parties or "drags" to which only homosexuals are admitted, and at these some generally appear in female dress.

Within their own group, too, there is considerable social discrimination. In the most respectable class are those who do no "cruising," i.e., picking up "friends" at random in the parks or streets. At the lower end of the scale are those who habitually solicit strangers in the manner of prostitutes. . . . A somewhat inferior status is held by passive homosexuals as compared with those who are exclusively active.

Choice of occupation is to a considerable extent determined by homosexuality. . . .

Thus we find many engaged in dressmaking, millinery, beauty parlor work, crocheting, embroidery, others work at window trimming, or in drapery, picture and art shops; still others are to be found among painters, sculptors, musicians, actors; others again in the army, navy, police, and among prison guards, male nurses, masseurs, and public bath attendants.

The clannishness of homosexuals has led to the development of special slang expressions among them:

Temperamental or queer, a homosexual person.

Turk, wolf, or jocker, an active sodomist.

Punk, lamb, queen, bitch, or prushun, a passive sodomist.

Trade, an active homosexual preferring irrumation [to have his penis sucked].

Fruit, fruiter, fairy, a passive homosexual who practices irrumation.*

Orchard, a park or other such place frequented by homosexuals.

*Why the male whose penis was sucked should be considered "active" (and by implication "masculine") while the male doing the sucking should be considered "passive" (and by implication "feminine"), was not explained, though the definition went against the common sense idea of activity and passivity. The basis for this 1927 definition of sucker as passive, suckee as active, was an essential association of each category with gender, rather than activity. That is, though "cocksucking" was activity, a moral categorization made it demeaning, therefore "feminine."

*Tea house,* a public lavatory frequented by homosexuals.

*Cruising,* going out in search of a partner.

*Peddling,* a punk or fairy "looking for something."

*A drag,* a social gathering of homosexuals at which some are in female
   dress; also an outfit of female dress worn by a homosexual.

*Dirt,* a pretended homosexual whose motive is blackmail.

*Sixty-nine,* position assumed for mutual irrumation.


♀ BOOK REVIEW

## 1928, January 8

### N. Y. Times Book Review Marcel Proust's *Cities of the Plain*

This *Times* review, headed "Proust's Harvest of Dead Sea Fruit," was an in-joke
pun ("fruit" was used at this time for homosexual; see 1927, Rosanoff).[36] The
novel completed Proust's "Study of the Relation of Vice to Society," said the
subhead.

This was the novel "in which the author commences on a large scale his
study of sexual inversion," began reviewer Rose Lee. Called in French *Sodome et
Gomorrhe,* it was published in English "under the veiled title" *Cities of the Plain.* But,
Lee assured readers, the "text is all there, complete and unbowdlerized and
perfectly safe from the censors." The publisher had "taken the precaution of
offering the much discussed work to a limited subscription public at the respectable price of $15" (a limited sale constituted the legal fiction of a "private" and
uncensorable transaction).

"There is nothing so horrifying or even so unexpected in *Sodome et Gomorrhe,*" the critic again reassured, assuming her readers' familiarity with literary
representations of inversion. The Baron de Charlus "stands revealed as what,
during . . . previous volumes, . . . we have already suspected him to be." The
female Albertine "is discovered to be the bosom friend of two girls whose practices the hero [Charlus] happened to observe" in the first book of *Swann's Way.*
Other characters

more or less tainted with the vice of Sappho or "of the shepherd Corydon,"*
pass in and out. Their relations to society are analyzed—their fears, their

---

*This reference to "the vice of Sappho" as "sexual inversion" is the earliest explicit naming
of such female-female eroticism to be found in *The Times.* It represents an historic recognition of the
reality of lust between women unlinked to any relationship with men. The "vice" of the shepherd
Corydon referred to Virgil's story of Corydon's love for Alexis, from which André Gide's homosexual
apologetic took its title; his *Corydon* was first privately published in 1911 in an edition of twelve copies,
in 1920 in a second edition of twenty-one copies, and in 1924 in a commercial edition (Paris:
Gallimard); in 1950 *Corydon* was first published in an American edition, in English, with an introduction by Frank Beach (N. Y.: Farrar, Straus); see Bullough, *Sexual Variance,* pp. 145, 156 n. 94; and
*National Union Catalog, Pre-1956 Imprints,* v. 199, p. 46. For the next *Times* reference to "Sapphic
women" see 1928, September 16.

conflicts, their jealousies, their concealments, the ambiguous and often tragic situations in which they are placed.

"Everywhere the treatment is delicate and not too somatic," the critic again assured her readers. The manner was also sometimes "symbolic, as where Proust writes of the biblical cities reuniting their scattered members by the aid of astral signs."

Proust's letter to a friend was quoted: " 'There are some improper passages' " in the first part of *Sodom et Gomorrhe*, " 'and even more' " such passages in the second part. But the work was " 'so serious and its tone so literary that this cannot really be an obstacle.' " "Undoubtedly," said the reviewer,

> that type of subject matter has done much to enhance the vogue of Proust in some quarters, as it has tabooed him in others. Many persons have probably been attracted by his reputation for pornography whom his merely literary qualities might have repelled. . . . it is hard to imagine they could have extracted much unlawful enjoyment from the pages of *Sodom et Gomorrhe*.

The novel's style was so "impersonal" as to put it "almost in the class of biological research," recalling "Fabre's famous studies of insect life." Fabre was sometimes "more exciting," she thought; his "pictures of scorpions embracing one another or of the female spider devouring her lover have a dramatic warmth that one never finds in Proust."

The "dominant figure" in Proust's present volume "is the Baron de Charlus, the grand seigneur tormented and violent, with his dyed mustaches and heavy, powdered face, his strange, shrill voice breaking out into paranoic diatribe or insult."*

Comparing Proust with Ruskin (whom the young Proust was said to have admired), the reviewer found the Frenchman's "themes more various, his humanity at once wider and more minute." Proust "is much more than a monument to departed drawing rooms." His "pages cannot help but give one fresh insight into familiar motives and impulses." Proust "can enrich permanently the understanding and perceptions" of those with "patience enough to follow him."

*For the literature presenting the homosexual as paranoic see 1913, Shockley, and 1933, May 31.

BOOK REVIEW

## 1928, May 20
### N. Y. Times: Book Review: Houston Peterson's *Havelock Ellis: Philosopher of Love*

Reviewing this study of Havelock Ellis's ideas, critic R. L. Duffas noted that Ellis had been "brought into cruel and damaging notoriety," in 1897, in England by the attack on the first of his *Studies in the Psychology of Sex,* the volume on *Sexual Inversion:* [37]

> The result was to associate him, in the minds of many persons who might otherwise have been sympathetic with his opinions, with a subject which even the liberal-minded frequently find obnoxious. The truth was . . . that Ellis was interested in the abnormalities of sex only as a necessary phase of an examination into the normalities.

Duffas thought that "When our generation is studied in historical perspective one of its most important characteristics will certainly be the new ways in which it has thought about sex"—and Ellis would be credited with his "hygienic and liberating" influence.*

♀ RESISTANCE/BLACK AMERICAN

## 1928, June
### Ma Rainey: "Prove It On Me Blues"

If it was true (as jazz historian Chris Albertson has asserted) that Gertrude "Ma" Rainey was inclined to women-loving, then self-affirmation as well as open defiance of white and middle-class sexual norms characterized "Prove It On Me Blues," written by this famous Black singer, and recorded by her in 1928—a "race record" sold to Black people.[38] If Ma Rainey's song involved public self-revelation it is almost unique in the history of American lesbianism before 1956 (when a few women began to write, using their own names, in *The Ladder,* the publication of The Daughters of Bilitis, the early emancipation organization).

Whatever this song's relation to Ma Rainey's own life and sexual persuasion, it is unique as an unambivalently affirmative, forceful statement by a woman-loving character who proclaims her proclivities and defiantly challenges the world to "prove it on me." This song of resistance was sung in the first person by Ma Rainey, in the character of a collar-and-tie-wearing, man-disdaining lesbian. It

---

*For other reviews which refer explicitly to the historical context of writings on sex and intimacy see "historical perspective" in the index.

was recorded by a major music corporation, suggesting that the popular Black culture of the 1920s could sometimes sustain a public, earthy affirmation of woman-to-woman love almost unknown in white, heterosexual society. Another recording for the Black working-class market, "It's Dirty But Good," expressed a somewhat similar affirmation of lesbians (see *GAH*, p. 77). A whole series of other recordings—for example, "Sissy Man Blues," "Freakish Man Blues," "B. D. [Bull Diker] Woman's Blues," and "Fairy Blues"—referred more ambivalently to female and male homosexuals. Other Black blues openly and enthusiastically celebrated the pleasures of female-male sex.

On the following recording Ma Rainey was accompanied by her "tub jug washboard band," including two kazoos, piano, banjo, and jug, "with moaning by the band." In "Prove It On Me Blues" Ma Rainey sang:

> Went out last night,
> Had a great big fight,
> Everything seemed to go a-wrong[?].
> I looked up,
> To my surprise,
> The gal I was with was gone.
>
> Why she went
> I don't know,
> I mean to follow everywhere she goes.
> Folks say I'm crooked[?],
> I don't know where she took it,
> I want the whole world to know.
>
> [Chorus]
> They say I do it,
> Ain't nobody caught me,
> You all got to prove it on me.
>
> Went out last night,
> With a crowd of my friends,
> They must bin womens
> Cause I don't like no mens.
> It's true I wear a collar and a tie,
> Make the women-folk[wind blow(?)]
> Go all wild.[All the while(?)]
> You all say I do it,
> Ain't nobody caught me,
> You sure got to prove it on me.
>
> [Chorus]
> They say I do it,
> Ain't nobody caught me,
> You all got to prove it on me.

I went out last night,
With a crowd of my friends,
They must bin womens
As I don't like no mens.
Wear my clothes
Just like a man[?],
Talk to the gals,
Just like any old man.
Cause they say I do it,
Ain't nobody caught me,
You sure got to prove it on me.


♀ NEWS REPORTS/RESISTANCE

# 1928, August 30
## *N. Y. Times:* Radclyffe Hall's
## *The Well of Loneliness* in England

A series of stories in *The New York Times* reported the controversy in England over Radclyffe Hall's novel of lesbianism, a term for which the *Times* still used a variety of euphemisms.[39]*

On August 30, 1928, a dispatch from London reported that the U. S. publisher Alfred Knopf had bought the American rights to Hall's "book on sex matters," a novel which treated "skillfully a seriously growing psychological problem."

The novel had been suppressed by its English publisher after a request from that country's Home Secretary (the equivalent of the U. S. secretary of state). The Secretary's request was interpreted to mean that "book censorship has been established in England." But the recent publication of Compton MacKenzie's novel *Extraordinary Women*, a satire on "the same problem" as *The Well of Loneliness*, had raised the question of why Hall's book was suppressed but Mackenzie's allowed.[36:2]

On October 6, *The Times* reported that George Bernard Shaw, H. G. Wells, and Radclyffe Hall herself, had protested English customs officials' seizure of copies of her "sex novel," published in France, and being imported into England.[6:4]

A story on November 4 explained that the Paris publisher of *The Well of Loneliness* had "produced the book at an increased price," had "advertised it extensively" in England and, because of a "big demand," a fifth reprinting was planned. The lawyer for the novel's defense "insisted that the book was a

---

*For the controversy in the U. S. over *The Well of Loneliness*, in 1929, see *GAH*, pp. 398–405. In *Almanac* see 1929, January 2.

sombre warning which could under no circumstances corrupt or deprave."[4:2]

Seven days later, on November 17, *The Times* reported that a London judge had found *The Well of Loneliness* "obscene." He had ordered the police "to destroy" copies "as an 'offense against public decency.' " The judge agreed that the novel was well written, but he said:

> The better an obscene book is written the greater is the public to whom it is likely to appeal. The more palatable the poison, the more insidious it is.

The judge "indicted the book in terms so scorching that Miss Hall, in court, protested." The judge then "silenced her sternly and added: 'If you cannot behave yourself in court, I will have to have you removed.' "[6:7]

On December 15, *The Times* reported the British publishers of *The Well of Loneliness* had "lost their appeal . . . against the decision that all copies of the book must be seized and destroyed by the police."

Poet Rudyard Kipling had been in court, prepared "to testify for the government in favor of the book's suppression." (He did not actually testify.) The government's lawyer had called the book " 'more subtle, demoralizing, corrosive and corruptive than anything ever written.' " He said:

> The book seeks to glorify vice or to produce a plea of toleration of people who practice it. It is propaganda.[4:3]

The British Home Secretary publicly suggested that his powers to prohibit "immoral literature are too limited." He had to prosecute an "indecent book" in court, and could not simply ban publication. Newspapers opposed the Home Secretary's suggestion that he should decide if a book could be published. Writer Conan Doyle supported the Home Secretary's right to ban books, stating:

> We do not want . . . to see this country in the same condition as France, which has a great quantity of pornographic literature in circulation. Personally, I hate all these sex novels. . . . The art of writing is in avoiding it [sex].

"Ireland, also," said *The Times,* is agitated over the censorship of books, newspapers, &c." A proposed Irish censorship bill would ensure:

> No newspaper or other publication which advocated or advertised birth control would be permitted to circulate in the Irish Free State. On that point the Government is inflexible.[6:7]

On November 10, *The Times* reported: "Forty distinguished witnesses" (mostly authors) had appeared in a London court, prepared to testify in favor of *The Well of Loneliness.* The judge had refused to hear any of these witnesses, on the grounds that the novel's literary quality was not the point: " 'The book may be a very fine piece of literature and yet be obscene.' "

The chief police inspector had testified that the book's "whole theme, which dealt with masculine women, was objectionable."[4:2]

On December 23, 1928, *The Times* reported that the British Home Secretary had said in reference to "the inhibition placed on a certain novel in the United Kingdom," that he and the police were

> not concerned with morals, but with crime. The police are not concerned with immorality in a private house, but if it takes place in a public park which belongs to the nation it is . . . the Parliament itself, which has decreed it a crime.
>     . . . in the same way as it is the duty of the police to take before the magistrate any one committing an indecent act in a public place so it is the law of the land that if an indecent book is published it is the duty of the police to take proceedings.*

The Home Secretary was " 'prepared to leave myself in the hands' " of England's authors, " 'for the overwelming majority of them desire to publish books which are uplifting and made for the welfare of the country.' "[III, 3:6]

♀ BOOK REVIEW

## 1928, September 16
### *N. Y. Times Book Review:* Compton Mackenzie's
### *Extraordinary Women*

Mackenzie's "style" and "subjects" had both "ripened with the years," said a *Times* reviewer.[40] The British author

> treats at exhausting length about the loves and hates and jealous bickerings of the Sapphic women who live on the Mackenzian Island of Sirene in the Bay of Naples.† He finds it necessary to intrude himself frequently in the chronicle to tell you what a frightfully daring subject he has chosen. But really, he excites himself unduly. That theme has grown hackneyed in recent years.‡

"Any latent electricity" the subject might contain was "insulated" by Mackenzie's "verbiage." The reviewer added: "In writing this story of women Mr. Mackenzie has developed an appropriately gossipy technique."

---

*The law criminalizing the sexual act of two males in a "public park" was used here to support the censorship of a lesbian novel as pornography.
    †For the next *Times* reference to "Sapphic intimacy," see 1935, August.
    ‡For other such comments referring to temporal changes in the response to homosexuality, see "historical perspective" in the index.

# 1928
## Claude McKay: *Home to Harlem*

Two scenes in McKay's book were set in Harlem bars in the years after World War I.[41] They provide a rare glimpse into a Black, working class, New York City culture which casually integrated divergent sexualities. In one Black bar, the Baltimore, it was said:

> All round the den, luxuriating under the little colored lights, the dark dandies were loving up their pansies. Feet tickling feet under tables, tantalizing liquor-rich giggling, hands busy above.
> "Honey gal! Honey gal! What other sweet boy is loving you now? Don't you know your last night's daddy am waiting for you?"[30–31]

When the cabaret singer moans a tune: "Dandies and pansies, chocolate, chestnut, coffee, ebony, cream, yellow, everybody was teased up to the high point of excitement."[32]

Another bar, the Congo, continued to prosper, despite increasing competition, and "formidable opposition."

> The Congo was a real throbbing little Africa in New York. It was an amusement place entirely for the unwashed of the Black Belt. Or, if they were washed, smells lingered telling the nature of their occupation. Pot-wrestlers, third cooks, W. C. attendants, scrub maids, dish-washers, stevedores.
> Girls coming from the South to try their future in New York always reached the Congo first. The Congo was African in spirit and color. No white persons were admitted there. The proprietor knew his market. He did not cater to the fast trade. "High yallers" were scarce there. Except for such sweetmen [pimps] that lived off the low-down dark trade.[29–30]

The Congo was described as

> thick, dark-colorful, and fascinating. Drum and saxophone were fighting out the wonderful drag "blues" that was the favorite of all the low-down dance halls. In all the better places it was banned. Rumor said it was a police ban. It was an old tune, so far as popular tunes go. But at the Congo it lived fresh and green as grass. Everybody there was giggling and wriggling to it.

Two lines from one "drag 'blues'" went: "And there is two things in Harlem I don't understan' It is a bulldycking woman and a faggotty man."[36]*

---

*This line is similar to one in "Foolish Man Blues," recorded by Bessie Smith in October 1927; quoted in *GAH*, p. 82; also see backnote to 1928, June.

♀  BOOK REVIEWS/RESISTANCE

# 1929, January 2
## *The Nation* and *The New Republic*:
### Radclyffe Hall's *The Well of Loneliness* in the United States

*The Nation* noted that the U. S. publisher Covici-Friede "has just issued an edition" of Radclyffe Hall's *The Well of Loneliness,* to be sold for $5.[42]

The Society for the Suppression of Vice had unofficially maintained that though the book's language and conclusions were both moral, "the subject is itself . . . criminally indecent." Previously, said *The Nation*, "No subject has been in itself taboo," questions of censorship had revolved around whether a book's treatment would "debauch the reader." Printed copies of *The Captive* had been "freely circulated," though the play had been suppressed under the New York State law of 1927.

*The Nation* argued that Hall's novel dealt in an "unsensational, and entirely proper way with the unhappy life of a woman struggling against perverse tendencies." It was "worthwhile to call public attention to the badly misunderstood plight of many, many men and women." Every attempt "to declare any subject of human interest and social significance undiscussable" promoted a "socially dangerous obscurantism."[5]

In *The New Republic* on January 2, reviewer Robert Morss Lovett wrote that Hall's purpose in *The Well of Loneliness* was

> to set forth the tragedy of those who, in consequence of sexual inversion, are deprived of the normal satisfactions of physical life, and then, by the uncomprehending cruelty of society, are driven into social exile.

In the book the heroine, Stephen Gordon,

> storms through life seeking fulfillment, a victim of the passion which she does not understand, which leads her into the valley of humiliation, a wretched love of an unworthy woman, jealousy, deceit, discovery, and banishment. . . .

Then, after Stephen won recognition as a writer, honor for ambulance service in the war, and a beautiful love, "the story ends in renunciation."

"The homosexual theme," said Lovett,

> is common today in Continental fiction. The English-reading public accepts Gide and Proust with a certain complacent wonder—"How different from the home life of our own dear Queen". . . .

But Hall's homosexual novel "offers a challenge," Lovett said, "as an appeal against the injustice and cruelty of society." The English had met that challenge by suppressing the book, and "In view of the prosecution of 'The Captive' it may be doubted whether the novel will escape in this country."

Though the "number of sexual inverts has been greatly under-estimated," and "is increasing, still the majority . . . find the homosexual theme dull." They "are interested in perversions of another sort"—Lovett quoted a recent comment by Aldous Huxley:

> The instinct of acquisitiveness has more perverts, I believe, than the instinct of sex. . . . People seem to me odder about money than about even their amours. Such amazing meannesses as one's always coming across, particularly among the rich.

Society's right "to protect itself against the invert by censorship" was the moral issue, Lovett believed. There was "something to be said" for the view that "the normal must be kept from knowledge of the invert lest the latter infect the former." Yet Proust's *Sodom and Gomorrah,* Gide's *The Counterfeiters,* and Bourdet's *The Captive* "can hardly be described as propaganda for the homosexual way of life." Similarly, over *The Well of Loneliness* "broods a persistent and deepening sadness."

Censorship of homosexual themes was futile, Lovett thought, and only advertised the subject. "If the invert is increasing in numbers, and becoming more prominent in the intellectual and esthetic experience of the world, then society will have to learn to live with this as with other forms of heresy."

Hall's book "sets forth the tragedy of the invert, in all relations of life," stressed Lovett, relieving it "from any suggestion of temptation." The book "is a plea to society for the rights of the individual," arguing that a "social attitude of ignorance and repulsion" had the "worst results" for both individual and society. Hall's treatment of her subject challenged the "crude mind of a class which sees no solution of social problems except prohibition and censorship."[195]

Ten days later, on January 12, *The New York Times* reported that *The Well of Loneliness* had been seized by the police.[3:6]*

In August 1929, Dr. Noah E. Aronstam of Detroit commented on *The Well of Loneliness* in a medical journal. He quoted the introduction to the novel by Dr. Havelock Ellis which called it a "completely faithful" picture of the sexual life presented.[542] (The link between medicine and fiction was complete.)

The historical context of Hall's novel was discussed, as was the social construction of new emotions:

> The world war with its great welter of blood and abundance of adventure, its exhaustion of all emotional centers, has left behind a populace unstable and undetermined as to subsequent standards. Human values have changed to such a degree that they can no longer be applied to an ever changing society. New traits, sensations and emotions have gradually developed in the social structure whose previously made laws are no longer able to combat them. The sexual sphere has also suffered a profound inversion. Heterosex-

*See *GAH,* p. 398.

"The Well of Loneliness" by Cosmo Clark, *The American Sketch*, March 1929, p. 4; reproduced from a  copy in The Library of Congress.

ual satiation has either given way to indifference or to the search for new
and hitherto unknown pleasures. Anything that will whet the dull edge of
the sensations is welcome. Small wonder then that this quest engenders new
feelings and new thrills in a population that fails to react as it formerly did
to old stimuli. Even our syncopated music has become more so—super-
syncopated. The jungle and the savage strive to force themselves into our
existence and the age of boundless hilarity and orgies has set in.

*The Well* chronicled "with painful accuracy" the history of a "male soul in
the vestments of a female body." Such people should not be condemned. "Formerly this inversion was designated as Lesbian love" (that term still needed to
be explained). The novel might help "homosexualists" to understand their "perverted sexual proclivities."

But "What shall the homosexualist do?" Hall's novel was quoted: " 'Acknowledge us, Oh God, before the whole world. Give us also the right to our
existence.' "[543]

In October 1929, *The Woman's Journal,* published in New York, reviewed
Kathleen Millay's novel *Against the Wall,* calling it "a bitter indictment of women's
colleges," and Radclyffe Hall's *The Unlit Lamp,* calling it "One of the best novels
this reviewer has read in a long time." The "novelty" of the story was that the
"conflict is between a mother and a woman friend, not as usual, between a mother
and a [male] lover." This novel "makes one suspect that *The Well of Loneliness*
. . . may have been misunderstood." A drawing of Hall was reproduced from *The
Well of Loneliness.* [33]The printing of Hall's picture, one of the more butch images,

CHARLES BUCHEL

*Radclyffe Hall*

was a rather daring act in light of the long history of innuendo concerning feminists and female inverts. Among *Woman's Journal* editors were such famous feminists as Carrie Chapman Catt and Alice Stone Blackwell.

♀ NEWS REPORT/CROSSING WOMAN

## 1929, April 26
### N. Y. Times: Mrs. Lillian Arkel-Smith/Colonel Sir Victor Barker

A wireless to *The Times* from London reported the sentencing there of "Mrs. Lillian Arkel-Smith, who masqueraded as 'Colonel Sir Victor Barker' for six years and actually went through a form of marriage with another woman."[43]

Arkel-Smith was sentenced to nine months in prison. She was convicted of

having entered a false statement in the marriage register and of having made a travesty of the wedding ceremony.

"You are an unprincipled, unscrupulous adventuress," said Sir Ernest Wild, the recorder, in passing sentence. "You have . . . profaned the House of God; you have outraged the decencies of nature and you have broken the law of man. You have set an example which, were you to go unpunished, others might follow."*

Mrs. Arkel-Smith had an amazing career as a man. She became a leader in various English organizations and deceived her acquaintances into believing she was a World War hero.

She had been sentenced in the same court in which, several years earlier, she had been tried in her male role, and acquitted of carrying a revolver without a license.

RESISTANCE/PERSONAL TESTIMONY

## 1929, April?
### F. K.: "Report from America,"
### a raid on the Lafayette Baths

An eyewitness report of a police raid on the Lafayette Baths in New York City was published in a periodical of the German homosexual emancipation movement,

---

*This outraged response to a woman marrying a woman contrasts with the much more calm, even tolerant response to such "eccentricity" documented in earlier newspaper accounts. The outrage in 1929 arose from the new understanding that a female-female marriage might imply an erotic consummation (competitive with male-female relations), not intense, romantic friendship.

the *Journal of Human Rights* (Berlin).[44] This report, expressing a sense of outrage and injustice, constituted a form of homosexual resistance. It is translated here for the first time.

New York City newspapers confirm that a huge police clean-up occurred on the first weekend in April 1929. Vagrants, gamblers, and other "suspicious" elements were arrested during a record-breaking heat wave.

On a "warm," "muggy" Saturday evening at nine o'clock the correspondent had gone to the Lafayette Brothers' Turkish Bath, "very well-known, . . . especially as a place where like-minded people meet (a quees place)"—*sic*, a "queens'" or "queers'" place. He had "already been there ten times." After paying "two dollars at the door," he undressed and went to the steam room: "the first thing happens there" (apparently, his first sexual encounter).

> At about ten-thirty I go up to the dormitory and look for a bed. Chance brings me together with a young, racy Sicilian. Unfortunately, we hadn't noticed that there were eight detectives among the customers of the baths. . . . now it's midnight, and I'm already asleep, my friend at my side.
>
> All at once there's a whistle, someone yells "Hallo," and everyone has to go to the front room. The bath is locked shut. Various people were struck down, kicked, in short, the brutality of these officials was simply indescribable. A Swede standing next to me was struck on the eye with a bunch of keys, and then he got hit in the back so that two of his ribs broke. There was a telephone call, and ten policemen, even more detectives, an inspector, and the captain of the detectives arrived. "Put on your clothes." Everyone, from the night manager to the most recent arrival, was put in the paddywagon ("cooler" [*sic*]), taken to the station, and jailed. By noon on Sunday we appeared before the magistrate's court at 2nd Avenue and 2nd Street and were charged with things we hadn't done. All of the forty-five people who were there were fined ten dollars or two days in the workhouse, except for four who were sentenced to six months, three weeks, two weeks, and one month.
>
> I must say that there's a huge difference between Germany and the United States when it comes to being arrested and charged. At any rate, this is the crudest treatment I've ever been through. I often remember my friend [lover?], Hans Schirmer, who died by suicide seven years ago. I almost did myself. I would place the blame for this on the terrible furtiveness and phoney shame which prevails here in America. It's bad enough that you can't even drink a glass of beer or wine here [this was the Prohibition Era]. I turned twenty-six on the eleventh of March, and I wouldn't have thought that something like this could happen to me. It's probably fair to say that there's more freedom in every European country, especially Germany and France, than in the famous and infamous U.S.A.

## 1929, May 4
### N. Y. Times: "Woman . . . Wed To One Of Her Sex,"
### Peter Stratford/Derestey Morton and Beth Rowland

A headline in *The Times* read: "Woman Lived As Man, Wed To One Of Her Sex."
The story, datelined Hollywood, California, reported:[45]

> Beth Rowland, a screen writer, admitted today that she was the "wife" in
> the strange case of Peter Stratford, whose death in Oakland yesterday [May
> 2] revealed "him" to be a woman masquerading as a man for many years.
>
> The screen writer said her first meeting with Stratford occurred sev-
> eral years ago in the Middle West when she was employed at secretarial
> duties. A friendship of two years, she said, was followed by marriage, im-
> mediately after which Stratford left her and went to the Pacific Coast in ill
> health. Later she [Rowland] followed and they were reunited at Niles, Cal.
>
> The secret of her "husband's" sex was not revealed to her until a few
> months ago, the screen writer said, and at that time she parted company and
> came here to do motion picture writing.
>
> From a packet of letters, a marriage certificate and other papers found
> in a hotel room at Niles today was pieced together a strange story of the
> misshapen life of Peter Statford.
>
> The correspondence revealed the determination of a woman, appar-
> ently possessed of all the mental attributes of the opposite sex, to become
> a man. Out of that determination, investigators said, was born Peter Strat-
> ford, a person with a gift for literary criticism and a follower of the cult of
> Sufi, an offshoot of an ancient Oriental religion.
>
> With the birth of Peter Stratford, the letters showed, died Derestey
> Morton, a British subject, who came to America from New Zealand twenty
> five years ago [1904].
>
> Peter Stratford married Miss Rowland in Kansas City, Mo., in 1925.
>
> In Hollywood, the letters revealed, Peter Stratford assisted nationally
> known playwrights and authors in their work.
>
> Other letters to a woman in Los Angeles, addressed only as "Alma,"
> revealed Peter's love for her as based on the tenets of the Sufi cult. . . .
>
> Yesterday Stratford, suffering from tuberculosis, was hurried to a hos-
> pital in Oakland.
>
> When doctors told the patient death was near, Stratford whispered her
> secret.

A follow-up story, in *The Times* of May 5, was headed: " 'Stratford's' Body
Remains Unclaimed." A story from Oakland, California, reported that "A grave
in Potter's Field" waited for the woman who had married another woman "and
worked at jobs varying all the way from heavy manual labor to writing critical

essays." It added: "No one claimed the body." A report from Hackensack, New Jersey, said that "Peter Stratford" had once boarded near there, and had " 'obtained a position with the government medical forces [in New York] during the war, . . . and because of his masculine walk and a voice that bordered on baritone, he was able to conceal his identity.' "

♀ MEDICAL

## 1929, May
## Dr. F. de Quervain:
### Castration "is indicated in cases of . . . homosexuality"

A summary of international writings on "Sexology" in a U. S. medical journal informed American doctors of a recent article in a German periodical.[46] Without comment the U. S. journal reported Dr. Quervain's "Results of Castration in Sexual Abnormalities":

> observations made upon some thirty-two patients, twenty-seven men and five women in whom castration had been carried out in the attempt to relieve some sexual abnormality. The libido was diminished more or less in every case. Out of eight cases of perverse sexual practices, a cure was secured in five cases. Psychic disturbances (depression, epileptic and schizophrenic disturbances) of transient nature were observed in nine cases; vasomotor disturbances, similar to those of the menopause, were seen in seven cases. The castrate body type developed in only seven cases. Twenty-three of the patients expressed themselves as very well satisfied with the results of the operation. The operation is indicated in cases of persistent exhibitionism, rape and homosexuality.

♀ MEDICAL

## 1929, August
## Dr. John F. W. Meagher:
### Some homosexuals "have a . . . psychopathic
### pride in their condition"

An article by Dr. Meagher, a psychiatrist at several New York City hospitals, asserted a theory of socially caused and acquired homosexuality—the sort of theory Radclyffe Hall's advocacy of congenital inversion was designed to combat.[47]

Meagher declared that "homosexual interest" in an adult "is normal within limits," and "forms the basis of deep friendships." It was "of course pathological

if any sort of physical relations are desired, or any sex excitement results."[505]
    There was "an incredible prevelance of all forms of homosexuality today."
There

> has been a particularly great increase of morbid homosexuality since the
> war, especially in Europe. This, in part, was due to the changed social
> conditions. . . .

"Not so many years ago this subject was only indifferently discussed in scientific
circles," but "it is a most important problem today in our social life.[505]
    Women were said to be

> often ignorant of this problem. I have examined many who did not know
> that their fundamental difficulty was homosexuality.[506]

"A woman who morbidly loves herself and is fixed on her own family, could not
really love a man."

> Studying this whole subject historically, you will notice that there has always
> existed a certain antagonism between the sexes. Sex made woman depend
> on man, so even normal women rebel against it, even if only symbolically.
> Homosexual women often exhibit open aversion or even hostility toward
> men. One reason for the woman resisting sex attraction is because of her
> unconscious fear of being dominated. Real love is never domineering; it
> leads to submission on the part of both. . . . The one thing that lessens the
> natural tension between man and woman is genuine reciprocal love.[507]

> Speaking of "Homosexual Traits," Dr. Meagher said: "A militant defense
> of homosexuality may be due to unconscious homosexual tendencies on the
> defender's part." "Many" homosexual "patients are vain, prudish, affected and
> prejudiced."

> Indulgent male inverts like pleasant, artistic things, and nearly all of them
> are fond of music. They also like praise and admiration. They are poor
> whistlers. Their favorite color is green. . . . Active male homosexuals are not
> prone to make sacrifices, personal or social, as was observed in the analysis
> of war neuroses. Some aggressive homosexual women wear male attire, and
> are often very proficient in business, sports, etc. The passive ones are of the
> clinging type, who like to kiss other girls.[508–09]

Dr. Meagher described a "submissive type" of male who

> had an orgasm when one of our surgeons in St. Mary's Hospital examined
> him for a varicocele [an enlargement of the veins of the spermatic cord], and
> the next day committed suicide after our urologist examined him. He said
> he felt "tortured"; and killed himself in a homosexual panic.[510]

Meagher claimed:

> Indulgent homosexual women often try to seduce innocent girls who are not
> acquainted with this problem. The latter may not realize that the kiss of an
> older woman is sometimes not innocent, thinking it only means friendship.

Also active homosexual women can do young women much harm by instilling perverted and untruthful sex ideas into them, thus ruining both their ideals and their character. There are enough other modern social conventional forces, kept up because of prudishness and prejudice which tend to ruin psychosexual development, without adding this factor. . . . Homosexual relations once experienced, produce a craving for repetition.[510]

The doctor warned: "Parents who *sissify* their sons tend to make homosexuals out of them."

There are certain families who cultivate interests which tend toward homosexuality. The women of this class who want a career, do not want to be subjected, and so avoid marriage, or are unhappy in it. . . . The driving force in many agitators and militant women who are always after their rights, is often an unsatisfied sex impulse, with a homosexual aim. Married women with a completely satisfied libido rarely take an active interest in militant movements. They have other interests, family and social, with which to use up their energy. Iwan Bloch said that the militant woman's movement was in part responsible for the diffusion of what he calls pseudo-homosexuality.* A few homosexual women feel depressed, thinking that they suffer because of their femininity, and because they cannot be men. Most of them would deny this, of course.[511]

A "woman who yearns only for higher education and neglects love, is usually of the frigid type," said Meagher.[508] To become "normal," a "frigid" woman

must transfer her interest from her self and her family, to the man. And she must change her childish aim, if she ever expects to assume the adult woman's role. A married woman is apt to remain anesthetic in the vagina unless the clitoris gives up some of its sensibility . . . to the vagina.[513]

Dr. Meagher declared: "Some homosexuals have a great aversion to physicians, fearing that their perversion will be found out; and some of them want to retain it." "Homosexual perversion" was best treated "at the psychic level, for drugs and surgery used alone are rarely beneficial."[515–16] "Perverted homosexuals," those who "gratify their cravings," should be "differentiated from ethical homosexuals" (those who do not act on their urges).

Many homosexual women have never had full sexual satisfaction (orgasm) in marriage. . . . So-called emancipated women are usually frigid, and usually have little unselfish maternal feelings. The best biological and social asset to society are the complete she-women, and the complete he-men. . . .[516]

In treating homosexual patients it is "necessary to have a knowledge of the history of mankind and of the age-old antagonism which has always existed between man and woman."

*Iwan Bloch, *The Sexual Life of Our Time In Its Relations to Modern Civilization* (N. Y.: Allied Book Company, 1908).

A cure for any form of homosexuality is possible only when it is desired. There is no treatment where an individual prefers his or her infantile attitude and does not want to progress and become psychosexually normal. Some want to be cured; others do not, but have a morbid, childish and psychopathic pride in their condition. Homosexual women who show such obstinate childish trends, as being unforgiving, resentful, and play-acting, are very difficult to manage.[517]

Dr. Meagher concluded: "If the pervert homosexual insists on not following advice, he knows society's attitude and must bear the responsibility for his conduct."[518] Some writers claimed that "perversions are not of social or legal concern

if the public is not injured; that they are only biological variations. But society and the law have a different viewpoint. The social must always prevail over the individual attitude. It might be interesting to note here that many homosexual kleptomaniac women are prone to steal silk underwear.[518]

♀ MEDICAL

## 1929, August
## Dr. Clarence P. Oberndorf:
## "Diverse Forms of Homosexuality"

Dr. Oberndorf of New York, a psychoanalyst and author of several articles on homosexuality, began one with a quote from the principal character in *The Well of Loneliness:* "'I am humble now; I'm some awful mistake—God's mistake—I don't know if there are any more like me, I pray not for their sakes, because it's pure hell.'"48

Although "homosexuality" had

ruffled civilized society since biblical times, only in recent years has it attracted the consideration of physicians interested in psychopathology. In the past few years in America, with the lifting of the barriers which had made all discussion of sex a question for hushed voices and closed doors, homosexuality, for perhaps the first time, has come to be accepted in restricted circles as a topic of general public interest, even after dinner chatter. . . . but popularization of the topic has not led very appreciably to its clarification.

Oberndorf criticized Dr. Joseph Collins and Radclyffe Hall as "widely read" writers who presented inaccurate views of "the present day interpretation of homosexuality."

The doctor explained: "Between the extremes of the sexual types of the

ultra womanly woman and the maximal manly man, one finds innumerable shades
. . . of sex inversion." All "psycho-analytic investigators" had found "the social
and mental traits of one sex in the body of the opposite"—the "amazing contradictions of masculine strivings in feminine bodies and *vice versa.* "[519]

"The "masturbator's . . . love and practices fall upon a body of the same
sex, therefore are homosexual," said Oberndorf.* Masturbation was "not dissimilar to the activities of two earth worms in copulation where each is active and
passive at the same time."[519]

In "both hospital and private practice" Oberndorf had found that the "active woman homoerotic" seemed "particularly content in her abnormality." The

> passive male homosexual may be annoyed by the social hazards of this
> inversion and seek some means of escaping from the ostracisim and legal
> jeapardy, but rarely wishes to be cured when he fully appreciates that the
> cure involves relinquishing of the inversion. . . . My own restricted experi-
> ence in attempting to alter continuous, voluntary, passive homosexuality in
> males through the administration of animal organ extracts, such as orchitic
> [testicular] substance adrenin, pituitary extract, and the like, has been uni-
> formly disappointing.[521]

The case was cited of a "mechanic" who had "indulged in overt passive
homosexuality with his brother." One of his symptoms was: "When in a mixed
group he found himself inevitably drifting among the women to assist them in the
kitchen to prepare refreshments."[522]

"Unconscious homosexuality" was said to be indicated by the "inability of
the male to lead in dancing or of the female to be led, desire on the part of the
male to be invited rather than invite the girl, [and] feeling of security on the part
of the male when underneath weights."[522]

Dr. Oberndorf warned that "Many persons" regarded adolescent
" 'crushes' " between persons of the same sex "merely as evidence of tenderness." But crushes were often "sexual." "In one American college for women I
am told they are colloquially designated by the girls as 'U. F.'s' (unhealthy friendships)."

This psychoanalyst pleaded "for a more tolerant and enlightened attitude"
toward the "psychopathology of homosexuality" on the part of "physicians, jurists, and laymen"—because "homosexuality is a diseased process." In "most
cases" the homosexual "sufferer" was "no more responsible" for the condition
"than for a crooked nasal septum." (A note added: "Operations on the . . . nasal
septum" were "very often followed by several hours of sexual eroticism.")[523]

---

*This aspect of society's masturbation taboo bears investigation in its relationship to its
homosexuality taboo. Oberndorf ignores the fact that while the material, practical object of all
masturbators is their own bodies, and thus homosexual, the fantasy object of masturbators may be
other-sexed.

♀ PLAY REVIEW

# 1929, November 13
## N. Y. Times: Thomas Dickinson's *Winter Bound*

A drama by play anthologist and former professor of English, Thomas H. Dickinson, produced by the Provincetown Playhouse in New York City, was reviewed.[49]

The unnamed critic reported that the theater-goer was "confronted" by "a theme of twisted impulses that wandered vaguely along the path of 'The Captive' ":

> Mr. Dickinson's play concerns two girls, Tony Ambler and Eunice Mackail, who have come to Tony's Connecticut farm-house for the Winter to see, as Tony says, if "women can be true to themselves," if they can attain a plane of life transcending sex. Tony, a sculptress, assertive, robust, "like a boy that never grows up," is dominant with a strength made expressive in pity, tenderness and contempt.

Complications ensue with the "invasion of a neighboring farmer, who is attracted to Eunice and whose passion is returned." In a "final revolt against Tony's authority, Eunice breaks away at last to marry Chet Williams, sending her companion off to a future that is not indicated."

The reviewer criticized Dickinson for never bringing his theme into focus, except perhaps in "moments of lucidity that follow the unrestrained storms of bitterness between the two women."

Another New York newspaper reviewer, Richard Watts, Jr., wrote that *Winter Bound* was "intended to treat of the pathological subject of what must be loosely, vaguely and inaccurately described as decadent love."

Beginning with two women planning to live for a winter on a farm, "without the complications that arise from association with men," the playwright was said to present a heroine (Tony Ambler) who might be either

> an abnormal person, a woman who wanted to idealize love and place it on a spiritual basis, or a girl who had been bruised in the past and therefore instinctively feared the entire idea. At the end she exits weeping with the cry that she is "a hundred years ahead of my time," but you never know just why.

And in another New York City newspaper John Mason Brown described *Winter Bound* as "lumbering down that brimstone path which leads to 'The Well of Loneliness.' " This theatrical "study in abnormality" portrayed the conflict between the "masculine" Tony Ambler and the "completely feminine girl" who is for the first time under Tony's "domination." The play recorded "the struggle for the possession" of the "girl," fought between Tony and a male farmer.*

*For comment on such struggles for "possession" see 1926, September 30; also see 1937, December.

# 1929
## Katharine Bement Davis:
### *Factors in the Sex Life*
### *of Twenty-Two Hundred Women*

The Bureau of Social Hygiene, a branch of the Rockefeller Foundation, issued a report on the "sex life of normal women," titled *Factors in the Sex Life of Twenty-Two Hundred Women,* by Katharine Bement Davis, a sixty-nine-year-old penologist and social worker.[50]

The "normal" woman studied was defined as she "who was not pathological mentally or physically and who was capable of adjusting herself satisfactorily to her social group." The study was based on questionnaires answered by 1,000 married women, and 1,200 single women who had graduated from college at least five years previously. This report on female sexuality was one of the most important published before that of Kinsey and his associates in 1953.

Using statistical methods Davis studied "such subjects as were important and timely."[xiii] Lesbianism among unmarried college women and among married women were the subjects of two chapters, written with Marie E. Kopp.

The survey of "Homosexuality" in "The Married Woman" found this group to be much more conflicted, negative, and puritanical about their lesbian experience than the single college graduates—who were more accepting and affirmative of their feelings.

The chapter on "Homosexuality" in "The Unmarried College Woman" reported that 1,200 single female college graduates were asked if they had ever had "intense emotional relations with any other girl or woman?" The character of such relations, the stage of life at which they occurred, their duration, their number, the respondent's "mental attitudes toward" them, and the "effect" of these relations were determined by follow-up questions.

Six hundred and five women, or slightly over 50 percent of all those who answered the questionnaire, said they had "at some time or other experienced intense emotional relations with other women." These respondents' experiences were accompanied by physical expressions recognized as sexual by 312 women, slightly more than half of the group. The three hundred and twelve who recognized their experience as sexual constituted 26 percent of the entire sample.[247–48; 277]

Of the above 605 women, 234 said their intense same-sex relations were "accompanied by mutual masturbation, contact of the genital organs, or other physical expressions recognized as sexual." Another group of 78 women said their intense emotional relations, though without physical expression other than hugging and kissing, were "recognized at the time as sexual." These two groups constituted the 312 women whom Davis and Kopp called "overt" homosexuals.

Another group of 293 women said their experience of intense same-sex relations was "unassociated with consciousness of a sex experience and unaccompanied by physical expression other than hugging and kissing."[247] (The distinction between "sex" and "hugging and kissing" reveals a dubious and unquestioned, culturally relative assumption. If the relations under study had been those of men with men, "hugging and kissing" would probably have been considered a "sexual" manifestation. This is pointed out to stress the influence of researchers' assumptions and categories in any analysis of behavior and feeling.)

Among the noteworthy results of this study is the high percentage of women who found their intense emotional relation with other women "helpful and stimulating."[255] The study found that "only 40 of the 312 overt homosexuals regarded their homosexual relationship in the light of a sex problem requiring solution."[271] Females attending coeducational schools experienced significantly fewer intense emotional relations with other women. But the "college crush," and even "overt" homosexual relations existed to a considerable extent at coeducational institutions.[258–60; 277–78]

As to a correlation between particular kinds of work and homosexual experiences—only in the group of "social service" workers was there a significant correlation between occupation and the experience of both overt lesbian activity and intense emotional relations with other women.[263]

A number of the women questioned used the opportunity to make statements in defense of active lesbian relationships—a form of resistance to traditional medical and theological condemnation.

The report included selected histories of single college women, including their experiences of same-sex intimacy.*

NEWS REPORT/EDITORIAL

# 1930, April 1
## N. Y. Times: Motion Picture Code, "Sex perversion . . . is forbidden"

"Respect for Flag Demanded in Movies" read a subhead. *The Times* reported that a new code of standards had been adopted by the Motion Picture Producers and Distributors Association, headed by Will Hays.[1]

Movies were now to reflect "the better standards of life." "Law, natural or human," was "not to be ridiculed," nor law violation portrayed sympathetically.

Hays explained: "The love of man and woman" was a proper theme,

---

*My plan to include excerpts from these histories was frustrated at the last moment by the inclusion in Davis's original contract with Harper of a clause specifying that the publisher was not, "under any circumstances," to clear material for reprint. Although Davis is deceased and there are no known heirs, the Harper and Row permissions manager felt the company had to abide by the original contract. The reader will find the excerpts I wished to reprint on the following pages of Davis's book: 279-93, 296.

but "all sex relationships" were to be treated "with due care." The code provided:

> That the sanctity of the institution of marriage and the home shall be upheld.
> That adultery shall not be explicitly treated or justified.

"Passion" was not to be depicted unless essential. And "Sex perversion or any inference of it is forbidden on the screen." "White slavery" was not to be treated. "Ministers of religion" were not to be pictured as "comic" or as "villains." The "use of the flag" was to be "respectful." And "Obscenity . . . is forbidden."

The large size of the film audience was cited by the industry as the basis for its new standards. *The Times* explained: "The new code is generally considered an outgrowth of severe criticism by prominent churchmen" that the "moral character of audiences" was being undermined by films.

A *Times* editorial on the same day explained further that "dramatists, educators, psychologists, church leaders, and representatives of many women's organizations" had been consulted in formulating the new code, which stressed "conformity to 'the wholesome instincts of life.' " American films "must afford our foreign friends a pleasant notion of us."

♀  BOOK REVIEW

## 1930, April 20
### *N. Y. Times Book Review:*
### André Gide's *The Immoralist*

"The world of André Gide," said Louis Kronenberger, "is a world of moral conflicts."[2] "No writer of our generation has wrestled more arduously with his own soul, or been less satisfied with his vision of life, than Gide." His "vision of evil," it was said, "enslaves him, allows of no ultimate release, and leaves him with an ineradicable sense of guilt."

Gide's character, Michel, the "immoralist" of the novel (translated by Dorothy Bussy) had been "Brought up to a scholarly and ascetic way of living." He "married to please his father, never possessed his wife," and while in North Africa on his wedding tour almost died of tuberculosis. The nearness of death made Michel realize "he had never experienced life." With this new "thirst for life" his "instincts began to reassert themselves," and *The Immoralist* "recorded Michel's transformation, step by step, from an ascetic to an abnormal." His "self-development" lead him from a happy relationship with his wife to

> a passive expression, in the company of handsome Arab boys, of homosexual love; at the end self-development has become so dominating that

Michel's wife, now tubercular herself, is not protected from death, and dies; and Michel proceeds from a heterosexual liaison to a homosexual one.*

Midway in Michel's development an old friend, Menalque, leads him "to abandon halfway measures and consider only himself."

Gide claimed in his preface neither to indict nor apologize for Michel. But the reviewer thought an "indictment falls . . . upon the egotistic philosophy which engulfed" the character. Michel's

adventure ends for him in a bitter unhappiness of soul. Thus moral judgment is not lacking. . . .

♀ BOOK REVIEW

## 1930, July 6
### N. Y. Times Book Review:
### Geoffrey Moss's That Other Love

In a review headed "A Puzzling Girl," a Times critic warned:[3]

Those who, after reading the inscription on the jacket, look for another "Well of Loneliness" in "That Other Love," will be somewhat disappointed. To be sure, the story concerns itself with the attraction of one woman for another, but this is only shown late in the book and never becomes graphic in its descriptions. Mr. Moss has made the attraction neither abnormal nor morbidly psychological, but neither has he provided any reason for it.

The reviewer explained: after the balked elopement of the "Tall, blond and handsome" Phillida Chard with a married man, "she has no further interest in members of the opposite sex." She is "best friends" with Huguette, whose "promiscuous" relations with men repel Phillida, but do not destroy the "friendship."

Then she becomes acquainted with a sculptress, Vera Coswell, whom she loves dearly. For a long time Vera repulses her efforts at friendship, finally, however, giving in, and the two women have a house together in France.

Nothing in Phillida's history accounts for the fact that she loves women more than men; and her subsequent decision to forsake Vera and marry in order to have children is also poorly motivated. Granted that in life people drift in and out of such relationships with little apparent reason, it is the duty of an author to create reasons for everything. As a child, Phillida sees nothing to disgust her with normal life. . . . Neither, as a child, does she show preference to women. . . . From the time she lives with her stepmother, her activity and thoughts are as normal as those of any other girl of her age, one instance when she is disgusted with a man who makes love to her disagreeably being not enough of an experience to leave any definite mark on her character.

*This is the first use of the "homosexual"/"heterosexual" dualism in The Times.

♀ BOOK REVIEW/RESISTANCE

## 1930, July 30
### N. Y. Times Book Review:
### André Birabeau's *Revelation*

This novel's translation from the French by Una, Lady Troubridge, lover of
Radclyffe Hall, may now be seen as a lesbian's act of resistance to the literary
portrayal of the homosexual as a revolting degenerate.[4] In the novel the mother's
change in response from "disgust" to "love" suggested the possibility of a similar
change in response in readers.

"This novel," said Louis Kronenberger, "differs from any previous treatment of sexual pathology in literature."

> Emphasis is thrown thrown not on the invert himself, young Dominique, but
> on his mother's reactions to the discovery, after he is killed in a motor
> accident, that he was homosexual.
>
> Dominique's father was a newspaper correspondent who was seldom
> in Paris, and his mother, living almost the life of a widow, was her son's
> inseparable companion. She lived for him, studied, loved, indulged and
> watched over him, rejoiced in what she believed his purity. . . .

When after his death she discovered his "tell-tale love letters," her "reaction is
one of violent disgust." These feelings shift from her son "to the unknown man
who she believes had corrupted him," and she goes to Avignon to "kill him."

> But confronted, not by a man who looks degenerate but by some one
> sympathetic to her and devoted to Dominique's memory, her feelings
> change again: She ceases to hate the man, and once more she loves her son.

This "study of Mme. Casse is morbid and painful." An inferior psychologist
and artist would have made explicit "how Mme. Casse's excessive devotion led
to a mother-fixation in her son," and how this "led to Dominique's sexual inversion." But author Birabeau left this to conjecture—"it may or may not be true"
—and made "the mother so utterly unconscious of what she perhaps has done
that she is not only shocked at discovering it, but revolted as well."

This was "a serious and dignified, if sometimes rather horrifying work."

♀ BOOK REVIEW

## 1930, September 14
### N. Y. Times Book Review:
### Radclyffe Hall's *A Saturday Life*

"The American publication" of this early, "amateurish" and "unimportant"
novel "can be explained on the basis of Radclyffe Hall's considerable personal

celebrity," said an anonymous critic.[5] But the book would disappoint readers interested in Hall's work because of her talent, as well as "the far larger group who hope for forbidden thrills after the manner of 'The Well of Loneliness.'"

BOOK REVIEW

## 1930, September 28
### N. Y. Times Book Review:
### Floyd Dell's *Love in the Machine Age*

The anti-puritanism of the 1930s is revealed in this review as "modern" in its advocacy of male-female sexual freedom, traditional in its anti-homosexuality.[6] Author Floyd Dell was known as a member of the Greenwich Village "bohemian" set.

In this book, said reviewer Henry James Forman, Dell set out to combat what he called "the patriarchal system." Dell referred to the system that prevented the young from choosing their own mates, "first by complete economic dependence upon their parents, and second by the inculcation of permanently childish states of mind in regard to work and love." The reviewer added:

> The train of evils in the wake of these disabilities of the young, the infantilism, prostitution and homosexuality, certainly present a depressing picture of our civilization.

Dell attacked "'the desperate makeshift happiness of oppressed human beings,'"—in particular that "Inculcation of purity" which he maintained "breeds distrust of the opposite sex." Dell argued that young people should be "'permitted to develop normally to hetero-sexual adulthood.'" But the reviewer thought that "such a state already exists, here and now."

In his introduction Dell argued

> that by the destruction of the patriarchal family and its accompanying social-sexual institutions, modern machinery has laid the basis for a more biologically normal family life than has existed . . . in the whole life of mankind.

The reviewer thought that the "patriarchal system" attacked by Dell was "already in ruins."

MEDICAL

## 1931, April 15
### Dr. Harry Benjamin:
### *"For the sake of morality"*

A recent New York City investigation of prostitution, resulting in "the stark tragedy of murder and suicide," caused Dr. Benjamin to decry the "puritanism" behind such attempts at suppression.[7] This relatively liberal doctor attacked restraint on male-female coitus because it allegedly fostered homosexuality— perceived as a "misfortune" under conditions of social "intolerance." Benjamin also suggested that a "normal polarization" led to "psychosexual differentiation" in a "heterosexual direction." His later theories of "transsexualism" (he coined the term), further developed his notion of a "normal" male-female polarity. His reference to "boys" who were "seventeen to twenty-five" and "older," documents the relativity of the concepts of adulthood and youth.

"Recently," said Benjamin,

A well-educated and rather refined man, a homosexual from Germany, visited me in New York. In the course of conversation he remarked: "Your New York here is just an Eldorado for us (homosexuals); the boys are so easy to get here, they fall for the least attention."

. . . I am afraid it is true. Many conversations with young boys, after sufficient confidence was gained, have added weight to the statement of my visitor, and have also provided me with an explanation.

During the period of puberty and for some years afterwards, the psychosexual differentation is not always complete. The homosexual phase . . . through which we all pass . . . before and during puberty, still leaves some traces in the mentality of boys between the ages of about seventeen and twenty-five. They are still nearer bisexuality than older boys. The testicular hormone may not have fully exerted its eroticizing influence in the heterosexual direction. . . .

I am speaking of the many boys who are not fully masculinized at that age, those who are not yet polarized on the woman. They have already their normal heterosexual libido and would like to satisfy it; but society has built up the barrier. If they could easily . . . procure normal relations they would do so. Normal polarization would then take place and all would be well.

. . . It is after all the lesser evil to visit a prostitute once in a while than to become a homosexual in our present time of intolerance against this deviation from the norm. But only too often the road to sex development in the normal direction is blocked. . . .

These boys, mostly sensitive and very emotional, are longing for more than physical gratification only. They are longing for love and sympathy. When at this stage a homosexual man enters their lives, their own receding or latent homosexual component is brought temporarily or even permanently to the surface again. I have heard this "history" many times, not only from normal men who were fortunate enough to escape these homosexual influences unharmed, but also from bisexuals and homosexuals who sometimes actually ascribe their misfortune to these early events. "If I could have had the right girls at the right time, I would still be for the girls," one expressed it.

Not only the growing boy, who is still nearer the bisexual state, is thus handicapped by our demands for "sex purity," but also the bisexual adult. One of our foremost judges fully confirmed my contention, that . . . homo-

sexual practices have been on the increase since the suppression of prostitution. These bisexual adults being unable . . . to procure heterosexual relations, . . . prefer to satisfy the other side of their sex constitution rather than
live without sex expression entirely.

Benjamin ended by wondering if "we shall ever grow up in sex matters and
arrange them according to biology and medicine and not according to theology
and to a sex perversion called puritanism."[381]


IMAGE

# 1931
## Blair Niles: *Strange Brother*

The jacket of a novel about Mark Thornton, a sexual "abnormal," conveys the
book's note of melodramatic tragedy.[8] The jacket also conveys the identification
with Thornton of a woman journalist, her recognition that her own suffering over
love (for a male) is similar to Thornton's—that he is her "strange brother."
Though *The New York Times* reviewed no less than fourteen of the prolific Niles's
other books, its failure to review *Strange Brother* (like its failure to review *The Well
of Loneliness*) suggests a conscious policy of silence concerning the relatively
sympathetic portrayal of the homosexual. This patterned silence is discussed in
the Introduction to the modern era, p. 164.


♀  BOOK REVIEW

# 1932, May 29
## *N.Y. Times Book Review:*
## Anna Elizabet Weirauch's *The Scorpion*

Under the heading "Chronically Miserable" a *Times* reviewer briefly evaluated
Weirauch's novel published in New York, and translated from the German by
Whittaker Chambers.[9] Considering Chambers's own homosexuality, his simultaneous sexual 'reformation,' political recantation, and religious conversion and his
later attack on an alleged former friend, Alger Hiss, Chambers's translation of this
early, melodramatic lesbian novel bears further study.

*The Times* review began:

For a novel peopled almost entirely by characters afflicted with abnormalities this book is singularly devoid of offensive detail. The atmosphere of
relative cleanliness sustained is due to the chief sufferer's delineation as a
border-line neurotic with yearnings for spiritual beauty and an ingrained
horror of the botched creatures with whom fate constantly brings her into

contact. This character, Metta, when she comes of age and into comfortable means, wanders disconsolately from city to city of her native land, the prey to consuming phobias and complexities, associating with people who do their utmost to drag her to their own level of iniquity. The idealist in her nature preserves Metta from the nether depths, though habitual despair tempts her relentlessly to end her distraught life. Just why it is that Metta should be so chronically miserable—bad companions and the evil influences to which she never wholly yields do not fully explain it—is never clearly established. This lack of definiteness in the girl's portrayal, combined with her unreasoning surrender to morbid wretchedness and introspection, weakens the story's logic, coherency and conviction.

♀ BOOK REVIEW

## 1932, September 11
### N. Y. Times Book Review:
### Arthur Weigall's *Sappho of Lesbos*

A *Times* review of a book about Sappho suggested a new moral and historical relativism in regard to her "homosexuality." In contrast, the review suggested an absolute aesthetic standard in regard to her poetry.[10]

Reviewer Florence Finch Kelly said that in this "first complete and detailed biography of Sappho," Weigall "handles frankly and scientifically that dark factor in Sappho's life and poetry that caused the early church to burn her books and since then has cast a shadow upon her reputation."

> There have been attempts, some of them in quite recent years, to explain away the homosexuality of much of her work and to prove that she has been outrageously maligned. But Mr. Weigall will have none of this. . . . She should be judged, he insists, not by the moral standards of many centuries later but by those of her own place and period. The Greeks, of course, had no sexual morals whatever, and not many of any other kind, and Sappho, in these respects, was simply the product of her environment. . . . The world as she knew it did not look upon homosexuality as reprehensible.

"Weigall brings this all out frankly and clearly," arguing that the beauty of Sappho's poems should be judged "without any regard for the conditions" that produced it; that these poems "ranked among mankind's greatest artistic achievements"; and that Sappho herself should be judged by her art.

♀ FILM REVIEW

## 1932, September 21
### N. Y. Times: *Girls in Uniform*

"The widely discussed" German film, which "enjoyed remarkable success in Berlin, Paris and London," had opened in New York.[11]\* *Times* film critic Mordaunt Hall reported:

> The New York State Board of Censors at first frowned upon the suggestion in this film of the "captive" theme, but recently they reconsidered their refusal to grant it a license.†

\*See reviews of the play *Mädchen in Uniform*, 1932, November 6, and the novel, 1933, November 19.

†For *The Captive* see 1926, September 30.

Hall praised the film as "a beautiful, tender, and really artistic cinematic work." The "suspicions of the severe principal" of the girls' school were "approached subtly," and the film was "actually more of a rap on the knuckles for the military notions than an exposition of unnatural affection."

PLAY REVIEW

## 1932, November 1
### *N. Y. Times:* John Lyman and Roman Bohnen's *Incubator*

A drama titled *Incubator* was set in a state training school for males in the Midwest.[12] The play was reviewed in *The Times* under the heading "Boys in Uniform" (a reference to the earlier film and the impending production of Christa Winsloe's *Girls in Uniform;* see 1932, November 6).

*Incubator* told the story of young Fred Martin who arrived in the school "a friendly, likable lad and leaves a toughened, bullying one, an almost certain criminal." In the school, the reviewer explained, "Fred has no easy time of it."

> Two of the boys develop an unnatural affection for him, and for a time the piece threatens to become a shocker dealing with twisted sex relationships.

But Fred saved himself, transferring to a school office evidently beyond the range of "unnatural affection."

"The boys in uniform who people this school . . . are extremely sex-conscious adolescents, and that fact is stressed." It was "sex in one form or another which occupies most of their thoughts."

♀  PLAY REVIEW

## 1932, November 6
### *N. Y. Times:* Christa Winsloe's *Mädchen in Uniform*

A dispatch from London discussed the English stage adaptation of Winsloe's *Mädchen in Uniform.*"[13] Charles Morgan said it had been a long time "since any serious piece" had been received with

> so much enthusiasm by audiences and critics. Although there is no man in the cast, no love story in the ordinary sense and not a gleam of happiness in the conclusion, I cannot but believe that this play will be a great commercial, as it is already a great artistic, success.

The play was set in a German girls' school "dedicated to the Prussian military ideal. The 'revolution has not touched it.' " The philosophy inspiring the school suggested the time will come when Germany will need soldiers again and the mothers of soldiers. The girls must be trained to be "women of iron."

A teacher, Fräulein von Bernburg, "divided within herself between loyalty to the system and a humane mistrust of its extreme rigors," kisses each of her charges "impartially"—"a deliberate freezing of personal emotion." So when Manuela, the schoolgirl heroine, kneeling on her teacher's bed, "flings her arms round the mistress's shoulders in passionate demand for affection Fräulein von Bernburg repels her with gentle firmness."

> The developing love between girl and mistress is, as the play presents it, almost a love between mother and child, though it is open to us to assume, if we will, that subconsciously it is inflamed in some degree by passion different in origin.

When Manuela publicly declared "that she and Fräulein von Bernburg love each other" this confession was heard by the headmistress, who condemned and punished her for it. Manuela was disgraced, and finally committed suicide, having been "deprived of love in a bleak and cruel world"—but not before her teacher had revolted against the headmistress's Prussian severity.

The writing of the play was said to communicate

> a superb, controlled indignation and pity—pity not for this girl only but [for] a starved and suffering humanity represented in her.[IX:1:3]

An American production of *Girls in Uniform* was praised in *The New York Times* later the same year. On December 31, 1932, Brooks Atkinson found it a "deeply touching" portrait of life in a Prussian girls' school "conducted on military principles." What upset the school's discipline, said Atkinson, was the

> sensitive imagination of Manuela, the motherless child of a Prussian officer, who finds in her teacher the first womanly tenderness she has ever known and who loses her head out of pleading, girlish ecstasy. In a moment of excitement . . . she shouts aloud the joy of her love for her teacher. "Scandalous!" exclaims the headmistress, who knows so much that she understands nothing. Manuela does not realize what she has done. . . . Bewildered and brokenhearted, she leaps out of a window and kills herself.

Atkinson called the "tired, forced knowledge" of the teachers in the play "one of the prime injustices of our regimented civilization." He liked the staging of the play for capturing "the dewy girlishness" of the students, who "gather in giggling groups and serendade each other with complete spontaneity."[10:3]

♀ IMAGES

## 1932
### N. Y. Tribune: "Mr. and Mrs."

A "Mr. and Mrs." cartoon in *The New York Tribune* derived its humor from the contrast between a traditional view of "maiden ladies" as "timid" and needing protection, and the reality of three independent women, quite able to fend for themselves.[14] (See next page.) The comic strip reflects the new middle-class awareness of "masculine" women moving together into view—and even into the neighborhood. (This cartoon was clipped by an anonymous individual and pasted into a scrapbook on lesbian themes now in The Institute for Sex Research.)

PLAY REVIEW

## 1933, January 8
### Cleveland Plain Dealer and N.Y. Times:
### Noel Coward's Design for Living

Coward's play, *The Times* noted, had been "cryptically announced" to concern " 'three people who love each other very much.' "[15] The play's pre-Broadway opening in Cleveland, Ohio, had been greeted enthusiastically. *The Times* reprinted a comment from the *Cleveland Plain Dealer:*

> The story is an unconventional variation of the triangle that would have shocked Queen Victoria and may even disturb some of her descendants.

Actress Lynn Fontanne played "an emancipated woman," uninterested in marriage, who lived successively with a playwright (Noel Coward) and an artist (Alfred Lunt).

> The artist and the playwright are devoted friends. Their friendship, deep and treasured as it is, does not cool the attraction the heroine has for them.

After many complications the three were said finally to display

> a forgiving indulgence for their own unconventionalities, and the feeling they leave at the last is that they belong, by right of their difference from herd, together."

Brooks Atkinson reported, in *The Times* of January 29, 1933, that although the Broadway production of *Design for Living* had

> a constant odor of sin, . . . it is no more sensual or erotic than a highly polished blade of steel. In conversation with Gilda, Leo succinctly describes the plot: "I love you. You love me. You love Otto. I love Otto. Otto loves you. Otto loves me."

## Mr. and Mrs.—

*Joe's Fears Prove Groundless*

♀  BOOK REVIEW

# 1933, January 29
## *N. Y. Times Book Review:* Sinclair Lewis's *Ann Vickers*

Although *The Times* review did not mention the lesbian episode in this novel, the critic's association of "tomboy," "feminist," and self-seeking woman implied an opposite ideal, the "normal" woman—selfless, dependent and man-loving.[16]

Reviewer J. Donald Adams placed Ann Vickers in historical perspective as

> one of that host of young women who came out of college in the years just before the war, intensely eager to have a part in the work of the world, somewhat self-consciously hopeful of doing something to make it a better place. And like so many of those young women, she is to find it hard to make the adjustment between her desire to count as an individual and the insistent demand of her emotional needs as a woman. Ann is 40 before she is at peace with herself. . . .

As a social worker Ann Vickers at different times participated in the "suffrage movement, the social settlement house, philanthropy and organized charity, [and] prison reform"—realizing finally that "there is no smooth path to perfection."

Lewis's novel "will not please uncompromising feminists." The "heart of the book is not the world of social service, but Ann's personal problem as a woman." As an "eager little tomboy" Vickers had become a "feminist" when she put out a fire while all the men were standing still in shock. Later in life Vickers found a "real man" and told him that "he and the son that he has given her have brought her 'out of the prison of ambition, the prison of desire for praise, the prison of myself.' " The reviewer thought that "the ultra-feminists" would "mock" those words "for the betrayal which they are." Yet at the end Vickers still wanted to work, and "is still a feminist, but one that has come to terms with life." Lewis's theorized that a woman's "career can never be an adequate substitute for a more fundamental need, even when that need demands the subordination of self," and "psychic dependence." Ann Vickers, the reviewer concluded, "is a woman first, a feminist afterward."*

---

*Sinclair Lewis's portrait of a woman torn between desire for achievement and subordination to a man is interesting in terms of his own deeply troubled marriage to journalist Dorothy Thompson, and Thompson's attraction to woman-loving; see *GAH*, pp. 556–62.

♀ INTIMACY

## 1933, March 5
## Eleanor Roosevelt and Lorena Hickock:
*"That soft spot just north-east of the corner of your mouth"*

Among their revelations, the love letters of Eleanor Roosevelt and Lorena Hickock indicate that, though certifiably heterosexual in the technical sense, this now most famous first lady and Franklin Roosevelt were not exactly a model of domestic intimacy.[17]* On October 16, 1936, in a letter to her lesbian friend, Eleanor Roosevelt wrote that she was alien to her husband and did not wish it to be otherwise.[221]† Such comments, together with biting interchanges between Eleanor and Lorena about men and politics, document a woman-to-woman intimacy whose ironies are grand. On August 7, 1940, after hearing of some particularly petty political intrigue, Hickock wrote to the president's wife:

> My God, dear—these men are children, small quarrelsome children. And we are expecting them to run the nation in a time of awful peril! I think they need someone to give them Hell—the whole gang of them, *both* sides [Democrats and Republicans]. They don't deserve to win this election if they keep on the way they've been going. . . .

That Hickock had several overt lesbian relationships, and that she had discussed these with Eleanor Roosevelt is clear from Doris Faber's recent mean-spirited biography of Hickock. This biography also indicates that any public association with the new, explicit fiction of lesbianism made Hickock nervous. About two or three years before becoming friends with Roosevelt, Hickock had met a young newspaperwoman carrying a copy of *The Well of Loneliness* and had spontaneously responded that *she* would not be seen in public with that book. On a later occasion a sexual overture by Hickock had shocked this same woman reporter.[78–79]

Eleanor Roosevelt's and Hickock's existing letters, those which were not destroyed, do leave it unclear exactly what relations the two engaged in beside kissing, hugging, lying in bed together, and sharing an intense love for several years, a less intense friendship for the rest of Eleanor Roosevelt's life. (It is curious to note that if two men were known to have engaged in exactly the same activities, and written the same love letters, there would be no question about the appropriateness of the label "homosexual"; it has, however, been strenuously

---

*The quotations from Eleanor Roosevelt's letters are taken from the excerpts of her letters quoted in articles in *The New York Times* and *Times Literary Supplement*. Lorena Hickock's letters were given by her to the government and are in the public domain.

†Raised numbers in brackets cite page references of information in Faber's *Life of Lorena Hickock*. For my comment on this biography see pp. 8–9.

denied that Roosevelt's and Hickock's relation was "lesbian." This double standard in the use of terms does not simply reflect cultural differences in the physical expressions permitted female and female, male and male. The differential attribution of "homosexuality" to men and to women is one aspect of the traditional denial of female eroticism.)

There is no doubt that Roosevelt's and Hickock's intimacy was, for both women, powerful, deep, and supportive. When one realizes that the moving love letters that still exist are those which were *not* destroyed, it is clear that that correspondence eliminated must have been intimate indeed.

That both Hickock and Roosevelt were completely conscious of lesbianism is revealed in various letters, for example, in Hickock's correspondence to Roosevelt, in 1936, about the suicide of of one woman after a failure in woman-loving. In letters to Roosevelt, Hickock also casually discussed contraception, prostitution, and a pathetic female strip-tease act she'd witnessed. Both Roosevelt and Hickock were modern women of the world.

Historian Arthur Schlesinger, Jr., has suggested that Eleanor Roosevelt and Lorena Hickock were completely formed by the sexually innocent ideology of the late Victorian era—and that their declarations of love expressed that ideology. Schlesinger thereby implied that the consciousness and emotions of both women ceased to develop after their childhoods. Though common, that idea of childhood determinism is stupid. Besides being insulting, it ignores the fact that by the 1930s in the United States, female and male homosexuality had become a common topic of plays, books, and articles, with even the staid *New York Times* speaking openly on the subject. Hickock, and to a lesser extent Roosevelt, actually worried about gossip concerning their relationship.

It is also doubtful that late Victorian girls were as sexually naive as a Victorian ideology of innocence would have us believe. Victorian girls' schools, for example, are referred to in numerous sources as a major institutional setting for "crushes" and sexual relations between boarders. Eleanor Roosevelt happens to have attended just such an English girls' school. This was headed by the same headmistress who had earlier presided over the institution pictured in Dorothy Strachey Bussy's *Olivia*, a lesbian's reminiscence of her first female love (see 1949, March 27). The same headmistress with whom Bussy had fallen in love was an important influence on Eleanor Roosevelt.[18]

Between 1958 and her death on May 1, 1968, Lorena Hickock donated 2,336 of Eleanor Roosevelt's letters to her, and 1,024 of hers to Roosevelt, to the National Archives. Hickock provided that they be opened to the public ten years after her death, with only references to living persons censored temporarily. She herself had already destroyed some of the most personal letters, and after her death her sister destroyed additional items. Hickock's unsympathetic biographer attributed her subject's failure to burn *all* these letters to a desperate desire for posthumous fame. It is clear, however, that these letters recorded the love that had been Lorena Hickock's greatest happinesses, and of much importance to

Eleanor Roosevelt's development as an independent person. In a spirited act of resistance against that deathly convention which provides that evidence of such love must be exterminated, Lorena Hickock bequeathed to the nation her precious tokens of loving. Hickock's gift allows us to look back on and know some of the historical qualities of one particular female-female intimacy dating from 1932.

Lorena Hickock became (as she said) " 'very close friends' " with Eleanor Roosevelt while the journalist was covering Franklin Roosevelt's 1932 presidential campaign. By the end of 1932, before the Roosevelts moved to Washington to occupy the White House, Eleanor Roosevelt and Lorena Hickock were spending many evenings together in New York City, dining out and going to Broadway plays.[102] (Among those plays they could have seen two with homosexual references, Lyman and Bohnen's *Incubator* and *Girls in Uniform,* Christa Winsloe's classic portrayal of a schoolgirl "crush.")*

On the night of February 16, 1933, after Eleanor Roosevelt spoke at Cornell University, she and Hickock stayed together in Ithaca, New York and Roosevelt may have for the first time told Hickock about Franklin's affair with Lucy Mercer. In any case, Eleanor and Lorena's own intimacy grew, and a few weeks later, on March 4, at Franklin Roosevelt's presidential inauguration, Eleanor Roosevelt was wearing a sapphire ring given her by Hickock, who had received it from a female opera singer she'd once interviewed.[110] The symbolism of the ring indicates that that presidential inauguration also inaugurated a less public engagement between the president's wife and her woman friend. After the inauguration Hickock returned to New York City, and the two friends were separated for the first time since the blossoming of their intimacy. But Eleanor Roosevelt had promised to write to Hickock every night.[118]

On March 5, 1933, the evening Hickock left, on stationery embossed in gold with the seal of the president of the United States, Eleanor Roosevelt wrote her first letter from the White House to Lorena Hickock:

> Hick my dearest, I cannot go to bed tonight without a word to you. I felt a little as though part of me was leaving tonight, you have grown so much to be a part of my life that it is empty without you even though I'm busy every minute [*N. Y. Times,* October 21, 1979].

On March 6, Roosevelt wrote to Hickock a few hours after they had talked on the telephone.

> Hick darling, Ah, how good it was to hear your voice. It was so inadequate to try and tell you what it meant. Funny was that I couldn't say je t'aime et je t'adore as I longed to do, but always remember I am saying it, that I go to sleep thinking of you. . . . [*N. Y. Times,* October 21, 1979]

---

*For *Incubator* see 1932, November 1; for *Girls in Uniform* see 1932, November 6. A year later, in 1933, Roosevelt and Hickock could have seen *The Green Bay Tree* and, in 1934, *The Children's Hour* (see 1933, October 31; 1934, November 21).

On March 7, Hickock's birthday, Eleanor Roosevelt wrote to her:

> Hick darling, All day I've thought of you & another birthday I *will* be with you. . . . Oh! I want to put my arms around you, I ache to hold you close. Your ring is a great comfort. I look at it & think she does love me or I wouldn't be wearing it [*Times Literary Supplement,* July 11, 1980].

On March 8, Roosevelt wrote:

> Just telephoned you. Oh! it is good to hear your voice, when it sounds right no one can make me so happy! [*Times Literary Supplement,* July 11, 1980]

On March 9, Eleanor told Lorena:

> My pictures are nearly all up & I have you in my sitting room where I can look at you most of my waking hours! I can't kiss you so I kiss your picture goodnight and good morning! [*Times Literary Supplement,* July 11, 1980]

On March 10 Eleanor Roosevelt wrote to Hickock:

> Remember one thing always. No one is just what you are to me. I'd rather be with you this minute than anyone else and yet I love many other people and some often can do things for me probably better than you could, but I never enjoyed being with anyone the way I enjoy being with you [*N. Y. Times,* October 21, 1979].

On March 11, Eleanor Roosevelt said:

> I couldn't bear to think of you crying yourself to sleep. Oh! how I wanted to put my arms around you in reality instead of in spirit. I went and kissed your photograph instead. . . .[*N. Y. Times,* October 11, 1979].

On November 22, after hearing that White House reporters were gossiping about someone's divorce, Eleanor Roosevelt wrote to Hickock that it was difficult to prevent such public talk. If Hickock was a male they themselves would be gossiped about. Hickock replied that there probably was some gossip about their relationship.[160]

On December 5, from the Minnesota timber country, Lorena Hickock wrote Eleanor Roosevelt a fourteen-page letter, counting the days and hours until they would be together—and adding:

> I've been trying today to bring back your face—to remember just *how* you look. Funny how even the dearest face will fade away in time. Most clearly I remember your eyes, with a kind of teasing smile in them, and the feeling of that soft spot just north-east of the corner of your mouth against my lips. I wonder what we shall do when we meet—what we'll say. Well—I'm rather proud of us, aren't you? I think we've done rather well.

Hickock ended:

Goodnight, dear one. I want to put my arms around you and kiss you at the corner of your mouth. And in a little more than a week now—I shall!

Two months later, on February 19, 1934, *Time* magazine mentioned that "Miss Lorena Hickock," a "rotund lady with a husky voice, a peremptory manner, [and] baggy clothes," had become "fast friends with Mrs. Roosevelt." Since before Franklin Roosevelt's election as president, Hickock "has gone around* a lot with the First Lady, up to New Brunswick and down to Warm Springs." It had recently become "known that Miss Hickock" would accompany Eleanor Roosevelt on a trip to Puerto Rico.[158–59]

On September 1, 1934, Eleanor Roosevelt wrote to Lorena Hickock, "I wish I could lie down beside you tonight & take you in my arms" [*Times Literary Supplement,* July 11, 1980].

♀  BOOK REVIEW

# 1933, April 9
## *N. Y. Times Book Review:*
## Maude Meagher's *The Green Scamander*

Penthesilea, the "warrior Queen" of the Amazons, was the heroine of Meagher's novel.[19] This, said a reviewer, was a "romance of the days when 'the artificial stunting of women's minds, bodies and spirits was a comparatively new thing in the world.' " Then "women enjoyed a degree of freedom and of equality with men which they were not to regain until the dawn of the present century." (Women's freedom had apparently been won about 1900.)

The story centered on the Amazon Queen and her "young and dearly loved friend, Camilla." It included "fascinating descriptions" of "ceremonies belonging to the worship of the moon and of the great mother-goddess, Kybelé" (or Cybele).†

NEWS REPORT

# 1933, May 7
## *New York Times:* "Nazi Students Raid Institute on Sex"

A "wireless" to *The Times* reported that about eighty students had attacked "Dr. Magnus Hirschfeld's 'Institute for Sexual Science' " in Berlin, at the start of a Nazi crusade against the " 'Un-German Spirit' in print and picture."[20] (Although *The*

---

*The slangy phrase "gone around," with its double meaning of accompanying and romantic dating, suggests the innuendo was quite consciously intended to hint at improper intimacy. *Time,* known for its Republican sympathies, meant to cast aspersions on the Democratic President's wife.

†For another view of "Amazons" see 1933, May 12.

*Times* did not say so, Hirschfeld and his Institute were famous and central in the German homosexual emancipation movement, which existed from 1897 to 1933, when the Nazis began their concerted attack on homosexuals.

The dispatch added that "In less than an hour" the student raiders

> had gathered about half a ton of books, pamphlets, photographs, charts and lantern slides, which they hauled away . . . [to be] sorted by medical experts and the scientific part reserved for legitimate use.
>
> The "Un-German" part will be consigned to the Nazi fires that are to light up the university campus Wednesday.
>
> The archives of the institute contained extensive correspondence with professional men in all parts of Europe and the United States. This correspondence, the students said, would be treated as confidential and would be destroyed later, since they are determined to root out the Hirschfeld establishment.

Bust of Magnus Hirschfeld carried by Nazis (from Victor Robinson, "In Honor of Magnus Hirschfeld," *Anthropos,* number 1 [January 1934], p. 51; copy courtesy of James Steakley).

FILM REVIEW

## 1933, May 12
### N. Y. Times: The Warrior's Husband

"Handsome women in shining armor stalk the screen" at the Radio City Music Hall, wrote critic Mordaunt Hall of this "Story of Amazons and Their Insignificant Spouses."[21]

The warrior's husband was named Sapiens (from *Homo sapiens*—J. K.). His wife, the warrior,

> is the redoubtable Hippolyta, Queen of the Amazons. The lot of the modern hen-pecked husband is to be envied compared with that of Sapiens, familiarly called Sap. He wears "the silks and satins" and his hair and beard are in corkscrew curls. He dares not say that his soul is his own in the hearing of either his wife or her lovely sister, Antiope. . . .*

In the film, said *The Times,* Hercules was presented as

> a timid creature who shudders at the thought of Antiope harming him. This perfect fool is even afraid of Sapiens and it is perhaps this fact that impels Sap to risk everything in order to make himself a domineering man.

The "worm turns." Sap sees to it that the Greeks are given "Diana's magic girdle" (from which the Amazons get their strength). One of the Amazons, Antiope, "is carried off by Theseus," a Greek who is struck by her beauty. "He kisses her and she resents it, but there is more kissing and she is not displeased."

Actor Ernest Truex, in the role of Sapiens, was said to be "too good a comedian to have to cope with female attire and corkscrew curls."

MEDICAL

## 1933, May 31
### Dr. A. A. Brill: "Homoerotism and Paranoia"

In a paper read at a joint meeting of The American Psychiatric Association and American Psychoanalytic Association in Boston, the influential Freudian psy-

---

*According to Vito Russo, when the Amazon queen congratulates the Greek men for being " 'like women of the world,' " Homer says to Theseus, " 'By the gifts that fortune hands me, she takes you for a pansy.' " (Late in 1933, the word "pansy" was banned from films by the censor.) Examining the Amazon warrior's effeminate husband, Sapiens, Homer asks: " 'What is this creature?' " He adds: " 'I abhor it. Why, even the Greeks have no word for it.' " After Sapiens greets a handsome Greek messenger, the latter takes a long look at him and says: " 'You find them wherever you go' "; see Russo, *The Celluloid Closet,* pp. 39–40.

choanalyst A. A. Brill contributed to the large literature on homosexuality and paranoia.[22]*

Brill distinguished homosexuality per se from paranoia, and his argument provided an implicit critique of the repression of homosexual feelings, a rationale for their free expression. But by discussing homosexuality and paranoia together, without stressing the social persecution of homosexual acts, Brill sometimes suggested that homosexuality and paranoia were inherently linked. In May 1933, after the start of the full-scale Nazi persecution of homosexuals in Germany (see 1933, May 7), the Freudian association of homosexuality and a "delusion of persecution" was irresponsible and malevolent. (Also see 1934, January; 1934, July 1.) The tendency within psychoanlaysis and other psychologies to reduce human responses to the subjective, denying social realities, was particularly outrageous in 1933 and '34.

Brill began by stressing a distinction between "normal" and "pathological homosexuality." Homosexuality itself was "a part of the normal sexual instinct," originating "in the polymorphous perversity of the infantile sexuality." In "sublimated form" homosexuality "plays a useful part in our social relationship." But homosexuality might become "accentuated" or "inhibited," resulting in "difficulties of everyday adjustment to which the sensuous performances of the frank homosexual are absolutely foreign." That homosexuality associated with "difficulties of . . . adjustment" Brill called "pathological."[957–58]

Freud, said Brill, had "correlated paranoia and homosexuality," tracing the origin of a *"delusion of persecution"* to *"a repressed homosexual wish phantasy."*[959] In the paranoia associated with pathological homosexuality the "destructive impulses" pushed the erotic instinct to the background," making way for the "death instinct."[973]

♀  BOOK REVIEW

## 1933, September 3
### N. Y. Times Book Review:
### Gertrude Stein's *The Autobiography of Alice B. Toklas*

In a mass fit of split perception reviewers across the United States managed to adore this book of Stein's, even though most of them drew back in horror at

---

*Brill's paper was published in March 1934; see backnote. He was prominent in America as the original translator of the first U. S. editions of Freud's books. His work for the American cigarette company executives who wished to create a demand for their product among women is discussed in Stuart Ewen's *Captains of Consciousness: Advertising and the Social Roots of the Consumer Culture* (N. Y.: McGraw–Hill, 1976), p. 160. My critique of Freud's and his followers' psychological reductionism regarding homosexuality and paranoia parallels recent critiques of Freud's interpreting as imaginary his patients' reports of childhood sexual molestation by adults; see *N. Y. Times*, August 25, 1981, C 1:1, C 2:1.

"lesbianism."[23] For example, just two weeks after a *Times* reviewer praised Stein's *Autobiography*, a *Times* review of Mario Praz's *Romantic Agony* mentioned "Lesbian and homosexual loves" in close association with "perversity," the "Decadent period," and the "Fatal Woman" (see 1933, September 17). Though critics with difficulty imagined Gertrude Stein or Alice B. Toklas as a "Fatal Woman," reviewers did have to ignore Stein's visible eccentricity. Critics made her book a popular success while somehow conspiring to ignore that its female author had a crew cut, and that its ostensible subject was her female lover. The remarkable workings of this double vision is a subject requiring further concentrated thought.

*Times* reviewer Edward M. Kingsbury explained that despite its title this book "is by and about a writer at once famous and obscure," Gertrude Stein. Her "travelings" and "settlements" were "almost always amusing. Drop in on Miss Stein—Alice B. Toklas with her—anywhere."

The reviewer ended with a word from Alice B. Toklas (as recorded by Stein):

> I met Gertrude Stein. I was impressed by the coral brooch she wore and by her voice. I may say that only three times in my life have I met a genius and each time a bell within me rang and I was not mistaken, and I may say in each case it was before there was any general recognition of the quality of genius in them.

Stein was one of the "geniuses" for whom the bell rang in Alice B.


♀ BOOK REVIEW

# 1933, September 17
### *N. Y. Times Book Review:*
### Mario Praz's *The Romantic Agony*

In a review of Praz's *Romantic Agony* a historical connection was explicitly made between "Lesbian and homosexual loves," a literary archetype, the "Fatal Woman" (including "vampires" and other monsters), and the "Fatal Man."[24]*

Praz's study of "sadism" as portrayed in a century of literature was reviewed at length by Eda Lou Walton. In one chapter Praz was said to trace how in the Decadent period

> Lust becomes intellectualized. Nor is it to be wondered that, as the Decadent period advances, Lesbian and homosexual loves are justified in a curiously pseudo-intellectual philosophy. . . . Perversity is more subtle than the most

---

*For discussion of the lesbian as "vampire," male and female homosexuals as monsters, see the Introduction to this period, p. 164 and backnote. For an example of the lesbian as vampire see 1936, May 18. For the male homosexual as monster see 1936, February 9. Also see "vampire" in the index.

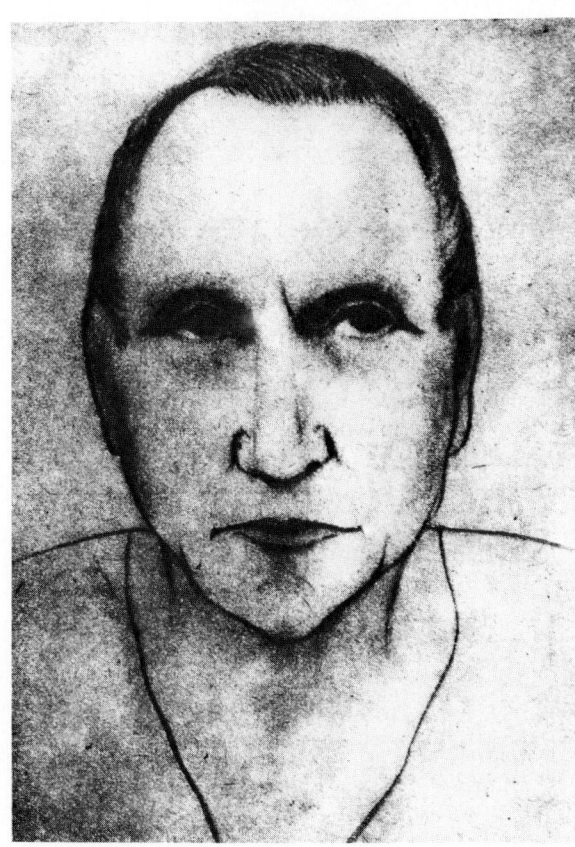

A drawing of Gertude Stein by Francis
Picabia, illustrating *The New York Times
Book Review*'s comments on *The
Autobiography of Alice B. Toklas* (1933).

violent action. Everywhere in this period the Byronic heroes grow feminine,
the Fatal Women masculine.

The "Fatal Woman" was a "type" established in Romantic literature, but "as old
as mythology; they are the harpies, the sirens, the gorgons, the vampires"—
"women capable of crime and enormous lust." The "Fatal Man" was, similarly,
a "literary type of outlaw or criminal" who appeared "in many disguises" in
Romantic and Decadent works. Byron's life and literature had focused "the portrait for the popular imagination."

♀ IMAGES

## 1933, October 11
### *Brevities:* "Queer Business"

Cartoons in a sensationalistic New York paper, *Brevities*, included images of effeminate men and masculine women as "queers."[25] Captions suggested that "feminine" male homosexuals were much interested in performing oral sex upon true he-men.

PICKLED CORNED BEEF

"*Rivalry!*"

*Brevities*, October 11, 1933, p. 12; copies of these cartoons courtesy of Allan Bérubé.

QUEER BUSINESS

"*A gentleman to see you, Mister Smith!*"

*Brevities*, January 15, 1934, p. 5.

A FAIRY NICE BOY

*"Were you calling for succor my good man?"*
*"Hell, no! I was yellin' for help."*

*Brevities,* November 23, 1933, p. 8.

SWEET BOY'S SWEET DREAM

*A guy who ate too much before going to bed.*

*Brevities,* December 10, 1933, p. 4.

NIZE BABY!

*"I want a policeman!"*

*Brevities,* February 12, 1934, p. 4.

PLAY REVIEW

## 1933, October 21
### N. Y. Times: Mordaunt Shairp's The Green Bay Tree

Brooks Atkinson reviewed the play *The Green Bay Tree,* which had opened in New York the night before.[26] He praised the "forcefully" told story

> of the relationship existing between Mr. Dulcimer, a rich hot-house sybarite, and Julian Dulcimer, whom he adopted at a tender age and has reared in emasculating luxury.* The relationship is abnormal, since Mr. Dulcimer, with all his petty sensuousness, is an abnormal person, but there is nothing in the play to indicate that the relationship is more than passively degenerate.

Mr. Dulcimer was " a possessive, selfish tyrant," who was "immured within luxuries," and "Julian is one of the luxuries he prizes most." When Julian "falls in love with a spirited young lady, Mr. Dulcimer withdraws the allowance." Julian "tries to prepare himself for earning a living," but "cannot face the shabbiness . . . of a life that is not heavily endowed." Though loving Leonora,

> he slinks back to his guardian. Leonora comes there to save him for herself and himself, also. His father comes there, crazy with evangelical zeal, and kills Dulcimer to free his son from corruption. That is how Julian comes to inherit all the wealth of Dulcimer's estate and . . . in the last act . . . sits down wearily to take up a rich, graceful, overcivilized life in Dulcimer's indulgent image.

> Actor James Dale's Dulcimer was called "a monster of fussiness and supercilious venom." Laurence Olivier's Julian was "an extraordinary study in the decomposition of a character."

> In another comment on October 29, Atkinson said that whether *The Green Bay Tree* was "a tragedy of sexual degeneracy is a technical question." In England it had reportedly been acted "from that point of view." In the American production, "Although the relationship existing between the two men is at least potentially degenerate," the director had focused on "the inhumanity of the dilettante's scheme of living," and had cut the text "to free it of morbid overtones."

BOOK REVIEW

## 1933, November 12
### N. Y. Times Book Review: Kay Boyle's
### Gentlemen, I Address You Privately

"Miss Boyle has invaded the harsh, dark, tangled precincts of the moral world where whole and merciless vision is demanded," said reviewer Louis Kronen-

---

*The idea that luxury emasculates suggests that poverty masculinizes.

berger.[27] Boyle

> has seized one man at a crisis in his development and, pinning him fast, hurled another man into contact with him. Munday, bred in the ascetic ways of the church, has broken with the church when the story opens, and turned to his music for compensation. At that moment, effeminate Ayton bursts into Munday's life and insists upon joining it to his own. Munday, his starved body answering before his mind is able, consents; and at once he is drawn into a homosexual relationship with Ayton. Soon he finds himself much more deeply drawn than he could possibly have foreseen: for Ayton has deserted his ship and committed thefts, and Munday is forced into hiding with him.

Ayton also impregnated Leonie, a female character. He was presented in the novel as an

> experimenter with life, a man who lives dangerously, wanting all sensations and experiences. In naive hands he would doubtless symbolize some spirit of evil, but realistically . . . he is simply unmoral, unprincipled and mischievous. He is merely the reef against which Munday founders.

BOOK REVIEW/RESISTANCE

## 1933, November 19
### N. Y. Times Book Review:
### Christa Winsloe's *The Child Manuela*

The English translation of Winsloe's novel *Mädchen in Uniform* was published in New York and reviewed in the *Times*. [28]*

The setting was a school where girls were supposed "to learn fortitude" and the "iron Prussian virtues, so that when they become officers' wives they will know how to train their soldiers' children." In this school the motherless Manuela "fastened her affection on Fräulein von Bemberg":

> It is this relationship that causes the explosion. Fräulein von Bemberg loves the child, but whether she feels that officers' daughters should not indulge in sentiment or whether she recognizes a latent homosexuality in herself is not defined. Although Manuela is often described as wishing she were a boy, what she seems to show is merely a hunger for mother-love and the thoroughly normal turbulence of the adolescent. Choosing either interpretation, the important fact remains that Fräulein von Bemberg's repression of her feelings and the school's suppression of Manuela's feelings led to a fateful frustration. And it is as a study of frustrations, in adulthood as well as childhood, that the latter half of this book becomes a social document that is moving and eloquent.

*For *The Times* review of the film *Girls in Uniform* see 1932, September 21; for the play see 1932, November 6. The teacher's name was "von Bernburg" in the play.

♀ FILM REVIEW/CROSSING WOMAN

## 1933, December 27
### *N. Y. Times:* Greta Garbo's *Queen Christina*

As described in *The Times*, Garbo's "Christina" was notable for her cross-dressing, assertiveness, and activity, characteristics comprising a popular stereotype of the lesbian.[29]* Male homosexuality was simultaneously hinted at in the "unusual interest" Don Antonio showed in the Christina he thought to be a young man. All the allusions to "perversion" were apparently allowed under the production code due to their ambiguity and a satisfactorily heterosexual ending.

*Times* reviewer Mordaunt Hall reported that Garbo was "forceful" as the queen, and "charming as Christina the woman":

> When Christina was born one is informed that her father . . . regretted that she was not a boy. He persuaded her as a child to wear knickerbockers.

The reviewer assumed that Christina's father had "insisted" that she "continue dressing as a boy after she was crowned Queen." Her "penchant for male attire" resulted in "a beguiling incident." In the film "Christina has a dominant personality," and "goes dashing on horseback over the snow-covered countryside." With her valet she fixed the broken coach of one, Don Antonio, who "thinks the Queen is quite an intelligent young man." At an inn Antonio again meets this "young man." Antonio and the disguised Christina

> become unusually interested in each other. Eventually, Don Antonio suggests that they share the room and after some hesitation—Christina agrees. In course of time Don Antonio realizes that his companion is a woman. It is a case of love and—they spend the night together.

Later Antonio learned that his female companion was the queen.


♀ BOOK REVIEW/CROSSING WOMAN

## 1934, January 7
### *N. Y. Times Book Review:*
### Margaret Goldsmith's *Christina of Sweden*

Reviewer Margaret Wallace thought: despite Queen Christina's lack of political importance, she "remains interesting" due to her "striking and eccentric personality."[30]† Christina's father had directed

*For *The Times* review of Goldsmith's biography *Christina of Sweden* see 1934, January 7.
†For *The Times* review of the Garbo film *Queen Christina* see December 27, 1933.

that she was to be brought up entirely as though she had been a boy. Nothing a prince should have learned was to be omitted from her curriculum. Military tactics and the science of government, fencing, shooting, and riding were to be taught her, and it was to be the aim of her tutors to install into her youthful mind "a masculine attitude toward life in general."

Christina's "appalling sense of personal inferiority" was attributed by the biographer to Christina's mother, "who never allowed the child to forget her culpability in having been born a woman, and an unattractive woman at that." Christina " 'watched and imitated men' " at an early age, learned to swear, and became one of the finest classical scholars in Sweden. "Most biographers,"

confronted with the mass of contradictions and concealments that go to make up what we know of Christina's character, have made rather a sorry and unconvincing business of explaining her abdication. Miss Goldsmith, franker than most, has laid a good deal of stress upon the strain of sexual abnormality more or less evident in Christina's nature, and attributes her determination to resign her crown to an unconquerable aversion to marriage.

The reviewer questioned the adequacy of this explanation, remarking in passing that "Miss Goldsmith . . . may occasionally be suspected of special pleading in behalf of her heroine."

Christina's later years, it was said, were "confused and unhappy," and she "scandalized Europe by her unconventional dress and behavior" (unspecified).


FILM REVIEWS

# 1934, January 17
## The Nation; The New Republic: Lot in Sodom

The film *Lot in Sodom*, by Dr. John S. Watson (and Melville Webber) was reviewed in *The Nation* by William Troy.[31] Watson's vision of the destruction of Sodom, said Troy, made "no undue exploitation of the contemporary fascination with the *moeurs* to which the Sodomites have given their name."[82–84]

In *The New Republic*, on March 21, 1934, Otis C. Ferguson said that in the

almost two months now that this two-reel film has been showing in New York City . . . it has been either so ignored by reviewers or so learnedly obscured with generalities that nobody seems to gather the least idea of what it is about, or why. Obviously it retells the Biblical fable of the fall of Sodom.

The film was technically important. "But . . . to speak plain truth, it also gets good and bawdy before it has done." Ferguson explained:

there is just enough concern for realism in the matter of how Sodom took its pleasure (Lot offering his daughter as an incentive to the Natural Life, and the boys indignant; the angel of the Lord arriving and they making what are called passes at him) . . . to suggest an exercise in seeing how much you can get away with.

"There have been several tongues in several cheeks during the film's execution" said Ferguson. And a viewer of the film knew that in this Sodom

you would be afraid. Not with the simple terror bred of war-whoops and maelstroms: you would be afraid of what the directors have captured here —possibly the Spirit of Evil. By casting types whose feminine bent is made only more sinister through its superimposition upon a brutal masculinity . . . the directors go beyond the fact of Sodom to their special feeling for it. Despite the pleasing absence of moral purpose, . . . the story makes sin very sinful, heartily repellent.

IMAGES

# 1934, January
## *Broadway Tattler: "Our great vaterland vill eliminate all pansies"*

A comic strip in a sensationalistic New York paper expressed an ambivalent attitude toward a recent Nazi law, passed November 24, 1933, providing "surgical castration as a therapy and crime prevention measure."[32] This was later used against homosexuals and others. On the one hand the comic strip implicitly criticized the Nazis' castration of homosexuals; on the other hand Hitler was presented as a "pansy," subject to his own eugenics surgery. The joke was less funny six months later, when on July 1, 1934, *The New York Times* reported Hitler's murder of his long-time henchman Ernest Roehm (a homosexual), an event that marked the start of full-scale Nazi arrests of homosexuals.

♀ BOOK REVIEW

# 1934, March 11
## *N. Y. Times Book Review:*
## Radclyffe Hall's *Miss Ogilvy Finds Herself*

Hall's "admirers will be disappointed if they expect any fresh titillation from this volume of distinctly mediocre short stories," said an anonymous critic.[33]

According to the author, the title story . . . contains the nucleus of those sections of "The Well of Loneliness" which dealt with Stephen Gordon's

youth. . . . Miss Ogilvy [is] a sexual invert who for the first time finds fulfilment in war work, and who is cruelly at a loss when the war ends. The tale, however, wanders off into a type of fantasy which is both fatuous and obscure and which destroys any poignancy it might otherwise have had.

Despite Hall's "fluency of style," the reviewer marveled "that 'The Well of Loneliness' could ever have created such a furor."

BOOK REVIEW

# 1934, April 1
## N. Y. Times Book Review:
## Edgar Calmer's Beyond the Street

That "sexual inversion" was part of the ordinary life of an urban educational institution was suggested by this review, headed: "As Life Goes On in a City School."[34] Critic Fred T. Marsh described this first novel, set in a large high school located on 47th Street and Eleventh Avenue in New York City. Ten teachers and five students were the novelist's subjects.

> Eros is the presiding deity and the story is one of many and complicated and unusual loves. Frustration and defeat for nearly all the players is the semi-tragic note on which the drama ends.

Among the minor figures a male Latin teacher is in love with a "Miss Gerstman"; a female English teacher pursues a "Mr. Norsworthy"; a domineering male teacher takes his bitterness out on his wife and colleagues. Among the eight major figures:

> Chemwitz, the music teacher, has learned sympathy and understanding through physical suffering, being born with that courage which admits of no self-pity. Therefore he understands the nature of that attraction which his most gifted pupil feels to the handsome little Mexican boy, Vincent.
>     The two boys have been friends. But Alex Sadowsky was born with that emotional intensity which is both the need and the curse of the artist temperament. He embarrasses Vincent with his jealousy, his abjectness, his protection, his eagerness, his changing moods. Vincent has no notion of what the matter is, but he drifts away to more normal companionship, feeling at the same time a little guilty for deserting his old friend.

Another love is that of "Miss Farge," a teacher, for a male student of eighteen. "There remains," said the reviewer,

> the triangle—Mr. Quent, the popular and respected English teacher; Miss Cassell, the Southern girl who is the belle of the faculty; and John West, [the high school's] star athlete. This is probably the most serious and successful of the stories running through the novel. It deals with the theme of sexual inversion.

## 1934, May
## George Ives to Dr. Joseph Wortis:
### *"Your work is of great interest to me"*

In 1934, Joseph Wortis, a young American doctor, was in London on a stipend to study homosexuality.[35] There he was introduced to George Cecil Ives who (though Wortis did not know it) was the founder of a secret homosexual liberation organization, and one of the major, early British homosexual emancipation pioneers.* Ives's letters to Wortis record the Englishman's attempt to reach out and influence an American doctor whose work might promote a more tolerant social response to homosexuals. Ives's previously unpublished letters provide evidence of the now little-known interaction between early British homosexual emancipationists and Americans. Ives's letters also document the concerns of one English homosexual at a time of grave social crisis in Europe: the retrenchment of sexual law reform in the Soviet Union and the rise of the Nazis in Germany. Ives's concern with the social situation of homosexuals contrasts sharply with contemporary doctors' concern with the alleged physiological and psychological causes and treatment of homosexuality, providing striking evidence of the conflicting interests of homosexuals and those who studied them. Of this conflict Ives, with his faith in "Science" and scientists was, ironically, unaware.

The activities of George Ives as a homosexual emancipation pioneer were first revealed in Jeffrey Weeks's history of homosexual politics in Great Britain. Weeks's work and additional original research by Michael Dunn in Ives's papers at the University of Texas, Austin, provide the basis for the following brief summary of Ives's achievement.

As a child, says Weeks, Ives had perceived men-loving men as wronged. Asked when he first joined "The Cause" he answered: "Oh, as far back as I can remember, when I was a boy and I *could* not understand why such a wonderful thing should not be sanctioned."[119] Ives had been called to "the War of Liberation" as a youth, he said.[122] In Edward Carpenter's poems, *Towards Democracy*, Ives, in 1892, found "The first grip of sense . . . I got from the outside world."[119] About 1892, Ives linked Carpenter's and Oscar Wilde's fight against middle-class respectability with homosexual emancipation: "the cause must be sacred and followed by all sorts of men, each to work in their particular sphere —the issue and the hope is great enough to bind even the most heterogeneous society and if only organised which we have never been before, we shall go on to victory."[120]

By July 1893, Ives's diary suggests that his secret homosexual emancipation

---

*For Ives's *History of Penal Methods,* published in the United States, see 1914; for Ives and The British Society for the Study of Sex Psychology, see 1925, June 4.

organization, the Order of Chaeronea, was in existence and expanding. The Order was named after the Battle of Chaeronea (338 B.C.), in which the "Sacred Band" of Thebes, an army of male lovers, was annihilated by the Macedonians. Ives's Order of Chaeronea was a mystically-defined homosexual brotherhood, support group, and social reform organization devoted to the interests (as Ives wrote in 1922) of a "persecuted minority." Initiation into the Order included a quasi-religious ritual and members learned secret signs and possessed special signet rings (reminiscent of the ceremony adopted, independently, by the leaders of the original U. S. Mattachine Society in the early 1950s, when the group was still an "underground" organization).

The prosecution and jailing of Oscar Wilde, in 1895, increased Ives's sense of the need to keep the Order's existence secret—a secretiveness so insistent it infuriated Wilde, whom Ives visited in jail. In 1898, Wilde wrote to Ives: "Yes: I have no doubt we shall win, but the road is long, and red with monstrous martyrdoms." Wilde thought that "nothing but" law reform "would do any good." Activities of the Order's members probably included lobbying, individually, for such law reform, and giving moral and, perhaps, legal and financial support to homosexuals in trouble. Membership in the Order was comprised mainly of literary men, and was never very large. The second most active member seems to have been Laurence Housman, a socialist, feminist, pacifist, and writer, and brother of the more famous poet, A. E. Housman.

Among Ives's published works were *The Book of Chains* (1897, poems), *The Classification of Crimes* (1904), *A History of Penal Methods* (1914, see), *The Continued Extension of the Criminal Law* (1922), and *The Graeco-Roman View of Youth* (1926, the original title of which was *The Graeco-Roman View of Paederasty*). Ives was pleased when his *Graeco-Roman* proved "a comfort" to a homosexual in the United States to whom Dr. Wortis lent it. An essay of Ives's was titled "A Socialist View of Liberty" (1898); Weeks says that, in 1904, Ives identified himself as that kind of socialist who "refuses all compromise with the religious parties, all compromise with existing sexual morality, all compromise with the class system in any shape."[126]

Ives's diary of 122 volumes, 20,000 pages, and three million words, covering sixty-three years (from 1886 to 1949, the year before his death), includes a number of references to Americans. For example, on October 6, 1922, he wrote:

> I hear that Edward Carpenter declares from personal knowledge that Walt Whitman was a homosexual. E. C. met him when he was over in the United States.

Whitman was referred to again on February 15, 1931, when Ives wrote:

> I still await the advent of the *young* Prophet, of him who shall take up the [homosexual emancipation] work of Carpenter (not to mention of Whitman and Symonds) and I have seen no trace of him. . . .

In 1932, Laurence Housman recommended that Ives read the American novel *Strange Brother,* a sympathetic plea for the tragic homosexual, by a woman, Blair Niles (see 1932, Niles). Ives read the book and sent Niles a copy of his own volume on *The Continued Extension of the Criminal Law.*

It was in 1934 that Ives met the young American, Dr. Joseph Wortis, who was traveling in Europe on a grant to study homosexuality. The dramatic details of the story behind Wortis's stipend were revealed in Phyllis Grosskurth's biography of Havelock Ellis:

> In the summer of 1932, Kingsley Porter, a professor of art history at Harvard, and his wife paid Ellis a visit. Porter was a homosexual and was suffering from a deep depression, as he was in danger of losing his job because of scandal. His wife was sympathetic.[418]

Ellis's exact advice is not known, but Ellis put Porter in touch with Alan Campbell, a young homosexual novelist (later married to the writer, Dorothy Parker). A few months later, says Grosskurth, Campbell moved into the Porters' home in Cambridge, Massachusetts. Grosskurth supposes that Ellis, having accepted (at least, intellectually) his own wife's female lovers, advised the Porters to adopt some similar arrangement. (Ellis's autobiography reveals him to be extremely insensitive to emotional relations, his own and others'.) The restless Alan Campbell left the Porters' house after a few months. On July 11, 1933, Campbell reported that Kingsley Porter had committed suicide.[419]

In her husband's memory, the "extremely wealthy" Mrs. Porter then provided funds for the study of homosexuality. In October 1933, Wortis was informed by Havelock Ellis, whom he had met in London the year before, that " 'a very large sum of money' " was " 'to be devoted to the scientific study of homosexuality . . . with the view of illuminating the subject and of promoting a rational and humane attitude towards it.' " Ellis arranged for Wortis to receive the money, and Wortis did so for seven years, during which time he traveled to Europe with his wife to study physiology, biochemistry, endocrinology, and to spend four months being analyzed by Freud. (Wortis stopped receiving the stipend when he turned to the study of insulin treatment for mental disturbance.)

On May 27, 1934, Havelock Ellis wrote to George Ives that "My young American friend Dr. Joseph Wortis," who was investigating "sex problems, especially homosexuality," was in London. "He knows your interest in these subjects, and would be pleased if you care to meet him."

In May 1934, Ives himself wrote to Wortis that

> your work is of great interest to me. I hope we shall meet as I have much to discuss and some books to show you.

Ives offerred to take Wortis and his wife to tea in the Zoological Gardens.

A letter of Ives to Wortis is dated "May 2272" (that is, 1934—members of the Order of Chaeronea employed a system of dating in which the year one was the year of the Battle of Chaeronea, 338 B.C.). Ives informed Wortis of several "important" English medical journal articles. He mentioned that his own book, *The Graeco-Roman View of Youth,* had been sent "to many foreign libraries but not, so far, to any in England." Ives apparently worried about his book's reception, and about his reputation in his native land.

On June 14, Ives wrote that he was "very pleased" that Wortis was reading his "Graeco-Roman."

On "June 22, 2272," Ives sent Wortis a notice about a meeting of the "delinquents society" (Ives had lectured on "The Plight of the Adolescent," and the treatment of juvenile delinquents apparently interested him.)

In a letter of "July 2272," Ives suggested that Wortis might like to attend a lecture by Harold Picton on "My Experiences in Republican and Nazi Germany." Ives added, "I like Picton, but hate all meetings."

On "1 August 2272," Ives told Wortis of "a book which is said to be too important for you to miss," René Guyon's *Sex Life and Sex Ethics,* with an introduction by Dr. Norman Haire (a homosexual, and a leader in the sex reform movement).* Ives said that to read Guyon's book in the British Museum Library required an endorsement "by one of the Library staff," but Wortis, a doctor, would have "no difficulty."

On a postcard of August 4, Ives mentioned hearing that Hans Licht's book on ancient Greek sexuality "is good," but expensive.

On August 5, Ives mentioned that he had "glanced at Guyon's book, and think it very sound." Guyon was defining "a new and rational moral code," as were "many of our best minds." Ives also recommended André Gide's *Corydon* (a defense of homosexuality) which he had read in French.

On September 25, 1934, Ives wrote that he was glad Wortis had met Sigmund Freud,

> one of the dynamic forces of the century. He has extracted more truth out of mendacious mankind than I ever expected to see revealed on this side of the grave! But my knowledge of psychoanalysis is rather limited.

Ives added: "I had a letter last week from Dr. Hirschfeld [the exiled German-Jewish homosexual emancipation leader], written from his Institute in Paris, a very kind note in common English."

On March 27, 1935, Ives wrote to Wortis, who was now back in the United States:

> I think things are going well in this country, but Germany, Italy, and Russia are, now, police states. I had some hopes about Russia, but it too has reverted to the Judeo-Pauline taboos upon sex questions, and after having

---

*Guyon's book, in England titled *Sex Life and Sex Ethics,* was published in the United States as *The Ethics of Sexual Acts,* trans. by J. C. and Ingeborg Flugel (N. Y.: Knopf, 1934). For Haire, see Weeks, *Coming Out.*

made a rational code at the revolution, re-imposed an unjust and unscientific law on March 7, 1934.

Many of the English Communists, at first, refused to believe it, the more since those in Germany used to appeal to the homosexuals for votes, saying, "then you will obtain liberty." A friend of mine, who will very probably be in office if there comes in a Labour Government wrote saying "This is very sad news, but there it is."

"In England," though, said Ives, "H. G. Wells, Bertrand Russell and even the rather puritanical Bernard Shaw are quite sound about liberty."

Russia has forgotten eternal justice and recent discoveries, and that has been a bitter disappointment to me and to all who had thought that the old taboos had vanished for ever—probably some "repressed" anti sex crank has been in power at Moscow, and we must all work to see this evil law is repealed. All the Dictators have one thing in common, a dislike of of liberty, said General Smuts;* and that is too true. And they are all wanting children, to play them as living pawns, in the statesmen's game, of war and aggression. But matters may not turn out according to their desires: we shall see what evolves.

Ives again recommended Guyon's *Sex Life and Sex Ethics,* saying "It is valuable, . . . you ought to have it, for it boldly questions many assumptions which are based upon prejudice." If Wortis knew "anybody who would like a copy" of Ives's *The Graeco-Roman View of Youth,* or if Wortis knew of a likely U. S. publisher, Ives would be "very glad."

And on "12 June 2273" (1935) Ives wrote to Wortis:

I wonder if you have yet heard of the death of the great and kindly Dr. Magnus Hirschfeld?

Ives enclosed an obituary, and added:

Mercifully, he had crossed the frontier [out of Germany], foreseeing the persecution that was to be inflicted on the Jews and the sex reformers. And I hear he carried away the best of his books to safety.†

A few months earlier Ives had "written an appreciation of Dr. H and his work . . . in the Freethinker, on the destruction of the 'Institute' [in Berlin] and received an affectionate acknowledgement of it from him at the time." Ives added:

I am so pleased to think that my Graeco-Roman has been a comfort to some one to whom you lent it. Please tell him that I greatly appreciate his message. I might be inclined to send him a copy if he cannot afford to buy one? But most of my books are in the New York Public Library. René Guyon's work

---

*The reference is to Christian Smuts, the South African field marshal—hardly a paragon of freedom. See Smuts's biography in the *Dictionary of National Biography.*

†For the Nazis' attack on Hirschfeld's Institute see 1933, May 7.

is remarkable for its open attack upon conventional views. He challenges the idea that the homosexuals are inferior, subnormal, or even abnormal, if Nature were left alone. And he complains that people have assumed prevailing customs and moral codes to be absolute standards, although they depend, to a great extent, on theology, and are slowly changing.

That Russia, having cast off Judaism and Christianity, should come under the sway of the Judeo-Pauline taboo, after a decade of liberty, is one of the most depressing facts I have ever heard of. I am no politician, but the English communists with whom I have spoken at first refused to believe such a law possible.

Most people say the motive is entirely political, and that it was at first intended to apply only to a portion of Asiatic Russia. I cannot see how this can be true. . . . It is just possible that one or two cranks have been active (as they perpetually are) and have got their way, through the indifference of their colleagues; one cannot tell. . . .

And, at the back of all persecutions, is the age-old instinctive jealousy of Age for Youth. The gods and the "divine" laws, generally reflect the weaknesses and desires of the old men!

(Ives apparently attributed anti-erotic laws and taboos to the envy of older males' desire, but inability, to indulge—a dubious theory, to put it mildly.)

One final recorded contact of George Ives with an American occurred on June 4, 1939, when Ives was visited in London by Dr. J. S—— of New York. Ives's diary says that he had not seen S——

for ten years or so. We had a long talk until past midnight on the O of C [Order of Chaeronea] Movement and particularly on Shakespeare and the origin of his sonnets—on which Dr. S—— is an authority. He wanted my new book [*Obstacles to Human Progress*] and *would* pay for it. . . .

He has left me some writings to look over, and I was able to give him some addresses and references. We have one, or more, acquaintances in common. . . .

Ives noted parenthetically that S—— was "(. . . *not* a member of the Order, tho he might be of use: I wonder?)."*

---

*S—— visited Ives again on June 10, and the two discussed S——'s new writings. On July 19, Ives records his "wading through" S——'s typescript on Shakespeare.

♀ BOOK REVIEW

## 1934, June 10
### N. Y. Times Book Review:
### M. J. Farrell's Devoted Ladies

Lesbian relationships were parasitic and poisonous, suggested this review by
Margaret Wallace.[36] She described this novel as opening in London, where Jane
and Jessica "seem to be headed for some spectacular trouble in their private
relations."

> Jane, a young and appealing and rather stupid American girl, widowed and
> wealthy, appears to be helplessly under the influence of her English friend,
> who is vastly more intelligent, selfish, and cruel.

At a party Jessica hurled a bottle at Jane; and at this party Jane met an "innocent
Irish gentleman," George Playfair.

> On a trip to Ireland, to aid Jane in recuperating from "an attack of acute
> alcoholism," Jane and Jessica met Hester and Piggy. Piggy, "hopelessly unpopu-
> lar and unattractive, lavishes the wealth of an unwanted attention" on one, Joan,
> "who makes unscrupulous use of Piggy and returns very small kindness for
> benefits received."

> Piggy finally took desperate measures to prevent the "poisonous" and "jeal-
> ous" Jessica from breaking George's proposed marriage to Jane.

> The reviewer called this "a witty tale." Its "sparkle and vitality" made it
> "brilliant."

NEWS REPORTS

## 1934, July 1
### N. Y. Times: The execution of Ernst Roehm

The Nazis' open declaration of war against homosexuals on a heretofore unprece-
dented scale began with the murder of Ernst Roehm on June 30, 1934, now
known as "the night of the long knives."[37] Hitler and Roehm had been close
friends for fifteen years; in 1919, Roehm had first helped make Hitler aware of
his political potential. During those years Roehm had become Chief of Hitler's
Storm Troops, transforming the brownshirt militia into a major instrument of
Nazi coercion. As part of a compromise with the Army leadership, says historian
James Steakley, Hitler allowed Goering and Himmler to murder Roehm and
dozens of other Storm Troop officers. To justify these murders Hitler alleged
Roehm's and others' involvement in a "radical" right-wing, "national bolshevist"

plot to overthrow him. Hitler also cited Roehm's homosexuality, though the Fuehrer had known of Roehm's sexual predilections for at least fifteen years. Roehm's homosexuality had become common knowledge in 1925, when Roehm, in court, charged a male prostitute with theft. Although Nazi Party public policy was from the first strongly anti-homosexual, Hitler had willingly put up with Roehm until Roehm stood in the way of the leader's plans to consolidate his absolute rule.

On July 1, 1934, *The New York Times* carried the first confused, inaccurate reports of recent events in Germany. A five-column headline on page one read: "Hitler Crushes Revolt By Nazi Radicals, . . . Roehm A Suicide." A dispatch from Berlin reported that Hitler himself had motored to Captain Roehm's country house and found Roehm ill, in bed. In a room across the hall Hitler had reportedly found Herr Heines, a Nazi leader,

> with a a youthful male companion.
> "The scene that took place on Chancellor Hitler's arrival," says the official account, "is indescribable." Herr Hitler's own indignation was overwelming. Herr Heines is listed tonight as among the dead. . . .[2:4]

The report that Roehm had committed suicide was false, as was the insinuation by Hitler that Roehm and other alleged anti-Hitler leaders had conspired with a " 'foreign power' " (Russia) and had aimed to establish "a new national bolshevism."

*The Times's* front page also printed a "Nazi Party Statement." This claimed that Roehm's "well-known unfortunate characteristic gradually led to intolerable burdens" which drove Hitler "into most serious conflicts of conscience." The "arrests" of Roehm and others, said the statement,

> revealed such immorality that any trace of pity was impossible. Some of these Storm Troop leaders had taken male prostitutes along with them. One of them was even disturbed in a most ugly situation and was arrested.
> Der Fuehrer gave orders for this plague to be done away with ruthlessly. In future he will not permit millions of decent people to be compromised by a few of such sick men.[1:7]

"Hitler Commands Nazi Abstinences" read another page-one headline. The sub-head added that Hitler had forbidden "Moral 'Debauches,' " and "Wants 'Men, Not Apes.' " Hitler demanded that Storm Troop leaders

> cooperate in preserving the Storm Troop as a clean and upright institution. Every mother should be able to place her son in a Storm Troop, in the party and in the Hitler Youth without any fear that he could be morally ruined. I expect accordingly that every Storm Troop leader will take the greatest care to secure the instant dismissal from the party and from the Storm Troop [of] any one guilty of a breach of [the German Penal Code's] Section 175 [dealing with homosexual crimes]. [The last bracketed explanation was in *The Times.*]

Hitler had told Storm Troop leaders: "I desire men in the party, not absurd apes."[1:5, 2:6]

Another *Times* story of July 1, headed "Roehm Case Recalls 1907 Court Scandals," said that "charges of homo-sexuality" against Roehm recalled those against Prince Eulenburg and his group. In 1907, "The German nation" had been "shocked at the revelation about the nature of the friendship which held the group together."[2:5]

Subsequent *Times* stories reported Roehm's execution before a firing squad, and clarified some of the politics behind Hitler's turning on his once-trusted aide. No more was said about Roehm's or others' sexuality, and nothing about the Nazis' current anti-homosexual terror.

♀ NEWS REPORT

## 1934, October 25
### *N. Y. Times:* Gertude Stein,
*"A gay hat [on her] close-cropped head"*

Gertrude Stein, a "square-shouldered woman of 60 with a constant chuckle in her throat and a rollick in her gait," had returned to lecture in America after a thirty-one year absence.[38] A *Times* story was accompanied by a photo. "Her feet were in thick woolly stockings, and round-toed, flat-heeled oxfords." A "cerise vest of voluminous proportions and a mannish shirt of cream and black stripes" were also mentioned, as was "a gay hat" on her "close-cropped head."

Stein parried a dozen reporters' questions for more than an hour. "No one enjoyed that interview more than Miss Stein, unless it might have been Miss Alice B. Toklas, her secretary and companion, who sat, dark and small, on the periphery of the attentive circle." Toklas "gazed raptly at Miss Stein," who was said to have "tried to make it plain that she was normal and intelligent, and 'born legitimate of two respectable parents.'" Questioned about her difficult style, Stein said: "I describe what I feel and think. I am essentially a realist."

> She could not be drawn into a discussion of politics and would say nothing about Hitler, Mussolini or art under the dictatorships, explaining that "these things are outside me. I concern myself chiefly with something I know. My business is writing." But naturally, she added, she has feelings about the world and "the most violent ideas" about politics.

Gertrude Stein returns to Paris, May 4, 1935. (Photograph similar to that which appeared in *The New York Times,* October 25, 1934; Associated Press/Wide World Photos.)

♀ PLAY REVIEW

# 1934, November 21
## *N. Y. Times:* Lillian Hellman's *The Children's Hour*

Brooks Atkinson praised Lillian Hellman's "venomously tragic play of life in a girls' boarding school" which had opened on Broadway the previous night.[39] But Atkinson thought the play should have ended "before the pistol shot" with which one of the heroines admitted her love for the other and killed herself. Atkinson wanted "the point" of the play to be that Karen Wright and Martha Dobie, the headmistresses of the school, "are innocent" of the rumors spread by a "diabolical adolescent," Mary Tilford. Hellman

> has drawn that evil character with brilliant understanding of . . . child nature. Purely as a matter of malicious vanity, Mary spreads the rumor that the headmistresses have an unnatural affection for each other. . . . The scandal destroys the school and turns the two headmistresses into social exiles. To recover their self-respect . . . they bring a libel action . . . but they cannot prove their innocence.

That "defeated situation" seemed to Atkinson "the logical" and "most overpowering conclusion to the play," and he instructed the author and producer to bring the curtain down before the play's present ending—before one woman's admission of guilt and her suicide had complicated the issue of "innocence."

Restating his argument on December 2, Atkinson praised Hellman's way of showing "how circumstances arouse public opinion" against the two female schoolmistresses, and "brand them as social exiles." Hellman, "having made that point," was criticized for ending her play with a "confession and a routine suicide."

♀ PLAY REVIEW/CROSSING WOMAN

# 1934, November 22
## *N. Y. Times:* James Bridie
## and Claude Gurney's *Mary Read*

The London production of a new play titled *Mary Read* was reported in *The Times* to be based on "the adventurous life of an eighteenth century amazon" who had been "Brought up as a boy," and had "passed as a man most of her life."[40] Read worked as a page-boy, sailor, soldier, and pirate. Actor Robert Donat "played her lover, an effeminate youth attracted by her masculinity."*

---

*For another couple consisting of "Amazon" and effeminate male see the film "The Warrior's Husband," 1933, May 12. A special affinity between a "masculine" woman and rather "feminine" male is also portrayed in the film *Bringing Up Baby;* see 1938, March 4.

# 1935, April 9
# Dr. Sigmund Freud:
## "Letter to an American Mother"

In 1935, Sigmund Freud wrote to an American mother who had asked him for advice about treatment for her son.[41] Freud's letter was first published in 1951, after its anonymous recipient sent the original to Dr. Alfred Kinsey along with this note: "Herewith I enclose a letter from a Great and Good man which you may retain.—From a Grateful Mother."

Freud's letter indicates his relatively tolerant view of homosexuality as an "arrest of sexual development," involving "blighted heterosexual tendencies." A value judgment placed heterosexuality at the end of any "mature" individual's development. On the basis of that judgment, Freud did not conclude that exclusive or predominant heterosexuality comprised an "arrest" of sexual development toward a mature homosexuality. For most homosexuals, Freud said, psychoanalysis could provide a means of living contentedly, uninhibitedly, and efficiently as homosexual. Freud wrote in English, commenting immediately on the mother's failure to explicitly name her son's alleged problem:

> Dear Mrs.———:
>
> I gather from your letter that your son is a homosexual. I am most impressed by the fact that you do not mention this term yourself in your information about him. May I question you, why you avoid it? Homosexuality is assuredly no advantage but it is nothing to be ashamed of, no vice, no degradation, it cannot be classified as an illness; we consider it to be a variation of the sexual function produced by a certain arrest of sexual development. Many highly respectable individuals of ancient and modern times have been homosexuals, several of the greatest men among them (Plato, Michelangelo, Leonardo da Vinci, etc.). It is a great injustice to persecute homosexuality as a crime and a cruelty too. If you do not believe me, read the books of Havelock Ellis.
>
> By asking me if I can help, you mean, I suppose, if I can abolish homosexuality and make normal heterosexuality take its place. The answer is, in a general way, we cannot promise to achieve it. In a certain number of cases we succeed in developing the blighted germs of heterosexual tendencies, which are present in every homosexual, in the majority of cases it is no more possible. It is a question of the quality and the age of the individual. The result of treatment cannot be predicted.
>
> What analysis can do for your son, runs in a different line. If he is unhappy, neurotic, torn by conflicts, inhibited in his social life, analysis may bring him harmony, peace of mind, full efficiency, whether he remains a homosexual or gets changed. If you make up your mind he should have

analysis with me—I don't expect you will—he has to come over to Vienna. I have no intention of leaving here. However don't neglect to give me your answer.

     Sincerely yours with kind wishes
           Freud


♀  BOOK REVIEW/RESISTANCE

# 1935, August 18
## *N. Y. Times Book Review:*
## Gale Wilhelm's *We Too Are Drifting*

Through the lens of various reviewers' responses to Gale Wilhelm's lesbian novel it is possible to gauge her book's resistant stance, her defiance in dignifying her characters at a time when the very subject of "Sapphic intimacy" evoked uneasiness.[42] The *Times* reviewer, for instance, condemned lesbianism as a "subject-matter" which necessarily limited the novel's appeal to "larger human impulses and values," a criticism often leveled against Jewish, Black, and other literatures focusing on a minority experience. The "human" was definitely not "Sapphic." Two universes, "normal" and "abnormal," were assumed here to be absolutely distinct, separate, and unequal.

   *Times* reviewer Stuart Young began:

> The problem presented in "The Well of Loneliness" and "The Children's Hour" is again before us in Gale Wilhelm's brief story of the Lesbian relationship of three young American women. It must be stated at once that this potentially disturbing subject-matter is carefully handled. By brevity and understatement . . . this author has given a skittish subject about as much dignity as it can hope for in normal society.
>
>    Unlike her predecessors, she has managed not to argue the matter psychologically or to hold up any general plea for the invert except that which is naturally inherent in her choice of subject. We simply see the thing which is Sapphic intimacy happen in the overwrought lives of Jan and Madeline and Victoria. The result is in no sense a full-sized view of life but rather a very vivid segment from the specialized milieu in which these characters move. To read about them is not a very pleasant, heart-warming experience. In fact, it is downright chilling, but the writing is so honestly conceived . . . as to bid for considerable recognition.
>
>    The fact that the author does not extend the emotional involvement of her unconforming characters so as to throw them into full contrast with the normal, accounts in great part for the balance of the work, and for what, I suspect, will be the general acceptance of it. The only real turbulence and conflict in this writing occur in the actual inner ordeal of the abnormal characters and not in their relation to the normal stratum of existence. One

small element of abnormal life is thereby made to stand momentarily for the whole.

The reader, said this reviewer, never saw the men in the story

thrown out of joint by the prim knowledge that the women whom they cherish will never quite give them emotional fulfillment. We suppose that they realize something is wrong, but the author never reveals how this realization affects them. Thus by limiting the conception to the private ordeal in the lives of three maladjusted women this novel achieves a certain unity and avoids the bitter, doubtful contest with the normal which might run the book emotionally amok.

But whether, according to the nature of our sensibilities, we writhe in distaste or accept the subject matter, we must recognize that this 26-year-old author can handle her delicate materials with a deft turn of phrase that exceeds the hard-boiled school from which she has learned so much. . . . Words are put forward with a brisk, knowing air that somehow makes the reader aware of larger areas of experience beyond the personal predicaments of such a character as Jan, loved persistently in this story by Madeline; of Victoria, loved as ardently by Jan.

The fact that these women carry about with them in their day-by-day meetings the self-conscious, we-are-the-damned, we-too-are-drifting air, and that they strike and maintain a kind of quietly hysterical attitude toward society which is arrogant and hard and overtense makes it difficult for us to understand their tenseness. There are moments, as when Jan is with Kletkin, the sculptor, in his studio, in which underneath the film of their moods a quick sense of life is felt. It is then that we get over the instinctive barriers erected by the unpleasant substance of the material and salute the sheer artistry of the writing.

But on the whole there is a frailty of conception in this work which is the fault of the subject-matter. Miss Wilhelm's brilliant technique working in a field of more varied experience would certainly create something of more than passing notice. To be sure, the present work goes further than the medical brochure and the document. It has moments of poetry. It indicates talent. But it can claim none of the distinction which comes from those novels which move the spirit and the intelligence to a new awareness of larger human impulses and values.

Reviewing Wilhelm's book in *The New Republic* Robert Cantwell said on October 2, 1935:

As a revelation of the way Lesbians regard their own affairs, the book is of some interest. . . . But in denying her characters any vital commerce with . . . the normal world, Miss Wilhelm has robbed her book of the only kind of conflict that could give it life.[221]

PLAY REVIEW

## 1935, April 21
### N. Y. Times: Maurice Rostand's
### The Trial of Oscar Wilde

The "invert" as victim allowed for a safe sympathy in response, as this review indicated.[43]

In a play review from Paris, Philip Carr called *The Trial of Oscar Wilde* an attempt "to restore the reputation" of its subject. The "history dealt with is recent," and "at least one of the characters represented on the stage, Lord Alfred Douglas, is still alive, while another, Frank Harris died only a short time ago." Whether it was "artisically permissible" for a playwright to portray real "people and incidents which were the occasion of so much scandal, may be doubted." "Moreover, there is little doubt" that this playwright, "far from deploring the scandalous associations of his subject, has deliberately exploited them, and that the success which his play will most probably obtain will be largely due to them."

The play's success would also be due to its "highly dramatic" subject, a drama "quite apart from the whole question of sexual inversion." This drama resided in the story of an "artist" struggling against the "incomprehending and hostile prejudice of prosaic and selfishly calculating materialists," and in the picture of "ruin caused by the fixed pursuit of an all-engrossing passion." The drama of Wilde's story also arose from the "commanding appeal of suffering," especially "when the sufferer is one who has stood high and has been brought low by his own fault."* Suffering was also "particularly moving" when it was shown to produce "a purification of the soul." The playwright had developed all these "dramatic qualities."

It was possible to believe that the historical Wilde "was not carried away by passion but was the slave of vice." The Wilde who came out of prison was possibly "a broken but still unrepentant sinner." But Wilde's "suffering" was clear in this play.

♀ NEWS REPORT/EDITORIAL/MEDICAL

## 1935, October 28
### N. Y. Times: "A general drift away
### from feminine . . . traits"

"Women's Personalities Changed by New Adrenal Gland Operation," declared a page-one headline in *The Times*.[44] "Abnormalities Causing a Drift Away from

---

*Whatever role Wilde played in his own fate, calling his downfall his "own fault" obscures others' responsibility.

Femininity Are Corrected and Attractiveness Restored by Surgery," said the subhead. Referring to an "abnormal" and "normal" "femininity" caused by glandular function, the story implied that any psychic deviation was a physical problem with, possibly, a surgical cure. An editorial reference to "Sappho" indicates that such assumptions were extended to psycho-sexual proclivities. The report indicates that hormone treatment was beginning to be spoken of in the press as a "cure" for gender nonconformity, including homosexuality.

The story told of Dr. Frank Hinman's report to a San Francisco conference of the American College of Surgeons. Dr. Hinman's operation on the adrenal gland was intended to correct an "overfunctioning" which caused "marked physical changes in physical appearance," "growth of beard on the face, and a deep masculine voice," as well as "aversion to marital relationship, despondency, suicidal tendency and a general drift away from feminine toward decidedly masculine traits." Hinman's adrenal gland operation reportedly restored "the normal feminine personality," correcting "impotence" and "frigidity."

An editorial in the following day's *Times* described the adrenal glands' secretion of cortin and adrenalin and said:

> Whether or not Napoleon owed his energy and willfulness to . . . adrenalin
> . . . and whether or not Sappho was the victim of her excessive cortin, as
> we have been assured by the more unrestrained endocrinologists, there can
> be no doubt that the glands help to make us what we are.

But the editorial warned: "The whole subject of hormones is still shrouded in mystery," and talk of " 'personality glands' " denied that "personality is something very complex," involving more than hormones.

> It is a question, therefore, how far what we vaguely call "personality" can
> be changed, and whether that change is always for the better. The surgical
> remedy . . . [for] physical and psychical defects is evidently the beginning
> of something important, but of what it is too early to predict.

BOOK REVIEW

## 1935, November 10
### *N. Y. Times Book Review:* André Gide's *If It Die*

Reviewer Louis Kronenberger said: "Perhaps it is well" that the publication in English of Gide's autobiography (translated from the French by Dorothy Bussy) "has been delayed until now."[45] (The book had been published privately in France in 1920, publicly in 1924.) Kronenberger thought the public is no longer so horrified by disclosures of homosexuality that it need regard the book—as it might have regarded it ten years ago [1925]—as something sensational.*

Gide's autobiography could now be "examined in the light" of all his other "important books." Kronenberger added:

> The notoriety achieved for this book by its homosexual passages has been exceedingly great; it has also been exceedingly disproportionate. The sexual episdoes recorded here had, it is true, a most significant rôle in Gide's moral development; it is no less true that they are described with the utmost frankness. But the book is for all that much less the confession of an invert than the story of a writer's early life. . . . For the most part, indeed, these memoirs wear rather a normal than a special air, and the reader will find here more recognitions than revelations.

> Gide came from a Protestant family, his father was a professor of Law; his mother "was a woman of much force and conviction, narrow-minded but selfless." From boyhood Gide loved his cousin Emmeline, and "It was perhaps her refusal to marry him which made his sexual life, later on, the prey of abnormal instincts; it was finally their betrothal which culminated his cure."
> After being introduced to French literary salons by Pierre Louÿs, Gide, a few years later, traveled with a friend, Paul Laurens, to North Africa where they "shared" a "little native girl," and where Gide

> entered into liaisons with several native boys. It was an occasion of profound moral crisis no less than of physical fulfilment. He had been brought up in a strict Puritan atmosphere where sin was real and concrete; he had felt shame at all falls from grace; he had regarded Satan as a living force. But for a time Gide derived from these liasons not ecstasy alone but a sense of well-being and triumph, instead of guilt and defeat.

In his novel *The Immoralist,* Gide had converted this moral crisis into a conflict between Christian "self-denial" and Nietzschean "self-indulgence." In that novel "the Nietzschean formula comes wholly to grief." In Gide's autobiography "the shift back from abnormality is less abrupt and less guilty."

---

*Such contemporary references to changes in response provide valuable evidence helping us specify basic periods in the history of heterosexual reactions to homosexuals. For other such references see "historical perspective" in the index.

♀ FILM REVIEW/CROSSING WOMAN

# 1936, January 10
## N. Y. Times: Sylvia Scarlett

The film starring Katharine Hepburn, adapted from a novel by Compton Mackenzie, and reviewed by André Sennwald, was said to collect "some odd characters"
and set them on an "odd sort of vagabond odyssey":[46]

> When Sylvia's father commits larceny and is forced to flee France, Sylvia
> joins him and becomes a boy for the occasion so as not to be a bother during
> their flight. . . . Sylvia's secret passion for a handsome artist finally causes
> her to abandon her disguise and attempt to recapture her girlhood. It is in
> the bitter-sweet indecisions of her romance with a man who refuses to take
> her seriously that Miss Hepburn is at her best.

Vague allusions in the film to homosexuality were ignored. The *Times* review did not mention that before Sylvia Scarlett gave up her male identity and
clothes, she (according to Parker Tyler)

> involuntarily snares the heart of a young lady, who thinks that this hand-
> some, dashing boy can improve his manly looks. Whereupon she draws a
> moustache on the submissive Hepburn, and charmed with the results, plants
> a lusty kiss on the lips beneath it.[212]

BOOK REVIEW

# 1936, February 9
## N. Y. Times Book Review: Murrell Edmunds's
## Sojourn Among the Shadows

"This Freudian nightmare," said reviewer Dorothea Kingsland, "drags one painfully through distorted passions and wild metaphysical speculations."[47] The male
homosexual appeared here as metaphorical monster in a mystical horror show.*

> It begins, familiarly enough, with two men on a park bench—the callow
> youth who is the author's mask and the strange, older man with the heavy
> head and sorrowful features whose gestures and mouthings alternately star-
> tle and fascinate his unwilling companion. The actual story comes from the
> stranger's lips. It is a revelation of half-mythical experience testifying hys-
> terically to the evil nature of creation and the immense burden of human
> suffering.

*For discussion of the homosexual as monster and vampire see the Introduction to this section,
p. 164; for a lesbian vampire of 1936 see May 18; and see "vampire" in the index.

It tells of a boy tortured by a lewd evangelical father and of a queer, kind old uncle who steals him away, comforts him with strange words and tries to send him down the long road of life alone. But the boy follows after the uncle, against the latter's wish, and as they wander through dark meadows and black forests and into strangely inhabited cabins the powers and the horrible weaknesses of the uncle's secret nature are fearfully unfolded to the listening, watching child.

It is this knowledge which has stitched eternal suffering upon the face of the one who tells the story. It is this knowledge which causes the callow youth to turn away in horrified repugnance when the story is done. But the youth, after his first instinctive flight, turns back, and, though the stranger has disappeared, would seem to look with compassion upon this thing which he has come to understand. Indeed, compassion appears to be the moving force in this peculiar fable. But one cannot be certain of its final meaning, for Mr. Edmunds, perhaps in self-defense, speaks only in riddles.

The author's thoughtfulness was compared with Wilde's in *De Profundis*. But Edmunds's novel was "a rather nebulous euphemism compared with such direct, even if disputable, interpretations of the same theme" as *The Well of Loneliness* (1929) and *We Too Are Drifting* (1935). Edmunds lost sight of "philosophical significance" in the "demoniacal climax of the story," yet the "frantic, groping shadows of men" did convey "sensations of wonder and horror."

BOOK REVIEW/MEDICAL/RESISTANCE

# 1936, March 9
## *Time; The New Republic:*
## Dr. Havelock Ellis's *Studies in the Psychology of Sex*

On a page headed "Medicine," *Time* magazine reported: "Until this week only doctors and lawyers could legitimately buy" Dr. Ellis's "compendious . . . survey of the vast, tangled jungles of sex activities," his *Studies in the Psychology of Sex*.[48] The history of that restriction was traced.

In 1897, when this "inquisitive Englishman published *Sexual Inversion* as his first volume, "London police promptly arrested the bookseller and confiscated all available copies of this volume." Later,

Frank A. Davis of Philadelphia, as a personal favor to Dr. Ellis, began printing his *Studies,* which eventually ran to seven volumes and retailed for $30 per set. Mr. Davis was very strict about selling only to the professions. Since the War [1918], however, there has been such a great change in the U. S. attitude toward sex that Bennett A. Cerf, head of Manhattan's Random House, felt safe in bringing out this week a new four-volume edition of *Studies in the Psychology of Sex* and selling them to all comers at $15 per set.

This unexpurgated edition, printed from the old Davis plates, had behind it a mass of U. S. court decisions which, to Mr. Cerf, seemed to remove the last effective restrictions on the popular publication of the Ellis masterwork.

When Ellis first "poked around London and Paris asking impertinent questions of men & women," he soon discovered "that most people like to talk about their sex life." He thereafter "let the concupiscent, the celibate and the sexually miserable beat a path to his study and tell him all."

The seventy-seven-year-old Ellis lived in London and was

aware that beyond the tangled fields which he long ago cleared, lie great rivers of hormones which irrigate the human body and profoundly affect the flowering of personality.

On April 15, 1936, historian Lewis Mumford reviewed Ellis's sex *Studies* in *The New Republic.* That the series "can be offered to the general public is proof of the great change" that Ellis had helped to bring about "in the attitude of the Western World toward sex."*

The "importance of Ellis's work" could be properly appraised only when

one realizes that among Western peoples sex had during the nineteenth century reached its nadir. The narrowing of the emotional life, attendant upon overindulgence in practical activities, had been abetted by the Victorian reaction against the coarse speech and easy animality of the eighteenth century.

In the 1800s, "normal sexual interests" were found "chiefly among the 'low,' such as professional prostitutes, or among country lads and lasses." Then "a paralyzing dualism" between lusting males and frigid females "pervaded the sexual habits of the middle classes."

Up to the time of Ellis's writing it is scarcely an exaggeration to characterize the normal sexual state of respectable married women as frigidity, and when men sought anything like an adequate response from women they turned to those who were "loose". . . .

"The need for sexual enlightenment during the nineteenth century was as great among the medical profession as among laymen: indeed, in all the more complicated aspects of sex this still holds true." Mumford referred to an (unnamed) "American founder of the birth-control movement" (Margaret Sanger) as one of the medical instructors whose doctrines were limited by their personal "erotic" problems.

*Here again follows a useful contemporary evaluation of changes in response to sex. Mumford's interpretation of Victorian middle-class society as uniformly repressive is now, though interesting, debatable. Though Mumford writes in this review as a sexual modernist who views sex simplistically as an unqualified good, his later comments on the relation between sexual and revolutionary politics were an early and quite amazing statement of ideas ignored in America until the 1960s.

In the nineteenth century, he continued,

"Normal" sexual life was confined ideally to the brief marital rape that took place, just before sleep, under the double cover of darkness and bedclothes in a legalized Victorian bed.

Though Ellis had "opened his original studies with a monograph upon homosexuality," his "great merit was to emphasize the normal expressions of sex, and to redefine the 'norm' in terms of a much wider historical, psychological and anthropological background than any previous writer had drawn upon."

"On the subjects of homosexuality, prostitution, asceticism, chastity, marriage," Ellis's "even sanity makes him a far better guide than those whose specialized researchers have contributed more to the subjects."

But Mumford criticized Ellis's treatment of "sex and society":

one could wish for some deeper exploration of the role of love, reproduction and parenthood in relation to the occupational strains, hours of labor, difficulties of nutrition and nurture, inequalities in economic rights and privileges: likewise for some inquiry into the relation of sex to environment, particularly as affected by urban and rural ways of living. But these are subjects for Ellis's successors. . . .

Mumford concluded: "Despite all fears to the contrary," the subject of sex,

probably still occupies far too small a place in the routine of men and women in the industrially more advanced countries today. Though superficial freedoms have been achieved, sex holds too small a place in life, and irradiates too narrow a field of the personality. Havelock Ellis's great work symbolically restores sex to the central position of importance it should have in every harmonious life. Indirectly, it should count eventually as a powerful stimulus toward radical changes in our economic order; for though our sterile masculine habits of thought usually tend to express revolutionary social changes in terms of seizing power and transforming the instruments of production, no valid social change will be consummated until it is expressed likewise in terms of its end-products—the creation of an environment friendly to love, and a transformation of all the agents of reproduction and nurture. That includes everything from housing to education.[281–82]

♀ FILM REVIEW/RESISTANCE

## 1936, March 19
### *N. Y. Times:*
## Lillian Hellman's *These Three*

The film *These Three,* adapted by Lillian Hellman from her play *The Children's Hour,* was reviewed by Frank Nugent.[49] This critic's repeated reference to the original content of *The Children's Hour* was an act of resistance against that censorship office and studio decree which tried to suppress all such comment on the original source. According to Vito Russo, "Any mention . . . that Wyler's 'These Three' had been based on 'The Children's Hour' was forbidden by the censors, and that prohibition was enforced by the studio with the cooperation of the press." A review in the film industry trade paper, *Variety,* said " 'it is verboten to ballyhoo the original source' " (see Russo, *The Celluloid Closet* p. 63).

*The Times* review began: "The Hays office," the film industry's own censorship board, "would not sanction" a film of the original "Children's Hour." So Hellman had written a "considerably amended" version for the screen." Though "brilliant," the film was said to lack "the biting, bitter tragedy" of the play. The film "chooses (or the censors chose for it) to ignore any implications of an abnormal relationship between the two women school teachers, . . . and it progresses to what must be considered a happy and romantic ending." (Heterosexuality triumphed on the screen; homosexuality was vanquished on the stage—J. K.) But the film preserved "the very heart of the original"—the "helplessness" experienced by three persons faced by the lies of a "venomous little girl." It was "immaterial" whether the "falsehood" told by that girl concerned an "unnatural affection" between two women, or that one woman's fiance had been " 'carrying on' " with her female friend and coworker. The film was about two women "in love with the same man."

♀ CROSSING WOMAN/RESISTANCE

# 1936, April 12
## Dr. Alberta Lucille/Alan Hart:
### *The Undaunted*

In 1917, the twenty-seven-year-old Alberta Lucille Hart adjusted to her earlier erotic and affectional experiences with women by taking steps to pass permanently as a male, Dr. Alan Hart.[50] Hart's early history was recounted (anonymously) in a detailed medical journal article, published in 1920 by Dr. J. Allen Gilbert, a Portland, Oregon, psychiatrist whom Hart had consulted to overcome a fear of loud noises. She ended her analysis with Gilbert by obtaining a hysterectomy, starting to pass as a male, and marrying (in Gilbert's words) a "normal woman" who was "fully cognizant of all the facts." Gilbert's account was excerpted in *Gay American History,* where his subject, whom he had referred to only by the initial "H," was identified as Alberta Lucille Hart—an identification made on the basis of details provided by Gilbert's article.

Further research has now established that the former Alberta Lucille, as Dr. Alan Hart, wrote and published five books, four novels, and a popular account of radiation treatment, a type of medicine in which s/he had specialized.

Alberta Lucille Hart as Dr. Alan L. Hart, from the dust jacket of Hart's *These Mysterious Rays* (New York: Harper, 1946).

Dr. Alan L. Hart's last book, *These Mysterious Rays* (Harper & Row, 1943), discussed X-ray, radium, and ultra-violet therapy. On its jacket was Hart's photograph. Under the photo a brief biography described Hart as "a roentgenologist [X-ray technician] of many years training and practice," and a novelist. "His experience has included X-ray work in tuberculosis hospitals in Albuquerque, N. M. and Rockford, Ill.," and in Spokane, Washington. "In 1928, he conducted a chest clinic in Idaho and later took charge of an X-ray laboratory in Tacoma, Wash." In 1938, he became Tuberculosis Consultant to the Idaho Tuberculosis Association and the State Department of Public Health. In 1943 Hart was "serving with the Army as a civilian employee in the Induction Center in Seattle, reading chest X-ray films." Hart's use of the middle initial "L" on the title page of *These Mysterious Rays* suggests a continuing desire to recall her female identity as "Lucille," despite her passing.

Dr. Alan Hart's first novel, *Doctor Mallory,* was published by W. W. Norton in 1935. Commenting on it in *The New York Times Book Review* on March 31, Rose Feld described it as "the saga of a country doctor," Robert Mallory, "who fought bravely against the odds of ignorance, prejudice and chicanery" in a poor Oregon fishing village. Feld added: "Whether or not one approves of . . . socialized medicine, one must grant Mr. Hart the point of making an excellent case for it." Even when his wife left him Dr. Mallory refused to give up his dream of making "the community conscious of the dignity of the human body. . . . One of the best parts of the book is his [Mallory's] public denunciation of the medical profession when it forgets that its purpose is to serve and to educate and not to profit out of the ills of man."[17]

On April 14, 1935, *The Oregonian,* a Portland newspaper, reported that "Dr. Alan L. Hart, University of Oregon medical school '17," author of *Dr. Mallory,* had recently spoken in Portland. Dr. Hart was said to have practiced in Oregon, in New Mexico, and was then living in Spokane. He was to speak on a Portland radio station. "His mother is a resident of Albany and Dr. Hart is to visit there this week."

Dr. Alan Hart's second novel, *The Undaunted,* was published in 1936 by Norton. Reviewing the book in *The New York Times* on April 12, Louise Munsell Field declared: "For anyone interested in the development of medical science" Hart's novel "will prove little less than fascinating." It told of the experiences of Dr. Richard Cameron, first at Seaforth (on the Puget Sound), "in a medical laboratory associated with the Safe Harbor Hospital," and later at the Fifer Research Institute at Northdevon (described in the book as one of the oldest, largest cities in the United States, on the Atlantic seaboard).[105] Dr. Cameron was portrayed "as capable of enjoying a triumph over his enemies as he is of championing poor Sandy Farquhar, the intelligent, even brilliant little Scotsman who felt himself an outcast, who was tormented, scorned, hounded from place to place." The reviewer did *not* indicate that Sanderson Farquhar was "hounded from place to place" because of his homosexuality.

A recent reading of the novel reveals that Hart presented Farquhar as victim; Hart's intention was clearly to win readers' sympathy. Farquhar, Hart stressed, could not help being what he was (and, in any case, had had only one active homosexual "affair"). Farquhar's history included some elements of Hart's own experience. In his article of 1920, Dr. Gilbert mentioned that "H" had been working in a hospital as a male doctor "until she was recognized by a former associate. . . . Then the hounding process began." The "diaries and notebooks" which in the novel Farquhar left to be published—because "He'd always wanted . . . to do something for people of his sort"—suggests the speculation that Hart perhaps left similar manuscripts.

In the novel Farquhar was introduced as a man who

> had had to develop an inordinate courage in order to live at all. Small and frail from infancy, fear took possession of him. He worried lest he fall ill and lest he fail his studies. . . . He was forever haunted by the fear of being without a job.
>
> He was dogged by other phobias as well. Loud noises had always terrified him. . . . But with an obstinacy equal to his fears, he stuffed his ears with cotton and practiced revolver shooting at a mark. . . .
>
> . . . He was afraid of himself, of certain quirks in his own personality. He dreaded the suggestive hints people dropped about his failure to marry after his mother's death; he fled from women and lived quite without inti-

mates of either sex. There seemed to be a sort of barrier between him and other people: it was as though there were a "No Admittance" sign over his private life. Most of the time he was unapproachable. . . . If he tried to tell a smutty story, he was so ill at ease himself that he made his listeners uncomfortable too.

Thus Farquhar's whole existence had been a mosaic of fear and inner conflicts and outer bravado.

The novel's main character, Richard Cameron, did not know all this, "but he had liked Sandy" from the moment he had seen him defying another doctor.[75–76]

Farquhar told Cameron about his past dismissals from jobs as X-ray technician, even though his work was superior. " 'If I have nerve enough to ask why, they say something vague about my personality.' " His employers had " 'the whiphand because they control the money while I haven't any.' " Farquhar said:

"People won't leave anybody alone who isn't just like them and just as stupid. They think—God help them!—that they're normal. They measure everybody else by themselves. If you want to read different books or live differently than they do, then you're dangerous or abnormal. You're a Bolshevik, a degenerate, and you must be suppressed—by all the good 110% Americans! Normal, average, wholesome! I'm sick of the words. Who knows what is normal? You think you're normal, and I think I am, and they think they are. My God, what a mess! It makes me want to vomit!"[81–82]

Later, Richard Cameron told Farquhar:

"You're an idealist, a reformer, at heart. You see the world and the people in it—how silly and stupid it all is. And you're outraged. . . .

". . . In spite of your thirty-nine years and all your experience, you still think maybe something might be done about it and you ought to try to do it. In other words, you don't think humanity is hopeless. You still believe people might be bribed or persuaded or bullied into using their brains and living decently. Then, when every attempt to get them to do any of these things fails, you get angry and rail at them, for their stupidity. You're a defeated uplifter, Sandy, berating the heathen because they won't be uplifted. . . ."[84]

The friendship between Cameron and Farquhar begins to cause comment. The evil Dr. Ascot mentions "that there 'was something funny' about Cameron's liking for Sandy Farquhar," about whom another doctor is also "busily gossiping."[101]

When Richard Cameron describes a prisoner used as a guinea pig in medical tests, and mentions his own refusal to continue the tests, Farquhar comments:

"There's nothing people won't do to other people, Rich—people that they hate. Men are cruel to—other men."[145]

When he starts a new job Farquhar displays a "bare hint of the confidence born of recognized skill." He looks hopeful. He prays: " 'Keep the hounds off me

—until I can dig myself in!' " He has "about him not a vestige of insignificance —only the passionate longing for life of a handicapped animal in a world of foes."[183]

But later, Farquhar muses disconsolately on his fate. Even if he gets credit for his work, no one could "make him a different man."

> Neither could he. He had tried. Yes, damn it, he had always tried. But the thing had been impossible from the first. Why not admit that, once and for all?
>
> In his pocket Farquhar could feel the little notebook he had carried for years. In it he set down now and then ideas that came to him. He remembered the first entry in the little book, made when he was twenty. "My body is an incubus [burden] and my fears are born of it. But it is possible for the possessor of a defective body to remain unbroken by the disasters that overcome it because he has it always in his power to escape his servitude, his subjection, to his body. And I think it is his right. What a horror life would be—all life!—if there was no end to it!"

Farquhar analyzes the Damon Fifer Research Institute:

> In that institution dedicated to the study of disease and the discovery of truth, the inevitable had occurred. People—all people—were short-sighted and selfish and greedy; scientists were no exception. . . . If men could only learn not to knife each other, not to hate each other! . . . If they could only work together, face things squarely as they were, set reason a guard over their conduct!

Four of the twenty men who worked at the Institute were different:

> They passed their knowledge on to others. They did not work for money. They were adventurers, crusaders, men nagged by an insatiable desire to know. . . . They were not intolerant of other men in search of truth.
>
> It was possible then for men like that to maintain an existence in the hostile modern world—precarious and impecunious, but still an existence. . . . And all the other men who reported at the Institute for work were sycophants, parasites.[196–97]

Farquhar finally resigns from the Fifer Institute, as he says, "before I could be fired."[245] Afterward, while attending a symphony concert, he realizes that "appearances were no longer of importance."[253] At intermission the women at the concert seem to be laughing at him:

> Women always alarmed him and tonight they terrified him. He was convinced that to them he seemed not a small inconspicuous man in a dinner jacket but a clown, an absurd and comical figure forever denied entrance to their world.
>
> He could see himself as he felt he must appear to them—a ridiculous person with the burden of the past upon him. . . .
>
> His own burden was large and heavy.[255]

A group of young men telling "smutty stories" look at Farquhar "with what he was sure was contempt." He feels hunted. "He had always been hunted, he always would be. There was no escape with the pack of his past on his back."[256]

> He felt nothing now but that sense of utter personal defeat. What little faith had survived the years was toppling in ruin tonight. He had been driven from place to place, from job to job, for fifteen years because of something he could not alter any more than he could change the color of his eyes. Gossip, scandal, rumor always drove him on. It did no good to live alone, to make few acquaintances and no intimates; sooner or later someone always turned up to recognize him. And then there was that wretched business of resigning by request to be gone through again, and after that the concoction of a plausible story to account for the resignation and the ordeal of hunting another job without explaining exactly why he had left the old one and . . . without lying about it. Each time he underwent these humiliations his self-respect seemed first to writhe and then to shrink.[257]

Farquhar thinks:

> he was shut out forever from the happy normal life for which he had always longed. He was alone, he would always be alone. He had no friend in all the world but Richard Cameron and he could not bother him asking for help.
>
> A stifling sense of isolation shut down over Farquhar. . . . He was an outcast; the pack, red-tongued and savage, was in pursuit. He had no defense against that mob—neither money nor prestige nor influential friends. He had only himself, his own personality such as it was, his love of beauty, and his passion for justice. But over himself he had a power that could defeat the world and deliver him. . . .[258]

After Farquhar is found dead Richard Cameron receives a letter and a package which his friend had addressed to him, and pieces together Farquhar's story. Although Farquhar had planned suicide, he had died while saving the life of a drowning boy.[260–61]

Cameron tells a sympathetic colleague Farquhar's early history:

> "He was always a hero, all his life! . . . He was a delicate youngster and the bigger boys bullied him at school and tormented him when he couldn't hold his own with them. That started him being afraid of things. . . .
>
> "He'd been an only child, . . . and his poor health kept him out of athletics and prevented him mixing much with other kids of his own age. I suppose there never was a boy who knew less about the workings of the human body than he did when he went away from home to college. And it was just after that he discovered he was a homosexual. . . .
>
> "Sandy took it hard. He felt that he must always be an outcast, and he never got a chance to change his mind. He stayed away from men and women both; after that one affair he never had another. He lived alone, made books and music . . . take the place of people. When he got to medical

school he found a fellow there who'd known him in college and [he] spread the word about Sandy.

"Well, he stuck it out and took his degree in spite of everything, but when it came to outrunning gossip he found he couldn't do it. He went into radiology because he thought it wouldn't matter so much in a laboratory what a man's personality was. But wherever he went, scandal followed him sooner or later."

If Farquhar could have started his own medical practice, Cameron thinks " 'he might have succeeded . . . for he was a grand man with sick people. But he had no capital and so he had to work for other doctors or hospitals all his life. That ruined all his chances because eventually his story would get around and then he'd be forced to leave.' "[262]

Cameron concludes: " 'The thing that killed Sandy' " was

"the thought that, no matter how clean and decent he was, he must always be an outcast. He left some diaries and notebooks and asked me to take what little insurance he had and publish them at my own discretion. He'd always wanted, he said, to do something for people of his sort, something to stop them being hounded and persecuted for things they can't help."

Cameron is angered that " 'a man like Sandy has to die while all sorts of filthy-minded people who weren't fit to tie his shoestrings go around being respectable. He was kind and honest and brave, he was a good doctor, he loved beautiful things, and, in spite of all that happened to him, he loved people.' "[263]

On the second from the last page of the novel Cameron thinks that Farquhar "ran from things it would have been better to face."[309]

In 1977, an inquiry to the public library in Albany, Oregon, elicited the information that as Dr. Alan Hart, Alberta Lucille had published a number of books and technical papers, that Hart's widow was still living in a Connecticut city, and that she corresponded with a friend in Albany. Subsequent attempts to learn more of Hart's life by contacting her widow were discouraged by her. The message passed on by her friend in Albany was: "Let that all be passed now. She is older and does not want any more heart ache now."

♀ FILM REVIEW

## 1936, May 18
### *N. Y. Times: Dracula's Daughter*

In this film a female vampire with a predilection for female victims was vanquished by a male psychiatrist—a cinematic parable of the lesbian and the doctor.[51] That parable was not spoken of in *The Times.*

In *Dracula's Daughter,* said reviewer Frank Nugent, "Miss Dracula manages to be lovely and deadly at the same time," always leaving "her bloodless victims with those two telltale marks on the throat." Among the film's "blood-curdling" scenes was one in which a "a young blond model screams with terror when the vampire flashes the hypnotic ring in her eyes and bares her gleaming teeth." In another scene the psychiatrist "almost surrenders himself to vampiricism to save the life of Marguerite Churchill, who is under the spell of the undead." The reviewer advised: "Be sure to bring the kiddies."*

*Dracula's Daughter;* an older female vampire contemplates younger female flesh.

NEWS REPORT

# 1936, June 3
## *N. Y. Times: "A shouting, jeering mob"*

The account in *The Times* did not say so but a rumor that someone in William Haines's party had molested a six-year-old boy was behind the Klan-like attack

*Some of the original ads for this film proclaimed: "Save the women of London from Dracula's Daughter"; and the film's lesbian overtones were noted in the New York *World-Telegram* which pointed out that Dracula's daughter went around " 'giving the eye to sweet young girls' "; see Russo, *Celluloid Closet,* pp. 49, 58.

on Haines, his lover James Shields, and their friends.[52] A local racist group, "The White Legion," apparently had a hand in this anti-homosexual, vigilante incident.

*The Times* printed an Associated Press dispatch from Los Angeles which reported: "A shouting, jeering mob, about 100 men and women, severely beat William Haines, former motion picture star, and Jimmie Shields, a companion, near Manhattan Beach, and drove them and nineteen friends out of town. . . ."

> At his antique and interior decorating shop in Hollywood . . . Mr. Haines declared he did not know the reason for the mob's acts.
>
> "It was a lynch mob all right," he said. "Some wild, untrue rumor must have stirred them up. It might have been some sort of clan or secret organization."
>
> Several men in the Manhattan Beach area said today they were members of an organization known as "The White Legion" and that they aided in the demonstration. Others openly boasted on the streets of participating in the disturbance.

"Haines was knocked down and both his eyes blacked, and Shields was cut and bruised severely." Friends of Haines's who were attacked included "five men in a house near the Haines beach place," and eleven men who were guests at a Haines party.

♀  BLACK AMERICANS/IMAGE

# 1936
## John Dos Passos:
### *"Pat was dancing with a . . . pretty mulatto girl. Dick was dancing with a softhanded brown boy"*

Dos Passos's novel, *The Big Money* (1936), included a scene in which a white woman and man on a date went to a Harlem night club where each danced with members of their own sex.[53] A drawing by Reginald Marsh (from the 1946 edition of the book) depicting two women and two men dancing together marks a historical change in the meaning of such dancing and such images, from a time when they represented, merely, a curious, quaint custom, to 1946 when the present sketch depicted a contact with explicit homoerotic connotations. Despite the present illustration, the image of two women dancing together probably retained its status as innocent amusement longer than did the image of two males dancing in a newly eroticized world.*

*For an earlier depiction of male-male dancing as an innocent entertainment in the New York Stock Exchange see 1885, November. For such male-male dancing at the U. S. Military Academy at West Point see the post card, p. 318. For A. Castaigne's engraving of "A Miner's Ball" (1891) and for a photograph of cowboys dancing in the American Wild West, see *GAH*, pp. 507, 510. For a written description of male-male dancing in the West see Clarence Mulford's *Tex* (1922), quoted in *GAH*, p. 510.

Dancing couples by Reginald Marsh, in John Dos Passos, *The Big Money* (Boston: Houghton Mifflin, 1946), p. 455.

In addition to the stereotype of lesbian leching after heterosexual woman, Dos Passos's scene included a little racist touch.

In *The Big Money* Pat has just asked Dick to take her to someplace "really low." A taxi carries them to "a dump he'd heard of," whose entrance is "an unpainted basement door with one electriclightbulb . . . above it."

They had a hard time getting in. There were no white people there at all. It was a furnace room set around with plain kitchen tables and chairs. The steampipes overhead were hung with colored paper streamers. A big brown woman in a pink dress, big eyes rolling loose in their dark sockets and twitching lips, led them to a table. She seemed to take a shine to Pat. "Come right on in, darlin'," she said. "Where's you been all my life?"

Their whiskey was gone, so they drank gin. . . .

The only music was a piano where a slimwaisted black man was tickling the ivories. . . .

Pat was dancing with a pale pretty mulatto girl in a yellow dress. Dick was dancing with a softhanded brown boy in a tightfitting suit the color of his skin. The boy was whispering in Dick's ear that his name was Gloria Swanson. Dick suddenly broke away from him and went over to Pat and pulled her away from the girl. Then he ordered drinks all around that changed sullen looks into smiles again. He had trouble getting Pat into her coat. The fat woman was very helpful. "Sure, honey," she said, you don't want to go on drinkin' tonight, spoil your lovely looks." Dick hugged her and gave her a tendollar bill.

In the taxi going downtown Dick tells the angry Pat: " 'I thought it was time to draw the line.' "[455–56]


♀ MEDICAL/BLACK AMERICAN

## 1937, January
### Dr. George Henry: *"A tenderness I have never known"*

A "report of a study of 100 socially well adjusted men and women whose preferred form of libidinous gratification is homosexual," was presented by Dr. Henry of the Payne Whitney Psychiatric Clinic New York City.[54] The homosexuals who had

> submitted themselves for examination came voluntarily after being acquainted by a field worker with the nature of the study. They have offered themselves because of their interest in a scientific investigation of a human relationship which they believe is unjustly frowned upon by society. Most of them belong to the professional class. . . .[889–90]

The individuals studied apparently agreed to detailed physical and mental examinations by Dr. Henry in the hope that their participation would contribute to psychiatrists' attempts to ameliorate the social intolerance of homosexuals.

Each of the four case histories related by Dr. Henry (two males, two females) contained extreme forms of childhood and familial trauma, of sometimes dubious connection with the individual studied. For example, the sister of one male homosexual had married an impotent man whose "chief interest was in pictures of beheaded women," and who had committed suicide "in a particularly gruesome manner."[891] Each of Dr. Henry's reports suggested that the individual's homosexuality had been determined by early trauma; later homosexual interests were linked causally with early disturbances. (It was not suggested that the childhood traumas of heterosexuals had caused their heterosexuality.) Despite Dr. Henry's claim that his subjects were "well adjusted," he concluded that "Well-adjusted overt homosexuals are rare," and that homosexuality was a condition best "prevented."

One of Dr. Henry's four histories was that of a Black lesbian, one of the earliest of the few reports of such lives found in U. S. medical journals. Despite Dr. Henry's racist and heterosexist biases, apparent in his wording, his history of "Mary Jones" portrays a woman who surmounted many familial and social hurdles to make an affectional and erotic relationship with another woman. Dr. Henry summed up this subject's story as "Case IV. Disillusioned in Marriage. Finds a Substitute in Homosexual Liasion."

Mary Jones is a successful negro actress who is now nearly 50 years old [born, then, about 1887]. She is well adjusted to her actual situation in life and has no regrets for having established homosexual relationships. She is at ease in any social group. Her soft, deep voice, friendly attitude along with an evident personal security has caused her to be sought after by both white and colored people.

　　Mary has little in her early life which she can look back upon with pleasure. She was an illegitimate child, the daughter of a 12-year-old colored nursemaid and of a white man in whose home her mother was employed. . . . Mary's skin was of such a light color that she was conspicuous in a colored neighborhood where other children called her a half-white bastard.

　　. . . Mary's step-father . . . used to beat up the mother and this relationship added much to Mary's unhappiness as a child. Her mother really seemed more like a sister and as a matter of fact in early childhood Mary had been led to believe that her grandmother was her mother.

　　Mary's early training, especially her moral training, came from her grandmother. "I've always been lectured about virtue. If I were not good my grandmother said she would come back and haunt me." As a result of this training she remained a virgin until after her marriage. . . . "When I was six I saw mother in bed with men. I remember mother putting rouge on her cheeks. I cried and cried because I thought only bad women did that."

　　. . . The grandmother died when Mary was 13 and she was then turned over to a maternal aunt, Louise. . . . "She was very stingy. She used to make me feel that I ate too much. She was very critical of me. She always prophesied that I was going to be a bad girl."

　　Three years later Mary was married to the spoiled son of a wealthy self-made negro. She was not especially in love with him but she and her family felt that she should not neglect this opportunity for advancing her social position. The marriage proved to be a failure. Her husband never worked, drank to excess, gambled and frittered away whatever income they had. She was entirely dependent upon her father-in-law for support. She tried to be a good wife to her husband and to influence him to give up his dissipated mode of living but her efforts were of no avail. Two pregnancies were terminated by abortion because she felt she could not afford to have children.

　　Five years after marriage Mary had become thoroughly disillusioned but "I put up with him until after mother's death." The mother developed general paresis [paralysis] and Mary tried to take care of her. Even after she had to be taken to a state hospital Mary made daily visits. Her husband's dissipation gradually increased and shortly after her mother died he developed tuberculosis. She returned to him to nurse him until his death.

　　At 28 Mary was a widow and employed as a demonstrator. The manager of the firm was a dour, taciturn and indifferent man. She had never encountered an individual of this sort and she was fascinated by his indifference. She took the initiative in their courtship and marriage. They have been married for more than 20 years now and she has never succeeded in getting him to offer any expression of affection for her. "He would lose some of his manliness if he made such an admission." For many years after marriage she believed he was faithful to her but he was in the habit of staying out all night without explanation and she learned that he was interested in other women. This made her very unhappy. Although no contraceptive measures were used she did not become pregnant by her second husband. "I regret having no children. It's the one great unhappiness, particularly as I feel I would have made a very good mother."

Soon after Mary remarried she took part in amateur theatricals. Her musical talents were soon recognized and her promotion was rapid. Her husband was jealous of her professional success but in recent years he has been dependent upon her for support.

Her prominence in theatrical work probably made her more attractive to women. She says, however, that all her life women had made advances to her but she would not consent "because it all seemed unnatural and abnormal." Finally at the age of 41 [about 1928], while dancing with a woman, "something very terrific happened to me—a very electric thing. It made me know I was homosexual." Since then she has had several alliances with both white and colored women and for the past five years she has been living with a white woman. This woman is "one of the finest women I have ever known. She has come to be very, very dear to me—not just for sex alone —it's a very great love." Mary has no regrets for having yielded to homosexual temptations. "This last relationship affords a tenderness I have never known." Nevertheless she believes she would have remained a conventional married woman if her second husband had not neglected her. "If marriage had been satisfactory I would never have had homosexual relations."[896–98]


♀ PLAY REVIEW

# 1937, February 21
## N. Y. Times: Stephen Powys's
## Wise Tomorrow in London, Baltimore, and New York

A story from London reported the opening there of Wise Tomorrow.[55] This play was about "an elderly retired actress who tried to recapture some of her former glory by sponsoring a young actress, and the independence of her vain protégée," a plot involving the "gradual undermining of the girl's character."[19:1]

The American premier of Wise Tomorrow in Baltimore was reported in 'The Times on October 5; Marylanders were said to have found the "sophisticated" comedy "provocative."[29:2]

Reviewing the Broadway opening of Wise Tomorrow in The Times on October 16, Brooks Atkinson called it the story of an evil-minded and treacherous old actress who falls in love with an attractive young actress and wrecks her life. At the opening of the play Joan Campion is a normal young lady of the stage who expects soon to marry. . . . But Diana\* Ebury, a retired harpy of the theatre, sees Joan on the stage, makes friends with her and breaks up her prospective marriage. Finally she dies, as blatantly as possible, and posthumously makes Joan hers by naming her as the heir to Ebury property.

The topic is sufficiently malodorous. The author does nothing to redeem it in the frowziness of his playwrighting. . . .[22:5]

♀ BOOK REVIEW

## 1937, March 7
### N. Y. Times Book Review:
### Djuna Barnes's Nightwood

"Sooner or later," said reviewer Alfred Kazin, "the thought must occur to any reader of this novel that its characters are freaks."[56]† This had occurred to T. S. Eliot, who had written an introduction to the book explaining that to believe the characters were freaks was to miss the point.

But what was "the point," Kazin asked, of a novel in which

a fantastic doctor from the Barbary Coast, a fantastic nobleman, the latter's wife and two lesbian women are thrown together some time after the war somewhere in Paris and Vienna. They are all, in their fashion, fakes.

The doctor had no license, the Baron no right to call himself a baron, and the three women "defraud themselves and each other in their romantic relationship."

The Baroness, having given birth to a sickly boy, leaves her husband; a wealthy, mousy little woman takes her away from another woman and goes to America with her. Thereafter nothing of any dramatic consequence occurs. . . .

The doctor was a figure of "monstrous stature," reflecting a "demonic sadness that is at once oppressive and moving." Each "distinctive" character had "a desperate lyricism" that set him or her off against an "unrelieved background of helplessness." This

is a background against which joy must be grotesque in its extravagance and exquisite self-torture is one of the conditions of existence, a background against which people move in a kind of angry stupor, without love, without

\*The name Diana has often signified lesbianism; see, for example, the book *Diana,* 1939.
†For the association of homosexual and "freak" see footnote to 1896, October 13.

trust, and never without some inhuman fear that all the pin points of their own making will fuse into a spear and stab the life out of the consciousness that alone sustains them.

INVESTIGATIVE FILES

# 1937, March 13
# J. Edgar Hoover: Private files

The private files of former FBI Director J. Edgar Hoover contain hundreds of pages of documents recording rumors about the sexual lives of numerous persons.[57] Brief summaries, made in 1975, of these voluminous files were obtained under the Freedom of Information Act. According to these summaries the first file containing allegations of homosexuality dates to 1937, the last such file to 1970. Efforts to obtain photocopies of the complete, original files are still underway. In regard to these documents, one interesting question is what J. Edgar Hoover, the longtime intimate of Clyde Tolson, made of the rumors concerning his own homosexuality. Another important question is to what use these files were put.

The summary of the earliest file to contain an allegation of homosexuality refers to a "First Communication," dated March 13, 1937, and a "Last Communication" dated October 18, 1967, a total of approximately forty-five pages, spanning thirty years. The file, described as "Congressional," is said to contain "Derogatory Information" ("unsubstantiated") that the subject of the file (name deleted) "was having an affair with a woman and also [an] allegation described as 'unfounded' that [name deleted] was a homosexual."

A second file contains a "First Communication" dated January 23, 1941, and a last dated September 14, 1943, a total of approximately 160 pages. The file, described as "Investigative," is said to contain "Derogatory Information," specifically, a

> report and memoranda of investigation re immoral activities of [name deleted]. Allegation was that [name deleted] was a homosexual.

The above file may refer to Sumner Welles, Under Secretary of State, and a close personal friend of Franklin and Eleanor Roosevelt. A lengthy memorandum, dated April 23, 1941, by William C. Bullitt, describes an interview with F.D.R. Bullitt brought to the President's attention reports of alleged homosexual acts by Sumner Welles. Two years later, in August 1943, the President, informed that Bullitt had been spreading rumors of Sumner Welles's "crimes," and that these rumors were about to be printed by newspaper columnists, was forced to request Welles's resignation; Welles resigned in September.

The "First Communication" in a third file of Hoover's is dated May 20,

1942, and a last dated June 27, 1942, a total of about eighty-five pages. The file, described as "Investigative," is said to contain "Derogatory Information." The dates and quotation below indicate that the file concerns Senator David I. Walsh (for details of this case see 1942, February). The contents of the file, the summary says,

> Contains results of investigation conducted based on allegations that [name deleted] was frequenting a house where homosexuals engaged in espionage activity visited. Investigation disclosed person thought to be [name deleted] was someone else.

A fourth file of Hoover's contains two pages of communications, both dated June 30, 1943. The file, categorized "Information," is said to contain "Derogatory Information," specifically, a "memorandum to [FBI official Clyde] Tolson from Robert C. Hendon, 6/30, 43, re gossip information [name deleted] had repeated to the effect Mr. Hoover was a homosexual."

And the last file, referring to the years covered by the present book, contains three pages, a "First Communication" dated June 27, 1944, and a last dated July 5, 1944. The file, called "Administrative," is said to contain "Report of interview by New York Office Agents with [name deleted] who reported he had heard a rumor to the effect Hoover was 'queer.' "

NEWS REPORTS/LEGAL CASES

## 1937, August 12
### *N. Y. Times:* "Sex crimes" in New York

Although all the reported sex crimes concerned adult males and little girls, news stories in *The Times* in 1937 used a genderless terminology referring to "sex criminals," "sex perverts," "sex delinquents," "sex offenders," "degenerates," " 'adult fiends'," "crimes of degeneracy," "abnormality," and a "wave of perversion"—a universalizing terminology which was elsewhere, at the time, extended to homosexuals.[58] The use of the same language to refer to coercive adult-child relations and homosexual relations between consenting adults confounded these behaviors in the public mind.

"Sex Criminal Gets 25 Years To Life" declared a *Times* headline on August 12, 1937, reporting the sentencing of an adult male for "assaulting two 10-year-old girls." The judge in the case agreed " 'with those officials who are decrying sex crimes.' " He added: " 'The talk of treating sex perverts as insane individuals I do not believe has much justification.' " He thought special legislation was required " 'to confine sex perverts in a special institution,' " and said: " 'Sex perverts are baneful enemies of society who should be segregated for the longest possible time in order to protect our little ones.' "[8:4]

The following day, August 13, a *Times* headline read: "Police Making List of Sex Criminals." The New York City "police are compiling a list of all known degenerates for future use," said the story, referring to a case in which a male adult had murdered an eight-year-old girl. "Already more than 300 names have been placed on the list in Brooklyn." Twelve adult males had been charged the previous day with "crimes of degeneracy" against girls age thirteen and under. The police list included men in all boroughs of New York City "charged with sex crimes during the last fifteen to twenty years." The police planned to "make a periodic check" of the persons listed.

One of the adult males charged with a sex crime said "the police had beaten him with blackjacks and rubber hose."

A few days later, on August 25, a *Times* headline read: "Sterilization Urged In Some Sex Cases." A New York Children's Court judge had recommended the "sterilization of certain types of sex delinquents." He said: "the 'adult fiends' " who committed " 'atrocities' " had themselves been "undetected child sex delinquents." If their "delinquencies" had been "discovered and properly treated, their vicious propensities might have been liquidated."* This judge added: "Some sex delinquents should be removed from the community and confined until their abnormalities are eliminated."

Two weeks later, on September 8, 1937, *The Times* reported a meeting of law enforcement officials in New Rochelle, N. Y., "to discuss methods of curbing the wave of perversion" which had that year allegedly doubled the number of "sex offenses against children." The legal officials, meeting in the parish house of an Episcopal Church, called for "the abolition of determinate sentences for sex offenders," and recommended that a board of "alienists" be appointed to decide when criminals were "fit to return to society."

♀  BOOK REVIEW/RESISTANCE

## 1937, August 15
### *N. Y. Times Book Review:*
### Elisabeth Craigin's *Either Is Love*

Craigin's novelistic defense of a "normal," "interfeminine" intimacy was met with skepticism by a *Times* critic, who said[59]:

> The woman who signs herself "Elisabeth Craigin" tells in this book the candid story of two loves. One was for the man to whom she was happily married. The other, earlier, but no less intense and absorbing, and on the

---

*The word "liquidation" may, in the 1980s, strike readers as ominous, perhaps more ominous than some of the older-younger relationships at which such moral outrage was directed.

other hand no less outgiving and generous, had been for another woman. And like Radclyffe Hall in "The Well of Loneliness," this pseudonymous author pleads here for an attitude of tolerance and understanding toward "interfeminine" romance.

The writer of this first-person narrative does not merely urge, however, that such an emotional relationship is not in itself degenerate or disgraceful; she takes a firm stand of her own in declaring also that it is not incompatible with the capacity for the deepest and most ardent "normal" devotion, that indeed it is not necessarily "abnormal" itself. The girl Rachel, in this record, was undoubtedly abnormal, and also unstable, emotionally, for all her clear mind, unselfish loyalty and good qualities. But the girl Elisabeth does not see herself as abnormal. And the book's most destructive neuroticism is that of the jealous and morbid [male] hypochondriac whose "normal" affection for Rachel is so mercilessly possessive, and who is so implacably determined to keep the two girls apart.

Elisabeth felt that the first relationship was something that must be confessed before her marriage. She feared a lessening of respect and affection, but she knew that she must face that danger. So she wrote down the whole story, every experience and reaction. This story . . . makes the main part of this little book.

It is not told sensationally nor lightly. Indeed, it has a weighty seriousness. And it is certainly not a story which lacks existing parallels. But it is so detailed in its frankness that its argument is weakened by minutiae. . . . But no one can deny that the author has stated her case with the utmost candor and earnestness.

NEWS REPORTS

## 1937, October 12
### N. Y. Times: Czech Nazis accused of "homosexuality"

"Czech Nazi Official Is Seized By Police," declared a *Times* headline.[60] A dispatch from Prague reported "A major political sensation" caused by the arrest, under the criminal code "dealing with homosexuality," of Hans Rutha,* a high official in the country's "camouflaged Nazi Party." The editor of the Nazi party newspaper and five others had also been arrested "on suspicion of homosexual offenses." The head of the Czech Nazi party "indicated that opposition within the party itself had been responsible" for Rutha's "having been denounced to the authorities."[7:1]

"14 Members of Czech Nazi Party Held For Morals Offenses," said a *Times* headline on October 17. The story announced more arrests under the law against

*Various *Times* stories referred to Rutha as Hans, Heinrich, and Heinz.

"homosexuality." Rutha, the "right hand man" of the Nazi party chief, was "involved in a scandal similar to that which cost the life of Ernst Roehm in Germany."[4:8]

On October 20, a long story from Prague analyzed the complex politics behind the arrest of Rutha and other Czech Nazis for "homosexual offenses." The arrests had done "incalculable harm" to the Czech Nazi movement; "mothers in the German area" of the country were said to now "fear to entrust their sons" to the party's youth movement.[13:1]

"Members of Youth Organization Face Homosexual Charges," declared a *Times* headline on December 3. Twelve members of the Czech Nazi party's youth movement had appeared in court to answer "charges of homosexuality"—directed chiefly against Rutha, who had "killed himself soon after his arrest early in November." The prosecutor charged the Nazi press with "attempting to prove the motives of the accusation are political."[17:6]

And on December 10, 1937, a *Times* story from Prague announced that fourteen Czechs, all the accused, had received "suspended sentences after trial on homosexual charges."[2:3]

♀ FILM REVIEW

# 1937, October 20
## N. Y. Times: Club de Femmes

The *Times* film critic Frank Nugent began[61]:

> That marvelously proper institution, the New York Board of Censors . . . has had its highly moral way with Jacques Deval's "Club de Femmes." . . . With a few decisive scissor strokes and a dialogue eraser, it has converted a naughty, but nice, French comedy into a gently amusing, but nice (in a nice way), companion piece to other girls' club tours as "Stage Door," "Girls' Dormitory" and "Mädchen in Uniform." The resemblance, of course, is merely one of theme, not of treatment. . . .
>
> It was this reviewer's good fortune to see both versions, the uncensored and the post-whitewashed. In the original we went . . . to a women's club-hotel in Paris, a sumptuous but virtuous establishment dedicated to the protection of lone females against the predatory male. . . .

In the original film, one case study was that of

> the lively minx who smuggled her fiancé into her room, had an affair and —came the dawn—a baby. Over this, naturally, there was a great to-do, satisfactorily silenced when the sympathetic house physician [a female] told the bewildered directress [of the club] that it was a girl child and therefore in order.

Among the cases "tinged with tragedy"—the "purple group"—was that of

> the borderline young woman, stiffling her impulse toward the innocent blond in the next room, but driven to murder when her vestal is outraged through the connivance of the club's serpent. . . .

But in the censored version the first young woman's fiancé "has become her husband," and the second female's "stifled passion has been changed to sisterly solicitude." The reviewer praised the actresses who played "the near affinities." He ended: "à bas les censeurs!"—down with censors.*

BOOK REVIEW

# 1937, December 5
## *N. Y. Times Book Review:*
## James Cain's *Serenade*

Cain's novel, said critic J. Donald Adams, told the story of opera singer John Howard Sharp, whose career was "interrupted by the loss of his voice" due to "his too intimate friendship with the wealthy amateur conductor, Winston Hawes."[62] (Loss of a singing voice was a new symptom among those said to be caused by homosexuality.)

> Sharp was normally attracted by women, and Hawes was the one man in his life who had aroused an abnormal response.

"It was the Indian girl, Juana," a "little Mexican three-peso prostitute," who "brought back to [Sharp's] voice its magnetic quality." The "reappearance of Winston Hawes," and "the battle for Sharp between Hawes and Juana" constituted the rest of the "tragic" story. The novel had its "weaknesses," but was "not easily laid aside."†

♀ PLAY REVIEW

# 1937, December 14
## *N. Y. Times:*
## Aimee and Philip Stuart's *Love of Women*

The two English playwrights did not "exploit" the scandal value of their "unconventional" subject, said Brooks Atkinson.[63] *Love of Women,* which had opened on Broadway,

---

*For a lesbian's response to *Club de Femmes* see entry of 1947, June, p. 622.
†For James Baldwin's comment on James Cain and *Serenade* see 1949, Summer.

is the story of two young women who have lived alone for five years and started the gossips to gabbling. They have just made their mark in the world by writing a successful drama. A brilliant surgeon has fallen in love with one of them. For her it is a choice between love and a successful career at dramatic collaboration. For her comrade of five industrious years it looks like calamity. It turns out that way, for the brilliant surgeon captures his bride and her comrade is left frightened and alone.*

All this is the subject for an intelligent play in the vein of "The Green Bay Tree" and "The Captive."

♀ MEDICAL

# 1938, January
# Marie E. Kopp: "Surgical Treatment
# As Sex Crime Prevention Measure"

An international survey of sexual surgery on males and females as a "sex crime prevention measure," appeared in a U.S. medical journal.[64] Marie Kopp was enthusiastic about sexual surgery as a mode of treatment for what she loosely referred to as "sexual overexcitation," "perversion of sex desire," "sexual aberrations," "sex abnormality," "sex crime," "unnatural offense," "rape, homosexuality, abuse of minors, etc."† Kopp also recommended sexual surgery for persons she referred to as the "hypersexed or pervert male and female," the "mentally and morally diseased," and the "asocial and abnormal."

Among penal codes mentioned approvingly as providing "surgical castration as a therapy and crime prevention measure" were those of Nazi Germany.[702]

A survey of the U. S. history of sexual surgery as crime preventive referred to Dr. Harry O. Sharp, who in Jeffersonville, Indiana, about 1889, had "utilized sterilization [vasectomy] for the purpose of reducing sexual over-excitation, a serious problem among the inmates of the State Institution for Delinquent Boys." Until 1907, Dr. Sharp, "without legal authority but guided by humanitarian and eugenic purposes, performed several hundred operations of vasectomy upon men before their release from custody." In 1889, Dr. Isaak Kerlin, superintendent of the State Training School for Delinquent Boys in Elwyn, Pennsylvania, had "obtained parental consent for the castration of a feebleminded inmate on eugenic grounds."[697] Vasectomies had also been performed on fifty-eight boys at the Institution for Feebleminded Children in Winfield, Kansas, by Dr. F. Hoyt Pilcher, "on avowed eugenical grounds." In Massachusetts, at the State Hospital

---

*"Captures his bride": for the metaphor of hunting and war applied to a male's pursuit of a female, see 1926, September 30; and 1929, November 13.
†For Marie Kopp's other work see 1929, Davis.

for Epileptics, "24 inmates were subjected to sterilization before regulation by statute."[697]

In 1907, "the first statute on eugenical sterilization in the world" had become law in Indiana. In 1938, thirty-two states of the Union had enacted sterilization laws. "Some 25,403 persons have been surgically treated up to January 1, 1937."[698]

FILM REVIEW/CROSSING MAN

## 1938, March 4
### N. Y. Times: Bringing Up Baby

Reviewing the film *Bringing Up Baby* (with Cary Grant and Katharine Hepburn) *Times* writer Frank Nugent criticized what he called the script's clichés, including "the one about the man wearing a woman's negligee."[65]

The reference was to a scene in which the Cary Grant character, having lost his own clothes, has donned a woman's frilly housecoat. Asked persistently why he's wearing that unusual outfit, he finally retorts in exasperation: "Because I just went gay all of a sudden." That quick throwaway is one of the earliest uses of "gay" for homosexual documented in the United States. *The Times* reviewer did not comment on the line.*

BOOK REVIEW

## 1938, March 20
### N. Y. Times Book Review:
### Elliot Paul's Concert Pitch

The first part of this book, said critic Louis Kronenberger, concerned "the launching of a young pianist and the courtship of his mother" by the male narrator.[66] The widowed mother of the twenty-year-old pianist, Robert, had lived entirely for him. But "a powerful Parisian music critic, a homosexual named Piot," has fallen in love with Robert. Realizing that the "inbred" relation of mother and son "must be broken," the narrator "permits Piot—whose motive neither mother nor son understands—to take the boy to America for a tour." The last part of the book was "all on a violently descending plane." With "such people as Piot and Robert," the author had "not only drawn a convincing picture of artistic temperament, but also created human beings whom it is teasing to investigate and possible to accept."

*For "gay" also see footnote to 1922, Stein; and footnote to 1933, October 12, p. 437.

♀ BOOK REVIEWS/RESISTANCE

# 1938, August 14
## N. Y. Times Book Review; Springfield Republican;
## Boston Transcript:
## Gale Wilhelm's Torchlight to Valhalla

A reviewer's perception that love between women was, in 1938, a "somewhat overworked" subject suggests that a little lesbianism went a long way.[67] But a non-sensationalistic treatment, like that in Gale Wilhelm's new novel, was still rare. A critic's calling lesbianism a commonplace literary theme does suggest an important historical change in the quantity of explicit representations, however negative most continued to be.*

Wilhelm's "deliberately mannered," sometimes "precious" style was "extremely effective" in "evoking mood," said *Times* reviewer Rose C. Feld. *Torchlight to Valhalla* was set in Berkeley, California, and

> tells the story of the conflict of emotions of a 21-year-old girl who realizes that she is unable to respond to the love of a man. The theme is not a new one for Miss Wilhelm; her first novel, "We Too Are Drifting," was concerned with the same problem. She handles her subject with a sensitive touch, achieving her effects by reticences rather than elaborations.
>
> The best part of the book, by far, is her description of the relationship between the girl, Morgen, and her father, Fritz.

When Morgen's father died the unhappy woman turned to Royal, a male suitor, hoping that

> in his arms she will find forgetfulness.
>
> The result of that union brings unhappiness and confusion to both of them. For Royal the answer is flight, for Morgen the discovery that her way of life is different. The introduction of the girl, Toni, resolves the problem for her.

The "final chapters of the book dealing with the 17-year-old Toni seem young compared with the maturity" of the earlier story. "Because of this weakness, the book becomes a problem of emotional adjustments of youth rather than of inversion."

A review in the *Springfield Republican,* on August 14, called *Torchlight to Valhalla* "important mainly because of the economy of style and the dignified handling of a delicate and now somewhat overworked subject."

*For Wilhelm's earlier lesbian novel see 1935, August 18.

In the *Boston Transcript* on August 27, A. B. Tourtellot declared that, however "advanced" Wilhelm was as an artist, "the substance" of her novel

> is in grave danger of stagnation. She treated this subject of woman's love for woman adequately and successfully in her first book. Now she can do nothing but repeat. . . .

♀ PERSONAL TESTIMONY

## 1938, August
### *The Forum:* Marion Joyce's "Flight from Slander"

*The Forum* magazine published the life story of a woman (born about 1888) who, from the age of eighteen, had been mistaken for "Lesbian."[68] Her history is all the more poignant because she completely accepted the moral judgment that the labels "Lesbian" and "abnormal" constituted "slander." Ironically, her reminiscence is now an important source for the social history of American lesbianism, providing, for example, a rare glimpse of women-loving interests among 'ordinary' housewives. This painful tale is all the sadder because of its apparent authenticity, and its subject's utter lack of defense against the dominant society's life-destroying judgments and acts. The author's uncritical acceptance of the standard condemnation of lesbianism illustrates the devastating effects of such views. Marion Joyce's need to assert her status as "normal woman," and the extremity of her anti-lesbian reactions—her making several major geographical moves—indicates some inner identification denied and distanced. Also illustrated is the disastrous effect which the delegitimation of the old female friendship had on some women whose lives spanned the era of transition from romantic friendship to erotic love, from the late nineteenth century through the first third of the twentieth.

An "Editor's Note" introducing Joyce's reminiscence claimed that neither the magazine nor author were "concerned with Lesbianism as a moral issue."

> But, as most observant people will have discovered for themselves, the craze for modern psychologies has infected a multitude of self-styled sophisticates . . . with a zeal for imputing homosexuality to any man or woman unfortunate enough to appear in some way effeminate or mannish. . . .

Such imputation was the worst kind of "cruelty."[90] Marion Joyce began:

> I was born with the belief that between two women there might be sincere affection and sympathetic understanding, the symbol of real friendship. Schoolgirl attachments were precious to me; the loyalty of my feminine friends and my mother's was unquestioned. As a child, I read with admiration of the heroic female friendships of history.
>
> I was eighteen [about 1906] before I learned that thoughtless remarks

could blast a normal companionship and make it a shameful thing. Public opinion, formed by cheap medical reprints and tabloid gossip, dubbed such contacts perverted, called such women Lesbians, such affection and understanding destructive.

I am 50 years old and single and never before have I had the courage to speak frankly, because a woman has no defense against the slander of perversion. But now I have reached the end of my personal endurance under the persecution that I have been forced to accept because I happen to have been born a woman well above the average in height, with a voice that is two octaves lower than it should rightly be, with hands that are broad at the knuckles and capable of swinging an ax or steadying a plow. Because I must earn my living, I am asking the right to live my life without the menace of ignorance made cruelly aware of misapplied clinical facts for commercial gain.

I had a normal childhood in . . . an isolated country district. My father had a farm, and there I was brought up with my brothers. . . . My best friend was the farmer's son, . . . with whom I planted corn, picked strawberries, and plucked chickens. The coachman taught me to harness horses, and I rode the work team when my father plowed in the spring.

Despite these tomboy activities I had a family of dolls, a silk dress which gave me a real little-girl thrill, and curls at the end of my short hair. . . .

When I was twelve [about 1900], my father lost his money, my mother died, and a secure world in which I had been living fell away from me. . . .

Social conditions in those days were vastly different from those of today. It is trite to recall that the adolescent girl of the better class was then protected to the point of becoming a virtual prisoner in the shelter of her home and immediate friends. Women ambitious for business careers were marked as curiosities. . . .

The social position which my family held brought me in contact with a girl whom I had known from childhood and whom I admired because her wealth brought her so much freedom. She had been educated in a high-grade Southern school, spent her winters with her family in the neighboring city, and had just returned from an extensive European tour. I was eighteen, and she was my only friend. . . . Why she sought my company I didn't know but I accepted it gratefully.

And then she told me of Lesbianism.

She had a hard time making me understand what she meant, because she gave me credit for a knowledge greater than I possessed. . . . All I knew of sex came from my father's books and from the writing on the basement walls of the public schools. Salacious and filthy as some of this wisdom was, it had nothing to say of the perverted love of one woman for another.

What this girl told me of herself and her friends I hardly understood, but when she plainly stated they were sure that I belonged with them, I was filled with terror and loathing.

The next morning I ran away.

I went to a neighboring city, hoping to find there a chance for individual progress as a normal woman. Nor have I since been back to that village. . . . Whenever I meet an acquaintance of my childhood, I take great care that ours shall be a passing contact . . . lest I be marked with the name that these women handle so deftly and so carelessly.

In the city I lived in a girl's club . . . which housed some 40 girls who were studying for careers or employed in offices. I had $10 a week and a bad case of fright. At night I studied in art school and by day I sold Bibles by house-to-house canvassing. . . .

One morning at the "club" I was awakened by the sound of muffled sobs in the adjoining room. My first impulse was to offer assistance, but something held me back. That night, when I came in from work, the girls were standing in hushed groups. The girl next door to me, the tall, slim Canadian, had committed suicide.

I started to ask questions, but the curious smile on the lips of the girls I spoke to stopped me. Then I remembered my neighbor's room-mate, a silly little blond who whistled popular songs and ran around in a disheveled pink negligee. Where was she?

"Flora was married last week," answered a girl bluntly. "Ann couldn't live without her."

I moved, this time to a small apartment. . . . I avoided the other roomers and enjoyed complete isolation.

Working in "publicity," Marion Joyce

was cautious, even in my business connections. Lesbianism was no subject of conversation there, but I found the idea lurking hidden here and there, particularly among men who had lost business opportunities to women. They could not accept women bosses gracefully. To rationalize their own failure it became necessary for them to distort the personalities of the women.

Then, too, I discovered that a certain type of woman was to be feared and avoided. Unfortunately I had made a business contact with one of these before I realized what the consequences might be.

One day she resented a luncheon engagement I had with an old friend. "What is the woman to you?" she demanded. "Are you married to her?"

I turned and started to empty my desk, stacking my possessions in a pile.

"What are you doing?" she asked, and started to cry.

"I'm quitting," I said flatly. "You can have what is left of the business."

During the war period [1916–18] of flaming youth and few scruples, Lesbianism became a common topic for conversation. I heard it discussed, saw it flaunted, felt it whispered. Gradually it became impossible for two women to live together and avoid slander. Few had the courage to brand such talk a lie, for denials brought smiles and further talk. "She protests too much," they would say.*

*Other sources suggest that in the teens erotic relationships of all kinds were becoming more common, recognized, and commented upon; see Daniel Scott Smith, "The Dating of the American Sexual Revolution: Evidence and Interpretation," in Michael Gordon, ed., *The American Family in Social-Historical Perspective* (New York: St. Martin's Press, 1973), pp. 321–35; and Christina Simmons, "Companionate Marriage and the Lesbian Threat," *Frontiers*, vol. 4, no. 3 (Fall 1979), pp. 54–59.

Those I knew avoided the subject with me. And, although *The Captive* was taking the theater public by storm, no women I knew went to see it. They were afraid. Strangely, having the instinctive knowledge of the disaster this tentative, secret publicity might bring to them as a whole, they had no desire to meet the curiosity of an awakening audience alone, much less subject a woman friend to such torture. During the period when this play had its run, a bunch of violets became the symbol of an unhealthy association between women, and few women dared buy the flowers at a florist's shop.*

About this time a woman for whom I had a very deep affection called me. . . . Before her marriage she had had a devoted woman friend, who was now dead. I had always admired both women. . . .

When I met her she was distraught. After nervous preliminaries, she said in a deadly monotonous voice: "I can't stand this any longer. I have come to you because you are the only sane person that I know and because you knew Sarah while she lived. You knew what we meant to each other as friends, that Sarah was decent and that I am decent. But someone has lied to my husband—and he believes the lies. He believes that our friendship was perverted. I have children—can't you help me? Don't you understand?"

How could I help her? What defense did she have against the accusation? Her word and her dead woman friend whom she had loved dearly. I talked to her for hours and left her, I vainly hoped, with a new faith in herself. She shot herself not long afterward.

In Chicago Marion Joyce worked hard toward a "major business position," under a woman boss.

One day I inadvertently entered my superior's office while she was in conference—a conference too personal in nature to bear intrusion. Nevertheless, I was given an unexpected chance at the coveted job. I was invited to become an intimate friend of the boss.

I spent sleepless nights walking the streets of Chicago. . . . I decided always to have a stenographer with me in the office when the woman made her daily visits. For weeks the struggle was intense, and my health broke down. I should have resigned before I did but somehow I couldn't take that licking. That job was the culmination of years of hard work and I had grown tired of running away.

I went to a nerve specialist who, on discovering that my pay envelope was in danger, sent me to a clinic. The clinic was dominated by a man who experimented with the human mind. . . . I waited for hours in a crowded room beside a woman who cried constantly because she saw dancing monkeys on the walls. . . . Then I was X-rayed and had a blood test made.

*For *The Captive* see 1926, September 30. Women's fear of being seen at the play, described by Joyce, is similar to Lorena Hickock's fear of association with *The Well of Loneliness;* see 1933, March 5. "Violets" became a "symbol of an unhealthy association between women" after the unseen captivator in *The Captive* was represented as sending her victim these flowers. "Pansies" were reportedly associated with male homosexuals as early as 1903; see Charles Washburn, *Come Into My Parlor: A Biography of the Aristocratic Everleigh Sisters of Chicago* (New York: Knickerbocker, 1934), p. 127.

I was tired and growing angry when I was put in charge of a woman doctor who held a paper with a list of questions which she asked me rapidly.

Half the time I didn't know what she was asking. What did I know of my mother other than that she was always near me? Of course I loved her. How could I feel about my women friends other than that I loved them and wished them well? What did I know of the voice with which I was born?

As I grew sullen, barely answering her, she became sharper and more eager. . . . I was frightened. "Every answer I give you you are using against me for some purpose of your own," I protested.

She smiled at my anger and continued her monotonous list. . . . I stuck it out, believing that the doctor heading the clinic would understand and help me.

When the woman finished, . . . she told me this man would see me immediately. She took me to the lecture hall and seated me under an arc light. All about in the shadowy, tiered seats men sat watching me.

Then the head doctor began to talk, and I realized he was talking about me.

He said my heart was too steady, my shoulders too broad, my weight too great, and my voice too deep. My thyroid was apparently deficient, and my adrenals overactive, judging by the uncontrolled resentment I had shown under preliminary examination. . . . I was a woman, he said, who must be made over if she were to be of value. He could do this if given time— he could raise my voice, make my heart beat more rapidly, reduce my weight, and narrow my shoulders. In fact he could make me a normal woman —at some future date.

I looked at those faces hemming me in. If I spoke, my deep voice would betray me; if I let my anger flare up, it would be my adrenal glands; if I made a protest, it would be brushed aside. The man desired to make his theories real; I was to be one of his ultimate experiments. His voice grew fainter as I felt a hard, cold ugliness grow inside of me. I couldn't hear him distinctly.

Finally another man came down out of the crowd and took me away. "I am sorry," he said. "You can go now if you wish."

I know I left that clinic at noon but I remember nothing else of what I did until much later.*

I went to a doctor who had taken care of me when a child, who knew my parents and knew me better than I did myself. That night he burst into profanity that came in an uninterrupted stream of staccato explosions, until he shook me by the shoulders and laughed in my face. "So they are going to change you—to make you over, are they? Well, don't let them! Get out of the city and away from these people!"

So I ran away again, this time seeking a place where my brain could rest, where my strength was an asset in earning my living, where my voice would not destroy my efforts, and where men were not afraid to give women

*Marion Joyce's experience in the clinic amphitheater is similar to that reported by E. Kraepelin in 1905, and quoted and analyzed by Dr. R. D. Laing in *The Divided Self: An Existential Study in Sanity and Madness* (Baltimore, Md.: Penguin, 1965), pp. 29–31.

credit for what they could do. I abandoned my business career, gave up a big salary and the years of effort it cost me to gain success. I searched for the most isolated spot I could find.

I bought a farm in Canada where the snow prevented sophisticated city people from reaching me except during the three brief summer months. For ten years I lived on this farm with my cows, chickens, and dogs; my associates were overalled natives and their women, lumberjacks and farmers who seemed to find my determined fight for existence something to be admired.

Four years ago [1934] the depression took away my small margin of financial safety, and I was forced to return to the cities. I had no choice. If I were to live, I had to come back to the industrial centers where my past training could be turned into cash. I started again as I had started 30 years ago [about 1908], selling books from door to door.

. . . The March I worked the lake meadows was a very rainy March. Doors were open to me because I was tired and wet. I came into women's houses, a stranger. No one knew where I belonged or where I was going. I stayed for an hour and then disappeared. But in that hour I learned more of a woman's secrets than her husband or sweet-heart ever knew. I was told many startling things, and the word *Lesbian* was never used, although I learned much of abortions, malformed children, and the shortcomings of men.

Now again I went from door to door, peddling an educational service. I was routed through suburban towns and discovered that the women had grown wise in a queer, abnormal way. In the 30 years that had elapsed, their attitude had become expectant, and their eyes held often a glistening look that I feared.

"Are you a man or woman?" one asked frankly. "I am very lonely here."

Did I run away? Not this time. I laughed and sold her my books, knowing she would never open them, then walked down her steps with a check and a date I never kept.

I find that I can sell anything—but not on the merits of the goods I handle. According to the sales manager, I must use "personality plus." That means, to a woman dealing with women, only one thing today. I find a majority of women eager for a dangerous experience never quite realized, which they may use to give a sharper edge to their poor lives.*

The last four years have been the hardest I have lived, because I am vividly conscious of the vicious distortion in the minds surrounding me. I am tired with an inertia of which you can have little conception. I must constantly fight against an overwhelming disgust with humanity.

I have sold books as a canvasser, diamond rings on the installment plan to laborers. I have been an art student and an illustrator. I have lived

*In her autobiographical account, "Mary Casal" describes selling house-to-house to rural women (1895–1900?). She remarks upon these women's "disapproval" of her "tailor-made suit," "man's shirt and tie," and Fedora—and the "thrill" she caused in "their restricted lives"; see Casal's *The Stone Wall* (Chicago: Eynecourt Press, 1930; reprinted N. Y.: Arno Press, 1975), pp. 139–41.

in Bohemian centers and in summer art colonies. I have worked on the desks of trade magazines and once became involved in a women's political organization. I have driven an automobile over lonely roads, stopping at tourist camps and lunchrooms. I have worked in restaurants, lived in city hotels, and run a farm. I learned how to swing an ax, to hoe, to keep books, to understand banking and the peculiarities of farm machinery and automobiles. I also know perfumes, the best silk stockings, the advantages of short-vamp shoes, and the price of a permanent wave. Somewhere I acquired knowledge of the proper feeding of children and their necessary education, learned how to identify measles, to boil cabbage, and to alter a coat. I never learned to spell.

Does this make me a Lesbian?

Must I strip my body to prove I am a normal woman? What more can I do than strip my soul naked in an attempt to protect other innocent individuals who, like myself, refuse much that would be of service to humanity because that same humanity will not let them be normal?


PLAY REVIEW

## 1938, October 6
### N. Y. Times:
### Chester Erskin's The Good

A play attacking the evil effects of small-town puritanism presented homosexuality as one of the evils such puritanism provoked.[69] In the 1980s the play's irony resides in its author's own puritanical equation of evil and homosexuality. Anti-puritans of the 1930s often argued for greater heterosexual freedom on the grounds that repression led to homosexuality and other "abnormalities."*

"Stripping the mask off an upstate town," playwright Erskin "has found a number of ugly things crouching in the darkness," began Brooks Atkinson's review of the Broadway production, The Good.

It "is Mr. Erskin's contention"

that all the misery in his play comes logically from the pitiless rectitude of Mrs. Harriet Eldred and her pious though, happily, deceased father. His implacable virtue was responsible for a few moral horrors that occurred some years before the curtain went up. Carrying on the venomous tradition, she is responsible for her husband's derelictions with a jaunty housemaid, the suicide of an unhappy high school student and the homosexual practices of her son. Possibly this review has inadvertently overlooked some of the small-town festers Mr. Erskin has located in Maytime along the Hudson

*For example, see The New York Times review of Floyd Dell's Love in the Machine Age, 1930, September 28, and Dr. Harry Benjamin's " 'For the Sake of Morality,' " 1931, April 15.

River. But the effect of his play is to make theatregoers content with the wholesomeness and nobility of New York City, the spotless island town downstream.

Erskin had "written his play with the weariness of a man shocked by human depravity," and had "accented the sorrowful" in his direction of the piece. Actor Jarvis Rice made "something palatable out of the unsavory character of the abnormal son." (The alimentary metaphor suggests the reviewer's own association to the "abnormal."*) Atkinson ended: playwright Erskin, "an old Hudson (N. Y.) boy," should "hesitate about visiting back home."

PLAY REVIEW

# 1938, October 11
## *N. Y. Times:*
## Leslie and Sewall Stokes's *Oscar Wilde*

Critic Brooks Atkinson ostensibly objected to the exploitation of an "unsavory" subject, Oscar Wilde's homosexuality. But Atkinson's objection now seems to reflect his own intense discomfort with a relatively sympathetic treatment of the theme.[70] His objection to the "persecution" of Wilde's spirit seems to mask his own opposition to the presentation of homosexuality as tragic and thus sympathy-deserving—a current liberal line stressing pity for piteous inverts. A scene between Wilde and a "handsome boy" also seems to have especially disturbed Atkinson; he mentioned it in two reviews.

"If the harrowing story of Oscar Wilde must be repeated more than forty years after it burst on the world," wrote Atkinson, "it is fortunate that an actor of Robert Morley's quality is chosen to play the part." Although the play "childishly enjoys the fetid odor of one of the world's most pitiable scandals," Morley "plays his part like an artist." Whatever Wilde's "pathological infirmities," Morley "does not forget that first of all he was a master of the writing profession."

"The prosecution and imprisonment of Wilde is still a matter of controversy," the story of Wilde's

undoing will not die. It is as though the world were still persecuting his spirit and preserving his ordeal.

The play did not make Atkinson "alter a wish" that Wilde "be permitted to rest in peace."

In one scene the playwrights showed Wilde dining "with a handsome boy of mean breeding"; the Stokeses had "not mercifully averted their eyes from the

*For Atkinson's association of food, eating, and sexual "abnormality" also see 1938, October 11.

squalid details of Wilde's sexual abnormalities." The revelations at Wilde's trial were still "unsavory," said Atkinson (employing his customary alimentary metaphor for "sexual abnormalities"; see 1938, October 6). Actor John Carol was said to play "as inoffensively as possible the part of one of Wilde's bizarre youths."

Atkinson concluded: In view of Wilde's "brilliant" writings, "perhaps the world can afford to be charitable now and let his tired bones lie quietly."[20:2]

Refusing to let tired bones lie, Atkinson devoted another long essay to the play in *The Times* of October 16. Wilde's was "a trial from which no one emerged with honor":

> The atmosphere in which he was prosecuted was as abnormal as he was; it was furious with rancor and rapacity, for the custodians of morality grow sadistic when the pack is aroused. Although rancor ultimately cools, the wonder over a malodorous scandal endures at least unto the second generation. . . . For the price of a theatre ticket you can see [Wilde] keeping a rendezvous with a handsome young groom; you can see him hounded in the Old Bailey, . . . and you can see him gibbering over his absinthe in a Paris cafe at the end.

Wilde's "private life," presented in the play, "was horribly degrading and on a tragically lower plane than his best work." In life Wilde was "a voluptuary in his tastes, a poseur and over-fastidious aesthete." But in Wilde's writings there was artistic genius, and there were "many years" of Wilde the writer "before disease began to eat away his character." (The "disease" of sexual "abnormality" again suggested an alimentary metaphor; "abnormality" and "eating" seem to have obsessed Atkinson.)

It was only two months after Wilde's celebration for *The Importance of Being Earnest* that his prosecution made him "a moral leper, hated for the rest of his disease-ridden life." It was ironic that Wilde "should be remembered principally for the malady that took possession of him"; that Wilde should be so portrayed was also in "bad taste." But that opinion the reviewer said was "not widely shared this week."

♀  BOOK REVIEW

# 1939, March 12
## *N. Y. Times Book Review:*
## Mary Renault's *Promise of Love*

Reviewer Edith H. Walton praised Renault's first novel as "a story of high-keyed passion" which did not lose touch with the world of work.[71] Renault's two lovers, a female nurse and a male medical researcher, were governed, "as most of us are, by financial stress and the kind of job they hold."

The nurse, Vivian Lingard, at twenty-six years old, had always

been somewhat overshadowed by her elder brother, Jan, who has the golden kind of charm which approaches the proportions of a legend. It is through Jan that she meets Mic Freeborn, a difficult, twisted, introspective young man who has just been appointed a pathologist at the hospital. As their friendship develops, Vivian discovers how greatly Mic is bound by his child-hood, which was scarred by poverty, loneliness and illegitimacy. Hence come his self-distrust and supersensitiveness. Hence, also, his homosexual tendencies. When Vivian realizes, in a moment of sudden, pained shock, that Mic was originally attracted to her because of her resemblance to Jan, their dawning romance very nearly founders.

Since she cares enough, Vivian surmounts this hurdle, knowing that she has it in her to heal Mic's wounds. The two become lovers and find themselves as perfectly matched physically as they are in intellect and heart. From the beginning, however, their love affair is cruelly hampered by the demands of their work and by hospital routine.

"Unable to marry for economic reasons," and "harried subtly by the ghosts of Mic's past," the two lovers "make a brave attempt to keep their love intact in the face of utter physical exhaustion."

OBITUARY/EDITORIAL

# 1939, July 11
## N. Y. Times: The death of Dr. Havelock Ellis

Responses in *The Times* to the death of Dr. Havelock Ellis express a smug self-congratulation concerning "present sane" attitudes toward sex.[72] (Belying this modernism are such anxious outbursts as those of the *Times*'s Brooks Atkinson; see 1938, October 11.)

A *Times* obituary recalled that Ellis had begun his "monumental" *Studies in the Psychology of Sex* with the volume on *Sexual Inversion*. That book's obscenity prosecution had associated him, "even in the minds of Victorian liberals, with an obnoxious and dangerous subject."

The current "popularity" of Ellis's "magnum opus" had become apparent shortly after Random House republished his *Studies* in 1936. "The first printing of 4,000 sets at $15 sold out within two weeks."

The same day a *Times* editorial declared that Ellis had "rationalized the subject" of sex, recovering for "the common intelligence a great obscure territory that had been shut off from it by senseless taboos." Ellis's sex *Studies* were "largely" responsible for "the present sane, reasonable and informed opinion, contrasting violently with that of forty years ago [1899]."

# 1939
## Diana Frederics:
### *Diana, A Strange Autobiography*

Though one may legitimately question the authenticity of this "autobiography" by the pseudonymous Diana Frederics, the book does seem to be an honest account of one lesbian's life, despite occasional melodramatic, larger-than-life episodes.[73] But if future research should prove *Diana* to be more fiction than fact, the book would still stand as an almost unique example of a relatively "advanced" lesbian defense. Though lesbianism is referred to throughout as a misfortune, due to a young girl's "improper" early "masculine" identification, the title character's main concern is to find a way to satisfy her erotic and affectional needs as an active lesbian, while living in a hostile society. The volume ends, as few other early homosexual stories did, on a note of "fulfillment." That may explain why it was not reviewed in *The New York Times*.

An "Author's Foreword" maintained that "The characters and events in this

Title page of *Diana* (1939).

book are real," although the writer had "made whatever changes were necessary to protect her characters' identities."[xi]

Frederics indicated that she was in her early twenties in the "first years of the Depression," suggesting that she was born around 1910. At age sixteen, after falling in love with a female classmate, Ruth, and experiencing a longing to caress her, Frederics discovered a book "explaining" such emotions. The setting was her family home in northern Kentucky. Her self-identification through a book suggests the emotional impact such a volume might have on a young lesbian; similar scenes have been reported by others.

> Browsing in my father's library one night, I came upon a book on sex. I had seen it many times, I had read parts of it, but now I saw a section I had never noticed before. One detailed chapter was on homosexuality. I read and reread, eager, fearful, and finally sick in the pit of my stomach.
>
> Such new phrases as "pervert," "nature will have her little joke," "queer mental twists," "Case A," "uranians," "crime against nature," jumbled on top of each other in my mind. I looked long minutes at a gruesome picture captioned "Homosexuals burned at the stake in Germany, 1494." It seemed to me that I could almost smell the burning flesh. I could reproduce that picture now from memory. There were two pairs of them: two women together, sitting, their backs against a log, faggots in their laps; and two men, standing together, faggots at their feet, their hands clasped. The executioners were jeering as flames licked at the victims.
>
> I took the book and went upstairs to my room; it seemed miles away. I believe that nothing could ever happen to me again which would match the despair of that hour. It stands etched in my memory as a nightmare of unspeakable terror.
>
> I felt like another "case" on file in a psychological laboratory. I was, then, a "pervert," "uranian," "homosexual"—no matter, all added up to the same thing. *I* was subject to arrest! *I* was grotesque, alienated, unclean!
>
> Suddenly I even doubted if my body were normal. With a nausea of apprehension I examined my body carefully for any indication of abnormality. There was none that I knew of, but perhaps I couldn't tell. My mind was white with fear. I could scarcely wait for morning to come and with it the opportunity to go down to a doctor's office for a complete physical examination. I would go to a doctor who didn't know me, and give a fictitious name. I would pay him out of my allowance.
>
> I couldn't sleep when I went to bed. The night seemed never-ending. I got up and turned on my night-lamp and read again until Mother saw my light and came to see if I were ill.
>
> The next morning I hurried downtown to a reputable physician who, I was sure, did not know me. It was too early for his office to be open; I had to wait an hour. Finally he came, a small grey man with a wrinkled face and a large nose. I have wondered many times since what he must have thought of the child who tried to hide her trembling as she asked for "a thorough examination for any possible abnormalities." My memories of his kind smile

are still vivid. His calm quieted my terror, and when I told him I was in a dreadful hurry he seemed to understand.

I was embarrassed when the nurse took me into a big room and told me to lie down with only a sheet to cover me. My mind had been too full of dread possibilities to wonder how I would be examined. Grimly I undressed and lay down, and the doctor came in. I shut my eyes against my mounting panic, telling myself that only his verdict was important.

After a stretch of time the doctor looked at me. He smiled and told me I was "perfectly normal and healthy." This knowledge, not doubted twenty-four hours before, was such a relief I was actually happy for a little while. Horrified at the thought of all kinds of impressions the book had given me, at least I now knew that my body was normal.

If only my mental turmoil could have been as easily calmed![20–22]

Frederics began "to hide," avoiding friends (especially Ruth), resigning the presidency of the senior class, refusing a music award because she would have had to acknowledge it publicly with a speech and a piano solo, and breaking a finger so as not to have to play in a planned recital. When an older brother, Gerald, asked what was wrong, Frederics finally had to tell him what she had discovered about her nature:

Very suddenly came the thought that he would be embarrassed by what I was going to say. But I had cut myself off from any retreat. I have no idea now how I did begin. Bit by bit, without being prepared or having the truth softened, Gerald heard the miserable acknowledgment of my homosexuality. I did not tell him of my physical examination, but I omitted nothing else. I made him understand, without daring to use the word "love," that I loved Ruth. I even told him why I had wanted to hurt my hand, that I couldn't stand making a show of myself before people who would scorn me if they knew. I wanted to be out of sight and mind. I hadn't worked out what I would do with my life, but I could get adjusted somehow if only I were let alone.

Then it was over, much sooner than I had thought it would be. I could not look at Gerald but I felt him staring at the wall above my desk.

When he spoke his voice was so low I had difficulty hearing him. I recall his words as if I had made a conscious effort to memorize them. He spoke carefully but very firmly. He denied outright that I was a homosexual. He explained that I was the victim of a school-girl crush, that crushes were common at my age, that I was hypersensitive, that the accidental discovery of homosexuality had made me accept a quick conclusion. He told me of other crushes he had heard of, and he admitted that he could understand my feeling: Ruth was very attractive. But there was nothing abnormal about it. I would outgrow it. Gerald sounded reasonable. Furthermore, he was studying to be a doctor, and to my mind doctors somehow knew the innermost secrets of all human behavior.

He was naturally upset that the book in question had treated homosexuality as a vicious social disease and criminal offense. I remember how he suddenly jumped up and, calling to [a brother] John, asked him to go to the library, six blocks away. I wondered why. Half an hour later John handed Gerald a volume of Havelock Ellis and a volume of Freud, the first I had ever seen. Gerald read to me a long time, first from one book then from the other, stopping here and there to explain. I was astounded. I hadn't known that homosexuals had ever been treated with reverence; I only knew that they had been burned at the stake. I hadn't known they might find a worthwhile place in society; I thought they were ostracized when they were discovered. I listened intently to every syllable Gerald read. And I hadn't known that the large majority of homosexuals are intellectually sound; I had thought they frequently had disordered minds, sometimes inclined to sexual insanity.

Before Gerald left me that night he looked at me and smiled. . . . He added . . . , "And even if you were what you thought you were, I think your dad would understand all right."

The revelation had been a godsend. I was not entirely convinced that I was not a homosexual; the core of my existence had been too abruptly displaced and the memory of Ruth had burned too deeply. But I was overjoyed to learn that even if I were, my nature would not doom me to the fate of witches nor to the insane asylum. It was wonderful to know that homosexuals were not a monstrous jest on nature's part, but a fairly common group of men and women for whom the normal was, incongruously, abnormal to so-called "normal" people. Intelligent people who understood were neither horrified nor shocked by them.

My saving grace was a feeling of rebellion.[26–28]

♀ BOOK REVIEW/RESISTANCE/INTIMACY

# 1940, January 14
## *N. Y. Times Book Review:*
## Vera Brittain's *Testament of Friendship*

Vera Brittain's biography of her friend, the English novelist and journalist Winifred Holtby, may now be seen as an attempt to reclaim that woman-to-woman intimacy which since the late 1800s doctors had called "abnormal."[1]

"Although this is the story of a novelist's very active life," said *Times* critic Katherine Woods,

it is well named a "Testament of Friendship." Miss Brittain points out with some indignation that, while strong friendship between men has been intelligently celebrated in history and legend, equally strong friendship between women has been scarcely even believed in. It has been regarded as something shallow and jealousy-ridden (not to say feline), or else unhealthily emotional (not to say abnormal); whereas, as most sensible people know, life abounds in women's sane, firm comradeships. Such a friendship was that between Winifred Holtby and Vera Brittain, whose children called Miss

Holtby "Auntie," and whose home she shared. But friendship was plainly one of Winifred Holtby's talents.

Holtby's close associations with numerous other women were cited, as was Holtby's "curious, intermittent, unfulfilled love affair" with a "charming, sensitive, unstable" male. The reviewer quoted Brittain's comment that Holtby's " 'tragedy lay in the responsiveness of her generous temperament, her disastrous willingness to put aside her permanent interests for the temporary convenience of others.' "

Holtby's enthusiasm for life and her work were stressed. "She was always writing" and "she was always busy over causes," an artist and a social reformer.

Reviewer M. L. Becker commented in *Books,* on January 14, that Brittain's biography of Holtby was valuable to students because it shows

> the trends of thought and action among women directly after the great war. . . . But most of all, the book is valuable for . . . proof out of life that friendship did not die with the generation of Emerson.

RESISTANCE

## 1940, January 27
## Henry Gerber to Manuel Boyfrank:
### *"Our proposed movement is of great social value"*

As the founder of the Society for Human Rights, Chicago, in 1924, Henry Gerber is one of the pioneers of the homosexual emancipation movement in the United States.[2]* In the following, previously unpublished letters, Gerber recalls that early organizing attempt, reveals something of the "philosophy" behind his resistance efforts, and conveys a few of the conflicts, contradictions, and crotchets of a man about whom little information has been available. Gerber's original cranky letters occasionally display an unpleasant self-righteousness and elitism and express a blanket condemnation of homosexuals and touches of misogyny. This forefather of gay liberation was an imperfect man of his time; his negative qualities do not need to be denied in order to recognize his contribution.

References scattered throughout Gerber's letters to Manuel Boyfrank, 1940–57, and in a few other sources, allow us to know something of his life. Gerber's letters reveal that he was born late in June 1892, in Bavaria, Germany. Despite youthful erotic episodes with both boys and girls, Gerber did not identify as homosexual when he left Bavaria in 1913, at the age of twenty-one. Gerber arrived in the United States in 1914 and the following year joined the U. S. Army

---

*For Gerber's and others' chartering of the Society for Human Rights, Chicago, see 1925, June.

Henry Gerber (from the National Gay Archives, Los
Angeles; courtesy of James Kepner).

under a provision admitting aliens. During World War I Gerber was "offered
internment" as an alien, and received, he said, three free meals a day. From 1920
to 1923, he served with the U. S. Army of Occupation in Europe, and in 1921
visited his home town. In Germany Gerber discovered the homosexual emancipation organizations then in existence.

On December 10, 1924, the State of Illinois chartered the Society for
Human Rights, founded by Gerber and six other men—the earliest documented
homosexual rights organization in the United States. Both the Society and *Friendship and Freedom,* the periodical its members twice published, were named after
German homosexual emancipation prototypes. The founding of the Society led
to the arrest of Gerber and several associates, and Gerber lost his job and savings.
Though he and the others were finally set free this failed organizing attempt was
recalled by Gerber in his letters with a mixture of bitterness and pride.

Between 1928 and 1930 (while Gerber lived in New York City), three contributions to homosexual emancipation periodicals in Germany were published
under his by-line. In one Gerber condemned the "hypocrisy" of those English
Christians responsible for suppressing Radclyffe Hall's *The Well of Loneliness.* He
said the lesbian drama, *The Captive* (see 1926, September 30), was also forbidden
in "many" U. S. cities. "But the better newspapers were generally not hostile to
the topic." And "In America, where the Christian religion is losing ground, the
horizon is growing brighter for homosexuals." Gerber's second report surveyed
the legal penalties in the forty-eight states for "sodomy" and the "crime against
nature." His third report told of a recent case in which an artilleryman had
received ten years for homosexual acts with another artilleryman.[3]

From 1930 through 1939, while still in the United States Army, working as
a proofreader, Gerber used military supplies and equipment to publish *Contacts,*
a mimeographed newsletter for pen-pals which also served, discreetly, to facilitate
introductions between male homosexuals.

In June 1932, Gerber, under a pseudonym, published an essay "In Defense of Homosexuality" in *The Modern Thinker.* In 1934, Gerber was circulation manager of a mimeographed monthly, *Chanticleer,* in which he published several essays on homosexuality under his own name.[4]

In 1936 and later, Gerber's own ad for pen-pals appeared in *Contacts.* Having been brought up a Catholic, he was "now an avowed atheist." Though believing in the "brotherhood of man," he thought "there is no hope for mankind to free itself from exploitation of the entrencht money changers." It was "not the business of Government to interfere in the sexual enjoyment of adults as long as the rights of others are not violated." He was "Immune to the alleged charms of the female sex, but do not 'hate' women; consider them necessary in the scheme of things." "Nature will always be in favor of procreation and is distinctly on the side of women in trapping man" into performing "his natural duties." A "genuine introvert," he considered "solitude" a blessing, and himself "truly civilized and self-sufficient, but always welcome people of like mind, . . . who can share the simple pleasures of discussion, music and travel."

Gerber's ad was answered by Manuel Boyfrank, of California, who in 1940 described himself as thirty-nine years old, a sailor and office worker. Picking up on Gerber's not-so-subtle hints, Boyfrank announced his own homosexuality, and proposed a scheme for a homosexual emancipation organization. Boyfrank had independently realized the need for some organization to counter the persecution of homosexuals. He apparently envisioned a commercially organized, all-male correspondence club (and, possibly, an erotic photo supply service) which would function simultaneously to locate homosexual males, facilitate sexual contacts, and organize members against their oppression. (Though these combined functions are those of the present gay newspaper, *The Advocate,* in the legal context of the 1940s the combination of erotic and political functions verged on the crackpot.) In the enthusiasm at first aroused by Boyfrank's proposal, Gerber did not immediately realize the basic difference between their visions.

On January 27, 1940, Gerber answered Boyfrank:

> I was surprised to find you a homosexual, too, but let me tell you from experience it does not pay to do anything for them. I once lost a good job in trying to bring them together. Most men of that type are too scared to give their names or to join any association trying to help them; the other half are only interested in physical contacts and have not the slightest interest to help their cause. I found that out to my own sorrow.[1]

Gerber was sorry Boyfrank was "not 20 years younger," so he would appeal to Gerber's erotic interest. But "it helps to have one homosexual to discuss live subjects." There were about twelve homosexuals in the *Contacts* correspondence club. Gerber gave Boyfrank their identification numbers so (through Gerber) Boyfrank could send them his proposal for an organization. Boyfrank should call on him again when I can help you. I would like to see such a service going, but you are more independent than I am, and [I] will not risk my job again. Once is enough.[1]

In his response Boyfrank asserted: "There is a need for an organization to conduct propaganda for our cause." He included ten letters for Gerber to mail to the homosexual *Contacts* members.

On February 19, 1940, Gerber wrote that he found Boyfrank's letter "very interesting"; he himself had long been "studying the problem" of organizing homosexuals. But, he warned, society "suppresses everything that does not lead to monogamy and procreation"—that should make them hesitate. "We can undermine the wall by little individual blasts and it will topple by and by." "Much has already been done" in that direction. The "origin" of society's "enmity" to homosexuals was "religious," thus "every knock at religion will help to free us." All "this morality business" was

a desperate effort of Society (business interests) to mate every sap so he will have a home and family and can easier be exploited.

As long as Gerber was still in the Army it was "too risky" for him to be associated with an all-male correspondence club of the sort Boyfrank proposed. But Gerber then advised:

Some organization to defend our cause would necessarily have to have much money, some medical authorities of note and lawyers to defend us. I tried it once in Chicago. . . . I lost my post office job and swore never to do another thing openly for the cause. You are safe in your job and could do that. That is have some sort of clipping bureau and prepare literature to send to newspaper editors. I would be glad to help you in this, but it would have to be entirely anonymously to be on the safe side.

Gerber stated his "philosophy": "Instead of trying to help others who do not appreciate it and only get you in trouble, use all your energy to get what *you* want." But he ended his letter:

If I can help you on any project you may decide to give birth to, let me know and [I] will be glad to assist you if I can.

Nothing further came of this discussion. The next letter to Boyfrank in which Gerber discussed the organizing of homosexuals was four years later, on March 12, 1944. Gerber suggested that Boyfrank start up the now defunct *Contacts* correspondence club. This club, had been "the Society for Human Rights over again but . . . with the sex element disguised."[2] (*Contacts* involved both women and men.)

Gerber agreed with Boyfrank:

homosexuality is nature's own birth control and therefore less of a perversion than artificial birth control. But try to tell that to the hypocrites who use artificial birth control to the extent of 100% and then turn around and

abuse homosexuals as perverts and [for] committing a crime against nature!
. . . now with the rubber shortage it is even patriotic to be a homosexual.

Homosexuality was a check to "overpopulation." But "Even homosexuals would
be glad to reproduce themselves if it was a patriotic duty for every man to have
a certain number of children." Two men "could have their particular sexual
enjoyment," then give their semen "to the laboratory where it would be injected
into a female willing to bear children for the state at the prevailing union wages
for procreation in a professional way."[4]

Later in this letter Gerber commented: "Yes, the word homosexual, which
was unknown about 50 years ago [1894], is now creeping even into 'decent'
literature, i.e. sex-repressed stuff." He had "even" seen homosexuality mentioned as a problem in a book on "the Family."[6–7]

Gerber claimed that, having arrived at the age of fifty-two,

I no longer believe in martyrdom for the sake of others; I even come to
believe that the individual or even a group cannot change the severely slow
progress of evolution, especially when religion and politics pull in the opposite direction.

But . . . every individual can at least do as he pleases and encourage
indirectly others to do as they please and to nullify all oppressive laws. The
homosexuals already have the most successful underground movement in
force by which all such silly laws as against sodomy are practically annulled.

A week later, on March 19, 1944, Gerber wrote to Boyfrank that he had
heard from an old friend, F. M., in New York, who ran a club for those "interested
in rockets" (Gerber called it "a camouflaged society for homosexuals.")* Gerber
then proposed to Boyfrank a new organization to combat anti-homosexuality (his
excitement is discernible behind his words):

What do you think of the inclosed? I am in dead earnest about it. This of
course is only a faint outline, the name, aims, system, membership method,
cost of printing, finding a reliable printer, etc. would have to be worked out
in detail. But I think [F.M.] would be interested, and it would be just the
thing for you and me to work on. All three of us of course are willing to do
all we can, and I am sure that millions the world over would be glad to give
their moral support, and perhaps we might find a rich bitch [male homosex-
ual] . . . who would give us the pennies to print a few pamphlets. . . .

Of course, one man can handle this alone, too. But let me know your
ideas. Somehow I feel you are enthusiastic about it. It requires no martyrdoms but a bit of courage.

Gerber enclosed a proposal for the "Society Scouting Sex Superstition, An
International Underground Movement Fighting Fascism in Sex." A note explained: "The word homosexual would nowhere appear, we fight any kind of sex
superstition."

*For an earlier reference to clubs serving as disguised homosexual contact services see c. 1908,
Stevenson.

The main idea of course would be to protect homosexuals against persecution. This could be done in two ways:
1. fighting persecution in law, in the press, personally.
2. keep homosexuals in touch with each other and thus protect them from outsiders.
   The three enemies of homosexuals are recognized as:
1. religious fanatics who spread the dogma that sexual intercourse is sinful.
2. imperialist and fascist politicians who want a big population for cannon fodder.
3. extortionists who take advantage of laws against homosexual acts.

The group would collaborate "with organizations who fight fascism in other fields," such as the atheist periodical, *The Truth Seeker.* The "Philosophy" of the new organization would be:

That it is nobody's business what two adults (at the age of 16) decide to do to enjoy themselves sexually, as long as they act in mutual agreement, without violating the rights of others. That every person has a right to decide whether he wants to marry or not, whether he wants to have children or not, and how to practice birth control, either artificially, by the use of instruments or devices, or naturally, by masturbation or other manual or onanistic (non-procreative) means.

This society would be a secret underground but perfectly legal as it would use only weapons of propaganda and education. There would be a nucleus of about 3–7 directors, men who could absolutely rely upon each other who would conduct the society without being known to the members at large. They would devise the literature to be sent to those who oppose liberty and democracy and try to force people to obey certain religious dogmas in matters of sex, i.e. fascist suppression of sex freedom. Pamphlets, such as "What is homosexuality," "who are the perverts?" etc. pointing out the facts about sex, would be printed by the society and sent directly to offenders, judges, legislators and authors writing against homosexuals, and would be distributed among the members to distribute discreetly where it is most needed. Membership would be strictly selective.

There would be three types of members:
1. the founders.
2. contributing members who want to contribute to the society for the expense of printing, etc.
3. active members who would serve as scouts detecting persecution of homosexuals and reporting these cases to the founders who would then act.

There would be no meetings and no dues to pay, no membership cards or anything identifying the members with the society.

It would be interesting to see some hypocrite who himself practices birth control get a letter from England or Canada, or California or Washington, pointing out to him that he is as much of a pervert as those whom he attacks and that he ought to be ashamed of his hypocrisy and mend his way or else—since it is no longer possible to attack a minority as the witches of old, since they now are organized and know how to defend themselves against fascists. . . .*

A note at the top of the proposal read: "Confidentially destroy after reading or making notes."

On March 28, 1944, Gerber wrote that he was glad Boyfrank had found his proposal "important,"

> and that you assure me of your keen interest in the scheme and your intention of doing all you can to further it. That is the main thing to know that I can count on your full support, morally and "spiritually."

Gerber thanked Boyfrank for praising his

> endeavors to do all that can be done for the defense of "our kind." The debt the human race owes us, as you put it, may never be paid adequately, but at least I feel that I am fully repaid by the thanks of a few whom I have directly or indirectly helped. After all, I have no reason to pat my own back for my unselfish altruism, for the work benefits me directly and is not altogether unselfish. . . .
>
> Yes, I believe that our proposed movement is of great social value. It stands on the same level as the efforts of other great liberators who in times past have worked against slavery and the abolition of punishment of "witches." I find this latter analogy of homosexuals to be very appropriate for all that keeps people persecut[ing] homosexuals is the superstitious belief that homosexuals are in some way "devils or witches" who defy "natural" laws. The fact is, however, that homosexuals simply practice the *natural* form of birth control.

The right to "enjoy sex regardless of procreation" was the crux of the matter. A man should have "the right to make up his own mind how he wants to waste his semen."

> I am, of course, also willing to invest money in the movement. I just collected $200 mustering-out-pay and that would be a nice contribution of Uncle Sam to our cause! Only after we have something to show will others put in their pennies.

Gerber said he had had "trouble getting a printer" years before in Chicago, when "I put out the homosexual magazine." He now envisioned a "nifty letterhead" to use when they started writing to editors or authors. He thought they should include in their organization "any type of person who values his sex liberty." To "work together with the 'birth controllers' would be natural," but most of them were not ready to support homosexuality as a non-procreative form

---

*For other early uses of this "minority" concept applied to homosexuals see 1922, Ives (quoted in 1934, May); 1925, Robinson; scattered references in Lisa Ben's *Vice Versa* (see entry of 1947, June); and 1949, June 19, a reference from the *N. Y. Times Book Review*. For others' use of the homosexual-witch analogy see witch in the index.

of sex. The character and name of the organization could always be changed later to make it more specifically homosexual—"in fact that is the approved underground tactic to change names and localities often."

> We might even use my old name I had once in Chicago—when we got raided and I lost my post office job—Society for Human Rights.

Gerber rejected Boyfrank's suggestions for the organization's name: "Band of brothers" ("band of sisters would be better"—or "band of queens"). "Children of light sounds silly." Greek-related names "would create a false impression" since Greeks "nowadays" have the "unsavory reputation" of being "boys-fuckers-in-the-assers" and "that would not do."[3]

"Whom else to include in our 'committee of correspondence'?" (Boyfrank had suggested that committee and Gerber adopted it "gladly.") A number of possible men were "in the army and may be overseas sooner or later." Others were "not interested in the cultural value of the movement but only in getting something that costs nothing" (sex).

> The homosexuals in the U. S. and elsewhere are in most respects too cowed to dare fight for their rights—incongruously as it may sound, considering that they go 6,000 miles to give the New Guinea cannibals the four freedoms while here at home they have none at all but go to jail!

There was "No martyrblood, I am afraid."

> Very few, I am afraid, would contribute anything financially, but the movement could be spread at little cost and accomplish many things without money. Any two people can start a "society" or movement. . . . There is that much liberty at least. Of course, our movement unlike the labor movements would absolutely not become a racket. . . . neither you or I or others in the committee would want a salary!
>
> So I guess that for the time being it is up to you and me to get started with preparatory plans and we can go ahead.

They could start with "bulletins" giving "information on what is going on in the world, . . . with a homosexual angle."

A week later, on April 5, Gerber wrote an anonymous letter to *Time* magazine, to correct "several grave misstatements" in an article on the recent case in which Wayne Lonergan had murdered his wife.*

Gerber argued that Lonergan was "*not a homosexual,* but a *bisexual.*" Besides,

---

*On April 3, 1944, a *Time* report on "The Lonergan Case," on a page headed "Medicine," called his trial "a clinical study of unusual interest to doctors and psychiatrists." For it was "obvious" that Lonergan's lawyer "would make some plea of insanity involving homosexuality." Newspaper headlines had already "billed Lonergan as a homosexual who seemed utterly unmoved by his wife's murder," and "There was already testimony about his perversion." Lonergan had allegedly confessed "to homosexual relations, both before and after his marriage. One of the men involved is said to have been . . . Lonergan's wife's father." *Time* said: "All this fits the classic definition of a homosexual." However, "To most people Lonergan does not look like a homosexual." Homosexuals were "not necessarily physically abnormal." "As a rule, homosexuals are made not born," said *Time,* citing two psychiatrists.[68–69]5 heterosexuals, bisexuals, and homosexuals sometimes committed crimes and should be treated equally, irrespective of sexual differences.

Gerber suggested that *Time* put his letter into their files:

> In a hundred years when this country, too, will become somewhat civilized, it may, perhaps, be printed. But till then I must remain just a prophet of things to come—if a bit optimistic.

Gerber also attacked the psychiatrists involved in the Lonergan case:

> The subsidized psychiatrist—yes-man—always wears a policeman's badge under his white frock. Psychiatry is a political device to drag those to the concentration camp—euphemistically camouflaged under the term "state hospital"—who have not committed a crime but who are guilty of the heinous offence of refusing to be suckers and to be exploited. Those who refuse to believe the political, religious and moral fairytales current in our conventions, are styled psychopaths, degenerates, perverts, radicals, infidels, etc.

"In all countries where fascism rules and people are oppressed by unjust laws," these people "form active underground movements opposing regimentation." And "Persecution of homosexuals is fascism of the worst kind." The "millions of homosexuals in this country are well-organized and resent being persecuted by hypocritical 'normal' people. . . ." Among the "enemies" of homosexuals were "religious fanatics,"

> imperialistic politicians who want a big turnover in population for the war mongering; extortionists and blackmailers who take advantage of futile sex laws; psychiatrists who wish to earn easy money "curing" them.[4]

Gerber ended: "Homosexuals, too, have rights, you know!"[5]

Boyfrank did not immediately reply to Gerber's proposal. When Boyfrank did reply Gerber began to see they had conflicting views. Boyfrank wanted to organize groups of homosexuals themselves, using a correspondence club as the means. Gerber wanted homosexuals to support a re-education program run by a few.

On April 12, 1944, Gerber wrote Boyfrank: "You misunderstood [my] proposition entirely." Using Greek terminology as a code, Gerber said:

> I have absolutely no confidence in dorian crowd [homosexuals], mostly a bunch of selfish, uncultured, ignorant egotists, who have nothing for the ideal side of life.
>
> What I was driving at was some sort of education committee, organized on a loose, wide basis, not necessarily exclusively doric architecture [composed of homosexuals], on the lookout for irresponsible remarks of uncultured propagandists for nondoric art [heterosexuality].

Boyfrank's plans for a large "doric society" were "splendid but impracticable." Gerber thought "a few trusted dorics must get together and work on it."

A few days later, in a letter of April 14, 1944, Gerber said he did agree on one point with Boyfrank:

Formal agitation is not effectual. I have never entertained the idea that one
could stand on Union Square and shout the gospel. That would be freedom
of speech and there ain't no such animal in these benighted states. . . . The
very impossibility of enforcing unrighteous laws is our best bet. . . .[2]

There was even a trend toward greater public discussion of homosexuality.

There is more and more reference to Doric love in books and magazines
now, which only 20 years ago [1924] was camouflaged as "unmentionable
love". . . . It only makes people more curious and they want to know why
it cannot be mentioned. . . . the reasons why it actually is suppressed don't
sound so good to reasonable ears.

Boyfrank's ideas "about reestablishing [the] Society for Human Rights, Inc.
and Contacts," were "interesting though very vague."[5] Gerber recalled again
the "debacle" of the Society for Human Rights, when other homosexuals had
"skipped out."[8] He thought "formal associations or clubs impracticable."[12]

On April 20, 1944, Gerber wrote to Boyfrank, arguing more emphatically
against the latter's organizing ideas. They "should stick to one wider object, all
inclusive." Their "aim would be to demand equal rights with heteros in everything." That goal "would be large enough."[1] "During the war with [the] fast
changing population, we can do almost nothing but lay the foundations for a
future society to spring up after the war."[2]

The following week, on April 25, Gerber wrote to F.M. In coded, religious
language, he urged their making national links: "That will take long work but
once we have this accomplished we have laid the groundwork and can send our
gospel to all." (Explaining his "underground language," Gerber said: "We have
seen so many movies with undergrounds in German-occupied countries that we
have a good idea how we can fight the sex-Hitlers here too.")[3]

One aim of the organization would be:

Fellowship of all true believers [homosexuals]. . . . Each to help and protect
the other. This will certainly come to pass when our organization is strong
enough.[4]

At this point Boyfrank apparently objected to Gerber's plan; and Gerber
finally realized that he, Boyfrank, and F.M. had fundamentally different ideas
about organizing homosexuals. On May 25, 1944, Gerber wrote in the past tense
to Boyfrank:

As my plan was, we would have some sort of loose society where the better
sort of homosexuals in each large city would be afforded opportunity to
meet their kind safely, and also to write to those lying heterosexual propagandists. . . .

Jesus had been

a rebel against law and order and was duly crucified. Just as I was crucified
for trying to help other homosexuals gain more freedom. It cannot be done.
Perhaps your backing out now is *a good thing for me* and has saved

me from the last remnant of *my delusion that homosexuals are worth saving.*
Bunk.

He told Boyfrank:

> Since we do not seem to have the same ideas about life, no use for you
> wasting time writing to me. I thought you and I could get up some *cultural
> project,* but that takes time and one must be independent.
>
> Having your excuses and the reluctant attitude of F.M. I have now
> forgotten the idea altogether and am out to enjoy myself, which is the real
> and natural purpose in life after all.

Gerber concluded:

> If you have time some day, let me know of what is going on and how you
> are making out. Too bad we could not work together.[4]

But a month later, on August 5, 1944, Gerber wrote to Boyfrank: "I was
greatly surprised to hear from you today as I had thought that we had drifted so
far apart that the rift was beyond repair." Gerber was "glad that you still have
our noble cause in your uppermost mind."[1]

Gerber responded to Boyfrank's "notes on our work." "In our work we
must not attack religion or marriage," although "Politicians and priests profit by
marriage and a man's settling down, because marriage is like a self-imprison-
ment."

"Having had plenty of experience in fighting for homosexuality," Gerber
knew

> we cannot get started by picking up fairies on the street and make them
> presidents or vice-presidents of our club—as I had stupidly done in my now
> defunct Society for Human Rights.
>
> They are only interested in getting as many pieces of trade as possible
> and have no solidarity or interest in helping others.

Gerber wanted to get "homosexuals to realize that the law looks at us as
outcasts and anti-social." He wanted "society to realize that we look at it as
persecuting innocent people."[3] He told Boyfrank:

> Our greatest point of difference so far is that I want to work *from top down*
> and you want to work *from the bottom up.*
>
> I can never agree to that. . . . You want to enlighten the people as to
> sex, while I want to enlighten the authorities that persecution of homosexu-
> als is anti-social and unjust and hypocritical as long as the perversions
> [non-procreative acts] of the heterosexuals are not punished.
>
> . . . my plan can bring some results, while your plan can only put you
> in jail.

Boyfrank wanted to use the interest of male homosexuals in erotic contacts
as a means of organizing them against their persecution. Gerber said, "It cannot
be done." Gerber wanted to convince the authorities to repeal anti-homosexual
and anti-erotic laws.[4]

In a letter of October 23, 1945, Gerber reported to Boyfrank that a correspondent in the U. S. military in Reims, France,

> tells me there are more queers there among the personnel, majors and captains and lieutenants and a few French queens, and they had an organization called Queers, Incorporated, and they had membership cards, etc.[1]

Gerber denounced those who

> with one breath . . . condemn crusading and with the other . . . say: "It's an outrage to put men in jail for such things; *something ought to be done about it!* " They are too stupid to see that if everyone wanted to keep aloof nothing would be done.[2]

Gerber said, "I use every opportunity in writing to others or speaking to them" to tell them the truth about "our cause." He had answered the ad of an "Atheneum Club" in Imboden, Arkansas. For one dollar he received addresses of fifteen "book lovers." The Club's "moving spirit," Bill Tullos, had sent him a pamphlet on a "Scientific Socialist Society." Gerber said: "I am not interested in politics though agreeing with socialism and some aspects of communism." Tullos, he said, had "the old-fashioned idea that homosexuals should be pitied." Gerber told him:

> homophiles want no pity from the heterophiles, but the equal right to enjoy birth control according to their own methods. . . .* There is always an opportunity to put our ideas before the public, one at a time, but the idea will spread. All great causes start from small nuclei. We have the nuclei of some 10 million homophiles in the U.S. and although most of them do not cooperate, and some of them even make our work harder by their antisocial deeds, we are nevertheless on the way.[3]

Later, Gerber added (somewhat uncharacteristically): "The best bet for us after all is human nature which is always open to friendship, sympathy and helpfulness."[4]

On February 18, 1946, Gerber wrote to Boyfrank:

> the older I get . . . the more I desire peace and relaxation and I have now about decided to withdraw from any work . . . that might disturb that calm. . . . the powers that be are too strongly entrenched [so as] to make any concerted movement impossible or only inducive to insecurity, enmity and frustration. I think the best thing is to let the coming generations fight for the things which we could not accomplish.

But that was not the end of Gerber's involvement in the struggle for homosexual rights. His correspondence with Manuel Boyfrank, touching on the organi-

---

*This is the earliest known usage of "homophile," a word used in the 1950s by members of the U. S. homosexual emancipation movement. Gerber's use of the word here, in 1945, suggests he may possibly have originated it. "Heterophile" remained an idiosyncratic usage.

zation of homosexuals, continued, sporadically, through 1948; Gerber wrote one
more letter to Boyfrank in 1957. Gerber also continued to work on the manuscripts of four books: one on ethics titled "Moral Delusions," one on the laws
relating to sex, one on religion, and the last, his autobiography. (What happened
to these manuscripts is unknown.)

On July 18, 1946, Gerber wrote a thirteen-page letter to Dr. Leopold Wexburg who, the Washington *Times-Herald* had reported, had called for stiffer legal
penalties for homosexuals.[6] In December 1946, Gerber was rewriting his translation of two German novels to include his "philosophy" about homosexuality;
their collective title was "Angels of Sodom."

In July 1947, *The American Mercury* magazine included Gerber's signed response to an earlier discussion of homosexuality. The magazine's editor then
asked Gerber for an article on homosexuality, but rejected the two he sent, "Is
Homosexuality Inborn or Acquired?" and "Can Homosexuality Be Cured?" The
latter included "three theoretical psychoanalyses" of homosexuals. The last
spoke "in defence of his homosexuality," pointing out that "the authorities encourage murder of homosexuals by their attitude."[7]

Early in September 1947, Gerber wrote to the *Washington Post* and the
*Times-Herald,* protesting recent anti-homosexual editorials, occasioned by a proposed new sex law. (Manuel Boyfrank also wrote to the *Times-Herald.*) On September 15, 1947, Gerber wrote to the editor of a conservative periodical, *National
Defense,* attacking its "red-baiting, Jew-baiting," and its declaration that military
men " 'guilty of homosexual offenses . . . should be de-sexed.' "[8]

In September 1948, *The American Freeman,* a periodical, published an anonymous response of Gerber's to an earlier letter from a homosexual who had been
jailed in Denver, Colorado.[9]

By February and March 1949, Gerber had translated into English several
chapters of Magnus Hirschfeld's major work, *Homosexuality in Man and Woman.* In
the 1950s, these translations were published in *ONE Institute Quarterly,* the scholarly journal of the new homosexual emancipation organization ONE, Inc. (Los
Angeles).[10]

In July 1953, Gerber contributed $10 to *ONE Magazine,* "to help you in our
struggle to get recognition," and the periodical printed a short, anonymous letter
in which he described his 1925 organizing attempt (see 1925, June 4). Gerber
continued to correspond with *ONE* editors, and on August 12, 1954, mentioned
that *Writer's Digest* had recently published his letter referring to homosexuals " 'on
the march' " (to which he received six replies).

In August 1956, Gerber sent $5 and several essays to the New York Matta-
chine Society, "to help along" the publication of its newsletter. In one essay,
"There Is Strength in Numbers," Gerber wrote that homosexuals "and other
minority groups," were "persecuted and locked up, beaten, extorted, and blackmailed because they are not organized." He added: "Minorities always have a
fight on hand, but if they sit down and meekly take this treatment . . . they cannot

expect it to stop." An editor of the New York Mattachine newsletter commented privately: "Excellent idea. A little too strong to go into print at this stage of the game."[11]

In his last letter to Manuel Boyfrank on June 18, 1957, Gerber mentioned the troubles of *ONE Magazine* (Los Angeles) and *The Mattachine Review* (San Francisco). The U. S. Post Office Department claimed the periodicals were obscene. Gerber told Boyfrank:

> I am now 65 and my libido is about gone. So I no longer worry much what the lot of other homosexuals may be.

Gerber then advised Boyfrank to "actively support" the existing homosexual organizations; he was surprised to hear that Boyfrank did not subscribe to *ONE Magazine* or *The Mattachine Review*. [2] Gerber had been in touch with a few homosexuals in Washington, D.C., who had had a Mattachine chapter. "But there was too much talking and no results at all, as well as "increased dues." He did not know if the group still existed. "In my old age I do not want to get mixed up with any trouble any more." But the following month, Gerber reported to a New York Mattachine officer that the German homosexual magazine *Der Kreis* had recently "published an article translated by Mattachine member 1205" (Gerber, apparently).

In September 1962, *ONE Magazine* published a long, *signed* reminiscence by Gerber of his attempt to organize the Society for Human Rights in 1925. His last letter to the *ONE* editors was dated January 24, 1966.[12]

On December 31, 1972, the eighty-year-old Henry Gerber died of pneumonia in the Washington, D.C., Soldier's Home. He had lived long enough to have heard of the 1969 Stonewall Rebellion, and the start of a new era of nationwide, activist gay and lesbian liberation organizations.[13]

♀ FILM REVIEW/CROSSING PERSONS

# 1940, July 27
## N. Y. Times: Turnabout

The film *Turnabout*, adapted from a novel by Thorne Smith, hinged on the reversal of female and male sex roles.[14] It suggested the emasculating effect on the male, and the masculizing effect on the female of any change in the sexual division of prerogatives, contentedly concluding with a return to "normal."* The film also played with stereotypical images of effeminacy elsewhere linked with homosexuality.

The *Times* reviewer found *Turnabout* to be an unfunny comedy-fantasy about

*For a lesbian's response to *Turnabout*, see 1947, June, p. 623.

"a husband and wife who reverse their biological status." The reviewer explained that when Mr. and Mrs. Willows "exchange their natural endowments and the sundry prerogatives thereof," Mr. Willows

> walks about like a sailor's jest, falsetto-voiced, hand on hip; the wife dons the family jeans and orders a phenomenal breakfast in a basso that stuns the chambermaid. There's the devil to pay at the office and in the home and, come evening, the penitential pair are content to retire to their respective marital corners.

The film was a "naughty joke" without "wit."

BOOK REVIEW

## 1941, February 23
### N. Y. Times Book Review:
### Harlan Cozad McIntosh's This Finer Shadow

The author of this first novel had committed suicide the previous year, at the age of thirty-two, said reviewer Marianne Hauser.[15] His novel seemed "born of an eminent inner compulsion." One felt "the author had to write this very book."

> McIntosh's novel is centered around homosexuality, which is about the most difficult and also most precarious theme for a writer. I do not know of any really outstanding novel on the subject. Proust's "Sodome et Gomorrhe," one of the finest studies of homosexuality, can hardly pass for an independent novel, being inseparably part of Proust's great cycle.
>     In writing of erotic abnormalities the author has to struggle against tradition and traditional tact, wherefore his narrative grows easily overwritten, sentimental or vague.

But this book included a "strange, unforgettable passion, burning brilliantly yet lonely, like a star far from life." The "mood" was of "emotional isolation." Though "outside of the accepted human circle," the characters were "real within their loneliness."

The central character, Martin, was a "neurotic, psychoanalytically speaking."* He was also "a mystic with strong muscles" and a sailor.

> He comes to New York, decides to live ashore, walking the streets jobless, moneyless. Searching for work, he meets Mr. Roberts. . . . The scene of their first meeting, Martin's immediate recognition of Roberts's one weakness, and Roberts's sudden, impassioned interest in the young sailor is written superbly. . . .

---

*The homosexual as "neurotic" was a Freudian-influenced concept typical of the 1940s and '50s, although it also appeared earlier and later.

# 568

Through Roberts, Martin is drawn into the precious, artificially scented atmosphere of sexual eccentricity. The pathological mixture of womanish masquerade and undisguised, deep love, of vulgarity and hyperestheticism is described with keen psychological insight. . . .

There was sometimes "a bit too much preciousness" and "a silky, silvery, oriental parade, reminiscent of Wilde." But this was balanced by the author's "critical observation," "sense of humor," and "profound, saddened understanding of human aberration."

On February 24, 1941, a twenty-four-year-old homosexual, Donald Vining, bought a copy of *This Finer Shadow,* looked through it, and noted in his diary:

I became convinced I had thrown good money away. It is very definitely not *the* book on homosexuality.

The next day Vining added:

The sixteenth chapter, about the party attended by men dressed as women, was the most horrible thing I ever read, despite the frequent humor in it. That men should dress as women, assume feminine names, and go to such stag affairs is beyond my capacity for tolerance and understanding. If it's women they want, why don't they get women? The psychology of it all is beyond me.

♀ BOOK REVIEW

## 1941, March 10
### *N. Y. Times Book Review:*
### William Davey's *Dawn Breaks the Heart*

"The real theme" of this book, said reviewer William Jay Gould, began with the marriage of the central character, Philip Bentham, to Vivian Ashley.[16] The two

quarrel constantly and bitterly, but their love for each other remains intact. It survives even Philip's shock when Vivian tells him that she is a Lesbian. (If this seems abrupt in this brief summary, it is no less abrupt in the novel.)

Philip's first—and lasting—reaction is disgust, but he can neither bring himself to leave her nor reconcile himself to her abnormality. The few moments of happiness they have together are snatched out of a chaos of struggle and torment. The end is inevitable. . . .

The "treatment of the central theme," the frustration of Philip's love for Vivian," failed "to make anything of the love story much more than a study of an inexplicable masochism."

# 1941, April
## F. A. McHenry: "Homosexuality,
## Crime, and the Newspapers"

A call for the franker reporting of crimes against homosexuals appeared in the *Journal of Criminal Psychopathology.* [17]

"Homosexuality as a factor in a reported crime" had long been "discreetly presented" in U. S. newspapers. But "only recently are the journals becoming more outspoken, said McHenry. However, the "casual reader" could still not usually tell that homosexuality had been "part and parcel" of a reported crime. While the papers' reticence "sometimes protects the reputation of the unlucky victim," it also served to perpetuate the public's illusion that an incident involved only "a simple assault or robbery." The "community would be better served, if the newspapers would report these matters in full."

"The press of any large city" in the United States reported what could be categorized as a "homosexual-crime" as often as every two weeks. Newspaper reports were quoted to illustrate kinds of crimes perpetrated upon or involving homosexuals: robberies and murders, blackmail, extortion, and suicide. (McHenry's alteration of "names and localities" diminishes the present historical usefulness of the quoted items.)

The "penalty and social ostracism" associated with homosexuality "have been unusually severe in comparison with other types of offenses." The public had unconsciously "sensed that the offense . . . is peculiarly a vicious one inasmuch as it aims at the very existence of the race itself." With an "ostrich-like attitude" the community ignored "the problem" of homosexuality, and punished severely only those cases involving "flagrant scandal." Therefore "a scientific approach" to the "control of homosexuality has never been developed." McHenry added:

> Few people realize that the homosexual is a deviate who suffers intensely by the social ostracism brought to bear upon his case and that his condition should be treated rather as a biological phenomenon than as an overt offense against the community.

In the future, he hoped, the same "clear attitude" would be brought to bear upon homosexuality as, in the last decade, had been brought to bear upon "the problem of syphilis."[534]

♀  BOOK REVIEW

## 1941, August 17
### *N. Y. Times Book Review:*
### Angela du Maurier's *The Little Less*

This novel dealt with incest and "Lesbianism," announced reviewer Jane Spence Southron.[18] And Angela du Maurier lingered "in a manner not unsuggestive of the curiosity of adolescence, around the burial ground of a theme that was done to death a decade or so ago."

The reviewer thought some themes were "alien to fictional purpose." But if all themes were to be treated "one can reasonably insist that exceptional subjects be treated exceptionally." Only "great tragedy" could deal adequately with the theme of incest. She added:

> It is surely time to concede that the subject of Lesbianism, if used otherwise than in the scientific investigation of human abnormality, should fall into a special category of its own, possibly as a minor subsidiary of tragedy. Miss du Maurier has developed her central idea along lines that rarely lift above melodrama.
>
> Oddly enough the novel needed little beyond the pruning away of its more sensational material to have been an interesting though not entirely satisfying study of inhibitions.

Du Maurier's heroine, Vivian Osborne, brought up by her father "without any display of affection and almost without friends," had become a woman whose "capacity for devotion might, you would think, have assured her supreme happiness as a wife and mother." Although she was a "dog and horse loving girl"— a "girl in no ways masculine," who "had never had any great liking for her own sex"—a woman suddenly "disrupts her life." Just when Vivian's marriage was "all but certain" she left home to "help Virginia." The latter, on learning of her husband's infidelities, "has left him and is struggling to earn a living for herself and her deaf-mute son." Virginia "sees nothing sinister" in Vivian's help.

Vivian finally married and had a son. She then

> cold-shoulders her husband and transfers to the boy the possessiveness that was understandably the result of early inhibitions and [which] should be taken into account . . . in assessing her devotion to Virginia.

♀ BOOK REVIEW

## 1941, November 2
### N. Y. Times Book Review:
### Felice Swados's *House of Fury*

"In this unusual story of girls in a penal institution, said reviewer George Froede,

> there is laid bare all the emotional relationships, the crushes, hates, come-
> dies, and even horrors, which are all the inmates have to compensate for the
> everyday life of the world on the otherside of the high picket fence.[19]

The novel portrayed female "prisoners trying to make lives behind the high
fence; their normal outlets for love and hatred checked; their aspirations
muffled."

On one side of the institution's grounds the white "girls" were housed. "On
the other are the Negro girls," who, like men, are "thought of as evil by the white
girls." An escape attempt by two of the Blacks set off "all the smouldering
tensions." The book ended "with the girls throwing off their restrictions and
yielding to the tempestuous overflowing of passion long suppressed."

♀ SLANG

## 1941
### Gershon Legman:
### "The Language of Homosexuality"

"An American Glossary" of homosexual slang was included in the first edition of
Dr. George Henry's study, *Sex Variants*.[20] One of the earliest extensive collections
of homosexual slang, this glossary was excluded from the 1948 edition of Henry's
book, and so is difficult to find.*

Legman's glossary included "only words and phrases current in American
slang, argot, and colloquial speech since the first World War, and particularly
during the period between 1930 and 1940." Terms were included from the
vocabularies of homosexuals and their "associates," and from the language of
heterosexuals referring to homosexuals. "Many terms are included which homosexuals never or almost never use." Much of the terminology of oral-genital sex
was used generally. "Every effort has been made to supply a complete and ex-
haustive record" of slang referring to homosexual erotic practices. Terms which
were "part of the slang sexual vocabulary of heterosexuals" were omitted ("al-

---

*For an earlier, briefer list of homosexual slang see 1927, Rosanoff.

though *pick up* and *proposition* are included"). Many terms listed had different sexual connotations when applied to heterosexual relations. "Terms used exclusively by homosexuals are marked with a single asterisk: *." Terms used "only by 'outsiders' are marked by the double asterisk: **." Most terms, unmarked, were used by both groups. Legman mentioned in this connection the "slow, fluid change of language." In this reprinting a female symbol (♀) has been placed next to those words which Legman says have explicit reference to lesbians. It also seems important to recognize that Legman's list, though of great historical value, contains words expressing an extreme misogyny, racism, and anti-homosexuality, as well as referring to what are often considered disgusting physical details.

Almost all types of male homosexuals, said Legman, "very commonly substituted feminine pronouns and titles for "properly masculine ones"; male homosexuals "use the terms *she, hers, Miss, Mother,* and *girl* (almost never 'woman') in referring to themselves and each other"—and sometimes to male heterosexuals with an "overtone" of "jocularity or mild contempt."

Legman said:

> Lesbians do not seem usually to refer to each other by masculine pronouns and titles, even though very many of them adopt masculine or semi-masculine names (such as Toni, Billie, Jackie, Jerry, etc.). However, note the entries *papa* and *daddy* in the glossary.
>
> Very noticeable too is the seeming absence of almost any but "outsiders' " slang in relation to female homosexuality. It is difficult to assign a reason to this absence, but, if there really is such an absence, and a concealed argot does not exist, two interrelated factors stand out particularly: The tradition of gentlemanly restraint among Lesbians stifles the flamboyance and conversational cynicism in sexual matters that slang coinage requires; and what little direct mention of sexual practice there is among female homosexuals is usually either gruffly brusque and vague, or else romantically euphemistic. This is largely due to the fact that Lesbian attachments are sufficiently feminine to be more often emotional than simply sexual, to which fact the practical non-existence of commercial Lesbianism is also largely due. There is certainly no Lesbian prostitution to compare with the prostitution existing for and among homosexual males.

An alleged "greater tolerance in America toward Lesbians than toward homosexual men" made "unlikely any feeling of criminality, let alone criminal community, among Lesbians"; these and other factors were not "conducive to the manufacture of slang." A "fairly extensive Lesbian argot is likely to be found" in prisons —but Legman had "not had the opportunity" to research it.*

Legman's lumping together of tramp, prison, prostitute, Black and other slang resulted in a list which indiscriminately combined the vocabularies of so-

---

*For some early examples of lesbian prison slang see the reference to "bull diking," 1921, August; and Charles A. Ford's report of 1929 in *GAH,* pp. 69–74.

cially disparate groups. The very size of his list suggests the increasingly detailed scrutinization to which some homosexual subcultures were being subjected. The extensiveness of this list also indicates, perhaps, the increasing size, visibility, differentiation, and cohesiveness of various homosexual subcultures, and the increasing consciousness of their existence in the dominant society.

It may be noted that "gay" appears in this glossary as a word used by homosexuals about themselves and their world. The still limited use of this word among homosexuals (or at least the limited knowledge of its use among heterosexuals) is indicated by its absence from the long list of "unconventional speech" first published in 1942 in *The American Thesaurus of Slang.* *

The meaning of Legman's own explanatory terms are now fairly clear. The mystified reader can consult his introduction for detailed definitions. A selection from Legman's glossary follows.

> **androgyne**  A homosexual man, particularly if effeminate. Colloquially pronounced in three syllables, the accent on the first. Compare *morphodite.*
> **\*angel with a dirty face**  A male homosexual who wishes to indulge in homosexual practices, but who is hesitant or inhibited. (In use since the motion-picture, "Angels with Dirty Faces," in the mid-1930's.)
> **\*auntie**  A derogatory term for a middle-aged or elderly homosexual. Also: aunty.
> **Avenue, the**  Fifth Avenue in New York City, a favorite locale of homosexual prostitution.
> **\*badge, To wear one's**  To wear a red necktie; in some localities considered the insignia of homosexuality. Obsolescent.
> **\*\*birdie**  An effeminate man, usually derogatory, and with the implication or actuality of homosexuality. (College slang)
> **\*bleeding dirt**  Professional criminals or underworld characters who try to provoke homosexuals to some overt homosexual act, and then extort money from them. This petty racket is known in underworld argot as *the mouse,* but this term does not seem to be known or used by homosexuals. Compare *dirt.*
> **blow**  To fellate or cunnilingue, the object being the person, and not the genital organ. Colloquial past participle: *blowed.* . . .
> **boy**  A male homosexual, especially if a prostitute. (Reported as hotel slang from Los Angeles in 1939.)
> **\*brilliant**  NOUN & ADJECTIVE: Congenitally homosexual male.
> **\*brought out, To be**  To be initiated into the practice of homosexuality. The active form of the phrase: *to bring (one) out* is rarely used, and in general this locution is losing its original connotation of initiation by another person, and circumstances or fate are coming to be considered the initiatory agents, the phrase therefore coming to be almost the equivalent of *come out,* q.v.

*See Lester V. Berrey and Melvin Van Den Bark, *The American Thesaurus of Slang.* . . . (New York: T. Y. Crowell, 1942). For other early uses of "gay" see that term in the index.

**bugger** A pedicator. The word is used in its actual meaning only by educated homosexuals and others such as seamen and persons of British birth or background. It is used in America usually without realization of, or reference to its true meaning, even by children, as a term of opprobrium; originally a British usage. In rural America *bugger* is used as a term of endearment applied especially to children, and often corrupted to *beggar,* as is done, for purposes of euphemism, in Britain. . . .

♀**bull-dike** A homosexual woman, particularly one who wears mannish clothes and is in other ways aggressively masculine. Also: **bull-dyke, bull-diker,** and **bull-dyker.** A common corruption is **bull-dagger.** VERBAL ADJECTIVE: **bull-diking** (also spelled: **bull-dycking**) Compare *dike.*

♀**bumper** A Lesbian, particularly one who is, or is thought to be an active tribade; usually applied only to Lesbians of the masculine type.

**buttercup** An effeminate male homosexual. A factitious and ephemeral term of the early 1930's; numerous other such terms have been omitted from this glossary.

*camp** To speak, act, or in any way attract or attempt to attract attention, especially if noisily, flamboyantly, bizarrely, or in any other way calculated to announce, express, or burlesque one's own homosexuality or that of any other person. As a NOUN, *camp* refers to such flamboyance or bizarrerie of speech or action, or to a person displaying it. The VERBAL NOUN, **camping,** is very common; it should be noticed that camping is largely a practice of male homosexuals, and is not very common among Lesbians. ADJECTIVE: **campy.**

*chicken** A young boy of about fifteen to twenty years, especially one with little homosexual experience; also a generic term for boys of this age and sort, fancied by many homosexuals, both pedicators and fellators, termed **chicken-fanciers.**

**circus** Any erotic performance or exhibition of living persons (that is, not motion-pictures) before an audience, particularly multiple homosexual or heterosexual coitus or oragenitalism; the performers usually being joined sexually in some way into a single unit. See *daisy-chain* for one type of joining. The term *circus* has also come to be used in reference to simultaneous or consecutive and open sexual relations of a group of more than two persons without any non-participating spectators being present, either in the same room or behind peep-holes. . . .

**clip** To rob a person, usually in connection with an intended or actual sexual act. **To make a clip** is to rob a homosexual or other client in this way, and is said of prostitutes male or female. A prostitute who is accustomed to robbing the homosexual client, usually before any sexual act occurs, is termed a **clip artist.** *Clipping* may be surreptitious, but in the homosexual sphere it is more often bare-faced and brutal robbery.

**cock-sucker** A fellator or fellatrice. The term has come to be the most insulting term of contempt used at present in America, replacing *son-of-a-bitch* and *bastard* which have been overworked to a point where the original pejorative flavor has been almost entirely lost, and the terms are even used as endearments. While *cock-sucker* has not yet been blunted that far, it is already losing much of its sting, and it is applied to inanimate objects in irritation at their innate perversity, and even children are already using the term without recognition of, or reference to, its actual meaning. Compare *bugger*.

\***cognoscenti** (Mispronounced in a variety of ways.) Collectively, all persons in the fraternity of homosexuality, including homosexuals, their prostitutes and friends (see *jam*), and others who understand the argot, are acquainted with the current popular meeting places, and share the homosexuals' fear and detestation of the police.

♀\*\***collar-and-tie** A female homosexual who wears mannish clothes, particularly tailored suits, shirt or shirt-waist and tie, soft felt slouch hats, and low-heeled oxford- or moccasin-type shoes.

**come** VERB: To experience orgasm, and—if a man—ejaculation. NOUN: The semen, a term commonly used by homosexuals.

\***come out** To become progressively more and more exclusively homosexual with experience. This meaning is currently being given also to *brought out*, q.v., which originally had a distinctly different shade of meaning.

**cop a bird** To perform fellation. (Prostitutes' and Negro slang.) Also: **To cop.**

**corn-hole** To pedicate. Also: **corn-haul**, which may be a corruption, but note the phrase *to get one's ashes hauled*, meaning to copulate.

\***cruise** To walk or drive in an automobile through the streets, aimlessly but in certain specific and likely areas, looking (if a *hustler*) for a customer, or (if a homosexual—*pay-off* or otherwise) for a companion for homosexual intercourse, whether for money or *pour le sport*. The verbal noun, **cruising,** is very common as a term for this type of street-walking and accosting, and a homosexual or hustler who practices it is termed a **cruiser.** . . .

**crush** An infatuation, especially with an older person of one's own sex, such as a teacher; homosexual overtones usually being discernible, although seldom actual and overt homosexuality. Verbally, **To have a crush on (one).**

♀**cunt-lapper** A cunnilinctor or cunnilinctrice. The term is becoming obsolescent, and is giving place to **cunt-sucker.** . . .

♀\***daddy** A Lesbian of the masculine type, especially one who lives or consorts with a Lesbian of the feminine type, a *mama*, q.v. Compare *papa*.

**daisy-chain** A spintry; a group of more than two persons—heterosexual, homosexual, or both—linked together in simultaneous sexual intercourse of any kind or combination of kinds. Usually effectuated standing, or lying on a floor, in a rough circle. (Note Caravaggio's picture of St. Rosario, showing a spintrian circle of thirty men.) A person participating in a spintry is termed a **daisy-chainer.**

**dash, To have** a To be slightly tinged with homosexual tastes or characteristics. See *lavender*.

\*\***degenerate** A common colloquialism for a homosexual or a pedicator. Compare *pervert*.

♀**dike** A female homosexual, especially if aggressive and masculine. Also: **dyke.** Compare *bull-dike.* The verbal noun, **diking,** is often used to refer to Lesbian intercourse, especially tribady; and also, infrequently, to the intercourse of two homosexual men with each other. This latter usage is encountered only among homosexuals, and carries an overtone of derogation. As a verb, *dike* is seldom used alone, being more often combined with a preposition, as *dike with* or *diking together.*

**dirt** Gossip or criticism, especially concerning sexual or sexo-social behavior. Among homosexuals *dirt* is also used to refer to a person who informs against a homosexual, or robs or blackmails him, or is likely to. In this latter sense the term is usually employed as a predicate nominative, e.g. "He's dirt, just dirt!" Compare *bleeding dirt,* in which the pejorative force of *dirt* is augmented by the intensifying connotation of *bleeding* (note the British *bloody*) and its denotation of extortion. See *dish the dirt.*

*****dish the dirt** To gossip about the sexual nature, adventures, and misadventures of another homosexual. Also, to criticize anyone who has "done dirt" to one of the homosexual fraternity; or to criticize anyone generally. Often contracted to **dish.** See *dirt.*

**dive** To practice cunnilinctus. The verb is intransitive, and usually refers to habitual cunnilinctus rather than to a specific instance of it. Also: **dive in the bushes** and **dive into it.** Compare *muff-diver.*

*****double-life man** An actively bisexual man, who can, and does, have pleasurable sexual relations with both sexes.

*****dowager** An elegant elderly homosexual. A **dirty dowager** is one not quite so elegant.

♀*****drag** Elaborate feminine clothing, used for transvestist dressing by male homosexuals. Also a party, dance, or costume ball where homosexual men go dressed as women, and to a lesser extent, homosexual women dressed as men. . . .

*****drag-queen** A professional female impersonator; the term being transferentially used of a male homosexual who frequently or almost invariably wears women's clothing, often for purposes of homosexual contact, posing as a female prostitute or as a loose girl, and fellating men picked up under this disguise, with the excuse that coitus is not practicable because of menstruation. *Drag-queens* are even said to strap their penises up on their abdomens and to submit—without undressing—to pedication in the face-to-face posture, the client thinking that he is having coitus with a woman! Or the penis and testicles, it is said, can be hidden under a menstrual pad, and pedication openly suggested as a substitute for the desired coitus. While many effeminate male homosexuals wear women's underwear—chemises or even panties and brassière—they are not for that reason called *drag-queens.*

♀**dyke** A Lesbian of the masculine type. See *dike* and *bull-dike* for extended definition.

**eat it** To perform cunnilinctus. Also: **eat cunt; eat fish; eat pussy;** and **eat hair-pie.**

**\*\*fag** A male homosexual; a derogatory term never used by homosexuals themselves, who use *faggot,* q.v. *Fag* is also used as an adjective, although not so often as *faggot,* of which it is a contraction.

**\*faggot** A male homosexual; a derogatory term, especially when used by homosexuals of each other. Compare *fag.* Also **fagot** and **faggart,** this latter being a Negro corruption, or perhaps it is the original term while the other forms are corruptions. *Faggot* is also used as an adjective (e.g. "a faggot walk"), another adjective form being **faggoty,** which is mainly used by Negroes (e.g. "a faggoty man").

**\*\*fairy** A male homosexual; the term most commonly used in America. Also used adjectivally, as "a fairy joint."

**\*fence, To be on the** To forsake homosexual practices for heterosexuality (or vice versa?). Compare *gender, To lose one's.*

**\*flaming** VERBAL ADJECTIVE: Obviously homosexual; using cosmetics, wearing flamboyant clothes and suede or high-heeled shoes, and generally affecting exaggeratedly feminine mannerisms in order to announce, and attract attention to one's homosexuality. Most used in the term **flaming queen,** a homosexual who attempts thus to attract attention and drum up trade. Both parts of this term may be modified, as, e.g. "a very flaming young queen." Compare *queen.*

**\*\*flit** A homosexual (College slang, recorded at Harvard in 1939.)

**\*\*flutterer** An effeminate male homosexual. One of many factitious and short-lived terms. Compare *buttercup,* a term of the early 1930's, *flutterer* appearing in the tabloid press in 1940 or not very much earlier.

**\*\*freak** A homosexual.

**fruit** Originally a fellator, but currently applied to any male homosexual. Also: **fruiter.**

**\*ga-ga** 1. The first of "seven recognized stages of homosexuality, from *ga-ga* to the 'deeper tones' of lavender." (There do not seem to be terms for each stage, and it is possible that seven distinct stages are not actually thought to exist, the phrase being merely a way of indicating the progressive nature of homosexuality.) 2. An immature or inexperienced homosexual. 3. The preliminaries of arousal between two homosexuals who enjoy sexual intimacy with each other and are therefore looked down upon by many experienced homosexuals (compare *ki-ki*).

**gash-eater** A cunnilinctor; *gash* referring to the vulva. Gash-eating is the verbal noun. Compare *muff-diver* and *cunt-lapper.*

**♀\*gay** An adjective used almost exclusively by homosexuals to denote homosexuality, sexual attractiveness, promiscuity ("camped" as *promiscruity,* on *screw,* meaning to copulate), or lack of restraint, in a person, place, or party. Often given the French spelling, *gai* or *gaie* by (or in burlesque of) cultured homosexuals of both sexes.

**\*gender, To discover one's** To *come out;* to become progressively more homosexual with experience. "One who 'hasn't discovered his (her?) gender' hasn't achieved the 'deeper tones' of lavender."

*  **gender, To lose**  To leave homosexual practices and become heterosexual. Compare: *fence, to be on the.*

**get down (on)**  To fellate or cunnilingue. See *go down.*

**get into**  To pedicate; also, to copulate with a woman.

**go down (on)**  To fellate or cunnilingue. The object of this verb phrase is the person and not his or her genitalia. Compare *get down.*

**gonsil**  A young pedicant. (Tramp slang.) Also *gunsel,* q.v.

**Greek**  A pedicator; the term perpetuating an ancient libel on the Greek race. Compare *Turk,* in which case the implication is perhaps not entirely libellous.

**gunsel**  A young pedicant. (Tramp slang.) Also *gonsil,* q.v., as well as **guncell** and, in prison slang, **gonzel** (a variant of the German gänzel).

*  **hair, To let down one's.**  To drop all restraint in displaying one's homosexuality, or to admit to being homosexual. The use of this phrase in common American slang, as meaning to drop all pretense or finally to tell the truth, seems to stem from the homosexual meaning.

*  **head**  A generic noun or predicate nominative referring to a fellator, as, e.g. "looking for head." Term reported from Montreal in 1940. Compare *head-worker.*

**head-worker**  A fellator. Obsolescent, recorded by Ellis during the First World War as an American term. Compare *mouth-worker.*

♀**  **he-she**  A Lesbian; an uncommon and probably factitious term.

*  **hidden queen**  A male homosexual who conceals, or tries to conceal the fact of his homosexuality. Compare *veil.*

♀  **high-diver**  A cunnilinctor or cunnilinctrice. See *muff-diver.*

**homo**  A colloquial contraction of *homosexual,* used as a noun and (predicate) adjective, and refers almost exclusively to male homosexuals.

♀**  **horsewoman**  An aggressive, masculine Lesbian. Usually plural and generic: **horsewomen** Possibly derived from the superior position of the aggressive Lesbian in tribady, or from the "horsy" masculinity of clothing and gait of this type of Lesbian.

♀*  **husband**  The normal or else more aggressive member of a homosexual liaison, male or female; a favorite lover who sees the homosexual regularly. Compare *wife.*

*  **hustler**  A male prostitute to homosexuals, especially so called if he is himself heterosexual. A common slang term for an accosting female prostitute.

**icing-expert**  A fellator. From the similarity of white cake-icing to semen. The term is fairly recent, probably no older than the American Civilian Conservation Corps camps, where it is used.

*  **it**  The usual pronoun of reference used by homosexuals, instead of "he" or "him" in speaking of heterosexual men accosted or *picked up. . . .*

*  **jam**  1. A non-homosexual male (the term is said to be an abbreviation of *just a m*an, but this derivation may be merely a *camp*), especially if he is acquainted with another person's homosexuality but does not divulge it.

♀*  **jockey**  A Lesbian, particularly one of the masculine type, who takes or is imagined to take the superior position in tribady. Compare *top-sergeant.*

*__John__ The regular lover—paid or paying—of a homosexual male prostitute.

*__ki-ki__ (Pronounced with both "i's" long, as in *ice,* and with both syllables stressed equally, or with only a slightly greater accent on the first syllable.) A homosexual male who is sexually attracted only to other homosexuals, or who engages in an affair with another homosexual for want of the money or personal attractiveness necessary for contact with heterosexuals. Such homosexuals are commonly considered to indulge in mutual fellation, simultaneous or turnabout, or, less commonly, in mutual pedication. Variant: **kiki.** As an adjective in **ki-ki queen;** and as a predicate adjective as, for instance, in *to go ki-ki. Ki-ki queens* are held in mild contempt by *pay-off queens* (q.v.), and vice versa.

♀**lady lover** A Lesbian.

♀**lavender** A term implying homosexuality in most contexts; a chapter in Gene Fowler's "The Great Mouthpiece" (1931), for instance, concerning the imputed homosexuality of a prominent penologist, is called "An Allegation in Lavender"; and novels and anthologies on Lesbianism, such as "Diana" (1939) and "The Imitation of Sappho" (1930) are bound in lavender cloth, although there may be some connection here with "purple passion." There are said to be "seven recognized stages of homosexuality, from ga-ga to the 'deeper tones' of lavender." See *ga-ga* for further elucidation. **To have a dash** (or **streak**) **of lavender** means to be somewhat homosexual or to have a tendency toward becoming more so or entirely so; often contracted **to have a dash.**

♀**Lesbo** A derogatory contraction of the noun, or less commonly, the adjective, Lesbian.

**lily** **1. A derogatory term for a male homosexual. *2. A "sissy," or timid, homosexual who is inhibited or morally restrained from overt homosexuality, or who fears the possible consequences of yielding to his desires.

**lizzie** A male homosexual. Current during the 1920's; now obsolescent.

*__lover__ A non-homosexual man who is sustaining, or has sustained sexual relations or a liaison with a homosexual or with several homosexuals. Many such men are bisexual rather than heterosexual, although the precise distinction between these two psychosexual states seems to be a matter of some question.

♀*__mama__ A Lesbian of the feminine type, especially one living or consorting with a *papa* or *daddy.*

*__man__ When pronounced emphatically by a homosexual, this term refers to a man who is definitely not homosexual. Also: **he-man** and **real man.**

♀**mantee** A female homosexual with very masculine characteristics. The etymology is obscure, although a French origin of an older form, mintée, seems probable. The very virile stride of such Lesbians is termed a **mantee walk.**

*__Miss__ A title imputing homosexuality to the man whose name follows. Compare *Ma* and *Mother;* and note the remarks preceding this glossary concerning feminine titles and pronouns as used among homosexuals. Note also that male homosexuals will call most anyone Bessie or Mary, e.g. "Oh, Bessie, you're a camp!" Furthermore, the more effeminate male homosexuals—particularly those given to feminine mannerisms and pursuits (such as needlework) and those who dress in women's clothes whenever possible—often assume feminine names such as "Mae West," "Spanish Annie," "The Duchess," and other similar appellations.

**morphodite** A colloquial illiteracy for *hermaphrodite;* pronounced in three syllables, the accent on the first, and referring to either a physical hermaphrodite (who is commonly thought to be far more perfectly physically ambisexual than is usually the case) or to a male homosexual. Compare *androgyne.*

**Mother Superior** An older homosexual who is very experienced, and who has *come out* all the way. (See *ga-ga.*)

**mouser** A homosexual. (Tramp slang.) It may be relevant to note that pedicants have been known to have a picture of a mouse tattooed just disappearing between their buttocks. Compare *the mouse* mentioned s.v. *bleeding dirt.*

**mouth-worker** A fellator (or fellatrice). Compare *head-worker.*

**muff-diver** A cunnilinctor. From *muff,* the external female genitals and hair. While there is also a verbal noun **muff-diving,** meaning cunnilinctus, I have never recorded the radical verb form: "to muff-dive," but compare the verbal forms *to dive in the bushes* and *to dive into it.*

**mustache** "Sodomy," according to Pollock. It is difficult to decide precisely what he had in mind, but note that to **have a mustache** is a jocular colloquial euphemism for cunnilinctus. (Compare *Oom Paul.*)

**\*\*nance** NOUN & ADJECTIVE: Homosexual, male type. Also, and lately less frequently, **nancy.** Compare *pansy* and *panz.*

**\*\*neuter** A homosexual male.

**\*one-way man** A male prostitute who, if himself heterosexual, will allow himself to be fellated but not pedicated; or, if himself homosexual, will allow himself to be pedicated but will not perform fellation. This is not a very stringent definition, and there are many exceptions, but in general it is correct. Compare *two-way man.*

**Oom Paul** A cunnilinctor. (Prostitutes' slang, possibly originating in the similar appearance of a man engaged in cunnilinctus—as viewed by the woman—and a man with a bushy "Oom Paul Kruger" chin-beard. Compare *mustache.*)

**pansy** NOUN & ADJECTIVE: Homosexual, male type. The noun is employed among homosexuals to refer only to an effeminate homosexual who has *come out* all the way. See *ga-ga,* and compare *Mother Superior.* The noun is sometimes facetiously and factitiously contracted to panz (compare *nancy* and *nance*). Other adjective forms are: **pansyish** and **pansified.**

♀**\*papa** A Lesbian of the masculine type, especially so called if living or consorting with a *mama,* q.v. Also *daddy.*

**party** An act of intercourse, homosexual or otherwise; or an evening or other period of time devoted to eroticism. Verbally: **have a party (with)** and **put on a party (with).** Note *50-50 party* s.v. *fifty-fifty.*

*\*pay-off queen* A homosexual who pays for the privilege of practicing his particular type of eroticism upon another man. This type of homosexual is held in great contempt by homosexuals who do not pay the other participant, who is coöperating simply for pleasure, and by homosexuals who are prostitutes and receive money for homosexual practice.

\*\***pervert** A colloquialism very current in America for a homosexual or for any other sex deviator: rapist, sadist, pederast, coprophile, etc. Compare *degenerate.*

\***phoney** A homosexual whom a male prostitute suspects or knows to be stingy, and likely to cheat or bilk him.

**pick up** To accost, and strike up an acquaintance with a stranger for homosexual purposes. As a noun, usually hyphenated: **pick-up,** a person so accosted. Also used heterosexually.

**pick up the soap (for)** To allow pedication. (Sea slang, from the soap used in swabbing decks, or in shower baths.)

\*\***pixie** A homosexual male. The term is factitious; note its similarity to *fairy* in literal meaning.

**powder-puff** An effeminate male homosexual. (Prison slang.)

\***proud** Having deserted homosexual company, and having discontinued homosexual practices. Compare *gender, to lose one's.*

**punk** A young pedicant, especially one who enjoys being pedicated, and does not merely submit to it. Anal eroticism is neither widely recognized nor well understood in America, and the term is therefore very derogatory and has been carried over into non-homosexual slang as a term of extreme contempt. The term is also applied—with equal contempt—to any non-homosexual male who submits to pedication for money, with or without pleasure. An even more derogatory variant term is punkie which is used of a very young *punk.*

**pussy, to eat** To perform cunnilinctus. See *eat.*

**queen** A male homosexual, especially one of the effeminate type, and a pedicant or fellator. The term is not applied to virile homosexuals or to pedicators. There are many combining-forms, such as *flaming queen, tea-room queen, railroad queen.*

**queer** NOUN & ADJECTIVE: Homosexual; more often used of male homosexuals than of Lesbians. As an adjective it is the most common in use in America. The noun is occasionally modified to the pejorative form: **queerie.** Note the combining form **queer for** colloquially used among homosexuals and their associates to mean "pervertedly fond of," e.g. "queer for little boys," "queer for dirty feet"; or followed by verb phrases, e.g. "queer for lighting matches to people's hair," or "queer for having his beard pissed in." *Queer* is also occasionally used as meaning a cunnilinctor or a fellatrix, the latter also being termed a **queer-woman.** These usages are often very confusing, as one would expect *queer-woman* to mean a homosexual woman.

♀*queer bird A female homosexual.

*railroad queen A homosexual who *cruises* the "jungles" where tramps live and congregate.

*R.F.D. queen A homosexual who lives in the country or in a small town, and who has homosexual impulses and desires, but who does not understand the argot and ways, or know the habits and places of congregation of the homosexual fraternity in cities and metropolitan centers. From *R*ural *F*ree *D*elivery, a term which immediately suggests the rustic scene to the urban mind.

*rough trade An uncultured, roughly-dressed and -spoken man "picked up" by a homosexual, or such men generically. See *trade.*

♀**Sappho A Lesbian; the term usually carries an overtone of tolerant and good-humored derogation.

*say a mouthful To reprove or reprimand another homosexual verbally, incisively, and at great length. This idiom has a slightly different meaning in popular slang, to which I have been informed that it was brought over from homosexual argot. Also: **To lay (one) for filth.**

♀*sil A Lesbian who is currently in love with another woman. A contraction of *silly,* meaning infatuated (usually in combination as *silly* about). Also: **sill.**

*sister in distress A homosexual male in trouble, usually with the police.

sixty-nine A term referring to simultaneous mutual oragenitalism, heterosexual or homosexual. Although seldom used as a specific noun, the verbal form, **sixty-nine (with),** and the verbal noun, **sixty-nining** are common; but see *hoop-snake.* A person engaged in, or having a taste for, this practice is called a **sixty-niner,** a term which derives much of its popularity from the term "forty-niner" for a prospector in the gold-rush of 1849. A corrupt form is **six-to-nine.** The reference in both cases is to the similar appearance of the numerals 69 and two bodies engaged in mutual oragenitalism, the circles in the numerals 6 and 9 representing the participants' heads, and the tails of the numerals representing their torsi and legs. The Zodiacal sign of Cancer is even more similar (since the symbols are here one above the other instead of side by side), and has been used as a tie-pattern by homosexuals and members of fast society.

slide, the "An establishment where male homosexuals dress as women and solicit men. Not to be confused with a *benny house,* which employs women. Some *benny houses* will provide a boy or man for special orders."—**Maurer** (Prostitutes' slang). . . .

*straight Not a *clip-artist* or a *phoney,* q.v. Also employed as meaning not homosexual. To **go straight** is to cease homosexual practices and to indulge—usually to re-indulge—in heterosexuality.

suck To fellate or cunnilingue, the former sense being more common.

*swish ADJECTIVE: Have male homosexual characteristics. Even inanimate objects may be referred to, e.g. "But dearie, isn't that tie too swish?" Also: **swishy.** The reference is to the peculiarly effeminate walk of many male homosexuals, suggesting the imaginary rustle of skirts; and *swish* is also used verbally to refer to this gait, the verbal noun being **swishing.**

\***tea-room queen** A homosexual who frequents toilet rooms to find persons amenable to his erotic or erotico-financial plans, or to scrawl homosexual dithyrambs or invitations on the walls. The ironic "tea-room" for toilet does not seem to occur in any other connection.

\***temperamental** Homosexual. Usually an adjective; as a noun the term is obsolescent.

♀\***top-sergeant** A Lesbian of the masculine type, who takes, or is imagined to take the superior position in tribady. Compare *jockey.*

\***trade** Generic for male prostitutes to homosexuals, or for heterosexuals to whom homosexuals prostitute themselves; the existence or direction of any exchange of money being irrelevant. **Do for trade** to have homosexual relations with a heterosexual male (prostitute or otherwise), usually referring to fellating him, the object usually being interpolated into the idiom, as, e.g. "to do him for trade." *Trade* may be used as a predicate nominative in referring to a single person generically, e.g. "He is trade," such a person also being called a piece of trade. Compare *rough-trade* and *uniform.*

♀**trapeze artist** A cunnilinctor or cunnilinctrice; the term is often used of a woman who participates in mutual cunnilinctus with another woman at a *circus* or *stag (party).*

♀\***triangle** The situation in which a man and a Lesbian are both in love with the same woman; or in which both have sexual relations with her without any jealousy. Probably also applied to similar situations involving a male homosexual, a woman, and a more or less normal man; but I have never personally heard the term so used. This usage of *triangle* derives directly from the colloquial usage of the term to refer to the rivalry of two men over a woman married to one of them, or of two women over a man married to one of them.

\***tricks, To do** To be willing to fellate or to submit to pedication; said of a male prostitute of any type and sexuality.

**Turk** A pedicator. See *Greek.*

\***turn the tables** To blackmail a heterosexual client, said of homosexuals; the term implies, and correctly, that it is more often the homosexual who is blackmailed. The tables may also be turned on a homosexual client, a homosexual who would blackmail another being considered the lowest kind of *dirt* by the fraternity.

\***veil, To wear a mourning** To attempt to conceal the fact of one's homosexuality. An obvious homosexual who tries ineffectually to conceal his state is said to wear a cut-glass veil, that is, his concealment is perfectly useless and transparent.

♀\***wife** The less aggressive member of a homosexual alliance, male or female. See *husband.*

\***wise** Acquainted with the fact, the practices, and the locales of homosexuality; said of boys and young men by homosexuals.

*words and music, To know the To use or recognize typically homosexual locutions (such as *gay* and *camp*), suggesting that one is homosexual or understands the other person to be so.

yodel in the canyon (of love) To practice cunnilinctus. Sometimes contracted to **yodel.** In spite of the flowery euphemism of these terms, they are quite commonly used, particularly in the western United States.

**yoo-hoo (boy) A homosexual, from the flamboyant greetings of those homosexuals who affect feminine mannerisms.

zanie A male homosexual. A term not commonly encountered, but in use in America since the middle of the 19th century. Also: **zany.**

NEWS REPORTS

# 1942, February
## N. Y. Times;
### N. Y. Post; The Nation: The case of Senator David I. Walsh and Gustave Beekman

Early in February 1942, three federal agencies began surveillance of a house of male prostitution at 329 Pacific Street, Brooklyn, near the Navy Yard.[21] The many sailors, soldiers, and marines visiting the house had drawn attention to it.

On March 14, city detectives and Naval Intelligence officers raided the house. On April 30, Gustave Beekman, operator of the house, was found guilty of what *The New York Times* later called "a statutory crime" ("sodomy," though *Times* stories never mentioned the exact nature of the crime). After the verdict Judge Samuel Liebowitz "told Beekman that he would receive the maximum sentence of twenty years unless he cooperated" with authorities investigating "espionage aspects of the case."*

Beekman signed an affidavit, parts of which were first published in the New York *Post* on May 1. This affidavit was said to give "full and unprintable details about orgies" at the house, named two Germans who brought soldiers, sailors, and marines there and questioned them about military movements, "and referred at some length to a United States Senator who was alleged to be a frequent visitor." The *Post* withheld the visitor's name, but ran a silhouette of "Senator X." Most other newspapers remained silent about the charge against a Senator. On May 2, *The Times* reported that a grand jury was continuing to investigate "the possibility that Beekman's home was used for espionage purposes."[3:8]

On May 6, the *Post* revealed that the Senator named by Beekman was David

*N. Y. Times, October 6, 1942, 16:6.

I. Walsh, of Massachusetts, chairman of the Senate Naval Affairs Committee, and prominent among those isolationists who, before the bombing of Pearl Harbor, had opposed U. S. entry into the war. Walsh denounced the charges as " 'a diabolical lie. . . . I have never in my life been in such a place.' "

On May 12, *The Times* reported that Gustave Beekman had pleaded guilty and would be sentenced on a second charge of "maintaining a house for immoral purposes."[13:7] For this crime Beekman was later sentenced to "an intermediate term in the city penitentiary."*

The charges against Senator Walsh were first publicly discussed in Washington, D.C. on May 20. The next day *The New York Times* reported that Senator Alben Barkley had addressed the Senate: an FBI report said there was "not the 'slightest foundation' for charges that Senator Walsh . . . visited 'a house of degradation' . . . and was seen talking to Nazi agents there." (According to *The Nation* of May 30, Beekman had recanted to the FBI his original charge against Walsh, admitting that "the man he had identified as Walsh was another elderly gentleman.") Four isolationist senators charged that the *Post*'s stories "were part of a 'diabolical' campaign to smear . . . all Senators who had opposed United States entry into the war."

Barkley explained that the *Post* articles grew out of the trial of Gustave Beekman " 'for an offense too loathsome to mention in the Senate or in any group of ladies or gentlemen.' "

Senator Bennett Clark, of Missouri, charged that Dorothy Schiff Backer, " 'the old hussy who runs The New York Post,' " should be investigated, with others who had publicized the charges against Senator Walsh.[6:1]

In response, the *Post* called the FBI report "a flagrant piece of whitewashing," and published a third affidavit by Beekman. This stated "that his recantation was made after hours of high-pressure questioning by FBI agents," and reasserted "his identification of Walsh as a frequenter of his establishment."

*The Nation,* of May 30, pointed out that if Walsh was indeed innocent the *Post* was "guilty of an atrocious libel"; it hoped all sides of the matter would be heard in court. *The Nation* also called for "a full and open investigation" of the house on Pacific Street for, it said, "the exploitation of sexual irregularities has been a favored Nazi method of gathering information."[617]

On October 6, 1942, *The Times* reported that Gustave Beekman had been sentenced by Judge Liebowitz "to serve five to twenty years in Sing Sing Prison" on the (unspecified) "morals charge."[16:6]

Beekman was released on April 1, 1963, at the age of seventy-eight.†

---

*N. Y. Times,* September 29, 1942, 16:6.
†See C. A. Tripp, *The Homosexual Matrix* (N.Y.: McGraw-Hill, 1975), p. 225. The twenty-one years of servitude is unexplained.

♀  BOOK REVIEW

# 1943, July 4
## *N. Y. Times Book Review:* Dorothy Baker's *Trio*

Critic Maxwell Geismar thought that Baker's novel *Trio,* begun in 1930, and first published in 1943, had "overtones of quite different, almost completely dissimilar literary decades—from 'The Children's Hour' to 'The Grapes of Wrath.' "[22]*

As the novel opened, Janet Logan, the "pet student, intellectual disciple and confidant" of Professor Pauline Maury, was arranging things for Professor Maury's party celebrating publication of her "brilliant" study of "the French 'decadents.' " The professor's cat, Arthur Rimbaud, "bites Janet, and the Filipino house boy hopefully brings forth Pauline's pearl-handled pistol."

A student helper, Ray MacKenzie, watched the "academic amenities," and the "increasingly strange human relationships . . . swirl and twist beneath the surface." The "disturbed background" of the chief characters was finally revealed: "Pauline controls Janet" and "her purposes are not not life-giving."† Through her "glamorous appeal to Janet's young imagination she has come to dominate Janet's mind."

When the "guilty" Janet tried to escape this "bondage" through friendship with Ray MacKenzie, the latter was caught up by "twisted currents of human behavior." A "rather difficult theme is treated honestly," said the critic.

♀  OBITUARY

# 1943, October 12
## *N. Y. Times:* The death of Radclyffe Hall

The death of the British author of *The Well of Loneliness* was reported in *The Times.*[23] When that "Best Seller" had appeared in England in 1928, said the obituary,

> *The Times* of London and other newspapers accepted the work, which deals with abnormal women, as a serious literary composition and an important

---

*For *The Times* review of the play *Trio,* see 1944, December 30. For a lesbian's response to the novel *Trio* see entry of 1947, June, p. 623.

†Though Pauline's purposes are "not life-giving" the female vampire remains implicit here. For another *Times* association of literary "decadents" and lesbianism see 1933, September 17, review of Mario Praz's *Romantic Agony.* For another (implicit) association of homosexuality and a Filipino house boy see *The New York Times Book Review* comment on Carson McCullers's novel *Reflections in a Golden Eye,* March 2, 1941, p. 6; the reviewer also refers to "murder," a "ghastly green" peacock, an "epicene penumbra," the "grotesque," "masks," "distortions," "horror and evil," and things "darkly hidden."

sociological and psychological study of a delicate problem, but a section of the English popular press called it obscene.

*The New York Times* obituary mentioned no surviving companion or friends.

MEDICAL/CROSSING MAN

## 1944, February
## Drs. D. M. Olkon and Irene Case Sherman:
### " 'I enjoy being embraced by men' "

Two doctors associated with Chicago psychiatric institutions reported the case of a physically normal male who loved men, perceived his feelings and himself as thoroughly "feminine," dressed as a female, and desired surgical castration and vaginal construction so he could live as a woman.[24]

Studying this report without labeling the individual described, we can see how a constellation of erotic desire and particular interests were associated by both subject and doctors with an essential "femininity." These desires and interests seemed illicit for a male. Especially interesting in this report are the implicit notions and value judgments of the doctors concerning manhood and womanhood, homosexuality, and cross-gender behavior. Their open hostility toward the subject is also remarkable.

A "Self Statement" by this man, M. M., age thirty-four, married to a woman, was taken on August 18, 1942:

> As far back as I can remember I was feminine. Although I was usually alone I preferred being in the company of and playing with girls their games. Whenever possible I wore a dress. I felt I was a girl and ought to have been raised that way. . . . Inwardly I preferred doing girls' duties but I did not show it outwardly. I am shy and sensitive to others' thoughts and actions.
>
> The boys considered me a sissy. . . . Mother kept me spotlessly clean as she would I were a girl. . . .
>
> In high school I did not take part in sports. . . .
>
> I am experiencing menstrual periods in the form of splitting headaches, sleepless nights, very trying days. Also . . . have strong desires to be handled by a man. I know what it is to be in love with and loved by a man.
>
> I want very, very much an operation for more reasons than one.[160–61]

This individual, self-designated "Mildred," said: "I longed to be loved as any woman is." As a male, he said, "I am at a loss, I do not fit anywhere." A "desire for relations" with males was reported. He said:

> When I have money I buy things feminine.
> My reactions to life are feminine.
> Looking for a woman's occupation as one.

I am honored to take upon myself the responsibilities and duties of a woman.
I can cook, sew, keep house, everything a woman should know. . . .
I am a woman and as such I will live."[163]

Doctors Olkon and Sherman commented:

In his so-called autobiography and in his talk he admitted homosexuality and even showed photographs to prove his unusual "interpersonal relationships." Indeed he can be diplomated [sic] as an unusual psychopath. He boasted of being richly endowed in all female attributes. His own words were, "I enjoy being embraced by men and love all other things of men."

His sadistic tendencies were manifested by his cruelty to his wife and his family. He boasted of his disregard for society or criticism. He said public opinion meant nothing to him.

. . . he showed evidence of being devoid of emotional content. There seemed to be utter lack of social sensitiveness seldom absent even in perverts and "hardened criminals." By no stretch of imagination could one discern in him evidence of shame, sensitivity to others' opinion, or concern as to impressions regarding him. He was presented before a senior class of coeducational medical students, stood before them for almost an hour elaborating on his way of living, referring to his perverse activities in great detail without any manifestation of timidity, shame or other affect, a combination of narcissism, exhibitionism and disregard for the onlooker. Such a degree of emotional frigidity or callousness is seldom encountered even in the psychopath.

This apparent composure (see photographs) showed the poverty of his emotional equipment and is only to be compared with the poverty of emotion of the low grade imbecile and "hardened criminal" seen in penitentiaries.

Moreover, he rejected all responsibility to society and to the present national draft call. He definitely affirmed that nothing could or would stop him from living the life he has chosen to live. His lack of social responsibility and emotional bizarreness are characteristics of the psychopath. . . . All obstacles were brushed aside to the exclusion of all social values, using other antisocial trends as secondary stepping stones for the attainment of the extreme goal of being a female.

. . . He possesses some abilities above average; for example, he held the attention of a group of medical students by his sustained composure and by his presentation notwithstanding his meager culture (of course, the bizarreness of the trends kept them interested to some extent). On the other hand, he seemed oblivious to absurdities, such as asking for certification to his femaleness, and his senseless, silly and asinine statements commensurate with mental deficiency; for example, he asked to have an amputation of his genitalia and a vagina constructed, and gave a description of his catamenia [menstruation]. . . .[165–66]

The following pictures of M. M. were captioned by Doctors Olkon and Sherman.

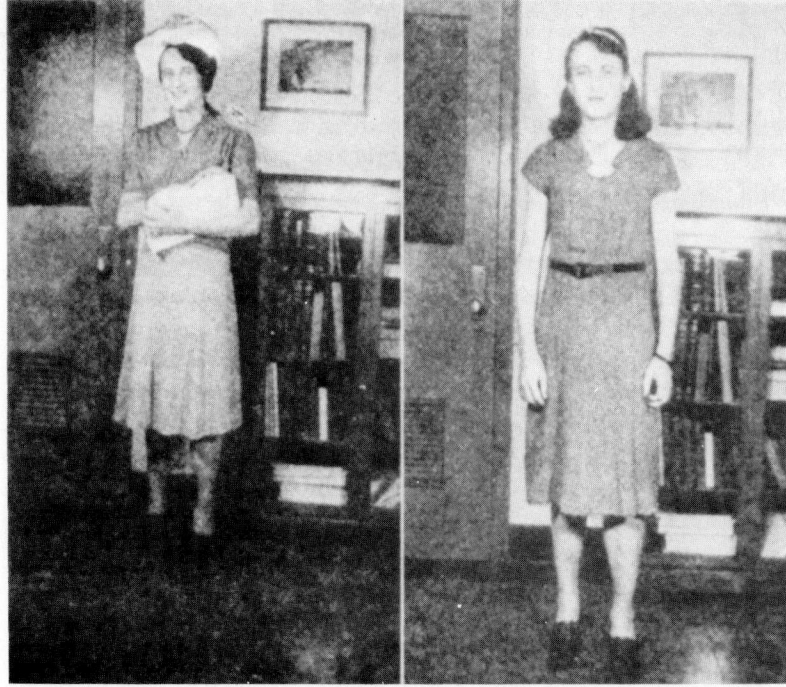

"Fig. 1 (*left*)—Note pose. He manifested no concern of bystanders' opinions of his change to female attire, denoting emotional stunting. Moreover, his smile portrays complete satisfaction in his exhibitionism and a happy mood. Fig. 2 (*right*)—He purposely arrayed himself in this dress to exhibit his 'girlish' figure, wearing a built-up brassiere to simulate the female bosom (not shown well in photograph). Note the ensemble of earring, neck lavalliere, breast pin, hair ribbon, bracelet and patent leather belt. Note also his facial expression of entire satisfaction with his exhibitionism."[161]

"Fig. 3 (*left*)—His posture of the woman at ease with facial expression of contentment. Fig. 4 (*right*)—Pose of a well-dressed, self-satisfied woman."[162]

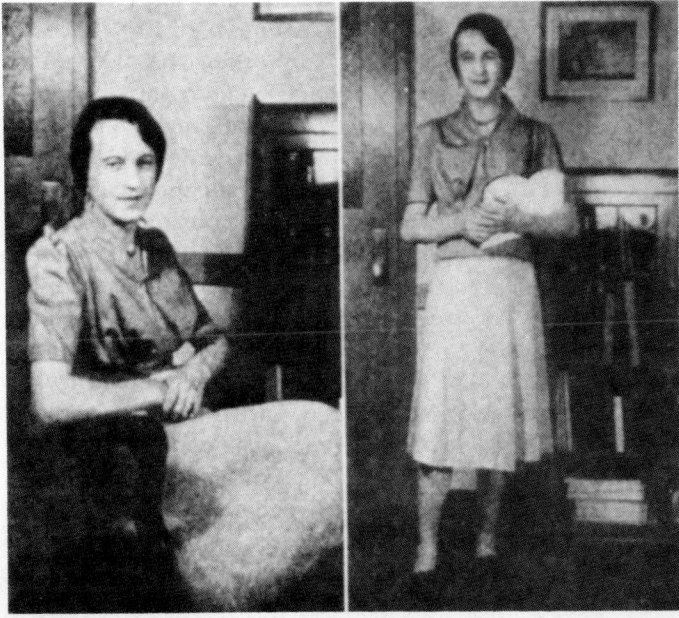

"Fig. 5 (*left*)—He pulled up the skirt to show the rolled-down stocking. Note his expression of entire satisfaction, notwithstanding his ill-shaped ankle. Fig. 6 (*right*)—Summer dress with Hollywood-like hair style."[163]

"Fig. 7 (*left*)—Something was said to displease him. Note the change of expression. Cruelty is spread all over his countenance. Fig. 8 (*right*)—His pose and facial expression denote dissatisfaction and cruelty, expressions quite at variance with those seen in the accompanying photographs of him in his female attire."[164]

## 1944, August
## Robert Duncan:
## "The Homosexual in Society"

The public acknowledgment of his own homosexuality by San Francisco poet Robert Duncan, in a published defense of the homosexual's humanity, was almost unique in works printed in the United States before the 1950s.[25] Only Edward Carpenter's autobiography, published in 1916 (see August 20), included a similar defense and self-revelation, though Gide's autobiography had also been self-revealing (see 1935, November 10).

Duncan's defense of homosexual humanity attacked both that group's "persecution" and that "homosexual cult" which claimed its members to be "different from, superior to, mankind." This aligned his essay philosophically with other homosexual defenses of the 1940s—for example Jo Sinclair's novel *Wasteland* (see 1946, February 17), and James Baldwin's essay "Preservation of Innocence" (see 1949, Summer). Each of those defenses devalued cultural differences of Jews, Negroes, and homosexuals to affirm their general humanity. To affirm the human, Duncan argued, required one to "disown *all* special groups." Throughout his essay the "special" and the different were considered second to the human. Duncan violently attacked that emotionally alienated cult of superiority and difference adopted by some homosexuals as a defensive response to social denigration. On the other hand, few other works of the time so clearly and forthrightly defended homosexuality "as but one of the many facets" of the human. That simultaneous owning of homosexual humanity, and disowning of homosexual difference remained an unresolved contradiction in Duncan's, Sinclair's, and Baldwin's defenses. Duncan published his essay in the periodical *Politics*.

A recent essay on the "Negro" was the background for Duncan's

discussing yet another group whose only salvation is in the struggle of all humanity for freedom and individual integrity; who have suffered in modern society persecution, excommunication; and whose "intellectuals," whose most articulate members, have been willing to desert that primary struggle, to beg, to gain at the price if need be of any sort of prostitution, privilege for themselves, however ephemeral; who have been willing rather than to struggle toward self-recognition, to sell their product, to convert their deepest feelings into marketable oddities and sentimentalities.

Discussing modern artists who were homosexual, Duncan said: "hostile critics have opened fire in a constant attack as rabid as the attack of Southern senators upon 'niggers.' " Other critics "who might possibly view the homosexual with a more humane eye seem agreed that it is better that nothing be said." In the case of "such an undeniable homosexual as Hart Crane," critics contended that he was great despite his "perversion"—"much as my mother used to say how much better a poet Poe would have been had he not taken dope." Or, "where it is possible they have attempted to deny the role of the homosexual in modern art."

But one cannot, in face of the approach taken to their own problem by homosexuals, place any weight of criticism upon the liberal body of critics. For there are Negroes who have joined openly in the struggle for human freedom, made articulate that their struggle against racial prejudice is part of the struggle for all; while there are Jews who have sought no special privilege of recognition for themselves as Jews but have fought for *human* recognition and rights. But there is in the modern scene no homosexual who has been willing to take in his own persecution a battlefront toward human freedom. Almost co-incident with the first declarations for homosexual rights was the growth of a cult of homosexual superiority to the human race; the cultivation of a secret language, the *camp,* a tone and a vocabulary that is loaded with contempt for the human. They have gone beyond, let us say, Christianity in excluding the pagan world.

Outside the ghetto the word "goy" disappears, wavers and dwindles in the Jew's vocabulary. But in what one would believe the most radical, the most enlightened "queer" circles the word "jam" remains, designating all who are not homosexual, filled with an unwavering hostility and fear, gathering an incredible force of exclusion and blindness. It is hard (for all the sympathy which I can bring to bear) to say that this cult plays any other than an evil role in society.

But names cannot be named. I cannot . . . name the nasty little midgets, the entrepreneurs of this vicious market, the pimps of this special product. There are critics whose cynical, back-biting joke upon their audience is no other than this secret special superiority; there are poets whose nostalgic picture of special worth in suffering, sensitivity and magical quality is no other than this intermediate "sixth sense;" there are new cult leaders whose special divinity, whose supernatural and visionary claim is no other than this mystery of sex. The law has declared homosexuality secret, non-human, unnatural (and why not then supernatural?). The law itself sees in it a crime, not in the sense that murder, thievery, seduction of children or rape is seen as a crime—but in an occult sense. In the recent Lonergan case it was clear that murder was a *human* crime, but homosexuality was non-human. . . .* It was lit up and given an awful and lurid attraction such as witchcraft . . . was given in its time. Like early witches, the homosexual propagandists have rejected any struggle toward recognition in social equality and, far from seeking to undermine the popular superstition, have accepted the charge of Demonism. Sensing the fear in society that is generated in ignorance of their nature, they have sought not to bring about an understanding, to assert their equality and their common aims with mankind, but

*On the Lonergan case see Henry Gerber's reference, and the quote from *Time* magazine, p. 560.

they have sought to profit by that fear and ignorance, to become witchdoctors in the modern chaos.

"To go about this they have to cover with mystery . . . the work of all these who have viewed homosexuality as but one of the . . . many eyes through which the human being may see"—those who, "admitting through which eye they saw, have had primarily in mind as they wrote . . . mankind and its liberation." (Melville, Proust, and Crane were cited.)

For these great early artists their humanity was the source, the sole source, of their work. Thus in *Remembrance of Things Past* Charlus is not seen as the special disintegration of a homosexual but as human being in disintegration, and the forces that lead to that disintegration, the forces of pride, self-humiliation in love, jealousy, are not special forces but common to all men and women. Thus in Melville, though in *Billy Budd* it is clear that the conflict is homosexual, the forces that make for that conflict, the guilt in passion, the hostility rising from subconscious sources, and the sudden recognition of these forces as it comes to Vere in that story, these are forces which are universal, which rise in other contexts, which in Melville's work have risen in other contexts.

It is, however, the body of Crane that has been most ravaged by these modern ghouls and, once ravaged, stuck up cult-wise in the mystic light of their special cemetery literature. The live body of Crane is there, inviolate; but in the window display of modern poetry, of so many special critics and devotees, is a painted mummy, deep sea green. One may tiptoe by, as the visitors to Lenin's tomb tiptoe by and, once outside, find themselves in a world in his name that has celebrated the defeat of all that he was devoted to.

"In all the homosexual imagery of Crane, in the longing and vision of love," Duncan noted the absence of "isolate sufferings" that converted "the poet's intangible 'nobility' into the private sensibility that colors so much of modern writing." The "Zionists of homosexuality" had "laid claim to a Palestine of their own, asserting in their miseries their nationality." In contrast,

Crane's suffering, his rebellion, and his love are sources of poetry for him not because they are what makes him different from, superior to, mankind, but because he saw in them his link with mankind; he saw in them his sharing in universal human experience.

How was one to respond to "those critics and artists, not homosexuals, who, however, are primarily concerned with all inhumanities, all forces of convention and law that impose a tyranny upon man"? And how to respond to

critics and artists who, as homosexuals, must face in their own lives both the hostility of society in that they are "queer" and the hostility of the homosexual cult of superiority in that they are human?

For the first group the starting point is clear, that they must recognize homosexuals as equals and as equals allow them neither more nor less than can be allowed any human being. For the second group the starting point is more difficult; the problem is more treacherous.

In the face of the hostility of society which I risk in making even the acknowledgment explicit in this statement, in the face of the "crime" of my own feelings, in the past I publicized those feelings as private and made no stand for their recognition but tried to sell them disguised, for instance, as conflicts rising from mystical sources. I colored and perverted simple and direct emotions and realizations into a mysterious realm, a mysterious relation to society. Faced by the inhumanities of society I did not seek a solution in humanity but turned to a second out-cast society as inhumane as the first. I joined those who, while they allowed for my sexual nature, allowed for so little of the moral, the sensible and creative direction which all of living should reflect. They offered a family, outrageous as it was, a community in which one was not condemned for one's homosexuality, but it was necessary there for one to desert one's humanity for which one would be suspect, "out of key." In drawing rooms and in little magazines I celebrated the cult with a sense of sanctuary such as a Medieval Jew must have found in the ghetto; my voice taking on the modulations which tell of the capitulation to snobbery and the removal from the "common sort"; my poetry exhibiting the objects made divine and tyrannical as the Catholic church has made bones of saints, and bread and wine, tyrannical.

After an evening at one of those salons where the whole atmosphere was one of suggestion and celebration, I returned recently experiencing again the after-shock, the desolate feeling of wrongness, remembering in my own voice and gestures the rehearsal of unfeeling. Alone, not only I, but, I felt, the others who had appeared as I did so mocking, so superior to feeling, had known, knew still, those troubled emotions, the deep and integral longings that we as human beings feel, holding us from violate action by the powerful sense of humanity that is their source, longings that lead us to love, to envision a creative life. "Towards something far," as Hart Crane wrote, "now farther away than ever."

Among those who should understand those emotions which society condemned, one found that the group language did not allow for any feeling at all other than this self-ridicule, this gaiety (it is significant that the homosexual's word for his own kind is "gay"), a wave surging forward, breaking into laughter and then receding, leaving a wake of disillusionment, a disbelief that extended to oneself, to life itself. What then, disowning this career, can one turn to?

What I think can be asserted as a starting point is that only one devotion can be held by a human being [committed to] a creative life and expression, and that is a devotion to human freedom, toward the liberation of human love, human conflicts, human aspirations. To do this one must disown *all* the special groups (nations, religions, sexes, races) that would claim allegiance. To hold this devotion every written word, every spoken word, every action, every purpose must be examined and considered. The old fears, the old special ties will be there, mocking and tempting; the old protective associations will be there, offering for a surrender of one's humanity congratulations upon one's special nature and value. It must be always recognized that the others, those who have surrendered their humanity, are not less than oneself. It must be always remembered that one's own honesty, one's battle against the inhumanity of his own group (be it against patriotism, against bigotry, against, in this specific case, the homosexual cult) is a battle that cannot be won in the immediate scene. The forces of inhumanity are overwhelming, but only one's continued opposition can make any other order possible, will give an added strength for all those who desire freedom and equality to break at last those fetters that seem now so unbreakable.

♀  PLAY REVIEW

## 1944, December 30
### N. Y. Times:
### Dorothy and Howard Baker's play Trio

Reviewer Lewis Nichols praised producer Lee Sabinson's persistence in trying to find a Broadway theater for the play based on Mrs. Baker's novel.[26]* "It would not have been well for the theatre had 'Trio' been denied a hearing . . . because of fears over its subject-matter." The producer's "cause was a good one," although the play itself was "not equally good."

The drama,

> concerns a woman college teacher, the young girl who has been living with her and the boy the latter hopes to marry. It had been scheduled for a New York opening last November, when various local theatre owners feared that its subject-matter of lesbianism might bring down the padlock features of the Wales law [see below]. Unable to find a house, the play suspended a tour in Philadelphia and the cast and all concerned stood by until Mr. Sabinson could use the Belasco [Theater].

The Wales law was the New York State statute of 1927 prohibiting the theatrical presentation of the theme of "sexual perversion" (see *GAH*, pp. 90–91).

The reviewer continued:

> "Trio" is not a censorable play. It is honest and it treats its subject with dignity and restraint.

In the second act,

*For *The Times* review of Baker's novel *Trio* see 1943, July 4.

the scene is the boy's room, when he discovers the relations between the two women. The third act goes over into melodrama, when the teacher, who had written a prize-winning book is discovered to have plagiarized it. At the end she prepares to kill herself, in a rather gaudy . . . scene.

As "the boy," actor Richard Widmark played "easily and casually until, at the time of his discovery of the women's relationship, he overacts." The critic concluded:

Because of the attention "Trio's" booking troubles earned it, Mr. Sabinson was afraid sensation seekers might seek out the play. They will find nothing there to amuse them. . . .

♀  BOOK REVIEW

## 1945, February 18
### *N. Y. Times Book Review:*
### Mary Renault's *The Middle Mist*

The setting of Renault's *The Middle Mist,* said reviewer Rebecca E. Pitts, "is England in the late Nineteen Thirties."[27]* The "boyish heroine has lived for five years with a very charming woman before she finally falls in love with an old friend, Joe."

The relationship between the two women, Leo and Helen, was "fragile, yet grave in its protectiveness." The "honesty and courage" of these women contrasted in the novel with the qualities displayed by Elsie. "Leo's abjectly conventional younger sister" runs away from "the domestic hell created by her parents (who nag over trivialities because they hate each other too coldly and fundamentally to quarrel over serious matters)."

Leo had earlier also run away, but with a difference:

Leo had gone "on her own," battling loneliness and starvation until she found Helen Vaughan and began, meanwhile, to succeed as a writer. Elsie, on the other hand, goes at the instigation of young Dr. Peter Bracknell, a meddling egotist who enjoys making his patients fall in love with him.

When the doctor pursues Leo, this "crushes Elsie" and "turns Leo's long comradeship with Joe Flint into a bewildering but moving and decisive love affair." The "boyish girl," Leo, with her "fear of men," was transformed into "the woman in love." There was "tenderness and fairness in Helen's acceptance of this change."

*For *The Times* review of Renault's first novel *Promise of Love* see 1939, March 12.

♀  BOOK REVIEW

## 1945, June 17
### *N. Y. Times Book Review:*
### Nora Lofts's *Jassy*

"As the heroine of a historical romance of nineteenth century England," said reviewer Ruth Schorer, Jassy

> is the daughter of a radical workingman who is killed and a gypsy mother who abandons her.[28] Her story is told by four people who are in a position to observe her—the boy whom she adores, a lesbian who reviles her, a nymphomaniac whom Jassy dislikes and an idiot servant girl who worships her and who committs the crime of which Jassy is accused.

Lofts's novel employed

> certain special interests of modern fiction—radicalism, sexual divagation, neurosis and madness—as trappings to heighten the sensational and melo-dramatic interest of her historical materials. . . .

♀  BOOK REVIEWS/RESISTANCE

## 1946, February 17
### *N. Y. Times Book Review* and *Time:*
### Jo Sinclair's *Wasteland*

*New York Times* reviewer W. McNeil Lowry described the theme of *Wasteland* as "the struggle of a few tormented people, the children of Jewish immigrants to the United States, toward self-knowledge, identification with the group and the nation, and the consequent peace and security which the sense of belonging can give them."[29]*

> On February 18, *Time* magazine described the novel as the story of

> a photographer on a Manhattan newspaper. His original name was Jake Braunowitz, but he called himself John Brown so that his colleagues would not know that he was Jewish.

His immigrant father had "nagged his simple wife into animal dullness and shirked his responsibilities." Therefore, "strong-willed daughter Deborah had backed up her mother and made herself the 'father' of the family—and a Lesbian to boot."

*For a lesbian's response to *Wasteland* see entry of 1947, June, pp. 627–28.

*Time* described *Wasteland* as the first novel "by a 32-year-old woman writer who was born in Brooklyn." Her book had reportedly "thrilled" novelist Richard Wright.[106] Sinclair's volume had won the $10,000 Harper Prize for 1946, and one edition had been printed for the Book Find Club.

Sinclair's novel includes a perspective on homosexuality similar to that of Robert Duncan and James Baldwin; all illustrate how the "melting pot" ideology of the time might be used to affirm the homosexual in the name of the human.*

In her novel Sinclair linked the social outcast status of several "minorities" —Jews, Blacks, homosexuals, and the physically disabled—suggesting their need, not for pity, but for a sense of their own and their group's value within the larger national and human family.† The ideology expressed was integrationist—the stress was placed on the individual's and minority group's need for affirmation within the context of a universal humanity. The "difference," "oddness," and ghetto life of the individual or group was associated with pain and alienation. Affirmation of self or of the "minority" was linked, not with individual or group uniqueness, but with the realization that those called "abnormal," "sick," "crippled," or "queer" were fully as valuable, as much a part of a common humanity, as any others. This integrationist ideal was accepted at the time by most progressive and radical thinkers as holding the most promise for a humane society. Not until the mid-1960s would militant Black leaders fundamentally question the goal of "integration," and stress the positive value of a minority's affirming its own unique culture, its difference from and opposition to the dominant, oppressive society.

In *Wasteland* Deborah Brown's lesbianism was presented as a product of a family situation in which she early took on the traditional male role of protector, losing in the process some of the positive qualities associated with females. But though a deviant psychosexual causation was indicated, the novel was unique in presenting lesbianism (and, by implication, male homosexuality) as modes of feeling and acting with as much value as any others. The vibrant, alive, socially-concerned Deborah Brown is probably the most complex, human, and affirmative portrait of a homosexual (female or male) to appear in American fiction before the publication in 1964 of Christopher Isherwood's *A Single Man*.

Deborah Brown was seen briefly in *Wasteland* with a group of white and Black women friends, with the suggestion that one of these friends, at least, was a lover. It was also suggested that a number of these women were passionately and actively concerned about social injustice, and in doing something about it.[31–32, 135–37] Deborah herself, a young, struggling writer, said she wanted only to write about

---

*For Duncan see 1944, August; for Baldwin see 1949, Summer.
†For the concept of the homosexual as a "minority" see that word in the index. The Jew/-homosexual analogy is also touched on in the entry of 1947, June 23, the discussion of the film *Cross Fire*.

unfortunates, the people who have wandered off into odd alleys. Physical, mental, or spiritual alleys, I mean. The strange people, the ones who are despised, or condemned, or lost.[194]

Deborah's first story was published in the *New Masses,* a radical left periodical of the 1930s; a second story was sold to the *Sketch.*

In *Wasteland* a wise psychiatrist was shown as helping both Deborah and Jake Brown to find and affirm themselves. The novel suggested the possibility of an empathetic doctor helping a homosexual come to full self-acceptance—against the aspersions of society. Some homosexuals in the 1930s and 1940s may have been lucky to discover such a humane psychiatrist, one working quietly against the tenets of more vocal and publicized anti-homosexual colleagues.

Late one evening, seeing her brother Jake depressed, Deborah Brown tells him she knows how he feels: " 'I used to feel a lot like that,' " and " 'I couldn't understand why. Why I was even living.' "

" 'What's there to understand?' " asks the unknowing Jake.

"Us," she said softly. "Ma and Pa. What's going on in our house. What's going on in the world, and what connection we have with it. Me." Again she hesitated, then she said, "Wouldn't you like to understand me?"[142]

Deborah advises Jake to see a psychiatrist, revealing to him that she had done so herself:

"I was sick. I needed a doctor. I had some kind of poison in my head, instead of in my blood or my lungs. Like germs. So I went to a doctor. Wouldn't you go to a doctor if you had flu?"[143]

She explains:

"I knew how sick I must be, because every moment of the day I felt ashamed. Not only of my family and our way of living, but of myself. I felt isolated, a part of a tiny minority of people who did not dare lift their eyes to the level of the rest of the world. No matter how clean I kept myself. No matter if I loved beautiful music and beautiful words. No matter if I tried myself to write such words. Wherever I went, I felt that people must be looking at me with repugnance and with laughter."[143–44]

She continues talking to her brother:

"I never thought I'd be telling you any of this," . . . and he knew she was watching him, waiting for him to say something. "I think I've known for a long time that you were suffering—inside of you. There wasn't any way to get near you. Even if I had known you wanted me to. I couldn't be talking this way to you now if I hadn't been to a psychiatrist. I know you feel odd about me, Jack" [she uses the Christianized name he's adopted].

"Well, Jesus!" he blurted out, but then he did not know what to say.

"I'm sorry," she told him quickly. "Don't feel badly about it. I don't. It's better if I say it out loud. Really it is. You see, I never said it out loud even to myself until I went to a doctor. I used to think it, and feel it. That I was like—a cripple. Something for people to draw away from. Terribly ashamed."[144]

After some thought Jake feels free enough to comment:

"I always wondered why you hung out with colored people. . . . That friend of yours. I suppose you have other colored friends, too."

"Yes, I have." Her voice, too, was relaxed, and the room seemed closed about both of them warmly. "I went to them first because they seemed—yes, wounded. I felt that way, too. Wounded. What I called, after a while, people with social wounds". . . .

"I guess," she said, "I had to go to them so that I could feel stronger. By feeling not so alone. My doctor helped me figure that out. In those days, I thought of myself as part of any group that was persecuted or looked down on. Any group of people wounded by the world. Jews. Negroes, cripples of any sort. I pitied them, I wanted to help them, I wanted to protect them and push them up to where the rest of the world was living."

She smiled. "It was myself I was pitying. It was my own crippled look I was protecting. That was how it started. After a while, I knew I was part of these people because they were part of the world. But not of a special world, you understand. The ordinary world, the whole world. Just as I was part of that world. Nobody had any right to keep that world from me."

"Jews, too," he said very softly.

She nodded. "You too."

". . . But besides the Jews, there were all the others who were hated and laughed at. The world belonged to all of them, as well as to me. All the odd ones, the queer and different ones. They were people. I was people. After a while, I knew I had to hang out with them. I was them."

"Why?" he asked, watching her intently. "You mean, your hair? The way you look?"

He saw her flush, her mouth twist for a second, but she did not look away. "The way I am," she said. Her voice shook for just a moment, then deepened and steadied. "The way I am inside. It's the way I've got to be. I'm a person in the world. There's got to be room for me, too."

She rubbed her cheek, and he studied the square, strong hand for a moment.

"I'd like to tell you exactly how I feel about it," she said after a while. The short, deep lines sprang out in her forehead and some of the youthful, boyish look seemed gone from her face. "It's hard to put into words. I hate that business of intolerance. They hurt me with it all the time. But I'll tell you, feeling it, I can feel how they hurt the others with the same thing. I can feel how I'm part of a person they call nigger, or dirty Jew, or cripple. Maybe it takes hurt to understand hurt, I don't know. But it's like I can understand all kinds of hurt now. Every kind there is."

He sat quietly under the monologue, feeling the closeness between them.

"If you went to my doctor," she said, her forehead wrinkled deeper. "If you talked to him, asked him questions. It's like being sick and needing medicine, is all."

When he did not answer, she went on. "Before I went, I used to feel that awful shame. Of what I was. So ashamed I couldn't see straight, or even think. I'd be so hurt all the time, so ashamed of being different, that finally I just couldn't make sense of anything. Everything I touched—it was like I was in a dark room all the time. Sick. Sort of—empty. Do you know what I felt like? Like I was being wasted. My brain and—and my heart, and everything decent I had ever wanted to do. I felt like a—a desert."

"I know how you felt," he broke in eagerly.

"After I went to the doctor, after I didn't feel ashamed, it was so different."[145–46]

Later, analyzing Jake's and Deborah's relation to their Jewish family and heritage, the psychiatrist speaks of Jake's "urge for roots, for the stable, cultural, racial, social roots of a people." And Deborah's "attempts to cling to the . . . strength of her ancestors (within the hostile, unstable world she knew)" were "even deeper" than Jake's: "She would never have children, never be able to perpetuate herself in them; her perpetuation would have to be through association rather than through blood: her association with her undying people, with their capacity to live despite persecution and hardship, with their capacity to live in the troublous present and into the mysterious future; ergo, she, as part of such a people, would live on, too."[180]

In a subsequent analytic session with Jake, the doctor asks him if, by being passive in his family, he had not helped to steal Deborah's

right to be soft and delicate? Who helped to steal her right to be a girl, a baby sister, the one to be protected? . . .[190]

Jake asks about Debby:

"Is it such a terrible way to be? Just because she isn't like most women?" . . .

"I mean, I used to think it was like being crippled, or sick! But it isn't. And she used to feel that way about herself! But it's Debby, it's her, the way she is. And Debby is—. Jesus, what's wrong with her? Anything, really?"

"You mean you feel that she's fine, sensitive? She's as worth while as all so-called normal people?"

"I mean—. Sure! I know a lot of people, and she's as good as any of them. Better than a lot of them. I mean, damn it, I don't want anybody laughing at her! Or making cracks. Don't think I'm nuts, please. I mean the way I rip into her, and then the next minute I say she's wonderful. That's just the way I feel! Exactly!"

"You want to protect her?"

"I want—. It's like I want to give her things. I want everybody to know she's wonderful. Now that I—. Oh hell, I don't know how to say it!"

"Now that you've recognized her? Is that what you mean? Now that you're proud of her, proud she's your sister, that you are both in the same family? Is that it, Jake?"[191]

Jake, a photographer, finally becomes able to take a revealing portrait of his sister, and shows it to his doctor.

"That's the one I was telling you about," Jake said fondly. *Young Writer.* Do you like that one?"

"That's a fine picture. Of a very fine-looking young woman."

"Debby takes a swell picture," Jake said. "I'm going to take plenty more of her. Notice the way her hands show up?"

"You know," the doctor said, his eyes still on the picture, "I'm glad you didn't title this differently."

"What do you mean? What other things could I have called it?"

"Oh, any number of things. *Young Lesbian,* for example. Or, *Portrait of a Degenerate.*"

Jake stared at him, his eyes blank.

"You might have used such words not too long ago," the doctor said, picking up another print. "If you had taken the picture at all."

Jake swallowed. "You mean if I'd titled it truthfully, the way I really felt?"

"Yes, that's what I mean."

"But that's the way I think of her now," Jake said painfully. "As a writer. As Debby. I don't think, she's a man, or she's a woman, or what in hell is she?"

"The way you used to?"

"That's right, the way I used to."[219–20]

Late in the novel, during World War II, Deborah tells Jake about having given blood to the Red Cross:

". . . I felt at one with everybody. Know what I mean? Just *like* everybody."

"The way I want to feel," he mumbled.

He asks her if that's why she wanted him to go with her to give blood.

". . . Because of how I want to be like any guy in America? Jesus, how I want to be like that! Nothing different about me. I'll bet you know that."

"Yes." Her voice was very low. "I know how it is to feel different, Jack."

He felt a small sinking sensation at that, but almost immediately she went on. "That's almost over with, isn't it? The way we've considered ourselves—low. Our family. Not as good as other people. Oh really, Jack, I've felt that way, too! The way Pa has always been. Our house. Low people, low peasant Jew. I got over it."

"I'm getting over it," he told her, his voice low and hoarse.

"But this blood business," she cried. "Really, Jack, I wanted you to do it, too. And feel the way I did. Not low. Not different. Really, you just can't feel anything but good, doing it. You'll see."

While driving with Jake to the Red Cross, Debby says:

> "When I give blood I feel as if I'm giving it for Jews, too. Jews like Ma, who
> never had a break. Never. And I'm giving the pint for Negroes."
>     Her voice dipped even lower. "For people like me. There are so many.
> It's like giving your blood against any kind of segregation there is in the
> world. Anybody who is slapped in the face, laughed at. Pushed into a corner
> —of society. They can have my blood. Sometimes, when you're giving that
> pint of blood, when you're lying there, its like you hear a sound of crying.
> Really."
>     He thought tremulously, And I'll give my blood against wasteland.
> That's like segregation.
>     She went on. "You know, where we're going now they keep Negro and
> white blood separate. Isn't that amazing? They make little ghettos for a
> thing like blood. When I give my pint, Jack, it's against that, too. Dead
> against it. Some day they'll know they can't do a thing like that. Part of my
> blood will show them that some day."

As he is giving blood Jake thinks of Debby's words:

> And I give my blood for people like me, she had said. Any kind of segrega-
> tion. Negroes, Jews. And my kind, too.[281–84]

Jake recounts to his psychiatrist his experience donating blood. The doctor
notes to himself that in giving blood Jake had seen that his sister Deborah,

> as "different," as "odd," as any one of the family . . . not only was accepted,
> by the Red Cross (in this instance, the world, America at war) but was
> welcomed praised, because it was her fourth blood donation. . . .
>     Interesting comparison of values of S[ubject] and his sister in their
> reasons for making blood offering. The poetic sister gives as a way of
> warding off, and fighting, evil: the sins of society against minorities, the evil
> of society's segregation of Jew, Negro, homosexual. Her blood is offered up
> against ghettos of any kind, physical and spiritual. When she lies there, in
> the act of giving, in her heart she hears the cries of subject peoples, tor-
> mented peoples.
>     Basically, S gave his blood for the same reason, to break down the
> walls of ghetto. With him, however, the reason was not the universal one
> of Deborah's; with him, it was his individual ghetto, and that of his family.
> Out of this small reason some day may come the greater issue; his thinking
> already has stretched to meet the horizons of his sister's. S is a follower of
> what he admires and respects, and Deborah's strength of belief, her hope
> for a future of any kind of people, will continue to broaden his own ideals.

Giving his blood, Jake had

> made a gesture directly opposite wasteland, a gift of life. He gave as a Jew,
> and a patriot to some degree; but, most important, he gave as Everyman.
> He wanted to be the anonymous man of America, the man who is as sane

as the next man, with as much to give and as much to be reckoned with. His acceptance in this role proved of more importance than the Jew and patriot roles, though they stem directly from it. Everyman is alive. He is a member of society, a working part of it; he belongs. Everyman . . . is not, and cannot be, a part of wasteland. Everyman is strong enough to say his right name out loud. He has asked his sister to call him Jake. And in the books of society, he has written his name correctly. . . .[288–91]

In the last pages of the book, talk is of the Nazis—" 'What they do to people, not only to Jews' "—how they burn down ghettos and make new ones.

"There are plenty of ghettos," Debby said. . . . "Anywhere you look you can see them. Maybe it takes a war to wipe them all out." . . .

"I'd like to wipe them out, all right," Jake said. "Any kind. Every single one of them."

In Debby's eyes he saw the words he was not saying: Negro, Jew, your kind of people. . . .[315]

Debby's "eyes were wonderful," thinks Jake.

He could not keep feeling afraid, looking at her eyes. They were full of different expressions, like the colors of a rainbow but not bright, just soft and changing. Her eyes were a lot like the voice of their father, sad and yet, a second later, hopeful, strong as the walls of sound and yet lamenting what had gone before, grave and devout and yet full of a passionate, searching look.

He wanted to nod to her that he knew, that he remembered how tormented her eyes could be sometimes, but that he remembered how strong they could be, too. He wanted to tell her that he remembered how her voice had sounded when she said the word "tomorrow."[320]

BOOK REVIEW

# 1946, February 17
### *N. Y. Times Book Review:*
## Christopher Isherwood's *The Berlin Stories*

Alfred Kazin reviewed the reissue of Isherwood's two novels, *The Last of Mr. Norris* and *Goodbye to Berlin,* in a one-volume edition titled *The Berlin Stories.*[30] The review documents a common literary and media association of "sexual perversities," social decadence, and German Fascism, an association whose general falsity is indicated by the Nazi's persecution of homosexuals.

The character Arthur Norris was a "fantastic, corrupt and masochistic char-latan, . . . who attaches himself to the German Communist movement and makes a little money by betraying its secrets to the French General Staff." Norris was "dissolute as Oscar Wilde might have been if he had begun life as a commercial traveler."

> Mr. Norris has some of the passive sexual habits of the Baron de Charlus [of Proust], the anxieties of an aged vamp* and the *recherché* snobberies of a businessman who dabbles in the *avant garde.* He is a scoundrel, but at the same time such a fraud . . . that he becomes fascinating rather than repellent. One cannot leave Arthur Norris, it is too important to discover what he means.

Like Sally Bowles (the leading character in *Goodbye to Berlin*), Arthur Norris was "fascinating" because "he so naturally finds his bearings in an atmosphere of impending dissolution."

> In this cold and somber Berlin, 1930–33, where as Fritz Wendle says, "Eventually we're all queer"; where the Communists are preparing for the last-ditch fight that never came off, and the Fascists are spreading their wings; . . . where the winter is bitter cold, the republic rotting away, and the sexual perversities and alcoholic gluttonies represent, in each human soul, the consoling fantasy of companionship and human warmth—in this sad last night of the German crisis, . . . Arthur Norris and Sally Bowles are only two more of "the lost."

> "Inevitably," said the critic, in the last days of the Weimar Republic, "everyone" had liked Christopher Isherwood. They had "trusted him, told him their stories—his landlady, the head of the Communists in Berlin, the aristocratic perverts and resigned middle-class Jews, Arthur Norris and Sally Bowles; the little Fräulein Landauer, who put aspirins into the plants to revive them, and the homosexual Nationalist minister who consoled himself with boys' adventure stories in which everyone was free, athletic and happy."

BOOK REVIEW/INTIMACY

# 1946, February 24
## *N. Y. Times Book Review:*
## Gay Wilson Allen's *Walt Whitman Handbook*

Malcolm Cowley reviewed a new edition of Whitman's poems and a new *Handbook* about the poet, his review touching on the meaning of male-male comradeship in post-War America.[31]

---

*The "aged vamp," Mr. Norris, a "fantasic, corrupt and masochistic charlatan," was a variation on the homosexual-as-vampire theme. The "vampire slayer," a male who murdered young men, had appeared in *The New York Times* on December 5, 1924 (see), and a female vampire who preyed on young girls had appeared on May 18, 1936, in a review of the film *Dracula's Daughter* (see). Also see "vampire" in the index.

"Should *Leaves of Grass* be studied as a textbook . . . of American democracy?" Crowley asked. The answer was "No, with qualifications." After the first 1855 edition of his poems Whitman "ceased to mention his real country." Among the "specialized abstractions" to which he turned was "the religion of athletic comradeship." Other abstractions included "American optimism, the belief in progress," and "an almost spiritual faith in material things." It did "not include the struggle for wealth and the cold-eyed men who survive it." And Whitman's

> American mothers are idealized breeding machines. His brawny American workingmen parade with their arms draped negligently over one another's shoulders, like the chorus of a patriot opera.

Whitman stood apart "from the main current of American writing," none of whose authors

> reports, as Whitman did, that America is now, or is about to become, a democracy of loving and athletic comrades. On the contrary, they depict their individual countrymen as bewildered, unhappy and alone.

"To pry into the personal life of a great poet," said Cowley,

> is sometimes a rather disgraceful occupation; but there is justification for it in Whitman's case. . . . He . . . wanted to become a national bard, a prophet of the future. . . . We have a right to examine his credentials carefully.

The known facts of Whitman's life, as summarized in Allen's *Handbook*, "will prove disturbing to the poet's more ardent disciples." Among these disturbing facts, Whitman

> gave a completely false picture of his sexual experiences, in the "Children of Adam" poems, as later he would defend himself from more serious charges by boasting to a biographer that he had six illegitimate children (who never existed even in his fancy, unless he was lying to himself).*

Such "concealments and misrepresentations and plain lies," the review stated, should "make us hesitate" before absorbing Whitman's ideas into America.

FILM REVIEW

# 1946, March 15
## *N. Y. Times: Gilda*

"It seems" that in *Gilda,* said film critic Bosley Crowther, "a fantastic female [Rita Hayworth] . . . turns up in a Buenos Aires casino as the wife of the dour proprietor [George Macready]."[32]

*For Whitman's claim to paternity see *GAH*, pp. 348–52, 364–65, 628–29 n. 32.

But it also seems that she was previously the sweetie of a caustic young man [Glenn Ford] who is quite a hand at gambling and is employed by this same proprietor. For reasons which are guardedly suggested, she taunts and torments this tough lad until, by a twist of circumstances, her husband is suddenly removed. Then she marries the laddie but continues to fight with him because of some curious disposition which is never properly explained.[27:2]

In 1972, in *Screening the Sexes,* Parker Tyler wrote of "the powerful mature 'patron' " as a masked figure in the "homosexual pantheon." Many "oblique affairs between older and younger men have appeared on the screen." The "hidden homosexual" who acted as a patron to "the young and luckless" was found in the "slyly insinuating eroticism" of *Gilda.* At the start the younger male character "has his skin saved by a gray-haired gentleman in evening clothes . . . who routs some thugs with a rapier plucked from his elegant cane." Even in the 1940s, said Tyler, "It wasn't hard for the worldly-wise to guess" that the rescuer "was a stand-in for the malign-benign homosexual patron."

♀ OBITUARY

# 1946, July 28
## *N. Y. Times:*
# The death of Gertrude Stein

"Gertrude Stein, famed woman writer" and controversial literary figure had died in Paris, reported a *Times* obituary.[33]

"At the bedside were Miss Alice B. Toklas," two relatives, and a doctor.

"Devotees of her cult" of literature spoke of Stein's "freshness and rhythm."

Medical authorities compared her effusions to the rantings of the insane. The Hearst press inquired, "Is Gertrude Stein not Gertrude Stein but somebody else living and talking in the same body." Sinclair Lewis concluded she was conducting a racket.

*The Times* reported (incorrectly) that Stein "removed in 1903 to Paris with Alice B. Toklas, a San Francisco friend, who was her lifelong secretary-companion." (Stein first met Toklas in Paris, in 1907; the two had not known each other in America.)

Stein's lectures were said to have been popular; her audiences had been "entertained by this roughly dressed woman, with close-cropped hair that set off her strong features."

MEDICAL

# 1946, July
## A. C. Cornsweet and Dr. M. F. Hayes:
### *"The true fellator [and] the malingerer"*

Cornsweet, a commander in the U. S. Naval Reserve and a Ph.D., and Hayes, a lieutenant commander and a physician, published a medical journal article titled "Conditioned Response to Fellatio."[34] Their essay reflected the interest of military officials in differentiating "true homosexuals" from others who were claiming homosexuality in order to receive quick discharges from the armed forces.

"Sexual oralism"—defined as the obtaining of pleasure from the application of the mouth to the male sexual organ—was "a common perversion in both heterosexual and homosexual."[76] (This "perversion" implied a prior "true," procreative sexuality.)

After questioning about "200 male homosexuals," ages 18 to 30, Cornsweet and Dr. Hayes claimed they had discovered "a specific type of reaction" common to those "confirmed to the practice of sexual oralism." The "satisfaction" of the "confirmed fellator" centered in the lips, mouth, and throat. This "localization of sensation" was "one of the diagnostic 'signs' that distinguishes the overt from the latent homosexual."[76, 78] Such localization, "may be useful in distinguishing the true fellator from the malingerer who apes homosexuality but does not have the knowledge to describe the same localized sensations found in the true homosexual." The authors speculated that the "female fellator's satisfaction" might come from the same "localized sensation of pleasure."[78]

BOOK REVIEW

# 1946, September 8
## *N. Y. Times Book Review:*
## Janet Shane's *The Dazzling Crystal*

The marriage of Judith and Nicky Hoffman proceeded well and "ardently" until "shades of the husband's past and old circle of friends fall ominously over their newlywed happiness," said reviewer "B. V. W."[35]

"The most frightening . . . shade" was Mark Sauter, "Nicky Hoffman's one-time publisher," a "charming, effeminate man, whose thought processes are, roughly, fascistically artistic and Yellow-Nineties" (a reference to the English 'decadent' writers around Wilde).

Unable to explain his past relations with Mark to Judy, though what they may specifically have been remains only a suggestion to the end, Nicky runs away from both.

Only when a young male poet "who is Mark's latest protégé" committed suicide did the book "reach for a climax."

In James Cain's *Serenade* (see 1937, December 5) "an unnatural triangle" had been "called by name," and "violence" had brought the book to a dramatic end. In the present book "the great problem that was hid within—love vs. friendship, and all the ramifications of that theme—is submerged." At "the risk of sounding old-fashioned," the reviewer declared that "fascination between males is best handled by gentlemen authors rather than the ladies."


BOOK REVIEW

## 1946, October 6
### *N. Y. Times Book Review:*
### Charles Jackson's *The Fall of Valor*

This novel, said critic Robert Gorham Davis, "tells the story of a couple ten years married who go to Nantucket during the war . . . to find their lost love for each other."[36] There, Professor John Grandin and his wife met a Marine, Cliff Hauman and his wife. The professor was "stirred through and through by a schoolboy worship of the dazzling uniform and the figure in it," described in heroic, adolescent terms.

In real life, said the reviewer, the professor, an "important teacher at Columbia," would have had at least "glanced at some of the texts of the Viennese school of psychology," and have had some understanding of his own feelings. In the novel, however, he was presented as an unknowing, "dreadful ninny."

"Obviously" the book "will be widely read."

> Such embarrassed discussion of an embarrassing subject has an uncomfortable, reminiscent fascination even for the psychologically sophisticated. But such cases have been studied with exhaustive particularity in the professional journals. More to the point, a number of important imaginative writers have not only shared John Grandin's peculiarity, but in recent decades have dealt with it at great length in literature. John Grandin's obsession with the Marine uniform must be compared with the . . . distractions of Proust's Baron de Charlus when foreign troops began appearing in the streets of Paris during the last war, and John's observations of Nantucket must be set beside André Gide's account of his journey to Algiers.

Author Charles Jackson "has hit upon a subject that has been treated by experts." And, "Such an expert, in the precise sense of the word, Mr. Jackson quite obviously is not—happily for himself, and unhappily for 'The Fall of Valor.' "

♀ PLAY REVIEW

## 1946, November 27
### N. Y. Times:
### Jean-Paul Sartre's No Exit

A Broadway production of Sartre's "fascinating and macabre play about three lost souls in hell," was reviewed by Brooks Atkinson.[37]

In the play adapted by Paul Bowles, Sartre "has sharply dramatized the loneliness and despair of souls that are lost, imprisoned and condemned to eternal torture in each other's company." The play was "a bitter and resentful comment on life" by a man "whose hopes have been shattered by the colossal disasters of recent experience."

In this "ingenious, ugly and scornful" play, "two women and one man are locked up together in one hideous room in hell." They first think they will be able to dwell in "the privacy of their thoughts." But they soon "wring out of each other the black secret of their squalid crimes on earth." Each at first "imagines that one of the others can save him," but none of these "dead souls," finally, "can escape from the acts they have committed, and must be damned by them forever." According to Sartre: "Man is alone in this world; he is responsible to his own . . . decisions; no one can save him from himself."

The picture Sartre drew

is as gruesome as the characters, who are in varying degrees unspeakable. The man has been a coward—probably a collaborator, certainly a sadistic tormentor of his wife. One of the women has been a cruel betrayer of her husband and her lover. The other is a loathsome homosexual who has poisoned and destroyed the life of a married woman of whom she had become enamored.*

"Beyond the trapped agony of the three doomed characters" lay "the intellectual climate" in which Sartre lived and wrote as "one of the prophets of the current vogue of a Parisian philosophy in which the individual dissociates himself from society (which has betrayed him) and acts for himself alone."

---

*The female homosexual as destroyer is explicit here, the vampire implicit.

# 1947, January 17
## · N. Y. Times:
## William Tilden sentenced in Los Angeles

The former tennis champion of the world, William (Big Bill) Tilden, had been sentenced in Los Angeles Juvenile Court to nine months in the county jail "for contributing to the delinquency of a 14-year-old boy."[38] Tilden had pleaded guilty.

> "You have been the idol of youngsters all over the world," the judge said, "It has been a great shock to sports fans to read about your troubles. I am going to make this an object lesson."
> The judge imposed a sentence of one year, but suspended it and put Tilden on probation for five years, the first nine months in jail. He also stipulated that on release Tilden should obtain psychiatric treatment and should not associate with juveniles except in the presence of responsible adults.[31:4]

On September 1, 1947, a small item in *The Times* reported that "Big Bill" Tilden, fifty-four years old, had been released from the Los Angeles County Jail, having served seven and one-half months at the County Farm, on a "morals charge."[17:3]
Two years later, on February 11, 1949, *The Times* reported that Tilden had been sentenced again for violating probation in the 1947 "morals case involving a 14-year-old boy." The former tennis champion had started serving one year in jail. The paper explained: under the terms of Tilden's original probation he "must never be in the company of a minor without the presence of a parent." Officers had "found a 17-year-old boy in Tilden's apartment." Tilden would also return to court to plead on "another charge of contributing to the delinquency of a 16-year-old youth."[18:6]
On February 18, *The Times* reported that Tilden had pleaded guilty to "molesting" the sixteen year old. Tilden had been sentenced to one year in jail, to run concurrently with his earlier punishment for parole violation."[18:6]
On December 19, 1949, *The Times* reported that Tilden had been released from jail, having served ten months and seventeen days.[44:4]

♀ BOOK REVIEW/MEDICAL

# 1947, January 26
*N. Y. Times Book Review:*
## Ferdinand Lundberg and Dr. Marynia F. Farnham's:
### *Modern Woman: The Lost Sex*

*Modern Woman: The Lost Sex* is said to have, in 1947, "aroused a storm of controversy for its thesis that women, in deserting their traditional homemaking and nurturing roles, had only made themselves, and society, the more unhappy."[39]

Reviewing the volume in the *Times,* anthropologist Margaret Mead discussed Lundberg's and Farnham's contention that "women as mothers transmit the psychological disorientation" fostered by contemporary society "to the next generation." Mead mentioned the authors' "great enthusiasm" for the male "role of patriarch," their assailing the doctrine that "women are to be regarded as potentially equal to men."

In the 1980s, Lundberg's and Dr. Farnham's authoritative formulation of a procreatively-defined masculinity and femininity may be seen as one expression of the post-war ideology of fecundity. Taken seriously and enacted by a large part of the population, this gave rise to the baby boom of the 1940s and '50s. The ideal of the true woman and man as prolific breeder is also reflected in the new, historically specific stress in the late 1940s on the homosexual as "sterile."*

In their book Lundberg and Dr. Farnham argued that it was "superficial" to define "masculinity" and "femininity" in terms of the "characteristics" allegedly predominating in each sex. According to the authors' own "deeply penetrating" definition, "basic masculinity and femininity" was

> *determined by the emotional attitude of any man or woman to his or her reproductive function. Basic masculinity or femininity is impaired in proportion as acceptance and assertion of the reproductive function is in any way qualified or denied. . . .*
> . . . Qualification may take the most basic form possible: refusal or inability to engage in heterosexual relations on any terms. Such inability is clearly seen in full-fledged homosexuals. The next most basic form [of qualification] is: engagement in heterosexual relations but with the complete intent to see to it that they do not eventuate in reproduction. . . . Bachelor and spinster both represent examples of impaired masculinity and femininity. . . .[381–82]

Historically, bachelors "were recognized as having among them a high percentage of masturbators and homosexuals."[336]

The basic "masculinity and femininity" of males and females could only be

---

*For the homosexual as "sterile" see *Parents' Magazine*'s response to the Kinsey Report in the entry of 1948, January 4. Also see 1949, June; and James Baldwin's comment on this notion, 1949, Summer.

determined by "uncovering inner feelings," how "fully they accept or reject their respective reproductive roles."[385]

The authors spoke of

> those who are completely unable to function with any person of the opposite sex, victims of a parental job very thoroughly accomplished. Such are both the passive and active homosexuals. The child unable to make the step to full genitality . . . does not stand still in development but goes back to earlier forms of gratification.

Such persons were "often quite infantile in character"—"preoccupied with anal and oral activities." Some 'sexually disturbed' women were "impervious to the sexual power of the normal male," and "some become overtly or covertly homosexual."[259–60]

Some celibate women "succeeded in diverting to some work activity psychic energy that would otherwise clamor for sexual outlet."

> In other cases, as with some celibate men, this sublimation . . . of sexual energy has not taken place and she is a homosexual, overt, covert or unconscious. Some such women have a good deal more to say about public and institutional policy than is socially desirable. The same holds true of certain homosexual men. Both, however, may be socially useful. Very often the free-living masculine or homosexual woman is a community asset, a "good neighbor." She will often perform better in social emergencies than the entirely feminine woman. In critically appraising them, therefore, we imply no condemnation. That they are distorted as personalities and project their distortion into society, however, cannot be doubted.[296]

♀ MEDICAL/PERSONAL TESTIMONY

# 1947, March
# Jane MacKinnon: "The Homosexual Woman"

The report of a self-described "homosexual woman" was presented, without comment, in *The American Journal of Psychiatry,* the "Official Organ of the American Psychiatric Association."[40]

MacKinnon accepted most of the dominant medical-moral judgments: that it was improper to act on her erotic feelings; that female homosexuals were necessarily "lonely" and often "disadvantaged"; that certain human qualities were essentially male or female; that psychiatrists could alleviate the general publics' "prejudice" by providing them with facts. Nevertheless, MacKinnon's essay indicates her identification with homosexual women as a group, and her desire to abolish the most blatant forms of heterosexual oppression.

It was "easy" to "conceal homosexual tendencies," especially for women, said MacKinnon, because a masculine woman attracts less attention than an effeminate man. In many cases, she is respected and admired for her manly qualities. As a woman and at the same time a homosexual and a member in good standing in her community and profession, I can vouch for the truth of this.

"Few people are at all conscious of our existence." The "general public" was more aware of male homosexuals.

Heterosexuals spoke of the homosexual "with scorn, pity or lasciviousness."

If you are not one of us, it is impossible to realize our feelings when this occurs. It is incredible to us that a well educated girl could make the following remark: "What do they look like? I wonder if I've ever seen one."

She denied that homosexuals had "secret means of recognizing one another:

Many women, not homosexual at all, wear suits a lot, cut their hair short and seem, . . . very unfeminine. The active homosexual often makes herself look very attractive. . . .[661]

"What is it like to be this way?" asked MacKinnon. "You are always lonely." Between "you and other women friends is a wall." And "Very few men desire platonic friendships" with women.

Unable to find love or its most acceptable substitute friendship, we frequently become psychiatric cases. You cannot keep a healthy state of mind if you are very lonely.
The inability to present an honest face to those you know eventually develops a certain deviousness. . . . Always pretending to be something you are not, moral laws lose their significance.[661]

"How do homosexuals feel about one another?" One of the "saddest facts" was that "we seldom like one another." This was because of conflicts between the four general types of homosexual women. "Type I" was "large," "tall," "successful in the business world." She "uses her manly qualities to advance her in her work." She "frequently wears tailored suits and dresses and does not care for fussy hair styles or frills of any kind." She desired an "emotionally dependent" partner. "Type II" was "small, feminine in appearance," and "aggressive." Types I and II "cannot be satisfied unless they dominate, that is, assume the role of the man." These types did not associate. "To a homosexual there is something incongruous, embarrassing, about making love to another like herself. The entire basis of the friendship is the pretense that one of the women is a man." It was "uncomfortable" to realize "that your associate feels just as you do instead of as a woman would." Type III "is not a real homosexual, but has strong tendencies that way." Although not the dominating type, Type III might take an active role, sexually. And some "real homosexuals" retained "just enough femininity to want to surrender themselves to another from time to time." Type IV were "those who capitalize on the curiosity of people who are willing to pay to see something disgusting," those "whose activities in night clubs in the larger cities attract many people looking for a thrill."[662]

Every homosexual had asked "Why do I have to be this way?" and searched for "peace of mind." MacKinnon had been nineteen and a sophomore in college, when she first heard the word "homosexual."

> The way it was mentioned in a conversation made me wonder if that was what was wrong with me. A quick look at the dictionary told me immediately that not only was I a homosexual, but that I was a most unpleasant individual, a person whom anyone decent would avoid like the plague. The next impressions I received of myself through reading were equally terrifying. I had heard of degenerates, but never realized that many would think me one. . . . Puzzled, bewildered, I could find nowhere a single kind word being said. Most of the writers of the books could not seem to understand that a homosexual is not a *term,* but a *person.* She has feelings just as anyone else. She has an additional burden—the necessity of being quiet about her troubles. She must occasionally be present when her friends talk about her and those like her in the most unpleasant terms. . . . Yet her friends and her employer, not knowing, like her a lot. If she were to say—and it is often a temptation—"I am a homosexual," the repercussions would be all that anyone could imagine.
>
> In college I lived in a dormitory for four years. . . . Every year I developed a terrific crush on some new girl, always an older one. . . . Had we known more about homosexuality, my friends probably would have recognized my situation. . . . they never did, any more than my parents did. The girls on whom I had the crushes enjoyed my infantile adoration. . . . When they became tired of it, they dropped me.[663]

Of a man's romantic interest, MacKinnon said, "a man's attentions bore us to such a point that we cannot even pretend to enjoy them." After relationships with men "I had proved to myself that there was nothing in it for me," and "I decided to have no more dates."[664]

"How do I fill my life?" she asked.

> I am well-to-do financially and can go places and travel. I take underprivileged children on outings, to circuses, etc. This satisfies my need for someone to be dependent on me. My energies, thus diverted, do not travel always in the same channel: that which develops sexual tension.
>
> Do we feel we have an advantage over the heterosexual person?
>
> From the point of view of leading a full and happy life, we are definitely at a disadvantage. No one is content who is so very lonely. No one is content who has to exercise so much will power to subdue sexual desire.
>
> However, there are advantages. We are frequently able to build successful careers in professions that are concerned with working with people. We are two-sided, often understand others better. Many of us are artistic, can act or write.
>
> The moods of depression to which I am subject may be brought on

by seeing someone very attractive who is equally unattainable. . . . [But] when feeling good, I am more than equal to anyone else. . . .[664]

"What can be done to correct our situation?" she asked. "Hardly anything has appeared in print which would warn parents of such tendencies in their children." "Like venereal disease and other hush-hush subjects, publications that deal with this problem are often banned."

The rapidly developing science of psychiatry, by bringing this out into the light, could help us by making available more facts of why we are as we are. Some of us torment ourselves with the idea that we are "evil." We are not degenerates, yet many refer to us in such terms. . . . Not only should people realize that there are lots of us, but they should have their attitudes toward us changed. Then the parent, instead of being horrified, will be able to help his child to adjust to a rather hard world.

She asked psychiatrists "to provide us with knowledge about our place in the order of things."

There will be fewer homosexual women in mental hospitals and psychiatric offices if we are recognized as human beings instead of as material for a chapter in a book on abnormal psychology.

BOOK REVIEW

# 1947, June 8
## *N. Y. Times Book Review:*
## John Horne Burns's *The Gallery*

Burns's nine "Portraits" of "persons involved, one way or another, with the Allied invasion of Italy," included the story of "a woman who runs a bar for homosexuals," said critic Richard Sullivan.[41]

In the sections called "Promenades" Burns's concern for peoples' "fumbling, perilous attachments and responsibilities" was evident. Also evident was a "bitterness against American crudity," and a "falling back upon sexual activity and a kind of vague, wistful brotherhood" as a "panacea" for the ills of war and mortality.

NEWS REPORT

# 1947, June 9
## *Newsweek:* "Homosexuals in Uniform"

"Although Army regulations strictly forbade the drafting of homosexuals, scores of these inverts managed to slip through induction centers," said a *News-*

*week* story.[42] "Homosexuals in Uniform," appeared on a page headed "Medicine."*

*Newsweek* reported:

> Between 3,000 and 4,000 were discharged for this abnormality; others were released as neuropsychiatric cases. Last week, with most of the records on homosexuals tabulated, Army medical officers, for the first time, summed up their strange story.
>
> To screen out this undesirable soldier-material psychiatrists in induction-station interviews tried to detect them (1) by their effeminate looks or behavior and (2) by repeating certain words from the homosexual vocabulary and watching for signs of recognition.

A "urinary hormone-secretion test" had been "too uncertain and too expensive to try on every inductee."

> Frequently, a latent homosexual, who had no knowledge of his predilection, was inducted, . . . only to develop alarming symptoms in camp and on the battlefield. Many of these men refused to admit homosexuality, even to themselves, and went to elaborate lengths to prove their masculinity. One of these ruses was regular and conspicuous absence without leave, always with female companions. Often the soldier's primary trouble was not discovered until he was hailed before Army psychiatrists on an AWOL [Absent Without Leave] charge.

The following "facts about homosexuality" were said to be gleaned from Army files:

> They [homosexuals] topped the average soldier in intelligence, education, and rating. . . .
>
> Including all ages, there were more whites than Negroes in this group. They came mostly from the cities, rather than the country.
>
> Although the majority had no family history of nervous or mental disease, many were from homes broken by divorce or separation. In many instances the man had been brought up by his mother as a girl, or had been an only son in a large family of girls. About half assumed a "feminine" role, the other half "masculine." Most were either unmarried or had made a failure of marriage.
>
> As a whole, these men were law-abiding and hard-working. In spite of nervous, unstable, and often hysterical temperaments, they performed admirably as office workers. Many tried to be good soldiers.

Once homosexuality had been detected, "the man was usually evacuated" to a general hospital

> where he received psychiatric treatment while a military board decided whether or not he was reclaimable. A good number begged to be cured, but doctors usually doubted their sincerity and recommended discharge. At

---

*For homosexuals and the World War II military also see 1946, July; and 1948, April.

least half of the confirmed homosexuals, one psychiatrist estimated, were well-adjusted to their condition, and neither needed nor would respond to treatment. The majority, therefore, were released.

"Early in the war,"

the homosexuals were sent up for court-martial, but in 1943–1944, the Army decided to separate most of them quietly with a "blue" discharge (neither honorable nor dishonorable . . .). Last week, however, the Army announced a stiff new policy, effective July 1.

Instead of leaving service with the vague and protective "blue" discharge, the homosexuals who had not been guilty of a definite offense would receive an "undesirable" discharge. A few of this group with outstanding combat records might receive an honorable discharge. Those found guilty of homosexual violence or of impairing the morals of minors would receive a "yellow" or dishonorable discharge.

♀ RESISTANCE

# 1947, June
## Lisa Ben: *Vice Versa*

In June 1947, in Los Angeles, a woman who identified herself as "Lisa Ben" (an anagram of "lesbian") began for the next nine months to type out twelve copies of a periodical called *Vice Versa,* "America's Gayest Magazine"—the earliest-known U. S. periodical published especially for lesbians.[43]

Interviewed, in 1978, by Leland Moss, Lisa Ben revealed that she had grown up on a farm in northern California. In high school, at age fifteen, a "mad crush" on a girl friend, Caprice, was spoken of openly and unselfconsciously by Lisa Ben until her mother asked her, " 'You and Caprice never did anything *wrong* together, did you?' "

In 1978, Lisa Ben said she was "not a militant feminist." But she had "always hated office work," which had been forced on her by her father. "I only went two years to college, and then . . . without discussing it with me at all, my parents enrolled me in business school." Later, during World War II, she settled in Los Angeles.

Then finally I got my own room with kitchen priveleges and from there I met some gay girls. They lived on the floor above me, and one day we were all sunbathing on the garage roof, and they got to talking and I got to listening and I thought, "Gee, I wonder if these are some of the girls that I would very dearly love to meet"—because by that time I realized my liaison with Caprice for what it was, and thought well gee, that's good, that's exactly what I want, I don't want boys. I would love to find somebody in L. A., but who? Maybe there's one in China, or one in Paris, but certainly none in

Lisa Ben (pseudonym), 1978 (photograph by Robert Haynes).

southern California—that's how dumb I was! So when I heard these girls talk, I started talking, and finally they asked me, "Do you like boys, or do you go out strictly with girls?" and I said, "If I had my rathers, I'd go out strictly with girls," and they said, "Have you always felt this way?" and I said, "Yes," and they said, "Well, then you're like we are," and I said, "You mean *you're* like that?" It was like a Victorian melodrama!

Then they took me to a girls' softball game; of course I wasn't the least interested in sports, but it gave me a chance to meet other gay girls. Then we went to the If Club, dancing, and ah! that was when I met lots of girls, and when I started up my magazine.

While working in a movie studio Lisa Ben "had a lot of time to myself" and twice each month typed out five carbons and one original of *Vice Versa.*

If anyone came around I had to zip it into my briefcase quick. . . . I would give it away to my friends. . . . I didn't want to make money off it, I just wanted to give it away. I had no idea how daring or dangerous this was. I used to mail them blithely out from the place where I worked, until somebody said, "Don't you know you could get in trouble for mailing this?" I didn't know why, there were no four-letter words or pictures in it. . . .

After that Lisa Ben distributed *Vice Versa* personally, asking readers to pass their copies on to others.

In June 1947, in the first issue of *Vice Versa,* an editorial asked:

Have you ever stopped to enumerate the many different publications to be found on the average news stands? There are publications for a variety of races and creeds. . . .

    Yet, there is one kind of publication which would, I am sure, have a great appeal to a definite group. . . .

But this "other type of publication" would cause "news stands carrying the crudest kind of magazines" to "find themselves severely censured."

Hence the appearance of *Vice Versa,* a magazine dedicated, in all seriousness, to those of us who will never quite be able to adapt ourselves to the iron-bound rules of Convention.

*Vice Versa* was "meant to be a medium through which we may express our thoughts, our emotions, our opinions"—as long as material was "within the bounds of good taste."[1–2]

Lisa Ben reviewed the film "Children of Loneliness," which she had gone to see "with great anticipation."* Newspaper ads had suggested it was based on *The Well of Loneliness,* "that most admirable novel." But the film "in no way resembled the book."

Despite the gaudy pictures outside the theatre displaying scantily-clad girls in amorous poses, the story concerned effeminate men as well as lesbians. Those in the audience who hoped to view scenes of lesbian love were sorely disappointed. There was not the slightest demonstration of affection between two women, . . . aside from a brief flash of one girl with her hand upon the shoulder of another. . . .

    Scenes of she-men were far more prevalent. . . .

    Prior to the story, a "scientific" preface to the film is delivered on the screen . . . by a doctor and social worker. . . . If this is the type of social worker to which our society is exposed, then Heaven help our civilization! The references to homosexuality as a "weakness" and an "evil" are an insult and an abomination to any clear-thinking and right-minded persons, whether normal or a member of what is so aptly referred to as the "third sex."

    "Let this picture be shown to every adult, so that he (or she) will know how to combat such abnormal love and will not be dragged into the depths of degradation" is the moral that the doctor preaches. Ah, self-styled judges, who smugly carve the standards for society! If only you would not condemn them as freaks, as weaklings, tragedies of nature, . . . despise, scorn, or laugh

*The seven-reel film *Children of Loneliness* was registered with the U.S. Copyright Office, November 8, 1934, by Jewell Productions, Inc. It was written and directed by Richard C. Kahn, screen adaptation by Howard Bradford; see *Motion Pictures 1912–1939. Catalog of Copyright Entries* (U.S. Government Copyright Office, Library of Congress, 1951). Also see Russo, *The Celluloid Closet,* pp. 104–07. Russo says the film was rejected for showing by the film industry censorship office in May 1939, because it "is about sex perversion."

at them. If only the third sex could be recognized and accepted as equally as "honorable" as their smug and uncomprehending fellows! . . .

The film told the complicated story of Eleanor Gordon's and Paul Van Tyne's struggles against homosexual attraction. Paul takes Eleanor to an "odd cafe." Eleanor asks: " 'What sort of people are these?' " Paul answers: " 'These are the Children of Loneliness, Nature's tragic mistakes, trying to forget—.' " Bobby Allen, a woman once in love with Eleanor, tries to throw acid in her face. Dave, a "young and promising lawyer" in love with Eleanor, intervenes, "accidently spilling the acid on Bobby, who runs screaming into the street and is killed by a speeding automobile." Dave and Eleanor's romance is rekindled: "Bobby's death shriek provides a background for their first kiss." Paul commits suicide, "clutching futilely at the flimsy feminine costume" he had worn to a "drag party."

The doctor reappeared to assert the film's redeeming social significance. " 'If, by showing this picture, *one person* has received benefit thereby, if *one person* has been reclaimed—.' "

Lisa Ben called the film

a vicious piece of propaganda. Homosexuals are shown in the most unfavorable light, and in the cafe scenes are depicted as a depraved, fiendish and drunken lot. The few close-up scenes of effeminate men in the cafe were met by wisecracks and snickers by quite a few in the audience. . . .

She admitted, there was "degrading" behavior associated with homosexuality, just as there was with "so-called 'normal' love." But wouldn't homosexuals "be less neurotic" if "convention did not force them to live a life of deceit and subterfuge, to seem to be what they are not?" Could not "homosexual love" be "as honorable, as respectable, and as clean and fine as heterosexual?"[13]

An editorial in the second issue of *Vice Versa,* in July 1947, ended with a plea to keep the periodical " 'just between us girls!' "[2]

A review of *The Well of Loneliness* (see 1928, August 30; 1929, January 2), said: "There are an increasing number of novels" about "lesbian relations," but the "most beautifully and comprehensively written" was Radclyffe Hall's. That author provided insight "into the problems that Stephen and her kind must face in this unsympathetic, heterosexual world."

The central female character, Stephen Gordon, was described by Lisa Ben as "physically feminine and mentally masculine," and as born "when women had more sheltered lives than they now do."[3] Stephen's love, as a child, for a housemaid, "will probably recall to the minds of the more sympathetic readers their own similar youthful crushes."[4] Lisa Ben quoted Stephen Gordon's speech to her mother in which Stephen admitted being " 'different,' " but affirmed: " 'what I will never forgive is your daring to try and make me ashamed of my love. I'm not ashamed of it, there's no shame in me.' "[6]

Stephen finally renounced her lover, Mary Llewellyn, so Mary could marry a man and lead a 'normal' life, dooming Stephen "to a desolate and lonely existence." But Lisa Ben "heartily recommended" the novel to "every reader of *Vice Versa.*"

> It carries a powerful message—a plea against senseless persecution and intolerance, and despite its tragic nature, the novel imparts words of hope and inspiration for members of the third sex. It is an incentive not to give way to despair, no matter how unsurmountable the obstacles, no matter how bitter the persecution.[10]

In the same issue Lisa Ben reviewed and recommended the French film *Club de Femmes* (see 1937, October 20), whose setting was a women's residence, "a veritable Paradise for some who have no particular craving for masculine company." In the club's gym one saw "energetic 'tom-girls' romping with boxing gloves, or at play on the trapeze."[12]

"Throughout the film, with serene dignity and grace, moves Alice, . . . who is aware that she is 'different,' but does not know why." In "a swimming pool scene" Alice's "eye's yearningly follow the progress of a young curvaceous blonde."[13]

Alice and the blonde become friends when Alice helps her with her spelling and grammar. "One of the most expressive scenes shows Alice, bending lovingly over her friend, dictating a passage from a poem. . . . 'Come away with me, we too shall live together.' " But Alice still does not understand "her own nature."

When the club's switchboard operator, a procuress for her male companion, dupes the blonde into becoming his victim, Alice murders the operator. She then confesses to the club's doctor who "denounces Alice as an unnatural monster" and banishes her "to a leper colony."

The film was "highly recommended . . . because the presence of a lesbian . . . is handled in a sane, intelligent manner rather than furnishing the usual subject for harmful propaganda or mere sensationalism."[14–15]

In the same July issue of *Vice Versa* appeared a letter from a male heterosexual friend of Lisa Ben's, who wrote: "As possibly the only 'jam' [straight] recipient of your first issue, I wish to thank you for the privilege of seeing this unique publication." He continued: "An amazing venture, this, like woman suffrage in its time, and other 'lost causes.' " Though *Vice Versa* was then circulated "in the 'Uranian underground' only," he felt

> the day may come when it may enjoy a wider distribution as a medium of propaganda for this lost cause. Who was it? Gary Cooper, I believe, in "Mr. Smith Does Good Deeds"—who once said, "It is only the Lost Causes that are worth fighting for."[17]

"Like nudism, another unpolitical 'ism,' " he followed the lesbian cause "with sympathetic interest." He thought the two causes were "akin" as both aimed "to correct the distorted vision of Society, which . . . sees a fancied evil in the human body." Of course "we may all be atomized before the world wises up on the confusions."

In the meantime—"The world is full of people, and the people are full of prejudice," as Charles Boyer so truthfully tragically stated in the filmplay, "Shanghai."

"It might prove a helpful form of emotional therapy," he suggested, "if the gay-born would repudiate the phrase 'Nature's tragic mistakes' and speak instead, say, of 'Nature's interesting experiments.' "[18]

In August 1947, the third issue of *Vice Versa* included a review of the film *Turnabout* (see 1947, July 27). Portraying "the mutual exchange of a wife's and a husband's personalities," the film was said to be "fraught with amusing innuendos."[9]

A production in the Los Angeles area of Jean-Paul Sartre's play "No Exit" was also reviewed (see 1946, November 27). The lesbian, Inez, "has been condemned to eternal torment for falling in love with a married woman and acquainting her with the lack of qualities in her husband, which presumably caused the bewildered wife to commit suicide." Of the play's three characters, Lisa Ben "thought Inez was the least deserving of being consigned to eternal damnation."[15] "The audience . . . was a motley lot," said the reviewer.

> There were quite a few nattily dressed lads who seemed to come together by pairs, or in groups. Here and there could be seen a neatly tailored woman, alone, or with a woman companion. Some of them who came together were not the tailored type. If they expected an exhibition of unreserved lesbian affection they were disappointed.

"It is refreshing indeed," Lisa Ben concluded, to find a lesbian character presented "without apology or subterfuge."[14]

A second letter from Lisa Ben's male heterosexual friend referred to her praise for *The Well of Loneliness:* "It must be heartening to you that it is everywhere available in a dollar edition, and not classified as something contraband to be sold covertly, under the counter at a premium price." He added: "Wouldn't it be strange if Hollywood should some day 'discover' the Third Sex and film a series of problem pictures around the subject? . . .[16]

In the fourth issue of *Vice Versa,* in September 1947, Lisa Ben reported that she was "astonished to find so many potential subscribers to 'America's Gayest Magazine.' " But "Since *Vice Versa* can only be reproduced six copies at a time, via typewriter and carbon paper, I am finding it extremely difficult to comply with requests" for copies.[1]

A review of Dorothy Baker's novel *Trio* (see 1943, July 4) concluded: "The characterization of the lesbian as a selfish, deceitful woman is not very likely to go far in promoting tolerance toward lesbianism."[3]

In a major essay Lisa Ben declared: "Whether the unsympathetic majority approves or not," the "Third Sex is here to stay." The world was becoming more aware of "those in our midst who feel no attraction of the opposite sex."

"It is not an uncommon sight to observe mannishly attired women, or even those dressed in more feminine garb, strolling along the streets hand in hand, or even arm in arm," indicating more than "mere friendliness."

> And bright colored shirts, chain bracelets, loud socks and ornate sandals are increasingly in evidence on many of the fellows passing by. The war had a great deal to do with influencing the male to wear jewellery, I believe, with the introduction of dog tags, identification bracelets, etc. Whether the war, by automatically causing segregation of men from female company for long periods of time, has influenced fellows to become more aware of their own kind, is a moot question.

For "quite some time," she added, "the majority of teen-aged girls seem to prefer jeans and boys' shirts to neat feminine attire." She asked: "might not the masculine garb influence them toward adopting boyish mannerisms? . . ."

> Night clubs featuring male and female impersonators are becoming increasingly prevalent. Even cafes and drive-ins intended for the average customer, when repeatedly patronized by inverts, tend to reflect a gay atmosphere. Such places are ever the center of attraction for a "gay crowd," and become known as likely rendezvous in which to meet those of similar inclinations.

Books with lesbian themes like *Diana* (see 1939) and *The Well of Loneliness* were "available in inexpensive editions," even in "the corner drug stores." With the dissemination of such "knowledge"

> homosexuality is becoming less and less a "taboo" subject, and although still considered by the general public as contemptible . . . I venture to predict that there will be a time in the future when gay folk will be accepted as part of regular society.[4]

Once tabooed subjects were now themes of films, and "the time will come" when Stephen Gordon will step from Hall's "admirable" *Well of Loneliness* "on to the silver screen." Even *Vice Versa*, perhaps, "might be the forerunner of better magazines dedicated to the Third Sex."

> Currently appearing in many popular magazines are comprehensive articles on psychological differences between the two sexes, which are enlightening many women as to the unbridgable gaps between the opposite sexes, and why most of them [women and men], in this rapidly changing world, are unable to come to terms with each other on a mental and emotional basis.
>
> In days gone by, when women's domain was restricted to the fireside, marriage and a family was her only prospect. The home was a little world around which life revolved. . . . But in these days of frozen foods, motion picture palaces, compact apartments, modern innovations and female independence, there is no reason why a woman should have to look to a man for food and shelter in return for raising his children and keeping his house in order, unless she really wants to. Today, a woman may live independently from man if she so chooses, and carve out her own career. Never before have circumstances and conditions been so suitable for those of lesbian tendencies.[5]

In the fifth issue of *Vice Versa,* in October 1947, Lisa Ben wrote of the meaning to her of Halloween. October thirty-first was often "referred to as 'All Saints' Day,' " the one day when "demons, vampires, lost souls and the forgotten of God, all those beings which civilization fears, holds in contempt, denies existence and despises, are said to be free to roam the earth unrestrained, uninhibited."

> The legend of these outcast creatures gathering together on this one Night of the year, casting aside their masks, chains and shackles and revelling in their own true guise, has always had a great appeal to me, even from earliest childhood. Although Hallowe'en is not set aside as such, I have always considered it an appropriate day for those of us who must masquerade the other three hundred and sixty-four days of the year.[1]

An item in *Vice Versa* quoted the lyrics of a "beautiful" record, "Pervertida," which Lisa Ben had first heard recently, played on a radio program devoted to Latin-American music. On this record a male sang in Spanish: "Perverted lady whom I adore/ . . . all my life I will love you,/Even though they call you 'Pervertida.' " (The record featured Chucho Martinez and the Columbia Broadcasting System Orchestra, conducted by Terig Tucci, music by Augustin Lara.)[13]

The sixth issue of *Vice Versa,* in November 1947, contained Lisa Ben's comment, in reference to Thanksgiving, that "those of us to whom this magazine is dedicated have an extra reason to be thankful—our ability to appreciate feminine beauty."

> This sensitivity to feminine loveliness I regard as a blessing, and not a misfortune. How much more beautiful, in every way, are women than men! . . . How thankful I am to have been born in womanly form and yet to possess the capacity of appreciating to the fullest extent feminine beauty![1]

A review of the book *Diana* (see 1939), the story of a lesbian that "purports to be an autobiography," endorsed the volume whether it was "fact or fiction."[1] Lisa Ben declared: "Though the trials and tribulations of Diana are by no means minimized, it is gratifying to see that this book concludes on an optimistic note." She added: "Paragraphs describing in detail Diana's love-life leave little more to be wished for."[7]

In a discussion of language, Lisa Ben declared: "We gay folk have long needed an adequate vocabulary to express . . . our way of life."[9] The "widely used" terms "butch" and "fluff" (for "masculine" and "feminine" lesbians) Lisa Ben thought were "lacking somewhat in dignity." She had been told that the terms "Masons" and "Orders" had once been used in reference to the same distinction. The word "femme," which was "common in gay parlance," was "more suitable." Lisa Ben herself had "introduced two original expressions" in *Vice Versa:*

> "Tykes," a modification of a similar term of questionable taste which is in common use now, is applicable to all gay girls without reference to specific

temperament. "Laddies" (which would be "ladies" without that extra "d") pertains to all gay fellows in general.

She explained, the "tyke . . . is at ease with either a passive or an aggressive partner. In New York, so I am told, the expression is 'ki-ki,' but no one elsewhere seems to be familiar with this peculiar term."* She suggested: "We also need special words for 'husband,' 'wife,' and the state of 'marriage.'" Lisa Ben thought "coupled" or "teamed" could replace "marriage."

> And how about a term to designate those who are prejudiced against us? One little friend of mine solves this problem by using the jive term "square" to signify persons with a hostile feeling.[11]

Elsewhere in the same issue Lisa Ben thanked "a blond, curly-topped tyke," a medical student, for a letter that said: "I, personally, felt that sought-after feeling of belonging to a group somewhere in 'society,' while reading with 'you.'" *Vice Versa* was intended to impart just such a "feeling of camaraderie" and "spiritual communion" said the editor.[12]

In the December 1947, issue of *Vice Versa*, Lisa Ben reported:

> Seven short months ago—when I originated *Vice Versa*—the circulation of this publication was limited to just *one* reader! I knew no others to whom the magazine might appeal. I never supposed that *Vice Versa* would enjoy such popularity, or lead to so many pleasant and stimulating friendships as I have since found.
> Christmas, so I'm told, is the time for "Peace on Earth and Good Will toward Men." In our case, I think we'd best amend that last statement to "Women"![1]

The January 1948 *Vice Versa* contained a satirical short story by Lisa Ben about a drunk and violent heterosexual male's adventures in the "Fruitvale Heights" district of "Jamiston."[2-11] (In this "odd" part of town the drunk notices a woman streetcar conductor and thinks: "The war was over. Why didn't these women stick to home? Women were only good for one thing, anyhow—.")[4] Lisa Ben also reported being "rather irked by recent sensational newspaper accounts containing derogatory remarks about us." Writing the satire had provided a "release for my outraged feelings".[15]†

---

*Re "ki-ki": A source whose citation I've unfortunately lost (possibly another issue of *Vice Versa*) suggested that the lesbian use of the term "ki-ki" derived from a Mary Pickford film of that title. *The New York Times* review of Pickford's *Kiki*, March 6, 1931 (16:1) spoke of the "inexhaustible energy and verve" which that actress brought to her interpretation of the "mischievous hoyden of the [Broadway musical] chorus." As "Kiki" Pickford was "busy raising general havoc." She played a "noisy little creature" who lost her coveted place in the chorus—for biting a sister worker, no less." (She also finally won the "grudging affection of the man she loves.") An earlier film version of *Kiki* starred Norma Talmadge; see *N. Y. Times*, April 6, 1926, 26:4. Both films were adapted from a David Belasco play *Kiki*; see *N. Y. Times*, November 30, 1921, 13:1; December 4, 1921, VII, 1:2; December 11, 1921, VI, 1:4. For a male homosexual use of "kiki" see 1941, Legman.

†It would be interesting to study those "recent sensational newspaper accounts," as they may have also played some role in provoking Henry Hay's first formulation in August 1948, in Los Angeles, of the idea for a homosexual liberation organization; see *GAH*, p. 408.

The ninth and final issue of *Vice Versa,* in February 1948, featured a review of *Wasteland,* the novel by Jo Sinclair.* *Vice Versa*'s reviewer said that *Wasteland* told the story of Jake Brown and "his boyish sister, Deborah," who has . . . accepted the place of the strongest and most responsible member of the family."[2] The reviewer explained:

> forced into the position of a man, Debby has developed naturally from a tow-haired tomboy who led the neighborhood gang of boys and helped her father fix his truck, into a Lesbian. In an attempt to understand herself and escape the shame she feels at her differentness, Debby has sought the help of a psychiatrist. . . .[3]

"Throughout the book" Debby's story runs as an undercurrent to Jake's."

> We see Debby first through Jake's eyes as a freak; someone he has seen the neighbor women point to and laugh [at]; someone he could not bear the thought of his friends . . . knowing as his sister. . . . he is afraid she is "bad" in some way he cannot bear to face.[4]

All Jake knows is that Debby is " 'different.' "

> In her perplexity Debby has turned to the defense of all persecuted peoples. She has sought friends among Negroes, has identified herself with the Jews as a persecuted group. In such subject matter she has found material for her writing, at which she is moderately successful. Having learned to understand herself through the psychiatric treatment, she has lost the sense of shame which formerly tortured her, and has classed the homosexual group with other underprivileged minorities as people with a cause to be defended, a place to carve for themselves in the social fabric of the nation. She has ceased to pity herself or members of any minority as cripples.

*Wasteland* depicted

> the homosexual as a citizen, as a person with a place to take, proudly, in a properly educated society, rather than as the victim of an affliction or as a case history. There is none of the mental sickness, the morbidity too frequently associated with such characters in most current fiction.
>     Nor is [there] any of the self-pitying, maudlin over-dramatization of the plight of the invert, too often found in the work of inverts themselves when writing on the subject. . . . The psychiatrist gives Debby a clean bill of mental health, and commends her adjustment to society. . . .[4]

The psychiatrist explained Debby to Jake: " 'She was the one who fought for the right of your mother not to weep.' " Debby had done all the

> things which should have been done by her father, by her brothers. Your family was on its way to defeat, but her insistence, her strength, fought for the life of it. She had to throw off all weakness and softness, all femininity.

---

*This review, by a contributor identified as "Kit," provides an interesting contrast to that in *The New York Times Book Review,* which did not mention the lesbianism of the second major character; see 1946, February 17.

. . . If she had despaired, or wept, or been soft—as a girl might have—the whole family would have crashed with her.

The reviewer concluded:

Whether or not the reader accepts this diagnosis, this . . . excellent psychological novel . . . has won an important literary prize [the Harper Prize, 1946]. It has doubtless also won a reasonable amount of thinking people to accept in part the view that the homosexual may be an intelligent, healthy, decent member of society rather than a degenerate.[5]

In a letter to Lisa Ben, "Kit," the reviewer of *Wasteland,* called the publication of *Vice Versa* "such a courageous venture—though perhaps not a very wise one"—a reference to the associated dangers. Kit praised Lisa Ben for continuing the publication, though there was "such a slight chance of ever receiving much credit." In answer, Lisa Ben admitted it took "courage of sorts" to continue the magazine without getting much response from the readers for whom it was intended. But she did not feel her work on *Vice Versa* was in vain: "there is a definite need for such a magazine among the gay folk. . . . It is my personal contribution to others of my ilk, meant to provide an outlet for the creative self-expression so often, of necessity, pent up within us."[13–14]

FILM REVIEW

# 1947, July 23
## *N. Y. Times: Cross Fire*

The film *Cross Fire* had been adapted from the novel *The Brick Fox Hole* by Richard Brooks.[44] Commenting on the novel in 1945, in *The New York Times Book Review,* Dan S. Norton had criticized it, saying: "Most of the characters are straight from the tough fiction factory: a lone wolf, full of irony and pity; a true wife; an imitation Circe; a prostitute with an undersized but genuine heart of gold; a sly, sadistic villain; a homosexual." In this literary genre "a homosexual" had become a stock character; that was not true of movies.

In the film *Cross Fire,* reviewed in *The Times* in 1947, the homosexual had been replaced by a Jew, an interesting substitution considering the new and developing consciousness of various "minority" group persecutions.* That interchangeability of Jew and homosexual indicates one of the limits of the minority concept. The equation of Jew and homosexual as minorities denied what is different and specific to each group's history. In this case, the transmutation of homosexual into Jew suppressed the recognition of a specific link between antihomosexuality, violence, and heterosexual masculinity. In 1947, the idea of the

*For the use of the "minority" concept see that heading in the index. For another equation of Jew and homosexual as minorities see 1946, February 17.

homosexual as victim of social intolerance was still too radical to screen. The film makers' substitution of Jew for homosexual simultaneously suggested an implicit analogy, and continued the dominant deathly silence about homosexuals as victims of oppression. In 1947, the Jew was a safe stand-in for the cinematically invisible homosexual; homosexuality was still the love they dared not film. Given this background, Bosley Crowther's review of *Cross Fire* in *The Times* takes on an ironic resonance.

In regard to the film's theme of "intolerance, supported by loyalty," there is a further irony. The director of *Cross Fire,* Edward Dmytryk, would later serve six months in jail as one of "The Hollywood Ten," a group of screen writers and directors who were found in contempt of Congress for refusing, in October 1947, to testify before the House Un-American Activities Committee about their associations with the U. S. Communist Party. While in jail Dmytryk would issue a statement attacking the Party. In 1951, after aligning himself with the toughest anti-Communists in Hollywood, he would be considered rehabilitated and loyal, and would begin to work again. *Cross Fire* opened a few months before the 1947 loyalty hearings in Hollywood.

In *The Times* Bosley Crowther praised producer Dore Schary and other contributors to *Cross Fire* for

> a frank and immediate demonstration of the brutality of religious bigotry as it festers and fires ferocity in certain seemingly normal American minds. . . . For here, without hints or subterfuges, they have come right out and shown that such malice—in this case, anti-Jewish—is a dark and explosive sort of hate which, bred of ignorance and intolerance, can lead to extreme violence.

In the film, a man

> suspected of murder, refers to the victim as a "Jew boy"—that is all. A little later, this same man—an ex-soldier—lets slip some further anti-Jewish prejudice. And then the audience comes to realize, as does the district attorney probing the case, that here is the sole motive for the murder: a vicious and drunken hate.
>
> But then . . . there emerges an equally-strong resistance to the unmasking of the suspected man. . . . And thus is evolved a drama in which intolerance, supported by loyalty, is pitted against social justice and the righteousness of humanity.

Crowther mentioned that the film was adapted from *The Brick Foxhole,* adding: "Incidentally, the motive for murder which was brought out in the book has been changed for this present film version—and to remarkably advantageous effect."

BOOK REVIEW

## 1948, January 11
### *N. Y. Times Book Review:* Gore Vidal's *The City and the Pillar*

Reviewer C. V. Terry began by suggesting that there were already too many novels about homosexuals:[45]

> Presented as the case history of a standard homosexual, this novel adds little that is new to a groaning shelf. Mr. Vidal's approach is coldly clinical: there is no real attempt to involve the reader's emotions, as the author sets down Jimmie's life story. . . . the over-all picture is as unsensational as it is boring. Jimmie comes through as a dull young ox indeed—a doomed young ox who seems suspiciously in love with his doom, and wearies the reader beyond endurance with his endless self-questioning.

Vidal's earlier novel *Williwaw* had been "more than promising: this time he has produced a novel as sterile as its protagonist."*

♀ RESISTANCE

## 1948, January 14
### *N. Y. Times Book Review; Time; Parents' Magazine:*
### Alfred Kinsey's and others'
#### *Sexual Behavior in the Human Male*

"Now, after decades of hush-hush, comes a book that is sure to create an explosion and to be bitterly controversial," declared Dr. Howard A. Rusk in a *Times* review.[46]

This "is by far the most comprehensive study yet made of sex behavior," and Alfred Kinsey was "a brave man." He had the "courage to fight taboos and prejudices, preconceptions based on ignorance and the confusion that comes from translating one's personal experience as universal practice." While gathering data Kinsey had faced "violent opposition from medical groups and school boards, psychiatrists and sheriffs, scientific colleagues and politicians." However, many other groups had cooperated in the study, and it had been funded by the Rockefeller Foundation.

"Cold, dispassionate fact" about the sexual behavior of males on "every level of our social strata" was presented in the report with "scientific objectivity" and "without moralizing."

The existence of "wide variations in sex concepts and behavior" were

---

*For the homosexual as "sterile" see that heading in the index.

demonstrated. "Most prejudices" about sexual activities were shown to result from "conflict between the attitudes of different social levels." The "wide range of human sexual behavior" raised questions about "what is 'normal' and 'abnormal,' and where such terms fit in a scientific study."

> Dr. Kinsey points out that homosexual experience is much more common than previously thought. He indicates, however, that this is an extremely difficult problem to analyze "as very few individuals are all black or all white," and that one homosexual experience does not classify the individual as a homosexual. He decries the use of the noun, and finds that there is often a mixture of both homo- and heterosexual experience.

The "stability of our sexual mores," deduced from a comparison of the sexual activities of older and younger generations, indicated there were not "constant changes in such mores," said Rusk.

"After the initial impact" of the Kinsey report, its results would be "healthy," leading to a reexamination of "the legal criteria by which we renounced and condemn individual sex behavior."

Rusk quoted Kinsey: "if circumstances be propitious, most individuals might have become conditioned in any direction, even into activities which they now consider quite unacceptable."

The "facts" presented by Kinsey "indicate the necessity to review some of our legal and moral concepts" in a spirit of "tolerance and understanding."[VII, 3:1]

On March 7, a *New York Times* subhead proclaimed: "The Now Famous Kinsey Report Is Criticized On Statistical and Sociological Grounds." Two University of Pennsylvania sociologists had questioned the report's finding that "37 per cent" of the male population "have had some homosexual experience between adolescence and old age." Criticism focused on Kinsey's method of obtaining a fair sample of the population. Also criticized was Kinsey's contrasting human sexual behavior "with 'normal mammalian behavior.' " Kinsey was said to dwell

> on the "Tyranny of the mores" on the "victims of the mores". . . . If we were to judge sexual practices in terms of "normal mammalian behavior," all culturally affected behavior would be "abnormal," [the two sociologists] point out.[IV, 9:6]

On June 4, *Time* magazine reported another "devastating scientific attack" on the Kinsey report by "a prominent psychiatrist," Dr. Lawrence S. Kubie. The psychiatrist said the report's

> "implication that because homosexuality is prevalent we must accept it as 'normal,' or as a happy and a healthy way of life, is wholly unwarranted."

*Time* also reported: "In a speech last week to the American Psychopathological Association, in Manhattan," Dr. Kinsey had argued that most sexual behavior considered "abnormal" was "part & parcel of our inheritance as mammals and is natural and normal biologically." It is, he said, scientifically sound to look to mammalian background "as sources of human behavior." He was seconded by Yale Psychologist Frank Beach who has studied sex habits from shrews (mouselike mammals) to humans. Dr. Beach reported that homosexuality is common among some animals.

Columbia University Psychiatrist Abram Kardiner attacked what he called Kinsey's plea for tolerance toward perversion. Moral laws that separate men from the other animals are not "historical happenstance"—they grew, he said, out of the necessity for control.[76–77]

"What Parents Can Learn from the Kinsey Report" was discussed in *Parents' Magazine* in October by Dr. O. Spurgeon English, a professor of Psychiatry at Temple University, and Constance J. Foster.

People who had not had "an adequate rehearsal for love in their early upbringing" often

> find themselves in dark alleys and on dead-end streets, seeking expression for their instinctual drives in socially unacceptable ways such as homosexual relationships or promiscuity in and out of marriage.

Such persons sought substitutes for the "rich creativity of sexual expression and the begetting of children in happy homes." These persons sought satisfaction

> in mistaken and unfortunate ways that run counter to the cultural standards we have set up for our civilization, which are the monogamous ones of marriage and the establishment of a family.[144]

The Kinsey report should provoke parents to ask: "Do we make our children feel as welcome and wanted as a May morning through all the days of their lives with us?" Did parents mistakenly isolate sex from other aspects of life? "Sex," it was suggested, properly "enters into history, literature, art, music, newspaper headlines and even into dinner table discussions," as much as it did into "biology."[145]

"The findings of the Kinsey report that bother parents most are the greater prevalence of homosexuality than we suspected, and the amount of premarital sexual activity engaged in by young people in their late teens."

"Homosexuality," it was explained,

> is not a reflection on sex but only a sign that it has been diverted into the wrong channels, according to our social and cultural standards. It is not wicked or unfortunate since it is often sterile instead of creative. . . .* To receive physical comfort and satisfaction without accepting the full responsibility of a relationship with a person of the opposite sex which involves the passing on of life is to go against what are judged civilization's best interests.

---

*For the homosexual as "sterile," the obverse of the heterosexual as fecund, see my comment on Lundberg and Farnham's expression of the post-War procreative imperative, 1947, January 26.

"But homosexuals are not born—they are made." They "are made in the home that rears them." Cited was a boy who's mother "shows dissatisfaction with his sex," and who's father "inhibits the process of identification with the male." This was

> fertile soil for the development of the homosexual character structure which, according to Dr. Kinsey's findings, affects an astoundingly large percentage of the masculine population.*

A second example was a girl whose father

> tries to make her as much like a boy as possible, encouraging her to climb trees, play baseball, and become aggressive and independent like a boy.

Her mother, if not interested in her daughter's "friendship," might inspire in her daughter "no wish to emulate a woman." This girl might grow up without "any wish to play a woman's role in life."[146–47]

The Kinsey report was said to pass "no judgment on homosexuality." It was "equally futile" for parents to "condemn or condone." Parents could "only realize the risks"—and know how to prevent the development of "the homosexual personality."

The authors advocated "understanding" of those who have "through no fault of their own been unable to fall in love with a person of the opposite sex." They "would like to if they could and they suffer from the rebuffs the world accords them."[147]

♀ BOOK REVIEW

# 1948, January 18
### N. Y. Times Book Review:
### Truman Capote's Other Voices, Other Rooms

Under the heading "Deep-South Guignol" critic Carlos Baker commented on the first book by a twenty-three-year-old author, Truman Capote.[47] The critic assumed the necessity of being "fully" "male or female," and discussed the "tomboy" as "nocturnal" swamp wanderer (a junior vampire?).

"The taste for the bizarre, the eccentric, the over-subtle and the attenuated has dominated one whole segment of southern writing," said the critic, citing

---

*Kinsey never spoke of a "homosexual character structure," and in fact opposed such concepts, stressing the wide variety of persons who sometimes participated in homosexual acts and/or experienced homosexual feelings.

among others, Poe, Kate Chopin, Carson McCullers, Eudora Welty, and Capote's "gothic inventiveness."*

One character in Capote's book was "Cousin Randolph, a middle-aged cherub in Chinese-silk pajamas, lost somewhere between the worlds of male and female and powerless to be fully born into either." The novel's "other grotesques" included a

> tomboy, Idabel, given to soft drinks and nocturnal roaming in the swamp. The interest is something like that of a spectator at a Mardi Gras parade: the wonder is what will be thought of next.

MEDICAL

# 1948, April
## Dr. William C. Menninger:
## Homosexuals and the military

Dr. Menninger had served as chief consultant in Neuropsychiatry to the surgeon general of the U. S. Army, 1943–46. A chapter on homosexuality in Menninger's book *Psychiatry in a Troubled World: Yesterday's War and Today's Challenge* is a concise historical summary of U. S. Army policy and actions toward homosexuals during World War II.[48] Menninger also hints at the enormous impact of the war as an experience of male-male intimacy. (The impact on female-female intimacy of the sexual segregation and work force transformations of both World War I and II are suggested elsewhere, as is the similar impact of other American wars.)† It is

---

*Kate Chopin's works and life include significant female-female intimacy; see her novel *A Heidelberg Romance;* and her relationship with Katherine Garesche, discussed by Per Seyersted, *Kate Chopin: A Critical Biography* (Baton Rouge, Louisiana: Louisiana State University Press, 1969), pp. 18–19, 48, 184. Carson McCullers's works and life include significant homosexual themes; for the 1940s see *The Heart Is A Lonely Hunter* (Boston: Houghton, Mifflin, 1940), and *Reflections in a Golden Eye* (Boston: Houghton Mifflin, 1941), reviewed in the *Times Book Review,* March 2, 1941, p. 6.

†For the American Revolution see Alexander Hamilton's love letters to John Laurens, *GAH,* pp. 452–56, and Deborah Sampson's war-time romances, *GAH,* pp. 212–14.

For the Civil War see Whitman's letters, prose, and poetry, and the bits of soldiers' letters to Whitman, in the New York University Press edition of Whitman's writings; for this war also see General Philip Sheridan's description of two Amazons in the Union army between whom "an intimacy had sprung up," *GAH,* pp. 227–28. Also see the romantic adventures of Sarah Emma Edmonds Seelye, entry of 1883, May 27, and *GAH,* pp. 599 n. 1, 601 n. 31.

For the U. S. war against the Filipino independence movement, 1898–99, see the "beastly acts between ourselves" cited by Edgar Lee Masters, *Spoon River Anthology* (1915; N. Y.: Collier Books, 1962), the poem of Harry Williams, pp. 220–21.

For World War I see "Homosexuality: A Military Menace," by Dr. Abrams, 1918; the comments of Dr. Constance Long, 1919; and references to female participation in the war cited in Radclyffe Hall's *Well of Loneliness.*

For World War II, see Pat Bond's narrative in the film *Word is Out;* also see Lisa Ben, 1947, June, p. 624; Allan Bérubé, "Marching to a Different Drummer: Lesbian and Gay GIs in World War II," *Advocate,* October 15, 1981, pp. 20–24; the war novels of the late 1940s and '50s discussed by Austen, *Playing,* pp. 158–70; and various documents of the 1940s concerning homosexuals and the military quoted in the present book.

For the Korean War, see Sanford Friedman, *Totempole* (N.Y.: Dutton, 1965).

ironic that same-sex camaraderie, affection, and eroticism should so commonly be experienced in the context of killing.

In his article Dr. Menninger referred to a "predominance of homosexual interests," defined as "emotional attachments to members of our own sex." These were a "quite normal" stage of development between ages eight and fifteen. "Youth organizations such as the Boy Scouts, the Girl Scouts, . . . and the Campfire Girls thrive because of this normal interest in persons of the same sex."[223]

The "participation of men and women in separated social groups, clubs, fraternal organizations, and religious societies" were also called a "form of sublimated homosexual gratification."[223]

> Certainly there is no better example than the wartime Army of an organization built on entirely masculine lines. Therefore, in a technical, psychiatric sense, it was fundamentally a homosexual society. Yet it was in no sense a pathological unit. Its success depended on the ability of men to get along with, live with, and work with other men, and to accept the almost total exclusion of women from their lives. The introduction of the Women's Army Corps did not change this situation to any great degree.[223]

During the war "we placed 50,000 to 100,000 healthy young men in a camp and in essence told them to forget the most powerful drive in their lives," the erotic.

> They were supposed somehow to adjust to an exclusively male society and remain completely continent and abstinent. This did not happen. . . .
> The physical substitutes were varied: Many men discovered satisfaction in a physical interest in other men, which often surprised them; others resorted to masturbation; still others, including many married men, found "women" to satisfy their need. The Army did not sit in moral judgment on the non-marital sexual relations of the soldier as long as these were with women, except when they interfered with his effectiveness. . . .

One "most important [psychological] substitute" for "normal sexual energies" was "the satisfaction the soldier derived from the comradeship and fellowship of his associates—his male friends—a disguised and sublimated homosexuality."[224]

Another form of "sublimation" was so common it had been named by one psychiatrist " 'homosexual buffoonery.' "

> In the barracks, usually when the men were getting undressed, one frequently observed play-acting in which various persons "kiddingly" assumed the role of overt homosexuals. One soldier, returning from the shower room in the nude was greeted with catcalls, salacious whistling, and comments like, "Hey, Joe, you shouldn't go around like that—you don't know what that does to me." Joe responded by coyly draping a towel around himself and wriggling his hips in feminine fashion. Some of the men joined in the buffoonery by playing the role of the appreciative spectator: "Ain't

he hot stuff though!" "C'mon, take it off." Others acted the part of active solicitors for sexual favors: "How much do you want for sleeping with me tonight?"; "Come into my bed and I'll give you the time of your life."[225]

This buffoonery "was carried to such extremes that no one participating in it ever considered in his own mind the disturbing possibility of any seriousness in it."[225]

The " 'problem' " of overt homosexual relations between soldiers "was not nearly so large as one might have judged from the emotional discussions of the subject by some officers."[225]

"Four types of homosexuality" had come to the attention of Army psychiatrists.

"Latent homosexuality" was manifested in men "who had never had any consciousness of particular interest in men or knowledge of this twist in their personality." When "placed in a strictly male communal life" they "became disturbed and anxious."

> The second type was the homosexual individual who, prior to his Army experience, had accepted his make-up and had satisfying contacts and sexual relationships with other men. He was able to do this without any distress or emotional concern to himself. Usually he remained discreet about it and very often got along well socially. Undoubtedly there were many such men in the Army. Only a few of them were detected by accident and thus brought to the attention of the psychiatrists.

A third group manifested homosexual interests only in "special situations, usually when under the influence of excess alcohol."[226]

A fourth, "small group," were

> a social menace in the use of their deliberately seductive tactics. Their judgment was so badly warped that they made open propositions or gave exhibitions of their interests and desires.

One "detailed, confidential survey" was reported of 183 men, known "from prewar studies" to be either homosexually active, probably active, or as "having a latent interest in homosexuality." One hundred and eighteen of these had served from one to five years in the armed forces. Fifty-eight percent

> were officers in the Army, Air Force, and Navy. The amazing fact is that they concealed their homosexuality effectively and, at the same time, made creditable records for themselves in the service.[227]

Another study of "270 patients" admitted to a hospital "for problems of homosexuality" noted "no difference in the incidence between Negro and white soldiers." A "predominance of skilled over semiskilled workers" was noted. None of these patients was illiterate. They were generally "law-abiding; arrests were very infrequent." The group included

10 master sergeants, 6 technical sergeants, 19 staff sergeants. Many others had ratings of considerable talent in clerical, musical, and dramatic ability.

But the "temperament and skills necessary for the combat soldier were infrequently seen."[228]

Dr. Menninger outlined the history of the Army's response to homosexuals:

The standards for admission to the Army as outlined . . . April 19, 1944, specifically state that "persons habitually or occasionally engaged in homosexual or other perverse sexual practices are unsuitable for military service and will be excluded. Feminine bodily characteristics, effeminacy in dress or manner, or a patulous [expanded] rectum are not consistently found in such persons but where present should lead to careful psychiatric examination. If the individual admits or claims homosexuality, or other sexual perversion, he will be referred to his local board for further psychiatric and social investigation. If an individual has a record as a pervert, he will be rejected."

All homosexuals discovered in the army who "were not tried by court-martial" for specific offenses were initially "given blue discharges," a discharge "without honor." Menninger explained:

A man on his own initiative, or because of noticeable difficulty in adjusting himself, might visit or be sent to a psychiatrist for consultation. When it was found that the basis of the difficulty was homosexuality, if this was reported to his commanding officer, the man probably received a blue discharge, or perhaps would be tried. Objections to this were raised by many homosexual individuals, whose request for help from a medical officer ended up in a discharge "without honor." This action undermined confidence in medical officers. Furthermore, the Army required that doctors report even those statements given in confidence in a consultation room. The homosexual was no more responsible for his personality difficulty than a mental defective was for his. Even so, the old procedure, based on prejudice, singled him out for punishment. This resulted in many instances of careful avoidance in the case records of the word "homosexual."

Some progress in the handling of the problem came with the publication . . . dated January 3, 1944. This directive applied only to those who were discovered or reported to have performed homosexual acts. . . . It provided hospitalization of those who were deemed reclaimable. It permitted the giving of a blue discharge to an offender who was deemed not reclaimable, in lieu of court-martial. Included in the category of "reclaimable" were those who were guilty of first offense, those who acted as the result of intoxication or curiosity, or "those who acted under undue influence, especially when such influence was exercised by a person of greater years or superior grade."

For this particular disability the commanding officer of the hospital was required to transmit to the Adjutant General . . . a full report of the diagnosis, treatment, results of treatment, and the recommendation as to the disposition of every homosexual patient. This information was to be kept on file. Depending upon the results of treatment, the individual was returned to duty, separated from the service, or tried by court-martial.

A probably insignificant number of "homosexual offenders were salvaged for further duty." But "many who were fundamentally homosexual were returned to duty with no mention . . . to commanding officers of the root of their difficulty."

As to "the homosexual who was not guilty of any offense" it had been "common practice . . . to give 'discharges without honor'" on the "premise that homosexuality constituted an undesirable trait of character."[230]

"Without the prior knowledge of the Office of the Surgeon General," army regulations were revised March 7, 1945, to the effect that "'the mere confession by an individual to the psychiatrist that he possesses homosexual tendencies will not in itself constitute sufficient cause for discharge.'"

This was amended after a "series of conferences" with Army leaders. A memorandum by the surgeon general, in July 1945, said:

> "personnel who were inadaptable for service by reason of homosexuality were entitled to honorable discharges, providing they were guilty of no offense and that their service had been honorable and faithful."

It was said that: "a person with homosexual tendencies, as the mental defective, is not responsible for his condition"—and mental defectives were "given honorable discharges when released because of ineptness."[230-31] This honorable discharge for non-offending homosexuals was formalized in a special order of October 31, 1945.

> This did not permit discharge merely on the basis of a confession of homosexuality. It required adequate evidence of an existing psychological maladjustment which rendered the individual inadaptable for service. . . .

Menninger recalled:

> Throughout the war, and increasingly in late 1945 and 1946, reports came to me of individual soldiers who had given months or even years of good service and had then received a blue discharge because of homosexuality. Many soldiers wrote me; many physicians wrote me. It was apparent that the blue discharge had sometimes been punitive and unfair, certainly nonmedical. An appeal for a reconsideration of their discharge can be addressed to the Secretary of War Review Board. It may be well for these men to recognize, however, that the odds are against them; the prejudice still exists!
> . . . Army regulations based on old prejudices were modified in favor of a more objective appraisal of the problem. Homosexuals, in the opinion of the psychiatrist, have immature personalities which make them and their lives and some of their personal relations grossly pathological. Like any sick person, they deserve understanding instead of condemnation. At the same time it is necessary to realize that as citizens they vary in their usefulness. Some have unusual talent and may make important contributions to society.

At the other end of the scale is the homosexual who is a menace, and society has a right to be protected from him. Persons afflicted with a homosexual make-up should not be condemned wholesale but instead should be considered individually.[231]

BOOK REVIEW

## 1948, July 11
### N. Y. Times Book Review:
### André Gide's The Immoralist

The novel *The Immoralist* "is a study of homosexuality," said critic Albert Guerard, Jr.[49]* But the book would be meaningless to readers unless they understood that "Gide's Michel never commits a homosexual act—and that in the end, he only half understands the origin of his 'immoralism,' of his suicidal effort to uncover his 'authentic self.'" In this review, Gide's oppositions, puritanism and anti-puritanism, repression and expression, self-punishment and self-affirmation, come clearly to the fore. But why the "recognition" of the homosexual in oneself should be associated with self-destruction was not explained; an implicit equation of the homosexual and the destroyer was apparently assumed.

The "key which opens every dark passage of the novel" was Michel's statement: "'Sometimes I am afraid that what I have suppressed will take its revenge.'"

> The vengeance of what has been suppressed touches every fiber of Michel's intellectual and moral life; determines . . . his "gratuitous" defense of Gothic barbarism, just as it determines his systematic destruction of his orderly Norman farm (that image of inherited prudence and parental example), or the reckless compulsive spending of his money. He must cut deeper and deeper . . . until the "authentic self" (the unrecognized homosexual) is revealed. This victimized authentic self exhibits a curious subconscious hostility toward the convention-bound and an abnormal sympathy for the free. It is attracted by all whom conscience considers guilty, and repelled by all the well-behaved.

In his hours of "order" and "self-control,"

> Michel must punish the "self" which orders and controls, the self that lingers on of childhood fears and rejections. But he must also punish another "self" . . . for every step taken toward actual liberation. . . . Aggressions directed outward in one symbolic act after another invariably and at

---

*This *Times* review does not cite Gide's translator. An earlier U. S. edition of *The Immoralist* (N. Y.: Knopf, 1930) was translated by Dorothy Bussy; see *N. Y. Times Book Review*, April 20, 1930, p. 9.

last turn back inward, the Huguenot to assail the homosexual and the homosexual to assail the Huguenot.

Michel's "drama of recognition and discovery" was a "drama of partial . . . suicide." It was a drama not " 'solved,' " a dilemma "more than sexual," a problem of the self which helped to make Gide's novel "one of the best of our century."

FILM REVIEW

## 1948, October 1
### *N. Y. Times: Red River*

Critic Bosley Crowther mourned the passing of the days when men were men, praising the idealized masculine images in the film *Red River*.[50] He also criticized the intrusion of a woman into this story of two male adversaries. It was this civilizing female who finally urged the two men (as Vito Russo reports): "Stop fighting! You two know you love each other."[78] The film's association of male camaraderie and violence also appeared in these cowboys' uniting (as Crowther said) "to beat the redskins off." A link between male-male antagonism, violence, and repressed male-male love was also discussed by James Baldwin; see 1949, Summer. Both Crowther's review and the film seemingly expressed a nostalgia for the lost masculine camaraderie of the war years. That Montgomery Clift's homosexuality is now public knowledge adds a certain retrospective irony to Crowther's praise of the "solidly masculine cast."

"Despite a big let-down . . . near the end," said Crowther, *Red River* was "on the way toward being one of the best cowboy pictures ever made." From the moment John Wayne and Walter Brennan cut away from a wagon train

> and strike off for their own realms, you know that you're riding with stout men.
>
> That's the big thing about this picture; for at least two-thirds of the way, it's a down-to-earth story of cow-pokes and the tough, dangerous lives they used to lead. . . . And it's a story of two strong-minded men, a hard-bitten veteran and a youngster—or Mr. Wayne and Montgomery Clift.
>
> So long as it sticks to cow-herding and the gathering clash between these two . . . it rings with the clang of honest metal and throbs with the pulse of real life.

Director Howard Hawks had filled "Red River" with "masculine ranginess"; he made the film "look raw and dusty, made it smell of beef and sweat." He had also got "fine performances out of a solidly masculine cast." John Wayne,

> a consistently able portrayer of two-fisted, two-gunned outdoor men, surpasses himself in this picture. We wouldn't want to tangle with him. Mr. Clift has our admiration as the lean and leathery kid who does. . . .

The entertainment continued until the "cattlemen meet a wagon-train which is being besieged by Indians and help beat the redskins off." Then "the cowboys —and the picture—run smack into 'Hollywood' in the form of a glamorized female." The "havoc" this "charmer" played with the hero "is almost complete":

> The characters turn into actors and the story turns into old stuff. It ends with the two tenacious cowboys kissing and making up.

BOOK REVIEW

## 1948, November 21
### *N. Y. Times Book Review:*
### Hubert Creekmore's *The Welcome*

An inauthentic marriage and social conformity were opposed in this novel to male-male "intimacy" and non-conformity.[51] But a reviewer thought these themes were not given universal enough embodiment to constitute a compelling critique of "modern marriage." This fictional critique was apparently aimed at the newly enforced heterosexuality of the late 1940s.

This novel, said critic Warren E. Preece, is "the story of Don Mason's return home" to a small Southern town "after an extended stay in New York." Don "is remembered in Ashton . . . as a member of the intelligentsia, . . . and as an intimate of Jim Furlow, who exchanged his friendship with Don for an unhappy marriage."

The author "is concerned with the relationships of Don, who escaped the patterns of Ashton life, and Jim, who 'qualified' for society through marriage." Also portrayed was "Don's relationship to his neurotic mother and to Isabel Lang, who loves him even though she thinks she knows the truth about his former intimacy with Jim."

"Marriage," the author maintained, "has failed because it has become something dictated by the necessity of social approval." The novel itself failed as an "examination of modern marriage" because its setting and characters "are hardly typical enough to provide a view of anything but a small section of society."

BOOK REVIEW

## 1949, March 13
### *N. Y. Times Book Review:*
### Isabel Bolton's *The Christmas Tree*

An author's pitting a humane homosexuality against a destructive heterosexual masculinity was not appreciated by a *Times* reviewer; the fictional formulation of such a sexual politic met with incomprehension.[52] But, in 1949, this allegory of heterosexual/homosexual war was prophetic of the patriotic, anti-homosexual witch hunts of the 1950s.

This book "as a whole is meant to be dominated by modern history," said critic Mark Schorer. The grandmother, Mrs. Danforth, "is in charge of the 6-year-old son of her son, Larry, a 'brilliant' homosexual, and his divorced wife, Anne." Anne's new husband is Captain Fletcher, "the All-American Extrovert." The author intended Larry's story to be "an allegory of the tortured modern intellectual, sensitive to humane values, but corrupted by a deep 'dis-ease,' in conflict with [Captain Fletcher] the healthy, well-meaning but willing agent of brutality and war."*

> Their struggle over the pitiful puppet-child, Henry, is presumably a struggle for control of the future. How one is to read the conclusion of this allegory I do not know: Larry shoves the Captain to his death from a terrace, . . . and then is . . . taken off to his death by the police.

The "private story" constitutes no analogy to the "public values" the author expected readers to see in it. Mrs. Danforth's "mistakes in raising her child, who lays his homosexuality at her door and wishes to talk it all over in his advanced years"—this is "irrelevant" to what the author "wishes it to mean."

♀  INTIMACY/RESISTANCE

# 1949, March 27
## *N. Y. Times Book Review:*
## [Dorothy Strachey Bussy's] *Olivia*

In the autobiographical novel, *Olivia,* published under a pseudonym, first by the press founded by Leonard and Virginia Woolf, then by a New York firm, Dorothy Strachey Bussy recalled her first romance with a woman.[53]† The book was reviewed in *The New York Times* by Hilda Osterhout:

> "Olivia," the author tells us, is an autobiography; the story of her first love. No romance in the ordinary sense, "Olivia" chronicles a 16-year-old English girl's awakening to life and tragedy through an unfortunate attachment to her French schoolmistress.

The reviewer commented on the book's "powerful" effect, calling it "a narrative of sheer emotion."

---

*For other conjunctions of heterosexual masculinity and violence see 1948, October 1 and 1949, Summer.

†For Dorothy Bussy's translations of Gide see *N. Y. Times Book Review* on *The Counterfeiters,* October 2, 1927, p. 2; *The Immoralist,* April 20, 1930, p. 9; and *If It Die,* see entry of 1935, November 10. For her translations of other Gide works see *The New York Times Book Review, Author Index,* under Bussy. For Bussy as a pupil at Les Ruches and a teacher at Allenswood when Eleanor Roosevelt attended that school see backnote to 1933, March 5.

Taking her theme from a maxim of La Bruyère, that one loves completely only the first time—the loves that follow being less spontaneous—the author eschews the analysis of emotion, a tendency which, she maintains, is not present in the abandon of first love. Like D. H. Lawrence she holds that to analyze a living thing is to kill it.

The reviewer quoted "Olivia's" introductory comment that poets, analytical novelists, and psychologists poisoned the "sources of emotion."

Minus analysis, a welcome relief from much of current writing, Olivia's feelings are none the less comprehensible in terms of adolescent rebellion. Transplanted from a Victorian household in England where duty, work and abnegation are the rule to a finishing school in Paris invested with the glamour of a salon, the girl's release is expressed in an overwhelming admiration for Mlle. Julie, brilliant headmistress of the establishment. As this fixation grows all normal values are inverted; hopelessness lends dignity to passion, and hope itself becomes a poison.

Never directly stated but projected through the lens of Olivia's emotions, the character of Mlle. Julie comes wonderfully alive as a cruel and tragic figure in an atmosphere of evil who causes the suicide of one woman, accepts the slavery of another, wounds Olivia by rejection and finally destroys herself.* The disaster of unnatural love is revealed in Mlle. Julie's own words: "My purest joys have been spoilt. Even my thoughts have been spoilt. Even my inmost self."

In . . . creation of feeling by the naming of an emotion, rather than the suggestion of it by situation, sensations, or imagery, "Olivia" achieves the purity of classic tragedy.

Though the style of the book was "occasionally marred by pedantism and sentimentality," these were "minor flaws." *Olivia* "remains a work of art; intensity controlled with a compact structure."

The reviewer's associating young Olivia's feelings for her schoolmistress with "adolescent rebellion," and the reviewer's reference to the "disaster of unnatural love" were not how Dorothy Strachey Bussy intended her themes to be interpreted. In her Introduction to *Olivia* Bussy stressed, not the tragedy of lesbianism, but the poignancy of a non-comprehended, deeply-felt first love, "a rare and beautiful memory." Bussy's Introduction may be read, in fact, as one of the earliest of the rare defenses of lesbianism published in the United States.

The novel had been written, said Bussy,

to please myself, without thought of my own vanity or modesty, without regard for other people's feelings, without considering whether I shock or hurt the living, without scrupling to speak of the dead.

The world, I know, is changing. I am not indifferent to the revolution that has caught us in its mighty skirts, to the enormity of the flood that is threatening to submerge us. But what could I do? In the welter of the

---

*For the homosexual as "destroyer" see that heading in the index.

surrounding storm, I have taken refuge for a moment on this little raft, constructed with the salvage of my memory. I have tried to steer it into that calm haven of art in which I still believe. . . .

This account of what happened to me during a year that I spent at school in France seems to me to fall into the shape of a story—a short, simple one, with two or three characters and a very few episodes. It is informed with a single motive, tends to a single end, moves quickly and undeviatingly to a final catastrophe. Its truth has been filtered, transposed, and, maybe, superficially altered, as is inevitably the case with all autobiographies. I have condensed into a few score of pages the history of a whole year when life was, if not at its fullest, at any rate at its most poignant—that year when every vital experience was the first, or, if you Freudians object, the year when I first became conscious of myself, of love and pleasure, of death and pain, and when every reaction to them was as unexpected, as amazing, as *involuntary* as the experience itself.

I know the difficulties that surround such an enterprise. I know, for instance, how careful the adjustment must be before the necessary, dry skeleton of fact can be clothed with the warm, round, living flesh of youth, with colour and movement. . . .

How should I hope to succeed in such an attempt? Why should I resist the desire to make it?

Love has always been the chief business of my life, the only thing I have thought—no, felt—supremely worth while, and I don't pretend that this experience was not succeeded by others. But at that time, I was innocent, with the innocence of ignorance. I didn't know what was happening to me. I didn't know what had happened to anybody. I was without consciousness, that is to say, more utterly absorbed than was ever possible again. For after that first time there was always part of me standing aside, comparing, analysing, objecting: "Is this real? Is this sincere?". . . . Was this stab in my heart, this rapture, really mine or had I merely read about it? For every feeling, every vicissitude of my passion, there would spring into my mind a quotation from the poets. . . . Comforting, perhaps, but enraging too. Nothing ever seemed spontaneously my own. As the blood dripped from the wound, there was always part of me to watch with a smile and a sneer: "Literature! Mere literature! Nothing to make a fuss about!". . . .

And there were not only the poets to poison the sources of emotion, there were the psychologists, the physiologists, the psycho-analysts, the Prousts and the Freuds. It was deeply interesting, this withdrawal of oneself from the scene of action, this lying in ambush, waiting and watching for the prowling beasts, the nocturnal vermin, to come creeping out of their lairs, to recognize this one and that, to give it its name, to be acquainted with its habits—but what was left of oneself after this relinquishing of one's property? Wasn't one a mere field where these irresponsible animals carried on their antics at their own free will? Irritation, disgust, cynicism and scepticism are bred of such thoughts—the poisonous antidotes of the poison of passion. But the poison that works in a girl of sixteen—at any rate in the romantic, sentimental girl I then was—has no such antidote, and no previous inoculation mitigates the severity of the disease. Virgin soil, she takes it as the South Sea islanders took measles—a matter of life and death.

How should I have known, indeed, what was the matter with me? There was no instruction anywhere. The poets, it is true (for even then I frequented the poets), had a way of talking sometimes which seemed strangely to illuminate the situation. But this, I thought, must be an illusion or an accident. What could these grown-up men and women with their mutual love affairs have in common with a little girl like me? My case was so different, so unheard of. Really no one had ever heard of such a thing, except as a joke. Yes, people used to make joking allusions to "school-girl crushes." But I knew well enough that my "crush" was not a joke. And yet I had an uneasy feeling that, if not a joke, it was something to be ashamed of, something to hide desperately. This, I suppose, was not so much a matter of reflection (I did not think my passion was reprehensible, I was far too ignorant for that) as of instinct—a deep-rooted instinct, which all my life has kept me from any form of unveiling, which has forbidden me many of the purest physical pleasures and all literary expression. How can one bathe, without undressing, or write without laying bare one's soul?

But now, after many years, the urgency of confession is upon me. Let me indulge it. Let me make my offering on the altar of—absence. The eyes that would have understood are closed. And besides, it is not my soul but that of a far-away girl of sixteen.

One more oblation to the gods! May they grant me not to have profaned a rare and beautiful memory![7–11]

BOOK REVIEW

## 1949, June 19
### N. Y. Times Book Review:
### Ward Thomas's *Stranger in the Land*

The concept of homosexuals as "ostracized" and a "minority" made its first appearance in *The Times;* the respectable middle class was discovering the invert as *Stranger in the Land,* a malign sexual foreigner.[54] This new "minority" idea was accompanied here by the old image of the homosexual as "demonic" destroyer. And that old destroyer was linked with the new notion of homosexual "sterility," an ideological formulation specific to The Fecund Forties.*

"In his first novel," said reviewer Hilda Osterhout, Ward Thomas "presents the dilemma of a moral man, afflicted with the curse of inverted love."

He is one of the first writers to deal with homosexuality, so recurrent a subject in modern letters, on a socially conscious plane as the problem of

---

*For the homosexual as "destroyer" see that heading in the index. For the homosexual as "sterile" see that term in the index.

a minority ostracized by the group. But "Stranger in the Land" is less a homosexual novel than the story of the demonic relationship between the hunter and the hunted. . . .

Thomas has accentuated the predicament of his protagonist Raymond Manton by placing him in a small New England town in wartime. In fact, one might call "Stranger in the Land" a war novel, for it is the story of the loneliness and humiliation of those who were left behind. Rejected by the Army as a "psychoneurotic,"* Manton teaches in the local high school, the sole support of his ailing mother, who has no cognizance of her son's abnormality.

Manton's only friend is Terry Devine, a handsome young man whose main preoccupation is to frequent the town's bars at someone else's expense. The relationship between these two forms the substance of the book. When Terry resorts to blackmail, threatening to turn Manton over to the police, a move which would mean death for his mother, Manton is faced with the prospect of life-long enslavement or suicide.

As Manton contemplates death he comes face to face with the real tragedy of his life—sterility. "He would go sterile to his grave, leaving no mark on his narrow little world that he had ever existed, neither a child of his loins, nor any enduring product of his imagination." The author extends Manton's plight to that of contemporary man trapped in "the awful sterility of life in the modern world, with its mechanized and regimented vulgarity, its rationalized God, and psychoanalyzed love and commercialized joy," a world in which science has dissected emotions to the point of destroying them.

The end result of such a process . . . is that of loneliness and dissolution. It is possible that the author is less concerned with the fate of the homosexual than he is with the fate of modern man himself and in this novel is merely using the homosexual as a symbol of the impotence and meaninglessness in modern life.

. . . The images, . . . the "moon brooding over its own luminous sterility," all suggest that the author is dealing with the negative, the night side of life. . . .

Manton is a credible hero whose state of acute anxiety breaking down into the cool psychosis of the murderer is superbly portrayed. . . . Unfortunately, [the author] tends to destroy his effects at times by excessive analysis and by weighting his sentences with the very clinical terminology he deplores. . . .

*For the homosexual as "neurotic" see that term in the index.

RESISTANCE/COMMENTARY

## 1949, Summer
## James Baldwin: A *"panic . . . close to madness"*

An essay titled "Preservation of Innocence; Studies for a New Morality" was published in Tangier, Morocco, in a small-circulation journal, *Zero,* by the twenty-five-year-old James Baldwin.[55]*

Probing the mutual implications of the "homosexual" and the relations of women and men, Baldwin's speculations are prophetic of themes that have become more ordinary in our own time, but were truly original in 1949. Compared, for example, to even the most sophisticated 1940s psychoanalytic theorizing, straitjacketed by thought-stopping references to fixations of emotional development, heterosexual "maturity," and old notions of the masculine and feminine, Baldwin's essay goes for the deep, complex, and human, criticizing the categories socially imposed to divide, conquer, and trivialize.

Baldwin points to a link between an uneasy, unfulfilled masculinity and violence, naming a "panic . . . close to madness" caused not, certainly, by "homosexuality," but by terror at "sexual activity between men." That terror is still too little understood in this society; it is the horror of the male who must annihilate the homosexual in order to destroy that possibility in himself.

"The problem of the homosexual," began Baldwin, "so vociferously involved with good and evil, the unnatural as opposed to the natural, has its roots in the nature of man and woman and their relationship to one another." But the "natural" and "unnatural," and the "nature" of the sexes, were difficult to know. A "natural state" was "perversely indefinable outside of the womb or before the grave." It was not even "altogether desirable." "We spend vast amounts of our time and emotional energy in learning how not to be natural." It was therefore "very difficult to know exactly what is meant when we speak of the unnatural." Whenever "nature is invoked to support our human divisions" we have "every right to be suspicious, nature having betrayed only the most perplexing and untrustworthy interest in man and none whatever in his institutions."[14–15]†

"The oldest, the most insistent and the most vehement charge faced by the homosexual" was that

> he is unnatural because he has turned from his life-giving function to a union which is sterile.‡ This may . . . be considered a heavy, even an

---

*For additional comment on Baldwin's essay see the Introduction to this section of documents, pp. 161–62, 171.

†For the "natural/unnatural" polarity see that heading in the index. For the superseding of natural/unnatural by "normal/abnormal" see the latter heading in the index.

‡For the homosexual as "sterile" see the *Parents' Magazine* review of the Kinsey report, entry of 1948, January 4; and 1949, June 19, and the index.

unforgivable crime, but since it is not so considered when involving other people, the unmarried or the poverty-stricken or the feeble, and since his existence did not always invoke that hysteria with which he now contends, we are safe in suggesting that his present untouchability owes its motive power to several other sources. Let me suggest that his present debasement and our obsession with him corresponds to the debasement of the relationship between the sexes; and that his ambiguous and terrible position in our society reflects the ambiguities and terrors which time has deposited on that relationship as the sea piles seaweed and wreckage along the shore.

For, after all, I take it that no one can be seriously disturbed about the birth-rate: when the race commits suicide it will not be in Sodom.[15–16]

"Natural" and "unnatural" had both become irrelevant designations. So "the Deity" had been set up, and a "duality of good-and-evil";

and now Sin and Redemption, those mighty bells, began that crying which will not cease until, by another act of creation, we transcend our old morality. Before we were banished from Eden and the curse was uttered, "I will put enmity between thee and the woman," the homosexual did not exist; nor, properly speaking, did the heterosexual. We were all in a state of nature.[16]*

"God" was "man's most intense creation,"

and it is not in the sight of nature that the homosexual is condemned, but in the sight of God. This argues a profound and dangerous failure of concept, since an incalculable number of the world's humans are thereby condemned to something less than life; and we may not, of course, do this without limiting ourselves.

"Experience" and "history" indicated "that it is not possible to banish or to falsify any human need without ourselves undergoing falsification and loss."[17]

"The nature of man and woman and their relationship with one another" had caused much "conjecture," and "no little discomfort." The "more we imagine we have discovered the less we know," and this relationship became "more and more complex."

Men and women seem to function as imperfect and sometimes unwilling mirrors for one another; a falsification or distortion of the nature of one is immediately reflected in the nature of the other. A division between them can only betray a division within the soul of each. Matters are not helped if we thereupon decide that men must recapture their status as men and that women must embrace their function as women; not only does the resulting rigidity of attitude put to death any possible communion, but, having once listed the bald physical facts, no one is prepared to go further and decide, of our multiple human attributes, which are masculine and which are feminine.[17]

*For the invention of the "homosexual" and "heterosexual" see those headings in the index.

"The recognition of this complexity is the signal of maturity; it marks the death of the child and the birth of the man."[18]

It was "the truly awesome attempt of the American to . . . preserve his innocence" concerning the undefinability of the sexes, and his simultaneous attempt to "arrive at a man's estate," that led to the creation of that "mindless monster, the tough guy,"

> whose masculinity is found in the most infantile and elemental externals and whose attitude towards women is the wedding of the most abysmal romanticism and the most implacable distrust.[19]

It was impossible, for example, to believe that the hero of any James M. Cain or Raymond Chandler mystery novel "loves his girl":

> he wants her, but that is not the same thing and, moreover, what he seems to want is revenge; what they bring to each other is not even passion or sexuality but an unbelievably barren and wrathful grinding. They are surrounded by blood and treachery; and their bitter coupling, which has the urgency and precision of machine-gun fire, is heralded and punctuated by the mysterious and astounded corpse. . . . Men and women have all but disappeared from our popular culture, leaving only this disturbing series of effigies with a motive power which we are told is sex, but which is actually a dream-like longing, an unfulfillment more wistful than that of the Sleeping Beauty awaiting the life-giving touch of the fated Prince. For the American dream of love insists that the Boy get the Girl, . . . and we are always told that this is what he *really* wants, to stop all this chasing around and settle down, to have children and a full life with a woman who, unhappily even when she appears, fails to exist.[19]

Novelist James Cain, said Baldwin,

> has achieved an enormous public and, I should hope, a not inconsiderable fortune on the basis of his remarkable preoccupation with the virile male. One may suggest that it was the dynamism of his material which trapped him into introducing, briefly, and with the air of a man wearing antiseptic gloves, an unattractive invert in an early novel, *Serenade,* * who was promptly stabbed to death by the hero's mistress, a lusty and unlikely senorita. This novel contains a curious admission on the part of the hero to the effect that there is always somewhere a homosexual who can wear down the resistance of the normal man by knowing which buttons to press. This is presented as a serious and melancholy warning and it is when the invert of *Serenade* begins pressing too many buttons at once that he arrives at his sordid and bloody end. Thus is that immaculate manliness within us protected; thus summarily do we deal with any obstacle to the union of the Boy and the Girl.[20]

*For *The N. Y. Times* review of *Serenade* see 1937, December 5.

When in such novels "the Boy and Girl" became "the Bride and Groom" the author left them, for "it is not for our eyes to witness the pain and temptation that will follow." For

> the boy cannot know a woman since he has never become a man.
>
> Hence, violence: that brutality which rages unchecked in our literature is part of the harvest of this unfulfillment, strident and dreadful testimony to our renowned and cherished innocence.* Consider, in those extravagant denouncements which characterize those novels—to be more and more remarked on the bookshelves—which are concerned with homosexuality, how high a value we place on this dangerous attribute. In [Gore Vidal's] *The City and the Pillar* the avowed homosexual who is the protagonist murders his first and only perfect love when at length they meet again for he cannot bear to kill instead that desolate and impossible dream of love which he has carried in his heart so long. In [William Maxwell's] *The Folded Leaf* the frail, introverted Lymie attempts suicide in an effort to escape the danger implicit in his love for Spud; a bloody act which, we are told, has purchased his maturity. In [Charles Jackson's] *The Fall of Valor* the god-like Marine defends his masculinity with a poker, leaving for dead the frightened professor who wanted him.† These violent resolutions, all of them unlikely in the extreme, are compelled by a panic which is close to madness. These novels are not concerned with homosexuality but with the ever-present danger of sexual activity between men.
>
> It is this unadmitted tension, longing and terror and wrath which creates their curiously mindless and pallid, yet smouldering atmosphere.[21]

The last three novels cited were not any different from novels by James M. Cain, Laura Z. Hobson, or Mary Jane Ward. All

> are wholly unable to recreate or interpret any of the reality or complexity of human experience; and that area which it is their self-avowed purpose to illuminate is precisely the area on which is thrown the most distorting light. As one may close [Hobson's] *Gentlemen's Agreement,* which is about Gentiles and Jews, having gained no insight into the mind of either; as [Ward's] *The Snake Pit* reveals nothing of madness and James M. Cain tells us nothing of men and women, so one may read any current novel concerned with homosexual love and encounter merely a procession of platitudes the ancestry of which again may be traced to The Rover Boys and their golden ideal of chastity. It is quite impossible to write a worthwhile novel about a Jew or a Gentile or a Homosexual, for people refuse, unhappily, to function in so

---

*For a link between violence, heterosexual masculinity, and repressed homosexual feelings also see the discussion of *Cross Fire* and *The Brick Foxhole,* 1947, July 23; Menninger, 1948, April; *Red River,* 1948, October. Baldwin's critique of heterosexuality would only become commonplace after the development of a militant feminist movement in the late 1960s; in 1949 it was almost unique.

†For Vidal's *City and the Pillar* see entry of 1948, January 11; for Maxwell's *Folded Leaf* see comment in *The New York Times Book Review,* April 8, 1945, p. 3; for Jackson's *The Fall of Valor,* see entry of 1946, October 6.

neat and one-dimensional a fashion. If the novelist considers that they are no more complex than their labels he must, of necessity, produce a catalogue, in which we will find, neatly listed, all those attributes with which the label is associated. . . .[21–22]

Baldwin ended:

A novel insistently demands the presence and passion of human beings, who cannot ever be labeled. Once the novelist has created a human being he has shattered the label and, in transcending the subject matter, is able, for the first time, to tell us something about it and to reveal how profoundly all things involving human beings interlock. Without this passion we may all smother to death, locked in those airless, labeled cells, which isolate us from each other and separate us from ourselves. . . .[22]

FILM REVIEW

# 1949, September 20
## N. Y. Times: Germany Year Zero

Roberto Rossellini's film about "the grief and demoralization of people in post-war Berlin," was said by critic Bosley Crowther to include "sordid details" in the life of a twelve-year-old boy.[56]

The "hard and depraved circumstances" in which the boy was forced to live "are not only shocking to witness but are a mockery to the decency of man." Rossellini "doesn't spare us," although "it looks as though the censor often does." The director,

shows us degradation and depravity at its most wretched and low. From . . . people in Berlin slicing meat off a dead horse in the streets to suggestions of vice among children, he puts post-war Berlin on the line.

"Crowded dwellings, petty thievery, prostitution, black marketing, perversion and vice—these form the background of the youngster that seems Mr. Rossellini's main concern."

BOOK REVIEW

# 1949, October 10
## Newsweek: "Queer People"

The equation of the "homosexual," the most violent sex murderer, and most peculiar sex "pervert" is found in a Newsweek book review.[57] An equation of punishment and rehabilitation may also be noted. Newsweek's pervert-baiting constituted a move toward the full-scale, national anti-homosexual witch hunts of the 1950s. On a page headed "Medicine," and subtitled "Queer People," the essay began:

> The sex pervert, whether a homosexual, an exhibitionist, or even a dangerous sadist, is too often regarded merely as a "queer" person who never hurts anyone but himself. Then the mangled form of some victim focuses public attention on the degenerate's work. And newspaper headlines flare for days over . . . details of the most dastardly and horrifying of crimes.

Dr. J. Paul DeRiver, a "criminal psychiatrist," was head of the Los Angeles Police Department Sex Offenses Bureau. Before his Bureau appeared "every person accused of a sex crime" in the city. The psychiatrist had written a "factual, scientific book," *The Sexual Criminal,* published that week. It included "43 actual case histories" and "reveals frank facts." Also included were "Lots of very queer people"—sadists, masochists, "the sadistic pedophile," "zoophiles, psychopaths who perform sadistic acts on animals, and the necrophiles, who . . . commit acts of moral degeneracy upon or in the presence of dead bodies." Details of lust murders were cited.

A "special assistant attorney general of California, Eugene D. Williams, had written an introduction to Dr. DeRiver's book. Williams was quoted:

> The semihysterical, foolishly sympathetic, and wholly unscientific attitude of any individual engaged in social work and criminology to regard sex perverts as poor unfortunates who are suffering from disease and cannot help themselves, has a tendency to feed their ego.

*Newsweek* added:

> A sterner attitude is required, if the degenerate is to be properly treated and cured. Williams suggests that the sex pervert be treated, not as a coddled patient, but as a particularly virulent type of criminal. "To punish him," he concludes, "he should be placed in an institution where the proper kind of rehabilitory work can be done so that, if capable of being brought to the realization of the error of his ways, he may be brought back to society prepared to live as a normal, law-abiding individual, rather than turned out as he now is from the penitentiary, confirmed in his perversion."

BOOK REVIEW

## 1949, November 6
### N. Y. Times Book Review:
### Nial Kent's *The Divided Path*

Critic Judith P. Quehl said: "This new addition to the psychopathic shelf, homosexual division, takes one Michael from early childhood—his mother had always wanted a little girl and used her son as a daughter substitute—to alleged man-hood as a pianist.[58]

> Given the almost typically textbook background, the reader can hardly be surprised when Michael makes his eventual choice. . . . What follows is . . . a dreary recital of half-hearted attempts to return from the divided to the beaten path. . . .

"As a serious study of aberration, this novel misses by a mile."

# Backnotes and
# Selected Bibliography

# Backnotes

The backnotes give the source of quotations or information referred to in the main text. Additional information and sources are given in chronological order throughout the backnotes.

In the Documents section to Part II, backnotes are numbered consecutively from 1, beginning with each new decade. Running heads at the top of the backnote pages, referring to page numbers in the corresponding text, will allow the reader to move easily between backnote and text.

## Introduction: Lesbian and Gay History—Theory and Practice

1. The original sources of the terms cited here and in the following paragraph may be found by consulting the index in Katz, *Gay American History* (abbreviated throughout the backnotes as *GAH*) and this *Almanac*. For the English vocabulary of love and lust also see Eric Partridge, *Shakespeare's Bawdy: A Literary and Psychological Essay and a Comprehensive Glossary* (New York: Dutton, 1960), Partridge's *Dictionary of Slang and Unconventional English*, 6th ed. (New York: Macmillan, 1967), *The Oxford English Dictionary*, and such early works as John S. Farmer and W. E. Henley's *Dictionary of Slang and Its Analogues* (1890–1909); reprinted with important introductory essay by Gershon Legman, "On Sexual Speech and Slang," and including the volume titled *Vocabula Amatoria* (New York: University Books, 1966). Also see the index to this *Almanac* for listings under "terminology," and individual terms (such as "crime against nature").

2. Vern L. Bullough and Martha Voght, "Homosexuality and Its Confusion with the 'Secret Sin' in Pre-Freudian America," *Journal of the History of Medicine*, vol. 28 (April 1973), pp. 143–54.

3. Carroll Smith-Rosenberg, "The Female World of Love and Ritual: Relations Between Women in Nineteenth-Century America," *Signs*, vol. 1, no. 1 (Fall 1975), pp. 1–29.

4. For the sexual "continuum," see Alfred C. Kinsey, Wardell B. Pomeroy, and Clyde E. Martin, *Sexual Behavior in the Human Male* (Philadelphia: Saunders, 1948), especially pp. 636–51 on "The Heterosexual–Homosexual Balance."

5. For "androgyny," see Carolyn Heilbrun, *Toward a Recognition of Androgyny*

(New York: Knopf, 1974) and "The Androgyny Papers" issue of *Women's Studies*, vol. 2, no. 2 (1974), which contains essays criticizing the ideal and ideology of androgyny.

6. For sexual "variations," "sexualities," "homosexualities," and "heterosexualities" see, for example, Vern L. Bullough, *Sexual Variance in Society and History* (New York: Wiley, 1976); John Gagnon, *Human Sexualities* (Glenview, Ill.: Scott, Foresman, 1977); Alan P. Bell and Martin S. Weinberg, *Homosexualities: A Study of Diversity Among Men and Women* (New York: Simon and Schuster, 1978).

7. Anna Mary Wells, *Miss Marks and Miss Woolley* (Boston: Houghton Mifflin, 1978).

8. Marjorie Housepian Dobkin, ed., *The Making of a Feminist: Early Journals and Letters of M. Carey Thomas* (Kent, Ohio: Kent State University Press, 1980). Also see the critical review by Helen Vendler, *New York Times Book Review*, Feb. 24, 1980, pp. 24–25.

9. Frederick Rudolph, *Curriculum: A History of the American Undergraduate Course of Study Since 1636* (San Francisco: Jossey-Bass, 1977), p. 170.

10. Anthony F. C. Wallace, *Rockdale, the Growth of An American Village in the Early Industrial Revolution* (New York: Knopf, 1978), pp. 104–13.

11. For an early, major analysis of the liability of a feminism fearful of lesbianism see "The Woman-Identified Woman," in Karla Jay and Allen Young, ed., *Out of the Closets: Voices of Gay Liberation* (New York: Douglas, 1972), pp. 172–77. A section of essays in this anthology focuses on lesbianism and feminism.

12. Doris Faber, *The Life of Lorena Hickock, E. R.'s Friend* (New York: Morrow, 1980).

13. E. M. Forster, *Maurice* (New York: Macmillan, 1971), p. 139.

14. Lisa Duggan to Jonathan Katz, personal communication, 1980.

15. Dr. Richard von Krafft-Ebing, *Psychopathia Sexualis, With Special Reference to the Antipathic Sexual Instinct, A Medico-Forensic Study.* Translated by Franklin S. Klaf (New York: Bell, 1965).

16. On "intimacy" as historical and as an object of historical research see Howard Gadlin, "Private Lives and Public Order: A Critical View of the History of Intimate Relations in the United States," *Massachusetts Review*, vol. 17, no. 2 (Summer 1976), pp. 304–30; and William J. Goode, "The Theoretical Importance of Love," *American Sociological Review*, vol. 24, no. 1 (Feb. 1959), pp. 38–47. That there exists a huge Marxist literature on the political economy of "alienation," and almost none on the history and social organization of "intimacy," suggests that intimacy, even in this most social of analytical modes, has been thought of as "natural," rather than a historical construct. An important exception is the Frankfort School; on Norbert Elias and Theodore Adorno see Susan Buck-Morss's review of Elias's *The Civilization Process* (New York: Urizen Books, 1978), in *Telos*, no. 37 (Fall 1978), pp. 181–98. As an explicit research project, the evidence for the existence of many, qualitatively different historical forms of erotic and/or intimate relationships has only recently started to be collected and interpreted, usually as an aspect of family history. For two ambitious but flawed histories of the changing forms of (mostly) male–female intimacy see Lawrence Stone, *The Family, Sex, and Marriage In England 1500–1800* (New York: Harper & Row, 1977) and Edward Shorter, *The Making of the Modern*

*Family* (New York: Basic Books, 1975). The diaries and correspondence quoted by Carroll Smith-Rosenberg and Lillian Faderman may be interpreted as evidence for the existence of qualitatively different, historically specific forms of female–female relationships, emotions, and interactions; see Smith-Rosenberg, "Female World" and Lillian Faderman, *Surpassing the Love of Men: Romantic Friendship and Love between Women from the Renaissance to the Present* (New York: Morrow, 1981). Further research in such "personal" sources is needed to bolster my argument for the historical relativity of love and lust.

17. Blanche Wiesen Cook, "The Historical Denial of Lesbianism" (review of *Miss Marks and Miss Woolley* by Anna Mary Wells), *Radical History Review,* (Spring/Summer, 1979), p. 64. For other recent, thoughtful statements of the "lesbian" as "woman-loving" see Faderman, *Surpassing*, pp. 17–18, 190, 328–31; Judith Schwarz, "Questionnaire on Issues in Lesbian History," *Frontiers,* vol. 4, no. 3 (Fall 1979), p. 4; Annabel Faraday, "Liberating Lesbian Research," in Kenneth Plummer, ed., *The Making of The Modern Homosexual* (London: Hutchinson, 1981), pp. 112–29; Adrienne Rich, "The Meaning of Our Love for Women Is What We Have to Constantly Expand," *Out and Out Pamphlet no. 1* (New York: Out and Out Books, 1977); and the classic statement by a group of Radicalesbians, "The Woman-Identified Woman," reprinted in Jay and Young, *Out of the Closets.* Audre Lorde's "The Erotic as Power" stresses the creative force of the shared erotic for all "woman-identified women," but she does not limit this to lesbians, and does not try to define that term; see Lorde's "Uses of the Erotic:

The Erotic as Power," *Out and Out Pamphlet no. 3* (New York: Out and Out Books, 1978).

In the early 1980s there is an ongoing debate within the lesbian-feminist community about the character, place, and value of the affectional, sensual, erotic, sexual, orgasmic, and genital in relationships between women, a debate about the present definition of "lesbian." Such debate implicitly assumes "lesbian" (and, I argue, "gay") to refer not to a fixed, universal entity, a thing, but to historically changing relationships constructed by those who live them within given conditions, with a vision of future possibilities. On one side of this debate are those lesbians who stress the importance of reclaiming a devalued and denied female eroticism, as well as a more general woman-loving. On the other side are those who stress the importance of rediscovering the history of a devalued and ignored woman-to-woman nurturing, support, friendship, and intimacy, as well as the specifically sensual and erotic. To some extent this difference in viewpoints amounts to a matter of emphasis, and neither side is mutually exclusive. However, in some of the "lesbian" as "woman loving" works the presence of a definite antisexual tone and tendency may be noted, a tendency to devalue the erotic for itself, apart from any link with "romance" and "love." This antisexual tendency originates, I think, as a response to a traditional reduction of the "lesbian" (and "gay male" and "homosexual") to the narrowly "sexual," and from an historically conditioned "feminine" devaluation of sexual pleasure not legitimized by affection.

In my own historical work I have tried to stress the importance of researching both "intimacy" and the specifically "sexual" in past relationships of women with women and men with men. In some instances it seems important to me to insist on the words "lesbian" and "gay" as overall, transhistorical names for those relationships (such as that of Eleanor Roosevelt and Lorena Hickock) in which a specifically erotic, sexual element may be detected. I also speak of a more general history of "friendship" and "intimacy" as of central "relevance" to "lesbian" and "gay" history. Such formulations are presented here as working definitions, by no means as absolute, essential, and conclusive. In any case, the basic work of "lesbian" and "gay" history research seems to me not a matter of our own present definitions and categories, but of ascertaining the historically specific qualities of past relationships, responses, and conditions. Our definitions are not the basic issue, but are simply tools of more or less usefulness in helping us to discover and understand the particular historical qualities of those past relationships, responses, and conditions. It now seems to me an open question whether the histories of "lesbians" and "gay men" are most usefully defined by us as histories of the specifically erotic or of a more general same-sex intimacy. In light of the ongoing lesbian-feminist debate, the complexity of the unresolved issues, and the necessity for anyone doing "lesbian" and "gay" history research to define provisionally the "lesbian" and "gay," I hope my own partisanship with the "lesbian" and "gay" as erotic school will be understood as an endeavor, in good faith, to respond dialectically and in an antisexist manner to a difficult situation.

According to my present and evolving understanding, the different histories of lesbians and gay men include, simultaneously, a number of relationships. These include: lesbians to lesbians/gay men to gay men; lesbians to heterosexual women/gay men to heterosexual men; lesbians to heterosexual men/gay men to heterosexual women; lesbians to gay men/gay men to lesbians.

A new perception of the historically specific construction of the categories "lesbian," "gay," "homosexual," and "heterosexual" also suggests that the past interactions at issue are more generally stated as the socially constructed erotic and intimate relationships of: female to female/male to male; female to male/male to female. A deep, complex understanding of lesbian and gay history will, I think eventually have to include research and analysis of all those strands.

For some recent lesbian-feminist works stressing the importance of recovering and affirming the specifically erotic in relationships of women with women (as well as female–female intimacy) see the "Sex Issue" of *Heresies: A Feminist Publication on Art and Politics*, vol. 3, no. 4, issue 12 (1981), especially Tee Corinne, "Study for a Book of Lesbian Erotic Images," p. 20; Amber Hollibaugh and Cherríe Morago, "What We're Rollin' Around in Bed With: Sexual Silences in Feminism; A Conversation toward Ending Them," pp. 58–62; J. Lee Lehman, "Lust Is Just a Four-Letter Word," pp. 80–81; and Joan Nestle, "Butch–Fem Relationships: Sexual Courage in the 1950s," pp. 21–24. For the importance of affirming female eroticism also see Paula Webster, "Pornography and Pleasure," pp. 48–51. Also see Pat Califia, *Sapphistry* (Tallahassee, Fla.: Naiad Press, 1980).

**18.** John Boswell, *Christianity, Social Toler-*

*ance, and Homosexuality: Gay People in Western Europe from the Beginning of the Christian Era to the Fourteenth Century* (Chicago: University of Chicago Press, 1980).

19. For "temperamental" and "kiki" see those terms in the index. The term "gay" (for homosexual) first appeared in the *New York Times Book Review,* June 30, 1963, p. 5, in a review of John Rechy's *City of Night.* The use of the word "gay" by homosexuals was first mentioned in the *New York Times,* Dec. 17, 1963, in a story by Robert C. Doty, "Growth of Homosexuality in City Provokes Wide Concern," 1:1, 33:1. Doty also used the word once himself, in reference to "gay periodicals." The *Times's* first mention of any homosexual emancipation organization was its reference to the "Homosexual League of America," headed by Randolph Wicker. Unbeknownst to the *Times,* this was a pseudo-group; Wicker was its only member (see *New York Times,* July 16, 1962, 47:-4.) For "Gay Liberation Front" see *New York Times,* March 9, 1970, 29:1.

20. Benkert's use of the word *Homosexualität* is discussed by James D. Steakley, *The Homosexual Emancipation Movement in Germany* (New York: Arno Press, 1975), pp. 10–12.

21. For Kinsey's mistaken assumption that the word "homosexual" was, "of course, patterned after and intended to represent the antithesis of the word heterosexual" (that "homosexual" followed the use of "heterosexual") see Kinsey, *Male,* p. 612.

22. The historical emergence of a "homosexual role" was first most clearly articulated by Mary McIntosh in "The Homosexual Role," *Social Problems,* vol. 16, no. 2 (Fall 1968), pp. 182–92.

23. Works in homosexual history have so far tended to stress subjective attitudes toward or of homosexuals, treating homosexual history as a history of consciousness, of the subjective. Even works which have also emphasized the changing objective conditions and historical forms of "homosexual behavior" have spoken of this behavior as a universal. For example, Jeffrey Weeks distinguishes "between homosexual behavior, which is universal, and a homosexual identity, which is historically specific" (*Coming Out; Homosexual Politics in Britain, from the Nineteenth Century to the Present* (London: Quartet Books, 1977), p. 3. American gay Marxist historians have approvingly quoted Weeks's formulation. In formulating my own Historical Theory of Sexual Relativity, I do not suggest the existence of a universal, abstract, ideal, biological "homosexuality" or "heterosexuality" (or even "sexuality") which manifests qualitatively different, historically specific forms. I do think that female–female, male–male, and female–male relationships are constructed socially so as to take essentially different historical forms; some include lust, or sensuality, or a diffuse sensuousness, or eroticism, or none of the above; some manifest a degree of alienation or of intimacy. According to this historical relativism, the word and concept "heterosexual" was produced and distributed in late-nineteenth- and early-twentieth-century America to express and to idealize qualitatively new relationships between men and women in which eroticism was defined as central and legitimate. Assuming "heterosexuality" (or "homosexuality") to be universal obscures the historically specific character of the relationships referred to, and the specific social uses of the categories.

## Part I
### Early Colonial Exploration,
### Agriculture, and Commerce:
### The Age of Sodomitical Sin, 1607–1740

*Introduction*

1. In addition to the sources listed in *GAH*, Native American "homosexuality" and cross-dressing are discussed in Trumbach, "London's Sodomites: Homosexual Behavior and Western Culture in the Eighteenth Century," *Journal of Social History*, vol. 11, no. 1 (Fall 1977), pp. 7–8, 26 n. 16, 27 n. 17, 28–29, notes 29–35; Thomas K. Fitzgerald, "A Critique of Anthropological Research on Homosexuality," *Journal of Homosexuality*, vol. 2, no. 4 (Summer 1977), pp. 385–97. Also see Martin Bauml Duberman, "Documents in Hopi Indian Sexuality: Imperialism, Culture, and Resistance," *Radical History Review*, Spring/Summer, 1979, pp. 99–130; and note 5 below.

2. The most profound, extended critique of the medical concept of "transsexualism" is Janice G. Raymond's *The Transsexual Empire: The Making of the She-Male* (Boston: Beacon Press, 1980). For other feminist critiques of "transsexualism" see Marcia Yudkin, "Transsexualism and Women: A Critical Perspective," *Feminist Studies*, vol. 4, no. 2 (June 1978), pp. 97–106, and my unpublished paper " 'Transsexualism': Today's Quack Medicine; An Issue for Every Body," Nov. 1, 1978. An historical study needs to be made of the medical and autobiographical literature on "transsexualism"; it will, I think, reveal the fundamentally sexist nature of the concept and of the associated medical treatments.

3. The relation between debates about the "rationality" of Native Americans and Spanish imperialism is discussed by Francisco Guerra, *The Pre-Columbian Mind: A Study into the Aberrant Nature of Sexual Drives, Drugs Affecting Behavior, and the Attitude Towards Life and Death, with a Survey of Psychotherapy, in Pre-Columbian America* (London: Seminar Press, 1971).

4. Guerra (see above), pp. 67–68.

5. Sociologist Kenneth Plummer asks: "Why should one even begin to contemplate the notion that the *berdache* has anything at all to do with homosexuality in our terms?" in his and Jeffrey Weeks's interview with Mary McIntosh, in Plummer, ed., *The Making of the Modern Homosexual* (London: Hutchinson, 1981), p. 48. Harriet Whitehead's recent thoughtful and important analysis, "The Bow and the Burden Strap: A New Look at Institutionalized Homosexuality in Native North America," tries to understand the meaning of the berdache in terms of native culture; however, her analysis fails to transcend the universalizing terminology of "homosexuality" and "heterosexuality," and is in that common anthropological mode that completely ignores historical change and time; in Sherry B. Ortner and Harriet Whitehead, ed., *Sexual Meanings: The Cultural Construction of Gender and Sexuality* (Cambridge: Cambridge University Press, 1981), pp. 80–115.

6. "Adultery" was generally defined by the marital status of the woman; that is, "adultery" was *not* committed when a married man had sexual intercourse with a single woman. "Adultery" was a capital crime in Massachusetts, Con-

necticut, Plymouth, and the New Haven colonies until the 1670s, when law reforms substituted whippings. See Lyle Koehler, *A Search for Power: The "Weaker Sex" in Seventeenth Century New England* (Urbana, Ill.: University of Illinois Press, 1980), pp. 146–52.

7. There were nineteen legal cases involving charges of "sodomy" or other erotic acts between men or between women, 1607–1740. 1624, Nov. 30: Virg.; Cornish executed. 1629, June 29: Higgeson; "5 beastly Sodomitical boys." 1635, Feb. 14: New Hamp.; "two men . . . committed sodomy." 1637, Aug. 6: Plym.; Allexander and Roberts, "lewd behavior and unclean carriage." 1641: Mass. Bay; "sodomy" (?) 1642, March 1: Plym.: Michell and Preston, "lewd and sodomitical practices." 1642, Dec. 5: Essex Co., Mass. Bay; Eliz. Johnson, "unseemly practices." 1646, June 25: New Neth.; Jan Creoli executed. 1646: New Haven; Plaine executed. 1649, March 6: Plym.; Norman and Hammon, "lewd behavior . . . upon a bed." 1649, Oct. 29: Plym.; Berry and Joanes, "sodomy" charge. 1653, March: New Haven; "sundry youths," "much wickedness in a filthy corrupting way." 1658, Aug. 26: New Neth.; Hillebrant, "sodomy" charge. 1660, May 13: New Neth.; Quistout executed for "sodomy." 1663, July 4: New Hamp.; Giles, "buggered her servant boy." 1677, May 22: Conn.; Sension, attempted "sodomy." 1712, Jan. 29: Mass.; Mingo, alias Cocke Negro, executed(?). 1718, March: N. Carolina; Clark vs. Winn. 1734, March 25: Georgia; three hundred lashes for "sodomy." Some additional cases of ambiguous character are mentioned in Robert Oaks, " 'Things Fearful to Name': Sodomy and Buggery in Seventeenth-Century New England," *Journal of Social History*, vol. 12, no. 2 (1979),

pp. 268–81; reprinted in Elizabeth H. Pleck and Joseph H. Pleck, *The American Man* (Englewood Cliffs, N.J.: Prentice-Hall, 1980), pp. 53–76. This is the major, recent essay on the subject. Also see Oaks's "Perceptions of Homosexuality by Justices of the Peace in Colonial Virginia," *Sexualaw Reporter*, vol. 4, no. 2 (April/June 1978), pp. 35–36; reprinted in *Journal of Homosexuality*, vol. 5, no. 1–2 (Fall/Winter), pp. 35–41; and Louis Crompton, "Homosexuals and the Death Penalty in Colonial America," *Journal of Homosexuality*, vol. 1, no. 3 (1976), pp. 277–94.

8. The four executed for sodomy, 1607–1740, were: 1624, Nov. 30; Virg.; Cornish. 1646, June 25: New Neth.; Jan Creoli. 1646: New Haven; Plaine. 1660, May 13: New Neth.; Quistout. The disposition of "sodomy" charges in two cases is unknown: see 1635, Feb. 14, New Hamp., and 1658, Aug. 26, New Neth. (Hillebrant case). A sixth man, Mingo, alias Cocke Negro, may have been executed for sodomy in this period in Massachusetts (see 1712, Jan. 29). For the 1566 execution see *GAH*, pp. 14–16.

In the following period an Irish doctor was reportedly "convicted of Sodomy, and executed" in 1743, at Fort Frederica, Georgia; see *The Journal of William Stephens, 1743–1745*, edited by E. Merton Coulter (Athens, Ga.: University of Georgia Press, 1958–59), vol. 2, p. 3. One execution for a "crime against nature" is reported to have occurred in Pennsylvania in 1785. This punishment is listed in a table of convictions and executions for various crimes committed in the new state, published by William Bradford. Upon examination, Bradford's information is confused: the Pennsylvania law of 1718, in effect in 1785, did *not* refer to the "crime against nature," but provided death for "sodomy and bug-gery," thereby distinguishing male–male "sodomy" from bestiality. An-other document, the *Minutes of the Supreme Executive Council of Pennsylvania,* for Dec. 1, 1785, reports: "A warrant was issued for the execution of Joseph Ross of Westmoreland, convicted of buggery at a late Court of Oyer and Terminer and General Jail Delivery, held at Hanna's Town for the said country, the said execution to take place on the twentieth instant." That use of the term "buggery" suggests that the execution in 1785 was for bes-tiality, not male–male sodomy. Brad-ford is quoted in Basil Montagu, *The Opinions of Different Authors upon the Pun-ishment of Death* (London: Hurst, Rees and Orne, 1809), p. 267. Also see: *Min-utes of the Supreme Executive Council of Pennsylvania . . .* (Harrisburg: Theo. Fenn, 1853), p. 588.

9. Edmund S. Morgan, *The Puritan Family: Religion and Domestic Relations in Seven-teenth Century New England,* revised and enlarged (New York: Harper & Row, 1966), p. 145.

10. Oaks, " 'Things Fearful,' " p. 272.

11. John Demos, *A Little Commonwealth: Family Life in Plymouth Colony* (London: Oxford University Press, 1971), p. 78.

12. Morgan, *Puritan Family,* p. 145.

13. Morgan, *Puritan Family,* pp. 145–46.

14. Demos, *Little Commonwealth,* pp. 50, 183–84.

15. For American Puritan use of the word "seed" for the raw material of offspring see Morgan, *Puritan Family,* pp. 6, 90, 180, 181; for the use of agricultural metaphors for persons, p. 9. For the use of "fruit" for offspring see Koehler, *Search,* p. 205. For the use of "crop," "cultivating," "fruit," and "plant," and for an agricultural metaphor for off-spring, see Greven, *Protestant Tempera-ment,* pp. 170–71, 175. For an American

Puritan reference to women as "fruitful vines" see Thompson, *Women,* p. 132. For men's "spilling" and "spending" their "seed" see 1637, Aug.; 1641–42, Mass.; 1656, March 1.

16. In the colonies the "act of procreation" and successful conception followed "the cycle of the agricultural year"; see James A. Henretta in *The Evolution of American Society, 1700–1815: An Interdis-ciplinary Analysis* (Lexington, Mass.: Heath, 1973), pp. 32–33, citing a paper by Kenneth A. Lockridge, "The Con-ception Cycle as a Tool for Historical Analysis," presented to the Stony Brook Conference on Social History, 1969.

17. The high rate of birth and population increase is discussed in Henretta, *Evo-lution,* pp. 9–13, 26, 57–60; Thompson, *Women,* pp. 54, 134. Also see Philip Greven, "Historical Demography and Colonial America, A Review Article," *William and Mary Quarterly,* vol. 24, no. 3 (July 1967), pp. 438–54 (especially p. 445); Wilson H. Grabill, Clyde V. Kiser, and Pascal K. Whelpton, "A Long View," pp. 374–96 in Michael Gordon, ed., *The American Family in Social Histori-cal Perspective* (New York: St. Martin's Press, 1973); Daniel Scott Smith, "The Demographic History of Colonial New England," pp. 397–415 in Gordon (see above).

18. On birth control and the early colonists see Koehler, *Search,* pp. 83, 103, 434; on abortion pp. 205, 329; on infanti-cide pp. 4, 83, 194, 199–205, 273, 274, 329, 433, 444, 471–73; on women's fear of death in childbirth pp. 34, 57, 204. On abortion also see Thompson, *Women,* pp. 205, 329.

19. On marriage and family as a means of property transfer see Philip Greven, *Four Generations: Population, Land, and Family in Colonial Andover, Massachusetts* (Ithaca, N. Y.: Cornell University Press,

1972), pp. 125–72; also see Greven's index on "land transmission," "paternal authority and control of land," "sons, delayed independence of."

20. On the French calling usurers *bougres* see Derrick Sherwin Bailey, *Homosexuality and the Western Christian Tradition* (Hamden, Conn.: Shoestring Press, 1975), p. 141; Boswell, *Christianity,* p. 290. Also see Michael Goodich, *The Unmentionable Vice: Homosexuality in the Later Medieval Period* (Santa Barbara, Calif.: Ross-Erikson, 1979), pp. 9, 128 n. 16.

21. On the Lombards and the English Parliament of 1376 see *Rotulia parliamentorum.* (Great Britain Record Commission.) . . . *Edward I* [to Henry VII, 1278–1503], 6 vols., edited by J. Strachey (London, 1767–1777), vol. 2, p. 332a. I thank Gordon McGregor for translating the original old French. On this 1376 protest also see François Lafitte, "Homosexuality and the Law: The Wolfenden Report in Historical Perspective," *British Journal of Delinquency,* vol. 9, no. 1 (July 1958), p. 13. Montgomery Hyde, *The Love That Dared Not Speak Its Name: A Candid History of Homosexuality in Britain* (Boston: Little, Brown, 1970), pp. 38–41. The economic rivalry between London traders and Lombard brokers is discussed in Ephraim Lipson, *The Economic History of England,* 9th ed. (London: Adam and Charles Black, 1947), vol. 1, ch. 10, p. 533, etc. and R. H. Tawney, *Religion and the Rise of Capitalism, A Historical Study* (New York: Penguin Books, 1947), pp. 33, 51.

22. On Henry VIII and the economics of the English Reformation see A. L. Morton, *A People's History of England* (New York: Random House, 1938), pp. 164–66. For the accusation of "manifest sin" see Michael E. Tigar and Madeleine R. Levy, *Law and the Rise of Capitalism* (New York: Monthly Review Press, 1977), p.

205. Historian John Richard Green says that in 1536 "Two royal commissions . . . were despatched on a general visitation of the religious houses, and their reports formed a 'Black Book' which was laid before Parliament" in that year. About two thirds of the religious houses were "charged with drunkenness, with simony, and with the foulest and most revolting crimes." Though some charges were exaggerated, "in the smaller houses at least indolence had passed into crime"; see Green's *History of the English People* (New York: Harper, 1899), vol. 2, pp. 162–63. It would be interesting to know more about the exact charges in that "Black Book."

23. For the text of the English buggery law of 1533, discussion of it, and of "benefit of clergy," see Bailey, *Homosexuality,* p. 147–50. Also see Hyde, *The Love,* pp. 38–41; Alex K. Gigeroff, *Sexual Deviations in the Criminal Law: Homosexual, Exhibitionistic, and Pedophile Offenses in Canada* (Toronto: University of Toronto Press, 1968), pp. 15–16.

24. For the early colonists and "rape" see Koehler, *Search,* pp. 91–101; Koehler (pp. 95, 97) reports seventy-nine rapes or attempted rapes in seventeenth century New England, and the hanging of at least six rapists. For the ambiguity of the Bible in regard to rape see Bullough, *Sexual Variance,* pp. 81, 88. Selectivity in Puritan capital law enforcement is also indicated by the failure to prosecute in Plymouth for youthful disobedience to parents; see Demos, *Little Commonwealth,* p. 102.

25. For Massachusetts Bay law requiring children to learn the capital laws see Morgan, *Puritan Family,* pp. 87–88; for similar Plymouth legislation see Demos, *Little Commonwealth,* p. 104.

26. The relations between the early colonial organizations of work, play, pro-

creation, and lust require further analysis. The Protestant (and specifically Puritan) work ethic and its relation to capitalism is discussed in Max Weber, *The Protestant Ethic and the Spirit of Capitalism*, translated by Talcott Parsons, foreword by R. H. Tawney (New York: Scribner's, 1958); R. H. Tawney, *Religion and the Rise of Capitalism, A Historical Study* (New York: Harcourt, Brace, 1926); Edgar A. J. Johnson, *American Economic Thought in the Seventeenth Century* (London: P. S. King, 1930); Robert W. Green, ed., *Protestantism and Capitalism: The Weber Thesis and Its Critics* (Boston: Heath, 1959); Gabriel Kolko, "Max Weber on America: Theory and Evidence," *History and Theory: Studies in the Philosophy of History*, vol. 1, no. 2 (1961), pp. 243–60; Edmund Morgan, "The Puritan Ethic and the American Revolution," *William and Mary Quarterly*, 3rd ser., vol. 24, no. 1 (Jan. 1967), pp. 3–43; C. Vann Woodward, "The Southern Ethic in a Puritan World," *William and Mary Quarterly*, 3rd ser., vol. 25, no. 3 (July 1968; Greven, *Protestant Temperament.*

27. See Edmund Morgan's revisionist interpretation in "The Puritans and Sex"; for Morgan's denial of Puritan asceticism see his *Puritan Family*, pp. 29, 33, 62–63. Also see William and Mallerville Haller, "The Puritan Art of Love," *Huntington Library Quarterly*, vol. 5, no. 2 (Jan. 1942), pp. 235–72. Philip Greven's distinction between Protestant "evangelicals" (including extreme, orthodox "Puritans"), "moderates," and the "genteel" provides a useful typology of colonialists; see his *Protestant Temperament.*

28. On marriage as chastity see Haller, "Puritan Art of Love," pp. 235, 236, 238–39, 243–44, 246, 256–57, 261, 264, 266, 269. If in the early colonies one was brought up *not* to fall in love and then marry, but to marry and then fall in love, the implications are interesting for what is now generally called "sexual orientation." It would seem that marriage then was undertaken, not only for economic reasons, but to control a kind of free-floating lust; "sexual orientation" in the early colonies may have been relatively objectless—the subject deserves more research.

29. On "original sin" as "natural corruption" see Greven, *Protestant Temperament*, pp. 63, 66, 99. The concepts "natural" and "unnatural" are most usefully analysed, I think, as the terms of a historically changing political ideology (related to the nature/culture, nature/nurture debate). For a feminist analysis see Sherry B. Ortner, "Is Female to Male as Nature is to Culture?" *Feminist Studies*, vol. 1, no. 2 (Fall 1972); reprinted in Michelle S. Rosaldo and Louise Lamphere, ed., *Woman, Culture, and Society* (Stanford, Calif.: Stanford University Press, 1972. For John Boswell's discussion of "Men, Beasts, and 'Nature' " see his *Christianity*, pp. 303–32.

30. The phrase "crime against nature" is first known to have appeared in legal commentaries published in America, and in statutes, in the 1770s. The "crime against nature" is referred to in the following sources, listed in chronological order: William Blackstone, *Commentaries on the Laws of England. Book the Fourth . . . Reprinted from the British Copy, Page for Page with the Last Edition* (Philadelphia: Robert Bell, 1772), ch. 15, part 4, pp. 215–17; William Bradford, *An Inquiry How Far the Punishment of Death is Necessary in Pennsylvania . . .* (New York: Dobson, 1793), pp. 20–21; New Jersey sodomy statute of March 18, 1796 in William Paterson, ed., *Laws of the State of New Jersey: Revised and Published Under the Authority of the Legislature* (Newark, N.J.: Matthias Day, 1800), pp. 208–09; François Marie Arouet Voltaire, *The Philo-*

sophical *Dictionary, for the Pocket; Translated from the French Edition* . . . (Catskill [N. Y.], Printed by T. and M. Croswel [sic] for selves and J. Fellows and E. Duyckinck, 1796), "Socratic Love, As It Is Called," pp. 217–22; New York sodomy statute of March 21, 1801, in James Kent and Jacob Radcliff, ed., *Laws of the State of New York* (Albany, N.Y.: Charles R. and George Webster, 1802), vol. 1, p. 253; Charles Louis de Secondat, baron de la Brède et de Montesquieu, *The Spirit of the Laws. Translated from the French . . . First American from the Fifth London Edition,* 2 vols. (Worcester, Mass.: Isaiah Thomes, 1802), book 12, ch. 6, "Of the Crime Against Nature," pp. 221–22; Massachusetts sodomy law of March 16, 1805, in Asahel Stearns, Lemuel Shaw, and Theron Metcalf, ed., *The General Laws of Massachusetts* . . . (Boston: Wells and Lilly and Cummings and Hilliard, 1823), 2 vols, vol. 2, p. 129; New Hampshire sodomy law of June 19, 1812, in Albert Stillman Batchellor, *Laws of New Hampshire* . . . (Manchester, N. H.: John B. Clarke, 1904), vol. 8, p. 130. *Coburn* vs. *Harwood,* Dec. 1822, in *Reports of Cases Argued and Determined in the Supreme Court of Alabama,* Henry Minor, ed., (New York: Collins & Hannay, 1829), vol. 1, pp. 93–95; Delaware sodomy law of Feb. 1826, in Willard Hall, ed., *Laws of the State of Delaware* (Wilmington, Del.: R. Porter, 1829), p. 139. On the phrase "crime against nature" as used by Saint Augustine see James W. Chesebro, ed., *Gayspeak: Gay Male and Lesbian Communication* (New York: Pilgrim Press, 1981), p. 32; and on Saint Thomas Aquinas as the originator of the phrase see Harold Beaver, "Homosexual Signs," *Critical Inquiry,* vol. 8, no. 1 (Autumn 1981), p. 111 n. 25.

**31.** Several uses of "buggerer" (a person who commits buggery) are listed in the *Oxford English Dictionary:* 1552 Huloet; 1571 Jewel; 1651 Baxter; 1704 *Faction Displ.* An additional use, 1736, by Matthew Hale, is cited by George Lee Haskins, *Law and Authority in Early Massachusetts: A Study in Tradition and Design* (New York: Macmillan, 1960), p. 271, n. 41.

**32.** On the Puritan "elect" being a "minority, probably no more than one-fifth of the total population," and on the fact that Puritan theorists "never thought that mere numerical majorities proved anything," see Perry Miller, *Errand into the Wilderness* (New York: Harper & Row, 1964), p. 150; also see his whole chapter on "The Puritan State and Puritan Society." The hierarchical power structure of the early colonies, and the lack of any developed democratic ideology, complicates our using the concepts majority/minority, normal/deviant, same/different to explain the reason for the condemnation of colonists who committed sodomy; they were not punished because they were considered members of a deviant, different, abnormal minority. It would be truer to say they were punished by the minority because their actions represented the unfettered impulses of the majority. For a problematic attempt to apply the modern "sociology of deviance" to the early colonies see Kai T. Ericson, *Wayward Puritans: A Study in the Sociology of Deviance* (New York: Wiley, 1966). John Boswell's ahistorical idea of "gay people" as a "minority" in every society involves his explaining the growing "intollerance" in the 1200s as due to "gay peoples'" increasingly visible "difference" from the majority population of the cities; see his *Christianity,* pp. 301–02.

**33.** On evangelical Puritans' condemnation of all forms of lusting, desiring, and self-assertion see Greven, *Protestant Temperament,* pp. 44, 83, 131, 133.

**34.** On the term "sexuality" (referring to

the quality of being sexual or having a sex, possessing sexual powers or feelings, or being conscious of our preoccupation with sex) as a Victorian rather than a colonial invention, the *OED* lists uses of "sexuality" starting in 1800, and including 1826, 1848, 1882–84, 1879, 1888, 1893, and 1899.

35. A Boston female's reference to women and men as "Different Sexes," dating to 1686, is quoted by Koehler, *Search*, p. 182. But stress on the differentiation of the two sexes, and on the similarity of each to itself, is rare in early colonial documents. Also see the introduction to the document dated 1724.

36. On human–beast intercourse resulting in part-human, part-bestial creatures see Oaks, "Things Fearful," p. 275, on the George Spencer case (1641); p. 276 on the Thomas Hogg case (1647). Because the early colonists closely associated human–animal sexual contacts and male–male sexual relations, the commentaries on bestiality cases often include revealing references to sodomy; a more detailed analysis of colonial bestiality would be relevant to the study of sodomy. The colonists' fear of the merging of the human and the bestial may be related to their fear of being overwhelmed by a hostile "nature."

37. In contrast to the resolution of the Hall case in 1629, a Victorian American report in 1839 of a doctor's response to alleged hermaphroditism suggests that "female" and "male" were then considered by him mutually exclusive. In 1839 the Philadelphia *Medical Examiner* reported an "interesting case" described by Dr. William Harris in a lecture on "The Clitoris" at the city's Medical Institute. This report makes it clear that even the definition of "female" and "male" sex-biology is a matter of what particular physical characteristics are socially chosen as essentially distinguishing. In this case three different sources reportedly offered competing, contradictory definitions of the same physically abnormal individual.

First, at the birth of an ambiguously sexed child in the late 1700s, women neighbors in Chester County, Pennsylvania, defined the child as a "hermaphrodite" whose "female" appearing "generative organs" led them to call it "her" and "Elizabeth." Second, when Elizabeth matured, developing physical characteristics usually associated with males, as well as a liking for "manly sports" and "the labours of the field," "she" publicly renamed "herself" Rees, and "now abandoned all the duties of a female." In the early 1800s she "married a woman" and reportedly experienced "the most consummate pleasure" in using her large clitoris "as a male organ"(?). Nothing in the document says that Rees ever called her/himself "male," and the adoption of the sexually ambiguous name "Rees" suggests an ambivalent sexual self-definition; Rees's public adoption of customarily male behavior was possibly concomitant with the private adoption of a more ambiguous self-conception. In the early 1800s, among farmers in rural Pennsylvania, a relative lack of rigidity in the sexual division of labor, and in the definitions of "female" and "male," may have made such sexual ambiguity socially permissible.

In 1839, Dr. Harris offered a third definition of Elizabeth/Rees, insisting on "her" unequivocal categorization as "female." Dr. Harris also denied the existence of hermaphrodites; a person was either male or female, he implied.

Each of the definitions has different theoretical implications for the perception and judgment of this individual's erotic life. Rees's public assumption of behavior customary for males in the early 1800s apparently permitted this individual to be socially accepted as "male," to marry, and to be known in the neighborhood to enjoy marital "coition." In contrast, Dr. Harris's 1839 definition of Rees as "female" implied that Rees's sexual activity with "her" wife involved two females, and perhaps that changing of the "natural use" prohibited by St. Paul (though nothing was said of this).

Dr. Harris's report documents a clear conflict between this professional man, his medical concept of "female" and "male," and those Chester County women he demeaned as "gossiping females," "gossips," and "the vulgar," and their popular concept of "hermaphrodite." Also evident is a conflict between Dr. Harris and Rees, whose dying request denied the physician the privilege of making any post-mortem examination—thus resisting in death a medicalizing definition. This report indicates Dr. Harris's concern with making absolute "distinctions" between the sexes, a concern which does not seem to have equally preoccupied Rees or the women of Chester County. See "Clinical Lecture. The Clitoris" ("From a lecture by Dr. William Harris") (Philadelphia) *Medical Examiner* vol. 2, no. 20 (May 18, 1839), pp. 314–15. This case is cited as being reported by Dr. Harris in the *Philadelphia Medical Examiner* (sic) in 1820 (sic), and as being "given world wide reputation by the great American forensic physician [Theodoric R.] Beck" in his volume *Medical Jurisprudence.* (No reference to this case is found in Beck's *Elements of Medical Jurisprudence,* 1823 ed.) Harris's case also reportedly "altered the European view as to the coitus procedure of

female inverts"; see James G. Kiernan, "Sexology," *Urologic and Cutaneous Review,* vol. 19, no. 6 (June 1915), p. 349, and same, vol. 20, no. 1 (Jan. 1916), p. 45.

More research is needed on the American social history of the "hermaphrodite." The category "hermaphrodite," claimed as a defense by one of the parties to a female–female marriage, was reported in a working-class newspaper in 1836. Although one party in this relationship tried to persuade a judge "that she was an hermaphrodite," it was said that medical "examination proves her statement to be false. She is a perfect female"; see *"A Female Husband," The National Laborer* (New York), Aug. 25, 1836; copies of this paper available on microfilm, Library of Congress. The story also refers to an earlier report of the same case. I thank David Roediger, who discovered this document in his research on labor history and brought it to the attention of the New Haven Lesbian and Gay History Project, and George Chauncey, who provided me with a photocopy.

For another 1839 report of a "hermaphrodite" see Thomas L. Nichols, *Journal in Jail, Kept During a Four Months Imprisonment for Libel, in the Jail of Erie County* (Buffalo: Dinsmore, 1840), p. 229. Also see Michel Foucault's introduction to *Herculine Barbine: Being the Recently Discovered Memoirs of a Nineteenth-Century French Hermaphrodite* (New York: Pantheon, 1980).

38. Mary P. Ryan, *Womanhood in America: From Colonial Times to the Present,* 2nd ed. (New York: New Viewpoints, Franklin Watts, 1979), pp. 28–29.

39. Laurel Thater Ulrich, "Vertuous Women Found: New England Ministerial Literature, 1668–1735," in Nancy F. Cott and Elizabeth H. Pleck, ed. *A Heritage of Her Own: Toward a New Social*

*History of American Women* (New York: Simon & Schuster, 1979). Ulrich's and Ryan's works are examples of a recent feminist history stressing the relative deemphasis on the differentiation of women and men in the early colonies. Thompson's *Women* argues similarly. Koehler's *Search* is a recent feminist history stressing the differentiation of males and females in the early colonies. I side with the Ryan and Ulrich interpretation. For my critique of Koehler's equation of "active"/"passive" with male/female see the present book, p. 53. In Ulrich's " 'A Friendly Neighbor': Social Dimensions of Daily Work in Northern Colonial New England," *Feminist Studies,* vol. 6, no. 2 (Summer 1980), pp. 392–405, she takes a different position, arguing that between 1650 and 1750 "the economic lives of women and men were clearly differentiated" and that this was linked to the social inequality of women. Ulrich here (p. 404, n. 2) also cites an attack on the "myth of the [colonial] golden age" by Mary Beth Norton and Carol Ruth Berkin, in *Women of America* (Boston: Houghton Mifflin, 1979).

Sexual differentiation and similarity, as they were socially constructed, perceived, and responded to by the early colonists, require further research. The absence in the early colonial evidence of any definite link between "sodomy," and "sodomitical," and femininity or masculinity contrasts with the English evidence from the late 1600s on. In an important early essay, "The Homosexual Role," Mary McIntosh (see) pointed out: "At this period references to homosexuals [sic] as a type and to a rudimentary homosexual subculture, mainly in London, begin to appear." McIntosh said these references stressed "effeminacy" and "transvestism," seeming to make no distinction between "transvestism and homosexuality." The "terms emerging at this period to describe homosexuals—Molly, Nancy-boy, Madge-cull—emphasize effeminacy."[187–88] In a recent essay, historian Randolph Trumbach argued that a link between male "homosexual behavior" and "effeminacy" had been established in England in the royal courts and the theatrical world well before the late 1600s. But the evidence provided by Trumbach detailed the emergence to public view, in the London of the early 1700s, of what he called a male "homosexual sub-culture" involving sodomy, effeminacy, prostitution, an argot, arrests, executions, blackmail, newspaper reports, published pamphlets and trial records, and the larger criminal underworld. His evidence documents the public consciousness of the " 'Gomorrean' " as a member of a group, and even acts of resistance, and what may have been an early published defense, *Ancient and Modern Pederasty Investigated and Exemplified,* by Thomas Cannon; see Trumbach, "London's Sodomites," pp. 1–33, especially 11–23.

Future analysis of the early American colonists' responses to the sexes' differences and similarities may profitably explore the following three points. (1) Clothes styles and cross-dressing; for a 1674 report of a woman cross-dressing as a sailor see Koehler, *Search,* pp. 122, 133 n. 71; for another female cross-dresser of 1679 see same, p. 195; for the requirement that women's heads be covered as a sign of their subordination see same pp. 196, 258. In 1691–92, in Massachusetts, Mary Henly was charged with wearing men's clothes, thus "seeming to confound the course of nature," and was placed under the charge of a family; see "Records of the Middlesex County

Court," vols. 1689–99, no pagination, quoted by Lawrence W. Towner, "The Indentures of Boston's Poor Apprentices: 1734–1805," *Colonial Society of Massachusetts Publications*, vol. 43 (1966), p. 422. I thank Stephen W. Foster for this reference. (2) Hair styles and lengths; see the comment in 1722 by Rev. Solomon Stoddard of Northampton, Mass., in Perry Miller and Thomas H. Johnson, ed. *The Puritans*, rev. ed. (New York: Harper & Row, 1963), vol. 2, pp. 454–57. Also see the English Puritan William Prynne's *The Unlovelinesse of Love-lockes. Or, A Summarie Discourse, Prooving: the Wearing, and Nourishing of a Locke, or Love-locke, to be Altogether Unseemly, and Unlawfull unto Christians. In which there are Likewise some Passages Collected out of Fathers, Councells, and Sundry Authors, and Historians, Against Face-painting; the Wearing of Supposititious, Poudred, Frizled, or Extraordinary Long Haire; the Inordinate Affectation of Corporall Beautie: and Womens Mannish Unnaturall, Impudent, and Unchristian Cutting of Their Haire; the Epidemical Vanities, and Vices of Our Age* (London: n. p., 1628). A modern description calls this a "diatribe on the wearing of long hair by men and that of short by women with proof given from the works of various historians and councils that the vanities of corporeal beauty in men and the vice of mannish attitudes in women lead to the world's destruction through homosexuality"; in *Catalogue 572* (Boston: Goodspeed's Book Shop, n. d.), p. 20. I thank Carol and Robert Joyce, Jr., for this reference. (3) The male Bride-of-Christ phenomenon in which men spoke unselfconsciously of their relation to a male Christ as that of a female lover; see Greven, *Protestant Temperament*, pp. 124–40.

The history of sodomy, buggery, and related matters in England, 1607– 1740, provides a useful contrast to early colonial America. Among the major published sources on English homosexual history in this era are Trumbach's "London's Sodomites," McIntosh's "Homosexual Role," Hyde's *The Love*, Weeks's *Coming Out*, Bullough's *Sexual Variance*, Stone's *Family*, Faderman's *Surpassing*, and Foster's *Sex Variant Women*. Alan Bray's *Homosexuality in Renaissance England* (London: Gay Men's Press, 1982) sounds promising.

40. Lyle Koehler, "The Case of the American Jezebels: Anne Hutchinson and Female Agitation during the Years of Antinomian Turmoil, 1636–1640," reprinted in Esther Katz and Anita Rapone, ed. *Women's Experience in America: An Historical Anthology* (New Brunswick, N.J.: Transaction Books, 1980), pp. 21–45.

41. John Cotton on Hutchinson quoted in Ben Barker-Benfield, "Ann Hutchinson and the Puritan Attitude Toward Women," *Feminist Studies*, vol. 1, no. 2 (Fall 1972), pp. 86; also see Koehler, "Jezebels," p. 30.

42. The relationship between the *idea* of women as the "weaker sex" and their *actual* susceptibility to death in childbirth is problematic. Norton's summary of demographic studies of colonial Ipswich and Andover indicates "no significant attrition of the female population during the years when . . . married women would be bearing children." And though in colonial Plymouth "there is significantly higher female than male mortality . . . during the years when women would be likely to bear children," it is "far from clear" that this difference in the female and male death rates is "due to maternal deaths"; see Susan L. Norton, "Population Growth in Colonial America: A Study of Ipswich, Massachusetts," *Population*

*Studies,* vol. 25, no. 3 (Nov. 1971), pp. 441–42, citing (for Andover) Greven, *Four Generations,* and (for Plymouth) Demos, *A Little Commonwealth.*

**43.** Morgan, "Puritans and Sex," p. 290.

**44.** Oaks, " 'Things Fearful,' " p. 271.

**45.** On St. Paul's prohibition against women changing "the natural use" see Boswell, *Christianity,* p. 107.

**46.** On a sodomy charge usually resulting in execution: although Mathew Giles's wife and young male servant had, apparently out of court, accused him of buggering this servant boy, that charge does not seem to have been brought against Giles in court (see 1663, July 4). For a list of executions for sodomy see backnote 8, above.

**47.** For the seven cases in which the crime was described as "tending to sodomy," "sodomitical," or as "lewd" and "filthy," or in which the charge was attempted "sodomy," see: (1) 1629, June 29: Higgeson. (2) 1637, Aug. 6: Plym., Allexander and Roberts. (3) 1642, March 1: Plym., Michell and Preston. (4) 1642, Dec. 5: Mass., Eliz. Johnson.

(5) 1649, March 6: Plym., Sarah Norman and Mary Hammon. (6) 1653, March: New Haven, "sundry youths." (7) 1677, May 22: Conn., Sension.

**48.** For a list of executions for sodomy see "Early Colonial," backnote 8, above.

**49.** The death penalty for sodomy was first abolished in Pennsylvania on Sept. 15, 1786; in New Jersey, March 18, 1796; in New York, March 26, 1796; in Rhode Island, 1798; in Virginia (for free persons), 1800 (slaves were still penalized by death); in Massachusetts, 1805; in Maryland, 1809; in New Hampshire, 1812; in Georgia, 1816; in Delaware, 1826; in North Carolina, 1869; in South Carolina, 1873; see Crompton, "Homosexuals," pp. 285, 287–88.

**50.** For Pareja see *GAH,* pp. 286–87.

**51.** For St. Paul's Epistle to the Romans, 1:26–27 see above, backnote 45.

**52.** On Africans as the second largest occupational group after yeoman farmers, in 1680, see Edwin J. Perkins, *The Economy of Colonial America* (New York: Columbia University Press, 1980), p. 71.

## Documents

**1.** 1607, June: John Smith et al., *A Map of Virginia. With a Description of the Country, the Commodities, People, Government and Religion* . . . (Oxford,: Joseph Barnes, 1612), in Philip L. Barbour, ed., *The Jamestown Voyages under the First Charter, 1606–1609: Documents Relating to the Foundation of Jamestown and the History of the Jamestown Colony Up to the Departure of Captain John Smith, Last President of the Council in Virginia Under the First Charter, Early in October 1609* (London: published for the Hakluyt Society by Cambridge University Press, 1969), 2 vols., vol. 2, ch. 2, p. 384 (p. 9 in original 1612 ed.). I thank Doug Thompson for informing me of this document. The *OED* also indicates that "love" was

used in the seventeenth century "In reference to illicit relations: A paramour; said of both men and women" (an example dates to 1613). The word "love" also signified "The personification of sexual attraction" (an example dates to 1667). The term "love-boy" (1656) meant a "catamite" (a "boy kept for unnatural purposes"). The reference is classical.

**2.** On the absence of females among the Virginia settlers in 1607 see Julia C. Spruil, *Women's Life and Work in the Southern Colonies* (Chapel Hill, N. C.: University of North Carolina Press, 1938), p. 3.

**3.** 1610, May 24: Virginia "Sodomy" law; background in Alden T. Vaughan,

*American Genesis: Captain John Smith and the Founding of Virginia* (Boston: Little, Brown, 1975), pp. 77–81. Law text in [William Strachey], *For the Colony in Virginea Britannia. Lavves Diuine, Morall and Martiall, &c.* (London: Walter Burr, 1612); reprinted in Peter Force, compiler, *Tracts and Other Papers, Relating Principally to the Origin, Settlement, and Progress of the Colonies in North America . . .* (1844) (New York: Peter Smith, 1947), pp. 9–10. This martial law is cited by Bullough, *Sexual Variance,* pp. 507, 526, quoting an unreliable secondary source. The adoption in Virginia, in 1661, of the laws of England is mentioned by Thomas Jefferson in *Notes on the State of Virginia* (New York: Harper & Row, 1964), p. 126.

4. 1613: New Netherland; sodomy law; see Louis Crompton, "Homosexuals and the Death Penalty in Colonial America," *Journal of Homosexuality,* vol. 1, no. 3 (1976), p. 282. It would be useful to know the exact term for the crime in the original Dutch, and its connotations.

5. 1624, Nov. 30; Virginia, Richard Cornish executed; H. R. McIlwaine, ed., *Minutes of the Council and General Court of Colonial Virginia, 1622–1632, 1670–1676 . . .* (Richmond, Va.: Colonial Press, 1924), pp. 34, 42, 78, 81, 83, 85. Fuller texts were reprinted in *GAH,* pp. 16–19, and are also included in an appendix to Crompton, "Homosexuals," pp. 290–92. The *Minutes* of this case were first printed with some useful footnotes in *The Virginia Magazine of History and Biography;* see vol. 21, no. 1 (Jan. 1913), p. 91; n. 2 (Apr. 1913), p. 144; in 1913 the character and "details" of this case were said to be "unprintable, even as part of an ancient record." Also see vol. 24, no. 3 (June 1916), pp. 243–45, etc. Footnote with data on Thomas Hatch and " 'Duty

boys' " vol. 25, no. 2 (Ap. 1917), p. 120. For background on this early period in Virginia see Edmund S. Morgan, "The First American Boom: Virginia 1618 to 1630," *William and Mary Quarterly,* 3rd ser., vol. 27, no. 2 (Apr. 1971), pp. 169–98. Cornish's execution was the subject of an apparently fictionalized, undocumented account, published in the gay press, a good example of how not to write gay history: see Dick Leitch, "America's First Protest Movement: Gay Zap 1624," *Gay* (N. Y.), vol. 4, no. 108 (Oct. 1973), pp. 11, 16, 20, 22. Leitch claims Thomas Jefferson commented on this case; I have found no documentation of this.

About 1626, according to William Bradford, Thomas Morton and the other male settlers at Merrymount were guilty of "great licentiousness." The men's consorting with Indian women is mentioned, along with "worse practices" associated with ancient Roman feasts. Bradford said that Morton and his men "set up a maypole, drinking and dancing about it many days together, inviting the Indian women for their consorts, dancing and frisking together like so many fairies, or furies, rather; and worse practices. As if they had anew revived and celebrated the feasts of the Roman goddess Flora, or the beastly practices of the mad Bacchanalians." It would be interesting to know just what feasts and "beastly practices" Bradford had in mind; see his *Of Plymouth Plantation,* pp. 204–06; Oaks, " 'Things Fearful,' " p. 269.

6. 1629, March 25: Virginia, Thomas/ Thomasine Hall; H. R. McIlwaine, ed., *Minutes of the Council and General Court of Colonial Virginia . . .* (Richmond, Va.: Colonial Press, 1924), pp. 194–95. A "crosscloth" is identified in the *OED.* Women's "head clothes" as a sign of their submission to male authority is

discussed by Koehler, *Search*, p. 196. "Coyse" is unidentified; also see Alden T. Vaughan, "The Sad Case of Thomas(ine) Hall," *Virginia Magazine of History and Biography*, vol. 86, no. 2 (Apr. 1978), pp. 146–48.

7. 1629, June 29: "Francis Higgeson's Journal, . . ." in *The Founding of Massachusetts* (Boston: Mass. Hist. Society, 1930), p. 71. On the General Court: Nathaniel B. Shurtleff, ed., *Records of the Governor and Company of the Massachusetts Bay Colony . . .* (Boston: Wm. White, 1853–54), vol. 1, pp. 52, 54 (courts of Sept. 19 and 29, 1629). On hanging: Edwin Powers, *Crime and Punishment in Early Massachusetts: 1620–1692* (Boston: Beacon Press, 1966), p. 43.

8. 1632: Maryland "buggery" law; Wm. Kilty, ed., *Report of All Such English Statutes as Existed at the Times of the First Emigration of the People of Maryland . . .* (Annapolis, Md.: John Chandler, 1811), p. 161. For the law of 1793: Wm. Kilty, ed., *The Laws of Maryland . . .* (Annapolis, Md.: Frederick Green, 1800), vol. 2, ch. 57 (no pagination).

9. 1635, Feb. 14: New Hampshire; "two men . . . committed sodomy"; Nathaniel Bouton, ed., *Provincial Papers: Documents and Records Relating to the Province of New Hampshire, from the Earliest Period of its Settlement:* 1623–1687 (Concord, N.H.: G. E. Jenks, 1867), vol. 1, p. 106.

10. 1636, Oct.: John Cotton "sodomy" law proposal; William R. Staples, ed., *The Colonial Laws of Massachusetts Reprinted from the Edition of 1672 . . .* (Boston: Rockwell & Churchill, 1890), p. 35 n.; *GAH* p. 20. For Cotton's sixteen capital crimes see: George L. Haskins, *Law and Authority in Early Massachusetts . . .* (New York: Macmillan, 1960), pp. 124–25.

11. 1636, Nov. 15: Plymouth "sodomy" law; David Pulsifer, ed., *Records of the Colony of New Plymouth in New England.*

*Laws. 1623–1628* (Boston: Wm. White, 1861), vol. 11, p. 12.

12. 1637, Aug. 6: Plymouth, Allexander and Roberts case; Nathaniel B. Shurtleff and David Pulsifer, eds., *Records of the Colony of New Plymouth* (Boston: Wm. White, 1855), vol. 1, p. 64. For charge of Oct. 2, 1637: same, vol. 1, p. 68. For charge of Jan. 5, 1642: same, vol. 2, p. 6.

13. 1641, Nov.: Massachusetts Bay sodomy law; Wm. H. Whitmore, ed., *The Colonial Laws of Massachusetts* (Boston: Rockwell and Churchill, 1890), p. 55; George L. Haskins, "The Capitall Lawes of New England," *Harvard Law School Bulletin*, vol. 7 (Feb. 1976), pp. 10–11; Charles M. Andrews, *The Colonial Period in American History* (New Haven: Yale University Press, 1934–38), vol. 1, pp. 454–59.

14. 1641–42: Massachusetts Bay: "sodomy"?: John Winthrop, *The History of New England from 1630 to 1649*, edited by James Savage (Boston: Little, Brown, 1853), vol. 2, pp. 54–58. Researchers should note that the 1908 edition of Winthrop's *"History"* (New York: Scribner's), edited by James Hosmer, is expurgated of sexual references. On the failure to categorize the crime committed in this case as "rape" see Robert Oaks, " 'Things Fearful to Name': Sodomy and Buggery in Seventeenth-Century New England," *Journal of Social History*, vol. 12, no. 2 (1979), p. 273. Bradford's, Rayner's, Partridge's, and Chauncey's opinions are in William Bradford, *Of Plymouth Plantation*, edited by Samuel Eliot Morison (New York: Knopf, 1952), pp. 317–20, 404–13. In *Gay/Lesbian Almanac*, Latin words in the three ministers' texts referring to specifics of sex acts are translated into English. I am deeply indebted to Jaime Vidal for translating the Latin, and for

writing an eighteen-page analytical "disquisition" on the ministers' comments. (The English and European tradition of rendering sexual specifics in Latin requires analysis: the implied dangerousness of words describing sexual details is interesting. For my comment on this see p. 166.) Researchers should note that the 1912 edition of Bradford's *History of Plimmoth Plantation*, edited by W.C. Ford, 2 vols. (Boston: Houghton Mifflin) has many useful footnotes referring to the old sources cited as authorities by the three ministers. For the legal records of this case see Shurtleff, *Mass.*, vol. 2, pp. 12–13, 21–22.

15. 1641: T. Shepard's "The Sincere Convert," in *The Works of Thomas Shepard, First Pastor of the First Church, Cambridge, Massachusetts. With a Memoir of His Life and Character*, edited by John Albro (Boston: Doctrinal Tract and Book Society, 1853); (reprinted N.Y.: AMS Press, 1967), vol. 1, pp. 28–29, 41. The *DAB* says "The Sincere Convert" was first published in 1641, but the first publication included in bibliographies of early American literature dates to 1665. Shepard's private journal quoted in Greven, *Protestant Temperament*, p. 56, from Shepard's *God's Plot: The Paradoxes of Puritan Piety: Being the Autobiography and Journal of Thomas Shepard* (Amherst, Mass.: 1972), pp. 41, 72.

16. 1642, March 1: Plymouth; Michell and Preston; Shurtleff, *Plymouth*, vol. 2, pp. 35–36. These records also report that Jonathan Hatch was arrested as a "vagrant" and, for his "misdemeanors" with his sister, sentenced to be whipped and sent to Salem. The proceedings of the same date also cite "Tristam Hull, of Yarmouth, for unclean practices" (unspecified). Hull's citation did not prevent him from being elected consta-

ble of Yarmouth six years later, in 1647 (vol. 2, p. 115).

17. 1642, Dec. 1: Connecticut sodomy law; J. Hammond Trumbull, ed., *The Public Records of the Colony of Connecticut . . .* (Hartford: Lockwood and Brainard, 1850), vol. 1, pp. 77–78; Mary Jeanne Anderson Jones, *Congregational Commonwealth: Connecticut 1636–62* (Middletown, Conn.: Wesleyan University Press, 1968), p. 101–02.

18. 1642, Dec. 5: Essex Co., Mass. Bay; Eliz. Johnson; George Francis Dow, ed., *Records and Files of the Quarterly Courts of Essex County . . .* (Salem, Mass.: The Essex Institute, 1911), vol. 1, p. 44.

19. 1642: Bradford, *Of Plymouth Plantation*, pp. 316–22.

20. 1644: Edward Coke, *The Third Part of The Institutes of the Laws of England . . .* (London: Printed by M. Flesher for W. Lee and D. Pakeman, 1644), ch. 10, pp. 58–59. The *DNB* says that *The Third Part* of Coke's *Institutes* was finished in 1628 and first published in 1644. On Coke also see Robert Oaks, "Perceptions of Homosexuality by Justices of the Peace in *Colonial Virginia*," *Sexualaw Reporter*, vol. 4, no. 2 (Apr./June 1978), p. 35; Alex K. Gigeroff, *Sexual Deviations in the Criminal Law* (Toronto: University of Toronto Press, 1968), pp. 7–12. On the Lombard money lenders see Part I, Intro., n. 21. I thank Jaime Vidal for identifying the "crying sins." In Catholic tradition the four crying sins are (1) voluntary homicide, Gen. 4:10; (2) the sins of Sodom and Gomorrah, Gen. 18:20–21; (3) oppression of widows and orphans, Exodus 22:22–24; (4) defrauding the laborer of pay, Letter of James 5:4: "But look, here is the pay of the reaper you hired and whom you cheated, and it is crying out against you! And the cries of the other laborers

you swindled are heard by the Lord of Hosts himself." The next verse adds: "Yes, you have had a magnificent time on this earth; you have fattened yourselves up—for the day of slaughter!" On the crying sins also see Goodich, *Unmentionable Vice,* p. 61.

21. 1646, June 25: New Netherland; execution of Jan Creoli; E[dmund] B. O'Callaghan, ed., *Calendar of Historical Manuscripts in the Office of the Secretary of State, Albany, N.Y.* (Albany: Weed, Parsons, 1865); reprinted as *Calendar of Dutch Historical Manuscripts* (Ridgewood, N.J.: Gregg Press, 1968), p. 103; *GAH* pp. 22–23, 570 n. 22.

22. 1646: New Haven; execution of Wm. Plaine; Winthrop, *History,* vol. 2, p. 324. Winthrop gives the year of Plaine's execution as 1646; Smith (below) says it was "about 1648." It would be interesting to know of any further documentation of this execution in New Haven or other records. The problem in exactly dating and documenting this execution suggests there may be other executions, severe punishments, or cases which are, so far, unknown to us. Also see Bernard Christian Steiner, *A History of the Plantation of Menukatuck, and of the Original Town of Guilford, Connecticut* (Baltimore: Steiner, 1897), pp. 25, 45, 53, 86, 227, 260; Ralph D. Smith, *The History of Guilford, Connecticut from its First Settlement in 1636. From the Manuscripts* (Albany: J. Munsell, 1877), pp. 11–12, 15.

23. 1647, May 19: Rhode Island "sodomy" law; Wm. R. Staples, ed., *The Proceedings of the First General Assembly of "The Incorporation of Providence Plantation," and The Code of Laws Adopted by That Assembly, in 1647, with Notes Historical and Explanatory* (Providence: Charles Burnett, Jr., 1817), pp. 31–32; John Russell Bartlett, ed., *Records of the Colony of Rhode Island and Providence Plantations, in New England* (Providence: A. C. Green, 1856), vol. 1, pp. 156–90. The incorporation of four towns referred to here as Rhode Island was also known at the time as "Providence Plantations."

24. 1648: Massachusetts Bay "sodomy" law; Max Farrand, ed., *Book of the General Lawes and Liberties of Massachusetts* (San Marino, Calif.: Huntington Library, 1929), p. 5. The list of capital crimes is the same as that printed on the 1643 London broadside; the sodomy provision cites Gen. 19:5 in the margin.

25. 1649, March 6: Plymouth; Sara Norman and Mary Hammon; Shurtleff, *Plymouth,* vol. 2, pp. 137, 148, 163; J. R. Roberts, " 'leude behaviour each with other upon a bed': The Case of Sarah Norman and Mary Hammond," *Sinister Wisdom,* no. 14 (Summer 1980).

26. 1649, Oct. 29; Plymouth; R. Berry and T. Joanes; Shurtleff, *Plymouth,* vol. 2, pp. 146–47, 148; vol. 3, p. 37, 176–77.

27. 1650, May: Connecticut sodomy law; George Brinley, ed., *The Laws of Connecticut: An Exact Reprint of the Original Edition of 1673* (Hartford: privately printed, 1865), p. 9.

28. 1653, Feb.: Michael Wigglesworth, *The Diary of, . . . 1653–1657; The Conscience of a Puritan,* edited with an introduction by Edmund S. Morgan (New York: Harper & Row, 1965). Also see Greven's comments on Wigglesworth in *The Protestant Temperament.*

29. 1653, March 23: New Haven; "sundry youths"; Franklin Bowditch Dexter, ed., *New Haven Town Records, 1649–1684* (New Haven: New Haven Historical Society, 1917), pp. 178–79.

30. 1656, March 1: New Haven "sodomy" law; *New Haven's Settling in New England and Some Lawes for Government* (London: printed by M. S. for Livewell Chapman, 1656), in J. Hammond Trumbull, ed., *The True-Blue Laws of Connecticut and New*

*Haven . . .* (Hartford: American Publishing Co., 1876), pp. 198–201.

31. 1658, Aug. 26: New Netherland; Nicolas Hillebrant; O'Callaghan, p. 201 (Fort Orange Records, vol. A, p. 91); p. 319 (Council Minutes, vol. 8, p. 992).

32. 1660, May 13: New Netherland; Jan Quisthout and Hendrick Harmsen; O'Callaghan, p. 211 (Council Minutes, vol. 9, p. 251), p. 213 (same, p. 294–96, 298), pp. 251–52 (same, vol. 10, p. 275).

33. 1661: Virginia buggery law; Jefferson, *Notes on the State of Virginia,* p. 126.

34. 1663, March: North and South Carolina "buggery" law; François Xavier Martin, ed., *A Collection of the Statutes of the Parliament of England in Force in North Carolina* (New Been, N. C.: The Editor's Press, 1792), p. 208, where the English statute of 1533 is cited as in effect as of 1792, suggesting it was in force during the early colonial period.

35. 1663, July 4: New Hampshire; Mathew Giles case; Otis G. Hammond, ed., *New Hampshire Court Records, 1640–1692; Court Papers, 1652–1668* (Concord, N. H.: State of New Hampshire, 1943), pp. 182–83; discussed by Kohler, *Search,* pp. 153–54. The preceeding entry suggests the Giles case was heard on July 4.

36. 1663: Rhode Island "sodomy" law; *Acts and Laws of His Majesties Colony of Rhode Island . . .* (Boston: Nicholas Boone, 1719), p. 6. This law, as first published in 1719, provided that those convicted of sodomy be punished by death "with benefit of Clergy." This was probably a printer's error for "without" benefit of clergy—an error which might theoretically have removed the mandatory death penalty for sodomy. "Benefit of Clergy" provided an exemption of the death penalty for the clergy and some others.

37. 1665, March 1: Duke of York's sodomy law; George Straughton and others, ed., *Charter to William Penn, and Laws of the Province of Pennsylvania . . .* (Harrisburg, Pa.: Lane S. Hart, 1879), p. 14. Also see Charles M. Andrews, *The Colonial Period of American History* (New Haven: 1934–38), vol. 3, pp. 106–07, 116–17.

38. 1668, May 30: New Jersey "sodomy" law; Aaron Leaming and Jacob Spicer, ed., *The Grants, Concessions, and Original Constitutions of the Province of New Jersey . . .* (Philadelphia: W. Bradford, 1758), pp. 77, 79.

39. 1671, June 6: Plymouth "sodomy" law; *The Book of the General Laws of the Inhabitants of the Jurisdiction of New Plimouth, Collected Out of the Records of the General Court, . . . Held at Plimouth the Sixth of June Anno Dom. 1671* (Cambridge, Mass.: Samuel Green, 1672), pp. 3–5.

40. 1672, Oct.: Connecticut "sodomy" law; *The Book of the General Laws for the People within the Jurisdiction of Connecticut . . .* (Cambridge, Mass.: Samuel Green, 1673), p. 9, reprinted in George Brinley, ed., *The Laws of Connecticut. An Exact Reprint of the Original Edition of 1673* (Hartford, Conn.: for private distribution, 1865). The 1750 revision is mentioned in a footnote to *The Public Statute Laws . . .* (see below). The 1796 law is in *Acts and Laws of the State of Connecticut* (Hartford: Hudson & Goodwin, 1796), p. 182. The 1808 revision (or reprinting) is in *The Public Statute Laws of the State of Connecticut, Book I* (Hartford: Hudson & Goodwin, 1808), pp. 294–95. The 1821 abolition of the death penalty for sodomy in Connecticut is reported by Louis Crompton (personal communication to Robert Oaks).

41. 1674: S. Danforth, *The Cry of Sodom Enquired Into; Upon Occasion of The Arraignment and Condemnation of Benjamin Goad For his Prodigious Villany. Together with A*

*Solemn Exhortation to Tremble at Gods Judgements and to Abandon Youthful Lusts* (Cambridge; Mass.: Marmaduke Johnson, 1674). Cited in Bullough, *SVISH,* p. 522; Oaks, " 'Things,' " pp. 277–78; Kohler, *Search,* pp. 72–73.

42. Theodosius and Arcadius are mentioned by Goodich, *Unmentionable Vice,* p. 75.

43. 1676, Sept. 25: Pennsylvania "sodomy" law; Harry Elmer Barnes, *The Evolution of Penology in Pennsylvania: A Study in American Social History* (Indianapolis: Bobbs-Merrill, 1927), p. 29; Crompton, "Homosexuals," p. 282.

44. 1677, May 22: Connecticut; N. Sension case; original manuscript depositions in "Crimes and Misdemeanors," vol. 1, document numbers 87–103, Manuscript Division, Connecticut State Archives, Connecticut State Library, Hartford. These records of testimony in the Sension case are written in various almost illegible hands. The transcriptions given here thus sometimes constitute a guess at the exact wording. A fascinating, detailed subject and name index exists for the 2,410 manuscript documents contained in the six volumes titled *Connecticut Archives, Crimes and Misdemeanors, 1662/63–1789.* For example, see headings: "Adultery," pp. 3–4; "Fornication," pp. 153–55; "Incest," p. 222; "Insane," p. 223; "Punishments. Castration," and "Death," p. 328; "Punishments. Mutilation," p. 329; "Rape," p. 332. For Nicholas Sension, pp. 361–62. For biographical details on Nicholas Sension, Nathaniel Pond, and others see Henry R. Stiles, *The History and Genealogy of Ancient Windsor, Connecticut . . . 1635–1891,* vol. 1, *History* (Hartford: Lockwood & Brainard, 1891), Sension, pp. 88, 166, 229, etc.; vol. 2, *Genealogies and Biographies* (same: 1892), N. Pond, p. 620; N. Sension, p. 676. Also see Linda A. Bissell, "Family, Friends, and Neighbors: Social Interaction in Seventeenth Century Windsor, Connecticut," Ph.D. dissertation, Brandeis University, 1973, pp. 123–28. I am deeply indebted to Lyle Koehler for first informing me of Bissell's work and the Sension case, and to Lisa Duggan for help in transcribing and understanding the documents. The transcriptions were made from photostatic copies and from a personal examination of the original manuscripts.

45. Sension case: Daniel Saxton also testified that John Enno had, on the above occasion, "waked him and told him Nicholas Sension had been with him and had wiped something off of him." Enno "showed him the sheet & there was something left wet on the sheet." Saxton "heard Sension pray God to turn him from this Sin he had so Long lived in. . . ."[96(b)]

46. 1680, March 16: New Hampshire "buggery" law; Albert Stillman Batchellor, ed., *Laws of New Hampshire, Including Public and Private Acts and Resolves and the Royal Commissions and Instructions, with Historical and Descriptive Notes . . .* (Manchester, N.H.: John B. Clarke, 1904), vol. 1, pp. 11–13.

47. 1681: West New Jersey "buggery" law; Barnes, *Evolution,* p. 28, citing Aaron Leaming and Jacob Spicer, ed., *The Grants and Concessions . . . of the Province of New-Jersey . . .* (Philadelphia: W. Bradford, 1752?), pp. 382–411; Andrews, *Colonial,* vol. 3, pp. 177–78; Crompton, "Homosexuals," p. 284.

48. 1682, Dec. 7: Pennsylvania "sodomy" law; George Straughton and others, *Charter to William Penn, and Laws of the Province of Pennsylvania . . .* (Harrisburg: Lane S. Hart, 1879), p. 110; Barnes, *Evolution,* pp. 31–36; Crompton, "Homosexuals," p. 282.

49. 1683,  March:  East  New  Jersey

"sodomy" law; Leaming and Spicer (1758), pp. 227, 237–39.

50. 1691: New York "buggery" law; Crompton, "Homosexuals," p. 282. For the New York State law of Feb. 14, 1787, which provided death for "buggery," see *Laws of the State of New-York, Comprising The Constitution and The Acts of the Legislature Since the Revolution from the First to the Twelfth Session, Inclusive* (Hanover: Hugh Gaine, 1789), vol. 2, p. 45.

51. 1693, June: Pennsylvania sodomy law; Straughton, pp. 539–58; James T. Mitchell and Henry Flanders, ed., *The Statutes at Large of Pennsylvania from 1682 to 1801* (Harrisburg: Clarence M. Busch, 1896), vol. 2, pp. 8, 79, 183–84; vol. 3, p. 202; Gail McKnight Beekman, ed., *The Statutes at Large of Pennsylvania in the Time of William Penn* (New York: 1976), vol. 1, pp. 9, 176.

52. 1697, May 26: Massachusetts "buggery" law; *Acts and Laws, Passed by the Great and General Council or Assembly of the Province of Massachusetts-Bay in New-England from 1692, to 1719* (London: J. Baskett, 1724), p. 110. Additional information on this law in Samuel Sewall, *The Diary of,* . . . edited by M. Halsey Thomas, 2 vols., (New York: Farrar, Straus & Giroux, 1973), vol. 1, p. 380. For the revision of 1785 see *Perpetual Laws of . . . Massachusetts Up to 1789* (Boston: Adams and Nourse, 1789), p. 178.

53. 1700, Nov. 27: Pennsylvania "sodomy" law; Mitchell and Flanders, vol. 2, pp. 8, 79; Barnes, *Evolution*, p. 36, says that though this law of 1700 was repealed by the English Crown it was reenacted on Jan. 12, 1706 (citing Mitchell and Flanders, vol. 2, pp. 171ff.).

54. 1701, June: Cotton Mather, *A Christian at his Calling. Two Brief Discourses. One Directing a Christian in his General Calling; Another Directing him in his Personal Calling* (Boston: Printed by B. Green & J.

Allen, for S. Sewall, June 1701). Discussed by Richard Bushman, *From Puritan to Yankee; Character and the Social Order in Connecticut, 1690–1765* (New York: Norton, 1970), pp. 23, 322.

55. 1702: New Jersey "buggery" law; Andrews, *Colonial*, pp. 177–78; Crompton, "Homosexuals," pp. 283–84, 287. For the law of 1796 see Wm. Patterson, *Laws of the State of New-Jersey; Revised and Published Under the Authority of the Legislature* (Newark: Matthias Day, 1800), p. 209.

56. 1706, Jan. 12: Pennsylvania "sodomy" and "buggery" law; Mitchell and Flanders, vol. 2, pp. 184, 235.

57. 1707, Feb. 9: L. Morris on Cornbury; E[dmund] B. O'Callaghan, ed., *Documents Relative to the Colonial History of the State of New York* (Albany: Weed, Parsons, 1855), vol. 5, pp. 38; *GAH*, p. 570 n. 23.

58. 1709: John Lawson, *History of North Carolina,* . . . edited by Frances Latham Harris (Richmond, Va.: Garrett & Massie, 1937), p. 208; *GAH*, p. 612 n. 8. For a biography of Lawson see *Catholic Encyclopedia*, vol. 8, p. 318.

59. 1712, Jan. 29: Massachusetts; execution of Mingo; Samuel Sewall, *The Diary of,* . . . *1674–1729; Newly Edited From the Manuscript at the Massachusettes Historical Society by M. Halsey Thomas*, 2 vols. (New York: Farrar, Straus & Giroux, 1973), vol. 2, pp. 677, 678. Additional references to Mingo: vol. 1, pp. 388, 446, vol. 2, p. 617. Reference to the Massachusetts "buggery" law of 1697, vol. 1, p. 380. I wish to thank Robert Joyce, Jr., for informing me of this document.

60. 1712: South Carolina "buggery" law; Thomas Cooper, ed., *The Statutes at Large of South Carolina . . .* (Columbia, S. C.: Johnston, 1873), vol. 2, p. 465. For the S. C. law of 1873 see Crompton, "Homosexuals," p. 28.

61. 1718, March: North Carolina; *Clark* vs.

*Winn;* Wm. S. Price, Jr., ed., assisted by Ruth Clow Langston and Donna Holmes Goswick, *The Colonial Records of North Carolina [Second Series]. Volume V. North Carolina Higher-Court Minutes 1709–1723* (Raleigh, N.C.: Department of Cultural Resources, Division of Archives and History, 1974), pp. 164–66. I thank Stephen W. Foster for informing me of this document and furnishing a photocopy.

62. 1718, May 31: Pennsylvania "sodomy" law; Mitchell and Flanders, vol. 3, p. 202; Barnes, *Evolution,* pp. 38–39. For the law of 1789 see Mitchell and Flanders, vol. 3, p. 281.

63. 1718: New Hampshire "buggery" law; Batchellor, vol. 2, p. 314. For the law of 1812 see Batchellor, vol. 8, p. 130.

64. 1719: Delaware "sodomy" law; *Laws of the State of Delaware . . .* (New-Castle, Pa.: Samuel and John Adams, 1797), vol. 1, p. 67. For the law of 1826: *Laws of Delaware* (Wilmington: R. Porter, 1826), p. 139.

65. 1724: *Onania; or, The Heinous Sin of Self-Pollution, and all its Frightful Consequences, in Both Sexes, Considered* (London, 1723; Boston for John Philips, 1924). Reprinted in *The Secret Vice Exposed! Some Arguements Against Masturbation* (New York: Arno Press, 1974).

66. 1732, June 20: Georgia "buggery" law; Horatio Marbury and Wm. H. Crawford, ed., *Digest of the Laws of the State of Georgia . . . 1755 to 1800 . . .* (Savannah: Seymour, Woohopter & Stebbins, 1802), pp. 400–01; for the law of 1777 see same.

67. 1734, March 25: Georgia; three hundred lashes for "sodomy"; Johann Boltzius and Israel Gronau, "Excerpts from the Original Diary of, . . ." Translated and annotated by Wm. H. Brown, in *Detailed Reports on the Salzburger Emigrants Who Settled in America . . . Edited by Samuel Urlsperger,* vol. 3, translated and edited by George F. Jones and Marie Hahn (Athens, Ga.: University of Georgia Press, 1972), p. 314. I thank Stephen W. Foster for informing me of this document.

## Part II
### The Modern United States: The Invention of the Homosexual, 1880–1950

### Introduction

1. On the response of the Salt Lake City lesbians to *The Well of Loneliness* see Vern Bullough and Bonnie Bullough, "Lesbianism in the 1920s and 1930s: A Newfound Study," *Signs,* vol. 2, no. 4 (Summer 1977), pp. 895–904.

2. On "Mädchen in Uniform" in amateur productions see Foster, *Sex Variant,* p. 301.

3. Barbara Welter, "The Cult of True Womanhood: 1820–1860," in Michael Gordon, ed., *The American Family in Social-Historical Perspective* (New York: St. Martin's Press, 1973), pp. 224–50. In the debate about whether the ideal Victorian woman was supposed to be (and was) asexual, or possessed a controlled, procreation-focused eroticism, Carl Degler argues against the existence of a single, monolithic asexual Victorian ideal and reality of womanhood; see his *At Odds: Women and the Family in America from the Revolution to the Present* (New York: Oxford University Press, 1980), especially ch. 11, "Women's Sexuality in Nineteenth Century America," pp. 249–78, and "What Ought to Be and What Was: Women's Sexuality in the

Nineteenth Century," *American Histori-cal Review,* vol. 79, no. 5 (Dec. 1974), pp. 1467–90. In contrast, Lillian Fader-man argues that the common, unself-conscious expression of passionate love between Victorian middle-class women, free of any perception of Sapphism, was possible only because they were presumed, and presumed themselves to be, asexual; see Fader-man's, *Surpassing,* especially, "The Asexual Woman," pp. 147–56. Sarah Stage argues that though Degler use-fully distinguished between contrasting Victorian sexual ideologies, and ideol-ogy and the actual behavior of females and males, he deemphasized the essen-tial way in which Victorian advice litera-ture "accorded women only a second-ary, second-hand sexuality"; see Stage's review of Degler's "What Ought to Be and What Was" (1974), Haller and Haller, *The Physician and Sex-uality in Victorian America* (1974), and Walters, *Primers for Prudery: Sexual Advice to Victorian America* (1974), in *American Quarterly,* vol. 27, no. 4 (Oct. 1975), pp. 480–85. In a very important essay, Wil-liam G. Shade argues that Degler may have overemphasized sexual similari-ties between Victorian and present-day women; that the Victorian "image of woman as the pious, asexual protector of the home and civilization came to dominate middle class values"; see his " 'A Mental Passion': Female Sexuality in Victorian America," *International Journal of Women's Studies,* vol. 1, no. 1 (Jan./Feb. 1978), pp. 13–29. Nancy F. Cott also differs with Degler, analyzing "that central tenet of Victorian sexual ideology which I call 'passionless-ness' "—the idea that "lustfulness" was uncharacteristic of women. Cott stresses women's pragmatic interest in adopting this idea. But Cott's major an-alytical term, "passionlessness," is a confusing misnomer. Victorian women could be and were intensely passionate without being thought carnal—passion and sexual lust were conceptually sepa-rated; see Cott's "Passionlessness: An Interpretation of Victorian Sexual Ide-ology, 1790–1850," in Cott and Eliza-beth H. Pleck, ed. *A Heritage of Her Own: Toward a New Social History of American Women* (New York: Simon & Schuster, 1979), pp. 162–82. Cott's study of Vic-torian female–female friendships also betrays a similar lack of perception of their overt passion and implicit eroti-cism, and she downplays evidence of this; see Cott's *The Bonds of Womanhood: "Woman's Sphere" in New England, 1780–1835* (New Haven: Yale University Press, 1977), ch. 5, "Sisterhood," pp. 160–96. In contrast, Carroll Smith-Rosenberg argues that Victorian mid-dle-class women's friendships were "sensual," "intense," "physical," and "romantic" though probably not geni-tally enacted; see her "Female World," pp. 4, 6, 25. My thesis is that though both Victorian women and men may have been perceived to have erotic feel-ing, this was conceptually isolated from passion and love as a result of the social division into separate spheres of erotic, procreative, and affectional relation-ships. I also stress a temporal distinc-tion; that the sexual ideology and sex of the early Victorian period differed es-sentially from that of the late Victorian era in which the erotic was perceived as breaking out of the ghetto to which it had earlier been assigned, and was ex-perienced as constituting part of every-day life, informing those hallowed in-stitutions of asexual "purity" The Family, The Home, The Child, The Mother, and The Woman.

4. On Victorian true manhood see Mi-chael Gordon, "The Ideal Husband as Depicted in the Nineteenth-Century

Marriage Manual," in Elizabeth H. Pleck and Joseph H. Pleck; *The American Man* (Englewood Cliffs, N. J.: Prentice-Hall, 1980), pp. 145–57, Ben Barker-Benfield, "The Spermatic Economy: A Nineteenth-Century View of Sexuality," reprinted in Michael Gordon, ed., *The American Family*, pp. 336–72; and Barker-Benfield's *The Horrors of the Half-Known Life: Male Attitudes Toward Women and Sexuality in Nineteenth-Century America* (New York: Harper & Row, 1976); Peter Gabriel Filene, *Him/Her/Self: Sex Roles in Modern America* (New York: New American Library, 1976), especially ch. 3, "Men and Manliness," pp. 68–93; Peter N. Stearns, *Be A Man! Male in Modern Society* (New York: Holmes & Meier, 1979), especially pp. 7, 9, 71ff., 114, 117, 121, 156.

5. On Frances Wright see Welter, "The Cult," p. 227.

6. On "semi women, mental hermaphrodites" see Welter, "The Cult," p. 241. For Dr. Clarke on a "hermaphroditic condition" of mind, etc., see Nancy Sahli, "Smashing: Women's Relationships Before the Fall," *Chrysalis*, no. 8 (Summer 1979), pp. 20–21.

7. For "unsexed females" (1853) see Ann Firor Scott, *The Southern Lady: From Pedestal to Politics, 1830–1930* (Chicago: Chicago University Press, 1970), p. 20. For "unsexed" women (twentieth century) see Filene, *Him/Her/Self*, p. 248, n.48. For "unsexed" applied to feminists and female sexual "perverts" (1880 on) see "unsexed" in the index. For Lucy Ann Lobdell see *GAH*, p. 222.

8. For Theodore Roosevelt's purity (1878) and Victorian chaste marriage see Filene, *Him/Her/Self*, p. 82.

9. On late Victorian sex radicals, free lovers, and birth controllers see Hal D. Sears, *The Sex Radicals: Free Love in High Victorian America* (Lawrence, Kans.: Regents Press of Kansas, 1977); Sidney Ditzion, *Marriage, Morals, and Sex in America: A History of Ideas* (New York: Bookman Associates, 1953); Linda Gordon, *Woman's Body, Woman's Right: A Social History of Birth Control in America* (New York: Penguin Books, 1977); David M. Kennedy, *Birth Control in America: The Career of Margaret Sanger* (New Haven: Yale University Press, 1970).

10. In *GAH* I coined the term "passing women" for females who dressed and worked and passed as men, women who passed beyond the limits of the domestic female role. I thank Frances Doughty for pointing out the sexist implications of the focus on women "passing" as men. I agree that these women's passing arose out of an original project of performing activities and crossing over into a world open only to men. Hence in the present book I use the terms "crossing person," "crossing woman," or "crossing man" in place of "passing." It is important that all our new uses of words be carefully examined before they become set and taken for granted.

11. On "transvestism" (1910), "cross-dressing" (1911), "sexo-aesthetic inversion" (1913) and "D'Eonism" (1920) see *GAH*, pp. 210, 599 n. 1.

12. As to "homovestism," I make no claim to the coinage. I believe I first read the term in a medical journal article, but have lost the reference.

13. On Ulrichs see Hubert Kennedy, "Gay Liberation 1864; Karl Heinrich Ulrichs, Pioneer of Homosexual Emancipation," *The Body Politic*, part 1 (March 1978), pp. 23–25; part 2 (April 1978), pp. 24–26; and James D. Steakley, *The Homosexual Emancipation Movement in Germany* (New York: Arno Press, 1975).

14. Carl von Westphal, "Die konträre Sexualempfindung," *Archiven für Psychiatrie und Nervenkrankheiten*, vol. 2 (1869), pp. 73–108; discussed and cited in Bul-

lough, *Sexual Variance*, pp. 639, 670 n. 12.

15. For Ellis's discussion see document cited in backnote 18, p. 693.

16. On Westermarck's *The Origin and Development of Moral Ideas* (1908) see *GAH*, p. 319–20, 618 n. 48.

17. On feminism and female "purity" see Linda Gordon, *Woman's Body*, pp. 116–26, 132, 205, 206, 356, 364, 409, and Shade, "A Mental Passion."

18. I hope in future to research and write an essay titled "The Invention of Heterosexuality: 1892–1930," detailing and analyzing the evidence for "heterosexuality" (the term, concept, feeling, act, and relationship) being a historically relative construction. For pioneering articles on the social enforcement of heterosexuality see Christina Simmons, "Companionate Marriage and the Lesbian Threat," *Frontiers*, vol. 4, no. 3 (Fall 1979), pp. 54–59; Adrienne Rich, "Compulsory Heterosexuality and Lesbian Existence," *Signs*, vol. 5, no. 4 (Summer 1980), pp. 631–60; and Lisa Duggan, "Women, Work, and Sexuality in the 1920s: The Limits of Change," 22 pp. typescript photocopy, draft #1, Spring 1981; an earlier presentation of this paper profoundly influenced my own ideas. Also see Ellen Ross and Rayna Rapp, "Sex and Society: A Research Note From Social History and Anthropology," *Comparative Studies in Society and History*, vol. 23, no. 1 (Jan. 1981), pp. 51–72 which presents a social-historical, constructivist concept of sex; and Ann Ferguson, Jacquelyn N. Zita, and Kathryn Pyne Addelson, "On 'Compulsory Heterosexuality and Lesbian Existence': Defining the Issues," *Signs*, vol. 7, no. 1 (1981), pp. 158–99. My own contribution is that "heterosexuality" was not only enforced but invented in the early twentieth century;

that is, its enforcement involved its invention.

19. For the American woman doctor on sexual feeling in friendships between females see *GAH*, pp. 371–73. This woman doctor, identified in *Sexual Inversion* only as "Dr. K," was probably Dr. Laura Keisker of Brookline, Mass., mentioned in Ellis's autobiography as corresponding with him for twenty years; see *My Life: Autobiography of Havelock Ellis* (Boston: Houghton Mifflin, 1930), p. 547.

20. Catherine Wells, "The Beautiful House," *Harper's Magazine*, vol. 124 (March 1912), p. 509. For further discussion of this story see Foster, *Sex Variant*, pp. 255; Faderman, "Lesbian Magazine Fiction in the Early Twentieth Century," *Journal of Popular Culture*, vol. 11, no. 4 (Spring 1978), pp. 806, 816; Faderman, *Surpassing*, pp. 305–07; 349, 466n.

21. The work and American influence of Sigmund Freud as it affected the U.S. history of homosexuality is a huge subject, the topic for a separate book, and I have dealt with it here only peripherally. See Nathan G. Hale, Jr., *Freud and the Americans: The Beginnings of Psychoanalysis in the United States, 1876–1917* (New York: Oxford University Press, 1971); and Ronald Bayer, *Homosexuality and American Psychiatry* (New York: Basic Books, 1981). A Freudian influence on perceptions of homosexuality can be detected in various *New York Times* book reviews excerpted here; see the index under "Freud" and "Freudianism" which list major explicit and implicit references.

22. For Benkert's use of *"Homosexualität"* (1869) see backnote 20, p. 661.

23. For Lucy Ann Lobdell see *GAH*, pp. 223–25.

24. For the doctor's report of 1902 see *GAH*, pp. 248–49.

**25.** Dr. George H. Napheys, *The Transmission of Life. Counsel on the Nature and Hygiene of the Masculine Function*, 9th ed. (Philadelphia: Fergus, 1871), p. 29. Rugoff says the passage in question appeared in an edition of 1870, but 1871 seems to be the earliest edition; see Milton Rugoff, *Prudery and Passion* (New York: Putnam's, 1971), pp. 269, 381. I thank Allan Bérubé for help with this research.

**26.** For the letter of 1882 on "our unfortunate class" see *GAH*, pp. 37–39.

**27.** On Earl Lind and the *Cercle Hermaphroditos* see *GAH*, pp. 366–71.

**28.** For two recent exponents of homosexual acts as "acts of revolution" see Charles Shively's essays in the Boston gay liberation newspaper *Fag Rag*, and John Rechy, *The Sexual Outlaw* (New York: Grove Press, 1977).

**29.** On the emigrant's letter of 1882 see *GAH*, pp. 37–39.

**30.** For reports from lovers of their own sex in the U. S. to Havelock Ellis see *GAH*, pp. 374–76; for a report to Magnus Hirschfeld see a letter from Boston (1906, April), *GAH*, pp. 382–83 (the date of publication printed in *GAH* is incorrect); for letters to Edward Carpenter see the present book, entry of 1921, April 4.

**31.** Ulrichs is mentioned in the following medical journal excerpts reprinted in this book: 1882, July; 1883, Apr.; 1884, May; 1884, July 19; 1884 Beard; 1888, Oct. (the 1882 letter); and 1888, Nov. In his *Prometheus*, published in Germany in 1869, Ulrichs cited "A young physician from North America," who had written to him on July 31, 1869: "Your writings . . . must be convincing for anyone who judges impartially."[15] Later in *Prometheus* Ulrichs listed individuals and publications supporting his views of Urnings, and believing in the repeal of the laws criminalizing

them. Among these supporters was "J. Hoffman, M.D. of Chicago (North America), presently of Würzburg, in repeated letters to me."[58] Ulrichs also referred in *Prometheus* to a communication to him from Julius Hoffman, "now of Würzburg," a doctor who had in 1868 worked in an insane asylum in "Jacksonville," in the U.S. (no state was listed).[30–32] Following Ulrichs's suggestion, Hoffman contemplated a blood transfusion from Ulrichs in order to study Uranianism in himself (see Ulrichs's *Argonauticus*, p. 83). Describing in *Prometheus* the circulation of his writings to the date of publication, Ulrichs reported that his publisher had, in 1868 and 1869, filled orders from New York, and that, by private means, his pamphlets had reached St. Louis and other North American cities[84]; see Ulrichs's *Argonauticus* and *Prometheus* (both originally published 1869), reprinted Leipzig: Max Spohr, 1898; reprinted New York: Arno Press, 1975. I thank Hubert Kennedy for a list of the U. S. references in Ulrichs's work, and James D. Steakley for a translation and information.

**32.** For "Dr. K," the American woman physician, see *GAH*, pp. 371–73; also see backnote 19 above. For "Miss S." see *GAH*, p. 374. On "Professor X" see *GAH*, pp. 374–75 and Hubert Kennedy, "The Case for James Mills Peirce," *Journal of Homosexuality*, vol. 4, no. 2 (Winter 1978), pp. 179–84. The first English edition of Havelock Ellis and John Addington Symonds's *Sexual Inversion* (which was suppressed and Symonds's name deleted as author) was reprinted New York: Arno Press, 1975.

**33.** For the distribution of Carpenter's pamphlets in the U. S. in the late 1890s see 1894, September 16.

**34.** For Emma Goldman's 1915 Portland

speech against the "social ostracism of the invert" see *GAH*, p. 377; also see Reb Raney, "Alexander Berkman in San Francisco," *Mother Earth*, vol. 10, no. 4 (June 1915), p. 152.

**35.** As for the "Conspiracy of Silence" (1870) my informant is Judith Walkawitz.

**36.** Alfred Douglas's poem "Two Loves" is quoted in part in Rubert Hart-Davis, ed., *The Letters of Oscar Wilde* (New York: Harcourt, Brace & World, 1962), p. 441 n. 3. The increasing public volubility of those speaking in England in defense of male–male love (and the quick backlash) is illustrated by a letter of George Ives to *The Humanitarian*, vol. 5, no. 4 (Oct. 1894), pp. 292–97; see Timothy d'Arch Smith, *Love In Earnest: Some Notes on the Lives and Writings of English "Uranian" Poets from 1889 to 1930* (London: Routledge & Kegan Paul, 1970), pp. 110–12, 156 n. 13. Also see Jeffrey Weeks, *Coming Out*, p. 120.

**37.** For the review by C. M. Bowra of *The Complete Poems of [C. P.] Cavafy*, translated from the Greek by Rae Dalven, introduction by W. H. Auden (New York: Harcourt, Brace & World, 1961) see *NYTBR*, May 28, 1961, pp. 3–4. The reviewer did refer to Cavafy's "highly unusual personality" and "errant appetites," but the unknowing reader would not have identified these poems as among the world's most beautiful male homosexual love lyrics. Patterned omission in positive reviews of works containing humane portrayals of homosexuality is also exemplified in the *Times* review by Stanley Moss of Edward Field's *Variety Photoplays* (New York: Grove Press, 1967), which explicitly cited the poem "Giant Pacific Octopus" as one of Field's "best," without indicating its homosexual content; see *NYTBR* Sept. 24, 1967, p. 56. It can be argued that the *homosexual revelation* as

plot device in such novels as Alan Hart's *The Undaunted* (1936) made it impossible for a reviewer to mention homosexuality without giving away one of the story's surprises. But in Jo Sinclair's *Wasteland* (1947) the lesbian revelation does not serve the purpose of surprise, and could have been discussed without giving away plot secrets. My point is that humane portrayals of homosexuality were not mentioned explicitly as such, at the same time as inhumane examples were explicitly cited in novels, reviews, and news reports.

**38.** For Dr. Kiernan on the "sex-invert homicide of Hattie Deuel at Pocomoke City, Md., in 1878," and the Alice Mitchell case (1892), see his column "Sexology: Increase of American Inversion," *Urologic and Cutaneous Review*, vol. 20, no. 1 (Jan. 1916), p. 46. In 1892, Dr. Rosse also referred to a case, "tried on the Eastern Shore of Maryland a few years ago," involving "Morbid love of two young women," one of whom murdered the other"; apparently the Hattie Deuel case. It would be useful to find newspaper reports or other records of that case.

**39.** For Dr. Hughes on Black "phallic fornicators" see *GAH*, pp. 42–43; for Hughes also see the present volume, document excerpt of 1893, Oct.

**40.** On Kinsey's writing, Masters and Johnson's ponderous prose, and the "history of sexological style" see Paul Robinson, *The Modernization of Sex: Havelock Ellis, Alfred Kinsey, William Masters, and Virginia Johnson* (New York: Harper & Row, 1976), pp. 123–27. Also see Martin Bauml Duberman's review of Masters and Johnson's *Homosexuality in Perspective* (1979), *New Republic*, June 16, 1979, pp. 24–31. My comment on "the higher abstractions of French Philosophy," a negative judgment of Foucault's dauntingly abstract level of discourse in his *History of Sexuality,* is definitely not meant as my total response to a provocatively useful work of genius from which I have learned much. My criticism is that Foucault's level of abstraction makes his work inaccessible to all but the most intrepid and experienced explorers of ideas. Foucault's unrelievedly high level of abstraction is also related to his elimination of the subject, his speaking as if you and I and the entrepreneurs of the erotic do not exist. I refer to his personification of "power," so that it appears to have interests, a will, activities, and a love life of its own.

41. For Ellis's American informant (1915) see *GAH,* pp. 52–53.

42. The relationship between the Protestant work ethic, capitalism, procreation, and eroticism is best expounded by Peter T. Cominos in "Late-Victorian Sexual Respectability and the Social System," *International Revue of Social History,* vol. 8 (1963), pp. 18–48, and pp. 216–50. Also see Steven Marcus, *The Other Victorians: A Study of Sexuality and Pornography in Mid-Nineteenth-Century England* (New York: Basic Books, 1966), on capitalism, money, and sex pp. 21–22, 25, 93, 99, 128, 149, 151, 155, 243–44, 282–83. The Cominos/Marcus linking of capital accumulation and sexual repression is contested by R. S. Neale, *Class and Ideology in the Nineteenth Century* (London: Routledge & Kegan Paul, 1972), pp. 127–29, 132–36; Lawrence Stone similarly contests the argument by P. Lejeune that early industrial society needed saving for investment and so banned masturbation as sexual spending, and that twentieth century consumer society promotes active sexual spending; see Lejeune, "Le 'dangereux supplement.' Lecture d'une aveu de Rousseau," in *Annales E.*

*C. S.,* vol. 29 (1974), p. 1020; cited by Stone in *The Family, Sex, and Marriage in England 1500–1800* (New York: Harper & Row, 1977), pp. 515–16, 741 n. 83.

43. "The New Hedonism" was the title of an essay by Grant Allen in *The Fortnightly Review* (London), new ser., vol. 55 (March 1894), pp. 377–92; it attacked Christianity and asserted that "in the sex-instinct [is] the origin and basis of all that is best and highest within us"; quoted by Timothy d'Arch Smith, *Love in Earnest,* p. 110; also see Weeks, *Coming Out,* pp. 120–21. For Charles A. Beard and Mary R. Beard on "the grand era of acquisition and enjoyment" see their *The Rise of American Civilization* (New York: Macmillan, 1930), ch. 23, p. 285.

44. "Pleasure Man" was the title of a risqué play by Mae West; see *NYT Theater Reviews,* Oct. 2, 1928. For feminine images of the 1920s see Mary P. Ryan, "The Projection of New Womanhood: The Movie Moderns in the 1920s," in Jean E. Friedman and William G. Shade, ed., *Our American Sister, Women in American Life and Thought,* 2nd ed. (Boston: Allyn & Bacon, 1976), pp. 366–84; and Russo, *Celluloid Closet.*

45. Though I suggest that the vampire was an archetypal image of the lesbian in the twentieth century, the female who preyed on women was a theme touched on earlier, and was given a changing, historically specific embodiment. The lesbian as vampire is explicitly discussed or implicitly touched on by Foster in *Sex Variant,* Faderman in *Surpassing* (see especially pp. 341–48), and Russo in *Celluloid Closet.* In chronological order, the lesbian vampire theme is touched on in:

Samuel Taylor Coleridge's poem "Christabel" (1816); see Foster, pp. 73–74; Faderman, pp. 277, 460n–461n, 462n–463n.

Christina Rossetti's poem "Goblin Market" (written 1859); see Foster, pp. 74–76; Faderman, pp. 108, 171–72.

Joseph Sheridan LeFanu's short story "Carmilla" (1872); see Faderman, pp. 288–89, 294.

Clemence Dane's (Winifred Ashton's) novel *Regiment of Women* (U.S. publication 1917); see Foster, pp. 257–60, 267, 269, 277, 283, 315, 330; Faderman, pp. 341–44, 392; *NYTBR*, Feb. 4, 1917 (excerpted).

Edouard Bourdet's play "La Prisonnière" (1925; translated and produced in the U.S. as *The Captive,* 1926); see Foster, pp. 208, 211–13; Faderman, pp. 347–48; *N. Y. Times,* 1926, September 30 (see).

Naomi Royde-Smith's novel *The Tortoiseshell Cat* (1925); Foster, pp. 273, 275–77, 293, 294, 320, 339; Faderman, p. 346.

Dorothy Sayers's mystery *Unnatural Death* (1927); Faderman, pp. 345–46.

G. Sheila Donisthorpe's novel *Loveliest of Friends* (1931); Foster, pp. 295, 308–09, 311; Faderman, p. 346.

Sinclair Lewis's novel *Ann Vickers* (1932–33); Foster, p. 300; Faderman, pp. 344–45.

Francis Brett Young's novel *White Ladies* (1935); Foster, pp. 315–16; Faderman, p. 343.

Francis Brett Young's novel *White Ladies* (1935); Foster, pp. 315–316; Faderman, p. 343.

The film *Dracula's Daughter* (1936); Russo, pp. 49, 58; *NYT Film Reviews,* 1936, May 18 (see).

Dorothy Baker's novel *Trio* (1943) and play (1944); Foster, pp. 325–26; Faderman, p. 343; *N. Y. Times Book Review,* 1943, July 4 (see); *N. Y. Times Theater Reviews,* 1944, December 30 (see).

Arthur Koestler's novel *Arrival and Departure* (1943); Foster, p. 325; Faderman, p. 345.

James Ronald's novel *The Angry Woman* (1948); Foster, p. 329.

Benjamin Karpman's study *The Sexual Offender and His Offenses* (1954; once lesbians "get hold of a victim they do not let go until she is bled dry"); Faderman, p. 330, 469 n. 47.

Roger Vadim's film *Blood and Roses* (1960); Russo, p. 49.

Joseph Laraz's film *Vampyres* (1974); Russo, p. 49.

In addition, on the homosexual vampire theme, the life, relationships, and writings of Bram Stoker, author of *Dracula,* bear investigation; see *GAH,* p. 605, n. 64.

46. I am aware that the U. S. history of lesbianism does not appear as enmeshed within the cash nexus as the history of gay males. Though there are major differences to be explored between the political economy of lesbianism and of gay males, I maintain that lesbianism has been and is as much subject to the imperatives of consumer capitalism as is male gayness. An indication of the fundamental mediation between the economy and present-day lesbian-feminist culture is suggested, for example, by Maida Tilchen's analysis of lesbian-feminist music, see "Women's Music: Politics for Sale," *Gay Community News Music Supplement,* June 6, 1981, pp. 1–5, 8, 12.

47. For Herbert Marcuse on "profitable conformity" and repressive desublimation see his *Eros and Civilization* (1955; New York: Vintage Books, Random House, 1961), pp. 86ff. For Foucault's argument against the "repressive hypothesis" see his *History of Sexuality.*

48. For the idea of "sexual scripts" and the theatrical metaphor see John Gagnon, *Human Sexualities* (Glenview, Ill.: Scott, Foresman, 1977).

49. For " 'sexual liberation' " movements as "movements of [sexual] affirmation" and as movements simultaneously "surmounting" the sexual see Michel Foucault in Bernard-Henri Lévy, "Power and Sex: An Interview with Michel Foucault," translated by David J. Parent from *Le Nouvelle Observateur,* March 12, 1977, in *Telos,* no. 32 (Summer 1977), pp. 152–61. For a critique of mechanical "reverse affirmation" as a tactic of "the homosexual rights movement" see Jeffrey Weeks, "Capitalism and the Organization of Sex," in Gay Left Collective, ed., *Homosexuality: Power and Politics* (London: Allison & Busby, 1980), p. 18. *The Healthy Homosexual* is the title of a book by a pro-gay psychologist, George Weinberg (New York: St. Martin's Press, 1972). An entire school of "scientific," prohomosexual psychology is devoted to demonstrating that homosexuals are just like heterosexuals and just as respectable; see especially the work of Evelyn Hooker described in Martin S. Weinberg and Alan P. Bell, *Homosexuality: An Annotated Bibliography* (New York: Harper & Row, 1972).

50. For a concrete, fictional, Utopian vision of a society without heteros, homos, masculines, feminines, bisexuals, or androgynes see Marge Piercy's *Woman on the Edge of Time* (New York: Fawcett, 1976). The "radical dissolution of the feminine/masculine dichotomy," and the "abolition of the gender system" is discussed by David Fernbach in *The Spiral Path: A Gay Contribution to Human Survival* (Boston: Alyson Publications, 1981), pp. 68, 99. For lesbian–feminist arguments for the extension of the category "lesbian" to include many forms of "primary intensity between and among women," and against the dissolution of the "lesbian" category, see Rich, "Compulsory Heterosexuality" and Jacquelyn N. Zita's comment on this cited in backnote 18 above.

## Documents

In Part II backnotes are numbered consecutively from 1, beginning with each new decade.

### 1880

1. 1880, Oct. 10: Alice Stone Blackwell to Kitty Barry Blackwell; "smashing"; see Nancy Sahli, "Smashing: Women's Relationships Before the Fall," *Chrysalis* no. 8 (Summer 1979), pp. 17–27.

   Professor August Howe Buck, of Boston University, is described in two biographical sketches sent to me by the Boston University Library without source citations.

   Alice Stone Blackwell letters to Kitty Barry Blackwell, Dec. 24–25, Dec. 31, 1877; Oct. 10, 1880; Feb. 20, 1881; March 12, 1882; in Blackwell Family Papers, Manuscript Division, Library of Congress.

   Alice Blackwell refers to her own crushes on several females in numerous letters. In 1884, when she was twenty-seven, she wrote to Kitty Blackwell: "I fell in love with Mrs. P. like a schoolgirl & feel rather ashamed of it. . . . I had supposed I was past that." Alice also declared, ardently and "jokingly," her hope of "marrying" Kitty, her cousin by adoption; she recalled, wistfully, how she and Kitty had once shared a bed. While at Boston University Alice was surprised by a nightwatchman as she and a female friend lay on a sofa in a darkened room: "I in Leila's arms—for she has a chronic desire to hug me, & indulges it when there is no one around to see"; A. S. Blackwell to K. B. Blackwell, letters 1873–1884, Blackwell Family Papers, Schlesinger Library, Radcliffe College, quoted by Peter Gabriel Filene, *Him/Her/Self: Sex Roles in Modern America* (New York: Mentor Book, New American Library, 1976), pp. 45–46, 252 n. 13. Filene says Alice Blackwell also discussed "heterosexual" feelings; also see Sahli, "Smashing," p. 23 for letter of 1884. Alice S. Blackwell wrote about the intimacy between her mother, Lucy Stone, and Antoinette Brown (begun in 1845); see her *Lucy Stone, Pioneer of Women's Rights* (Boston: Little, Brown, 1930). Also see biography of A. S. Blackwell in *Notable American Women.*

2. 1881, Feb.: Dr. William Dickinson, "A Case of Sodomy," *St. Louis Medical and Surgical Journal,* vol. 40, no. 2, pp. 196–97.

3. 1881, Aug. 20: Dr. E. T. Spitzka, "A Historical Case of Sexual Perversion," *Chicago Medical Review,* vol. 4, no. 4, pp. 378–79.

4. 1882, June 23: Dr. William A. Hammond delivered paper, "The Disease of the Scythians (Morbus Feminarum) and Certain Analogous Conditions," *American Journal of Neurology and Psychiatry,* vol. 1, no. 3 (Aug. 1882), pp. 339–55.

5. 1882, July: Dr. G. Alder Blumer, "A Case of Perverted Sexual Instinct. (*Conträre* [sic] *Sexualempfindung*)," *American Journal of Insanity,* vol. 39, pp. 22–35.

6. 1882: Dr. Henry N. Guernsey, *Plain Talks on Avoided Subjects* (Philadelphia: Davis), pp. 80–83. Numerous later editions.

7. 1883, March: Dr. William A. Hammond, *Sexual Impotence in the Male* (New York: Bermingham, 1883); expanded ed. *Sexual Impotence in the Male and Female* (Detroit: George S. Davis, 1887; reprinted New York: Arno Press, 1974),

pp. 55–70; paging identical to 1883 ed.

8. 1883, April: Drs. J. C. Shaw and G. N. Ferris, "Perverted Sexual Instinct," *Journal of Nervous and Mental Disease,* vol. 10, no. 2, pp. 185–204. *Casper's Vierteljahrschrift, 1852* is the earliest source cited here on sexual perversion; see p. 186. This was the German Johann Ludwig Casper, discussed by Bullough, *Sexual Variance,* pp. 590, 628 n. 11; 638, 670 n. 9.

9. For Westphal see backnote 14, p. 682.

10. 1883, May 27: *Detroit Post and Tribune,* Sarah Edmonds Seelye, "The Story of a Remarkable Life," signed "A. M. G.," p. 16: 2–5; Detroit Public Library. I thank Steven Kowalik and Barry Adam for help in obtaining a typed copy. This newspaper story is cited by Sylvia G. L. Dannett, *She Rode With the Generals: The True and Incredible Story of Sarah Emma Seelye, Alias Franklin Thompson* (New York: Nelson, 1960), pp. 19 (n. on p. 301), 42 (n. on p. 302); the interview with Seelye by a female reporter, "A. M. G.," is discussed on pp. 246–49, 253. For two differently titled editions of Seelye's autobiography see S. Emma E. Edmonds, *Unsexed: or, The Female Soldier. The Thrilling Adventures, Experiences, and Escapes of a Woman, as Nurse, Spy, and Scout, in Hospitals, Camps, and Battlefields* (Philadelphia: Phila. Pub. Co., [186?]), and her *Nurse and Spy in the Union Army: Comprising the Adventures and Experiences of a Woman in Hospitals, Camps, and Battlefields* (Hartford, Conn.: W. S. Williams, 1864), listed under Edmundson, Sarah Emma, in the *National Union Catalog, Pre-1956,* vol. 155, p. 291, and under Edmonds, p. 662. For additional references to Edmonds/Seelye see *GAH,* pp. 599 n. 1, 601 n. 31; and notes in Dannett. For references in the 1880s, in the *New York Times* to crossdressing see that paper: November 11, 1883, 3:7; January 26, 1884, 2:6; November 6, 1885, 2:4; August 9, 1887,

4:7. For a Colorado women's colony see *N.Y. Times* November 6, 1885, 4:7.

11. 1883: Dr. James G. Kiernan, see 1892, May, p. 208 in original document. In another place Kiernan reported: "The elopement of a married woman of Brandon, Wisconsin, with a young girl, in 1883, led to a discovery of a similar case [apparently, that in Belvidere, Ill.]. The couple were 'married' by a minister and set up in life for themselves. A recent [Dec. 1888] incarceration of a burglar in the Madison, Iowa, penitentiary, led to the revelation of a like case. The allegations which so often appear in divorce cases that a certain woman has alienated the wife's affections are an indication that cases of this type are far from infrequent"; see Kiernan, 1888, Dec., p. 171 in original document, n. 23 below.

12. 1884, Jan.: M., L. H., "Chicago Medical Society," *Chicago Medical Journal and Examiner,* vol. 48 (March 1884), pp. 263–65. Kiernan's lecture of Jan., 1884 was printed; see 1884, May.

13. 1884, April: E. J. H., "Correspondence," *Alienist and Neurologist* (St. Louis), vol. 5, no. 2, pp. 351–52. The author wrote in response to a paper by "Dr. Rice" on "Sexual Perversion." This is probably a mistaken reference to the article by Dr. Wise (Jan. 1883) about Lucy Ann Lobdell Slater; see *GAH,* pp. 221–23.

14. 1884, May: Dr. James G. Kiernan, "Insanity. Lecture XXVI.—Sexual Perversion," *Detroit Lancet,* vol. 7, no. 11, pp. 481–84. Kiernan also discussed Lucy Ann Lobdell Slater.

15. 1884, July 19: [Dr. George F. Shrady], "Perverted Sexual Instinct," *Medical Record* (New York), vol. 26, pp. 70–71.

16. 1884, July: Dr. B. Salemi Pace [review of Dr. P. Moreau's (de Tours) book *On Aberrations of the Genesic Sense* (Paris, 1880), translated by Joseph Workman

of Toronto, with introductory comments], *Alienist and Neurologist* (St. Louis), vol. 5, no. 3, pp. 367–85.

17. 1884: Dr. George M. Beard, *Sexual Neurasthenia. Its Hygiene, Causes, Symptoms, and Treatment, With a Chapter on Diet for the Nervous* (New York: Treat), pp. 98–107. I thank George Chauncey for providing a photocopy. On Beard's renown see John S. Haller, Jr., and Robin M. Haller, *The Physician and Sexuality in Victorian America* (New York: Norton, 1977).

18. 1885, Apr. 18: Dr. Charles K. Mills, "A Case of Nymphomania, With Hystero-Epilepsy and Peculiar Mental Perversions—The Results of Clitoridectomy and Oophorectomy—The Patient's History As Told by Her-Self," reported by Dr. William H. Morrison, *Philadelphia Medical Times* vol. 15, pp. 534–40.

19. 1885, Nov. 18: *Harper's New Monthly Magazine,* "Christmas Carnival In The New York Stock Exchange" (illustration), p. 845 in R. Wheatley, "The New York Stock Exchange," vol. 71, no. 426, pp. 829–53. I thank John D'Emilio for this reference.

20. 1886, Aug. 14: Dr. Randolph Winslow, "Report of an Epidemic of Gonorrhea Contracted from Rectal Coition," *Medical News* (Philadelphia), vol. 40, pp. 180–82.

21. 1886, Nov.: Drs. Philip Leidy and Charles K. Mills, "Reports of Cases of Insanity from the Insane Department of the Philadelphia Hospital; Case III.—Sexual Perversion," *Journal of Nervous and Mental Disease* (New York) vol. 13, no. 11, pp. 712–13.

22. 1888, Oct.: [Dr. Richard] von Krafft-Ebing, "Perversion of the Sexual Instinct.—Report of Cases," translated by H. M. Jewett, *Alienist and Neurologist* (St. Louis), vol. 9, no. 4, pp. 565–81.

23. 1888, Nov.: Dr. James G. Kiernan, "Sexual Perversion and the White-

chapel Murders," *Medical Standard* (Chicago), vol. 4, no. 3, pp. 129–30 (reprinted from Chicago Medical Society Transactions). Also see Kiernan, "Sexual Perversion," *Medical Standard,* vol. 4, no. 4 (Dec. 1888), pp. 170–72.

24. 1888, Dec. Dr. E. C. Spitzka, "The Whitechapel Murders: Their Medico-Legal and Historical Aspects," *Journal of Nervous and Mental Disease,* vol. 13, no. 12, pp. 763–78. Sexual "inversion" references: p. 765 Julian Chevalier's *Inversion of the Sexual Sense;* p. 768 "paederasts" and lust murder; p. 773 n. 22 Lord Cornbury; p. 775 *Numa Numantius;* p. 778 Princess Lamballe and Marie Antoinette.

25. 1889, May 11: *Aspen* (Colorado) *Times,* "Mad Infatuation," p. 4; *Denver Times,* July 6, 1889, p. 1. For a similar report see *Aspen Weekly Chronicle,* July 8, 1889, p. 4. I thank James Foshee for informing me of these documents and providing photocopies. A few inconsequential misspellings in the originals have been silently corrected.

26. 1889, Sept. 7: Dr. G. Frank Lydston, "Clinical Lecture. Sexual Perversion, Satyriasis and Nymphomania," *Medical and Surgical Reporter* (Philadelphia), vol. 61, no. 10, pp. 253–58. Continued, no. 11 (Sept. 14, 1889), pp. 281–84.

27. 1889, Nov. 17: *N. Y. Times,* The London Scandal on Cleveland Street, 1:1; Nov. 27, 1889, 2:6; Jan. 10, 1890, 2:6. Allan Bérubé informs me that the Cleveland Street or West End Scandal was covered prominently in San Francisco newspapers. For a recent book on the scandal see Colin Simpson, Lewis Chester, David Leitch, *The Cleveland Street Affair* (Boston: Little, Brown, 1976). On the *Paul Maul Gazette* and the social purity movement see Weeks, *Coming Out,* pp. 17–18.

1889, Nov. 24: *N. Y. Times;* "A Woman Marries A Woman. Money The Motive—Passing Successfully For A Count" [Sandor/Sarolta Vay], 11:6, from the London *Standard;* first published by a Vienna newspaper. Contrast this *Times* report of "eccentricities" with the medical-sexual version given by Havelock Ellis and John Addington Symonds, *Sexual Inversion* (London: Wilson and Macmillan, 1897; photo reprint N.Y.: Arno Press, 1975); there Vay's was called "The most completely recorded case of sexual inversion in a woman," p. 94n; also see Appendix F, "Countess Sarolta V.," pp. 279–87.

28. 1889: Frances E. Willard, *Glimpses of Fifty Years: The Autobiography of an American Woman, . . . Written by Order of the National Woman's Christian Temperance Union* (Chicago: H. J. Smith [for the Woman's Temperance Publication Association]). Willard also describes her "love" for two men, feelings which, from her published account, do not appear to have rivaled the intensity and depth of her feeling for women. Also see Mary Earhart Dillon, *Frances Willard: From Prayers to Politics* (Chicago: University of Chicago Press, 1944), p. 82. On Willard's intimacies also see her brief biography in *Notable American Women.*

### 1890

1. c.1890: Dr. Charles Torrence Nesbitt, "sexual perverts"; see his Papers, Duke University Library; for a photocopy of the library card file on Nesbitt, which includes a brief biographical summary, I thank Paul I. Chestnut, Assistant Curator for Reader Services. I thank Dennis Lampkowski for informing me of Nesbitt's Papers, which are listed and described in the Library of Congress Catalog of Manuscripts.

2. 1891, Aug. 15: Dr. Charles L. Dana,

"Clinical Lecture. On Certain Sexual Neuroses," *Medical and Surgical Reporter* (Philadelphia) vol. 65, no. 7, pp. 241–45.

3. 1892, Jan. 26: *N. Y. Times*, etc., Alice Mitchell murders Freda Ward; see *Times* stories and medical journal articles cited in text. I am informed that the Mitchell–Ward case was reported in the *Memphis Public Ledger*, Jan. 26 through Feb. 27, 1892, and the *Memphis Weekly Commercial*, July 27, 1892. A story in the *Ledger* on Feb. 11, 1892, 2:3, includes an account of Marie Hinkle (or Hindle) who had married another woman in Memphis, 1869–70. The *Ledger* of Feb. 18, 1892, 1:4, carried a story headed: "He Was A Woman," about an East Tennessee settler, Henry Armstrong, who was discovered to be Mira Lawrence. On the Mitchell–Ward case also see the sex radical Dr. Edward Bliss Foote in *Lucifer*, September 23, 1892, cited in Sears, *Sex Radicals*, p. 226.

4. 1892, Jan.: Dr. Graeme M. Hammond, "The Bicycle in the Treatment of Nervous Diseases," *Journal of Nervous and Mental Diseases*, vol. 17, no. 1, pp. 36–46. For Hammond's "masturbation drawers" see Dana, 1891, Aug. 15, p. 244 in original; I thank Bert Hansen for informing me of this document.

5. 1892, Feb.: Dr. H. C. Hughes; suicide in St. Louis, Missouri; see 1893 Oct.

6. 1892, March 27: *N. Y. Times*; the death of Walt Whitman, 4:7, 10:1.

7. 1892, April 27: Mary Grew to Isabel Howland, Sophia Smith Collection, Smith College. Discussed by Smith-Rosenberg, "Female World" p. 27. Also see biography of Grew in *Notable American Women* (I, pp. 91–92) which says: "She never married, but lived for many years with a close friend, Margaret Burleigh." This is inadequate as a description of an important close relationship.

8. 1892, May: Dr. James G. Kiernan, "Responsibility in Sexual Perversion," *Chicago Medical Recorder*, vol. 3, pp. 185–210; read before the Chicago Medical Society, March 7, 1892. Discussed case described by Dr. Wise (Lucy Ann Lobdell Slater and her wife; see n. 13, p. 690.

9. 1892, Nov. Dr. Irving C. Rosse, "Sexual Hypochondriasis and Perversion of the Genesic Instinct," *Journal of Nervous and Mental Disease*, vol. 17, no. 11, pp. 795–811; read at Medical Society of Virginia, Allegheny Springs, Sept., 1892; partial reprint *GAH* pp. 41–42; also in *Virginia Medical Monthly* vol. 19 (1892), pp. 633–49.

10. c. 1892: Lincoln Steffens on Jacob Riis and "fairies"; in *The Autobiography of Lincoln Steffens* (New York: Literary Guild, 1931), pp. 223–24.

11. 1893, May 8: Frederik Hammerich; Danish emigrant to the U. S.; the details of Hammerich's life were provided by Wilhelm von Rosen, who discovered Hammerich's letters in the archives of his brother, Kaj Hammerich, in Rigsarkivet (National Archives), Copenhagen (priv. ark. nr. 5529).

The interrogation of Martin Kok, Frederik Hammerich, and Anders Andersen is recorded in the documents of the Criminal Chamber, Police and Criminal Court of Copenhagen, now in the Provincial Archives of Copenhagen. The allegation in a Copenhagen newspaper (*Kobenhavn*, Feb. 21 1893) about Hans Christian Andersen's sexual relationship with "M. K." (Martin Kok, 1850–1942) had no foundation in fact. Andersen's diary reveals that the two were barely acquainted, and Kok denied the allegations in a letter to Andersen's executor, March 1, 1893. It seems quite probable, however, that Andersen was homosexual, although nonpracticing. But Danish public opinion in 1893 was horrified. A reader ended a long letter of protest to a newspaper with the words: "Much that was dear to our country has been lost," and asked was it possible to steal "the memory of our great men?" Andersen's homosexuality was asserted in an article in the *Jahrbuch für sexuelle Zwischenstufen* (Leipzig) vol. 3 (1901) by Albert Hansen, pseudonym of a homosexual Danish police officer and author, Carl Hensen Fahlberg. Later, in 1906, during one of Denmark's biggest homosexual purges, Fahlberg was arrested. Since he had not committed any provable crime he was released, but fired from the police force. He immigrated to the U.S. and lived as a farmer in Arkansas; very ill, he returned to Denmark in 1934. He wrote several novels with homosexual themes. He committed suicide in 1939. For Hammerich's obituary see unidentified newspaper cutting of Jan. 11, 1919 in the archives of Kaj Hammerich.

I thank Wilhelm von Rosen for this research and the translations.

12. 1893, June 27: Dr. C. H. Hughes, Delia Perkins and Ida Preston, Indianapolis, see 1893, Oct., pp. 558–59.

13. 1893, July: Dr. Edward C. Mann, "Medico-Legal and Psychological Aspects of the Trial of Josephine Mallison Smith," *Alienist and Neurologist,* vol. 14, no. 3, pp. 467–77; section on "Morbid Sexual Perversions," pp. 471ff.

14. 1893, July: T., "Reviews, Book Notices, Etc. [review of Krafft-Ebing's *Psychopathia Sexualis, with Especial Reference to Contrary Sexual Instinct. A Medico-Legal Study . . . Authorized translation of the Seventh . . . German edition. By Charles Gilbert Chaddock, M.D. . . .* (Philadelphia: Davis, 1892), and German ed. (1893)], *Alienist and Neurologist,* vol. 14, no. 3, pp. 526–27.

15. 1893, Aug. 16 Dr. F. E. Daniel, "Should Insane Criminals or Sexual Perverts be Permitted to Procreate?" read at the Joint Session of the World's Columbian Auxiliary Congress—Section of Medical Jurisprudence—and the International Medico-Legal Congress, Aug. 16, 1893; also before the American Medico-Legal Society, New York, Oct. 11, 1893; published in *Medico-Legal Journal* (Dec. 1893); *Psychological Bulletin* (New York), date unknown; *Texas Medical Journal* (Aug. 1893); reprinted as "Castration of Sexual Perverts," *Texas Medical Journal,* vol. 27, no. 10 (Apr. 1912), pp. 369–85. The last publication is the source of quotations cited here.

16. 1893, Oct. 21: *The* (New Orleans) *Mascot:* "Sodom and Gomorrah Discounted," cover and editorial page.

17. 1893, Oct.: Dr. C. H. Hughes, "Erotopathia—Morbid Eroticism," *Alienist and Neurologist,* vol. 14, no. 4, pp. 531–78; read at Pan-American Medical Congress, Sept. 1893. Also see Hughes's "Postscript to Paper on 'Erotopathia,'" same, pp. 731–32, reporting lurid details of "An Organization of Colored Erotopaths" in Washington, D.C.; reprinted in *GAH* pp. 42–43.

18. 1894, April: Dr. Havelock Ellis, "The Study of Sexual Inversion," *Medico-Legal Journal* (New York), vol. 12, pp. 148–57. Also in *Bulletin of the Psychological Section of the Medico-Legal Society* (New York), vol. 2 (1894), pp. 47–56. Reprinted with minor revisions in Ellis's *Sexual Inversion* (1897).

19. 1894, June: Dr. James G. Kiernan, "Psychical Treatment of Congenital Sexual Inversion," *Review of Insanity and Nervous Disease* (Milwaukee, Wisc.), vol. 4, no. 4, pp. 293–95.

20. 1894, Sept. 16: Robert Allan Nicol to Edward Carpenter; letters in the Carpenter Collection, Department of Local History, Central Library, Sheffield, England.

21. Nicol and the independent socialists of Bristol, England, are discussed by Sheila Rowbotham in her section on Carpenter in her and Jeffrey Weeks's *Socialism and the New Life: The Personal and Sexual Politics of Edward Carpenter and Havelock Ellis* (London: Pluto Press, 1977), especially pp. 74, 116.

22. Materials on Miriam Daniell and Helena Born are in the Helen Tufts Bailie Papers, Tamiment Collection, New York University Library, which also holds a copy of Carpenter's pamphlet *Homogenic Love* (1894) inscribed as follows from "W. H. R." to "H. B." (Helena Born): "I shall not forget you. I know the truth, the tenderness, the courage; I know the longings, hidden guilt there. So right on. Have good faith yet. Keep that, your unseen treasure untainted. Many shall bless you. To many yet, tho no word be spoken, your face shall shine as a lamp. It shall be remembered & that which you have desired—in silence—shall come to you abundantly. 28/July/95 Heatherbrae" [England?]. Born published "Poets of Revolt: Shelley, Whitman, Carpenter" in *The Conservator*, May 1896; reprinted in Born's *Whitman's Ideal Democracy and Other Writings* (Boston: Everett Press, 1902). Born was active in the Boston branch of the Walt Whitman Fellowship International, the American counterpart to the Carpenter circles described by Rowbotham, see above. Also see Joseph Interrante, "From the Puritans to the Present: 350 Years of Lesbian and Gay History in Boston," in Richard Burns, Neuma Crandall, Eric Rofes, ed., *Gay Jubilee: A Guidebook to Gay Boston—Its History and Resources* (Boston: Lesbian and Gay Task Force of Jubilee 350, Summer 1980), p. 25. For references to Carpenter see *Guide to Periodical Literature, 1890–99*, p. 431.

23. I find only two listings that may refer to works published by this Edmund Russell in the Library of Congress Catalogue, vol. 510, pp. 478–79.

24. 1894, Oct.?: Sarah Stein to Gertrude Stein, letter beginning "Dearest Girl/ Oh! I have just had such a splendid talk," from 1118 O'Farrell (San Francisco), no date, five pp. Second letter dated Monday, Oct. 29 (1894, according to a perpetual calendar), in Sarah Stein Letters, 1893?–1911, Folder I, Beinecke Library, Yale University. Mentioned by Linda Simon, *The Biography of Alice B. Toklas* (Garden City, N.Y.: Doubleday, 1977), pp. 28, 288 n. 60. Sarah Stein's doctor, Oscar J. Mayer, was the author of a fifteen-page article which may further elucidate Sarah Stein's comments to Gertrude: see Mayer's "Massage in Gynecology," read in the section on obstetrics and diseases of women, American Medical Association, San Francisco, June 5–8, 1894; published (Chicago: A.M.A., 1894); reprinted *Journal of the A.M.A.;* see listing *Nat. Union Cat. Pre-1956*, vol. 371, p. 618.

25. 1894: Dr. Charles Gilbert Chaddock, "Sexual Crimes," in Allan McLane Hamilton and Lawrence Godkin, ed., *A System of Legal Medicine*, 2 vols. (New York: E. B. Treat, 1894), vol. 2, pp. 525–72.

26. 1894: Dr. Allan McLane Hamilton, "Insanity in its Medico-Legal Bearings," in Hamilton and Godkin's *A System of Legal Medicine* (see 1894 Chaddock), vol. 2, pp. 49–50. A note adds: "The reader is referred to Krafft-Ebing's *Psychopathia Sexualis;* Taxtil's *La Corruption Fin de Siècle*, and various French romances, among them *Mademoiselle du Maupin* or *Mademoiselle Giraud ma Femme.*" Dr. Hamilton's editing of Alexander Hamilton's love letters to John Laurens is interesting in light of the doctor's

writings on "sexual perversion"; see *GAH* pp. 452–56.

27. 1895, March 3: *N. Y. Times* and *N. Y. Tribune:* Oscar Wilde; see date and page citations in main text. The indexes for the *Times* and *Tribune* list the reports of the scandal under "Wilde." But the *Tribune Index* lists some stories with no page or column citation. And the *Times Index* lists a number of stories with page and column citations which, for some reason, I was not able to locate on the microfilm edition consulted. On the American reaction to the Wilde case: sex radical Lillian Harmon assailed the treatment of Wilde in *Lucifer,* Aug. 2, Dec. 13, 1895; cited in Sears, *Sex Radicals,* pp. 227, 312 n. 40. Also see Willa Cather, "The Aesthetic Movement: 'fatal and dangerous,'" Lincoln, Nebraska *Journal,* May 19, 1895; reprinted in William M. Curtain, ed. *The World and the Parish: Willa Cather's Articles and Reviews, 1893–1902* (Lincoln, Neb.: University of Nebraska Press, 1970), pp. 153–54; and Cather, "Oscar Wilde: Helas," *Journal,* Sept. 28, 1895; in Curtain, pp. 263–66.

28. 1895, March: Marc-André Raffalovich, "Uranism, Congenital Sexual Inversion. Observations and Recommendations," translated by C. Judson Herrick, with the assistance of Prof. G. F. McKibben, *Journal of Comparative Neurology* (Granville, Ohio), vol. 5, pp. 33–65. The French version of Raffalovich's paper was "L'uranisme; inversion sexuelle congénitale; observations et conseils," *Arch. d'anthrop. crim.* (Lyon and Paris), vol. 10 (1895), pp. 99–127. The terms used in the American translation of Raffalovich are historically significant. Terms referring to a psychosexual condition: "Uranism"[33]; "con genital sexual inversion"[33]; "homosexuality"[33]; "homosexuality in children"[33]; "heterosexual sexual-

ity"[39, 45]; "heterosexuality"[59]; and "psychic hermaphroditism" (referring to what is now called "bisexuality").[59] Also included was one of the earliest American references to "homosexuality" and "heterosexuality" as equivalent, polarized conditions.[59]

Persons referred to were: "congenital sexual inverts"[35]; "uranistic children"[34]; "heterosexual children" [40]; "unisexuals" (vs. "true men")[35]; "unsexed women"[37]; "inverts"[35]; "superior" and "inferior inverts"[50]; the "homosexual" and "heterosexual"[39]; "pederasts" (as distinct from "inverts")[49]; "women [who are] homosexual and heterosexual at the same time"[55]; and "the man-woman"[59]. The act, "sodomy," was referred to once[49].

29. 1895, Apr.: Dr. Havelock Ellis, "Sexual Inversion in Women," *Alienist and Neurologist* (St. Louis), vol. 16, no. 2, pp. 141–58.

30. For the execution of the female weaver (1580), of Catharine Lincken (or Linck, 1721), and others, see Faderman, *Surpassing,* pp. 51–54, 424 n.15, 424 n.16. Faderman also cites Louis Crompton, "The Myth of Lesbian Impunity: Capital Punishment from 1270 to 1791," *Journal of Homosexuality,* vol. 6, no. 1/2 (Fall/Winter 1980/81).

31. 1895, June 24: *N. Y. Times,* "Friendships of Women" and "Woman's Emancipation," 4:7.

32. 1895, Summer: Dr. Austin Flint's photos of this subject and another male cross-dresser were first published anonymously in "Some Human Documents," *Post–Graduate: A Monthly Journal of Medicine and Surgery* (New York), vol. 11, p. 362, plus three pages of photos facing p. 370. Flint's longer case history and full nude photo of the subject were published in "A Case of Sexual Inversion, Probably with Complete Sexual

Anaesthesia," *New York Medical Journal*, vol. 94, no. 23 (Dec. 2, 1911), pp. 1111–12.

33. 1895, Sept. 26: Dr. John Wesley Carhart, *Norma Trist; or Pure Carbon: A Story of the Inversion of the Sexes* (Austin, Tex.: Eugene von Boeckmann). The date is that of copyright. I am deeply indebted to Eric Garber for informing me of *Norma Trist* (which he had found listed in an old science fiction bibliography), and for supplying a photocopy; the novel is in the Library of Congress.

34. Mary Wilkins Freeman, *The Long Arm . . . and Other Detective Stories . . .* (London: Chapman & Hall, 1895); "The Long Arm" reprinted in Carolyn Wells, ed. *American Detective Stories* (New York: Oxford University Press, 1927); see Faderman, *Surpassing*, pp. 292–93, 464, n. 51. Also see Mary R. P. Hatch, *The Strange Disappearance of Eugene Comstock* (New York: G. W. Dillingham, 1895); see Faderman, *Surpassing*, pp. 293–94, 464 n. 53.

35. 1895, Sept.: Dr. James Weir, Jr., "The Effects of Female Suffrage on Posterity," *American Naturalist*, vol. 24, no. 345, pp. 815–25. This document is discussed in John S. Haller, Jr., and Robin M. Haller, *The Physician and Sexuality in Victorian America* (New York: Norton, 1977), p. 77. Weir's terminology is historically significant: he referred to the psychosexual condition "homosexuality"[815]; "masculo-femininity (viraginity)"[819]; "gynandry"[820]; and "psycho-sexual aberrancy"[819]. He also referred to persons called the "New Woman"[818]; the "tomboy"[820]; "viragints, gynanders, [and] androgynes"[824]; "unsexed individuals"[821]; "female psycho-sexual aberrants"[821]; and an "unfeminine android"[820].

36. 1895, Dec.: Dr. Havelock Ellis, "Sexual Inversion: With an Analysis of Thirty-three New Cases"; read before the Medico-Legal Congress, Sept. 1895, and before the Medico-Legal Society, Dec. 1895; in *Medico-Legal Journal* (New York), vol. 13 (Dec. 1895), pp. 255–67. Also in *Bulletin of the Medico-Legal Congress, 1895* (New York: 1898), pp. 111–23.

   1895: *The Gay Brothers* (movie of two men dancing a waltz); directed by William Dickson at Thomas Edison Studio; see Russo, *Celluloid Closet*, p. 6.

37. 1896, Feb.: Angelina Weld Grimké, "Under the Days"; see Gloria T. Hull, "'Under the Days': The Buried Life and Poetry of Angelina Weld Grimké," *Conditions*, vol. 2, no. 2 (Autumn 1979), pp. 17–25.

38. 1896, Oct. 13: *N. Y. Times*, Archibald Gunter's "A Florida Enchantment," Oct. 13, 5:4; Oct. 18, sect. IV, 10:1. Unidentified clipping of Oct. 1896 headed: "Mr. Gunter Wrestles With a Question of Sex," in Harvard Theater Collection. The play first opened in New York in April; see reviews of Apr. 28 in *The Journal* and *The Herald;* also see review of Oct. 14 in *The Herald* and Oct. 18 in the *New York Sun;* all in Harvard Theater Collection. I thank Laurence Senelick for help with this research. Another review of the play is in *Critic: An Illustrated Monthly Review of Literature, Art, and Life* (New York), vol. 26; new ser., vol. 29 (Oct. 17, 1896), p. 234. The play was adapted from the novel *A Florida Enchantment*, coauthored by Gunter and Fergus Redmond (New York: Hurst, 1891; Home Publishing Co., 1892; microfilm reprint; see Roberts, *Black Lesbians*, p. 32). For reviews of the novel see *Saturday Review* (London), vol. 88 (Oct. 1899), p. 462; *The Athenaeum* (London), vol. 114 (Aug. 5, 1899), p. 189. Also see Foster, *Sex Variant*, pp. 109–11, 247,

366. For the movie *A Florida Enchantment* (1914) see Russo, *Celluloid Closet*, pp. 11, 13, 251. A brief biography of Gunter is in Stanley Kunitz and Howard Haycroft, ed., *American Authors 1600–1900* (New York: Wilson, 1938), p. 323.

39. 1897, May 23: *N. Y. Times*, "Woman. Calls Them Andromaniacs. Dr. [Charles] Parkhurst So Characterizes Certain Women Who Passionately Ape Everything That Is Mannish. Woman Divinely Preferred. Her Supremacy Lies in Her Womanliness, and She Should Make the Most of It—Her Sphere of Best Usefulness the Home," 16:1.

40. 1898, May: Dr. Francis W. Anthony, "The Question of Responsibility in Cases of Sexual Perversion," read; published *Boston Medical and Surgical Journal*, vol. 139, no. 12 (Sept. 22, 1898), 288–91.

41. 1898: Dr. Mary Wood-Allen, *What a Young Woman Ought to Know* (Philadelphia: VIR Publishing Co.), pp. 147–54, 173–76.

42. 1899, Jan.: H. Sturt, [review of] Edward Carpenter, *An Unknown People* (London: A. & H. B. Bonner, 1897, 37 pp.) and Havelock Ellis, *Sexual Inversion*, vol. I, *Studies in the Psychology of Sex* (London: Watford; The University Press, 1897), in *International Journal of Ethics* (Philadelphia), vol. 9, no. 2, pp. 261–62. For evidence that *The International Journal of Ethics* served as an information exchange for sex radicals and liberals in the U.S. and England see backnote 21, p. 704. Also see index for reviews and essays in *The International Journal of Ethics.*

43. 1899, Apr. 8: New York State Report; testimony at Mazet Committee hearings in *Report of the Special Committee of the [N. Y. S.] Assembly Appointed to Investigate the Public Offices and Departments of the City of New York . . .* 5 vols. (Albany: James B. Lyon, 1900); testimony of Police Chief William Devery, Apr. 8, vol. 1, pp. 173–76; Apr. 10, p. 278; George P. Hammond, Nov. 3, vol. 5, pp. 5125–6. I wish to thank Joel Honig for these references. In *GAH* also see testimony of May 17, pp. 44–45; May 31, pp. 45–46; June 1, pp. 46–47.

44. 1899, Apr. 30: *N. Y. Times*, "Hypnotism The Cure-All," 12:1. I thank Allan Bérubé for providing a photocopy. On Dr. John D. Quackenbos also see *GAH* pp. 144–45.

45. 1899, June: Nettie Miller shoots Charles Seibert, Chicago: a case of probable contrary sexual feeling; *Chicago Daily News* report, no date, described and quoted in "Forensic Medicine. A Case of Probable Conträre [sic] Sexualempfindung," *Medicine. A Monthly Journal of Medicine and Surgery* (Detroit), vol. 5, no. 6 (June 1899), pp. 526–28.

46. 1899: Dr. George J. Monroe, "Sodomy—Pederasty," *Saint Louis Medical Era*, vol. 9 (1899), pp. 431–34,

### *1900*

1. 1900, May 5: Dr. William Lee Howard, "Effeminate Men and Masculine Women," *New York Medical Journal*, vol. 77, (May 5, 1900), pp. 686–87. This is *not* a reprint of Howard's "Psychical Hermaphroditism" (1897), as the *Index Catalogue* indicates.

2. c. 1900: Mary Casal (pseud.), *The Stone*
*Wall* (Chicago: Eyncourt Press, 1930; reprinted New York: Arno Press, 1975).

3. 1902, Apr. 5: *N. Y. Times*: Oscar Wilde's "The Importance of Being Earnest," 5:1.

4. 1902, July 5: *NYTBR*, p. 541; Edward Carpenter, *Ioläus: An Anthology of Friend-*

*ship* (Boston: Goodspeed). Also see review in *Poet Lore*, vol. 14, no. 2 (Jan. 1903), pp. 33–34.

5. 1902, Dec. 18: Dr. William S. Barker, "Two Cases of Sexual Contrariety," *St. Louis Courier of Medicine*, vol. 28, (1903), 269–71; read Dec. 18, 1902.

6. 1903, Feb.: Dr. E. H. Smith, "Masturbation in the Female," *Pacific Medical Journal* (San Francisco), vol. 96, no. 1 (Feb. 1903), 76–83.

7. 1904, Jan.: Dr. William Lee Howard, "Sexual Perversion in America," *American Journal of Dermatology and Genito-Urinary Diseases* (St. Louis), vol. 8, no. 1 (Jan. 1904), pp. 9–14.

8. 1904, June 18: *NYTBR*, p. 402; Charles Godfrey Leland, *The Alternate Sex: or, The Female Intellect in Man and the Masculine in Women* (New York: Funk & Wagnalls). Prepared for the press by Leland's niece, Elizabeth Robbins Pennell, whose own life bears investigation.

9. c. 1905–20s: Postcards, mostly from the collection of Marshall Weeks, to whom I am deeply grateful. For the cards "What It Will Come To" (1910) and "When We Dance" (1918) I thank Allan Bérubé and the San Francisco Lesbian and Gay History Project.

10. 1906, June 4: Dr. William Lee Howard, "The Sexual Pervert in Life Insurance," *Medical Examiner* (New York), vol. 16, (July 1906), pp. 206–07; this includes typographical errors, with parts out of sequence, but the essay is complete as printed; read June 4, 1906.

11. 1906, July 24: Dr. Robert W. Shufeldt, "Biography of a Passive Pederast," *American Journal of Urology and Sexology*, vol. 13, no. 10 (Oct. 1917), pp. 451–60; reporting case of transvestite, "Loop-the-loop," interviewed and photographed 1906, July 24 (see) and Nov. 4, 1906 (the text for the latter date says 1916, evidently a misprint).

12. 1906, Sept. 8: Dr. T. H. Evans, "The Problem of Sexual Variants," *St. Louis Medical Review*, vol. 54, no. 10, pp. 213–15.

13. 1906, Nov.: Dr. Harold N. Moyer, "Is Sexual Perversion Insanity?" *Alienist and Neurologist*, vol. 28, no. 2 (May 1907), pp. 193–204, reprinted from *Transactions, Chicago Academy of Medicine*, Nov. 1906.

14. 1907, May 30: *N. Y. Times;* the Moltke–Eulenburg scandal in Germany; see the *Times Index* for 1907, 1908, 1909 for specific stories. Quotations contained in this account appeared in the following *Times* stories: 1907, December 31 (3:5); 1908, January 1 (4:2), April 30 (6:5), July 5 (3/1:2), July 15 (6:7); 1909, June 19 (4:3), July 8 (5:2). Eulenburg's obituary appeared in the *Times,* Sept. 20, 1921, 17:5. For background on the Moltke–Eulenburg scandal see Isabel V. Hull, "The Entourage of Kaiser Wilhelm II, 1888–1918," dissertation (Yale, 1978); (includes three chapters on Eulenburg, his circle, and his political importance); also Hull's "Kaiser Wilhelm and the 'Liebenberg Circle,'" in John C. G. Röhl and Nikolaus Sombart, ed., *Kaiser Wilhelm II: New Interpretations* (Cambridge: Cambridge University Press, 1981). I thank Isabel Hull for help with this research.

15. 1907, Nov. 11: *The Trinadad* (Colorado) *Advertiser*, "Woman Who Posed as Man 60 Years, Dead,/ Born in France/ Only Reason Was to Secure Man's Work" (Katherine Vosbaugh), pp. 1, 4. I thank James Foshee for informing me of this item and supplying a photocopy.

16. 1908, Apr. 2: *N. Y. Times;* Fischer-Hansen tried for extortion; Apr. 2, 14:4; June 12, 16:1; June 13, 4:2; June 16, 5:3; June 17, 5:5; June 18, 16:4; June 19, 6:6; June 20, 5:3. I thank Wilhelm von Rosen for providing a translation of Joakim Reinhardt's letter of

1908, an account of his life, including his first and his second, permanent, immigration to the U. S., and quotes from his other letters from America. Reinhardt's letter to Karl Larsen is in the Larsen collection, The Royal Library, Copenhagen, Manuscript Collection (NkS 4630, 4°). Reinhardt's letters to Larsen, and Larsen's papers, indicate that Reinhardt was homosexual.

17. 1908: Xavier Mayne (pseud. of Edward Stevenson), *The Intersexes: A History of Similisexualism as a Problem in Social Life* (Rome: privately printed, preface dated 1908; reprinted New York: Arno Press, 1975); parts reprinted in *GAH,* pp. 146–47, 253. An item dated Apr. 1909 (*Intersexes,* p. 521), indicates that the book was published after 1908.

18. 1909, March 13: *NYTBR,* p. 142; Clarissa Dixon, *Janet and Her Dear Phebe* (New York: Stokes).

## *1910*

1. 1910, Aug.: Dr. James G. Kiernan, "A Medico-Legal Phase of Auto-Erotism in Women," *Alienist and Neurologist,* vol. 31, no. 3, pp. 329–38.

2. 1911, Jan. 14: *NYTBR,* p. 14; Theodore Stanton, ed., *Reminiscences of Rosa Bonheur* (New York: Appleton, 1910).

3. 1911, Apr. 5: Vice Commission of Chicago, *The Social Evil in Chicago: A Study of Existing Conditions/With Recommendations* (Chicago: Gunthorp-Warren); includes other references to various kinds of "sex perversion," see pp. 39, 56, 73, 125, 126, 139, 240, 247, 290–91, 305, 348.

4. 1911, July: *International Journal of Ethics,* vol. 21, no. 4, pp. 502–03; Edward Carpenter, *The Intermediate Sex: A Study of Some Transitional Types of Men and Women,* 2nd ed. (London: Swan Sonnenschein, 1909).

5. 1911: Dr. William Lee Howard, *Confidential Chats With Boys* (New York: Edward J. Clode, 1911). I thank Jeffrey Escoffier for informing me of this and providing a copy.

6. 1912, Nov. 2: Dr. Douglas C. McMurtrie, "Some Observations on the Psychology of Sexual Inversion in Women," *The Lancet-Clinic* (Cincinnati, Ohio), vol. 108, no. 18, 487–90. The last mentioned female, G., sounds much like "Mary Casal," case VIII, "D.," like "Juno" and case "IX," like Juno's homosexual husband; see c. 1900, and *GAH,* pp. 548–56. In McMurtrie's essay of 1912, G. is said to be forty-eight, which would make her year of birth 1864, the same as Casal's.

7. 1913, March 30: *NYTBR,* p. 175; J. Lionel Taylor, *The Nature of Woman* (New York: Dutton); Taylor was a Lecturer on Biology and Sociology, London University.

8. 1913, October 19: *NYTBR,* p. 56; Walter Heape, *Sex Antagonism* (New York: Putnam's).

9. 1913: Dr. Douglas C. McMurtrie, "Notes On Homosexuality: An Attempt at Seduction; An Example of Acquired Homosexuality in Prison; A Commentary on the Prevalence of Inversion in Germany," *Vermont Medical Monthly,* vol. 19, pp. 66–68; reference to Berkman's *Prison Memoirs,* see *GAH,* pp. 530–38.

10. 1913–14: Dr. Francis M. Schockley, "The Role of Homosexuality in the Genesis of Paranoid Conditions," *Psychoanalysis and the Psychoanalytic Review,* vol. 1, pp. 431–38.

11. 1914, Jan.: Dr. Douglas C. McMurtrie, "Notes On Pederastic Practices in Prison," *Chicago Medical Recorder,"* vol. 36, pp. 15–17.

12. 1914, Feb. 21: Dr. Bernard S. Talmey, "Transvestism: A Contribution to the Study of the Psychology of Sex," *New*

*York Medical Journal,* vol. 99, pp. 362–68; read before the Society of Medical Jurisprudence, Dec. 8, 1913.

13. 1914, March 27: Jack London and wife to Edward Carpenter; in Carpenter Collection, Sheffield, England.

14. 1914, June: Dr. Douglas C. McMurtrie, "Department of Sexual Psychology. . . . An Indigenous American Sexual Phenomenon. The Berdache. Courtship by a Berdache. The Woman Dance Among the Musquakie. Lesbian Love and the Lexicographers. Tribadism in a French Dictionary, . . ." *American Journal of Urology,* vol. 10, no. 6, pp. 295–97.

15. 1914, July: Dr. Douglas C. McMurtrie, "Department of Sexual Psychology. . . . Homosexual Infatuation Between Women," *American Journal of Urology,* vol. 10, no. 7, p. 351.

16. 1914, Aug.: Dr. Wilhelm Stekel, "Masked Homosexuality," translated by Dr. S. A. Tannenbaum, *American Medicine* (Burlington, Vt.), vol. 9, no. 8, pp. 530–37.

17. 1914, Sept.: Dr. Douglas C. McMurtrie, "Department of Sexual Psychology. Lesbian Assemblies. Hirschfeld, Champion of Homosexuality. The Bible and Feminine Inversion. A Crime of Lesbian Love. Case of Perverted Sexual Tastes. . . . The Berdache Among the Illinois. Moral Conditions Among Seamen," *American Journal of Urology,* vol. 10, no. 9, pp. 432–36. Also see Russell B. Herts, "Visits to Three Scientists: Haeckel the Monist; Bloch the Syphilologist; Hirschfeld, Defender of Homosexuality," *Medical Review of Reviews* (New York), vol. 19 (1913), pp. 490–96. This is an early American defense of homosexuality as an inborn condition with various forms of expression.

18. 1914, Oct.: *International Journal of Ethics,* vol. 25, no. 1, pp. 110–13; Edward Carpenter, *Intermediate Types Among Primitive Folk: A Study in Social Evolution* (London: Allen; New York: Kennerley); review by T. Whittaker.

19. 1914, Nov.: Dr. Douglas C. McMurtrie, "Sexually Inverted Infatuation in a Middle-Aged Woman," *Urologic and Cutaneous Review,* vol. 18, no. 11, p. 601.

20. 1914: George Cecil Ives, *A History of Penal Methods: Criminals, Witches, Lunatics* (New York: Stokes).

21. 1914: Dr. William J. Robinson, "My Views On Homosexuality," *American Journal of Urology,* vol. 10, pp. 550–52.

22. 1914: Dr. Irving D. Steinhardt, *Ten Sex Talks to Girls (14 Years and Older)* (Philadelphia: Lippincott); on masturbation pp. 57–63

23. 1915, Feb.: Edith Lees Ellis; lecture in Chicago, and Margaret Anderson's response; on Edith Ellis's U. S. tours in Havelock Ellis, *My Life: Autobiography* . . . (Boston: Houghton Mifflin, 1939); first U. S. tour, pp. 468, 478–84; second U. S. tour, pp. 494–95; on Chicago and Edith's Feb. 4, 1915 talk on "The Abnormal in Eugenics" (as Havelock mistakenly calls it), see especially pp. 504–05, 508–09, 511–12, 517; on Edith's speech on homosexuality, "Abnormality and the Spiritual," and on her extended, boldest speech on homosexuality, "Eugenics and Spiritual Parenthood" (which Havelock says was delivered in the U. S.), see pp. 447–48. The latter speech is published with Edith's Feb. 4 speech, "Sex and Eugenics" (publication title "Eugenics and the Mystical Outlook") in Edith Ellis, *The New Horizon in Love and Life,* preface by Edward Carpenter, introduction by Marguerite Tracy (London: A. & C. Black, 1921), a collection said to be "written originally as essays and lectures," and published "without the author's final revisions." Additional homosexuality reference p. 158. Edith's comments on Edward Carpen-

ter in her *Three Modern Seers: James Hinton, Nietzsche, Edward Carpenter* (Berkeley Heights, N. J.: privately printed by Free Spirit Press, 1924, New York: Kennerley, 1910); in her *Personal Impressions of Edward Carpenter* (Berkeley Heights, N.J.: Free Spirit Press, 1922); and in her *Stories and Essays, . . .* prefaces by Charles Marriott and George Ives (founder of the secret homosexual emancipation organization in England, 1890s; see Weeks, *Coming Out*). *Stories* also contains Edith's essay "Oscar Wilde," and reminiscences by "Mrs. Clifford Bax" and F. W. Stella Browne (the English socialist-feminist).

Biographies of Havelock Ellis which have data on Edith include Isaac Goldberg, *Havelock Ellis; A Biographical and Critical Survey . . . With a Supplementary Chapter on Mrs. Havelock Ellis* (New York: Simon & Schuster, 1926); Arthur Calder-Marshall, *Havelock Ellis . . .* (London: Rupert Hart Davis, 1959); Phyllis Grosskurth, *Havelock Ellis: A Biography* (New York: Knopf, 1980).

As for Edith Ellis's Feb. 4 talk: *Chicago Daily Tribune*, Feb. 4, 1915, p. 10; "300 Brave Men Hear Mrs. Ellis . . . ," same, Feb. 5, 1915, 1:2. Also "Men Hear Ellis Sex Talk . . . ," *Chicago Daily News*, Feb. 5, 1915, 7:3. I thank James Monahan for researching and providing these accounts.

"Editorials and Announcements; Mrs. Havelock Ellis," *Little Review*, vol. 1, no. 10 Jan. 1915, p. 32; Herman Schuchert, "Mrs. Havelock Ellis's 'The Love of Tomorrow,' " same, pp. 34–35. Edith Ellis, "Heaven's Jester . . . ," *LR*, vol. 1, no. 11 (Feb. 1915), pp. 8–13. Mary Adams Stearns, "Mrs. Ellis's Gift to Chicago," *LR*, vol. II, no. 1 (March 1915), pp. 12–15; Margaret Anderson, "Mrs. Ellis's Failure," same, pp. 16–19 (both collectively titled "Two Points of View"). Also, E. C. A. Smith, letter to

*LR* from Grosse Ile, Michigan, vol. II, no. 2 (Apr. 1915), pp. 54.

24. 1916, Feb.: Dr. James G. Kiernan, "Sexology. Androphobia. Bearded Women and Inversion. Tomboyism and Inversion. . . . Psychic Evolution and Inversion. Homosexuality Among Harlots . . . ," *Urologic and Cutaneous Review*, vol. 20, no. 2, pp. 103–08.

25. 1916, June: Dr. James G. Kiernan, "Sexology. . . . Theory of Inversion. . . . Classification of Homosexuality," *Urologic and Cutaneous Review*, vol. 20, no. 6, pp. 345–46, 348–50.

26. 1916, Aug. 20: Edward Carpenter, *My Days and Dreams. Being Autobiographical Notes* (New York: Scribner's); *NYTBR*, Aug. 20, 1916, p. 328; *International Journal of Ethics* (Oct. 1916), vol. 27, pp. 124–25, review by F. W. S. Browne; on the very interesting Browne see Sheila Rowbotham, *A New World for Women: Stella Browne, Socialist Feminist* (London: Pluto Press, 1977); *GAH*, pp. 337, 383–85; and Weeks, *Coming Out*, pp. 99–100, 132, 134.

27. Carpenter's own sexual history, written by himself and beginning "My parentage is very sound," appears as "Case VI" in the 1897 edition of Havelock Ellis's *Sexual Inversion*, and as "Case VII" in other editions; see Emile Delavenay, *D. H. Lawrence and Edward Carpenter: A Study in Edwardian Transition* (London: Heinemann, 1971), p. 271. That "Case XVII" in the 1915 edition (1936) is George Merrill, is my own conclusion based on my knowledge of Merrill, and Carpenter's hint.

28. 1916: Dr. Emil Oberhoffer, "The Influence of Castration on the Libido," *American Journal of Urology and Sexology*," vol. 12, pp. 58–60.

29. 1917, Feb. 4: *NYTBR*, p. 33; Clemence Dane, *Regiment of Women* (New York: Macmillan); Foster, *Sex Variant*, p. 257; Faderman, *Surpassing*, pp. 341–44, 392;

*Book Review Digest,* 1917, p. 137. "Dane" was Winifred Ashton.

30. 1917, Apr.: Dr. Edward J. Kempf, "Social and Sexual Behavior of Infra-Human Primates with Some Comparable Facts in Human Behavior," *Psychoanalytic Review* (Washington, D. C.), vol. 4, no. 2, pp. 127–54.

31. 1917, Aug.: Dr. Alfred Adler, "The Homosexual Problem," *Alienist and Neurologist,* vol. 38, no. 3, pp. 268–87.

32. 1917, Sept. 2: *NYTBR,* p. 322; J. D. Beresford, *House-Mates* (New York: George H. Doran).

33. 1918, March: Dr. Horace Westlake Frink, *Morbid Fears and Compulsions; Their Psychoanalytic Treatment,* introduction by James J. Putnam (New York: Dodd, Mead); discussed by Mary Ryan, *Womanhood* (2nd. ed., 1979), pp. 163–64.

34. 1918, June: Dr. E. S. Shepherd, "Contribution to the Study of Indeterminacy," *American Journal of Urology and Sexology,* vol. 14, no. 6, pp. 241–52. Also see Shepherd's article on "the meaning of normal as applied to the sex impulse," same journal, vol. 13, (1917), pp. 64ff.

35. 1918, Nov.: Dr. Lilburn Merrill, Diagnostician of the Seattle Juvenile Court, "A Summary of Findings in a Study of Sexualism Among a Group of One Hundred Delinquent Boys," *Journal of Delinquency,* vol. 3, pp. 255–67; reprinted in *American Journal of Urology and Sexology,* vol. 15 (1919), pp. 259–69.

36. 1918: Dr. Albert Abrams, San Francisco: "Homosexuality—A Military Menace," *Medical Review of Reviews,* vol. 24, pp. 528–29. Abrams refers to his method of testing for "Electronic Reactions" in *International Clinics,* vol. 1, 27th ser. (1917); also see his *New Concepts in Diagnosis and Treatment: Spondylotherapy,* 6th ed. (1918).

37. 1919, Apr.: Dr. G. Sherman Peterkin, "Cultivation and Control as Against Suppression of Sexual Instinct," *Urologic and Cutaneous Review,* pp. 201–04.

38. 1919, June 29: *NYTBR,* p. 353; Sherwood Anderson, *Winesburg, Ohio* (New York: B. W. Huebsch); also see Austen, *Playing,* pp. 33–34.

39. 1919: Dr. Constance Long, "A Psycho-Analytic Study of the Basic of Character," *Proceedings of the International Conference of Women Physicians 1919,* 6 vols., vol 4 *Moral Codes and Personality* (New York: The Woman's Press, 1920), pp. 67–90. In the same volume also see Dr. Eleanor Bertine, "Health and Morality in the Light of the New Psychology," pp. 5–14; Dr. Beatrice Hinkle, "Arbitrary Use of the Terms, 'Masculine' and 'Feminine,'" pp. 100–18.

### 1920

1. 1920, Jan.: Dr. W. C. Rivers, "A New Male Homosexual Trait(?)," *Alienist and Neurologist* vol. 41, no. 1, pp. 22–27.

2. 1920, Nov.: Emory Holloway, "Walt Whitman's Love Affairs," *The Dial,* vol. 69, no. 5, pp. 473–83. It is interesting to note that *The Dial,* as a journal of "advanced" sexual thought, also first published D. H. Lawrence's *The Fox,* in 1922; see Faderman, *Surpassing,* pp. 350–51.

3. Emory Holloway, ed., *The Uncollected Poetry and Prose of Walt Whitman, Much of Which Has Been But Recently Discovered, With Various Early Manuscripts Now First Published and Collected,* 2 vols. (Garden City, N.Y.: Doubleday, Page, 1921).

4. Emory Holloway, *Whitman: An Interpretation in Narrative* (New York: Knopf, 1926).

5. 1920: Dr. Edward Kempf, *Psychopathology* (St. Louis: Mosby); especially chapter 10 "The Psychology of the Acute Homosexual Panic," pp. 477–

515; and other scattered references to homosexuality and mental disturbance.

6. 1921, Jan. 24: "Earl Lind" and *The New York Times:* the death of Kermit Engelhart; see "Earl Lind" (Ralph Werther/Jennie June), *The Female Impersonators. A Sequel to the Autobiography of an Androgyne,* ed. with an introduction by Dr. Alfred W. Herzog (New York: Medico-Legal Journal, 1922; reprinted New York: Arno Press, 1975), p. 209; *N. Y. Times,* Jan. 24, 1921. I thank Allan Bérubé for informing me of the *Times* coverage and providing a photocopy.

7. 1921, Apr. 4: Anonymous Detroiters to Edward Carpenter; letters in the Carpenter Collection, Sheffield, England.

8. 1921, Spring: Gertrude Stein, "The song of Alice B.," p. 12 in "A Sonatina Followed by Another," pp. 3–32 in Stein's *Bee Time Vine and Other Pieces,* preface and notes by Virgil Thomson (New Haven: Yale University Press, 1953).

9. 1921, July 20: *N. Y. Times;* Franklin D. Roosevelt and the scandal at Newport, R.I., 4:7. For the committee's report, whose details the *Times* called "unprintable," see U. S. Senate, 67th Congress, First Session. Committee on Naval Affairs, *Alleged Immoral Conditions at Newport (R.I.) Naval Training Station, Report of the Committee of Naval Affairs . . .* (Washington, D.C.: Govt. Printing Office, 1921; reprinted in *Government Versus Homosexuals* [New York: Arno Press, 1975]). Besides the Freidel book mentioned in the footnote to this document, also see Elliot Roosevelt, ed., *FDR, His Personal Letters,* 3 vols. (New York: Duell, Sloan and Pearce, 1947–50), vol. 2, pp. 517, 519–22; and Earl Looker, *This Man Roosevelt* (New York: 1932), pp. 93–100.

10. 1921, Aug. 12: *N.Y. Times;* Harry Gribble's play "March Hares"; reviewed by Alexander Woollcott, 8:3; further comment Aug. 21, 1921, VI, 1:1. For the English production see *N. Y. Times,* Jan. 1, 1928, VIII, 1:3.

11. 1921, Aug. 28: *NYTBR,* p. 27; comment by J. O'London on D. H. Lawrence's essay on Walt Whitman published in *The Nation* (London).

12. 1921, Aug.: Dr. Perry M. Lichtenstein, "The 'Fairy' and the Lady Lover," *Medical Review of Reviews,* vol. 27, no. 8, 369–74. Ralph Werther (Jennie June), "A Fairie's Reply to Dr. Lichtenstein," same, vol. 27, no. 11 (Nov. 1921), 539–42. For Werther's other writings in defense of "androgynes" (effeminate male homosexuals) and "gynanders" (masculine lesbians), see: *GAH,* pp. 336, 366–71, 575 n. 47, 592 n. 17 and 26.

13. 1921, Dec. 16: *N. Y. Times;* Ethel Kimball/John Hathaway, 5:3; same, Dec. 21, 1921, 6:6. The first story says that Ethel Kimball (spelled once as Kemball) had been arrested for auto theft. The second story says that she (as James Hathaway) had been arrested for "masquerading."

14. 1922: Gertrude Stein, "Miss Furr and Miss Skeene"; written 1908–1912; first published in *Geography and Plays* (Boston: The Four Seas Co., 1922) pp. 17–22; reprinted *Vanity Fair,* July 1923. On "Miss Furr and . . . ," Maud Hunt Squire, and Ethel Mars see James R. Mellow, *Charmed Circle: Gertrude Stein & Company* (New York: Praeger, 1974), pp. 131, 133–34 and n. on p. 488 which thanks Virginia Zabriskie of the Zabriskie Gallery, N.Y., for supplying an unpublished memoir by Anne Goldthraite. Mellow is incorrect in saying that the Miss Furr character has left her "husband"; it is clearly her father (and mother) whom she has left. On "Miss Furr and . . ." also see Richard Bridgman, *Gertrude Stein in Pieces* (New York: Oxford University Press, 1970), pp.

94–96, 366. Bridgman's interpretation of Miss Furr as "the weaker of the two women" has no basis in the story. He also says that Miss Furr's gaiety at the end "turns ragged and hysterical as Miss Furr tries to endure her rejection, making this a pathetic portrait rather than as both Elizabeth Sprigge and Carl Van Vechten have found it, a 'charming' one. . . ." Bridgman is wrong factually, obtuse analytically, and sexist. For Squire's letter to Stein (Fall? 1933) see Donald Gallup, ed., *The Flowers of Friendship: Letters Written to Gertrude Stein* (New York: Knopf, 1953), p. 269.

15. 1923, June 23: *N. Y. Times*, Fred G. Thompson/Mrs. Frances Carrick, 21:12; same, Oct. 4, 1923, 12:1. I thank James Foshee for informing me of this item and for a photocopy.

16. 1924, May 4: *NYTBR*, 2:2; Sylvia Stevenson's *Surplus* (New York: Appleton). The Greensboro (North Carolina) *Daily News*, and Forrest Reid in the *Literary Review of the New York Evening Post*, are both quoted from *Book Review Digest*, 1924, pp. 566–67.

17. 1924, Sept.: F. O. Matthiessen to Russell Cheney. Summary of Matthiessen's life by Joseph H. Summers and U. T. Miller Summers, in *The Dictionary of American Biography, Supplement Four* (1975), pp. 559–61. Explanation of the bracketed deletions to the Skull and Bones Society in Harry Levin's review of the published letters, *N. Y. Review of Books*, July 20, 1978, p. 43. Letters published as *Rat & the Devil: Journal Letters of F. O. Matthiessen and Russell Cheney*, edited by Louis Hyde (Hamden, Conn.: Archon Books, 1978).

18. 1924, Dec. 5: *N. Y. Times;* on Fritz Haarmann, the "vampire slayer"; see *Times* of 1924, Dec. 5, 3:5; Dec. 7, 30:2; Dec. 12, 4:8; Dec. 13, 17:7; Dec. 14, 10:1; Dec. 16, 12:3; Dec. 18, 24:1; Dec. 19, 14:1; Dec. 20, 1:2. On Dec. 18, 1924 a *Chicago Herald and Examiner* headline read: "Vampire Slayer Held Legally Sane," 3:5; in the same paper also see stories of Dec. 19, 7:4; Dec. 20, 4:4; Dec. 21, 10:3.

19. 1925, Feb. 22: *NYTBR*, p. 9; Thomas Mann, *Death in Venice and Other Stories*, translated from the German by Kenneth Burk (New York: Knopf).

20. 1925, May 31: *NYTBR*, p. 8; Cyril Hume, *Cruel Fellowship* (New York: Doran).

21. 1925, June 4: The Society for Human Rights, Chicago; see sources cited in the text and footnotes. My information about the references to the Society for Human Rights contained in George Ives's minutes of the British Society for the Study of Sex Psychology, and the manuscript and printed version of the Society's annual report of 1925, is based on pp. 24–25 of a twenty-seven page research paper prepared by Michael Dunn, and based on his research at the Humanities Research Center, University of Texas, Austin, which holds The George Ives Collection, including all the documents mentioned in the text. I am deeply grateful to Michael Dunn for his hours of research work.

Contacts between Americans and the British Society are documented as early as Jan. 25, 1918 when Richard G. Badger, head of the Gorham Press, Boston, wrote to Stella Browne in England that he had read her note about the Society in the *International Journal of Ethics* (indicating this journal's function as a major information exchange for early sex reformers). See F. Stella Browne, "A New Psychological Society," *International Journal of Ethics*, vol. 28 [Jan. 1918], pp. 266ff., cited in Weeks, *Sex, Politics, and Society*, p. 196.) Badger said "we are publishing a number of advanced sex books which are meeting with a very remarkable reception in this country. . . ." The British Society might distribute Badger's publications in England, and he might distribute theirs in the U. S., he suggested (information in Dunn's report cited above, p. 22). Among Badger's publications were Dr. Sandor Ferenczi's *Contributions to Psycho-analysis* (1916), with sections on homosexuality; Badger Clark's *Sun and Saddle Leather* (1919), including a homoerotic cowboy poem (*GAH,* p. 511); and the homoerotic *Sonnets of Karl August . . . von Platen-Hallermunde* (1923).

22. On Oct. 13, 1920, George Ives noted in his diary that at a meeting of the British Society for Sex Psychology he had met the Americans Margaret Sanger "of the Birth Control Movement" and David Thompson of the U.S. Library of Congress. "We do no end of good," said Ives, "by bringing all these advanced and distinguished people together!" In 1922, Dr. William Robinson's American Sexanalytic Press informed the British Society that it would send it the *Journal of Sexology and Psychoanalysis* at no charge (Dunn, p. 22). The same year Magnus Hirschfeld mentioned that the British Society for the Study of Sex Psychology had established "a branch in the United States," headed by Dr. Robinson and Margaret Sanger (*GAH,* p. 632, n. 89). In 1923, Sanger's *Birth Control Review,* printed in New York by the Women's Publishing Company, ordered several copies of the British Society's pamphlet "The Sexual Life of the Child." About 1924, the "American Society for the Study of Sex Psychology" was said to have approved the publication of a verse anthology titled *Men and Boys,* compiled by Edmund Edwinson (pseud., New York: privately printed, 1924). And in 1925 The New York Public Library requested a copy of the British Society's pamphlet "The Social Problem of Sexual Inversion" (Dunn, pp. 22–23).

23. 1925, July 5: *NYTBR,* p. 8; Marcel Proust, *The Guermantes Way,* 2 vols., translated by C. K. Scott Moncrieff (New York: Thomas Seltzer).

24. 1925, July 19: *NYTBR,* p. 4; Marion Mills Miller and David Robinson, trans. and ed., *The Songs of Sappho . . .* (Lexington, Ky.: Maxwelton). Another edition of the same text was published the same year in New York by Frank-Maurice.

25. 1925, Dec. 23: *New Republic,* vol. 45, p. 143; *NYTBR,* Nov. 15, 1925, p. 8; *Book Review Digest* for 1925, pp. 608–09; Naomi Royde-Smith, *Tortoiseshell Cat* (New York: Boni & Liveright); also see Foster, *Sex Variant,* pp. 273, 275–77, 293, 294, 320, 339.

26. 1925: Jessie Binford, "The Year's Work—1925," in *Annual Report of the Juvenile Protective Association* (Chicago: 1926). If the "detailed description of the performances at "a certain West Side theatre," in the records of the Juvenile Protective Association, still exist, they would provide rare documentation of an interesting homosexual culture, as would the "paper" published by the "homo-sexual" men and boys headquartered in Grant Park. Also see Walter Reckless, *Vice in Chicago* (Chicago: Chicago University Press, 1933; reprinted Montclair, N. J.; Patterson Smith, 1969), pp. 262–66. I thank James Foshee and Gregory Sprague for help with this research and for supplying photocopies.

27. 1925: Dr. William Robinson, "Nature's Sex Stepchildren," *Medical Critic and Guide* (New York), vol. 25, pp. 475–77.

28. 1926, May 9: *NYTBR,* p. 8; Dimitri S. Merezhkovsky, *The Birth of the Gods,* translated from the Russian by Natalie A. Duddington (New York: Dutton).

This review appears among several under the heading "Portrait of a Flapper in the New Fiction."

29. 1926, June 20: *NYTBR*, p. 5; Thomas Burke, *East of Mansion House*, including the story, "The Pash" (New York: Doran).

30. 1926, Sept. 30: *N. Y. Times;* Edouard Bourdet's *The Captive;* see citations in text.

31. 1926, Oct. 24: *NYTBR*, p. 152; Dr. Joseph Collins, *The Doctor Looks at Love and Life* (New York: Doran).

32. 1926, Dec. 15: *N. Y. Times;* Carl Dryer's *Chained (The Invert)*, 30:4. The invert was played by Benjamin Christensen; his protégé by Walter Slezak. Also see Russo, *Celluloid Closet*, p. 22.

33. 1927, Sept. 4: *NYTBR*, p. 7; Rosamund Lehmann, *Dusty Answer* (New York: Henry Holt); also see *Book Review Digest* 1927, pp. 429–30; Foster, *Sex Variant*, 278–79, 288, 308.

34. 1927, Nov. 13: *NYTBR*, p. 6; Compton Mackenzie, *Vestal Fire* (New York: Doran); *Book Review Digest*, 1927, p. 467.

35. 1927: Dr. Aaron J. Rosanoff, "Sexual Psychopathies," pp. 193–208 in *Manual of Psychiatry*, 6th ed. (New York: Wiley); reprinted as "Human Sexuality, Normal and Abnormal, From a Psychiatric Standpoint," in *Urologic and Cutaneous Review*, vol. 33, no. 8 (Aug. 1929), pp. 523–29. The list of slang does not appear in the 5th (1920) edition of this book.

36. 1928, Jan. 8: *NYTBR*, p. 15; Marcel Proust, *Cities of the Plain*, translated by C. K. Scott Moncrieff, 2 vols. (New York: A. and C. Boni).

37. 1928, May 20: *NYTBR*, p. 5; Houston Peterson, *Havelock Ellis: Philosopher of Love* (Boston: Houghton Mifflin).

38. 1928, June: Gertrude "Ma" Rainey, "Prove It On Me Blues" recorded; reissued on "AC/DC Blues, Gay Jazz Reissues," ST-106, Stash Records, P. O. Box 390, Brooklyn, N. Y. 11215; liner notes by Chris Albertson, author of *Bessie* (New York: Stein & Day, 1972), a biography of blues singer Bessie Smith which refers to Ma Rainey as lesbian; Albertson also describes Smith's lesbian relations (excerpt in *GAH*, pp. 76–82, which cites other black lesbians, and prints lines from "It's Dirty But Good," "The Boy in the Boat," and "Foolish Man Blues"). The words of "Prove It On Me Blues" as printed in this *Almanac* were deciphered to the best of Chris Albertson's, Rudy Grillo's, and my abilities from the unclear Stash recording. A version of the lyrics accompanying the Stash album includes some significantly different interpretations of the lines.

On Rainey see the brief biography by Charles Edward Smith in *Notable American Women*, and Derrick Stewart-Baxter, *Ma Rainey and the Classic Blues Singers* (London: Studio Vista, 1970). Besides "Prove It On Me," the Stash record "AC/DC Blues, Gay Jazz Reissues" includes "Buffet Flat Story," part of Chris Albertson's interview with Ruby Smith, Bessie Smith's niece; "Sissy Man Blues" (recorded Apr. 1936); "Foolish Man Blues" (Bessie Smith, Oct. 1927); "Garbage Man" (Apr. 1936); "It's Tight Like That" (Nov. 1928); "Sissy Man Blues" (Jan. 1935); "Boy in the Boat" (Oct. 1931); "Freakish Man Blues" (Oct. 1930); "B. D. [Bull Diker] Woman's Blues" (Bessie Jackson, March 1935); "Dirty Dozens" (Sept. 1929); "Ain't That a Mess" (Feb. 1936); "Fairy Blues" (Apr. 1928); "Freakish Rider Blues" (Apr. 1927); and "Sissy Man Blues" (March 1935).

A second Stash record (ST-118), "Strait and Gay," contains among others, "Sissy Man" (1935), "Sissy Blues" (Ma Rainey, 1926); and "Two Old

Maids in a Folding Bed" (Monette Moore, 1936).

**39.** 1928, Aug. 30: *N. Y. Times:* Radclyffe Hall's *The Well of Loneliness* in England; see citations in text.

**40.** 1928, Sept. 16: *NYTBR*, p. 16; Compton Mackenzie, *Extraordinary Women* (New York: Macy-Masius); *Book Review Digest,* 1928, p. 496; Foster, *Sex Variant,* pp. 279, 282–83.

**41.** 1928: Claude McKay, *Home to Harlem* (New York: Harper ); see Roberts, *Black Lesbians,* item 336, p. 72.

**42.** 1929, Jan. 2: *The Nation* and *The New Republic,* Radclyffe Hall's *The Well of Loneliness* in the U.S.; see citations in text and Dr. N. Aronstam, "The Well of Loneliness—An Impression," *Urologic and Cutaneous Review,* vol. 33, no. 8 (Aug. 1929), pp. 542–43.

**43.** 1929, Apr. 26: *N. Y. Times:* Mrs. Lillian Arkel-Smith/Colonel Sir Victor Barker, 8:5.

**44.** 1929, Apr. ?: F. K.: "Report from America," a raid on the Lafayette Baths; discovered and translated by James Steakley from "Der Bericht aus Amerika," *Blätter für Menschenrecht (Journal for Human Rights)* (Berlin), vol. 7, no. 5 (May 1929), pp. 8–9.

**45.** 1929, May 4: *N.Y. Times:* "Woman . . . Wed to One of Her Sex"; Peter Stratford/Derestey Morton and Beth Rowland, 40:4; same, May 5, 1929, 21:6.

**46.** 1929, May: Dr. F. de Quervain, "Results of Castration in Sexual Abnormalities," *Urologic and Cutaneous Review,* vol. 33, no. 5 (May 1929), p. 351; original in *Schweizerische Medizinische Wochenschrift,* March 2, 1929).

**47.** 1929, Aug.: Dr. John F. Meagher, "Homosexuality: Its Psychobiological and Psychopathological Significance," *Urologic and Cutaneous Review* vol. 33, no. 8, 505–18.

**48.** 1929, Aug.: Dr. Clarence P. Oberndorf, "Diverse Forms of Homosexuality," *Urologic and Cutaneous Review,* vol. 33, no. 8, pp. 518–23.

**49.** 1929, Nov. 11: *N.Y. Times;* Thomas Dickinson's *Winter Bound,* 24:6; other reviews by Richard Watts, Jr., and by John Mason Brown in a lesbian scrapbook, c. 1920s–1930s in the collection of the Institute for Sex Research, Bloomington, Ill.

**50.** 1929: Katharine Bement Davis, *Factors in the Sex Life of Twenty-Two Hundred Women* (New York: Harper; reprinted New York: Arno Press, 1972); ch. 10, "Homosexuality. The Unmarried College Woman" (written with Maria E. Kopp), pp. 238–96; ch. 11, "Homosexuality. The Married Woman," pp. 297–328. For a biography of Davis see *Notable American Women,* vol. 1, pp. 439–41.

### 1930

**1.** 1930, Apr. 1: *N. Y. Times,* Motion Picture Code, 1:7; editorial, same day, 30:3.

**2.** 1930, Apr. 20: *N. Y. Times Book Review,* p. 9; André Gide, *The Immoralist,* translated by Dorothy Bussy (New York: Knopf).

**3.** 1930, July 6: *NYTBR*, p. 6; Geoffrey Moss, *That Other Love* (New York: Doubleday, Doran).

**4.** 1930, July 30: *NYTBR*, p. 7; André Birabeau, *Revelation,* translated by Una, Lady Troubridge (New York: Viking).

**5.** 1930, Sept. 14: *NYTBR*, p. 9; Radclyffe Hall, *A Saturday Life* (New York: Cape and Smith). Also see *Book Review Digest,* 1930, pp. 455–56.

**6.** 1930, Sept. 28: *NYTBR*, p. 11; Floyd Dell, *Love in the Machine Age* (New York: Farrar & Rinehart).

**7.** 1931, Apr. 15: Dr. Harry Benjamin, " 'For the Sake of Morality,' " *Medical*

*Journal and Record,* vol. 133, pp. 380–82. Also see Benjamin, "An Echo and an Addendum to 'For the Sake of Morality,'" same, vol. 134, (Aug. 5, 1931), pp. 118–20. As to the term "transsexual," in Dec. 1949, Dr. David O. Caudwell in *Sexology* magazine, is said by Benjamin to have described "the strange case of a girl who wanted to be a man and called the condition 'psychopathia transsexualis.'" In Aug. 1953, after the publicity concerning Christine Jorgensen, Dr. Benjamin published an article on the subject and used the term "transsexualism"; see Benjamin, *The Transsexual Phenomenon* (1966; New York: Warner Books, 1977), pp. 29–30.

8. Blair Niles, *Strange Brother* (New York: Liveright; reprinted New York: Arno Press, 1975). This novel contains valuable and fascinating references to the social history of homosexuals in the U.S.: on a Black lesbian couple, Sybil and Amy, 57, 155; the "bond" between homosexuals and Blacks, 151–52; Mark reads *The New Negro,* an anthology, and likes Countee Cullen's poem "Heritage," 234; references to homosexual slang: a "Drag Ball" in Harlem at which Jack Johnson had been a judge, pp. 210ff., "fairies," pp. 100, 213; Mark wants to throw off his "mask," p. 105; "Nellies," pp. 195–96; "queer," p. 136; "temperamental," meaning "queer," p. 156; on language, p. 123; on homosexuals as metaphorical "freaks," p. 184; (the use of the phrase "gay charm" without any connotation of homosexual indicates that "gay" was unknown to the author in that sense, 159); the trial and sentencing of an effeminate male, Nellie, pp. 63, 100; homosexual life on Welfare Island, pp. 288ff.; on "Crimes Against Nature" in a book on Penal Law, p. 122; on homosexuals as "modern witches," p. 133;

homosexuality used to be unmentionable, now it's joked about, pp. 156–57; on "Irwin Hesse," a Jewish sex reformer who believes in hormonal determinism, pp. 164, 172–73; Dr. Steinach, p. 173; a "female extract" is on the market which "can feminize a tomboy"; Dr. Benjamin is experimenting with male extract, p. 179; June recognizes her suffering over heterosexual love is the same as Mark's over homosexual love—he is her brother, p. 193; a Fifth Avenue restaurant where homosexuals meet and are "flaunting" themselves, pp. 195–96; Broadway movie houses for "rough" types, p. 196; meeting places for male homosexuals, streets, lavatories, the zoo, Central Park, p. 196; blackmail, pp. 196, 198; "no real connection between sex and reproduction," pp. 202–03; Carpenter's *Love's Coming of Age,* pp. 78, 123; Plato's *Symposium,* p. 206; Whitman's *Leaves of Grass,* p. 78; Mark plans an anthology of what poets, philosophers, scientists have written about man's love for man, to be titled *Comrades and Lovers* or *Manly Love,* and to include Forel's *The Sexual Question,* H. Ellis, Hirschfeld, Ulrichs (who is quoted), Carpenter (who is quoted), and Whitman (who is quoted), pp. 230, 235, 299; on the history of homosexuality, p. 307; on J. A. Symonds's letter to Whitman, and Whitman's disavowal, pp. 308–11; a homosexual party, p. 312; a plea for tolerance, p. 318.

9. 1932, May 29: *NYTBR,* p. 15; Anna Elizabet Weirauch, *The Scorpion,* translated by Whittaker Chambers (New York: Greenberg). On Chambers's homosexuality and communism, and his sexual, political, and religious conversion see Allen Weinstein, *Perjury: The Hiss–Chambers Case* (New York: Random House, 1979), pp. 307, 400; on Chambers's translations from the Ger-

man, p. 183; on *The Scorpion,* p. 378; also see pp. 67–69, 71–72, 84, 102, 104, 108, 114, 118–19, 165–67, 170, 176, 181–84, 270, 281, 283, 305, 335, 379–84, 399–401, 557, 561, 577, 582–84, 598, 633.

10. 1932, Sept. 11: *NYTBR,* p. 4; Arthur Weigall, *Sappho of Lesbos. Her Life and Times* (New York: Stokes).

11. 1932, September 21: *N. Y. Times,* review of the film *Girls in Uniform,* 25:4. For a discussion of this film see B. Ruby Rich, *"Mädchen in Uniform:* From Repressive Tolerance to Erotic Liberation," *Radical America,* vol. 15, no. 6 (Nov.–Dec. 1981), pp. 17–36, and Russo, *Celluloid Closet,* pp. 56, 57, 58, 131.

12. 1932, Nov. 1: *N. Y. Times,* John Lyman and Roman Bohnen, "Incubator," reviewed by "J. B.," 23:3.

13. 1932, Nov. 6: *N. Y. Times,* Christa Winsloe, *Mädchen in Uniform* in London, reviewed by Charles Morgan, Sect. 9, 1:3; New York production, Dec. 31, 1932 reviewed by Brooks Atkinson, 10:3.

14. 1932: *N. Y. Tribune:* "Mr. and Mrs."; clipping in lesbian scrapbook, Institute for Sex Research, Indiana.

15. 1933, Jan. 8: *Cleveland Plain Dealer* and *N. Y. Times,* Noel Coward's "Design for Living," Sect. 9, 3:2; reviewed by Brooks Atkinson, *Times,* Jan. 29, 1933, Sect. 9, 1:1. Also see George Jean Nathan, "Design for Loving," *The American Spectator* (New York), vol. 1, nos. 2, 3 (Apr. 1933), cited by Foster, *Sex Variant,* p. 301.

16. 1933, Jan. 29: *NYTBR,* p. 1; Sinclair Lewis, *Ann Vickers* (New York: Doubleday). Also see *Book Review Digest* 1933, pp. 561–62.

17. 1933, March 5: Eleanor Roosevelt and Lorena Hickock; page citations in text.

18. For Roosevelt's relationship with Marie Souvestre, headmistress of Allens-wood, in England, see Joseph P. Lash, *Eleanor and Franklin* (New York: Norton, 1971), pp. 74–85, 729 n. Lash says: "Because of an internal crisis precipitated by her co-principal Marie Souvestre had given up Les Ruches," the girls' school near Paris which she had earlier headed. Lash adds: "A fictional account of the crisis at Les Ruches and a vivid portrait of Mlle Souvestre" are found in the anonymous *Olivia* (see 1949, March 27), by Dorothy Strachey-Bussy, sister of Lytton Strachey, a pupil at Les Ruches, and a teacher at Allenswood when Eleanor Roosevelt was there. Eleanor Roosevelt's cousin, a fellow student at Allenswood, recalled that Roosevelt was "beloved by everybody. . . . Young girls have crushes and you bought violets or a book and left them in the room of the girl you were idolizing. Eleanor's room . . . would be full of flowers because she was so admired" (Lash, p. 84). On Roosevelt at Allenswood also see Michael Holroyd, *Lytton Strachey: A Critical Biography* (London: Heinemann, 1967), vol. 1. pp. 38–39. Eleanor Roosevelt's *This Is My Story* (1937) mentions Souvestre in her account of Allenswood, pp. 54–65. Also see Dolores Klaich, *Woman Plus Woman, Attitudes Toward Lesbianism* (New York: Morrow, 1974), p. 161.

Relevant to Eleanor Roosevelt's intimacy with Hickock are Roosevelt's close friendships with several other females, Elizabeth F. Read and Esther E. Lape, Nancy Cook and Marion Dickerman; see Lash, *Eleanor and Franklin,* pp. 260–61; Elliot Roosevelt and James Brough, *An Untold Story: The Roosevelts of Hyde Park* (New York: Putnam's, 1973), which refers to Read and Lape as "she-males," p. 132, also pp. 187, 200–01, 203, 211, 237; James Roosevelt, *My Parents: A Differing View* (Chicago: Playboy Press, 1976), pp. 37, 39–80, 111–

12. I thank Stephen W. Foster and Judith Schwarz for help with this research.

Also relevant to interpreting Eleanor Roosevelt's response to Hickock's lesbianism is FDR's involvement in two homosexual scandals; see 1921, July 20; and see ER's and FDR's response to the Sumner Welles case in 1941–43, *GAH*, p. 580 n. 96; *Almanac*, p. 530.

19. 1933, Apr. 9: *NYTBR*, p. 7; Maude Meagher, *The Green Scamander* (Boston: Houghton Mifflin).

20. 1933, May 7: *N. Y. Times*, "Nazi Students Raid Institute on Sex," 12:3.

21. 1933, May 12: *N. Y. Times, The Warrior's Husband,* 20:3. The film was adapted from a play of the same title by Julian Thompson.

22. 1933, May 31: Dr. A. A. Brill, "Homoerotism and Paranoia," paper read at the joint meeting of The American Psychiatric Association and the American Psychoanalytic Association, Boston; in *American Journal of Psychiatry*, vol. 90 (March 1934), pp. 957–74; includes bibliography on homosexuality and paranoia.

23. 1933, Sept. 3: *NYTBR*, p. 2; Gertrude Stein, *The Autobiography of Alice B. Toklas* (New York: Harcourt, Brace). Also see *Book Review Digest*, 1933, pp. 895–96.

24. 1933, Sept. 14: *NYTBR*, pp. 2, 12; Mario Praz, *The Romantic Agony,* translated from the Italian by Angus Davidson (New York: Oxford University Press). Also see *Book Review Digest*, 1933, p. 758.

25. 1933, Oct. 11: *Brevities* (New York: New Broad Publishing Co.); see citations in text. *Brevities* described itself as "America's First National Tabloid Weekly." The front-page headline on the issue of Oct. 12, 1933 reads: "Sexy Sailors Blow!/Bawdy Boys Run Riot on High Seas as Fags Stir Emotions of Rollicking Rovers/Gay Decks Reek with Lust when Briny/Deep Bohunks Practice Funny Business." That is one of the earliest documented uses of the word "Gay" in association with homosexuals. I thank Allan Bérubé for providing me with copies of *Brevities*.

26. 1933, Oct. 21: *N. Y. Times*, Mordaunt Shairp, *The Green Bay Tree*, reviewed by Brooks Atkinson, 11:5; also Oct. 29, Sect. 9, 1:1

27. 1933, Nov. 12: *NYTBR*, p. 9; Kay Boyle, *Gentlemen, I Address You Privately* (New York: Smith & Haas).

28. 1933, Nov. 19: *NYTBR*, p. 9; Christa Winsloe, *The Child Manuela*, translated by Agnes Neill Scott (New York: Farrar & Rinehart). Also see *Book Review Digest*, 1933, p. 1031.

29. 1933, Dec. 27: *N.Y. Times;* Greta Garbo's *Queen Christina*, rev. by Mordaunt Hall, 23:3. Also see Parker Tyler, *Screening the Sexes: Homosexuality in the Movies* (New York: Holt, Rinehart and Winston, 1972), p. 223; Russo, *Celluloid Closet*, pp. 15, 58, 63, 64, 65.

30. 1934, Jan. 7: *NYTBR*, p. 5; Margaret Goldsmith's *Christina of Sweden* (New York: Doubleday, Doran).

31. 1934, Jan. 17: *The Nation*, vol. 138, pp. 82–84; *Lot in Sodom*. Also see *The New Republic*, vol. 78 (March 21, 1934) pp. 160–61; Tyler, *Screening*, pp. 129–30; Russo, *Celluloid Closet*, p. 30.

32. 1934, Jan.: *Broadway Tattler*, comic strip, "Our great vaterland vill eliminate all pansies," p. 2. Laws providing "surgical castration as a therapy and crime prevention measure" were enacted as an amendment to the Penal Code in Germany by the Nazis, on Nov. 24, 1933, and later, as a "eugenical section" of the Public Health and Social Welfare Law of June 14, 1935, amended July 18, 1935 (cited by Marie

E. Kopp, see 1938, Jan., p. 702 in original document).

**33.** 1934, March 11: *NYTBR*, p. 24; Radclyffe Hall, *Miss Ogilvy Finds Herself* (New York: Harcourt, Brace).

**34.** 1934, Apr. 1: *NYTBR*, p. 9; Edgar Calmer, *Beyond the Street* (New York: Harcourt, Brace). For an early male homosexual's review of this novel see Henry Gerber, "A Study in Pessimism," *Chanticleer*, vol. 1, no. 7 (July 1934), p. 5; copy at Harvard Library.

**35.** 1934, May: George Ives to Dr. Joseph Wortis; see citations in text. For information that Ives wrote to Wortis I am deeply indebted to Michael Dunn's research in Ives's diary now in the Ives Collection, University of Texas, Humanities Research Center, Austin; for Dunn's research also see backnote 21, 1925, June 4. For providing me with photocopies of Ives's letters to him I thank Dr. Joseph Wortis. On Ives and the Order of Chaeronea see Weeks, *Coming Out*, pp. 61, 115, 118–20, 122–24, 125–26, 130–31, 134–36, 141, 156, 162, 168. For Oscar Wilde's letters to Ives see Weeks, p. 115, and Wilde, *Letters*. Ives's works are listed in "A Catalogue of the George Ives Collection," at the Humanities Research Center. For Havelock Ellis and Wortis's stipend see Phyllis Grosskurth, *Havelock Ellis. A Biography* (New York: Knopf, 1980), pp. 387, 392, 408–09, 417–22. On Alan Campbell see Grosskurth, pp. 418–19 and John Keats, *You Might As Well Live: The Life and Times of Dorothy Parker* (New York: Simon & Schuster, 1970), pp. 205–06; 242–43. Dr. Wortis's study of homosexuality resulted in "A Note on the Body Build of the Male Homosexual," *American Journal of Psychiatry*, vol. 93, no. 5 (March 1937), pp. 1121–25; and "Intersexuality and Effeminacy in a Male Homosexual," *American Journal of Orthopsychiatry*,

vol. 10 (1940), pp. 567–69. Also see Wortis's *Fragments of an Analysis with Freud* (New York: Simon & Schuster, 1954), which touches, as does Grosskurth, on Wortis's complex, interesting friendship with the rivals Freud and Havelock Ellis.

**36.** 1934, June 10: *NYTBR*, p. 7; M. J. Farrell (pseud. of Mary Lesta Skrine), *Devoted Ladies* (Boston: Little, Brown). A reviewer in *Books* (June 10, 1934, p. 8) called *Devoted Ladies* "a very high achievement . . . in the handling of its subject matter: morbid sexual relationship." Also see *Book Review Digest*, 1934, p. 867.

**37.** 1934, July 1: *N. Y. Times*, the execution of Ernst Roehm; see citations in text. Also see James D. Steakley, *The Homosexual Emancipation Movement in Germany* (New York: Arno Press, 1975), pp. 108–09.

**38.** 1934, Oct. 25: *N. Y. Times;* Gertrude Stein, 25:4.

**39.** 1934, Nov. 21: *N. Y. Times:* "The Children's Hour," 23:2; Dec. 2, sect. 10, 1:1. On Dec. 2, Atkinson mentioned that the story of *The Children's Hour* was said to be based on "an actual law case reported in a book by William Roughead." That book, *Bad Companions* (New York: Duffield & Green, 1931), contains a summary of the case of Marianne Woods and Jane Pirie, the heads of a girls' school in Scotland, who sued Helen Cumming Gordon for libel in 1811. This fascinating original case included a racial and class antagonism not retained in Hellman's play. For the voluminous record of the original trial see *Miss Marianne Woods and Miss Jane Pirie Against Dame Helen Cumming Gordon* (reprinted New York: Arno Press, 1975). For a fairly detailed account of the case see Faderman, *Surpassing*, pp. 147–55. For further comment in the *Times* on *The Children's Hour* see 1936, June 7, sect. 9, 1:1; November 13, 27:3;

November 29, Sect. 12, 2:1. The *N. Y. Times* of Nov. 13, 1936, described a London production of *The Children's Hour* at a "private" theater "untroubled" by censorship. A London *Times* reviewer said the production emphasized "the less important" of the play's themes, "the tragedy of personal ruin rather than the tragedy of Martha's love for Karen." Only in a final brief scene did the actress playing Martha have " 'a chance to communicate that depth of passion which is hinted at in the opening.' " If this passion " 'had been fully developed,' " it would have " 'made the play even more moving than it is.' " [27:3]

On November 29, Charles Morgan, a *N. Y. Times* critic in London, explained that *The Children's Hour* had been "banned by the censorship" for production in the "public," commercial theater, "presumably on account of its Lesbian implications." Although Morgan could see no reason against the play's "public" performance, he doubted it would be permitted. The play's "theme" and its "burden of gloom" also made him "doubt its wide popularity over here."[XII:2:1]

**40.** 1934, Nov. 22: *N. Y. Times*, review of London production of James Bridie and Claude Gurney's play *Mary Read*, 26:7.

**41.** 1935, Apr. 9: Dr. Sigmund Freud, "Letter to an American Mother," in *American Journal of Psychiatry*, vol. 107 (1951), pp. 786–87. Reprinted in *International Journal of Psychoanalysis*, vol. 32 (1951), p. 331, and elsewhere. The original publication reproduced a photostat of the original letter, in English, in Freud's handwriting, and included a somewhat incorrect transcription, corrected here. A postscript by Freud is here excluded.

**42.** 1935, Aug. 18: *NYTBR*, p. 6; Gale Wil-

helm, *We Too Are Drifting* (New York: Random House; reprinted New York: Arno Press, 1975). *The New Republic*, Oct. 2, 1935, p. 221, quoted from *Book Review Digest*, 1935, p. 1071.

**43.** 1935, Apr. 21: *N. Y. Times*: Maurice Rostand's *The Trial of Oscar Wilde*, sect. 9, 2:1.

**44.** 1935, Oct. 28: *N. Y. Times*, "Women's Personalities Changed by New Adrenal Gland Operation," 1:2, 5:2; editorial, Oct. 29, 1935, 20:3.

**45.** 1935, Nov. 10: *NYTBR*, pp. 8, 24; André Gide, *If It Die. . . . An Autobiography*, translated by Dorothy Strachey Bussy (New York: Random House).

**46.** 1936, Jan. 10: *N. Y. Times*, *Sylvia Scarlett*, 16:2. Also see Tyler, *Screening*, pp. 212–13.

**47.** 1936, Feb. 9: *NYTBR*, p. 21; Edmund Murrell, *Sojourn Among the Shadows* (Caldwell, Idaho: The Caxton Printers).

**48.** 1936, March 9: *Time*, "Medicine: Studies for All", vol. 27, pp. 59–60; comment on Dr. Havelock Ellis's *Studies in the Psychology of Sex*, 4 vols. (New York: Random House) *New Republic*, vol. 86, pp. 281–82. Also see *Book Review Digest*, 1936, p. 308. A review of Ellis's *Studies* by Ernest Boyd in *The American Mercury*, May, 1936, informed readers that the British Museum Library had once classified Ellis's volumes as "erotic or pornography, and therefore did not admit them to the catalogue."[121] One of Ellis's important "clarifications" was said to be his "analysis of the loose and unjustified way in which such words as 'normal,' 'abnormal,' and 'pathological,' have been bandied about by people unequipped to pass judgments." Boyd stressed Ellis's "formidable challenge to conventional morality, as defined by orthodox theology." Ellis's *Studies* patiently demonstrated "the innumerable fallacies, misunderstandings, and the superstitious ignorance underlying most of our sexual concepts."[122] Ellis, it was said, defined "love" as a "synthesis" of "lust" and "friendship." "Love" included more than "sexual desire." This sex love was also different from simple "friendship." "Sexual love" included "lust," the "affections and the social feelings";[123] see *American Mercury*, vol. 38, n. 149 (May 1936), pp. 120–24.

**49.** 1936, March 19: *N. Y. Times:* Lillian Hellman's *These Three*, 22:4.

**50.** 1936, Apr. 12: Dr. Alberta Lucille/Alan Hart, *The Undaunted* (New York: Norton). The date of the entry is that of the *NYTBR* comment, p. 7. Also see *Book Review Digest*, 1936, p. 444. See the information about Alberta Lucille Hart in *GAH*, pp. 258–79, p. 606 notes 68–71. *The Library of Congress Catalog, Pre-1956 Imprints*, lists Alan Hart's book publications and year of birth (1890). The director of the Albany (Ore.) Public Library, Wayne L. Suggs, reports that "The Albany *Democrat Herald* of 1920 or 1921 ran an article on Dr. Hart and his sex change." My guess is that this story appeared sometime between Jan. and Sept., 1920, as Dr. Gilbert (see *GAH*) mentions Hart's exposure in his medical journal article of Oct., 1920. A microfilm of the Albany *Democrat Herald* is in the Albany, Ore., Public Library. Mr. Suggs also reports that Lucille Hart is listed in the Albany City Directory, 1911–12, as a student, Albany College, rooms 234S Calapooia. Suggs reports that a citizen of Albany recalls Alberta Lucille Hart as belonging to the White Spires United Presbyterian Church: "Wore masculine pin-striped suits. . . . Changed sex and became Alan Hart. Local doctors ran her out of town." Hart reportedly became "a successful doctor in Seattle, Washington area," later in Hartford, Connecticut.

Hart's "technical papers" remain to be researched. Dorothy Joan Zornman of the Literature and History Department, Library Association of Portland, reports that Alan Hart was mentioned in the newspaper *The Oregonian*, April 21, 1935, sect. 3, p. 7 (a review of *Dr. Mallory*), and March 29, 1936, magazine sect., p. 6 (a one-sentence citation of Hart as an Oregon author), and in the *Oregon Journal*, Apr. 14, 1935, sect. 1, p. 11 (on Hart speaking in Portland). I thank the Library Association of Portland, and Ted Stroll for providing copies of these items. I also thank Emily Rubin Weiner for her help with this research.

Alan Hart's novel, *In the Lives of Men* (New York: Norton, 1937), was reviewed in the *N. Y. Times* on May 16, where Lucy Tomkins called it "a doctor's eye view of the social and economic history of the Pacific Northwest from 1890 to 1909." Focusing on Fairharbor, "a frontier lumber city on Puget Sound," the novel traced Dr. Jim Winthrop's nineteen years of practice in a place where the "lumber king" and a "one-time saloonkeeper and political boss ran the town, ran the press, ran the workers," and almost everyone was motivated by "Greed and lust."[6–7]

*In the Lives of Men* presents a detailed picture of class structure and conflict, and the social history of Fairharbor, including references to prostitution, marriage, male–female relationships, violence against women, eroticism, puritanism, birth control, childbirth, the history of surgery, health care, and radiation treatment, the anti-Chinese agitation, worker discontent, democracy and the lack of it, American imperialism, capitalism, populism, and socialism.

A few passing references allude vaguely to homosexuality, or the suspicion of it. Mrs. Deborah Winforth of Fairharbor attends a Purity Congress at which prostitution is discussed and, it is said, "Even the hint that Catholic choir boys were given to abominable though anonymous practices did no more than give her a temporary shock."[171] (The word "abominable" hints that the reference is to what was called "mutual masturbation.") Speaking of venereal disease among Alaskan Klondikers, a character says: " 'It's just when there aren't many women in a country things get spread around pretty fast.' "[231] Another character wonders why Dr. Winthrop never married, and spends most of his time with another confirmed bachelor.[328] Dr. Winthrop remarks to this same bachelor on the difference in sexual values between 1907 and 1895: " 'In the good old days our religious friends would have accused you of being a second Oscar Wilde.' "[376]

A close friendship between two boys, Malcolm and Geoffrey, is portrayed as having homoerotic elements; see pp. 192; 310–11, 315–16; 360; 426. Geoffrey, born without one arm, is brought up by a father who refuses to turn his son into a "mollycoddle" or "sissy." [191; 202] Geoffrey learns to accept his "deformity," but feels strongly the "unfair discrimination" and "injustice" of the treatment accorded those physically different.[208–09; 224] Of "Miss Ballantine," Geoffrey's teacher, it is said: "For reasons of her own she had never married and had, consequently, a fund of affection which she found . . . going out to the crippled boy."[337] As a young man Geoffrey identifies and sides with the workers against his capitalist father, becomes "a radical, a Socialist," and a public soapbox speaker for the Interna-

tional Workers of the World (the Wobblies), who urges: " 'proletarians unite.' "[342; 402–03] Once, in the woods, Geoffrey spies carved on a log the words: " 'Passing the love of women, 1891.' "[359; 426–27] Geoffrey eventually falls in love with a woman, but always feels different, an outsider who identifies with workers and outcasts. Geoffrey tells Dr. Winthrop: " 'It's enough to drive a fellow crazy to be different, to know he can't ever be like other men. . . . I see people looking at me, with a funny expression on their faces. And that makes me hate them. It's like having a pack of dogs after you. You run and run, and all the time you know that in the end the pack will get you, because you're different.' "[416] When Malcolm wants to interfere with Geoffrey's radical political involvement, Dr. Winthrop urges that Geoffrey be left alone: " 'The big struggle of the future . . . is going to be between the haves and the have-nots. Maybe Geoffrey has picked the right side, maybe the long pocketbook won't always have the power it has today.' "[427] Geoffrey is finally shot to death while urging " 'Workers of the World, unite!' "[444]

Alan Hart's fourth and last published novel, *Dr. Finlay Sees It Through* (New York: Harper, 1942), reviewed in the *N. Y. Times* on May 31, by Louise Munsell Field, included the photo of Hart. The reviewer described the book as recording the "triumphs and trials of a varied assortment of doctors working in neighboring towns on Puget Sound during the difficult years of the depression." The story focused on Dr. John Finlay, a man in his early fifties, whose struggle to create "a cooperative, voluntary health insurance association" is "bitterly resented and opposed by all the mercenary and many of the admirable members of the local medical society."[7]

51. 1936, May 18: *N. Y. Times, Dracula's Daughter,* 14:2.

52. 1936, June 3: *N. Y. Times,* "A shouting jeering mob," 46:2. Also see Richard Lamparski, *Whatever Became Of?* (New York: Crown, 1973), pp. 180–81. I thank James Foshee for this reference.

53. 1936: John Dos Passos, *The Big Money* (New York: Modern Library); drawing by Reginald Marsh, p. 455.

54. 1937, Jan.: Dr. George Henry, "Psychogenic Factors in Overt Homosexuality," *American Journal of Psychiatry,* vol. 93, no. 4, pp. 889–908; discussion Dr. E. E. Mayer of Pittsburgh, Pa.; Dr. Ben Karpman of Washington, D.C. Dr. Henry's study of male and female homosexuals was one of the projects sponsored by the Committee for the Study of Sex Variants, established by Dr. Eugen Kahn in 1935. Dr. Henry's final report on his study is in his book *Sex Variants: A Study of Homosexual Patterns* (New York, London: Hoeber, 1941).

55. 1937, Feb. 21: *N. Y. Times;* Stephen Powys, "Wise Tomorrow," see citations in text.

56. 1937, March 7: *NYTBR,* p. 6; Djuna Barnes, *Nightwood,* introduction by T. S. Eliot (New York: Harcourt, Brace). See *Book Review Digest,* 1937, p. 58. Reviewing *Nightwood* in *The Nation,* Apr. 3, 1937, Mark Van Doren said: "For brilliance and formal beauty few novels of any age can compare with [this]. But one must also say how desperate it is. Mr. Eliot condemns in advance any reader who feels superior to the three chief persons of the narrative, all of whom belong to the third sex. This, however, is not the point. The point is that Miss Barnes has

strained rather than enriched our sensibilities."

57. 1937, March 13: J. Edgar Hoover; private files; censored summaries of Hoover's files obtained under the U.S. Freedom of Information Act. These files are discussed in the following news stories: John M. Crewdson, "Files From Hoover Backers Reported," *N. Y. Times,* Feb. 2, 1974, 52:1; "Censored Version Issued of Secret Hoover Files on Official's Misconduct" (AP) *N. Y. Times,* Nov. 24, 1976, L 13:3; and John M. Goshko, "Inside Hoover's Sex Files," (from *Washington Post*) *N. Y. Post,* Nov. 24, 1976, 5:1.

58. 1937, Aug. 12: *N. Y. Times,* "Sex Crimes" in New York, 8:4; Aug. 13, 19:8; Aug. 25, 3:7; Sept. 8, 17:6.

59. 1937, Aug. 15: *NYTBR,* p. 14; Elisabeth Craigin, *Either Is Love* (New York: Harcourt, Brace), reprinted New York: Arno Press, 1975). See *Book Review Digest,* 1937, p. 231. A review in *The Nation,* Aug. 14, 1937, by L. Paul Love, said: "In trying to convince us that both these loves are possible for her heroine," Craigin made the "grave" error of insisting "too often and against all evidence that this Lesbian love was not Lesbian but a pure love heretofore unnoted by psychoanalysts. . . ."[177]

60. 1937, Oct. 12: *N. Y. Times,* Czech. Nazis accused of "homosexuality," 7:1; Oct. 17, 4:8; Oct. 20, 13:1; Dec. 3, 17:6; Dec. 10, 2:3.

61. 1937, Oct. 20: *N. Y. Times, Club de Femmes,* 27:2.

62. 1937, Dec. 5: *NYTBR,* p. 4; James Cain, *Serenade* (New York: Knopf).

63. 1937, Dec. 14: *N. Y. Times,* Aimée and Philip Stuart's *Love of Women,* 33:2.

64. 1938, Jan.: Marie E. Kopp, "Surgical Treatment as Sex Crime Prevention Measure," *Journal of Criminal Law and*

*Criminology,* vol. 28 (Jan.–Feb. 1938), pp. 692–706.

65. 1938, March 4: *N. Y. Times, Bringing Up Baby,* 17:5.

66. 1938, March 20: *NYTBR,* p. 7; Elliot Paul, *Concert Pitch* (New York: Random House).

67. 1938, Aug. 14: *NYTBR,* p. 7; Gale Wilhelm, *Torchlight to Valhalla* (New York: Random House, reprinted New York: Arno Press, 1975). The *Springfield* (Mass.) *Republican,* Aug. 14, 1938, p. 7; and the *Boston Transcript,* Aug. 27, 1938, quoted from *Book Review Digest,* 1938, p. 1039–40.

68. 1938, Aug.: Marion Joyce, "Flight from Slander," *The Forum,* pp. 90–94.

69. 1938, Oct. 6: *N. Y. Times,* Chester Erskin's *The Good,* 27:2.

70. 1938, Oct. 11: *N. Y. Times:* Leslie and Sewall Stokes's *Oscar Wilde,* 20:2; Oct. 16, sect. 9, 1:1. Two years earlier, the *Times* had reported on an English production of the Stokes's *Oscar Wilde.* On Sept. 30, 1936, a dispatch from London by A. V. Cookman reported the opening there of the play—which some critics felt "left a slightly unpleasant taste." (The alimentary metaphor used again in reference to sexual "malady" suggests that such oral associations were not idiosyncratic to the *Times*'s Brooks Atkinson; see footnote to 1938, October 6.) A *Times* of London critic was quoted as declaring that the play " 'merely relates what had best be forgotten.' "[29:4] Another dispatch from London, in the *N. Y. Times* of Oct. 18, 1936, described the play as "an objective picture" of Wilde's career. The audience saw him "ridiculing the notion that it would be safer to ignore the Queensberry insult"—the reviewer assumed *Times* readers knew that Queensberry had insulted Wilde by accusing him of posing as a sodomite. Wilde was also shown in the play "giving champagne suppers to grooms." The reporter said: "Only once, . . . when Wilde has little left to hide and directly defends his malady, has the play a hint" of the dramatic potential it would have had if Wilde's "inner life" had been expressed.[Sect. 10, 3:8]

71. 1939, March 12: *NYTBR,* p. 7; Mary Renault, *Promise of Love* (New York: William Morrow). Also see *Book Review Digest,* 1939, p. 813.

72. 1939, July 11: *N. Y. Times,* the death of Havelock Ellis, 19:1; editorial, 18:3.

73. 1939: Diana Frederics, pseud., *Diana: A Strange Autobiography,* introduction by Dr. Victor Robinson (New York: Dial Press; reprinted New York: Arno Press, 1975).

*1940*

1. 1940, Jan. 14: *NYTBR,* p. 2; Vera Brittain, *Testament of Friendship: The Story of Winifred Holtby* (New York: Macmillan); *Books,* Jan. 14, 1940, p. 2 quoted from *Book Review Digest,* 1940, pp. 111–12.

2. 1940, Jan. 27: Henry Gerber to Manuel Boyfrank; see citations in text; Gerber's letters to Boyfrank (and Boyfrank's to Gerber), 1940–57, are in the collection of James Kepner, now in the Natalie Barney/Edward Carpenter Library, National Gay Archives, Hollywood. I am deeply indebted to James Kepner for providing photocopies, and for information about Gerber. Other Gerber documents cited are now in my own collection, to which they were donated by Tony Segura. In the 1950s, while working with the New York Mattachine Society, Segura corresponded with Gerber, and kept these documents for years in his closet.

3. For Gerber's three comments under his own name in German homosexual

emancipation movement periodicals I thank James D. Steakley who discovered and translated them. They are cited in *GAH*, pp. 632–33, n. 94.

4. For Gerber's issuance of *Contacts*, 1930–39, see *GAH*, p. 633, n. 98; for his pseudonymous essay of June, 1932, see Parisex, "In Defense of Homosexuality," *Modern Thinker;* and for his essays in *Chanticleer* (1934), see *GAH*, pp. 393–97, 633–34 nn. 99–104.

5. Gerber's letter of Apr. 5, 1944, to *Time* is in the Kepner collection. Also see "The Lonergan Case," *Time*, vol. 43 (Apr. 3, 1944), pp. 68–69; and *N. Y. Times Index*, 1944, pp. 913–14.

6. A copy of Gerber's anonymous thirteen-page letter of July 18, 1946, to Dr. Leopold Wexburg, was in Tony Segura's collection, now in my own collection; it was accompanied by a clipping from the Washington *Times-Herald*, July 4, 1946, headed "2 Doctors Urge Long Sentences For Sex Perverts."

7. For Gerber's published response under his own name to Bergan Evans's comment on the statement: "That homosexuals are always effeminate" (*American Mercury*, vol. 68, [May 1947], p. 598) see *American Mercury*, July 1947, which includes Evans's reply. In Oct. 1947 the same magazine published four letters in response to Gerber. Copies of Gerber's two rejected manuscript essays, "Is Homosexuality Inborn or Acquired?" and "Can Homosexuals Be Cured?" were in the Segura collection. Gerber discusses this rejection in a letter to Boyfrank on Aug. 9, 1947.

8. Copies of Gerber's letters to the Washington *Times-Herald*, Sept. 4, 1947, and the Washington *Post*, headed "A Plea For Sex Sanity," undated, signed "Psychoanalyst" (though Gerber included his name and a box number) are in the Kepner collection. Gerber's letter to *National Defense*, Sept. 15, 1947, Kepner collection.

9. Clipping of Gerber's anonymous letter in *American Freeman*, Sept. 1948, from Segura collection.

10. Gerber's translations of Hirschfeld in *ONE Institute Quarterly*, vol. 5, no. 2–4, iss. 17 (Spring-Fall 1962), pp. 41–53; vol. 6, no. 1–2, iss. 18 (Winter-Spring 1963), pp. 22–30.

11. Gerber to New York Mattachine, Aug. 1956; and copies of essays, from Segura collection. Gerber to *ONE*, Aug. 12, 1954, in Barney-Carpenter Library.

12. Gerber's letter to *ONE* editors, Jan. 24, 1966, in *ONE* collection, now in Barney-Carpenter Library.

13. The date of Gerber's death was reported in a letter to me on March 20, 1974, by Dr. Daniel G. Monaghan, from the U.S. Soldiers' Home, Washington, D.C.

14. 1940, July 27: *N. Y. Times; Turnabout*, 17:6.

15. 1941, Feb. 23: *NYTBR*, p. 24; Harlan Cozad McIntosh, *This Finer Shadow* (New York: Dial).

16. 1941, March 10: *NYTBR*, p. 24; William Davey, *Dawn Breaks the Heart* (New York: Howell, Soskin). Also see *Book Review Digest*, 1941, pp. 224–25. Also see Donald Vining, *A Gay Diary, 1933–1946* (New York: The Pepys Press, 1979), p. 171. Vol. 2 of Vining's diary (1946–1954) also includes interesting comments on novels with homosexual themes, *End as a Man, The Fall of Valor, The City and the Pillar, Quatrefoil*, etc.

17. 1941, Apr.: F. A. McHenry, "Homosexuality, Crime, and the Newspapers," *Journal of Criminal Psychopathology*, vol. 2, no. 4, pp. 533–48. McHenry was identified as an M.A. from New York City.

18. 1941, Aug. 17: *NYTBR*, p. 15; Angela du Maurier, *The Little Less* (New York: Doubleday). *Book Review Digest*, 1941.

19. 1941, Nov. 2: *NYTBR*, p. 20; Felice Swados, *House of Fury* (New York: Doubleday); *Book Review Digest*, 1941, p. 876.

20. 1941: Gershon Legman, "The Language of Homosexuality," pp. 1149–1179 in Dr. George Henry, *Sex Variants: A Study of Homosexual Patterns* (New York and London: Hoeber).

21. 1942, Feb.: *N. Y. Times, N. Y. Post*, and *The Nation*, the case of Senator David I. Walsh and Gustave Beekman; see citations in text, and *Time*, June 1, 1942, pp. 50–52; *Newsweek*, June 1, 1942; *Christian Century*, June 3, 1942.

22. 1943, July 4: *NYTBR*, p. 6; Dorothy Baker, *Trio* (Boston: Houghton Mifflin).

23. 1943, Oct. 12: *N. Y. Times*, the death of Radclyffe Hall, 27:3.

24. 1944, Feb.: Drs. D. M. Olkon and Irene Case Sherman, "Eonism with Added Outstanding Psychopathic Features: A Unique Psychopathological Case," *Journal of Nervous and Mental Disease*, vol. 99, no. 2, pp. 159–67.

25. 1944, Aug.: Robert Duncan, "The Homosexual in Society," *Politics*, vol. 1, pp. 209–11. For an interview with Duncan see *Gay Sunshine, A Journal of Gay Liberation*, no. 40–41 (Summer/Fall 1979), 8 pp. unpaginated. Also see Michael Rumaker, "Robert Duncan in San Francisco," *Credences* vol. 5, no. 6 (March 1978), pp. 12–55. For copies of the above documents I thank John D'Emilio. Although Henry Gerber published pro-homosexual essays in the U.S. under his own name in 1934 and later, he never, to my knowledge, explicitly and publicly identified himself in these as homosexual.

26. 1944, Dec. 30: *N. Y. Times*, Dorothy and Howard Baker's play *Trio*, 13:4.

27. 1945, Feb. 18: *NYTBR*, p. 10; Mary Renault, *The Middle Mist* (New York: William Morrow); published in England as *Friendly Young Ladies*; *Book Review Digest*, 1945, pp. 588–89.

28. 1945, June 17: *NYTBR*, p. 20; Nora Lofts, *Jassy* (New York: Knopf); *Book Review Digest*, 1945, pp. 437–48.

29. 1946, Feb. 17: *NYTBR*, p. 5; Jo Sinclair, *Wasteland* (New York: Harper). Jo Sinclair is the pen name of Ruth Seid; see *Book Review Digest*, 1946.

30. 1946, Feb. 17: *NYTBR*, pp. 1, 33; Christopher Isherwood, *The Berlin Stories* (*The Last of Mr. Norris* and *Goodbye to Berlin*) (New York: New Directions).

31. 1946, Feb. 24: *NYTBR*, pp. 1, 36; Gay Wilson Allen's *Walt Whitman Handbook* (Chicago: Packard), and Whitman, *Leaves of Grass*, introduction by Bernard Smith (New York: Knopf).

32. 1946, March 15: *N. Y. Times, Gilda* (film), 27:2; the screen play, by Marion Parsonnet, was adapted by Jo Eisinger from a story by E. A. Ellington. It was directed by Charles Vidor and produced by Virginia Van Upp. See Tyler, *Screening*, pp. 166–67.

33. 1946, July 28: *N. Y. Times*, the death of Gertrude Stein, 40:1.

34. 1946, July: A. C. Cornsweet and Dr. M. F. Hayes: "Conditioned Response to Fellatio," *American Journal of Psychiatry*, vol. 103, pp. 76–78.

35. 1946, Sept. 8: *NYTBR*, p. 16; Janet Shane, *The Dazzling Crystal* (New York: Reynal & Hitchcock).

36. 1946, Oct. 6: *NYTBR*, p. 14; Charles Jackson, *The Fall of Valor* (New York: Rinehart).

37. 1946, Nov. 27: *N. Y. Times*, Jean-Paul Sartre, *No Exit* (play), 21:1.

38. 1947, Jan. 17: *N. Y. Times*, William Tilden sentenced; see citations in text; also see Frank Deford, *Big Bill Tilden: The Triumphs and the Tragedy* (New York: Simon & Schuster, 1975).

39. 1947, Jan. 26: *NYTBR*, p. 18; Ferdinand Lundberg and Dr. Marynia F.

Farnham, *Modern Woman: The Lost Sex* (New York: Harper). The controversy over the book is mentioned in the *N. Y. Times* obituary of Farnham, May 30, 1979, A19:1.

40. 1947, March: Jane MacKinnon, "The Homosexual Woman," *American Journal of Psychiatry*, vol. 103, no. 5, pp. 661–64.

41. 1947, June 8: *NYTBR*, p. 7; John Horne Burns, *The Gallery* (New York: Harper).

42. 1947, June 9: *Newsweek*, "Homosexuals in Uniform," p. 54.

43. 1947, June: Lisa Ben, *Vice Versa;* page citations in text. For help in obtaining copies of *Vice Versa* I thank Barbara Grier, "Lisa Ben," and Leland Moss, who also provided the photo by Robert Haynes. For Moss's interview with Lisa Ben see *Gaysweek* (New York), Jan. 23, 1978, pp. 15–16.

44. 1947, July 23: *N. Y. Times*, "Cross Fire" (film), 19:2.

45. 1948, Jan. 11: *NYTBR*, p. 22; Gore Vidal, *The City and the Pillar* (New York: Dutton).

46. 1948, Jan. 4: *NYTBR*, *Time*, *Parents' Magazine*, Alfred Kinsey et al., *Sexual Behavior in the Human Male* (Philadelphia: Saunders); page citations in text.

47. 1948, Jan. 18: *NYTBR*, p. 5; Truman Capote, *Other Voices, Other Rooms* (New York: Random House).

48. 1948, Apr.: Dr. William C. Menninger, "Homosexuality," ch. 16, pp. 222–31 in *Psychiatry in a Troubled World: Yesterday's War and Today's* Challenge (New York: Macmillan, 1948). The medical report on "homosexual buffoonery" is by Dr. I. L. Janis, "Psychodynamic Aspects of Adjustment to Army Life," *Psychiatry*, vol. 8, (May 1945). The other medical report cited is by Dr. L. H. Loeser, "Sexual Psychopathy in the Military Services: A Study of 270 Cases," *American Journal of Psychiatry*, vol. 102, (July 1945), 92–101.

49. 1948, July 11: *NYTBR*, p. 21; André Gide, *The Immoralist* (New York: Knopf).

50. 1948, Oct. 1: *N. Y. Times*, *Red River*, 31:2. Also see Russo, *Celluloid Closet*, p. 78.

51. 1948, Nov. 21: *NYTBR*, p. 42; Hubert Creekmore, *The Welcome* (New York: Appleton-Century-Crofts).

52. 1949, March 13: *NYTBR*, p. 4; Isabel Bolton, *The Christmas Tree* (New York: Charles Scribner).

53. 1949, March 27: *NYTBR*, p. 4; Olivia [Dorothy Strachey Bussy], *Olivia* (New York: William Sloan, ; reprinted New York: Arno Press, 1975). *Book Review Digest*, 1949, p. 700.

54. 1949, June 19: *NYTBR*, p. 7; Ward Thomas, *Stranger in the Land* (Boston: Houghton Mifflin).

55. 1949, Summer: James Baldwin, "Preservation of Innocence: Studies for a New Morality," *Zero* (Tangier, Morocco), vol. 1, no. 2, pp. 14–22. I thank Larry Van Heusen for informing me of this document and providing a photocopy.

56. 1949, Sept. 20: *N. Y. Times*, *Germany Year Zero*, 35:2.

57. 1949, Oct. 10: *Newsweek*, vol. 34, *Queer People*, pp. 52, 54. Also see J. Paul DeRiver, *The Sexual Criminal* (Springfield, Ill.: Charles C. Thomas).

58. 1949, Nov. 6: *NYTBR*, p. 28; Nial Kent, *The Divided Path* (New York: Greenberg).

# Selected Bibliography

My interest in analyzing links between the particular historical terms and concepts referring to female–female and male–male eroticism and intimacy, actual historical instances of such relationships, the responses to them, and the particular socioeconomic structure, was inspired by Mary P. Ryan's *Womanhood in America: From Colonial Times to the Present* (New York: New Viewpoints, Franklin Watts, 1975; 2nd ed., 1979). There Ryan traces the relationship between different historical ideals of femininity, actual historical responses to and forms of female behavior, and the political economy. See my review of Ryan's first edition, *The Body Politic* (Toronto), Dec./Jan. 1977, pp. 19, 21. Also see my comments in "Why Gay History?" *The Body Politic,* August 1979, pp. 19–20; condensed from a keynote address delivered at the New York University conference, "Constructing a History of Power and Sexuality," March 31, 1978.

## *Theoretical Works*

Analysis of the theoretical implications of lesbian and gay history, of heterosexual history, and of the history of sex and intimacy in general, is still in its early stages. Among the works with an explicit theoretical focus, or which I have found useful and provocative for their implicit theoretical assumptions are the following.

Boswell, John. *Christianity, Social Tolerance, and Homosexuality: Gay People in Western Europe from the Beginning of the Christian Era to the Fourteenth Century.* Chicago: University of Chicago Press, 1980. Reviews by Martin Duberman, *New Republic,* Oct. 18, 1980, pp. 32–35; Keith Arrowsmith (pseud. of Walter Kendrick), *Village Voice,* March 11–17, 1981, pp. 44–45; Jeffrey Weeks, *History Today,* July 1980, p. 49; Scholarship Committee, Gay Academic Union, New York City (Warren Johansson, Wayne Dynes, John Lauritsen), "Homosexuality, Intolerance, and Christianity," Gai Saber Monograph No. 1 (P. O. Box 480; Lenox Hill Station, New York, N. Y. 10021); Paul Robinson, *New York Times Book Review,* Aug. 10, 1980.

Bullough, Vern L. *Sexual Variance in Society and History.* New York: John Wiley, Interscience, 1976. This is the most comprehensive international survey of homosexual history, superseding Arno Karlen's *Sexuality and Homosexuality* (1971), but Bullough's naive empiricism, unexamined assumptions, and reliability of sources should be questioned. The naive empiricist claims (mistakenly) to do without theory, without essential presumptions about a "field" of research, believing it is possible simply to go out and collect "facts." See, for example, Bullough's comment that to avoid the danger of unexamined assumptions "I have not adopted any theory about sexuality, whether Freudian, Marxian, or Augustian, but have accepted sexuality as a biological fact. . . ."[xi] Also see John Boswell's similar claim "to provide data" with "little built-in theoretical bias."[5] On the contrary, both authors make basic theoretical assumptions of a biological order.

D'Emilio, John. "Gay Politics, Gay Community: San Francisco's Experience," *Socialist Review*, No. 55, vol. 11, no. 1 (January/February 1981), pp. 77–104.

——. *Sexual Politics, Sexual Communities: The Making of a Homosexual Minority in the United States, 1940–1970*. Chicago: University of Chicago Press, 1983.

Faderman, Lillian. *Surpassing the Love of Men: Romantic Friendship and Love between Women from the Renaissance to the Present*. New York: William Morrow, 1981. Reviews by Benjamin DeMott, *Atlantic Monthly*, March 1981; Carolyn Heilbrun, *New York Times Book Review*, April 5, 1981, pp. 12–13, 19; Phyllis Grosskurth, *New York Review of Books*, May 28, 1981, pp. 12–14; Joanna Russ, (New York) *Daily News*, May 7, 1981, p. M8; Amy Hoffman, *Gay Community News Book Review*, June 27, 1981, pp. 4–5, 7.

Faraday, Annabel, "Liberating Lesbian Research," pp. 112–29 in Plummer, ed. (see below).

Foucault, Michel. *The History of Sexuality: Volume I: An Introduction*. Translated from the French by Robert Hurley. New York: Pantheon Books, 1978.

Hansen, Bert. "The Historical Construction of Homosexuality" (review of Weeks's *Coming Out* [see below]), *Radical History Review*, 20 (1979), pp. 66–73.

Interrante, Joseph. "Ahistorical Perspectives" (review of Vern L. Bullough, *Homosexuality: A History from Ancient Greece to Gay Liberation* [New York: New American Library, 1979] and Martin P. Levine, ed., *Gay Men: The Sociology of Male Homosexuality* [New York: Harper & Row, 1979]), *Gay Community News Book Review*, vol. 7, no. 33 (March 1980), pp. 3, 8.

——. "The Etiology of the Closet" (review of Weeks's *Coming Out* [see below]), *Gay Community News Book Review*, vol. 6, no. 33 (March 1979), pp. 2, 6.

——. "From Pathology to Lifestyle" (survey of *Time* magazine homosexuality surveys), *Gay Community News*, vol. 6, no. 47 (June 23, 1979), pp. 14, 17.

——. "From the Puritans to the Present: 350 Years of Lesbian and Gay History in Boston," in Richard Burns, Neuma Crandall, and Eric Rofes, ed., *Gay Jubilee: A Guidebook to Gay Boston—Its History and Resources* (Boston: Lesbian and Gay Task Force of Jubilee 350, Summer 1980).

——. "The History of Masculinity" (review of Elizabeth H. Pleck and Joseph H. Pleck, ed., *The American Man* [Englewood Cliffs, N.J.: Prentice-Hall, 1980]), *Gay Community News Book Review*, vol. 7, no. 39 (April 1980), pp. 4, 6.

——. "Homosexuality, Sexual Identity, and Masculinity in Historical Perspective." Typescript draft, October 23, 1981.

——. "No Papa, Yes Mama" (review of Zillah Eisenstein, ed., *Capitalist Patriarchy and the Case for Socialist Feminism* [New York: Monthly Review, 1979]), *Gay Community News Book Review*, vol. 6, no. 44 (May 1979), pp. 3, 7.

—— and Lasser, Carol. "Victims of the Very Songs They Sing: A Critique of Recent Work on Patriarchal Culture and the Social Construction of Gender," *Radical History Review*, (see Hansen above), pp. 25–40.

Lévy, Bernard-Henri. "Power and Sex: An Interview with Michel Foucault." *Telos*, no. 32 (Summer 1977), pp. 152–61.

Lynch, Michael. "Here Is Adhesiveness: From Friendship to Homosexuality." Typescript draft, December 1980.

McIntosh, Mary. "The Homosexual Role." *Social Problems,* vol. 16, no. 2 (Fall 1968), pp. 182–92; reprinted with additional comment in Plummer (see below).

Neuman, R. P. "Recent Work on the History of Sexuality" (review of Eric Trudgill, *Madonnas and Magdalens* [1976]; Stephen Kern, *Anatomy and Destiny* [1975]; Paul Robinson, *The Modernization of Sex* [1976], *Journal of Social History,* vol. 11, no. 3 (Spring 1978), pp. 419–25.

Padgug, Robert A. "Sexual Matters: On Conceptualizing Sexuality in History," *Radical History Review* (see Hansen, above), pp. 3–23.

Plummer, Kenneth, ed. *The Making of the Modern Homosexual.* London: Hutchinson, 1981.

Rubin, Gayle. "The Traffic in Women: Notes on the 'Political Economy' of Sex," pp. 157–210 in Rayna R. Reiter, ed., *Toward an Anthropology of Women.* New York: Monthly Review Press, 1975. Rubin's pioneering work speaks of the "sex/gender system," the "set of arrangements by which a society transforms biological sexuality into products of human activity, and in which these transformed sexual needs are satisfied." For the sake of clarity I prefer more functionally differentiated term/concepts such as the "social organization of lust," the "historical mode of procreation," the "social construction of gender" or "mode of engendering."

Sahli, Nancy. "Smashing: Women's Relationships Before the Fall." *Chrysalis,* no. 8 (1979), pp. 17–27.

Smith-Rosenberg, Carroll. "The Female World of Love and Ritual: Relations between Women in Nineteenth-Century America." *Signs,* vol. 1, no. 1 (Autumn 1975), pp. 1–29.

Weeks, Jeffrey. "Capitalism and the Organization of Sex," pp. 11–20 in Gay Left Collective, ed., *Homosexuality: Power and Politics.* London: Allison and Busby, 1980.

———. *Coming Out: Homosexual Politics in Britain, from the Nineteenth Century to the Present.* London: Quartet Books, 1977.

———. "Discourse, Desire and Sexual Deviance: Some Problems in a History of Homosexuality," in Plummer (see above), pp. 76–111.

———. "Inverts, Perverts, and Mary Annes: Male Prostitution and the Regulation of Homosexuality in England in the Nineteenth and Early Twentieth Centuries," *Journal of Homosexuality* vol. 6, nos. 1/2 (Fall/Winter 1980), pp. 113–34.

———. "Movements of Affirmation: Sexual Meanings and Homosexual Identities." *Radical History Review* (see Hansen, above), pp. 164–79.

———. *Sex, Politics, and Society: The Regulation of Sexuality Since 1800* (London: Longman, 1981).

———. " 'Sins and Diseases': Some Notes on Homosexuality in the Nineteenth Century." *History Workshop,* no. 1 (Spring 1976), pp. 211–19.

Other works on lesbian and gay male history, on a more empirical level, often contain important theoretical implications. These are listed in the following sources and in the backnotes.

### *Other Useful Works on Lesbian and Gay American History*

Austen, Roger. *Playing the Game: The Homosexual Novel in America.* Indianapolis: Bobbs-Merrill, 1977.

Bérubé, Allan. "Lesbian Masquerade," *Gay Community News,* Nov. 17, 1979, pp. 8–9.

———. "Marching to a Different Drummer: Lesbians and Gay GIs in World War II," *Advocate*, Oct. 15, 1981, pp. 20–24.

Bullough, Vern L., et al. *An Annotated Bibliography of Homosexuality.* 2 vols. (New York: Garland, 1976. Unreliable data, but useful anyway.

Common Women Collective. *Women in U.S. History: An Annotated Bibliography.* Cambridge, Mass.: Common Women Collective, 1976. Annotations from a lesbian feminist perspective.

Duggan, Lisa. "Lesbianism and American History: A Brief Source Review." *Frontiers,* vol. 4, no. 3 (Fall 1979), pp. 80–85.

Foster, Jeannette H. *Sex Variant Women in Literature: A Historical and Quantitative Survey.* New York: Vantage Press, 1956. Reprinted Baltimore: Diana Press, 1975.

*A Gay Bibliography: Eight Bibliographies on Lesbianism and Male Homosexuality.* New York: Arno Press, 1975. Especially important for the annotations; reprints bibliographies published 1958–1966.

"Gay history? Lesbian history?" *Gay Archivist: Newsletter of the Canadian Gay Archives,* no. 4 (Sept. 1981), pp. 5–7. (CGA, P.O. Box 639, Station "A," Toronto, Ontario, Canada, M54 1G2.) Useful recent bibliography.

Gay Task Force, American Library Association. "A Gay Bibliography" (Gay Task Force of the American Library Association, Box 2383, Philadelphia, Pa. 19103.) Published annually; includes recent, major works on gay and lesbian history and biography.

Grier, Barbara. *The Lesbian in Literature.* 3rd ed. Foreword by Maida Tilchen. Tallahassee, Fl.: Naiad Press, 1981.

Katz, Jonathan. *Gay American History.* New York: T. Y. Crowell, 1976.

———. "Melville's Secret Sex Text" [decoded the novel *Redburn*]. *Village Voice Literary Supplement,* Apr., 1982.

Kuda, Marie J., ed. *Women Loving Women: A Select and Annotated Bibliography of Women Loving Women in Literature.* Chicago: Woman Press, 1975.

Licata, Salvatore, and Petersen, Robert, eds. "Historical Perspectives on Homosexuality" issue of *Journal of Homosexuality,* vol. 6, nos. 1/2 (Fall/Winter 1980/81).

Parker, William. *Homosexuality: A Selective Bibliography of Over 3,000 Items.* Metuchen, N.J.: Scarecrow Press, 1971.

———. *Homosexuality Bibliography: Supplement, 1970–1975.* Metuchen, N.J.: Scarecrow Press, 1977.

Roberts, J. R., compiler. Foreword by Barbara Smith. *Black Lesbians: An Annotated Bibliography.* Tallahassee, Fla.: Naiad Press, 1981.

Russo, Vito. *The Celluloid Closet: Homosexuality in the Movies.* New York: Harper & Row, 1981.

Schwarz, Judith, ed. "Lesbian History" issue of *Frontiers,* vol. 4, no. 3 (Fall 1979).

Young, Ian. *The Male Homosexual in Literature.* Metuchen, N.J.: Scarecrow Press, 1975.

# INDEX

Abbreviations used: BSSSP, British Society for the Study of Sex Psychology; *NYT, New York Times; NYTBR, New York Times Book Review.*

The backnotes are not indexed.

Specific cities and towns are listed under their state, except for Boston, Chicago, Detroit, Los Angeles, New York, Philadelphia, San Francisco, Washington, D.C.

The three main analytical sections of this book are indexed under "homosexual history"; "colonial America"; and the "modern U.S."

Analysis and examples of terminology are indexed under "terms." From the two lists of terms (Rosanoff, 1927, pp. 438–40; Legman, 1941, pp. 571–84) only those words are indexed to which a second reference is made elsewhere in the text.

Titles of medical journals and of articles in them are not indexed.

Names of *New York Times* reviewers appearing once are not indexed, unless of unusual interest.

Pseudonyms appear in quotations.

# Copyright Acknowledgments

# COPYRIGHT ACKNOWLEDGMENTS

"Eonism with Added Outstanding Psychopathic Features" by Drs. D. M. Olkon and Irene Case Sherman, *Journal of Nervous and Mental Disease*, vol. 99, no. 2 (February 1944), pp. 159–67; reprinted by permission of The Williams and Wilkins Co., Baltimore.

Sarah Stein to Gertrude Stein, two letters, one beginning "Dearest Girl/Oh! I have just had such a splendid talk," from 118 O'Farrell (San Francisco), no date, and letter dated Monday, Oct. 29 [1894], in Sarah Stein Letters, 1893?–1911, Folder I, Beinecke Library, Yale University; reprinted by permission of the Collection of American Literature, Beinecke Rare Book and Manuscript Library, Yale University, and the Estate of Gertrude Stein.

"Miss Furr and Miss Skeene" by Gertrude Stein in *Geography and Plays* (Boston: The Four Seas Company, 1922); reprinted by permission of the Estate of Gertrude Stein.

Edith Lees Ellis about 1914, photograph in Havelock Ellis, *My Life . . .* (Boston: Houghton-Mifflin, 1939), opposite p. 578; reprinted by permission of Professor F. Lafitte, Trustee of the Havelock Ellis Estate.

Excerpts from manuscripts of the British Sexological Society and George Ives in the Collection of The Humanities Research Center, University of Texas, Austin; quoted with the permission of the Faculty Committee on the Use of Historical and Literary Manuscripts.

Excerpts from Charles Torrence Nesbitt's typescript autobiography quoted with the permission of the Manuscript Department, William R. Perkins Library, Duke University, Durham, North Carolina.

# About the Author

Jonathan Katz is a self-taught, independent researcher-writer with an interest in history. He is the author-compiler of *Gay American History: Lesbians and Gay Men in the U. S. A.* (1976), *Resistance at Christiana,* the history of an American fugitive slave rebellion (1974), and General Editor of the Arno Press–New York Times reprint series "Homosexuality: Lesbians and Gay Men in Society, History, and Literature" (1975). He is coauthor of *Black Woman,* a fictionalized biography for young people about a Black pioneer woman (1973). Katz's documentary play *Coming Out!* about lesbian and gay life and liberation in the U. S. A. was first performed in 1972 and published in 1975. His article, "Melville's Secret Sex Text," about the novel *Redburn,* appeared in *The Village Voice Literary Supplement* in April 1982. Katz has prepared scripts for two educational phonograph albums for Caedmon Records, *Black Pioneers I and II.* His documentary plays on Black American history were produced on WBAI-FM, New York. Katz, a codirector of The Institute for the Study of Sex in Society and History, lives in New York City.